SAGE was founded in 1965 by Sara Miller McCune to support the dissemination of usable knowledge by publishing innovative and high-quality research and teaching content. Today, we publish over 900 journals, including those of more than 400 learned societies, more than 800 new books per year, and a growing range of library products including archives, data, case studies, reports, and video. SAGE remains majority-owned by our founder, and after Sara's lifetime will become owned by a charitable trust that secures our continued independence.

Los Angeles | London | New Delhi | Singapore | Washington DC | Melbourne

Industrial Relations and Labour Laws for Managers

Industrial Relations and Labour Laws for Managers

Parul Gupta

Faculty of Law, Management Development Institute (MDI), Gurgaon

SAGE | TEXTS

Los Angeles | London | New Delhi
Singapore | Washington DC | Melbourne

First published in 2019 by

SAGE | TEXTS

SAGE Publications India Pvt Ltd
B1/I-1 Mohan Cooperative Industrial Area
Mathura Road, New Delhi 110 044, India
www.sagepub.in

SAGE Publications Inc
2455 Teller Road
Thousand Oaks, California 91320, USA

SAGE Publications Ltd
1 Oliver's Yard, 55 City Road
London EC1Y 1SP, United Kingdom

SAGE Publications Asia-Pacific Pte Ltd
18 Cross Street #10-10/11/12
China Square Central
Singapore 048423

Published by Vivek Mehra for SAGE Publications India Pvt Ltd and typeset in 10/12.5 pt Minion Pro by AG Infographics, Delhi.

Library of Congress Cataloging-in-Publication Data

Names: Gupta, Parul (Law teacher), author.
Title: Industrial relations and labour laws for managers / Parul Gupta, Assistant Professor (Business & Corporate Law, Public Policy & Governance), Management Development Institute (MDI), Gurgaon.
Description: New Delhi, India : SAGE Publications India Pvt Ltd, 2019. | Includes index.
Identifiers: LCCN 2019005413 | ISBN 9789353281830 (pbk.)
Subjects: LCSH: Labor laws and legislation—India.
Classification: LCC KNS1220 .G87 2019 | DDC 344.5401—dc23 LC record available at https://lccn.loc.gov/2019005413

ISBN: 978-93-532-8183-0 (PB)

SAGE Team: Amit Kumar, Indrani Dutta, Vandana Gupta and Kanika Mathur

Contents

Detailed Contents

Preface

Economic transactions occur when two parties agree on the value or price of the transacted good or service, commonly expressed in a certain currency. However, monetary transactions account only for a small part of the economic domain, and major constituents are human resources participating in economic activities. Thus, the most important parties for economic and industrial activities are the workers and the employers. Both the parties have a common interest in industry, but many a time they are found to be pulling in different directions. This pull in different directions leads to industrial unrest. Therefore, to ensure a sustainable economic growth, it is necessary to secure cooperation of both the parties to improve the relationship between them, which is termed 'industrial relations'. Cordial and healthy industrial relations are a precondition to growth and stability of the industry.

Industrial relations are considered to be the most delicate and complex problem of modern industrial society, and here the government plays an important role in establishing harmonious labour–management relations. It is mainly because the government has enacted a vast body of legislation to ensure that the rights of industrial workers in industrial establishments are suitably safeguarded. These legislations are termed 'labour laws' or 'labour legislations'. Thus, labour legislations are enacted by the government to provide economic and social justice to the workers in industries. These laws provide guidelines to the employers/industrialists to deal with the matters of wages, wage incentives, facilities for workers and working conditions of labourers.

This textbook provides the insights into labour legislations in force in India and their application in maintaining peaceful and healthy industrial relations. The book covers legislations dealing with industrial relations, wages, work conditions and social security, and also the legislations regulating the employment of women and children in industrial activities. Aiming to provide not only the knowledge about various provisions of different labour laws but also the application of these provisions in industrial activities, the book compiles a number of legal cases and their judgements. The author has tried to develop an understanding of the application of labour laws in business activities by providing relevant examples, case details, and judgements and caselets at appropriate places.

Acknowledgements

I would like to express my gratitude to my family, friends and colleagues who saw me through this book, and to all those who provided support, talked things over, read, wrote, offered comments and helped in completing this project. Because of their cooperation and continuous encouragement, my dream to get my book published has come true today.

I would also like to thank the entire team of SAGE for helping me in the process of selection, proofreading and editing.

About the Author

Parul Gupta is a Faculty of Law at Management Development Institute (MDI), Gurgaon. She has been teaching law courses to management students for the last 15 years. Before joining MDI, she served at Army Institute of Management & Technology, Greater Noida, for more than a decade. Her special expertise lies in labour law, business law and environmental law. She is a Visiting Faculty of various Indian Institutes of Management (IIMs), Indian Institute of Foreign Trade (IIFT), New Delhi, and Indian Institute of Technology Delhi (IIT Delhi), delivering the course of business and corporate laws and employment law. In the past, she has been the programme director and trainer of a management training programme for the judicial officers of the state of Uttar Pradesh and for court managers, wherein she imparted training to more than 1,000 judicial officers within a span of 3 years. In 2012, she was awarded the prestigious Vice Chief's Commendation Card by the Western Command of the Indian Army for her significant contribution to the growth of the institute and commitment for work. Dr Gupta is a seasoned trainer, imparting training to executives of various public sector units, such as Indian Oil Corporation Limited (IOCL), Bharat Electronics Limited (BEL) and National Thermal Power Corporation (NTPC).

She has authored three books and a number of case studies. Her research interest lies in corporate environmental responsibility, social entrepreneurship, public policy and corporate governance. Dr Gupta writes regularly in journals of repute and has written a number of research articles in various journals of international repute.

1

CHAPTER

Fundamental Aspects of Industrial Relations

LEARNING OBJECTIVES

Upon completing this chapter, the reader would be able to:

LO1. Understand the nature of industrial relations.
LO2. Describe various approaches to industrial relations.
LO3. Know about the emergence and growth of trade unions in India and also their participation in industrial relation activities.
LO4. Explore the role of state and employer/management in industrial relation activities.

Introduction

The maintenance of cordial and peaceful industrial relations is an important and delicate function of an organization for attaining and maintaining high levels of production, and peaceful and sound industrial relations. The main aim of every organization is to produce maximum at minimum cost. This aim can be achieved if peace and continuity remain in the industry. Machinery, material and so on are the inactive factors of production and not able to change without the efforts of the active factor, that is, human factor. This factor can think, can understand, can have desires and can work. Good industrial relations increase the morale of the workers and motivate the workers to work more. It is important not only from the point of view of the organization but also for the prosperity of the community in particular and the nation in general. Prior to the Industrial Revolution, the problem of industrial relations was literally non-existent, as the owners were themselves producers or the production was carried out by the family members themselves. But, with the passage of time, the situation started changing. With the liberalization of Indian economy, the management relations have become important.

LO1: Nature of Industrial Relations

Industrial relations can be defined as the relations between managements and unions or between representatives of employees and representatives of employers. The term 'industrial relations', in its widest sense, includes relations in all aspects of work and employment between the parties to an employment contract.

The term 'industrial relations' has a broad as well as a narrow outlook. Originally, industrial relations was broadly defined to include the relationships and interactions between employers and employees. From this perspective, industrial relations covers all aspects of the employment relationship, including human resource management, employee relations and union–management (or labour) relations. Now its meaning has become more specific and restricted. Accordingly, industrial relations pertains to the study and practice of collective bargaining, trade unionism and labour–management relations, while human resource management is a separate, largely distinct field that deals with non-union employment relationships and the personnel practices and policies of employers.

The relationships which arise at and out of the workplace generally include the relationships between individual workers, the relationships between workers and their employer, and the relationships between employees. The relationships employers and workers have with the organizations are formed to promote their respective interests, and the relations between those organizations, at all levels. Industrial relations also includes the processes through which these relationships are expressed (such as collective bargaining, workers' participation in decision-making, and grievance and dispute settlement), and the management of conflict among employers, workers and trade unions, when it arises.

Thus, we can say that the term 'industrial relations' refers to the study of relations among employees, employers, the government and trade unions. Industrial relations include the following:

- Indian labour market.
- Trade unionism.
- Collective bargaining.
- Industrial conflicts.
- Workers' participation in management.
- Quality circles.

The need of industrial relation has arisen to defend the interest of workers for adjusting the reasonable salary or wages. It also helps the workers to seek perfect working conditions for producing maximum output. Workers/employees are concerned with social security measures through this. Industrial relations are also needed for achieving democracy by allowing workers to take part in management, which helps to protect human rights of an individual.

According to National Commission on Labour (NCL), industrial relations affect not merely the interests of the two participants—labour and management—but also the economic and social goals to which the state addresses itself. To regulate these relations in socially desirable channels is a function, which the state is in the best position to perform. In fact, industrial relations encompasses all such factors that influence the behaviour of people at work.

Important Aspects of Industrial Relations

There are two important aspects of the industrial relations seen in a modern industrial society:

- **Cooperation:** Modern industrial production is based upon cooperation between labour and capital. Here, labour stands for the workers who manage the factories, mines and other industrial establishment or services. Capital stands for the owners of business enterprises who supply the capital and own the final product. The cooperation between the two is one of the basic requirements for the smooth functioning of modern industries and the growth of industrialization.
- **Conflict:** The second aspect of the system of industrial relations obtaining today is the existence of conflict; conflict, like cooperation, is inherent in the industrial relations set-up of today. The prevailing industrial unrest, the frequency of work stoppages resulting either from strikes or lockouts and the slowing down of production are the occasional expressions of the ever-present and latent conflict between workers and the management.

Managing Employer–Employee Relationships

Some of the major approaches to employer–employee relations are as follows:

1. **Psychological approach:** According to psychologists, differences in the perceptions of employers and workers give rise to problems of employer–employee relations. The two parties view and interpret situations and issues involved in employer–employee conflict in different ways.

   Employer and employee consider each other less appreciative of the other's position and less dependable than him/herself. Similarly, the perceptions of trade unions are different from those of employers' associations. In addition, dissatisfaction with pay, working conditions, nature of job and so on causes frustration and aggression on the part of workers. These in turn lead to strikes, gheraos, boycotts, works to rule and so on. Similarly, employers resort to lockouts and other forms of protest on account of frustration over market conditions, government policies and other constraints.
2. **Sociological approach:** Industry is a part of society and it is a community made up of individuals and groups with different family backgrounds, educational levels, personalities, emotions, likes and dislikes and so on. These differences in individual attitudes and behaviour create problems of conflict and cooperation in industry.

   The value systems, customs, status symbols and institutions of the society in which industry functions affect relations between the parties involved. Urbanization, housing and transport problems in industrial areas, disintegration of joint family system and other social problems cause stress and strain among workers. The social and cultural changes shape behaviour patterns and cause adjustments in employer–employee relations. There cannot be harmony and peace in industry when the society is in turmoil.
3. **Human relations approach:** Industry consists of living human beings who want freedom of thought and expression and control over their lives. When employers treat workers as inanimate objects and encroach upon their interests and desires, conflicts and disputes arise. Workers want security of service, good pay and working conditions, recognition for a job well done and the

opportunity to participate in decision-making. Employers must understand the needs, attitudes and aspirations of workers. Human relations approach explains the behaviour of individuals and groups at work and helps in modifying or utilizing such behaviour towards the achievement of organizational objectives. If management and labour both understand and apply the human relations approach to their mutual relations, industrial conflict can be minimized. Human relations approach is interdisciplinary in nature because knowledge drawn from several disciplines such as psychology, sociology, anthropology, economics and political science is used in it.

4. **Giri approach:** According to Shri V. V. Giri, the late President of India, collective bargaining and mutual negotiations between management and labour should be used to settle industrial disputes. He suggested that there should be bipartite machinery in every industry and every unit of the industry to settle differences from time to time with active encouragement of government. Outside interference should not encroach upon industrial peace. Giri's stress was on voluntary efforts of the management and the trade unions to wind up their differences, through voluntary arbitration. He was against compulsory adjudication which cuts the very root of the trade union movement. He advocated collective bargaining for securing industrial peace.

   Thus, the Giri approach to employer–employee relations implies the encouragement of mutual settlement of disputes, collective bargaining and voluntary arbitration. The essence of this approach is internal settlement in preference to compulsion from outside, and voluntary arbitration and collective bargaining rather than compulsory arbitration.

5. **Gandhian approach:** Gandhian approach to employer–employee relations is based on the fundamental principles of truth, non-violence and non-possession. If the employers follow the principle of trusteeship, there is no scope for conflict of interests between them and labour. Workers can use non-cooperation (Satyagraha) to have their grievances redressed. Gandhiji accepted the workers' right to go on strike, but they should exercise this right in a peaceful and non-violent manner. Workers should resort to strike for a just cause and after the employers fail to respond to their moral appeals. Gandhiji suggested that in the process of resolving disputes, the following guidelines should be observed:
   a. Workers should avoid forming unions in philanthropic organizations.
   b. Workers should seek redressal of their reasonable demands only through collective action.
   c. They should avoid strikes as far as possible in industries of essential service.
   d. Workers should resort to strikes only as a last resort after all other legitimate measures have failed.
   e. If they have to organize a strike, trade unions should seek authorization from all workers to do so by way of ballot, use non-violent methods and remain peaceful.
   f. When direct settlement fails, workers should, as far as possible, take recourse to voluntary arbitration.

LO2: Approaches to Industrial Relations

The concept of industrial relations has a very wide meaning and connotation. In the narrow sense, it means that the employer–employee relationship is confined to the relationship that emerges out of the day-to-day association of management and labour. In its wider sense, industrial relations includes the relationship between an employee and an employer in the course of the running of an industry and may project itself into spheres which may transgress into the areas of quality control. However, the term 'industrial relations' is generally understood in the narrow sense.

An industry is a social world in miniature. The association of various persons, workmen, supervisory staff, management and employers creates industrial relationships. This association affects the economic, social and political life of the whole community. In other words, industrial life creates a series of social relationships which regulate the relations and working together of not only the workmen and management but also the community and industry.

Industrials relations are, therefore, inherent in an industrial life. These include the following:

- Labour relations, that is, relations between union and management (also known as labour–management relations).
- Employer–employee relations, that is, relations between management and employees.
- Group relations, that is, relations between various groups of workmen.
- Community or public relations, that is, relations between industry and society.

The term 'industrial relations' is used to denote a specialist area of organizational management and study which is concerned with a particular set of phenomena associated with regulating the human activity of employment. It is, however, difficult to define the boundaries of this set of phenomena—and, therefore, the term itself—in a precise and universally accepted way. Any more specific definition must, of necessity, assume and emphasize a particular view of the nature and purpose of industrial relations; consequently, there are as many definitions as there are writers on industrial relations. For example, the two most frequently used terms of 'industrial relations' and 'employee relations' are, in most practical sense, interchangeable; yet they have very different connotations.

The former, more traditional, term reflects the original historical base of unionized manual workers within the manufacturing sector of the economy, while the latter has come into greater use with the development of less unionized white-collar employment and the service and commercial sectors of the economy. (The term 'industrial relations' is used because it is the more commonly known and used term.) The terms may be used in a very restrictive sense to include only the formal collective relationships between management and employees (through the medium of trade unions) or in an all-inclusive sense to encompass all relationships associated with employment (those between individuals at the informal level as well as those of a formal collective or organizational nature).

However, it is doubtful whether the two approaches can, or should, be separated so easily—informal, interpersonal or group relationships are influenced by the formal collective relationships which exist within the industrial relations system, and it may be argued that the formal collective relationships are themselves, in part, determined by the nature of individual relationships. Clearly, the border between formal and informal or individual and collective relationships within organizations cannot provide a natural boundary for the subject matter of industrial relations. The way we perceive the overall nature of this area of organizational study determines, to a very large extent, not only how we approach and analyse specific issues and situations within industrial relations but also how we expect others to behave, how we respond to their actual behaviour and the means we adopt to influence or modify their behaviour. While examining the different approaches, it is useful to differentiate between those approaches which are concerned with the general nature of employment organizations and those which specifically deal with the industrial relations system itself.

However, it is important to keep in mind that they are primarily analytical categorizations rather than causative theories or predictive models, and there is no one 'right' approach; rather, each approach emphasizes a particular aspect of industrial relations, and taken together, they can provide a framework for analysing and understanding the diversity and complexity of industrial relations, that is, the complexity of the human aspects of work-organizations.

Let us understand industrial relations from different perspectives.

1. Unitary perspective

Unitary perspective is based on the assumption that the organization is—or if it is not, then it should be—an integrated group of people with a single authority/loyalty structure and a set of common values, interests and objectives shared by all members of the organization. Managements' prerogative (i.e., its right to manage, make decisions) is regarded as legitimate, rational and accepted, and any opposition to it (whether formal or informal, internal or external) is seen as irrational. The organization is not, therefore, regarded as a 'them and us' situation—as Farnham and Pimlott put it.

> [There is] no conflict between the interests of those supplying capital to the enterprises and their managerial representatives, and those contributing their labour…the owners of capital and labour are but complementary partners to the common aims of production, profits and pay in which everyone in the organization has a stake. (Singh, B. D. (2009). *Industrial Relations—Emerging Paradigms*. Excel Books, 2)

The underlying assumption of this view, therefore, is that the organizational system is in basic harmony, and conflict is unnecessary and exceptional.

This has following two important implications:

a. Conflict (i.e., the expression of employee dissatisfaction and differences with management) is perceived as an irrational activity.
b. Trade unions are regarded as intrusions into the organization from outside which compete with management for the loyalty of employees. The unitary perspective is found predominantly among managers—particularly line management—and, therefore, is often regarded as a management ideology. Fox has argued that management clings to this view because:
   i. It legitimizes its authority by protecting the interests of management and employees as being the same and by emphasizing management's role of 'governing' in the best interests of the organization, as a whole.
   ii. It reassures managers by confirming that conflict (dissatisfaction), where it exists, is largely the fault of the government rather than the management.
   iii. It may be projected to the outside world as a means of persuading them that the management's decision and actions are right and the best in the circumstances and that any challenge to them is, at best, misguided or, at worst, subversive.

2. Pluralistic perspective

Fox believes that this view of the organization 'probably represents the received orthodoxy in many Western societies' and is often associated with a view of society as being 'post-capitalist'; that is, there is a relatively widespread distribution of authority and power within the society, a separation of ownership from management, a separation of political and industrial conflict, and an acceptance and institutionalization of conflict in both spheres.

This perspective is based on the assumption that the organization is composed of individuals who coalesce into a variety of distinct sectional groups, each with its own interest, objectives and leadership (either formal or informal). The organization is perceived as being multi-structured and competitive in terms of groupings, leadership, authority and loyalty, and this, Fox argues, gives rise to 'complex of tensions and competing claims which have to be "managed" in the interests of maintaining a viable collaborative structure'. The underlying assumption of this approach, therefore, is that the organization is in a permanent state of dynamic tension resulting from the inherent conflict of interest between the various sectional groups and it requires to be managed through a variety of roles, institutions and processes. The implications of this view for the nature of conflict and the role of the trade unions are very different to those of the unitary approach.

3. Radical perspective/Marxist approach

The radical perspective, which is also often referred to as the Marxist perspective, concentrates on the nature of the society surrounding the organizations. It assumes and emphasizes that the organization exists within a capitalist society where, Hyman argues, 'the production system is privately owned...; profit...is the key influence on company policy...; and control over production is enforced downwards by the owners' managerial agents'. The Marxist general theory of society argues that:

- Class (group) conflict is the source of societal change; without such conflict, the society would stagnate.
- Class conflict arises primarily from the disparity in the distribution of, and access to, economic power within the society—the principal disparity being between those who own capital and those who supply their labour.
- The nature of the society's social and political institutions is derived from this economic disparity and reinforces the position of the dominant establishment group, for example, through differential access to education, the media, employment in government and other establishment bodies, and so on.
- Social and political conflict in whatever form is merely an expression of the underlying economic conflict within the society.

4. The social action approach

The social action approach is a variant of the system approach. In the system approach, society plays a dominant role while the actors such as employers, employees and their representatives keep a low profile and play a passive role in the process. On the contrary, the social action approach assigns an active role to the actors of the industrial relations. The actors' understanding of the work situation becomes more important than the social factors, and their independent views gain a greater weightage in deciding their behaviour towards industrial relations. The social action theory primarily considers bargaining as an important tool for the resolution of a conflict. The actors, according to this approach, are willing to cooperate with other actors in the resolution of conflicts, and bargaining forms the basis for such cooperation.

5. Industrial sociology approach

The aim of the industrial sociology approach is to investigate the underlying trends and patterns in the cause and effect of industrial disputes, both intended and unintended. Unlike most other approaches which focus only on the resolution of conflict as a means of achieving industrial relations, the industrial sociology approach focuses on the prevention of industrial conflict by tracing the cause of the disputes and then avoiding it. This approach provides a conceptual framework for investigating, analysing and specifying the structure and process within the organization that often produce conflicts. As per this approach, the job context and content, the technological characteristics and human interaction often result in the distributive, structural and human relations conflicts in the internal environment. In case these conflicts are not resolved within the organization, they may assume larger dimensions and become external conflicts. The removal of the causes of the disputes, according to this approach, facilitates a more effective maintenance of industrial relations.

LO3: Trade Unions: The Participants of Industrial Relation Activities

'Trade union' means any combination, whether temporary or permanent, formed primarily for the purpose of regulating the relations between workmen and employers, between workmen and workmen or between employers and employers, or for imposing restrictive conditions on the conduct of any trade or business, and it includes any federation of two or more trade unions, provided that this act shall not affect:

- Any agreement between partners as to their own business.
- Any agreement between an employer and those employed by him as to such employment.
- Any agreement in consideration of the sale of the goodwill of a business or of instruction in any profession, trade or handicraft.

Trade Unionism in India

Industrial relations in India are closely linked with trade unionism. This is true with regard to both public and private sectors, since trade unionism is inherent in the Indian economy as a whole. Trade unionism is a rationale and united movement of working class which seeks to make improvement of the economic and social status of the wage earners through united action (Michael, 1987).

Trade unionism is a by-product of industrialization in both developed and developing countries, and over a period of time, trade unions have grown to the stage of being considered as formal organizations yielding considerable influence on the socio-economic and political life of the nation. Trade unions were born at a time when the Industrial Revolution started in England. Later, the concept of trade unions spread all over the world. At present, the trade unions play a mature and vital role in developing countries. In India also, trade unionism has reached a high position, though it was in its early stages before Independence.

Origin and Growth of Trade Unions in India

Origin of Trade Unions

Trade unionism marked its way to India during the 1880s. The reasons for this lateness can generally be given as the slow progress of industrialization of the country, the special difficulties arising out of the literacy of the workers, their migratory habits and heterogeneous composition of the labour force in the industrial centres. The pattern of growth and character of the movement during different periods was shaped by the existing social, economic and political characteristics of each period.

In the pre-First World War period, the labour movement was humanitarian in nature and aimed at the enactment of factory legislations. In the post-war and pre-Independence period, the movement took a political character. Under the influence of nationalism, the labour movement played a vital role in the freedom movement. In the post-Independence period, the character of the labour movement further changed on the one hand, and competition for political power among the parties has led to the formation of union organization on a political basis; on the other hand, the planning for rapid national development has necessitated a rethinking on the part of unions and leadership about their activities. While they are committed to the development planning, conflicts have arisen sometimes related to the means achieving the goals but mostly reflecting struggles for power.

Regulatory Framework to Maintain Labour Relations in Early Days of Trade Unionism

During the early period of industrial development, efforts towards organizing the workers for their welfare were made largely by social workers, philanthropists and other religious leaders, mostly on humanitarian grounds. In 1875, a few social reformers, under the leadership of Shri Sorabji Shapurji Bengali, started an agitation in Bombay to draw the attention of the government to the appalling conditions of workers in factories, especially those of women and children, and to appeal to the authorities, to introduce legislation for the amelioration of their working conditions. Consequently, Bombay Factory Commission was set up in 1875.

The first Factories Act was passed in 1881 on the basis of the recommendations of the Bombay Factory Commission. But, this Act could not adequately address the concerns of the workers and Bombay workers protested against the Act. Moreover, no provision was made to regulate the working conditions of women workers. This has given rise to a great disappointment to workers. Later in 1884, Shri Narayan Meghji Lokhande, a factory worker who was said to be the founder of the organized labour movement in India, organized an agitation and called for a conference of workers in Bombay to make representations to another Factory Commission and thus, in the year 1884, another Factory Commission was appointed, the year, which according to V. B. Karnik (Indian Trade Unions—A Survey 1960), may be said to mark the beginning of trade unionism in India. As no redress was effected by government, Lokhande convened a mass meeting of about 10,000 workers in Bombay on 21 April 1890 and drew up a memorandum containing the following demands:

1. A complete day of rest on every Saturday.
2. Half an hour's rest at noon.
3. Working hours should cease at sunset.
4. The payment of wages not later than the 15th of the month in which they were earned.
5. Payment to injured workers until they recovered together with suitable compensation, if they are permanently disabled. The year 1884 can legitimately be regarded as the beginning of the labour movement.

The mill owners agreed to grant a weekly holiday to workers, and encouraged by this success, Bombay Milibands Association was formed in 1890 by Shri Narayan Meghji Lokhande. The purpose was to provide a clearing house for the grievances of mill workers and to help in drawing public attention to the cause of labour. This was the first union in India which earned for its founder the title of being the 'first trade unionist' of the country. In order to provide effective organ to the labourers, a working-class newspaper, *Dinbandhu*, was published by N. M. Lokhande.

Origin of Labour Associations

After 1890, a large number of labour associations were started in the country such as the Amalgamated Society of Railway Servants of India (regarded as quasi-labour union by the Bombay Labour Gazette) started in 1897, the Printers' Union, Calcutta, in 1905, the Bombay Postal Union in 1907, the Kamgar Hitwardhak Sabha and the Social Service League in 1910; however, such labour associations organized during this period were essentially labour welfare organizations and could hardly be regarded as modern trade unions since they wanted to mitigate the evils of modern factory systems and improve the lot of the workers.

The few attempts that were made during this period were simple manifestations of some local grievances that were felt strongly and once they were solved or decided, the unions or labour associations became extinct or nonentities. Thus, the trade union movements in this period used to be for the workers rather than by the workers. The labour organizations formed during this period lacked definite aim and constitution and leaders worked mostly in an advisory capacity. Mr Narayan Meghji Lokhanday whose efforts during the period were commendable was 'more a philanthropic promoter of labour legislation and workers welfare than a pioneer of labour organisation or labour struggle'. This period has been characterized as the social welfare period of our early trade union movement.

Organized Labour Movements in India

The outbreak of the First World War saw the beginning of the labour movement in the modern sense of the term. The then economic, political and social conditions largely influenced the growth of trade union movement in India. It was also responsible for mass awakening especially among the industrial workers. The new consciousness produced restlessness, discontent, a spirit of defiance as well as a new ideal and aspirations.

The success of the Russian Revolution of 1917 and the establishment of the International Labour Organization (ILO) in 1919 were other important factors that contributed to the growth of the Indian trade union movement during this period. The Madras Labour Union—the first union in India to be formed on systematic lines—was established by Mr B. P. Wadia in 1919. Altogether, 17 new unions were formed between the end of 1917 and the end of 1919. Due to the agitation of workers in the Buckingham and Carnatic Mills, the management declared a lockout in 1920.

Between 1919 and 1923, scores of unions came into existence. At Ahmedabad, under the inspiration of Mahatma Gandhi and Shrimati Ansuyaben, occupational unions such as Spinners' Union and Weavers Union came into existence, which later on federated into an industrial union known as the Ahmedabad Textile Labour Association (Mazdoor Mahajan Sangh). The association, ever since its inception, has been a model of sound unionism in India, based on the Gandhian philosophy of mutual collaboration and non-violence.

Formation of All India Trade Union Congress (AITUC) The year 1920 was of crucial importance in the history of the Indian trade union movement. AITUC was formed in 1920, and it claimed 64 affiliated unions at the time of its inception with a membership of 140,854. Out of this membership, 91,427 represented railway employees and 19,800 were from the shipping industry. All the other industries throughout the country could account for less than a membership of 30,000. State-wise, Punjab accounted for a membership of 70,000, while Bombay of 47,000 and Uttar Pradesh of 15,000. All the other provinces including Bengal and Madras could account for a membership of only ₹8,000.

Textile Labour Association of Ahmedabad remained outside the AITUC from the beginning. The inaugural meeting of AITUC was attended, among others, by such eminent national leaders as Pandit Motilal Nehru, Mrs Annie Besant and M. A. Jinnah, and Lala Lajpat Rai, who presided over the special session of the Indian National Congress at Calcutta in the previous month, also presided over the inaugural conference of AITUC. Col. J. C. Wedgewood of the British Trade Union Congress was present as a fraternal delegate.

Lala Lajpat Rai was elected the first president of AITUC and among the vice presidents elected were C. F. Andrews and Mrs Besant, and Diwan Chaman Lal was elected as the general secretary. Lala Lajpat Rai was also elected by the conference as the Indian Workers' delegate to ILO. B. P. Wadia, Diwan Chaman Lal and N. M. Joshi were elected as advisers. For many years, AITUC functioned only at the time of the annual conferences. It met once in a year when the delegates made speeches, passed resolutions including representation in the legislative councils and in ILO.

Efforts were made to bring about unity within AITUC, and it was in 1934 that a compromise was reached through the efforts of the office bearers of the railwaymen's federation and consequently the Red Trade Union Congress was dissolved. The National Trade Union Federation also merged with AITUC in 1938. The annual session of the unified AITUC was convened at Nagpur in 1940, of which Suresh Banerjee and N. M. Joshi were president and general secretary, respectively. But the unity did not last long as was envisaged.

Split of AITUC The Second World War brought in its wake several problems; while one section in AITUC was in favour of an all-out support for the war effort, the others were opposed to it. In November 1941, the former group established their own central organization called the Indian Federation of Labour. Jamnadas Mehta and M. N. Roy became its president and general secretary, respectively. A further split took place in June 1947. The deteriorating economic condition of the workers arising out of the rapid increase in the cost of living during and after the war made workers conscious of the need of making organized efforts for securing the relief, and there was a marked increase in the number of unions and organized workers. At this time, the Hindustan Mazdoor Sevak Sangh (HMSS), which was the offspring of the labour subcommittee set up by the Gandhi Seva Sangh in 1937 to organize labour throughout the country on Gandhian principles, was acting as an advisory body and not as a federation of unions.

Rise of Indian Trade Union Congress Realizing the need for the greater production and with a view to restore normal conditions in the country, the Central Board of HMSS called upon its various member unions to affiliate themselves to AITUC and to promote through that body of the policy and programme of Congress party. Since their attempts to change the policy of AITUC proved futile, the labour leaders in the Congress party felt the necessity to a new central trade union organization. Thus, the Indian National Trade Union Congress (INTUC) was formed in May 1947 after the setting up of INTUC; the Communist-dominated AITUC suffered considerably in both prestige and membership. INTUC has now been the largest federation of trade union and, therefore, it is the most representative organization of workers in the country. The objective of this organization was claimed to be an attempt to explore the solution of labour problems by peaceful means.

Meanwhile, there came another split when the socialists separated and formed the Hind Mazdoor Sabha (HMS) in 1948. The Indian Federation of Labour formed in 1941 merged with this body. Some of the radicals, under the leadership of K. T. Shah and Mrinal Kanti Bose, formed another organization in 1949, known as the United Trade Union Congress (UTUC). Thus, by 1949, the trade union movement was split again with INTUC, AITUC, HMS and UTUC representing the four rival groups and a few national federations and unions remaining unaffiliated with any of them. The close relationship of NTUC with the Congress party, of HMS with the Socialist party, of AITUC with the Communist party and of UTUC with the Revolutionary Socialist Party and other splinter parties of the left was and is indicative of the continuing political involvement of the trade union movement.

Emergence of Labour Associations After Independence Thus, soon after Independence, the trade union movement in the country was split up into four distinct central organizations of workers. In addition, some other organizations of workers came into existence such as the Bharatiya Mazdoor Sangh (BMS, 1955), the Hind Mazdoor Panchayat (1962) and the Centre of Indian Trade Unions (CITU, 1970). UTUC was split up in the subsequent years into two federations, namely, UTUC and UTUC (Lenin Sarani). With the split of the Congress party in 1969, there was a split in INTUC also and a new body known as the National Labour Organization (NLO) came into existence with the initiative of mainly the Textile Labour Association, Ahmedabad.

There are some other federations also functioning as all India federations, for example, All India Bank Employees Association, National Federation of Post and Telegraph Workers, National Federation of Indian Railwaymen, All India Mine Workers' Federation and so on. In addition, there are many unions which are not affiliated to any central body. Besides, many of the unions affiliated to some of these federations are also members of one or the other recognized central organization. A number of trade unions as well as their federations operate as separate units, though at times they may collaborate with one organization or the other.

Growth of Trade Unions in India

By the year 1924, there were 167 trade unions in India. Out of these, 148 trade unions were located in Bombay, Bengal and Madras. During 1924–1947, the number of registered trade unions rose very sharply. Growth rate of membership during 1924–1947 was 15% per annum. This growth of membership of trade unions could be facilitated because of:

1. Passing of the Trade Unions Act, 1926.
2. Setting up of the popular governments in 1936 under the British India Act, 1935.
3. The outbreak of Second World War in 1939 which intensified the economic activity. The post-war period has been marked by the most rapid strides so far made by the trade union movement in India.

The most important factors are:

1. The constant inflow of outside and international influences.
2. The pressure of trade union rivalries, often based on political or ideological differences.
3. Government's industrial relations policy with its provision for compulsory adjudication machinery.
4. The enactment of labour laws conferring special privileges on registered trade unions.
5. Desire of workers to unite for safeguarding their interest especially to face harder conditions for labour, such as retrenchment lay-off and so on.
6. Attempts made by some employers to set up unions under their influence.

Structure and Types of Trade Union in India

In India, the structure of trade union consists of three levels: plant/shop or local, the state and the centre. It is generally from the central level that the ideology of the important central federations of labour in India percolates down to the state and local levels. Every national or central federation of labour in India has state branches, state committees or state councils, from where its organization works down to the local level.

There are two types of organizations to which the trade unions in India are affiliated:

1. **National federations:** The national federations have all the trade unions in a given industry as their affiliated members. Every trade union, irrespective of the industry to which it belongs, can join a general national federation. Such federations are at the apex of the trade union structure. The main objective of these federations is to coordinate the activities of trade unions and to provide a national perspective to trade union policies. The central union organizations are national federations of labour based on different political ideologies. Because of their political leanings, the affiliated trade unions in the field of labour relations follow either a militant policy or a policy of cooperation with the employers and the government, or a policy of continuous strife and litigation. The trade union leadership to these national organizations is generally provided by the politicians. Such leaders are found leading a dozen or more unions in a particular state. The national/central federations are empowered to decide the question of jurisdiction of the various local and national unions.

   A majority of these federations allow their affiliates to bargain independently with their respective employers. The federations only act as coordinating authorities for different unions under their control. They also select delegates to represent workmen in international conferences organized by ILO or the International Confederation of Free Trade Unions. The All India Federation of Trade Unions has a regular structure.

   For example, INTUC consists of a central organization, affiliated unions, industrial federation, regional branches and councils functioning under the direct control or supervision of the central organization, the assembly of delegates, the general council and the working committees. INTUC functions through its affiliated unions, delegates, assembly, general council (including office bearers), the working committees of the general council and the Pradesh bodies. UTUC consists of the general body (delegates' assembly), general council and the working committee of general council. HMS works through the general council, the working committee and affiliated organization.
2. **Federations of unions:** These are combinations of various unions for the purpose of gaining strength and solidarity. They can resort to concerted action, when the need for such action arises, without losing their individuality. Such federations may be local, regional, state, national and international. There are a few organizations which are local in character, such as the Bharatiya Kamgar Sena, the Labour Progressive Federation, Chennai, the National Front of Indian Trade Unions (NFITU) and the coordinating Committee of Free Trade Unions.

Organizational Structure of National Trade Unions

Organizational structure of trade unions consists of four levels which are as follows:

1. **Conventions/sessions:** National convention/conferences are held at periodic intervals, say annually or biannually. This is the highest policymaking body. This is presided over by the president of the union attended by the delegates such as chairmen of state units, representatives

of specialized services, legal experts and delegates from international bodies and special invitees. Office bearers are also elected by this conference.

2. **General council:** General council consists of president, vice president, secretary and other office bearers. It carries out policy decisions taken by convention. Various standing committees are set up on rendering study, analysis and recommendations on various aspects such as legislative measure, research and publications and international services.
3. **Provincial bodies:** State units are headed by chairman of state/regional areas. State units also liaise with national headquarters (HQ), and they keep a close watch of faithful implementation of labour legislation and practices. They assist/influence state governments to pass labour-friendly legislation and executive/administration actions. They are also responsible for membership of various unions representing workers in industrial undertakings (units) and/or representing trade and industrial units affiliated to the central trade union. These state units get themselves attached to state/provincial/HQ/regional unions/units. HQ unions are responsible for welfare of their members and membership drive. As bargaining agents, they are involved in collective bargaining with central government and/or state government and assist passing legislative measures.
4. **Local bodies:** Apart from the central and state governments, there also exist local governments that provide assistance to the state governments to efficiently cater to the needs of the people. These local bodies work independent of the state government, supervising the specified areas assigned to them. These local bodies can be classified into three types in an urban area.
   a. **Municipal corporation:** To cater to the needs of the people of larger urban areas.
   b. **Municipal councils and committees:** To cater to the needs of people of smaller urban areas.
   c. **Nagar panchayats:** To cater to the needs of the people of areas in transition from a rural to an urban area.

Finance of Trade Unions

Finance is the most important resource to carry out different activities not only in industries but also of unions. An organization needs financial resources to survive, grow and meet the needs of its members in attaining their objectives. For a variety of reasons, the finances of many trade unions have not been sound. Funds are needed for attracting and retaining competent members. Funds, therefore, are needed to pursue activities, which will in turn benefit the union members. Finance has become a problem to the unions in India. This may be because of the poor economic status of their members. The employees would hardly meet family expenditure because of the large nature of their family structure with the low salaries. They do not find excess money to spare to union.

The decisive nature of Indian trade unions has also led to the dissipation of funds among a large number of organizations; consequently, there are many small unions without much financial backing and without much staff to do substantial work. The generation of funds has been inadequate. In some cases, subscriptions are not collected promptly or are paid by members only when they have a problem. In the former case, it is overlooked by the trade union management for fear of losing membership, and on the other hand, some members do not mind paying subscription to more than one union in order to protect their interests in times of need. Another mechanism employed, besides the usual collections, is the special levy at the time of distribution of bonus. Some unions collect donations during the bonus period, while other unions collect donations during the strike and lockout period. Some national federations and independent unions often generate some reserves to pay the workers during strike period or to employ research staff to keep abreast of current trends, but this is not the case with all the unions.

Leadership in Trade Unions

As formal organizations, trade unions are goal-oriented organizations and they have evolved certain institutionalized practices to realize their goals. This does not come by a process of socialization. It operates in order to secure the right type of leaders. The leadership role in a trade union has a variety of demands placed on it. Not only does it require a certain amount of technical knowledge of the nature of business of the particular organization but also a sympathetic understanding of the workers, their attitude and their problems. A certain amount of commitment and empathy for a cause, even in uncertain conditions, is necessary. Till now the attraction for persons entering this occupation has been the possibility of a political career in the future.

Some unions follow union leadership where the leader's task is to make the union effective, by improving the terms and conditions of employment of the worker and also by being concerned with the liability of the enterprise. The trade union organization, based as it is, in many cases on individuals or the national federation and their ideologies, has not been able to evolve professional cadre of leadership at the grass roots to the desired extent. In fact, quite often, a single union executive leader is responsible for running a large number of unions.

In some trade unions, outside and internal leadership can also be seen. In fact, the Trade Unions Act of 1926 makes a provision for this and allows for 10% of the leadership to be from outside the sphere of the organization. An outside leader is one who is not a full-time employee of the organization, whereas the internal leader is a person who is part of the organization. The chief feature of the trade union movement in Kerala has been the continued dominance of outside leadership even to the present day. In every country, outside leaders have guided the trade union movement in the initial stages, but the leadership gradually passed on to the workers themselves. When the trade union movement had attained maturity, the outside element liquidated itself leaving the leadership in the hands of the workers. Very few trade unions have been organized by the workers.

There are advantages and disadvantages in both the systems. The 'outsider' leader has a knowledge of industrial practices in comparable organization and therefore has more experience when he comes to the negotiating table to bargain. If he is a politician or a person with strong political links, then he may be able to set some advantages either in terms of policy or in terms of implementation of administrative action, especially if he belongs to or has linkages with the ruling party. On the other hand, his involvement with the plant-level problems is much less as he is not on the shop floor to understand the intricate issues applicable to a particular plant, has not been an employee of the enterprise or an insider, and lacks the required depth of understanding of local issues and specifics.

The outsider is a professional who has many units under his wing, all of which demand his time, including the larger function of liaison. The insider would not only have greater knowledge of the enterprise but also more time for sustained work, being concerned as he is with just one enterprise. Also, external issues and ideologies are not unnecessarily included which could happen when outside leaders are in control for whom ideology may be more important than getting the best deal under the circumstances.

A group of thought leaders believe that leadership must come from the rank of labourers themselves. That outsiders may use trade unions as passing the game of power politics is also true. Another disquieting feature of trade union is the 'outside' leadership, that is, cadreship of trade union by persons who are professional politicians and lawyers and doctors and who have no history of physical work in the industry. This is leadership by 'intellectuals' rather than by workers. It applies at the local as well as at the national level.

Trade Union Recognition and Registration

Trade unions are the group's set-up with the aim of trying to create fairness and job security in a workplace. A trade union is an organization of workers who have banded together to achieve common goals in key areas such as wages, hours and working conditions.

Basically, a trade union bargains with the employer on behalf of union members and negotiates with employers. Freedom of association has been the cornerstone of society. This freedom finds its expression in a democratic form of government. Trade unionism has been a movement launched against the concentration of economic power in the hands of a few individuals of society and for the purpose of promoting the welfare of working class. Trade union movement is not confined to the premises of one nation or country, but it has widened to the international field as well. It may be desirable to mention that besides trade unions in specific countries, there is one international organization of working class known as ILO for promoting labour welfare.

Registration and Legal Status of a Registered Trade Union

Registration of a trade union is not compulsory but is desirable since a registered trade union enjoys certain rights and privileges under the Act. Minimum seven workers of an establishment (or seven employers) can form a trade union and apply to the registrar for registration. A registered trade union is a body corporate with perpetual succession and a common seal. It can acquire, hold, sell or transfer any movable or immovable property and can be a party to contracts. A trade union can sue and be sued in its own name and no civil suit or other legal proceeding can be initiated against a registered trade union in respect of any act done in furtherance of a trade dispute under certain conditions. It is worth noting here that no agreement between the members of a registered trade union shall be void or voidable merely on the ground that any of its objects is in restraint of trade.

(**Note:** Legal aspects of trade union registration have been covered in Chapter 14.)

White-Collar Unionism

The history of trade union movement in India reveals that since its inception from the First World War, it remained confined among the blue-collar workers of large-scale industrial concerns. But, in the twentieth century, the concept of trade unions has changed. All categories of blue- and white-collar workers (including high executive officers) of government, private concerns and institutions are increasingly taking advantage 'of trade union movement'. The evolution of the blue collar unions and then the white collar unions is just an effect of the development of an economy. A number of attempts were made to explain the meaning and special attributes of white-collar workers.

Exploring the historical origin of this term, it is found that the term white collar stood for the office workers who put on cleaner and whiter clothes in contrast to factory workers. Blue-collar workers receive their remuneration in the form of daily wages, whereas white-collar workers usually receive their remuneration in the form of monthly salaries. White-collar work involves intellectual or brain work, whereas blue-collar work (manual labour) involves only physical labour. White-collar workers have a special intellectual character, whereas wage earners are concerned with blue-collar workers.

White-collar workers are the executive employees of public and private concerns, doctors, engineers, teachers of school, colleges and universities, research workers, scientific and technical personnel, bank employees and so on who are engaged in white-collared jobs. Thus, the white collar denotes a different type of social group, whose work behaviour and way of life signify their deep-rooted divergence in their socio-economic background. Levels of education, manner of speech, social custom and ideology as contrasted with the 'blue collar', the tasks performed by the white-collar workers and their physical conditions of work have also traditionally been contrasted with blue-collar workers. They have been engaged and paid over relatively longer intervals, enjoying longer holidays and other privileges too. The attitudes of the management towards white-collar workers have been far from being hostile. All these special attributes of white-collar workers make them different in terms of their willingness to unionize.

Factors Responsible for the Late Start of Trade Unionism of White Collar

In almost all countries, the white-collar trade union movement started later than the general trade union movement. There were several factors which hindered the early unionization in the white-collar jobs. In the early nineteenth century, white-collar workers used to enjoy better conditions of work and life in comparison to the blue-collar workers. The work was leisurely and pay scales of the white-collar employees were relatively good. There was a large measure of security of job. The idea of greater job security made the 'white-collar employees reluctant to join unions'.

Because of the monopolistic and urgent character of most public services, the white-collar workers were expected to owe an unquestioned loyalty to the government and the public; they kept themselves away from the trade unionism with the impression that unions were meant only for the blue-collar or industrial workers.

In the nineteenth century, the white-collar jobs received higher social status and the white-collar employees were drawn mostly from the affluent sections of the society. They were treated as members of the 'governing class'. The relative nearness of the white-collar employees to the seat of authority and their identification with the management group gave them an opportunity to enjoy higher status in organization and society as compared with the blue-collar workers.

The growth of large-scale enterprises required the establishment of a supervisory hierarchy, the lower ranks of which gradually found themselves drifting away from the management side and lost the identification which they earlier had with that. They also found themselves being squeezed between the two, that is, the organization of the blue-collar workers pressing from below and the top supervisory level from above. It was essential for them to organize in such a condition. The narrowing of pay differentials between the blue-collar workers has pinched the white-collar workers. This pinch has been felt not only because of the slow rise in their pay scales but also because of other amenities, that is, sick leave, long service leave, annual leave, working environment and adequate remuneration available to the blue-collar workers and denied in many cases to the white-collar employees. The absence of uniform pay scales among white-collar employees under different state and central governments was another contributory factor for its growth.

Trade Unionism in the Unorganized Sector

Labour in India refers to employment in the economy of India. In 2012, there were around 487 million workers in India, the second largest after China. Of these, over 94% worked in unincorporated, unorganized enterprises ranging from pushcart vendors to home-based diamond and gem-polishing operations. The organized sector includes workers employed by the government, state-owned enterprises and private sector enterprises. In 2008, the organized sector employed 27.5 million workers, of which 17.3 million worked for government or government-owned entities. Over 94% of India's working population is part of the unorganized sector.

In local terms, organized sector or formal sector in India refers to licensed organizations, that is, those who are registered and pay GST. These include the publicly traded companies, incorporated or formally registered entities, corporations, factories, shopping malls, hotels and large businesses. Unorganized sector, also known as own account enterprises, refers to all unlicensed, self-employed or unregistered economic activity such as owner-manned general stores, handicrafts and handloom workers, rural traders and farmers.

Categorization of Labour in Unorganized Sector

India's Ministry of Labour, in its 2008 report, classified the unorganized labour in India into four groups. This classification categorized India's unorganized labour force by occupation, nature of employment, specially distressed categories and service categories. The unorganized occupational groups include small and marginal farmers, landless agricultural labourers, sharecroppers, fishermen, those engaged in animal husbandry, beedi rolling, labelling and packing, building and construction workers, leather workers, weavers, artisans, salt workers, workers in brick kilns and stone quarries, workers in saw mills and workers in oil mills.

A separate category based on nature of employment includes attached agricultural labourers, bonded labourers, migrant workers, contract and casual labourers. Another separate category dedicated to distressed unorganized sector includes toddy tappers, scavengers, carriers of head loads, drivers of animal-driven vehicles, loaders and unloaders.

The last unorganized labour category includes service workers such as midwives, domestic workers, barbers, vegetable and fruit vendors, newspaper vendors, pavement vendors, handcart operators and the unorganized retail. The unorganized sector has low productivity and offers lower wages. Even though it accounted for over 94% of workers, India's unorganized sector created just 57% of India's national domestic product in 2006, or about nine-fold less per worker than the organized sector.

Trade Union Federations of Workers in Organized and Unorganized Sectors

In 1995, India had 10 central federations of trade unions, namely (arranged by number of member unions in 1980): INTUC, CITU, BMS, AITUC, HMS, NLO, UTUC, AIUTUC (All India United Trade Union Centre), NFITU and TUCC (Trade Union Coordination Centre). Each federation had numerous local trade union affiliates, with the smallest TUCC having 65 and INTUC having 1,604 affiliated unions. By 1989, BMS had become India's largest federation of unions with 3,117 affiliated unions, while INTUC remained the largest federation by combined number of members at 2.2 million. The largest federation of trade unions, INTUC, represents about 0.5% of India's labour force in organized sector and unorganized sector. In 2010, over 98% of Indian workers did not belong to any trade union and were not covered by any collective bargaining agreement.

LO4: State and Employer/Management: The Participants of Industrial Relation Activities

The Role of the State in Indian IR Regulative and Participative Bodies

In recent years, in many underdeveloped countries, the state has assumed an important role in the sphere of industrial relations. This has raised several questions pertaining to the propriety and desirability of state action in this field which, in the advanced countries of the West, has traditionally remained outside the purview of state regulation. Such questions have become more prominent in India as state intervention was given. As the Third Five Year Plan indicated, government intervention was necessary during the decade (1951–1961) of the first two plans, because of the failure of the parties to settle industrial disputes, in order to check the growth of industrial unrest and to gain for the working class some measure of improvement and security.

At the same time, the Third Plan recognized that intervention has produced widespread dissatisfaction, because of the increased recourse to litigation with attendant legal delays. Hence, a new approach to industrial relations is advocated—a marked shift from compulsory adjudication to voluntary arbitration, from legal to moral sanctions, from courts to codes. Unfortunately, this policy has not been adequately implemented. The increased intervention of the state has become a matter of concern to both labour and management. Labour contends that state measures adversely affected the growth of strong unionism and collective bargaining; management's view is that its freedom is restricted by the state's attempt to regulate industry through labour legislation and administration. The intervention of the state in labour matters is not new in India. As in many advanced countries, it dates back to the early days of industrialization. What makes intervention highly controversial is its magnitude. Whereas in the early stages of industrialization the state tried to protect the interests of labour by legislation, it now seeks to improve opportunities for the worker, giving him a partnership status, so that he has a sense of belonging to the industry. This shift in the approach to problems of labour marks the beginning of a positive state policy in the social field. India is a good example of a state endeavouring to direct labour–management relations to achieve social goals within a democratic framework.

Employers' Associations/Organizations

Just like trade unions being represented by workers for promoting their economic and social interests, employers join employers' organization (EO). An EO or employers' association is a collective organization of manufacturers, retailers or other employers of wage labour. EOs are formal groups of employers set up to defend, represent or advise affiliated employers. The EOs seek to coordinate the behaviour of their member companies during negotiations with trade unions or government bodies. Main objectives of EOs are summarized as follows:

Objectives of EOs

The objectives of EOs are as follows:

- Develop healthy and stable industrial relations.
- Promote collective bargaining at different levels.
- Bring a unified employers' viewpoint on the issues of industrial relations to the government in a concerted manner.
- Represent in the meetings of Indian Labour Conference (ILC) and Standing Labour Committee (SLC) boards in conformity with tripartite approach to labour matter. Employers' associations are formed to promote and protect interests of employers in trade and industry.
- Promote and protect the interest of employers engaged in industry, trade and commerce in India.
- Study, analyse and disseminate information relating to labour policy, labour–management relations, collective bargaining and so on.
- Offer advice concerning various aspects of labour policy.
- Liaise with union government and initiate steps that are representative and legislative in nature.

The EOs also aim at:

- Training and developing staff and members.
- Obtaining data on wages and conditions of work in industries attached to them. Come out with surveys, research-based reports on issues of importance to both labour and management.
- Taking up projects for social and family welfare.
- Dealing with safety and health at workplace and working environment.
- Initiating steps to improve public image and public relations.
- Educating the public regarding the character, scope, importance and needs of trade, industry and commerce represented by members.

EOs operate at following three levels:

1. **Local organizations:** They serve the interests of local businessmen. The Bombay Mill Owners Association, for example, has been formed to protect the local interests of manufacturing units operating within the city. Such bodies operate through the local chambers of commerce.
2. **Regional organizations:** The regional outfits such as Employers' Federation to South India, Employers' Association, Calcutta, are affiliated to central EO. They offer consultancy service and take care of training, safety and welfare measures on behalf of their members. They even have special committees for specific regions or industry-related problems.
3. **Central organizations:** All India Organisation of Employers (AIOE), Employers' Federation of India (EFI) and All India Manufacturers' Organisation (AIMO) operated as apex bodies governing the affairs of several regional, local associations. To have better coordination, a super structure called the Council of Indian Employers (CIE) was formed in 1956, bringing AIDE and EFI under one umbrella.

Different EOs in India

There are a number of EOs operating in India. Few most prominent and influential ones are discussed as follows:

- **The All India Organisation of Employers (AIOE):** AIOE is a unitary type of organization, set up in 1953; its members hail from manufacturing, banking, insurance and commercial establishments; and it has no sub-organization on an industrial or geographical basis. The president is elected every year.
- **The Employers' Federation of India (EFI):** It has a federal structure formed in 1933, and it has a governing body executive committee and the secretariat. The governing body formulates policies, the executive committee implements policies and the secretariat with its own permanent staff is responsible for carrying out the decisions of the governing body. It had only four presidents in over 50 years. The EFI was registered as a trade union in 1963 under the Indian Trade Unions Act of 1926.
- **International Organisation of Employers (IOE):** IOE represents the interests of employers in all social and labour matters at the international level. Founded in 1920 with HQs in Geneva, it has a membership of Employers' associations from over 100 countries. The Central Council of Indian Employers is a matter of IDE.
- **Standing Conference of Public Enterprises (SCOPE):** The objectives of SCOPE cover a wider ambit. SCOPE looks upon its tasks as both internal and external to the public sector. Internally, it would endeavour to assist the public sector in such ways as would help improve its total performance. Externally, it would help improve its total boundary role in conveying such information and assist the public sector in such ways as would help improve its total performance and advice to the community and the government as would generally help the public sector in its role.
- **Council of Indian Employers (CIE):** The main object in setting up CIE was to ensure closer cooperation and coordination between the two bodies which together represent particularly the interests of large-scale industry in India. In the year 1973, SCOPE joined CIE.

Summary

1. Industrial relations can be defined as the relations between managements and unions or between representatives of employees and representatives of employers.
2. The term 'industrial relations', in its widest sense, includes relations in all aspects of work and employment between the parties to an employment contract.
3. There are two important aspects of the industrial relations seen in a modern industrial society: cooperation and conflict.
4. In a wider sense, industrial relations include the relationship between an employee and an employer in the course of the running of an industry and may project itself into spheres which may transgress into the areas of quality control. Industrial relations are, therefore, inherent in an industrial life.
5. Various approaches to industrial relations are unitary perspective, pluralistic perspective, radical perspective/Marxist approach, the social action approach and industrial sociology approach.

6. The various participants of industrial relations are trade union, the state and employers/ management.
7. Trade union means any combination, whether temporary or permanent, formed primarily for the purpose of regulating the relations between workmen and employers or between workmen and workmen, or between employers and employers, or for imposing restrictive conditions on the conduct of any trade or business, and includes any federation of two or more trade unions.
8. The state institutions of governance—the Parliament, the President, the Judiciary, the Executive and so on—get their power from the Constitution and are bound by it.
9. With the aid of the Constitution, India is governed by a parliamentary system of government with the executive directly accountable to the legislature.
10. The Constitution of India states that there shall be a President of India who shall be the head of the executive, under Articles 52 and 53. The president's duty is to preserve, protect and defend the Constitution and the law under Article 60 of the Indian Constitution.
11. Article 74 of the Indian Constitution provides that there shall be a prime minister as the head of union cabinet which would aid and advise the president in performing his constitutional duty. Union cabinet is collectively responsible to the House of the People per Article 75(3).
12. Just like trade unions being represented by workers for promoting their economic and social interests, in the same manner employers join EOs.
13. An EO or employers' association is a collective organization of manufacturers, retailers or other employers of wage labour.
14. EOs seek to coordinate the behaviour of their member companies during negotiations with trade unions or government bodies.

Descriptive Questions

1. How important is it for the organizations to maintain industrial relations in the current time?
2. Throw light on different perspectives to understand the nature and concept of industrial relations.
3. Write a note on the origin and growth of trade unions in India.
4. What do you understand by white-collar unionisms? What were the factors responsible for its growth in India?
5. What is the role of state in the maintenance of cordial industrial relations? Discuss in detail.

References

Michael, V. P. (1987). *Industrial Relations in India and Workers' Involvement in Management.* Bombay: Himalaya Publishing House.

Singh, B. D. (2009). *Industrial Relations—Emerging Paradigms.* Excel Books, 2.

2

CHAPTER

Evolution of Labour Legislation in India

LEARNING OBJECTIVES

Upon completing this chapter, the reader would be able to:

LO1. Understand the history of labour legislation in India.
LO2. Know the objectives and principles of labour legislation in India.
LO3. Describe the types of labour legislations in India.
LO4. Explore the constitutional provisions for the protection of labour workforce in India.
LO5. Explain the rights of woman workers.

Introduction

Indian labour laws refer to laws regulating labour in India. Traditionally, Indian governments at federal and state levels have sought to ensure a high degree of protection for workers, but in practice, legislative rights only cover a minority of workers. India is a federal form of government, and because labour is a subject in the concurrent list of the Indian Constitution, labour matters are in the jurisdiction of both central and state governments. Both central and state governments have enacted laws on labour relations and employment issues.

Labour Policy in India and Labour Legislation

Labour has a vital role in increasing productivity, and management has to help create conditions in which workers can make their maximum contribution towards this objective. In free India, the labour movement and trade unions should be in a position to assume larger responsibilities in the context of new scenarios and challenges which are coming up in the twenty-first century. One of the tasks in the Five Year Plans is to evolve practical ways in which they can make an increasing contribution to national development and national policy. The growth of the public sector provides opportunities for working out new concepts of labour relations and the association of labour in management in industry. Economic progress of a country is bound up with industrial peace. Industrial relations are, therefore, not a matter between employers and employees alone, but a vital concern of community which may be expressed in measures for the protection of its larger interests.

The NCL, however, preferred to describe its approach as one in quest of industrial harmony rather than industrial peace. It emphasizes the absence of strike and struggle. The concept of industrial harmony is positive and comprehensive, and it postulates the existence of understanding, cooperation and a sense of partnership between the employers and employees. A quest for industrial harmony is indispensable, when a country plans to make economic progress. It may sound platitudinous but is nevertheless that no nation can hope to survive in the modern—the technological—age, unless it becomes strong, great and prosperous, and it is wedded towards industrial development and technological advancement.

Economic progress is bound up with industrial harmony for the simple reason that industrial harmony inevitably leads to more cooperation between employers and employees, which results in more productivity and thereby contributes to all-round prosperity of the country. Healthy industrial relations, on which industrial harmony is founded, cannot therefore, be regarded as a matter in which only the employers and employees are concerned; it is of vital significance to the community as a whole. That is how the concept of industrial relations involves the cooperation not only of the employers and employees but also of the community at large. This cooperation stipulates that employees and employers recognize that though they are fully justified, and if they are safeguarding their respective rights and interests, they must also bear in mind the interests of the community.

Evolution of Labour Legislation in India

Labour legislation in India has a history of over 125 years. Beginning with the Apprentice Act, passed in 1850, to the labour laws regulating not only the conditions of work of industrial establishments, but also industrial relations. This was followed by the Factories Act of 1881 and the first State act was the Bombay Trade Disputes (and Conciliation) Act, 1934, followed by the Bombay Industrial Disputes Act, 1938, which was amended during the war years and was replaced by the Bombay Industrial Relations (BIR) Act, 1946. The central government at this time introduced the Industrial Employment (Standing Orders) Act, 1946. In 1947, the government replaced the Trade Disputes Act with the Industrial Disputes Act, which was later modified. This law is the main instrument for government intervention in industrial disputes. After Independence, many laws concerning social security and regulation of labour employment were enacted, such as the Employee's State Insurance (ESI) Act, 1948, Employees' Provident Fund and Miscellaneous Provisions Act (EPF & MP Act), 1952, Payment of Gratuity Act, 1972, Equal Remuneration Act, 1976, payment of wages, registration of trade unions and certification of standing orders.

In India, all laws emanate from the Constitution of India. Under the Constitution, labour is a concurrent subject, that is, both the central and state governments can enact labour legislation, with the clause that the state legislature cannot enact a law which is repugnant to the central law. A rough estimate places the total number of enactments in India to be around 160.

LO1: History of Labour Legislation in India

The history of labour laws in India dates back to pre-Independence British Era as these labour and industrial laws were enacted by the British administration to protect the interests of British employers and industrialists. The post-Independence enactment of important legislations in the areas of employee security and welfare derives their origin partly from the vision of independent India's leaders and partly from the provisions in the Indian Constitution and international conventions like the ILO. The labour legislations were also enacted keeping in mind the international standards on human rights and United Nations (UN) protocols.

Post First World War, labour reforms were discussed internationally and its impact was seen in India with the introduction of the Trade Unions Act of 1923 and Industrial Disputes Act of 1929. The need was to regulate the relationship between employees and employers. In these Acts, provisions were laid down to regulate the workers' right to form unions for collective bargaining and to protest via strikes and lockouts.

Initial periods of imperialism were based on exploitation of the worker class. With the emergence of ILO at an international level and with the inhumane treatment meted out to workmen being replaced with an outlook of dignity of labour, the whole scenario of labour legislations began in pre-Independence India. After Independence, legislations related to worker welfare such as Provident Fund (PF) Act, Employee State Insurance Act, Payment of Bonus Act and Payment of Gratuity Act were enacted with the intention of providing security and retirement benefits to workmen.

Over a period of time, several amendments have been made to the existing labour legislations as per the needs of the industry. The latest amendment to the Factory Act allows women workers to work between 7 PM and 6 AM. Such amendments have been done after industry associations such as the National Association of Software and Services Companies (NASSCOM) and the Associated Chambers of Commerce and Industry of India (ASSOCHAM) made recommendations to the labour ministry. Now the BPO and IT sector which employs a large women workforce during its nightshifts benefits tremendously from this amendment to the Factory Act.

Pre-Independence: Concurrent Authority, Introduction of Individual Workers' Rights and Constraints on Collective Rights

The pre-Independence years discussed in this section begin post First World War and continue till Indian Independence in 1949. In this period, labour regulations in India were influenced by several factors that together altered the industrial and political landscape of the nation. Significant forces include communist influence in the labour movement following the Bolshevik Revolution in Russia in 1917, the establishment of the ILO in 1919 and the rapid development of trade unions, including the formation of the AITUC in 1920.

The pre-Independence framework of employment regulation introduced core concepts that continue to shape labour regulation in contemporary India. First, since 1919, India's central and state governments have maintained shared legislative authority over labour and employment relations. Concurrent authority was carried into the Constitution of India in 1949 and remains the legal arrangement to date. Second, from the 1920s through the Second World War, labour legislation under British colonial authorities did, to a degree, strengthen individual workers' rights within industrial establishments. This period was also characterized by strict legislative control over collective rights, including but not limited to restrictions on the right to strike. Third, labour protections did not extend beyond industrial establishments, thereby excluding many categories of workers from the ambit of protection.

Beginning in the early 1920s, labour legislation focused on regulating working conditions in factories. Laws of the period strengthening rights of individual workers within factories included the following:

- The Factories (Amendment) Act, 1922.
- Workmen's Compensation Act, 1923.
- Payment of Wages Act, 1936.
- Employment of Children Act, 1938.

These measures have been attributed to the influence of international labour conventions, including the following:

- The Hours of Work (Industry) Convention, 1919 (No. 1).
- Night Work (Women) Convention, 1919 (No. 4).
- Night Work of Young Persons (Industry) Convention, 1919 (No. 6).
- Workmen's Compensation (Occupational Diseases) Convention, 1925 (No. 18).

The regulatory framework under guiding industrial relations in present-day India was also introduced during the 1920s. Significant legislation included the Trade Unions Act, 1926, and the Trade Disputes Act, 1929. The Trade Unions Act, 1926, provided for registration of trade unions, gave unions legal status and extended some protection against civil and criminal liability in the course of industrial disputes. However, both the Trade Unions Act, 1926, and Trade Disputes Act, 1929, remained limited in their protection of freedom of association and collective bargaining.

Unregistered unions were excluded from protection, and the legislation did not obligate employers to bargain with registered unions. The Trade Disputes Act, 1929, severely limited the right to strike and required referral of industrial disputes to a conciliation board or court of enquiry—although the outcomes of a referral were not binding upon the parties. Both pieces of legislation faced strong criticism by the emerging trade unions, including the AITUC.

In the context of the late 1920s and 1930s global economic depression and unemployment, mass dismissals of workers in 1928 and 1929 were met with a wave of strikes. Against this backdrop, the British government established the Royal Commission on Labour in India in 1929. Recommendations of the Royal Commission contributed to legislation passed from 1931 onwards, including legislation protecting individual rights and defining collective rights. The Indian labour movement, however, boycotted the commission in protest of legislative restrictions on the trade union movement by the British Imperial government.

In response to industrial unrest against the conditions and effects of the Second World War, regulation of employment relations by British colonial authorities during the war years further restricted strikes and other forms of industrial action. Legislation of this period included Section 49A of the Bombay Industrial Disputes Act, passed in 1941. The Bombay Industrial Disputes Act granted the Bombay government the authority to refer industrial disputes to compulsory arbitration by an industrial court and banned all strikes and lockouts prior to arbitration. The central government's Essential Services Act, 1941, and Defence of India Rules (Rule 81-A of 1942 and Rule 56-A of 1943) laid down further restrictions against strikes and industrial action. The Services Act, 1941, and Defence of India Rules (Rule 81-A of 1942 and Rule 56-A of 1943) laid down further restrictions against strikes and industrial action.

The pre-Independence period set the legislative groundwork for central features of India's contemporary labour law regime that persist to this day. Shared legislative authority between India's central and state governments, simultaneous promotion of individual rights and limitation of collective rights, and exclusion of non-industrial workers from the ambit of protection remain prominent features of India's contemporary labour law landscape. However, legislation that protects individual rights at work expanded significantly in the post-Independence period as the central government was explicitly tasked with strengthening workers' rights consistent with constitutional articulations of social justice and the role of the welfare state. This proliferation of rights, however, did not extend to collective rights and continued to exclude non-industrial workers.

Post-Independence: State-led Industrialization, Expansion of Individual Rights and Restrictions on Collective Bargaining

This discussion of the post-Independence period includes the years from 1950 to 1991. This time frame is further divided into three sub-phases of industrialization: phase one of industrial relations covers from the 1950 to mid-1960s; phase two covers from the mid-1960s to 1979 and phase three covers from 1980 to 1991. The logic of India's legal framework governing employment relations, drawing from colonial precedents and extending through the 1980s, has been described as the 'logic of industrial peace'. However, the third phase of post-Independence industrial relations (1980–1991) begins a shift within Indian state regulation of the economy and labour relations from the 'logic of industrial peace' to the 'logic of competitiveness of firm and the economy'.

Post-Independence: First Phase of Industrial Relations (1950 to Mid-1960s)

In the first phase of industrial relations following Independence, corresponding to the first three Five Year Plans (1951–1956, 1956–1961, 1961–1966), India entered a period of 'national development'. Following Independence, in order to advance government-directed nation-building, the State took on the principal role of ensuring uninterrupted industrial production. The shift to state-led industrial policy was pursued through import substitution and formation of large, employment-intensive public sector enterprises concentrated in production of capital and intermediate goods. India built up a diversified industrial base, and the public sector expanded to provide crucial infrastructure, raw materials and capital goods sufficient to sustain industrial growth.

The development of large public sector enterprises led to employment growth in the organized economy and to the formation of public sector unions. While AITUC continued to expand and consolidate its position within the union movement, the growth of the public sector provided further scope for large-scale unionization. The Congress Party-affiliated INTUC developed and expanded with clear links in authority between party and union.

Post Independence, the pursuit of harmony in labour relations was articulated as Gandhian doctrines of trusteeship and non-violence. Harmonious industrial relations were pursued through measures to avoid strikes and lockouts by channelling dispute resolution into governmental dispute settlement machinery. This labour relations regime has been referred to as 'responsible unionism', attendant to the maintenance of industrial peace. Although articulated as consonant with themes of post-Independence nation-building, it has been widely recognized that the evolution of labour law in India post 1945 largely followed the pattern established by British colonial authorities. Significant features of this colonial pattern include a significant expansion of individual rights, however, limited to formal sector workers, exclusion of informal sector workers and restrictions on collective bargaining.

Strengthening protection for individual workers' rights was articulated as the responsibility of the central government. The central government was tasked with 'dealing with all phases of the worker's life', including 'housing, welfare, work, better working conditions and fair wages'. Ideas of social justice and the role of the welfare state, articulated by the national movement for Independence and enshrined in the Indian Constitution, were articulated as the grounds for labour regulations aimed at advancing workers' rights in this period. Consistent with these articulated objectives, a range of protective legislation was introduced between 1946 and 1962. Highlights include the following:

- Industrial Employment (Standing Orders) Act, 1946, requiring employers to provide employees with clear terms of employment as set down by a certified employment schedule.
- Factories Act, 1948, regulating conditions of work in manufacturing establishments to ensure adequate safety, sanitation, health, welfare measures, hours of work and leave parameters for workers employed in factories.
- Minimum Wages Act, 1948, establishing wage standards by fixing distinct rather than universal minimum wages for scheduled forms of employment.
- Employees State Insurance Act, 1948, providing a system of insurance in cases of sickness, maternity, injury, disablement and death.
- Plantations Labour Act, 1951, and Mines Act, 1952, regulating conditions of work on tea and rubber plantations and in the mining sector.
- The EPF & MP Act, 1952, providing retirement benefits to employees through PFs, pension funds and deposit-linked insurance funds.
- Maternity Benefit Act, 1961, providing both prenatal and postnatal leave entitlements and wage allowances for female employees.
- Payment of Bonus Act, 1965, securing payment of an annual bonus to all employees receiving wages below a specified limit. Parallel to this advance in individual workers' rights within industrial establishments, however, regulation of industrial relations also excluded numerous workers from protection.
- The Industrial Disputes Act, 1947, applies only to 'workmen' in 'industries'. The term 'industry', however, has been progressively expanded to include an increasing but still limited range of employment under subsequent amendments to the Act.

While individual workers' rights were expanded post Independence, collective bargaining rights were circumscribed through legislative measures, strong state intervention in industrial relations and judicial precedents. Trade unions were legally sanctioned but strikes and lockouts were strictly regulated. The Industrial Disputes Act, 1947, applied conditions under which workers were allowed to strike and distinguished between legal and illegal strikes.

The Act also designated no procedures to determine the representative union in a particular bargaining unit. Since employers were under no legal obligation to bargain with unions, there was no incentive for collective bargaining. Instead, privileging strong state intervention in industrial disputes, compulsory arbitration lies at the core of the Industrial Disputes Act, 1947, permitting the state to force any conflict into compulsory arbitration and to declare any strike or lockout illegal. These provisions allowed the state to intervene in industrial disputes and direct industrial relationships through civil dispute mechanisms. For the most part, under these provisions, disputes were referred to conciliation, then to the Labour Commissioner—and if these mechanisms failed, disputes were settled in industrial courts, labour courts or through binding arbitration. While during the late 1950s attempts were made to introduce labour legislation promoting collective bargaining, these attempts ultimately failed.

The system of interest representation that held sway during this period, including interactions between unions, politics and the state, exemplifies what has been called 'state pluralism'. Under this framework, the state also intervened in determining wages and working conditions. Central and industrial wage boards and the Bureau for Public Enterprises were responsible for setting wages—except in cases of dispute in which adjudicators were called upon to mediate. Collective bargaining was centralized, for the most part, at the national level but also, in some cases, at the industry and regional levels. This structure for determining wages, referred to as 'tripartism', ultimately resulted in wages rising at a slower rate than labour productivity.

Although this period is marked by a significant rise in registered unions, due to strong state intervention in labour relations, collective bargaining remained underdeveloped. Reinforcing limitations on avenues for collective bargaining, in *All India Bank Employees' Association v. National Industrial Tribunal* (1962), the Supreme Court expressly circumscribed the boundaries of the constitutional right to form a union. The Court held that the constitutional right to form a union does not carry with it the right of collective bargaining and the right to strike. Under this line of reasoning, while the right to strike is a legal right, it does not amount to a fundamental right and can, therefore, be circumscribed.

In summation, from the 1950s to the mid-1960s, the state pursued uninterrupted industrial production through pursuit of harmonious industrial relations. This dual approach of conferring individual rights and restricting collective rights, rooted in British colonial frameworks, has been described as a paternalistic approach towards workers. Although this approach to workers' rights was propelled through post-Independence public articulation of 'socialist' principles, it has also been critiqued as ultimately aimed at promoting the narrow goal of industrial harmony.

Post-Independence: Second Phase of Industrial Relations (Mid-1960s to 1979)

The second phase of post-Independence industrial relations corresponds with the 1967–1969 Annual Plans, the Fourth Five Year Plan (1969–1974) and the Fifth Five Year Plan (1974–1979). From the mid-1960s to 1979, state policy persisted in the mode of extending individual rights at work. However, this period also reflected two crises that began to reshape the landscape of collective bargaining: economic deceleration under state led industrialization, and a crisis of legitimacy for the state pluralism model of industrial relations, characterized by state mediation of interactions between workers and employers. These forces prompted the growth of left unions and informed decentralized bargaining in growth sectors.

However, although trade union strategies diversified, the government and centralized unions simultaneously proceeded in the mode of state pluralism. The period from the mid-1960s to 1979 is associated with overall industrial stagnation, falling wages, falling productivity, rising inflation (above

10% in 1966–1967 and 1967–1968) and severe food price inflation (around 20%). There have been various explanations posited for this period of stagnation, including the following:

- Deceleration in public investment; unequal terms of trade between agriculture and industry; inefficient state regulation in the public sector.
- Despite socialist rhetoric, little progress in redressing asset and income inequality, leaving rural land monopolies and industrial sector asset concentration largely intact. The economy also suffered from oil price shocks in 1973 and 1978.

Between 1966 and 1974, this downturn in the economy led to a sharp rise in industrial disputes (strikes and lockouts) and the number of workers involved in industrial disputes. Many workers also turned away from party-aligned leadership and towards more radical union leaders, including lawyers and student activists.

Rising union activity came to a peak during the all-India Railway Strike of 1974. In response to the Railway Strike, Indira Gandhi declared an internal emergency from 1975 to 1977—suspending a range of civil rights and liberties. State insistence on industrial peace and discipline was reasserted, trade union rights were suspended and industrial conflict was suppressed.

This second phase of industrialization saw legislative changes in the structure of collective bargaining practices and industrial relations. The 1965 amendments to the Industrial Disputes Act, 1947, facilitated a new pattern in bargaining: coalition bargaining between multiple unions and an employer led to settlements; and conciliation proceedings were then sought to convert these agreements into legally binding documents. Particular states, including Gujarat, Madhya Pradesh, Maharashtra and Rajasthan, also enacted state-level laws regarding union recognition. Following earlier legislation on union recognition, Maharashtra, for instance, passed the Maharashtra Recognition of Trade Unions and Prevention of Unfair Labour Practices Act, effective in 1975, making failure to bargain with a representative union an unfair labour practice. Real wage gains beginning in the late 1970s have been attributed to the acceleration of union activity and shifts in the structure of collective bargaining from the mid-1960s through the 1970s.

Further, changing the landscape of collective bargaining, the 1976 amendments to the Industrial Disputes Act, 1947, brought closure, retrenchment and layoff into the ambit of regulation—further strengthening state authority and extending it to somewhat limit the impact of market forces in determining employment status. These amendments, however, led to a sharp spike in lockouts. In 1976, the number of working days lost due to lockouts exceeded the number of days lost due to strikes. Consistent with the raft of legislation protecting individual workers' rights that began in the colonial era and extended rapidly in the first post-Independence phase of industrialization, the 1970s saw the passage of a series of central laws protecting extraordinarily vulnerable workers.

The Contract Labour (Regulation and Abolition) Act, 1970, regulated the employment of contract labour and prohibited its use in perennial activities engaging 20 or more workers. Other legislation of the period, protecting particularly vulnerable workers, included the following:

- Limestone and Dolomite Mines Labour Welfare Fund Act, 1972.
- Bonded Labour System (Abolition) Act, 1976.
- Equal Remuneration Act, 1976.
- Iron Ore, Manganese Ore and Chrome Ore Mines Labour Welfare Fund Act, 1976.
- Interstate Workmen (Regulation of Employment and Conditions of Service) Act, 1979.

This string of laws conferring progressive protection of individual workers culminated in passage of the Child Labour (Prohibition and Regulation Act), 1986, which abolishes child labour in particular operations and strictly regulates working conditions where child labour is present.

In explaining the impetus of the neoliberal economic reforms that began in the early 1990s, both advocates and critics of neoliberal reform take as their reference the development impasse of this second phase of industrial relations, from the mid-1960s through the 1970s. The emerging dual crises that characterize this period—a crisis in state-led industrialization and simultaneous crisis in state pluralism as a mode of industrial relations—extended into the third phase of industrial relations, from 1980 to 1991.

Post-Independence: Third Phase of Industrial Relations (1980–1991)

The third phase of post-Independence industrial relations corresponds to the Sixth and Seventh Five Year Plans (1980–1985, 1985–1990) and the 1990 and 1992 Annual Plans. During this period, the economy suffered from severe internal and external shocks, including the 1979 drought—one of the worst droughts since Independence; political instability in the northeast, a recession in 1980–1981, rising inflation and increasing oil import bills. These factors, together, led towards India's balance of payment crisis. By the mid-1980s, the economy began to move away from inward-looking growth strategies and towards export promotion and domestic competition.

The massive public sector strike in Bangalore in 1980–1981 and the definitive Bombay textile strike of 1982—the longest strike in post-Independence labour history—mark a period of significant changes in the landscape of the union movement. The rise and proliferation of 'independent' unions operating in major industrial centres have been recognized as a defining feature of this phase. Due to segmented and uneven developments in the industrial sector, plant-level bargaining by independent unions was often able to deliver higher wages and benefits packages than party-affiliated unions. However, the structure of labour–management relations varied widely between cities: for instance, the Mumbai labour movement experienced a proliferation of labour leaders who disclaimed allegiance to political parties, while in Kolkata, the industrial relations regime remained highly politicized with strong links maintained between CITU and the ruling community party.

In 1984, the Bhopal gas disaster—the accidental release of 40 tonnes of toxic methyl isocyanate (MIC)—killed an estimated 10,000 people and caused massive poisoning of more than 500,000 others. This catastrophe, which continues to have severe impacts upon successive generations, had no parallel in the world's industrial history. The horror of the Bhopal gas disaster shattered the silence on exposure of workers and communities residing in the vicinity of industrial establishments to hazardous waste within factories. The 1987 amendment to the Factories Act, 1948, gave workers the right to information about the nature and extent of workplace hazards and held directors of companies responsible for risks imposed by hazardous waste and other dangers.

This period also saw the rise of judicial intervention in interpretation and application of labour rights through public interest litigation (PIL). The PIL facilitated access to the courts for disadvantaged sectors of society by modifying traditional standing requirements, procedure to file writ petitions and evidentiary processes—including by appointing fact-finding commissions and amicus curiae. The introduction of PIL in 1979 provided a new avenue for the Supreme Court to vindicate constitutional commitments to social welfare. This platform, oriented to remedial innovation and large questions of policy, facilitated cases on behalf of marginalized groups, including industrial and other workers. Famous cases in which the Supreme Court protected workers' rights include *People's Union For Democratic Rights v. Union of India* (1983), ruling that working for less than minimum wage falls within the scope of forced labour prohibited by the Constitution; *Bandhua Mukti Morcha v. Union of India* (1984) tackling the bonded labour system and *Vishaka v. State of Rajasthan* (1997) laying down detailed guidelines on sexual harassment at the workplace.

The period from the late 1970s through the 1980s has been distinguished as the first phase of PIL, characterized by litigation by public-spirited lawyers, journalists, social activists and academics that addressed the rights of disadvantaged sections of society, including child labourers, bonded labourers, prisoners, persons with intellectual disabilities, pavement dwellers and women. The rise of PIL has been seen to correspond to the extent and level of judicial activism shown by the Supreme Court, including in interpretation and application of labour law.

During the three phases of industrialization post Independence (1949–1991) discussed above, India saw a robust period of state-led industrialization and experienced deceleration of the economy with the inability to sustain this model. These shifts in the economy precipitated a shift from the 'logic of industrial peace' that in large part governed the years immediately post Independence to the 'logic of competitiveness of firm and the economy'. Despite this significant evolution in the economy, however, throughout this period, labour laws and Supreme Court jurisprudence expanded constitutionally protected individual workers' rights. At the same time, the central government maintained strict legislative control over collective rights—although by the second phase of industrialization (mid-1960s–1970s), particular states began enacting state-level laws pertaining to union recognition. It is against this regulatory backdrop that neoliberal economic reforms unfolded, beginning in 1991 and continuing through contemporary proposals for labour law reform.

National Commission on Labour

The first NCL was set up on 24 December 1966 under the chairmanship of Justice P. B. Gajendragadkar. The Commission submitted its report in August 1969 after detailed examination of all aspects of labour problems, both in the organized and unorganized sectors. The objective was to study and review the living conditions of labour and the labour legislations since 1947. In pursuance of this legacy which involves industrial relations and economy, the Second NCL was brought into existence after a long gap of 33 years based on the recommendation of Indian Labour Conference held in September 1992. It consisted of 10 members.

While developing the framework for its recommendation, the Commission took into account the emerging economic environment involving rapid technological change, globalization of economy, liberalization of trade and industry, need for bringing existing laws in tune with future labour market needs and demands. Study groups were formed for detailed study and review of various laws, umbrella legislation for unorganized sector workers, globalization and its impact, social security, women and child labour, skill development training and workers education.

Recommendations of National Commission on Labour on Industrial Relations

The Commission recommended new labour laws on labour management relation, wages, occupational safety and health, small enterprise, hours of work, leave and other working condition of work place, child labour and unorganized sector etc.

The Commission suggested that there is no need for any wage board for fixing wage rates for workers in any industry. It had an opinion that each state or union territory should have the authority to fix minimum rates of wage not less than national level. It also recommended linking of child labour with education by enactment of Child Labour (Prevention and Education) Act. The Commission recommended that there should be a policy framework in the unorganized sector that ensures the generation and protection of jobs, access to jobs, protection against the exploitation of poverty and lack of organization, protection against arbitrary or whimsical dismissal and denial of minimum wages. It also suggested that a system of welfare should include access to compensation for injuries suffered while engaged in work, PF, medical care, pension benefit, maternity benefits, childcare shelter and old age support. Following is the summary of the major recommendations of the Commission:

1. Compulsory adjudication of disputes should be used only as a last resort.
2. Both organizationally and financially, trade unions need to be strengthened.
3. Workers' education should be intensified for building up internal union leaderships and making workers more knowledgeable and conscious about their rights and obligations.
4. The idea of one plant or one industry should be popularized.
5. Government should encourage the parties to settle their industrial disputes by negotiation and bipartite consultation.

Second National Commission on Labour

The second NCL was set up on 15 October 1999 under the chairmanship of Ravindra Varma which submitted its report to the then Prime Minister Atal Bihari Vajpayee on 29 June 2002. The first NCL recommended that a works committee be set up in any unit which has a recognized union.

The first NCL was constituted on 24 December 1966 which submitted its report in August 1969 after detailed examination of all aspects of labour problems, both in the organized and unorganized sector. The need for setting up of the Second NCL had been felt for the following reasons:

1. During the period of three decades since setting up of the First NCL, there has been an increase in number of labour force and so on because of the pace of industrialization and urbanization.
2. After the implementation of new economic policy in 1991, changes have taken place in the economic environment of the country which have in turn brought about radical changes in the domestic industrial climate and labour market.
3. Changes have occurred at the work places, changes in the industry and character of employment, changes in hours of work and overall change in the scenario of industrial relations. These changes have resulted in certain uncertainties in the labour market requiring a new look to the labour laws.

In light of the above position, the government decided on 24 December 1998 to set up the Second NCL so that a high-powered body could dispassionately look into these aspects and suggest appropriate changes in the labour legislation/labour policy.

The NCL is a high-powered body comprising of a chairman and two full-time members. In addition, there are seven part-time members representing government, industry and workers. The Commission was required to give its final report in 24 months from the date of its Constitution. The detailed terms of reference of the Second NCL were as follows:

1. To suggest rationalization of existing laws relating to labour in the organized sector.
2. To suggest an umbrella legislation for ensuring a minimum level of protection to the workers in the unorganized sectors.

In developing the framework for its recommendations, the Commission took into account the following:

1. Follow-up implications of the recommendations made by the Commission set up in May 1998 for review of various administrative laws governing industry.
2. The emerging economic environment involving rapid technological changes, requiring response in terms of change in methods, timings and conditions of work in industry, trade and services, globalization of economy, liberalization of trade and industry and emphasis on international competitiveness, and the need for bringing the existing laws in tune with the future labour market needs and demands.
3. The minimum level of labour protection and welfare measures and the basic institutional framework for ensuring the same, in a manner which is conducive to a flexible labour market and adjustments necessary for further technological changes and economic growth.
4. Improving the effectiveness of measures relating to social security, occupational health and safety, minimum wages and linkage of wages with productivity and in particular the safeguards and facilities required for women and handicapped persons in employment.

The resolution setting up the Commission was issued on 15 October 1999 after completion of formalities connected with the setting up of the Commission and elections to the 13th Lok Sabha.

LO2: Objectives of Labour Legislation

From time immemorial, we find that a constant struggle has been going on between labour and capital. We may say that the history of labour struggle is nothing but a continuous demand for fair return to labour expressed in different forms, for example, increase in wages, resistance to decrease in wages, grant of allowances and other benefits. The mutual conflict between the employer and the employees over the question of adequacy of their respective shares in the social produce constituted the crux of the labour problem. Capital has been exploiting the labour to their own maximum benefit for they have better economic footing and power and further stand in better position to dictate their terms.

With the emergence of new problems arising out of industrial revolutions, the new ideas of social philosophy, national economy and social justice have taken the roots in industrial order which are discussed here before. After the First World War, the cost of living considerably increased. The increase in cost of living and countrywide political upsurge found its way in economic discontent among the masses, particularly in industries. The industrial unrest and economic discontent led to a number of strikes and labour troubles. Labour problems constituted as serious menace to the society and needed solution so that wheels of industry may be kept moving. Employers devoted their sole attention to the maintenance of machines and improvement of the technical know-how to the utter neglect of workers employed to run the machines, because they were available in large numbers and could be replaced in no time. The contribution of the capital and labour in any industry is equally important. Therefore, the prosperity of an industry depends on the cooperation of the capital and labour. As disputes between capital and labour are inevitable, the object of industrial legislation is to ensure the smooth relationship between the two.

The objectives of labour legislation are a developing concept and require ceaseless efforts to achieve them on a continuous basis. In its landmark judgement in Hindustan *Antibiotics v. The Workmen* (A.I.R. 1967, S.C. 948; (1967) 1, Lab.L.J.114), the Supreme Court of India made a significant observation. The object of the industrial law, said the Court, was to bring in improvements in the service conditions of industrial labour by providing them the normal amenities of life which would lead to industrial peace. This would accelerate the productive activities of the nation, bringing prosperity to all and further improving the conditions of labour. Labour legislation in India has sought to achieve mainly the following objectives:

1. Establishment of justice—social, political and economic.
2. Assurance of social welfare of workers. These laws help the employees to improve their social status, that is, material and morale of the workers by providing adequate wages and safety measures, ensuring appropriate working hours and health facilities.
3. Contribution to the growth of national economy. Labour legislations, by satisfying worker's needs, are able to increase their efficiency. Thus, efficient industry finally contributes a lot to improve national economy.
4. Facilitating the opportunities to all workers, irrespective of caste, creed, religion, beliefs, for the development of their personality.
5. Protection of the weaker section in the community.
6. Maintenance of industrial peace.
7. Creation of conditions for economic growth.
8. Protection and improvement of labour standards.
9. Protection of workers from exploitation.
10. Guarantee right of workmen to combine and form association or unions.
11. Assurance of right of workmen to bargain collectively for the betterment of their service conditions. Introduction to labour legislation.
12. Interference of state as a protector of social well-being than to remain an onlooker.
13. Assurance of human rights and human dignity. Proper regulation of employee–employer relationship is a condition precedent for planned, progressive and purposeful development of any society.

Principles of Labour Legislation in India

Labour legislation in India derives its philosophy and content from the Directive Principles of the Constitution and has been evolving in response to specific needs of the situation to suit requirements of planned economic development and social justice. It has been envisaged that growth of the economy would not only increase production but also absorb the backlog of unemployment and under-employment and a substantial proportion of additional labour force. Salient features of labour legislation are based on certain fundamental principles. Following is a brief discussion on the principles guiding the labour legislation in India:

1. **Principle of protection:** The principle of protection suggests enactment of labour legislation to protect those workers who are not able to protect their interests on their own and also workers, in particular industries, against the hazards of industrial processes.
2. **Principle of social justice:** The principle of social justice implies establishment of equality in social relationships. It aims at removing discrimination suffered by particular groups of labour. History is replete with examples where certain groups of society or labour have been subjected to various sorts of disabilities as compared to other groups or workers in general.
3. **Principle of regulation:** The principle of regulation generally seeks to regulate the relationships between the employers and their associations, on the one hand, and workers and their organizations, on the other hand. As the relationships between the two groups have repercussions on the society, the laws enacted on this principle also aim at safeguarding the interests of the society against the adverse consequences of collusion or combination between them. Thus, the principle of regulation seeks to regulate the balance of power in the relationships of the two dominant groups in industrial relations.
4. **Principle of welfare:** Although the protective and social security laws have the effect of promoting labour welfare, special labour welfare or labour welfare fund laws have also been enacted, with a view to providing certain welfare amenities to the workers, and often to their family members also. The main purpose behind the enactment of labour laws on this principle is to ensure the provision of certain basic amenities to workers at their place of work, and also to improve the living conditions of workers and their family members.
5. **Principle of social security:** Lord William Beveridge, the pioneer in initiating a comprehensive social security plan, mentioned five giants in the patch of social progress, namely, 'want', 'sickness', 'ignorance', 'squalor' and 'idleness'.

   One of the outstanding measures to mitigate the hardship is to make available social security benefits under the coverage of legislation. Social security legislation may be kept under two broad categories—social insurance legislation and social assistance legislation. In social insurance, benefits are generally made available to the insured persons, under the condition of having paid the required contributions and fulfilling certain eligibility conditions.

   In social assistance also, the beneficiaries receive benefits as a matter of right, but they do not have to make any contributions. The finance is made available by the state or a source specified by the state. Social assistance benefits are generally paid to persons of insufficient means and on consideration of their minimum needs.
6. **Principle of economic development:** Labour laws have also been enacted keeping in view the need for economic and industrial development of particular countries. Improvement of physical working conditions, establishment of industrial peace, provision of machineries for settlement of industrial disputes, formation of forums of workers' participation in management, prohibition of unfair labour practices, restrictions on strikes and lockouts, provision of social security benefits and welfare facilities, certification of collective agreements and regulation of hours of work have direct or indirect bearing on the pace and extent of economic development.
7. **Principle of international obligation:** This principle postulates enactment of labour laws with a view to giving effect to the provisions of resolutions, adopted by international organizations such

as ILO, UN and similar other bodies. In general, the countries ratifying the resolutions or agreements are under the obligation to enforce them. One of the instruments of doing so is the enactment of laws. The basic principles of the labour policy of ILO are as follows:

- Labour is not a commodity.
- Freedom of expression and of association are essential to continued progress.
- Poverty anywhere constitutes a danger to prosperity everywhere.
- War against want requires to be carried on with unending vigour within each nation and by continuous effort in which the representatives of workers and employers enjoying equal status with those of governments join with them in free discussion and democratic decisions with a view to promoting of common welfare.
- In enacting labour legislation, the general economic situation of the country has to be borne in mind lest the very objective of the legislation be defeated. The state of national economy is an important factor in influencing labour legislation in the country. Legislation is essential to safeguard the interests of the labouring classes. In the absence of legislation, the factory worker is bound to be exploited by the employer. Labour legislation provides essential safeguard to workers in matters of conditions of work, hours of work, safety in the factories, minimum wages, bonus, equal wages for men and women for the same work, prohibition of employment of children and that of women in hazardous industries.

LO3: Types of Labour Legislations in India

A large number of labour legislations have been enacted to promote the condition of labour, keeping in view development of industry and national economy. The labour legislations can be broadly categorized in following three categories:

1. **Protective and employment legislation:** The laws of this category either are concerned with the health and safety of the worker at his workplace or aim at protecting the worker by ensuring that he gets paid for the work done at the end of each month. Some of the Acts belonging to this category are the Factories Act, 1948, the Contract Labour (Regulation and Abolition) Act, 1970, and so on.
2. **Social security legislation:** The social security measures are meant to protect workers against risks of undue hardship and privation. The ESI Act, for example, provides medical care, accident compensation and compensation to a worker when he is unemployed or ill. The PF and gratuity schemes are meant to provide to the worker with some income after his retirement.
3. **Regulatory legislation:** The main objective of regulatory acts is to provide for a just settlement of disputes by negotiations, conciliation, mediation, voluntary arbitration and compulsory adjudication. The Industrial Disputes Act, 1947, Industrial Employment (Standing Orders) Act, 1946, and the Trade Unions Act, 1926, and so on come under this category. The Industrial Disputes Act, 1947, basically provides for the investigation and settlement of industrial disputes. The Act places constraints on strikes and lockouts. It provides for a works committee at the plant level to ensure that management and worker contribute to the efficient day-to-day working of the enterprise. The Industrial Employment (Standing Order) Act, 1946, requires management to specify the terms and conditions of employment and communicate these to the workers. The Trade Unions Act, 1926, is the enabling legislation for the formation of trade unions.

A further refined categorization of labour legislations is presented as follows:

1. Legislation related to industrial relations:

- The Trade Unions Act, 1926, and The Trade Union Amendment Act, 2011
- The Industrial Employment (Standing Orders) Act, 1946
- The Industrial Disputes Act, 1947

2. Legislation pertaining to wages:

- The Payment of Wages Act, 1936, and the Payment of Wages (Amendment) Act, 2005
- The Minimum Wages Act, 1948
- The Payment of Bonus Act, 1965
- The Equal Remuneration Act, 1976

3. Legislation related to work conditions:

- The Factories Act, 1948
- The Contract Labour (Regulation and Abolition) Act, 1970
- The Shops and Establishment (SEA) Act, 1953
- The Dock Workers (Regulation of Employment) Act, 1948
- The Plantation Labour Act, 1951
- The Mines Act, 1952
- The Merchant Shipping Act, 1958
- The Building and Other Construction Workers (Regulation of Employment & Conditions of Service) Act, 1996

4. Legislation pertaining to women and children:

- The Maternity Benefit Act, 1961
- The Child Labour (Prohibition and Regulation) Act, 1986

5. Legislation pertaining to social security:

- The Workmen's Compensation Act, 1923, and The Workmen's Compensation (Amendment) Act, 2000
- The Employees' State Insurance Act, 1948
- The EPF & MP Act, 1952, and the EPF & MP (Amendment) Act, 1996
- The Payment of Gratuity Act, 1972
- The Unorganised Workers' Social Security Act, 2008

For industrial regeneration, it is necessary that the partners of industry must cure their respective defects. Since Independence, a lot has been done by legislation and public opinion to improve the conditions of workers. The employers are now realizing that it is their duty as a citizen of a democratic country to forego their acquisitive tendencies of the past and set a new ideal for the future of the country. At the same time, it is the duty of the workers to realize their responsibility in improving the work efficiency and help in stepping up production resulting in greater profits, and prosperity of the industry to be ultimately shared by the management, workers and community at large. Workers are the dominant partners in the industrial undertaking and without their cooperation, good work, discipline, integrity and character the industry will not be able to produce effective results or profits.

The machine touch in the industry may be efficient, but if the human element refuses to cooperate, the industry is bound to fail in the long run. Therefore, the profits of the industry must be shared by employers, workers and the community, the workers claiming a dominant share, being the producers of wealth. Modern industrialization and economic growth, envisaged in the planning would, of necessity, call for increased use of legislation not only for tackling the social and economic problems that are existing but also for creating such industrial conditions as would seem to be conductive for establishing a healthy and just social order.

LO4: Constitutional Provisions for the Protection of Labour Workforce in India

The Indian Constitution is the world's longest. At its commencement, it had 395 articles in 22 parts and 8 schedules. It is made up of approximately 145,000 words, making it the second largest active constitution in the world. In its current form (September 2012), it has a preamble, 25 parts with 448 articles, 12 schedules, 5 appendices and the latest of which came into force on 8 September 2016.

As discussed before, labour is a concurrent subject in the Constitution of India. Indian Constitution mentions the subject matter for the welfare of labour including conditions of work, PFs, workmen's compensation and pensions, and governments are competent to legislate on labour matters and administer the same. The bulk of important legislative acts have been enacted by the Parliament.

The Constitution of India has conferred innumerable rights on the protection of labour. Indian Constitution through various articles, though not directly but indirectly, protects, supports and acts as a guideline to various labour laws for their effective implementation and functioning. The relevance of the dignity of human labour and the need for protecting and safeguarding the interest of labour as human beings has been enshrined in Chapter III (Articles 16, 19, 21, 23 and 24) and Chapter IV (Articles 39, 39-A, 41, 42, 43, 43A, 46, 47 and 54) of the Constitution of India keeping in line with Fundamental Rights and Directive Principles of State Policy which set an aim to which the activities of the state are to be guided. These Directive Principles provide:

- For securing the health and strength of employees, men and women.
- That the tender age of children is not abused.
- That citizens are not forced by economic necessity to enter avocations unsuited to their age or strength.
- Just and humane conditions of work and maternity relief are provided.
- That the government shall take steps, by suitable legislation or in any other way, to secure the participation of employee in the management of undertakings, establishments or other organizations engaged in any industry.

Let us discuss some of the important articles of Indian Constitution protecting the labour rights.

1. Article 14—Equality before law

Article 14 states that the state shall not deny to any person equality before the law or the equal protection of the laws within the territory of India prohibition of discrimination on grounds of religion, race, caste, sex or place of birth. The concept of equality does not mean absolute equality among human beings which is physically not possible to achieve. It is a concept implying absence of any special privilege by reason of birth, creed or the like in favour of any individual, and also the equal subject of all individuals and classes to the ordinary law of the land. As Dr Jennings puts it,

> Equality before the law means that among equals the law should be equal and should be equally administered, that like should be treated alike. The right to sue and be sued, to prosecute and be prosecuted for the same kind of action should be same for all citizens of full age and understanding without distinctions of race, religion, wealth, social status or political influence. (https://www.legalbites.in/law-notes-constitution-right-to-equality-under-article-14-of-constitution/, accessed 25 November 2017)

It only means that all persons under similar circumstances shall be treated alike both in the privileges conferred and in the liabilities imposed by the laws. Equal law should be applied to all in the same situation, and there should be no discrimination between one person and another. As regards the subject matter of the legislation, their position is the same.

2. Article 21—Protection of life and personal liberty

Article 21 states that no person shall be deprived of his life or personal liberty except according to procedure established by law. The sweep of the right to life, conferred by Article 21, is wide and far reaching. 'Life' means something more than mere animal existence. It does not mean merely that life cannot be extinguished or taken away as, for example, by the imposition and execution of the death sentence, except according to procedure established by law. That is but one aspect of the right to life. An equally important facet of that right is the right to livelihood because no person can live without the means of living, that is, the means of livelihood. If the right to livelihood is not treated as a part of the constitutional right to life, the easiest way of depriving a person of his right to life would be to deprive him of his means of livelihood to the point of abrogation. Such deprivation would not only denude the life of its effective content and meaningfulness but it would also make life impossible to live. There is thus a close nexus between life and the means of livelihood, and as such that which alone makes it possible to live, leaving aside what makes life liveable, must be deemed to be an integral component of the right of life.

3. Article 23—Prohibition of traffic in human beings and forced labour

Article 23 of the Constitution prohibits traffic in human being and beggar and other similar forms of forced labour. The second part of this Article declares that any contravention of this provision shall be an offence punishable in accordance with law. Clause (2), however, permits the state to impose compulsory services for public purposes provided that in making so it shall not make any discrimination on grounds only of religion, race, caste or class or any of them. 'Traffic in human beings' means selling and buying men and women like goods and includes immoral traffic in women and children for 'immoral' or other purposes. Although slavery is not expressly mentioned in Article 23, it is included in the expression 'traffic in human being'. Under Article 35 of the Constitution, the Parliament is authorized to make laws for punishing acts prohibited by this article. In pursuance of this article, the Parliament has passed the

Suppression of Immoral Traffic in Women and Girls Act, 1956, for punishing acts which result in traffic in human beings. Article 23 protects the individual not only against the state but also against private citizens. It imposes a positive obligation on the state to take steps to abolish evils of 'traffic in human beings' and beggar and other similar forms of forced labour wherever they are found. Article 23 prohibits the system of 'bonded labour' because it is a form of force labour within the meaning of this Article.

4. Article 39—Equal justice and free legal aid, and Article 41—Right to work to education and to public assistance in certain cases

The principles contained in Articles 39(a) and 41 must be regarded as equally fundamental in the understanding and interpretation of the meaning and content of fundamental rights. Article 39(a) directs the state to secure that the operation of the legal system promotes justice, on a basis of equal opportunity, and shall, in particular, provide free legal aid, by suitable legislation or schemes or in any other way, to ensure that opportunities for securing justice are not denied to any citizen by reason of economic or other disabilities. Article 41 states that the state shall, within the limits of its economic capacity and development, make effective provision for securing the right to work, to education and to public assistance in cases of unemployment, old age, sickness and disablement, and in other cases of undeserved want.

If there is an obligation upon the state to secure to the citizens an adequate means of livelihood and the right to work, it would be sheer pedantry to exclude the right to livelihood from the content of the right to life. The state may not, by affirmative action, be compellable to provide adequate means of livelihood or work to the citizens. But, any person, who is deprived of his right to livelihood except according to just and fair procedure established by law, can challenge the deprivation as offending the right conferred under the Article 21. Certain principles of policy to be followed by the state and the state shall, in particular, direct its policy towards securing the following:

- That the citizen, men and women equally have the right to an adequate means of livelihood.
- That the ownership and control of the material resources of the community are so distributed as best to subserve the common good.
- That the operation of the economic system does not result in the concentration of wealth and means of production to the common detriment.
- That there is equal pay for equal work for both men and women.
- That the health and strength of workers, men and women, and the tender age of children are not abused and that citizens are not forced by economic necessity to enter avocations unsuited to their age or strength.
- That children are given opportunities and facilities to develop in a healthy manner and in conditions of freedom and dignity and that childhood and youth are protected against exploitation and against moral and material abandonment.

LO5: Rights of Woman Workers

Over the years, several enactments have been passed for the welfare of the working people and protection of Indian employee rights. Some of these enactments carve out special provisions for the women workforce. In recent times, we have seen an increase in the number of women professionals in organizations, both public and private, due to the immense opportunities available and with the booming of specific industries like IT and start-ups.

Labour Laws in India for the Protection of the Working Woman

There are various labour laws in India which exist as on date, which provide benefits and security to all employees (whether male or female). However, for this article, we will touch upon a few of the important laws and will provide you a gist of these laws. Women constitute 50% of our population and if they do not come out and work, then our country will never grow at the pace we all envision it to grow, and for that very reason, governments over time have taken special care to enact and amend laws to ensure greater participation of women in the growth story of India.

The Maternity Benefit Amendment Act, 2017

Prior to this, the previous Maternity Benefit Act was passed in 1961. This amendment has not only expanded the term of the leave but rather has additionally prompted the presentation of numerous new provisions. A portion of the key arrangements in the altered Maternity advantage act are as follows:

- The maternity leave after the correction has been raised from the present 12 weeks to 26 weeks. Prenatal leave has likewise been increased from 6 weeks to 2 months. However, a lady with effectively at least two kids is qualified for 12 weeks' maternity leave. The pre-birth leave, for this situation, stays a month and a half.
- The correction has likewise broadened the advantage of the old represent supportive moms. A leave period of 12 weeks will be allowed to a lady who has adopted a child younger than 3 months. An authorizing mother is likewise qualified for a 12-week leave from the date the youngster is given over to her. An authorizing mother is characterized as a 'Biological mother who utilizes her egg to make a foetus embedded in some other lady' (the lady who brings forth the youngster is called host or surrogate mother).
- The Act has now made it necessary for businesses to educate a female employee of her rights under the Act at the time of appointment. The data must be given in written and in electronic form (email).
- Female government employees are qualified for maternity leave for a time of 180 days for their initial two live conceived kids.
- The new Act has additionally presented the choice of telecommuting/work from home for new moms. Ladies could practice this arrangement after the completion of the 26-week leave period. Contingent on the idea of work, lady representatives might have the capacity to profit from this advantage on terms that are commonly concurred with the business.
- Crèche facility has been made obligatory under the change for each foundation utilizing at least 50 representatives. Lady workers would be allowed to visit the crèche four times amid the day.

The old Maternity Act, despite its existence, was not able to give sufficient leave for new moms. Ladies needed to battle to get from the latest relevant points of interest, with numerous leaving their jobs. Execution issues are one of the numerous issues that ladies confront when they join work too early. Thus, it was about time ladies were given the advantages they required. The new Act will not just positively affect working ladies but will likewise prompt a more advantageous and upbeat work culture.

The Sexual Harassment of Women at Workplace (Prevention, Prohibition and Redressal) Act, 2013 (SHA)

Sexual harassment at work is not uncommon and we come across various cases dealing with harassment in the workplace. India finally enacted its law on prevention of sexual harassment against female employees at the workplace in 2013. The statute was enacted almost 16 years after the landmark judgement of the Supreme Court of India, in the matter of *Vishaka and others v. State of Rajasthan* (Vishaka Judgement). The Vishaka Judgement laid down guidelines making it mandatory for every employer to provide a mechanism to redress grievances pertaining to sexual harassment at work and enforce the right to gender equality of working women (guidelines). Till the enactment of the Sexual Harassment Act, organizations were expected to follow the guidelines, but in most instances, they fell short. The enactment of the sexual harassment act has brought the much-needed relief to the women workforce.

The definition of sexual harassment in the Sexual Harassment Act is in line with the Supreme Court's definition in the Vishaka Judgement and includes any unwelcome sexually determined behaviour (whether directly or by implication) such as the following:

- Physical contact and advances.
- Demand or request for sexual favours.
- Sexually coloured remarks.
- Showing pornography.
- Any other unwelcome physical, verbal or non-verbal conduct of sexual nature.

Apart from dealing with sexual harassment complaints, an employer has additional obligations in the nature of:

- Providing a safe working environment.
- Displaying conspicuously at the workplace, the penal consequences of indulging in acts that may constitute sexual harassment and the composition of the Internal Complaints Committee (ICC).
- Organizing workshops and awareness programmes at regular intervals for sensitizing employees on the issues and implications of sexual harassment in the workplace and organizing orientation programmes for members of the ICC.
- Treating sexual harassment as a misconduct under the service rules and initiating action for misconduct.

The Factories Act, 1948 (Factories Act)

The Factories Act is a legislation securing health, safety, welfare, proper working hours, leave and other benefits of the workers employed in a factory.. The Act aims at protecting workers employed in factories from unfair exploitation by their employers. The Factories Act also has exclusive provisions for women workers.

- The Factories Act stipulates the working hours for all adult workers. It also provides for overtime pay to workers who work beyond the prescribed hours of work.
- It also contains provisions pertaining to intervals or rest period during a working day, weekly off, annual leaves and so on.

- Generally, in factories, it is observed that work happens on a shift basis, and there are requirements for workers to work night shifts. However, night shifts are required to be on a rotational basis. Further, shift timings and hours of work are required to be fixed beforehand by the management and displayed on the notice board of the factory.
- No woman worker shall be allowed to work in a factory except between 6 AM and 7 PM. The state governments may, by notification, vary the limits as set out in this point, but in no circumstance will women employees be allowed to work between 10 PM and 5 AM.
- The shift timing of a woman worker cannot be changed except after a weekly holiday or any other holiday. Hence, women employees are entitled to get at least a 24-hour notice for their shift timing change.
- There are prohibitions for women workers to work in a hazardous occupation, in pressing cotton where a cotton opener is at work and limits to the maximum permissible load.
- The Factories Act also stipulates the employers employing 30 or more women workers to provide for crèches for children of the women workers, aged 6 years and below.
- There are various other facilities which are required to be given to workers in a factory such as washing and bathing facilities for women, toilets (latrine and urinals separate for women), restrooms and canteens.

State governments from time to time issue notifications for amending provisions of the Factories Act, which would be applicable to workers in factories in that particular state. For instance, on 1 December, former President Pranab Mukherjee gave his assent to the Maharashtra Factories (Amendment) Bill, 2015, wherein, among other amendments, it allows women to work in factories in night shifts. Prior to the amendment, the Factories Act did not allow women employees to work in the factories in night shift between 7 PM and 6 AM. With this amendment, it also makes mandatory for factory management to ensure the security of women working night shifts.

The Equal Remuneration Act, 1976 (Equal Remuneration Act)

The time again came across discussions and instances of pay discrimination, where women workers are getting paid lesser than their male counterparts. This is a story across the globe, even in developed nations. Article 39 of our Constitution directs that states shall, in particular, have policies towards securing equal pay for equal work for both men and women.

Under the Equal Remuneration Act:

- Employers shall pay equal remuneration to its male and female employees who are carrying out the same or similar work.
- Employers cannot discriminate between men and women while recruiting unless there is a restriction under the law to employ women in certain industries.

Shops and Establishments Act

The state governments enact their respective SEAs, regulating the working conditions of employees in a shop or commercial establishment. The SEAs provide for various provisions including provisions pertaining to (a) notice period for termination, (b) leave entitlement and (c) working conditions such as weekly working hours, weekly off and overtime. The Maharashtra Shops and Establishment Act, 1948 (MSEA), is the applicable law in case of establishments in the state of Maharashtra and while the Delhi Shops and Establishment Act, 1954, is the applicable legislation in case of establishments based in the state of Delhi.

However, due to the nature of work of certain industries, they may require their female employees to work beyond the prescribed limits, for which they will need to take prior permission from the authorities. The approvals for allowing women to work late nights always comes with special conditions and obligations, on the part of the employer, such as, providing a safe working environment, providing adequate security during the night hours, providing transport to their residence after the late working hours, women employees should be placed in a group while working at nights and not alone, etc. The IT sector has seen an exponential growth in the recent past and this sector is one which typically has huge manpower. We see an equal number of men and women working in the IT sector, and they work late into the nights for their shift work, due to catering to countries across the globe, with varied time differences. In order to address the safety of women workers in this sector, apart from the provisions under the SEA, the state governments have their independent IT/ITES (information technology enabled services) policies, which address the issues of women working night shifts and the various measures to be undertaken by the employer to ensure their safety.

Other Enactments

Apart from the laws discussed above, there are other laws for the welfare and safeguard of employees. Additionally, women employees must also be aware of various enactments which provide for social security for employees such as the EPF & MP Act, 1952, the ESI Act, 1948, Payment of Gratuity Act, 1972 and Payment of Bonus Act, 1965.

Summary

1. Labour legislation in India has a history of over 125 years. Beginning with the Apprentice Act, passed in 1850, to the labour laws regulating not only the conditions of work of industrial establishments, but also industrial relations.
2. In India, all laws emanate from the Constitution of India. Under the Constitution, labour is a concurrent subject, that is, both the central and state governments can enact labour legislation, with the clause that the state legislature cannot enact a law which is repugnant to the central law.
3. A rough estimate places the total number of enactments in India to be around 160.
4. The history of labour laws in India dates back to pre-Independence British Era as these labour and industrial laws were enacted by British administration to protect interests of British employers and industrialists.
5. The post-Independence enactment of important legislations in the areas of employee security and welfare derives their origin partly from the vision of independent India's leaders and partly from the provisions in the Indian Constitution and international conventions like the ILO.

6. The pre-Independence framework of employment regulation introduced core concepts that continue to shape labour regulation in contemporary India. First, since 1919, India's central and state governments have maintained shared legislative authority over labour and employment relations.
7. In the first phase of industrial relations following Independence, corresponding to the first three Five Year Plans (1951–1956, 1956–1961, 1961–1966), India entered a period of 'national development'. Following Independence, in order to advance government-directed nation-building, the state took on the principal role of ensuring uninterrupted industrial production.
8. Post Independence, pursuit of harmony in labour relations was articulated as Gandhian doctrines of trusteeship and non-violence. Harmonious industrial relations were pursued through measures to avoid strikes and lockouts by channelling dispute resolution into governmental dispute settlement machinery.
9. The second phase of post-Independence industrial relations corresponds with the 1967–1969 Annual Plans, the Fourth Five Year Plan (1969–1974) and the Fifth Five Year Plan (1974–1979). From the mid-1960s to 1979, state policy persisted in the mode of extending individual rights at work.
10. The third phase of post-Independence industrial relations corresponds to the Sixth and Seventh Five Year Plans (1980–1985, 1985–1990) and the 1990 and 1992 Annual Plans.
11. The first NCL was set up on 24 December 1966 under the chairmanship of Justice P. B. Gajendragadkar. The objective was to study and review the living conditions of labour and the labour legislations since 1947.
12. The second NCL was set up on 15 October 1999 under the chairmanship of Ravindra Varma which submitted its report to the then Prime Minister Atal Bihari Vajpayee on 29 June 2002.
13. Salient features of labour legislation are based on certain fundamental principles: social justice, social equity and uniformity.
14. The Constitution of India has conferred innumerable rights on the protection of labour. Articles 14, 19, 21, 23 and 24 form part of the fundamental rights guaranteed under Part III of the Constitution. Articles 38, 39, 39-A, 41, 42, 43, 43-A and 47 form part of the Directives Principle of the State Policy under Part IV of the Constitution.

Multiple Choice Questions

1. Labour legislation in India has a history of over ____________.
   - a. 200 years
   - b. 125 years
   - c. 100 years
   - d. 65 years
2. The ____________ was the first Act passed to regulate the industrial relations in India.
   - a. Apprentice Act
   - b. Factories Act
   - c. Bombay Trade Disputes Act
   - d. Industrial Disputes Act
3. Under the Indian Constitution, labour is a ____________ subject.
   - a. State
   - b. Union
   - c. Concurrent
   - d. None of the above

4. In the pre-Independence period, labour regulations in India were influenced by ________ that altered the industrial and political landscape of the nation.
   a. Significant forces including communist influence in the labour movement following the 1917 Bolshevik Revolution in Russia
   b. Bolshevik Revolution in Russia
   c. The rapid development of trade unions in the country
   d. All of the above
5. In relation to Indian labour legislations in the pre-Independence era, which of the following statements is not true?
   a. Unregistered unions were excluded from legal protection
   b. The legislation obligated the employers to bargain with registered unions
   c. The legislations limited the right to strike and required referral of industrial disputes to a conciliation board or court of enquiry
   d. The outcomes of a referral to conciliation board or court of enquiry were not binding upon the parties
6. The 1965 amendments to the Industrial Disputes Act, 1947, facilitated new pattern/patterns in collective bargaining that included ________.
   a. Coalition bargaining between multiple unions
   b. Leading an employer to settlements
   c. Seeking out the conciliation proceedings to convert the agreements into legally binding documents
   d. All of the above
7. The 1970s saw the passage of a series of central laws protecting extraordinarily vulnerable workers that included ________.
   a. The Sanding Orders Act
   b. The Industrial Disputes Act
   c. The Contract Labour (Regulation and Abolition) Act
   d. The Factories Act
8. The first NCL was set up in the year ________ under the chairmanship of Justice P. B. Gajendragadkar.
   a. 1948 c. 1966
   b. 1959 d. 1975
9. ________ belongs to the category of laws relating to the association of workers.
   a. The Trade Unions Act, 1926
   b. The Employees' State Insurance Act, 1948
   c. The Bonded Labour and System (Abolition) Act, 1976
   d. The Workmen Compensation Act, 1923
10. ________ of the Indian Constitution prohibits the discrimination on grounds of religion, race, caste, sex or place of birth.
    a. Article 19 c. Article 21
    b. Article 14 d. Article 26

Descriptive Questions

1. In the pre-Independence era, which factors majorly influenced the labour relations and changes in political and legal landscape in India?
2. What was the role played by NCL in reformation and evolution of labour legislations in India?
3. What are the guiding principles of labour legislation in India.
4. Write a detailed note on development and reformation of industrial relations and labour legislations in the post-Independence era.
5. Throw light on the constitutional provisions for the protection of labour rights in Indian Constitution.

Annexure A: Labour Laws in India

Pre-Independence

- Factories (Amendment) Act, 1922, No. 11 of 1922 (25 January 1922)
- Workmen's Compensation Act, 1923, No. 8 of 1923 (5 March 1923)
- Payment of Wages Act, 1936, No. 4 of 1936 (23 April 1936)
- Employment of Children Act, 1938, No. 26 of 1938, (1 December 1938)
- Trade Unions Act, 1926, No. 16 of 1926 (25 March 1926)
- Trade Disputes Act, 1929, No. 7 of 1929 (8 May 1929)
- Industrial Employment (Standing Orders) Act, 1946, No. 20 of 1946 (23 April 1946)
- Factories Act, 1948, No. 63 of 1948 (23 September 1948)
- Minimum Wages Act, 1948, No. 11 of 1948 (15 March 1948)
- Employees' State Insurance Act, 1948, No. 34 of 1948 (19 April 1948)
- Plantations Labour Act, 1951, No. 69 of 1951 (2 November 1951)
- Mines Act, 1952, No. 35 of 1952 (15 March 1952)
- EPF & MP Act, 1952, No. 19 of 1952 (4 March 1952)
- Maternity Benefit Act, 1961, No. 53 of 1961 (12 December 1961)
- Payment of Bonus Act, 1965, No. 21 of 1965 (25 September 1965)
- Industrial Disputes Act, 1947, No. 14 of 1947 (11 March 1947)

Post-Independence

- Contract Labour (Regulation and Abolition) Act, 1970, No. 37 of 1970 (5 September 1970)
- Limestone and Dolomite Mines Labour Welfare Fund Act, 1972, No. 62 of 1972 (2 December 1972)
- Bonded Labour System (Abolition) Act, 1976, No. 19 of 1976 (9 February 1976)
- Equal Remuneration Act, 1976, No. 25 of 1976 (11 February 1976)
- Iron Ore Mines Manganese Ore Mines and Chrome Ore Mines Labour Welfare Act, 1976, No. 61 of 1976 (10 April 1976)
- Inter-state Migrant Workmen (Regulation of Employment and Conditions of Service) Act, 1979, No. 30 of 1979 (11 June 1979)
- Child Labour (Prohibition and Regulation) Act, 1986, No. 61 of 1986 (23 December 1986)

3

CHAPTER

The Factories Act, 1948

LEARNING OBJECTIVES

Upon completing this chapter, the reader would be able to:

LO1. Understand the objectives, scope and important definitions of the Act.
LO2. Get the insights of the rules governing approval, licensing and registration of factories provided by the Act.
LO3. Explain the provisions for ensuring the health and safety of workers provided by the Act.
LO4. Know the provisions related to hazardous processes.
LO5. Explore the details of provisions for the employee welfare and working hours of employees provided under the Act.
LO6. Describe regulations related to the employment of young persons and women.
LO7. Understand the rules for annual leaves with wages laid down by the Act.
LO8. Get the details of rules dealing with penalties and contingence for offences against the Act.

Introduction

In the eighteenth century, with the industrial revolution taking place, the methods of producing goods changed forever. One of the most important changes was the substitution of machines for people. This resulted in the organization of work into large units called 'factories', followed by direct supervision of the manufacturing process and efficient division of work among the labour. The rapid growth of industrial revolution and unsafe production methods exacted a heavy toll on the workforce in terms of job-related injuries and deaths. Subsequently, in the twentieth century, as technology grew by leaps and bounds, associated hazards also grew with it. All this drew the attention of law- and policymakers towards collective efforts and thinking in the direction of controlling work-related hazards and accidents and safety of labour employed in factories.

The Indian Constitution extends fundamental rights to every citizen of India which also protects the rights of labour, and it ensures humane work conditions and the right to a dignified life. In the form of Directive Principles, the Indian Constitution directs the appropriate government to ensure the safety of the life and health of workers employed in industry. Thus, the Constitution of India guides the country to remain committed to regulate all economic activities for the management of safety and health of every working man and woman in the country. The law relating to the regulation of labour employed in factories in India was embodied in the Factories Act, 1934. The application of this Act revealed a number of defects and weaknesses which hampered effective administration. On the other hand, the industrial activities in the country were growing to a very large extent, and it became essential to overhaul the factories law. To achieve this objective, the Factories Bill was introduced in the legislature, and the Factories Act, 1948 (Central Act 63 of 1948), came into force on 1 April 1949.

LO1: Objectives, Scope and Important Definitions

Objectives and Scope of the Act

The Factories Act, 1948 (the Act), is a central enactment, which means that the Act is enacted and amended by the central government and enforced by the state government. The Act deals with occupational health and safety as well as welfare of workers employed in a factory. It applies to factories, as defined in the Act all over India, including the state of Jammu and Kashmir. Unless otherwise provided, the Factories Act applies to factories belonging to the central or any state government.

The main objective of the Act is to regulate the conditions of work in manufacturing establishments coming within the definition of the term 'factory' as used in the Act. It aims at ensuring the healthier and safer work atmosphere for the workers and for improving the general welfare of workers. The act sets out the broad outline of the measures for achieving the object of protecting the workers from industrial and occupational hazards and for their welfare. The state government is entrusted with the power to frame rules regarding the details of the measures for various types of factories so that the local conditions prevailing in the state are appropriately reflected in the enforcement.

Important Definitions

Factory (Section 2[m])

The term 'factory' is defined in the Act as follows:

'Factory' means any premises including the precincts thereof:

a. Whereon 10 or more workers are working, or were working, on any day of the preceding 12 months, and in any part of which a manufacturing process is being carried on with the aid of power or is ordinarily so carried on, or
b. Whereon 20 or more workers are working, or were working on any day of the preceding 12 months, and in any part of which a manufacturing process is being carried on without the aid of power, or is ordinarily so carried on.

Worth-noting points: Some important points to be noted in the definition of factory are elaborated as follows:

- The term 'factory' does not include a mine which is subject to the operation of the Indian Mines Act, 1952, a mobile unit belonging to the armed forces of the union, a railway running shed or a hotel, restaurant or eating place.

- For computing the number of workers for the purposes of this clause, all the workers in different relays in a day shall be taken into account.
- The state government (Section 85) is empowered to declare any establishment carrying on a manufacturing process to be a factory for the purposes of the Act even if it employs less than the prescribed minimum number of workers, provided that the manufacturing process is not being carried on by the owner only with the aid of his family.

Test for considering an establishment as factory: If we analyse the definition of factory laid down under Section 2(m) of the Act, we find that an establishment falls under the definition of a factory if the conditions stated below are met:

a. It is a place where a 'manufacturing process' is carried on.
b. The place employs the prescribed minimum number of 'workers'. That is 10 if 'power' is used, and 20 if no 'power' is used. To attract the application of this Act, it is sufficient if the prescribed number of workers was employed on any day of the preceding 12 months.
c. It is not a mine coming within the purview of the Indian Mines Act of 1952, a railway running shed, mobile unit belonging to the armed forces of the union or a hotel, restaurant or eating place.

Different departments to be separate factories or two or more factories to be single factory (Section 4): Either on receiving the application by the occupier directly in writing or on its own motion, the state government may decide to treat different departments or branches of a factory of the occupier specified in the application as separate factories or two or more factories of the occupier specified in the application as a single factory. Such a decision is subject to the conditions the state government finds fit for any of the purposes of this Act. It is to be noted here that no order under this section can be made by the state government on its own motion unless an opportunity of being heard is given to the occupier.

Exemption during public emergency (Section 5): In any case of public emergency, the state government may decide to (by notification in the Official Gazette) exempt any factory or class or description of factories from all or any of the provisions of this Act (except Section 67) for a fixed period and subject to such conditions as it may think fit. No such notification can be made for a period exceeding 3 months at a time. Here, 'public emergency' means a grave emergency whereby the security of India or of any part of the territory thereof is threatened, whether by war or external aggression or internal disturbance.

Certain premises deemed to be a factory (Section 85): The state government may (by notification in the Official Gazette) declare that all or any of the provisions of this Act apply to any place wherein a manufacturing process is carried on with or without the aid of power or is so ordinarily carried on, notwithstanding that:

a. The number of persons employed therein is less than 10, if working with the aid of power and less than 20 if working without the aid of power, or
b. The persons working therein are not employed by the owner thereof but are working with the permission of, or under agreement with, such owner.

The application of this section is subject to the condition that the manufacturing process is not being carried on by the owner only with the aid of his family.

Manufacturing Process (Section 2[k])

Under the Act, the term 'manufacturing process' is defined in a very wide sense. It includes the following processes:

a. Making, altering, ornamenting, finishing, packing, oiling, washing, cleaning, breaking up, demolishing, or otherwise treating or adopting any article or substance with a view to its use, sale, transport, delivery or disposal; or
b. Pumping oil, water, sewage or any other substance; or
c. Generating, transforming or transmitting power; or
d. Composing types for printing, printing by letter press, lithography, photogravure or other similar processes, or book binding; or
e. Constructing, reconstructing, repairing, refitting, finishing or breaking up ships or vessels; or
f. Preserving or storing any article in cold storage.

Some of the undertakings which have been held to be manufacturing processes are as follows: bidi making; conversion of raw films into finished products; the preparation of eatables in the kitchen of a restaurant; and use of a refrigerator for adapting any article with a view to its sale. The scraping out of salt and grading them also is covered under the definition of manufacturing process, even though it is done by manual labour. Let us discuss a case (Case 3.1) to get the deeper insights of the term 'factory' under the Act.

Case 3.1: Customs, Excise and Gold Tribunal—*Delhi Grauer and Weil (India) Ltd. v. Collector of Central Excise*[1]

On 1 March 1983, the Central Excise Preventive Officers of Bulsar Division (the officers) paid a surprise visit to the factory premises of M/s Growel Chromates, a division of M/s Grauer and Weil (India) Ltd., Bombay (the appellants). It was found that sodium dichromate manufactured by them was removed on payment of duty under gate passes for captive consumption to their chromic acid sections, situated adjoining their manufacturing premises for the manufacture of chromic acid flakes. The chromic acid flakes were found to be manufactured with the aid of power and removed under the delivery challans of the appellants without payment of duty.

The officers detained 98 drums of chromic acid flakes lying in the chromic acid section for enquiries. On the next visit of the officers, 126 drums (this included the 98 drums detained earlier) of chromic acid flakes in fully manufactured condition were seized in the belief that the goods were liable to confiscation as the appellants were not entitled to duty exemption. The goods were subsequently released to the appellants against a bond. On investigation of the case, the department found that the appellants had wrongfully availed the duty exemption on the basis that the chromic acid section was not a 'factory' within the meaning of the term in Section 2(m) of the Factories Act, 1948, though, according to the department, the said section was part and parcel of the appellant's factory.

Subsequently, a notice was issued to the appellants, charging them with contravention of various rules of central excise. The appellants were called upon to explain why penalty should not be imposed on them, why the goods confiscated and subsequently provisionally released should not be confiscated and why they should not be called upon to pay duty on detained chromic acid flakes illicitly manufactured and cleared.

[1] ECR 297 Tri Delhi, 1986 (25) ELT 338 Tri Del.

The officers argued that the chromic acid section was nothing but a part of the appellant's factory since it was served by common electric and water connections, the payments for the same and the salaries of the staff and workers were paid by the appellants, and further the raw material was supplied by the appellants and the final product was removed on the delivery challans of the appellants. On the other hand, the appellant contended that chromic acid could be manufactured out of sodium dichromate brought from outside (and not from the appellant's production) and that, therefore, the manufacture of chromic acid could not be said to be a manufacturing activity dependent on that of manufacture of sodium dichromate.

Thus, the appellants denied the charges and contended that the chromic acid section was not a part of the appellant's factory and did not fall in the category of factories as defined by the Factories Act, 1948, under Section 2(m).

Discussion Point

In light of the definition of factory as stated under the Act, could the chromic acid section of the appellant be treated a part of the appellant's factory?

Judgement and Explanation

The court observed that the appellants were engaged in the manufacture of sodium dichromate, which was a vital input for manufacture of chromic acid and the appellants were using it as such. Thus, the two activities could not be said to be independent of each other, especially considering the other features of the case, that is, common water and power connections, common payments for these facilities, common payments to workers, common delivery challans, and so on. This was not, therefore, a case in which it could be said that the activities in the chromic acid section were not connected with but were totally independent of the activities in the rest of the premises.

The court referred to Section 2(3)(a) of the Factories Act, 1911, which defined 'factory' as: 'Any premises wherein or within the precincts of which on any one day in the year not less than twenty persons are simultaneously employed and steam, water or other mechanical power or electrical power is used'.

In the light of above-mentioned facts and observation, it was held that the chromic acid section was clearly a part of the appellants' factory.

From the above discussion, it is clear that Section 2(3)(a) of the Act was intended not to cover merely incidental business in any premises but was intended to denote any premises as a composite whole with a central source of power, and that a saw mill and a ginning factory under the same roof and worked by the same motive power was a factory.

Worker (Section 2[1])

After considering the amendments of the year 1976, Section 2(1) of the Act defines 'worker' as under:

> A person employed, directly or by or through any agency (including a contractor) with or without the knowledge of the principal employer, whether for remuneration or not in any manufacturing process, or in cleaning any part of the machinery or premises used for a manufacturing process, or in any other kind of work incidental to, or connected 'with, the manufacturing process or the subject of the manufacturing process but does not include any member of the armed forces of the Union.

The definition of worker is very wide in scope and clearly states that 'worker' under the Act means any person engaged in any work connected with or incidental to a manufacturing process. The persons engaged directly as well as those who are engaged through an agency (including a contractor with or without the knowledge of the principal employer) are considered to be workers under the Act. The term also includes clerical workers and persons paid by piece rates in a factory. Apprentices, whether remunerated or not, are workers within the meaning of the Act. However, the term 'worker' does not include any member of the armed forces of the union. Case 3.2 covers the definition of worker under the Act.

Case 3.2: *Indian Petrochemicals v. Shramik Sena and Ors*[2]

The workmen of the factory of Indian Petrochemicals located at Nagothane (the petitioner workmen), District Raigad in the state of Maharashtra, filed the a writ petition before the High Court of Bombay for a declaration that the petitioner workmen, who were the workmen of the management, were entitled to have the same pay scales and service conditions as were applicable to regular workmen of the management. It was further requested in the petition that a direction be given to the management to absorb the appellants as regular workmen with effect from the actual date of their entering into the service of the canteen of the management and to pay them all consequential benefits including arrears of wages and so on.

The petitioner workmen of the factory contented that the management was treating them as persons employed on contract basis through a contractor named M/s. Rashmi Caterers. They further stated that the factory of the management, where the appellant workmen were employed, was governed by the provisions of the Factories Act, 1948, and the canteen, where the said workmen were employed, was a statutory canteen established by the management as required under the said provisions of the Act. It is further contended that the said canteen was maintained for the benefit of the workmen employed in the factory, and the management had direct control over the appellant workmen and the contractor, although M/s Rashmi Caterers, who was shown as a contractor, had no control over the management, administration and functioning of the said canteen. The work carried on by them in the said canteen was perennial in nature and the canteen was incidental to and was connected with the establishment of the management. Therefore, the petitioner workmen working in the canteen were the workmen of the said management. The petitioner workmen alleged that despite all these facts, the management was denying the status of the appellant workmen as that of a regular workman and was treating them as contract employees, contrary to the statutory provisions and judicial pronouncements of this court.

On behalf of the management, it was contended that the company was a public sector undertaking and it could not appoint any person in contravention of the recruitment policy which required the management to follow a roster system. Therefore, apart from the fact that the workmen were not in the regular employment of the said management, the absorption or regularization of the services of the petitioner workmen would contravene Article 16(4) of the Constitution and would also contravene the reservation policy which was applicable for recruitment in the establishment managed by it.

Discussion Point

Were the petitioner workmen in fact the employees of the management and their services had to be regularized?

Judgement and Explanation

It was found by the court that the initial appointments of the workmen were not in accordance with the rules governing the appointments or the established policy of recruitment of the management. The said recruitments could also be in contravention of the various statutory orders including the reservation policy. Further, the company was an instrumentality of the state and had an obligation to conform to the requirements of Articles 14 and 16 of the Constitution. Thus, the workmen could not be treated as the employees of the management. In spite of the same, the court directed the management to regularize the services of the

[2] *Indian Petrochemicals v. Shramik Sena and Ors* on 4 August 1999.

workmen, not as a matter of right of the workmen arising under any statute but with a view to eradicate unfair labour practices and in equity to undo social injustice and as a measure of labour welfare. It was further added by the court that it was necessary that in this process, suitable guidelines or conditions be laid down to regularize the services of the workmen so concerned depending upon the facts of each case.

Relationship of a master and servant: The word 'employed' used in the definition of the worker means that the relationship of master and servant must exist. It is immaterial here whether the wages are paid to the worker or not or wages rate paid on time-rate basis or piece-rate basis. The terms of the contract of employment decide whether the person is the employee or not. Here, an independent contractor, his collies and servants who are not under the direct control and supervision of the employer are not considered as workers.

Let us discuss a case to see in what all circumstances the relationship of employer and employee is presumed by the court for the purpose of this Act (Case 3.3).

Case 3.3: *Workmen employed in the Canteen v. Government of Tamil Nadu and Ors*[3]

The SRF Company (the company) had a factory which was registered under the Factories Act, 1948, at Manali, Madras. The company was engaged in the manufacture of fibres, synthetic yarn and so on, having 1,500 workers on their rolls. Under Section 46 of the Factories Act, the company was obliged to run a canteen which stated that the canteen was supposed to be provided and maintained by the occupier for the use of the workers. The canteen was established in the year 1990 and was being run through a contractor. The canteen was run in the very premises where the factory was situated and the building which belonged to SRF Company.

The services of 119 canteen employees working in the canteen were terminated. The employees being dissatisfied with this termination filed a writ petition challenging the termination on the grounds that the SRF Company dispensed with the services of 119 employees without prior permission as per S. 25N of the Industrial Disputes Act, 1947 (the Act). According to the employees of the canteen, the workers in the canteen were employed through the contractor on the terms prescribed by SRF Company. It was the SRF Company which organized the canteen. The furniture, utensils, electricity and so on for the canteen also were provided by the SRF Company. The canteen employees (the petitioners) claimed that the contractor was only a device and the contract between the SRF Company and the contractor could not be relied on by the SRF Company to deny the employer and employee relationship between SRF Company and the canteen employees.

On the basis of above-mentioned grounds, the petitioners further stated in their petition that the canteen employees were working directly under the SRF Company and that since the canteen was a part of the industrial establishment of SRF Company, they had to take permission under Section 25N of the Act before the services of the canteen workers were dispensed with and that admittedly, the SRF Company had not applied for such permission.

The SRF Company rejected the claims of the petitioners and contended that the statutory requirements of Section 46 of the Factories Act are that the company should arrange to provide the canteen facility for its workers and there is no obligation that it should run the canteen by employing its own workmen. It was further added that the company was entitled to entrust the work of preparation of food stuffs and its supply to its workmen through the contractor and that in doing so, the only requirement was that the company should register itself as principal employer and the contractor had to take out a licence under the provisions

[3] *Workmen Employed in the Canteen v. Government of Tamil Nadu and Ors* on 25 January 1995.

of the Contract Labour (Regulation and Abolition) Act, 1970. The contract between SRF Company and the contractor entered into in the year 1980 was periodically renewed, and all the canteen employees were appointed by the contractor. The company argued that the petitioners could not have any claim against SRF Company merely because the contractor was making use of the services of the canteen employees in the premises of SRF Company. Thus, the SRF Company disagreed with the relationship of employer and employee between the company and the canteen employees.

Discussion Point

Whether there existed the employer–employee relationship between the proprietor of the factory and the canteen employees?

Judgement and Explanation

It was held by the court that the question whether there exists the employer–employee relationship between the company (the proprietor of the factory) and the canteen employees was not a matter of presumption, but it was a question of fact, which had to be decided in each case on the facts and circumstances of such case. In the above case, Section 46 of the Factories Act could not make the company automatically the employer of the canteen employees in all cases and for all purposes. The court rejected the argument that even if the statutory canteen was run by a contractor, in view of the statutory obligation to provide and maintain the canteen under Section 46, the company was presumed to run the canteen and by a legal fiction, the relationship of employer and employees was created between the proprietor and the canteen employees.

It was further explained in the judgement when the occupier of the factory who was a registered principal employer under Section 7 of the Contract Labour Act entrusted the responsibility of running canteen to a contractor, who had taken out a licence under Section 12 of the said Act. As in the above case, the workmen employed in the canteen by such contractor could not be treated as workmen of principal employer, namely, occupier or proprietor of the factory. In such a case, there was no employer–employee relationship between the proprietor of the factory and the canteen employees.

It is clear from the above discussion that in the cases where the canteen is run by the contractor or cooperative societies, the employer in relation to the workers engaged in the canteen will be the contractor or the society, as the case may be, and not the proprietor of the factory, and in such cases, all the claims of the canteen employees are required to be met by the contractor or the cooperative societies as the case may be.

Obligations of a Worker (Section 111)

The Act under Section 111 states that no worker in a factory:

1. Shall wilfully interfere with or misuse any appliance, convenience or other things provided in a factory for the purposes of securing the health, safety or welfare of the workers therein.
2. Shall wilfully and without reasonable cause do anything likely to endanger himself or others.
3. Shall wilfully neglect to make use of any appliance or other things provided in the factory for the purposes of securing the health or safety of the workers therein.

The Section further provides that if any worker employed in a factory contravenes any of the provisions of this section or of any rule or order made thereunder, he is punishable with imprisonment for a term which may extend to 3 months, or with fine which may extend to ₹100, or with both.

Rights of a Worker (Section 111A)

The Act extends to every worker a right to:

1. Obtain from the occupier, information relating to workers' health and safety at work.
2. Get trained within the factory wherever possible, or to get himself sponsored by the occupier for getting trained at a training centre or institute, duly approved by the chief inspector, where training is imparted for workers' health and safety at work.
3. Represent to the inspector directly or through his representative in the matter of inadequate provision for protection of his health or safety in the factory.

Other Important Definitions

Some other important definitions include the following:

1. **Adult (Section 2(a)):** Under the Act, adult means a person who has completed his 18th year of age.
2. **Adolescent (Section 2(b)):** The act defines adolescent as a person who has completed his 15th year of age but has not completed his 18th year.
3. **Calendar year (Section 2(bb)):** Under the Act, calendar year is the period of 12 months beginning with the first day of January in any year.
4. **Child (Section 2(c)):** Child under the Act means a person who has not completed his 15th year of age.
5. **Competent person (Section 2(ca)):** Competent person in relation to any provision of this Act covers a person or an institution recognized as such by the Chief Inspector for the purposes of carrying out tests, examinations and inspections required to be done in a factory under the provisions of this Act having regard to:
    a. The qualifications and experience of the person and facilities available at his disposal.
    b. The qualifications and experience of the persons employed in such institution and facilities available therein, with regard to the conduct of such tests, examinations and inspections, and more than one person or institution can be recognized as a competent person in relation to a factory.
6. **Hazardous process (Section 2(cb)):** The Act explains the hazardous process as any process or activity in relation to an industry specified in the First Schedule where, unless special care is taken, raw materials used therein or the intermediate or finished products, by-products, wastes or effluents thereof would:
    a. Cause material impairment to the health of the persons engaged in or connected therewith, or
    b. Result in the pollution of the general environment.

    Section 2 (cc) 'hazardous substance' means any substance as prescribed or preparation of which by reason of its chemical or physiochemical properties or handling is liable to cause physical or health hazards to human being or may cause harm to other living creatures, plants, micro-organisms, property or the environment (The Factories (Amendment) Bill, 2014).

    The Section further provides that the state government is empowered to (by notification in the Official Gazette) amend the First Schedule by way of addition, omission or variation of any industry specified in the said Schedule.
7. **Young person (section 2(d)):** Under the Act, young person is a person who is either a child or an adolescent.

8. **Day (Section2 (e)):** The Act defines a day as a period of 24 hours beginning at midnight. References to the time of the day in the Act are to the Indian Standard Time (IST). Section 3 further elaborates on this issue and states that in areas where the IST is not observed, the state government can by rules define the local mean time.
9. **Week (Section 2(f)):** According to Section 2(f) of the Act, week covers a period of 7 days beginning at midnight on Saturday night or such other night as may be approved in writing for a particular area by the Chief Inspector of Factories.
10. **Power (Section 2(g)):** Power under the Act means electrical energy, or any other form of energy, which is mechanically transmitted and is not generated by human or animal agency.
11. **Prime mover (Section 2(h)):** Prime mover under the Act means any engine, motor or other appliance which generates or otherwise provides power.
12. **Transmission machinery (Section 2(i)):** Transmission machinery includes any shaft, wheel, drum pulley, system of pulleys, coupling, clutch, driving belt or other appliance or device by which the motion of a prime mover is transmitted to or received by any machinery or appliance.
13. **Machinery (Section 2(j)):** Machinery includes prime movers, transmission machinery and all other appliances whereby power is generated, transformed, transmitted or applied.
14. **Occupier (Section 2(n)):** As laid down by Section 2(n) of the Act, the person who has ultimate control over the affairs of the factory, and where the said affairs are entrusted to a managing agent, such agent shall be deemed to be the occupier of the factory.

    The Factories (Amendment) Act, 1976, added that in case of a ship, which is being repaired or on maintenance work is being carried out in dry dock which is available for hire, the following persons for certain section of the Act are considered to be:
    a. The occupier.
    b. The owner of the dock.
    c. The owner of the ship or his agent or master or other officers-in-charge in the ship or any person who contracts with such owner, agent or master or other officers-in-charge to carry out the repair or maintenance work.

    The Act imposes several duties and responsibilities on the occupier of the factory. An occupier of factory may be an owner, a lessee or a mere licensee, but he must have the right to occupy the property. He is also responsible to control the management.
15. **Shift and relay (Section 2(r)):** Where work of the same kind is carried out by two or more sets of workers working during different periods of the day, each of such sets is termed as a relay and each of such periods is called a shift.

LO2: Approval, Licensing and Registration of Factories

Licence (Section 6)

The Act mandates to obtain a licence before a factory is started. Section 6 of the Act empowers the state government to make rules requiring, for the purposes of this Act. Under the provisions of the Act, the state government may make rules:

- Requiring submission of plans of any class or description of factories to the Chief Inspector or the state government and also requiring previous permission in writing of the state government or the Chief Inspector to be obtained for the site on which the factory is to be situated.

- Requiring for the purpose of considering applications for such permission the submission of plans and specifications.
- Prescribing the nature of such plans and specifications and by whom they are to be certified.
- Requiring the registration and licensing of factories and prescribing the fees payable for such registration and licensing and for renewal of licences.

Timeline for granting the permission: The Act further provides that if after sending an application to the state government or Chief Inspector by registered post, for permission referred to in 3[clause (aa)] of Subsection (1) accompanied by the plans and specifications as required by the Act, no order is communicated to the applicant within 3 months from the date on which it is so sent, the permission applied for in the said application shall be deemed to have been granted.

Replacement and addition to the factory: The Amendment of 1976 added that any replacement and addition to the factory will not be permitted if it does not reduce the minimum clear space required for safe working around the plant or machinery or adversely affect the environmental conditions from the evolution or emission of steam, heat or dust or fumes injurious to health.

Notice by Occupier (Section 7)

Section 7 of the Act states that the occupier of a factory must, at least 15 days before he begins to occupy or use any premises as a factory, send to the Chief Inspector of Factories, a written notice disclosing the following information:

1. The name and situation of the factory.
2. The name and address of the occupier.
3. The name and address of the owner of the premises or building (including the precincts thereof).
4. The address to which any communications relating to the factory may be sent.
5. The nature of the manufacturing process to be carried on in the factory during next 1 year.
6. The total rated horsepower installed or to be installed in the factory, which shall not include the rated horsepower or any separate standby plant.
7. The name of the manager of the factory for the purposes of this Act.
8. The number of workers likely to be employed in the factory.
9. Such other particulars as may be prescribed.

The above-stated rules are enforced to ensure that the plans and specifications of the factory do not ignore proper measures of health, safety and welfare of the workers.

General Duties of Occupiers (Section 7A)

The Act directs every occupier to ensure, so far as is reasonably practicable, the health, safety and welfare of all workers while they are at work in the factory. Without prejudice to the generality of the provisions, the matters to which such duty extends are given as follows:

1. The provision and maintenance of plant and systems of work in the factory that are safe and without risks to health.
2. The arrangements in the factory to ensure safety and absence of risks to health in connection with the use, handling, storage and transport of articles and substances.

3. The provisions of such information, instruction, training and supervision as are necessary to ensure the health and safety of all workers at work.
4. The maintenance of all places of work in the factory in a condition that is safe and without risks to health and the provision and maintenance of such means of access to, and egress from, such places as are safe and without such risks.
5. The provision, maintenance or monitoring of such working environment in the factory for the workers that is safe, without risks to health and adequate as regards facilities and arrangements for their welfare at work.

Except in such cases as prescribed, every occupier is required to prepare and, as often as appropriate, revise a written statement of his general policy with respect to the health and safety of the workers at work and the organization and arrangements for the time being in force for carrying out that policy, and to bring the statement and any revision thereof to the notice of all the workers in such manner as may be prescribed.

General Duties of Manufacturers and so on (Section 7B)

The Act directs every designer, manufacturer and importer of an article for use in any factory to:

1. Ensure, so far as is reasonably practicable, that the article is so designed and constructed as to be safe and without risks to the health of the workers when properly used.
2. Carry out or arrange for the carrying out of such tests and examination as may be considered necessary for the effective implementation of the provisions of clause (a).
3. Take all necessary steps to ensure that adequate information will be available:
   a. In connection with the use of the article in any factory.
   b. About the use for which it is designed and tested.
   c. About any conditions necessary to ensure that the article, when put to such use, will be safe and without risks to the health of the workers.

If an article is designed or manufactured outside India, it is obligatory on the part of the importer to see:

1. That the article conforms to the same standards if such article is manufactured in India.
2. If the standards adopted in the country outside for the manufacture of such article is above the standards adopted in India, and that the article conforms to such standards.

A person who undertakes to design or manufacture any article for use in any factory is free to carry out or arrange for the carrying out of necessary research with a view to the discovery and, so far as is reasonably practicable, the elimination or minimization of any risks to the health or safety of the workers to which the design or article may give rise.

The Section further provides if it is reasonable for a person to rely on the results of the testing examination and research for the purposes of the subsections discussed above, then nothing contained in above-mentioned subsections be constructed to require a person to repeat such test or research. The duty imposed on any person by this section extends only to things done in the course of business carried on by him and to matters within his control.

Subsection (5) states where a person designs, manufactures, imports or supplies an article on the basis of a written undertaking by the user of such article to take the steps specified in such undertaking to ensure, so far as is reasonably practicable, that the article will be safe and without risks to the health of the workers when properly used, such undertaking has the effect of relieving the person from the duty imposed for conforming to the same standards of the article if such article is manufactured in India to such extent as is reasonably having regard to the terms of the undertaking.

Here, an article is not regarded as properly used if it is used without regard to any information or advice relating to its use which has been made available by the person who has designed, manufactured, imported or supplied the article.

The Inspection Staff

Inspector (Section 8): The Factories Act permits the state government to appoint inspectors, Chief Inspectors of Factories, Additional Chief Inspectors, Joint Chief Inspectors and Deputy Chief Inspectors to implement the provisions of this Act. Every District Magistrate is an inspector for his district. The Act further provides that a person cannot act as an inspector if he is or becomes directly or indirectly interested in a factory or in any process or business carried on therein or in any patent or machinery connected therewith.

Powers of inspectors (Section 9): Section 9 of the Act extends some powers to an inspector which may be exercised within the local limits for which he is appointed. The inspector is authorized to:

1. Enter, with such assistants being persons in the service of the government or any local or other public authority, as he thinks fit, and place which is used, or which he has reason to believe is used as a factory.
2. Make examination of the premises, plant and machinery.
3. Demand the production of any prescribed register and any other document relating to the factory, and take on the spot or otherwise statements of any person which he may consider necessary for carrying out the purposes of the Act.
4. Exercise such other powers as may be prescribed for carrying out the purposes of this Act.

However, no person can be compelled under this section to answer any question or give any evidence tending to incriminate himself. It is the duty of factory inspectors to enforce the provisions of the Factories Act and other industrial laws. For this purpose, they inspect factories periodically. If any rule is violated, they take steps like prosecuting the guilty persons and so on. Section 91 of the Act empowers the inspector to take a sample of any substance, used or intended to be used in a factory, for the purpose of finding out whether the substance is injurious and if the factory is violating any of the provisions of the Act.

Additional powers (Section 75): The Act extends additional powers to the inspector if the inspector is of opinion that confirms any of the following views:

1. Any person working in a factory without a certificate of fitness is a young person, or
2. A young person working in a factory with a certificate of fitness is no longer fit to work in the capacity stated therein.

Thus, in any two of the above-mentioned situations, the inspector is empowered to issue a notice to the manager of the factory, requiring that such person or young person to be examined by a certifying surgeon. He may also direct that such person or young person must not be employed, or permitted to work, in any factory until he has been so examined and has been granted a certificate of fitness or a fresh certificate of fitness, under Section 69, or has been certified by the certifying surgeon examining him not to be a young person.

Obstructing an inspector (Section 95): According to Section 95 of the Act, the person obstructing the inspector in the exercise of his powers as provided by the Act attracts a penalty. The Section states that a person who wilfully obstructs an inspector in the exercise of any power conferred on him by or under this Act, or fails to produce on demand by an inspector any registers of other documents in his custody kept in pursuance of this Act or of any rules made under the Act, or conceals or prevents any worker in a factory from appearing before or being examined by an inspector, shall be punishable with imprisonment for a term which may extend to 3 months or with fine which may extend to ₹300 or with both. However, the onus is on the prosecution to show that a person has obstructed an inspector.

Certifying surgeon (Section 10): Section 10 of the Act allows the state government to appoint qualified medical practitioners to be certifying surgeons for specified local areas or for specified factories or class of factories. Section 10(3) further states that a person cannot be a certifying surgeon for a factory or industry in which he is interested directly or indirectly. The state government may exempt any person or class of persons from the provisions of this subsection in respect of any factory or class or description of factories by issuing an order in writing which may subject to specified conditions.

The certifying surgeon appointed for the purpose of this Act is required to carry out the following duties under the Act:

1. The examination and certification of young persons under this Act.
2. The examination of persons engaged in factories in such dangerous occupations or processes as may be prescribed.
3. Exercising of such medical supervisions as may be prescribed for any factory or class or description of factories where:
   a. Cases of illness have occurred and it is reasonable to believe that the reason behind the illness is the nature of the manufacturing process carried on, or other conditions of work prevailing in the factory.
   b. By reason of any change in the manufacturing process carried on or in the substances used in the factory there is a possibility of injury to the health of workers employed in that manufacturing process.
   c. Young persons are, or about to be, employed in any work which is likely to cause injury to their health.

Procedure for Registration of Establishment

The employer of an establishment has to apply to the inspector of the local areas concerned in the prescribed form along with the prescribed fees to get the establishment registered under the Act. On receipt of the application and the fees, the inspector examines the correctness of the particulars contained in the application. On being satisfied about the same, the inspector registers the establishment and issues a registration certificate. Following are the required documents for registration:

- Memorandum of Association and Articles of Association/Trust Deed.
- Premises purchase agreement.

- List of Directors/Managers.
- First bank account opening proof/bank account no. details.
- First income tax assessment order.
- Self-declaration.
- Date of commencement of business.

Subsequent to the registration, the employers have to notify the changes made in the above-mentioned particulars to the inspector by applying in the prescribed form accompanied by prescribed fees to get the registration certificate suitably amended. The registration certificate has to be renewed every year by applying to the inspectors in the prescribed form.

LO3: Health and Safety of Workers

The Factories Act is the principal legislation, which ensures the health, safety and welfare of workers in factories. The Act addresses the issues of safety, health and welfare of workers at length. Many amendments were aimed to keep the Act in tune with the developments in the field of health and safety. However, it was not until 1987 that the elements of occupational health and safety, and prevention and protection of workers employed in hazardous process, were truly incorporated in the Act. The object brings the Act, within the competence of the Central Legislature to enact. However, the state governments have been empowered under certain provisions of this Act, to make rules, to give effect to the objects and the scheme of the Act.

Provisions Related to Worker's Health (Sections 11–20)

Sections 11–20 of the Act contain specific provisions intended to ensure that the conditions under which work is carried on in factories do not affect the health of the workers injuriously. Following are the main provisions under the Act relating to the health of workers:

1. **Cleanliness (Section 11):** The Act specifies that every factory has to be kept clean and free from dirt and the outflow of drains and so on. The floors must be cleaned and proper drainage must be provided. Inside walls, partitions and ceilings must be repainted at least once in 5 years. If washable water paint is used, then they must be painted once every 3 years and washed at least every period of 6 months (as amended in 1976). Where they are painted or varnished or where they have smooth impervious surfaces is required to be cleaned at least once in every period of 14 months. Further in any other case, where the inside walls are to be kept white-washed or colour-washed, the white washing or colour washing must be carried out at least once in every period of 14 months.
2. **Disposal of wastes and effluents (Section 12):** The Act mandates the effective disposal of the waste materials produced from the manufacturing process. The state government is empowered to make rules for the arrangements of the disposal of waste material from the factory. The management must make such prescribed arrangements and get those approved by prescribed authority.
3. **Ventilation and temperature (Section 13):** There must be a provision for adequate ventilation by the circulation of fresh air. The Act further provides that the temperature must be kept at a comfortable level and hot parts of machines must be separated and insulated.

4. **Dust and fume (Section 14):** If the manufacturing process used gives off injurious or offensive dust and fume, then necessary steps must be taken so that the harmful dust and fume are not inhaled or accumulated. The exhaust fumes of internal combustion engines must be conducted outside the factory.
5. **Artificial humidification (Section 15):** The Act states that the water used for this purpose has to be pure and it must be taken from some source of drinking water supply. The state government is empowered to frame rules regarding the process of humidification and so on.
6. **Overcrowding (Section 16):** The Act specifies that there must be no overcrowding in a factory. In factories existing before the enforcement of the Act, there must be at least 350 cubic feet (cft) of space per worker. For factories built after the Act came into force, there must be at least 500 cft of space per worker. In calculating the space, an account is to be taken of space above 5 m from the floor.
7. **Lighting (Section 17):** Factories must be well lit. Effective measures have to be adopted by the employer to prevent glare or formation of shadows which might result into eyestrain.
8. **Drinking water (Section 18):** The Act mandates proper arrangements to be made to provide sufficient supply of wholesome drinking water in the factory. All supply points of such water must be marked 'Drinking Water'. No such points shall be within 20 feet (or 7.5 m) of any latrine, washing place and so on. The Act further states that in factories employing more than 250 workers there must be arrangement for cold water during the hot weather.
9. **Latrines and urinals (Section 19):** Every factory must provide sufficient number of latrines and urinals. Latrine and urinals must be kept in a clean and sanitary condition, and there must be separate provision for male and female workers. In factories where more than 250 workers are employed, latrines and urinals shall be of prescribed sanitary types.
10. **Spittoons (Section 20):** In every factory, there has to be provided a sufficient number of spittoons in convenient places and they shall be maintained in a clean and hygienic condition.

Provisions Related to the Safety of the Workers (Sections 21–41)

Sections 21–40A, 40B and 41 of the Act deal with the safety of the workers in a factory. These sections lay down the rules for the purpose of securing the safety of workers. Following is the summary of the provisions of the Factories Act regarding the safety of the workers:

1. **Fencing of machinery (Section 21):** All dangerous machinery must be securely fenced. Here, the dangerous parts include the moving parts of prime movers, flywheels connected to every prime mover and electric generators and so on.
2. **Work on or near machinery in motion (Section 22):** Only the specially trained adult male workers wearing tight-fitting clothes must carry out the work on or near machinery in motion.
3. **Employment of young persons on dangerous machines (Section 23):** No young person (as defined under the Act) shall work at any dangerous machine unless he has been specially instructed as to the dangers and the precautions to be observed and has received sufficient training about the work. Even after receiving the training, such young person must work under the supervision of some person having thorough knowledge and experience of the machine.
4. **Striking gear and devices for cutting off power (Section 24):** Suitable devices have to be provided in every factory for cutting off power in emergencies from running machinery and maintained in every workroom.

5. **Self-acting machines (Section 25):** According to the provisions of this section, moving parts of a self-acting machine must not be allowed to come within 45 cm of any fixed structure which is not part of the machine.
6. **Casing of new machinery (Section 26):** This section is applicable on all machinery installed after the commencement of the Act. It provides that in all such machinery certain parts must be sunk, encased or otherwise effectively guarded, for example, set screw, bolt, toothed gearing and so on.
7. **Women and children near cotton openers (Section 27):** Women and children must not be allowed to work near cotton openers, except in certain cases.
8. **Hoists and lifts (Section 28):** Every hoist and lift must be so constructed as it remains safe to the users. There are detailed rules as to how such safety is to be secured. There are similar provisions regarding lifting machines, chains, ropes and lifting tackle.
9. **Lifting machines, chains, ropes and lifting tackles (Section 29):** In respect of every lifting machine (other than a hoist and lift) and every chain, rope and lifting tackle for the purpose of raising or lowering persons, goods or materials, the Act directs every factory to comply with following provisions:
    a. All parts, including the working gear, whether fixed or movable, of every lifting machine and every chain, rope or lifting tackle shall be:
        i. Of good construction, sound material and adequate strength and free from defects.
        ii. Properly maintained.
        iii. Thoroughly examined by a competent person at least once in every period of 12 months, or at such intervals as the Chief Inspector may specify in writing; and a register shall be kept containing the prescribed particulars of every such examination.
    b. No lifting machine and no chain, rope or lifting tackle shall, except for the purpose of test, be loaded beyond the safe working load which shall be plainly marked thereon together with an identification mark and duly entered in the prescribed register; and where this is not practicable, a table showing the safe working loads of every kind and size of lifting machine or chain, rope or lifting tackle in use shall be displayed in prominent positions on the premises.
    c. While any person is employed or working on or near the wheel track of a travelling crane in any place where he would be liable to be struck by the crane, effective measures shall be taken to ensure that the crane does not approach within 6 m of that place.
10. **Revolving machinery (Section 30):** In the factories where grinding is carried on, the maximum safe working speed of every revolving machinery connected therewith must be notified. Necessary steps are required to be taken to see that the safe speed is not exceeded.
11. **Pressure plant (Section 31):** Where any operation is carried on at a pressure higher than the atmospheric pressure, required steps must be taken to ensure that the safe working pressure does not exceed.
12. **Floors, stairs and means of access (Section 32):** All floors, steps, stairs, passage and gangways have to be of sound construction and properly maintained. Handrails are required to be provided where necessary. Safe means of access also has to be provided to the place where the worker will carry on any work.
13. **Pits, sumps, openings in floors etc. (Section 33):** Pits, sumps, openings in floors and so on must be securely covered or fenced.
14. **Excessive weights (Section 34):** The Act specifically mentions under Section 34 that no worker shall be made to carry a load so heavy as to cause him injury.

15. **Protection of eyes (Section 35):** The eyes of the worker have to be protected from fragments thrown off in course of any manufacturing process and from excessive light, if any, by providing them effective screen or suitable goggles.
16. **Precautions against dangerous fumes (Section 36):** No person shall be allowed to enter any chamber, tank and so on where dangerous fumes are likely to be present, unless it is equipped with a manhole or other means of going out.
17. **Precautions reading the use of portable electric lights (Section 36A):** The Section further provides that in such space no portable electric light of more than 24 volts can be used. Only a lamp or light of flameproof construction can be used in such space. The people entering such space have to be provided with a suitable breathing apparatus, reviving apparatus and so on. Such places shall be cooled by ventilation before any person is allowed to enter.
18. **Explosive or inflammable gas and so on (Section 37):** Where a manufacturing process produces inflammable gas, dust, fume and so on, necessary steps have to be taken to enclose the machine concerned, prevent the accumulation of substances and exclude all possible sources of ignition. Extra precautionary measures are required to be taken where such substances are worked at greater than the atmospheric pressure.
19. **Precaution in case of fire (Section 38):** Fire escapes have to be provided in a factory. Windows and doors must open outwards. The means of exit in case of the fire must be clearly marked in red letters. There must be arrangements in the factory to give warning in case or fire.
20. **Specifications of defectives and so on and safety of buildings and machinery (Sections 39 and 40):** If any building or machine is in a defective or dangerous condition, the Inspector of Factories can ask to test such machine or building to determine how they can be made safe. He is also authorized to direct the adoption of the measure necessary to make them safe. In case of immediate danger, the use of the building or machine can also be prohibited.
21. **Maintenance of buildings (Section 40):** If the Inspector of Factories finds any building in a factory, or any part of it, in such a state of disrepair that it is likely to affect the health and welfare of the workers, he may serve on the occupier or manager or both in writing specifying the measures to be done before the specified date.
22. **Safety Officers (Section 40B):** This Section of the Act empowers the state government to notify to the occupier to employ a number of safety officers in a factory:
    a. Wherein 1,000 or more workers are ordinarily employed or
    b. Wherein any manufacturing process or operation which involves the risk of bodily injury, poisoning, disease or any other hazard to health of the persons employed in the factory.
23. **Power to frame rules supplement to the above provisions (Section 41):** The state government is empowered to make rules providing for the use of such further devices for safety as may be necessary.

LO4: Provisions Related to Hazardous Processes

Site Appraisal Committees (Section 41A)

Under provisions of Section 41A of the Act, the state government is empowered to constitute a Site Appraisal Committee to examine the application for establishment of a factory involving hazardous process and send its recommendations to the state government. The Section provides for the constitution, powers, duties and functions of the Committee in a detailed manner. When the proposal for establishment or expansion of a factory is approved by the state government, it has to be further approved by the authorities mentioned in the section. Duties and responsibilities of the occupier of such a factory have been specified in Sections 41B and 41C.

Constitution (Section 41A(3)): Site Appraisal Committee is appointed by the state government for purposes of advising it to consider applications for grant of permission for the initial location of a factory involving a hazardous process or for the expansion of any such factory. The Committee consists of the following:

1. The Chief Inspector of the state who is appointed as the chairman of the Committee.
2. A representative of the Central Board for the Prevention and Control of Water Pollution appointed by the central government under Section 3 of the Water (Prevention and Control of Pollution) Act, 1974 (6 of 1974).
3. A representative of the Central Board for the Prevention and Control of Air Pollution referred to in Section 3 of the Air (Prevention and Control of Pollution) Act, 1981 (14 of 1981).
4. A representative of the State Board appointed under Section 4 of the Water (Prevention and Control of Pollution) Act, 1974 (6 of 1974).
5. A representative of the State Board for the Prevention and Control of Air Pollution referred to in Section 5 of the Air (Prevention and Control of Pollution) Act, 1981 (14 of 1981).
6. A representative of the Department of Environment in the State.
7. A representative of the Meteorological Department of the Government of India.
8. An expert in the field of occupational health.
9. A representative of the Town Planning Department of the State Government, and not more than five other members who are co-opted by the state government who are as follows:
   a. A scientist having specialized knowledge of the hazardous process which will be involved in the factory.
   b. A representative of the local authority within whose jurisdiction the factory is to be established.
   c. A many more than three other persons as deemed fit by the state government.

Functions (Section 41A (2-4)): As its main function, the Site Appraisal Committee examines an application for the establishment of a factory involving hazardous process and makes its recommendation to the state government within a period of 90 days of the receipt of such application in the prescribed form.

The Section further provides for a process that relates to a factory owned or controlled by the central government or to a corporation or a company owned or controlled by the central government. In such cases, the state government must co-opt in the Site Appraisal Committee a representative nominated by the central government as a member of that Committee. The Site Appraisal Committee has power to call for any information from the person making an application for the establishment or expansion of a factory involving a hazardous process.

No further approval (Section 41A (5)): Where the state government has granted approval to an application for the establishment of expansion of a factory involving a hazardous process, it is not necessary for an applicant to obtain a further approval from the Central Board or the State Board established under the Water (Prevention and Control of Pollution) Act, 1974 (6 of 1974) and the Air (Prevention and Control of Pollution) Act, 1981 (14 of 1981).

Compulsory Disclosure of Information by the Occupier (Section 41B)

Disclosure to whom (Section 41B(1)): The Act directs the occupier of every factory involving a hazardous process to disclose in a prescribed manner to the workers employed in the factory all information regarding dangers including health hazards and the measures to overcome such hazards arising from the exposure to or handling of the materials or substances in the manufacture, transportation, storage and other processes. The above-mentioned information is required to be disclosed also to the Chief Inspector, the local authority, within whose jurisdiction the factory is situated, and the general public in the vicinity.

Policy to ensure health and safety of workers (Section 41B(2)): The Act further instructs the occupier to, at the time of registering the factory involving a hazardous process, lay down a detailed policy with respect to the health and safety of the workers employed therein. Such policy is required to be intimated also to the Chief Inspector and the local authority and, thereafter, at such intervals as may be prescribed, inform the Chief Inspector and the local authority of any change made in the said policy.

On-site emergency plan and disaster control measures (Section 41B(4)): As directed by the Act, with the approval of the Chief Inspector, every occupier has to draw up an on-site emergency plan and detailed disaster control measures for his factory and make known to the workers employed therein and to the general public living in the vicinity of the factory. The safety measures are required to be taken in the event of an accident taking place.

Information to the Chief Inspector before commencement (Section 41B(6)): If any occupier of a factory contravenes the provisions of Subsection (5), the licence issued under Section 6 to such factory is liable for cancellation. But the cancellation of licence is subject to any penalty to which the occupier of the factory is subjected to the provisions of this Act.

Handling, usage, transportation of hazardous substance (Section 41B(7)): With the previous approval of the Chief Inspector, the occupier of a factory involving a hazardous process is directed by the Act to lay down measures for handling usage, transportation and storage of hazardous substances inside the factory premises and the disposal of such substances outside the factory premises and publicize them in a prescribed manner among the workers and the general public living in the vicinity.

Specific Responsibility of the Occupier for Handling Hazardous Processes (Section 41C)

Every occupier of a factory involving any hazardous process is directed to take following measures that includes the:

1. Maintenance of accurate and up-to-date health records or, as the case may be, medical records, of the workers in the factory who are exposed to any chemical, toxic or any other harmful substances which are manufactured, stored, handled or transported and such records must be accessible to the workers subject to such conditions as may be prescribed.
2. Appointment of persons who possess qualifications and experience in handling hazardous substances and are competent to supervise such handling within the factory and to provide at the working place all the necessary facilities for protecting the workers in a prescribed manner. Where any question arises as to the qualifications and experience of a person so appointed, the decision of the Chief Inspector shall be final.

3. Providing for medical examination of every worker:
   a. Before such worker is assigned to a job involving the handling of, or working with, a hazardous substance.
   b. While continuing in such job, and after he has ceased to work in such job, at intervals not exceeding 12 months in such manner as may be prescribed.

Powers of Central Government to Appoint Inquiry Committee (Section 41D)

Section 41D empowers the central government to appoint an Inquiry Committee to enquire whether such a factory is observing the standards of health and safety of workers as well as of the general public as prescribed and make recommendations. Its recommendations are, however, of advisory nature; the Committee has a chairman and two members and the central government determines the tenure of office of the members.

Emergency Standards (Section 41E)

Section 41E directs the central government to take certain steps for laying down emergency standards and enforcement thereof in case no standard of safety has been prescribed for hazardous processes. If the central government is satisfied that no standards of safety have been prescribed in respect of a hazardous process or class of hazardous processes, or where the standards so prescribed are inadequate, it may direct the Director General of Factory Advice Service and Labour Institutes or any institution specialized in matters relating to standards of safety in hazardous processes to lay down emergency standards for enforcement of suitable standards in respect of such hazardous processes.

The Section further provides that the emergency standards laid down as discussed above remain enforceable and have the same effect as if they had been incorporated in the rules made under this Act until they are incorporated in the rules made under this Act.

Permissible Limit of Exposure of Chemical and Toxic Substances (Section 41F)

Section 41F enjoins that the maximum permissible limits of exposure of chemical and toxic substances in manufacturing processes (whether hazardous or otherwise) in any factory shall be of the value indicated in the Second Schedule. The section allows the central government to make suitable changes in the said Schedule by notification in the Official Gazette.

Rights of Workers to Warn about Imminent Danger (Section 41H)

Section 41H extends the right to workers of a factory in which a hazardous process takes place to bring to the notice of the occupier, agent, manager or any other person who is in-charge of the factory or the inspector of the area of their apprehension about any imminent danger and the person or persons informed must enquire immediately on receipt of the information and take remedial action.

LO5: Employee Welfare and Working Hours

Employee Welfare

Employee welfare refers to the facilities provided to workers in and outside the factory premises such as canteens, rest and recreation facilities, housing and all other services that contribute to the well-being of workers. Welfare measures are concerned with general well-being of workers that affects their efficiency. In the early stages of industrialization, employee welfare activities did not receive adequate attention and employers were not ready to accept the financial burden of welfare activities. Wherever employers provided for such amenities, it was more with a paternalistic approach to workers rather than recognition of their needs. This resulted in the intervention of state in discharge of employer's responsibility for employee welfare, by using its persuasive powers and/or by enforcing legislation, where persuasion failed. Thus, some compulsory provisions were incorporated in the Factories Act, 1948, with respect to welfare of workers engaged in the manufacturing process.

Provisions for the Employee Welfare (Sections 42–50)

Sections 42–50 deal with the issues related to employee welfare. Summary of these provisions of the Act is stated as follows:

1. **Washing (Section 42):** Adequate and suitable facilities for washing have to be provided for the use of workers in the factories. There must be separate provisions for male and female workers. The workers who live in crowded areas have inadequate facilities for washing at their homes, and bathing facilities add to their comfort, health and efficiency. All such facilities must be conveniently accessible and have to be kept clean.
2. **Storing and drying (Section 43):** There has to be a suitable place for keeping clothes not worn during working hours in every factory. Facilities shall also be provided for the drying of wet clothes. The state government may make rules requiring the provision of suitable facilities for storing and drying clothing.
3. **Sitting (Section 44):** The Act directs that for workers who have to work in a standing position suitable arrangement for sitting shall be provided in the factories so that they may take rest when possible. This is to enable workers to take advantage of any opportunity for rest which may occur in the course of their work. When work can also be done in a sitting position efficiently, the Chief Inspector may direct the provision of sitting arrangements.
4. **First aid (Section 45):** Every factory must provide first aid boxes or cupboard for the use of workers. Such a box must be equipped with the required contents and they must be in charge of persons trained in first aid treatment. The in-charge of the first aid box must be available during the working hours of the factory. The box should be readily accessible to them during all working hours. The number of such first aid boxes must not be less than one for every 150 workers employed in the factory. In factories employing more than 500 workers, there has to be an ambulance room. It should contain all the prescribed equipment and be in the charge of such medical and nursing staff as may be prescribed.
5. **Canteens (Section 46):** Where more than 250 workers are employed, the state government may issue the instructions to open a canteen or canteens for workers. Rules may be framed regarding

the food served, charges to be made, constitution of a managing committee for the canteen and representation of the workers in the management of the canteen.

6. **Shelters (Section 47):** In factories employing more than 150 workers, there must be provided adequate and suitable shelters or restrooms and a lunch room (with drinking water supply) where workers may eat meals brought by them. The rest and lunch rooms shall be sufficiently lighted and ventilated. Such rooms shall be maintained in cool and clean conditions. The standards for shelters may be set by the state government.
7. **Crèches (Section 48):** In every factory employing more than 50 women workers, provision has to be made for suitable and adequate room for the use of children under the age of 6 years of such women. Such a room shall be of adequate size, adequately lighted, ventilated and maintained in clean and sanitary conditions under the charge of a woman trained in the care of children and infants. The standards for the crèches shall be laid down by the state government.
8. **Welfare officers (Section 49):** In every factory where 500 or more workers are employed, the factories Act also provides for appointment of welfare officers with prescribed qualification to look into the implementation of various facilities provided for the welfare of employees. The state government may prescribe the duties, qualifications and so on of such officers.
9. **Power to frame rules (Section 50):** The state government is empowered to make rules regarding the welfare of workers.

Provisions to Regulate Working Hours of Employees (Sections 51–55)

The Act regulates the working hours for adult workers employed in the factories. The important provisions related to working hours are discussed as follows:

1. **Weekly hours (Section 51):** The Act clearly mentions that no adult worker is required or allowed to work in a factory for more than 48 hours in any week.
2. **Daily hours (Section 54):** Section 54 of the Act provides that an adult worker is not required or allowed to work in a factory for more than 9 hours in any working day. The daily maximum may be exceeded only with the previous approval of the Chief Inspector to facilitate change of shifts.
3. **Intervals for rest (Section 55):** The Act fixes the periods of work of adult workers in a factory in a manner that each day it is so fixed that no period exceeds 5 hours so that no worker works for more than 5 hours before he has had an interval for rest of at least half an hour. However, the state government or the Chief Inspector may, by order in writing, and for reasons stated therein, increase the work period to 6 hours.

Provisions Relating to Spreadover, Night Shifts and Overlapping Shifts (Sections 56–60)

There are specific regulations relating to health and safety of women and young employees under the Act. Provisions relating to employment of young persons and women are stated as follows:

1. **Spreadover (Section 56):** The periods of work of an adult worker in a factory have to be arranged in a manner that is inclusive of his intervals for rest under Section 55, they do not spread over more than 10.5 hours in any day. The Chief Inspector is empowered for specified reasons to increase the spreadover up to 12 hours.

2. **Night shifts (Section 57):** Where a worker in a factory works on a shift which extends beyond midnight, following are important rules to be kept in mind:
   a. His weekly holiday and compensatory holiday cover a period of holiday for 24 consecutive hours beginning when his shift ends.
   b. The following day for him shall be deemed to be the period of 24 hours beginning when such shift ends and the hours he has worked after midnight shall be counted in the previous day.
3. **Overlapping shifts (Section 58):** The Act specifies that work must not be carried on in any factory by means of a system of shifts so planned that more than one relay of workers is engaged in work of the same kind at the same time. However, the state government or the Chief Inspector is empowered to grant exemption from this rule.
4. **Double employment (Section 60):** In any factory, no adult worker is required or allowed to work on any day on which he has already been working in any other factory, in such circumstances as may be prescribed.

Case 3.4 discussion clarifies the intention of law makers while extending various benefits to the workers through different provision of this Act.

Case 3.4: *Petroleum Employees Union v. Bharat Petroleum Corporation*[4]

In this case, the union of petroleum employees was agitating the point as to the number of working hours in connection with 65 workers who were working as Retail Outlet Technicians, originally their nomenclature called as Retail Outlet Fitters (ROF) must be fixed to 8 hours a day. These 65 workers were employees of the Bharat Petroleum Corporation (the company) in its marketing division. The company was dealing with petroleum products and was also a successor of erstwhile Burmah Shell, a foreign company. It has inherited along with the assets of the said company a certain work force which also included the ROF as originally employed by the said foreign company.

As stated by the employees, ROF was required to attend to the need of the retail outlet dealers known as petrol pumps. The petrol pumps had underground tanks from which the petroleum products were pumped out with the aid of pumping machine which had a built-in device of measuring the quantity being dispensed through it and also indicating the total price of the sale. It may or may not have provision for showing and calculating the total price of the sale transaction, but it did have metering device to indicate the quantity that was sold. In order to see that this pumping devices work properly, the aforesaid ROF had to attend to pumps situated in their allotted territories. For this purpose, the system worked out was that one of the pumps in their area used to act as a hub or a reporting station where the ROF would go to find out as to which of the pumps had developed problem, necessitating his visit. Apart from this, ROF had to visit all the pumps at regular intervals just to check that they were working properly and, if need be, to service them. These pumps might require repair which this ROF had to carry out.

The demand of the workmen was that like any other workers they should also have fixed hours of working. For this purpose, they were relying on the provisions of the Factories Act which stated this number to be 8 hours. The reason for them to so rely was a notification that had been issued by the state government in its Official Gazette. The company was also issuing necessary circulars to see that its retail outlet dealers were made aware of this notification. It was therefore an admitted position that the retail outlet where the product of the company was being given to the public at large had become a factory as per the said state notification and it was also an agreed position under the provisions of Factories Act that there has to be a fixed working hours which usually has 8 hours and that was what the workmen were demanding as stated above.

[4] BomCR 267, (1999) IILLJ 389 Bom, 1999 (2) MhLJ 926.

The company contended that the workmen were all employed in the marketing division of the company and there was no question of their being treated as factory workers. Consequently, the provisions of the Factories Act would not apply to them. On the other hand, the workmen by way of the petition contended that they were very much factory workers as they were working in the retail outlets which were the factory.

Discussion Point

In the above-mentioned circumstance, could the ROFs be treated as factory workers?

Judgement and Explanation

The court admitted the position that for working into the retail outlets in the manner stated above, the ROF had nothing to do with the factory as such. It was their working place that would determine whether they were factory workers or not. In this case, the nature of duty and place of work did not support the claim of the workers to be the factory workers. It was further stated by the court if the argument was to be accepted that 8 hours working per day was to be fixed because of the Factories Act and its applicability, it would necessarily mean that only that provision of the Factories Act would apply and rest of it would not be applicable to the workmen by the very nature of the duty. Therefore, it was decided by the court that there could not be any question of Factories Act being made applicable to the limited extent of fixing the working hours only.

In light of the above discussion, it is clear that the Factories Act is no doubt a beneficial piece of legislature meant essentially for the safety and well-being of the workers in general as also obligation being cast on the factory owners to take care of the interest of the public at large so far as safety standards are concerned. It has therefore made provisions for the purpose of achieving all or any objection keeping in mind the welfare of the workmen employed by the factory as also the member of the public and the provisions of having 8 hours a day and a weekly off is just one of the elements of the aforesaid exercise of looking after the welfare of the workmen.

Notice of Periods of Work for Adults (Sections 61–63)

Display of Notice (Section 61)

A notice must be displayed in every factory showing periods of work of adults, classification of workers in groups according to nature of their work, shifts and relays and so on. If there is any change made in the system of work, the same must be notified to the inspector before change. The manager of every factory must maintain a register of adult workers which shows the name of each worker, the nature of his work, the group in which he is included, the relay in which he is allotted and so on. The Act further provides that the hours of work of an adult worker must correspond with the notice and register referred above.

Register of Adult Workers (Sections 62 and 63)

The manager of every factory has to maintain a register of adult workers and such register is to be made available to the inspector at all times during working hours, or when any work is being carried on in the factory. The register must show:

a. The name of each adult worker in the factory.
b. The nature of his work.

c. The group, if any, in which he is included.
d. Where his group works on shift, the relay to which he is allotted.
e. Such other particulars as may be prescribed.

Where the inspector is of opinion that any muster roll or register maintained as a part of the routine of a factory gives in respect of any or all the workers in the factory the particulars required under this section, he may, by order in writing, direct that such muster roll or register to the corresponding extent is to be maintained in place of the register of adult workers in that factory. The same register is treated as the register of adult workers in that factory after such replacement.

Under Subsection (1A), it is clarified that no adult worker is required or allowed to work in any factory unless his name and other particulars have been entered in the register of adult workers. It is further stated that the state government may prescribe the form of the register of adult workers, the manner in which it is required to be maintained and the period for which it is to be preserved.

Hours of work to correspond with notice under Section 61 and register under Section 62 (Section 63): No adult worker is required or allowed to work in any factory otherwise than in accordance with the notice of periods of work for adults displayed in the factory and the entries made beforehand against his name in the register of adult workers of the factory.

Limitation of work (Section 64(3)): Following are the limitations of work inclusive of overtime placed by the Act:

1. The total number of hours of work by an adult worker in any day cannot exceed 10.
2. The work spreadover inclusive of intervals for rest must not exceed 12 hours in any one day.
3. The total number of hours of work by an adult worker in a week, including overtime, must not exceed 60.
4. Under the Act, quarter is a period of 3 consecutive months beginning on the 1st January, the 1st of April, the 1st of July or the 1st of October.

Confidential position (Section 64(1)): The state government is empowered to make rules defining the persons who hold positions of supervision or management or are employed in a confidential position in a factory or empower the Chief Inspector to declare any person, other than a person defined by such rules, as a person holding position of supervision or management or employed in a confidential position in a factory if, in the opinion of the Chief Inspector, such person holds such position or is so employed, and the provisions of this Chapter, other than the provisions of clause (b) of Subsection (1) of Section 66 and of the proviso to that subsection, shall not apply to any person so defined or declared, provided that any person so defined or declared shall, where the ordinary rate of wages of such person does not exceed the wage limit specified in Subsection (6) of Section 1 of the Payment of Wages Act, 1936 (4 of 1936), as amended from time to time, be entitled to extra wages in respect of overtime work under Section 59.

Rules for working hours (Section 64(4)): According to Subsection 4 of Section 64 of the Act, while making rules under Section 64, the state government shall not exceed (except in respect of exemption under clause (a) of Subsection (2)), the following limits of work inclusive of overtime:

1. The total number of hours of work in any day shall not exceed 10.
2. The spreadover, inclusive of intervals for rest, shall not exceed 12 hours in any one day:

   Provided that the State Government may, in respect of any or all of the categories of workers referred to in clause (d) of Subsection (2) (workers engaged in any work which for technical reasons must be carried on continuously from the provisions of Sections 51, 52, 54, 55 and 56), make rules prescribing the circumstances in which, and the conditions subject to which, the restrictions imposed by clause (i) and clause (ii) shall not apply in order to enable a shift worker to work the whole or part of a subsequent shift in the absence of a worker who has failed to report for duty

3. The total number of hours of work in a week, including overtime, shall not exceed 60.
4. The total number of hours of overtime shall not exceed 100 (The Factories (Amendment) Bill, 2016) for any one quarter. (Here, 'quarter' has the meaning as explained above.)

Section 64(5) further directs that rules made under this section shall remain in force for not more than 5 years.

Hours and spreadover (Section 65(2)): The exemption under Section 65 (2) can be granted only if following conditions are met:

1. The total number of hours of work in any day must not exceed 12.
2. The spreadover, inclusive of intervals for rest, must not exceed 13 hours in any one day.
3. The total number of hours of work in any week, including overtime, must not exceed 60.

   Provided that the Central Government or the State Government or the Chief Inspector with the prior approval of the State Government, as the case may be, may, by order, further extend the total number of hours of overtime work in any quarter up to one hundred and twenty-five in the public interest (The Factories (Amendment) Bill, 2016).

4. No worker must be allowed to work overtime for more than 7 days at a stretch, and the total number of hours of overtime work in any quarter must not exceed 115. (The Factories (Amendment) Bill, 2016).

The Factories (Amendment) Bill, 2016—Statement of Objects and Reasons (Bill No. 216 of 2016)

1. The Factories Act was enacted in 1948. Its main object is to ensure adequate safety measures and to promote the health and welfare of the workers employed in factories. The Act has been amended in the years 1949, 1950, 1951, 1954, 1970 and 1976. The last amendment to the Factories Act, 1948, was made in the year 1987, wherein a separate Chapter was inserted relating to hazardous process.
2. There have been several developments over the last 20 years since the last amendment was made. These include changes in the manufacturing practices and emergence of new technologies, ratification of ILO conventions, judicial decisions, recommendations of the committees and decisions taken in the conferences of Chief Inspectors of Factories. In order to give effect to those changes, a comprehensive Factories (Amendment) Bill, 2014 including the amendments presently proposed to Sections 64 and 65 of the said Act was introduced in Lok Sabha on 7 August 2014. The said Bill was referred to the Department-related Parliamentary Standing Committee on Labour for examination and report, which presented its report on the said Bill on 22 December 2014 to Parliament, which is under examination.
3. Since consideration and passing of the aforesaid Bill in Parliament may take some more time, with a view to boost the manufacturing sector and to facilitate ease of doing business so as to enhance employment opportunities, it has been decided to amend Sections 64 and 65 of the Factories Act, 1948, urgently to

extend the total number of hours of work on overtime. The salient features of the Factories (Amendment) Bill, 2016, inter alia, are to:

a. Enhance the limit of overtime hours from the present limit of 50 hours per quarter to 100 hours per quarter under Section 64.
b. Further increase the limit of overtime hours to a maximum of 125 hours per quarter in public interest under Section 65.
c. Empower the central government, in addition to the state governments, to make exempting rules and exempting orders in respect of total number of hours of work on overtime in a quarter, which would ensure uniformity in its application by various state governments and union territories.

4. The need for increasing the total number of hours of work on overtime in quarter is based on the demand from industries, so that factories can carry out the work on urgent basis.

Source: http://www.prsindia.org/uploads/media/Factories/Factories%20(A)%20bill,%202016.pdf, accessed on 8 February 2016.

Exemptions (Sections 64 and 65): The Act empowers the state government and also the central government (The Factories (Amendment) Bill, 2016) to exempt for limited periods certain factories from compliance with some of the provisions relating to hours of work and employment. Such exemptions are granted in special cases, for example in the case of workers engaged in urgent repairs or in preparatory and complementary work or the nature of the work in certain industries requires exceptional treatment, for example, workers engaged in engine rooms and boilers or in the printing of newspapers. However, the state government or central government (The Factories (Amendment) Bill, 2016) may exempt persons holding positions of supervision and management or in confidential positions in a factory from the operation of the rules regarding working hours. But the rule against the employment of women at night cannot be changed by the state government.

LO6: Employment of Young Persons and Women

Employment of Young Persons and Children

Rules regarding child workers are enumerated in the Factories Act, Mines Act and so on. The Children (Pledging of Labour) Act (Act 11 of 1933) prohibits the making of agreements to pledge the labour of children and the employment of children whose labour has been pledged. On the other hand, the Children Act of 1938, 1960 and 1978 prohibit the employment of a child who has not completed 15 years of age in any occupation connected with the transport of passengers, goods or mails by railway or connected with a part authority within the limits of any part. The Act also does not permit the employment of a child, who has not completed his 14th year of age, in the processes set forth in the Schedule to the Act. The Factories Act, 1948, also provides different sections dealing with the employment of children between 15 and 17 subject to certain restrictions as regards their periods of rest and so on.

Following are the provisions dealing with the employment of young persons and children under Factories Act:

1. **Prohibition on employment of children (Sections 67 and 68):** Section 67 of the Act mentions that any child who has not completed his 14th year is not required or allowed to work in any factory. Section 68 adds that a child who has completed his 14th year or an adolescent shall not be required or allowed to work in any factory unless:
   a. He has been granted a certificate of fitness which is in the custody of the manager.
   b. Such child or adolescent carries a token giving a reference to such certificate.
2. **Certificate of fitness (Section 69)**: The above-mentioned certificate of fitness is a certificate granted to a child or adolescent by a certifying surgeon after being satisfied that he has completed his 14th year and has attained the prescribed physical standards. In case of an adolescent, the certificate is granted if the surgeon is satisfied that he has completed his 15th year and is fit for a full day's work in a factory. The certificate is valid only for a period of 12 months. The certifying surgeon must have sufficient knowledge of the intended place of work and of the manufacturing process involved. It may also be granted subject to conditions (e.g., that of periodical re-examination). The certificate may be renewed and revoked if necessary. The occupier of the factory has to pay the fee for the certificate and all must not be recovered from the young person or his parents or guardian (Section 69).
3. **Effect of certificate of fitness (Section 70):** An adolescent who has been granted a certificate of fitness and who carries a token is deemed to be an adult for the purposes of calculating the hours of work of an adult and annual leave. However, any adolescent who has not attained the age of 17 years cannot be employed or permitted to work in any factory during night. An adolescent who has not been granted a certificate of fitness has to be treated as a child for the purposes of the Act (Section 70).
4. **Working hours for children (Section 71):** Section 71 of the Act deals with the working hours for children as stated below:
   a. No child shall be employed or permitted to work in any factory
      i. For more than 4.5 hours in any day.
      ii. During the night.

   'Night' for the purpose of this section means a period of at least 12 consecutive hours which shall include the interval between 10 PM and 6 AM. The Act further states that the period of work of all children employed in a factory must not exceed to two shifts which do not overlap or spreadover more than 5 hours each. Each child can be employed in only one of the relays which cannot be changed more frequently than once in a period of 30 days. However, with the previous permission in writing of the Chief Inspector, above frequency can be changed.
5. **Notice and register (Sections 72–74):** Section 72 directs that a notice must be displayed showing clearly the periods of work of children in the factory. No child shall be required or allowed to work in any factory on any day on which he has already been working in another factory. Section 73 of the Act deals with the maintenance of register of child workers by the factory manager. Such register of child workers must show the name of each child worker, the nature of his work, the group (if any) in which he is included, the relay to which he is allotted and the number of his certificate of fitness. The Section further elaborates that no child worker shall be required or allowed to work in any factory unless his name and other particulars have been entered in the

register of child workers (Section 73 (IA)) as added by the Factories (Amendment) Act, 1976. The hours of work of a child must correspond with the notice and the register (Section 74) mentioned above. The provisions of Section 52 which relate to weekly holidays apply also to child workers.

6. **Medical examination (Section 75):** If the inspector is of opinion that a person working as an adult is either a young person or the young person is not fit to work, he is authorized to direct the manager of the factory to have the person medically examined by a certifying surgeon.
7. **Power to Frame Rule (Section 76):** Under Section 76, the state government is empowered to make rules that:
   a. Prescribe the forms of certificate of fitness to be granted under Section 69, providing for the grant of duplicates in the event of loss of the original certificate, and fixing the fees which may be charged for such certificates and renewals thereof and such duplicates.
   b. Prescribe the physical standards to be attained by children and adolescents working in factories.
   c. Regulate the procedure of certifying surgeons under this Chapter.
   d. Specify other duties which certifying surgeons may be required to perform in connection with the employment of young persons in factories, and fixing the fees which may be charged for such duties and the persons by whom they are payable.

Other Rules Regarding the Employment of Young Persons

Following are some other rules regarding the employment of young persons:

1. As laid down by Section 23, the Act does not permit a young person to work at any dangerous machine unless he has been fully instructed as to the dangers arising in connection with the machine and the precautions to be observed, and
   a. Has received sufficient training in work at the machine.
   b. Is under adequate supervision by a person who has a thorough knowledge and experience of the machine.

   The state government may prescribe what machines are dangerous for the purpose of this section.
2. Section 76 of the Act empowers the state government to make rules regarding the forms of the certificate of fitness, the procedure relating to their issue and the physical standards to be attained by children and adolescents.
3. Another important Section to be discussed here is Section 77, which mentions that the provisions relating to the employment of young persons are in addition to and not in derogation of the provisions of the Children Act of 1938, 1960 and 1978.

Restrictions on the Employment of Women Workers (Section 66)

By Section 66 of the Act, following restrictions have been imposed to the employment of women workers:

1. **Maximum daily work is 9 hours (Section 54):** The provisions of Section 54 (which lays down that the maximum daily hours of work shall be 9 hours) cannot be relaxed and exemption cannot be granted in respect of any women worker.
2. **Prohibition of night work:** Any woman worker is not required or allowed to work in any factory except between the hours of 6 AM and 7 PM. However, the state government may, by notification in the official gazette, vary the limits for any factory or group or class or description

of factories. But in any case such variation cannot authorize the employment of women between the hours 10 PM and 5 AM.

3. **Change of shift only after holiday:** The Act does not permit the change of shifts for women except after a weekly holiday or any other holiday. However, for the women workers of fish-curing or fish-canning factories, the state government may make rules providing for the exemption from the aforesaid restrictions (wholly or partially or conditionally). Such an exemption is granted because in factories, as mentioned above, the employment of women beyond the hours specified is necessary to prevent damage to or deterioration in any raw material. But such rules will remain in force for not more than 3 years at a time.
4. **Other restrictions:** Following are other restrictions on the employment of women workers:
   a. **Work on or near machinery in motion (Section 22(2)):** Any woman or young person cannot be allowed to clean, lubricate or adjust any part of the machinery while the prime mover or transmission machinery is in motion or to work between moving parts, or between fixed and moving parts of any machinery which is in motion.
   b. **Cotton openers (Section 27):** The Act states that no woman or child can be employed in any part of a factory for pressing cotton in which a cotton opener is at work. Women and children may be employed on the side of the partition where the feed end is situated only if the feed end of the cotton opener is in a room separated from the delivery end by a partition extending to the roof or to such height as the inspector may in a particular case specify in writing.
   c. **Excessive weights (Section 34):** The Act empowers the state government to make rules prescribing the maximum weights which may be lifted, carried or moved by adult men, adult women, adolescents and children employed in factories or in any class or description of factories or in carrying on any specified process.
   d. **Crèches (Section 48):** If a factory employs more than 30 women workers, there must be provided and maintained a suitable room or rooms for the use of children under the age of 6 years of such women.
   e. **Dangerous operations (Section 87):** The state government may make special rules to control and regulate the factories which carry on operations exposing women, young persons and other workers to a serious risk of bodily injury, poisoning or disease.

LO7: Annual Leaves with Wages

The Factories Act provides directions for weekly holidays, compensatory holidays and annual leave with wages according to certain rules. The provisions regarding these holidays are explained as follows:

1. **Weekly holidays (Section 52):** The Act states that every adult worker must have a holiday on the first day of the week. But the manager of the factory is allowed to fix the holiday on any other day which is 2 days before or after the first day of the week. In case of such substitution, notice has to be given to the Inspector of Factories and also to be displayed in the factory premises. However, no such substitution can be made which will result in any worker working for more than 10 days consecutively without a holiday for a whole day. The state government is authorized to make rules providing for exemption from the above section in certain cases, for example, for urgent repairs.
2. **Compensatory holidays (Section 53):** The provision for compensatory holiday is applicable where as a result of the exemption of factory from the operation of the role regarding weekly

holidays, a worker is deprived of any weekly holiday. In such a case, he shall be allowed within the month in which the holidays were due, or within 2 months immediately following that month, compensatory holidays of equal number to the holidays lost.

Rules Governing the Annual Leaves with Wages

Entitlement of annual leaves with wages (Sections 78–84): There is provision of the grant of a certain period of leave with wages to workmen in the Act. Every such worker who has worked for a period of 240 days or more in a factory during a calendar year is allowed during the subsequent calendar year leave with wages. The number of days of such leaves is calculated by applying following rule:

1. **If the worker is an adult**—one day for every 20 days of work performed by him during the previous calendar year.
2. **If the worker is a child**—one day for every 15 days of work performed by him during the previous calendar year.

Section 79: Following are some important rules laid down by Section 79, to be followed while considering the annual leaves with wages:

1. **Computation of working days:** While counting the number of days of work performed by a worker, the following are to be included:
   a. Days of lay-off.
   b. Maternity leave to a female worker, not exceeding 12 weeks.
   c. The leave earned in the previous year. But the worker shall not earn leave for these days.

   The leave admissible under the rule mentioned above has to be exclusive of all holidays whether occurring during or at either end of the period of leave.
2. **Computation of period of 240 days:** A worker whose service commences on a day other than on the first day of January is entitled to leave with wages at the rate laid down above if he has worked for two-thirds of the total number of days in the remainder of the calendar year.
3. **Discharge dismissal, superannuation, death or quitting of employment:** The Act states if a worker is discharged or dismissed from service or quits his employment or is superannuated or dies while in service, during the course of the calendar year, he or his heir or nominee, as the case may be, shall be entitled to wages in lieu of the quantum of leave to which he was entitled immediately before his discharge, dismissal, quitting of employment, superannuation or death calculated at the rates specified above (Subsection (1)). This entitlement remains unaffected even if such a worker had not worked for the entire period specified in Subsection (2).
4. **Treatment of fraction of leaves:** While calculating the leave period, a fraction of leave for half a day or more has to be treated as 1 day and fractions of less amount shall be omitted.
5. **Treatment of earned leaves:** Leave earned, but not taken by an adult worker, can be carried forward to a succeeding year subject to a limit of 30 days. In the case of a child worker, the limit for carried forward leave is 40 days. However, earned leave not allowed because of any scheme for leave in operation can be carried forward without limit.
6. **Application for leaves:** Application for leaves must be submitted to the manager not less than 15 days before the date of commencement of leave. However, in the case of public utility service, it must be

made not less than 30 days before such date. In case a worker falls sick and wants to avail himself of the annual leave during the period of illness, he shall be granted leave even though the application is not made before the period specified above. The application for leave may be for the whole of the leave due or part of it. However, earned leave cannot be taken more than three times during the same year.

7. **Grant of leave:** To ensure the continuity of work, the occupier or manager of the factory may draw up a scheme for regulating the grant of leave. However, such a scheme has to be agreed by the works committee, if any, or the representatives of workers in the factory. It must be lodged with the Chief Inspector and displayed in the factory.
8. **Refusal of leave:** An application for leave submitted in proper time cannot be refused unless the refusal is in accordance with any leave scheme in operation.
9. **Payment of wages to worker for leave for to workers for leave period if he is discharged or if he quits:** If the employment of a worker who is entitled to leave under the Act is terminated by the occupier before:
   a. He has taken the entire leave to which he is entitled, or
   b. If having applied for and having not been granted such leave, the worker quits his employment before he has taken the leave

   The occupier of the factory is directed to pay him the amount payable under Section 80 in respect of the leave not taken, and such payment is to be made, where the employment of the worker is terminated by the occupier, before the expiry of the second working day after such termination, and where a worker who quits his employment on or before the next pay day.
10. **Treatment of unavailed leaves while computing the period of notice:** The unavailed leaves of a worker cannot be taken into consideration while computing the period of any notice required to be given before discharge or dismissal.

Payment in Advance (Section 81)

A worker who has been allowed leave for not less than 4 days, in the case of an adult, and 5 days, in the case of a child, has to be paid the wages due for the periods of the leave allowed before his leave begins.

Mode of Recovery of Unpaid Wages (Section 82)

Any sum required to be paid by an employer, under this Chapter but not paid by him, is recoverable as delayed wages under the provisions of the Payment of Wages Act, 1936 (IV of 1936).

Power of State Government to Frame Rules and Exempt the Factories (Sections 83-86)

The state government may exempt a factory from the operation of the above rules if it is satisfied that factory's own leave rules extend benefits (the totality of benefits) which are not less favourable to the workers than the statutory leave rules. If a worker by virtue of any award, agreement (including settlement) or contract of service is entitled to a longer period of leave than that provided by the aforesaid rules, then he will be entitled to such longer leave.

The workers of railway factory administered by the government are beyond the scope of the rules contained in these sections. These workers are governed by leave rules approved by the central government.

If an award, agreement (including settlement) or contract of service provides for a longer annual leave with wages than provided in the sections discussed above, the quantum of leave, which the worker is entitled to, has to be in accordance with such award, agreement or contract of service. However, in relation to matters not provided for in such award, agreement or contract of service or matters which are provided for less favourably therein, the provisions of above-mentioned sections (Sections 79–82), so far, as may be, are applicable (as added by the Amendment of 1976).

Provisions for Wages and Salary

Wages and salary are the terms used to denote payment made for service. Conceptually, there is no difference between salary and wages both being a recompense for work done or services rendered; however, ordinarily the former expression is used in connection with services of non-manual type while the latter is used in connection with manual services. Thus, the word 'salary' is used for payment of services of a higher class, and 'wages' is confined to the earnings of labourers and artisans. The High Court of Madras shared the opinion on the term 'wages' and stated that if the remuneration is to be paid daily or weekly, it can be called wages, but where there is monthly payment and is fairly high, considering the general standard of payment, it is to be called salary. According to the Payment of Wages Act, any amount over ₹1,000 may be considered as salary for the purposes of Factories Act.

Following is the discussion on important provisions dealing with wages and salary:

1. **Wages during leave period (Section 80):** According to rules laid down by Section 80 of the Act, for the period of leave allowed to a worker, he is entitled to be paid at a rate equal to the daily average of his total full-time earnings for the days on which he actually worked during the month immediately preceding his leave. While calculating the average rate, any overtime or bonus is excluded but dearness allowance and the cash equivalent of the advantage accruing through the concessional sale to the worker of food grains and other articles are included. The cash equivalent, referred to above, is to be computed by applying the same method as was used when calculating the extra wages payable for overtime work.
2. **Wages, if the worker is terminated or quits the service (Section 79):** When the employment of a worker who is entitled to leave is terminated by the occupier of the factory before he has taken the entire leave to which he is entitled, he has to be paid wages for the leave period not taken and such wages must be paid before the expiry of the second working day after such termination. In the same way, if the worker quits his service after having applied for and obtained leave, he must be paid wages for the leave period and the amount of wages payable is to be calculated according to the provisions of Section 80.

Provisions for the Extra Wages for Overtime

1. **Wages for overtime work (Section 59(1)):** If a worker works in a factory for more than 9 hours on any day or for more than 48 hours in any week, he is, in respect of overtime work, entitled to wages at the rate of twice his ordinary rate of wages.
2. **Ordinary rate of wages (Section 59(2)):** For the purpose of Subsection (1), 'ordinary rate of wages' stands for the basic wages plus such allowances, including the cash equivalent of the advantage accruing through the concessional sale to workers of food grains and other articles, as the worker is for the time being entitled to. However, it does not include a bonus and wages for overtime work.

3. **Time rate of the work (Section 59(3)):** If the workers in a factory are paid on a piece rate basis, the time rate of their work is computed by applying the following rules:
   a. If the worker had been paid on the same or identical job during a month immediately preceding a month during which overtime work was done, the time rate has to be equivalent to the daily average of their full-time earnings for the days of the overtime work. Also, such time rates shall consider being the ordinary rates of wages of those workers.
   b. But if a worker had not worked in the immediately preceding calendar month on the same or identical job, the time rate shall consider being equivalent to the daily average of the earning of the worker for the days on which he actually worked in the week in which the overtime work was done.

   For the purposes of this subsection while computing the earnings for the days on which the workers actually worked, the allowance also includes the cash equivalent to buy food grains and other articles through concessional sale as the worker is for the time being entitled to. However, any bonus or wages for overtime work payable for the period with reference to which the earnings are being computed are not be included.
4. **Cash for advantages to workers (Section 59 (4)):** The cash equivalent of the advantage extended to the workers through the concessional sale of food grains and other articles shall be computed as often as may be prescribed on the basis of the maximum quantity of food-grains and other articles admissible to a standard family.

   'Standard family' here means a family consisting of the worker, his or her spouse and two children below the age of 14 years requiring in all three adult consumption units.

   'Adult consumption unit' stated above means the consumption unit of a male above the age of 14 years, and the consumption unit of a female above the age of 14 years and that of a child below the age of 14 years is to be calculated at the rates of 0.8 and 0.6, respectively, of one adult consumption unit.

Power of State Government to Frame Rules

Section 59(5), empowers the state government to frame rules prescribing the manner in which the cash equivalent of the advantage accruing through the concessional sale to a worker of food grains and other articles has to be computed, and the register that is to be maintained in a factory for the purpose of securing compliance with the provisions of this section.

LO8: Penalties and Contingence of Offences

Sections 92–106 of the Act deal with the rules regarding penalties for offences against the Act. Following are the brief discussions on major provisions laid down for penalties for the offences under the Act.

General Penalty for Offences (Section 92)

The Act declares the owner or the manager of the factory responsible for the contravention of the provisions of this Act or of any rules made there under or of any order in writing given there under, unless otherwise expressly provided in this Act and subject to the provisions of Section 93, if in, or in respect of. In such a case, the occupier and manager of the factory both are considered guilty of an offence and punishable with imprisonment for a term which may extend to 2 years or with fine which may extend to ₹100,000 or with both, and if the contravention is continued after conviction, with as further fine which may extend to ₹1,000 for each day on which the contravention is so continued.

Case 3.5 will throw more light on the responsibility of managers and provisions for penalty where the manager is found guilty of contravention of the provisions of the Act.

Case 3.5: *Superintendent and Remembrancer ... v. H. E. Watson*[5]

The Inspector of Factories inspected a factory, the Statesman Printing Press (the factory), on 15 and 19 October 1933 and found that one printer, five proof readers and seven compositors in the advertisement section were employed on different dates beyond the time limit of 11 hours per day, as prescribed by Section 28, Indian Factories Act. The Inspector further stated in his report that the register of persons employed as directed and prescribed under Section 35 of the Act was not correctly maintained, regard being had to the facts that no entries were made in the register after 17 October 1933. The specified hours of work of the persons employed were also not entered in the register and that different shifts in which the workers were employed were not shown there. The Inspector lodged a complaint against Mr Watson for the violation of the provisions of the Act on the basis of the direction issued by Section 33(3) of the Act, which stated that the occupier was to be deemed as manager for the purposes of the Act, and he was jointly and severally responsible for any violation of the law.

Mr Watson, the manager of the factory, stated in his defence that during the dates between which the offences were alleged to have been committed, he was not in the country, and he had given over charge to Mr Hemmin, the Director of the Statesman Ltd. He argued that no charge could lie against him in respect of matters which took place in his absence and without his knowledge. It was further argued that he was not the occupier of the premises. It was therefore pleaded in defence that no penalty could be inflicted under the Indian Factories Act, on the accused, placed on his trial. So far as the charge under Section 28 read with Section 41(a) was concerned, it was stated on the side of the defence that the 13 persons referred to in the petition of complaint were not manual labourers; that they were persons who used their educational qualifications, were experts and were engaged in work of supervision or confidential work. It was further added the persons working in the advertisement department, the printer, the readers and copyholders mentioned in the petition of complaint, were all outside the scope of Section 28, Indian Factories Act.

Discussion Points

1. Could the penalties prescribed by the Factories Act be imposed on Mr Watson against whom complaints were lodged, and he was absent from the duties as manager, as contemplated by law, at the time when there was the alleged infringement of the law?
2. Did the infringement of the law by the manager of the factory assuming that there was infringement of the law involve want of good faith on the part of the manager?

Judgement and Explanation

To settle the first issue, it was held that Mr Watson was not the person against whom complaints could be lodged or the person who could be charged with any of the offences or the infringement of the law complained of, and on whom penalty could be imposed under the law for infringement of the law at a time when he was not the manager responsible for the working of the factory. For the second issue, the court found that

[5] AIR 1934 Cal 730, 152 Ind Cas 566.

a claim by the manager in good faith, in view of the difficulty, felt in interpreting the different provisions of the Factories Act, that the persons mentioned in the petition of complaint were not persons to whom Section 28 could be held to be applicable. The manager's view in this behalf was placed before the authorities for consideration, and no opinion was expressed by the authorities themselves. The only reply that was vouchsafed by them was the launching of the prosecution by a complaint before the criminal court, which has resulted in an acquittal of the person against whom the complaint was lodged, on the interpretation of the provisions of the law applicable to the case. It could not therefore be said that there was absence of good faith on the part of the manager of the factory.

Liability of Owner (Section 93)

The owner of any premises, let out for use as different factories, is responsible for the provision and maintenance of common facilities and services, for example, approach roads, drainage, water supply, latrines.

Enhanced Penalty after Previous Conviction (Section 94)

The act further provides if any person who has been convicted of any offence punishable under Section 92 is again found guilty of an offence involving a contravention of the same provision, then he is liable for a stricter punishment. Such a person is punishable on a subsequent conviction with imprisonment for a term which may extend to 3 years or with fine, which is not less than ₹10,000 but which may extend to ₹200,000 or with both.

Accident causing death: Where contravention of any of the provisions of Chapter IV of the Act or any rule made there—under or under Section 87—results in an accident causing death or serious bodily injury, the fine is not less than ₹1,000 in the case of an accident causing death, and ₹500 in the case of an accident causing serious bodily injury.

'Serious bodily injury' mentioned in the above lines stands for an injury which involves, or in all probability will involve, the permanent loss of the use of, or permanent injury to, any limb or the permanent loss of, or injury to sight or hearing, or the fracture of any bone, but does not include the fracture of bone or joint (not being fracture of more than one bone or joint) of any phalanges of the hand or foot.

Penalties

The penalties for the major offences are mentioned below:

Offences	*Imprisonment*	*Fine*
Obstructing Inspector (Section 95)	Up to 6 months and/or	Up to ₹10,000
Wrongfully disclosing result of analysis of sample under Section 91 (Section 96)	Up to 6 months and/or	Up to ₹10,000
Contravention of any duty or liability by a worker (Section 97)	Nil	₹500
Using false certificate of Fitness (Section 98)	Up to 2 months	₹1,000
Permitting double employment of child (Section 99)	Nil	₹1,000

Exemption of Occupier or Manager from Liability in Certain Cases (Section 101)

In most cases, the occupier or manager of the factory is charged for the offences committed against the Act. But the occupier or the manager is exempted from liability if he can prove in the court that he has used due diligence to enforce the execution of the Act and that some other person committed the offence without his knowledge, consent or connivance.

Cognizance of Offences (Section 105)

No court can take cognizance of an offence under the Act except on a complaint by or with the previous sanction of an inspector in writing. Only a Presidency Magistrate or a magistrate of the first class can try the offences under the Act.

Limitation of Prosecution (Section 106)

The complaint has to be filed within 3 months of the date when the commission of the offence came to the knowledge of an inspector. However, for disobeying a written order of an inspector, complaint may be filed within 6 months of the date when the offence was committed.

Appeals (Section 107)

The manager or the occupier of a factory on whom an order in writing has been served by an inspector can appeal against it to the prescribed authority within 30 days.

Display of Notices (Section 108)

In certain cases, as prescribed by the rules, abstracts of the Act and the rules are required to be displayed in the factory. All such notices under the Act must be displayed in English and in a language understood by the majority of the workers employed therein. The notices must be displayed in a conspicuous and convenient place at or near the main entrance of the factory and must be maintained in a clean and legible condition. The Chief Inspector may also instruct to display the posters relating to the health, safety and welfare of workers.

Summary

1. Indian Constitution has detailed provisions for the rights of the citizens and also the Directive Principles for securing the health and strength of employees and humane conditions of work.
2. The Factories Act, 1948, is a central enactment and deals with occupational health and safety as well as welfare of workers employed in a factory.

3. The main objective of the Act is to regulate the conditions of work in manufacturing establishments coming within the definition of the term 'factory' as used in the Act.
4. The Act mandates to obtain a licence before a factory is started. Section 6 of the act empowers the state government to make rules requiring for the purposes of this Act.
5. The Act directs every occupier to ensure, so far as is reasonably practicable, the health, safety and welfare of all workers while they are at work in the factory.
6. The Factories Act permits the state government to appoint inspectors, Chief Inspectors of Factories, Additional Chief Inspectors, Joint Chief Inspectors and Deputy Chief Inspectors to implement the provisions of this Act.
7. Section 10 of the Act allows the state government to appoint qualified medical practitioners to be certifying surgeons for specified local areas or for specified factories or class of factories.
8. Employer of an establishment has to apply to the inspector of the local areas concerned in the prescribed form along with the prescribed fees to get the establishment registered under the Act.
9. Sections 11–20 of the Act contain specific provisions intended to ensure that the conditions under which work is carried on in factories do not affect the health of the workers injuriously.
10. Sections 21–40A, 40B and 41 of the Act deal with the safety of the workers in a factory. These aforementioned sections lay down the rules for the purpose of securing the safety of workers.
11. The state government is empowered to constitute a Site Appraisal Committee to examine the application for establishment of a factory involving hazardous process and send its recommendations to the state government.
12. The Site Appraisal Committee examines an application for the establishment of a factory involving hazardous process and makes its recommendation to the state government within a period of 90 days of the receipt of such application in the prescribed form.
13. Section 41D empowers the central government to appoint an Inquiry Committee to enquire whether such a factory is observing the standards of health and safety of workers as well as of the general public as prescribed and make recommendations.
14. Employee welfare refers to the facilities provided to workers in and outside the factory premises such as canteens, rest and recreation facilities, housing and all other services that contribute to the well-being of workers.
15. Sections 42–50 deal with the issues related to employee welfare.
16. The Act regulates the working hours for adult workers employed in the factories. The important provisions related to working hours are discussed under Sections 51–55.
17. There are specific regulations relating to health and safety of women and young employees under the Act. Provisions relating to employment of young persons and women are stated under Sections 56–60.
18. A notice must be displayed in every factory showing periods of work of adults, classification of workers in groups according to nature of their work, shifts and relays and so on.
19. The Act also does not permit the employment of a child who has not completed his 14th year of age in the processes set forth in the schedule to the Act.
20. The provisions under Sections 67–75 deal with the employment of young persons and children under Factories Act.
21. By Section 66 of the Act, a number of restrictions have been imposed to the employment of women workers.

22. The Factories Act provides for weekly holidays, compensatory holidays and annual leave with wages according to certain rules.
23. The Act states that every adult worker must have a holiday on the first day of the week.
24. Every such worker who has worked for a period of 240 days or more in a factory during a calendar year is allowed during the subsequent calendar year leave with wages.
25. The state government may exempt a factory from the operation of the above rules if it is satisfied that the factory's own leave rules extend benefits (the totality of benefits) which are not less favourable to the workers than the statutory leave rules.
26. Conceptually, there is no difference between salary and wages, both being a recompense for work done or services rendered, though ordinarily the former expression is used in connection with services of non-manual type while the latter is used in connection with manual services.
27. Section 59(5) empowers the state government to frame rules prescribing the manner in which the cash equivalent of the advantage accruing through the concessional sale to a worker of food grains and other articles has to be computed.
28. Sections 92–106 of the Act deal with the rules regarding penalties for offences against the Act.
29. The Act provides if any person who has been convicted of any offence punishable under Section 92 is again found guilty of an offence involving a contravention of the same provision, he is liable for a stricter punishment.
30. No court can take cognizance of an offence under the Act except on a complaint by or with the previous sanction of an inspector in writing.
31. In certain cases as prescribed by the rules, abstracts of the Act and the rules are required to be displayed in the factory.

Multiple Choice Questions

1. The Act regulates the conditions of work in ________.
   a. All types of domestic manufacturing establishments
   b. All types of domestic and foreign manufacturing establishments
   c. Only manufacturing establishments coming within the definition of the term 'factory'
   d. All of the above
2. The term 'factory' does not include
   a. A mine which is subject to the operation of the Indian Mines Act, 1952.
   b. A mobile unit belonging to the armed forces of the union.
   c. A railway running shed or a hotel, restaurant or eating place.
   d. All of the above.
3. ________ of the Act contain specific provisions intended to ensure that the conditions under which work is carried on in factories do not affect the health of the workers injuriously.
   a. Sections 11–20
   b. Sections 42–50
   c. Sections 92–106
   d. None of the above

4. Sections 21–40A, 40B and 41 of the Act deal with ____________ in a factory.
   a. The employee welfare
   b. The safety of the workers
   c. The annual leave and wages
   d. The rules regarding penalties for offences against the Act
5. The state government notifies to the occupier to employ a number of Safety Officers in a factory, wherein ____________ are ordinarily employed.
   a. One hundred or more workers
   b. Five hundred or more workers
   c. One thousand or more workers
   d. Five thousand or more workers
6. Sections 42–50 deal with the issues related to ____________.
   a. The employee welfare
   b. The safety of the workers
   c. The annual leave and wages
   d. The rules regarding penalties for offences against the Act
7. The number of first aid boxes must not be less than one for every ____________ employed in the factory.
   a. 100 workers
   b. 150 workers
   c. 250 workers
   d. 500 workers
8. Where more than ____________ are employed, the state government may issue instructions to open a canteen or canteens for workers.
   a. 100 workers
   b. 150 workers
   c. 250 workers
   d. 500 workers
9. In every factory employing more than ____________, provision has to be made for suitable and adequate room for the use of children under the age of 6 years of such women.
   a. 50 women workers
   b. 100 women workers
   c. 150 women workers
   d. 500 women workers
10. In every factory where 500 or more workers are employed, the Factories Act also provides for the appointment of ____________.
    a. A welfare officer
    b. A medical officer
    c. An education officer
    d. None of the above
11. No adult worker is required or allowed to work in a factory for more than ____________ in any week.
    a. 60 hours
    b. 24 hours
    c. 48 hours
    d. 10 hours
12. Any women worker is not required or allowed to work in any factory except between the hours of ____________.
    a. 6 AM and 10 PM
    b. 8 AM and 7 PM
    c. 6 AM and 8 PM
    d. 6 AM and 7 PM

13. If a factory employs more than ____________ a suitable room or rooms for the use of children under the age of 6 years of such women must be provided and maintained.
    a. Thirty women workers
    b. Fifty women workers
    c. Eighty women workers
    d. Hundred women workers

14. No child shall be employed or permitted to work in any factory ________.
    a. For more than 4.5 hours in any day
    b. During the night
    c. Both (a) and (b)
    d. Neither (a) nor (b)

True/False Questions

1. The Factories Act, 1948, contains different sections dealing with the employment of children between 15 and 17 subject to certain restrictions as regards their periods of rest and so on.
2. Section 67 of the Act mentions that any child who has not completed his 16 years is not required or allowed to work in any factory.
3. If a worker works in a factory for more than 6 hours in any day or for more than 24 hours in any week, he is, in respect of overtime work, entitled to wages at the rate of twice his ordinary rate of wages.
4. Sections 92–106 of the Act deal with the rules regarding penalties for offences against the Act.

Descriptive Questions

1. Write the salient features of Factories Act, 1948.
2. What are the provisions regarding health, safety and welfare or workers laid down in Factories Act, 1948?
3. Throw light on different provisions related to hazardous processes under the Factories Act, 1948.
4. What are the provisions regarding hours of work, periodic rest and overtime of a worker under the Factories Act, 1948?
5. What are the rules governing hours of work and overtime of a worker employed in a factory as provided under the Factories Act, 1948?
6. Throw light on specific provisions for the employment of young persons and women laid down by Factories Act, 1948.
7. When does an employee get the entitlement for the annual leave and how is it calculated? Discuss in detail.
8. Discuss the provisions for penalty for different offences under the Factories Act, 1948.

ANNEXURE A Highlights of Changes in the Factories (Maharashtra Amendment) Act, 2015

Section/Particular	*Prior to Amendment*	*Post Amendment*	*Effect of Change*
Section 2(m)/Definition of 'Factory'	Term 'factory' has been defined to mean premises where: i. manufacturing process is carried on with the aid of power and 10 or more workers work on any day in the preceding 12 months; or ii. manufacturing process is carried on without the aid of power and 20 or more workers work on any day in the preceding 12 months.	Factory means premises where: i. manufacturing process is carried on with the aid of power and 10 or more workers or such number of workers as may be specified by the state government by notification, from time to time work on any day in the preceding 12 months. **Provided that the number of workers to be specified by state government shall not exceed 20 workers.** ii. manufacturing process is carried on without the aid of power and 20 or more workers **or such number of workers as may be specified by the state government by notification, from time to time** work on any day in the preceding 12 months. **Provided that the number of workers to be specified by state government shall not exceed 40 workers.**	Pursuant to this amendment, the state government is empowered to declare any premises as 'factory' even when: i. the manufacturing is with the aid of power and less than 10 workers are working therein; or ii. the manufacturing is without the aid of power and less than 20 workers are working therein. Conversely, pursuant to this amendment, the state government is also empowered by issuing a notification, not classify any premises as 'factory' even if: i. the manufacturing is with the aid of power and 19 or less workers are working therein; or ii. the manufacturing is without the aid of power and 39 or less workers are working therein.

Section/Particular	*Prior to Amendment*	*Post Amendment*	*Effect of Change*
Section 65(2)/Power to Make Exempting Orders	The state government or the Chief Inspector was empowered to exempt any or all adult workers of any factory or group/class of factories from compliance of any or all Sections 51 (weekly hours), 52 (weekly holidays), 54 (daily hours), 56 (spreadover). This exemption was made available to enable the factory or factories to deal with an exceptional press of work. For this purpose, the state government or the Chief Inspector was required to pass a written order stipulating the conditions for exemption.	In order to deal with exceptional press of work, any or all adult workers of the factories shall be exempted from compliance of any or all Sections 51 (weekly hours), 52 (weekly holidays), 54 (daily hours), 56 (spreadover). The terms and conditions for aforesaid exemption shall be **prescribed in the rules**.	Now, the terms and conditions for availing exemption from compliance under Sections 51 (weekly hours), 52 (weekly holidays), 54 (daily hours), 56 (spreadover) **would be prescribed under Maharashtra Factories Rules, 1963**. Thus, there would be no requirement to approach authorities under the Principal Act and instead the terms and conditions for the exemption will also be prescribed in the rules. Note: At present, the rules for the exemption have not been notified. Once the state government notifies the rules, it would become clear as to when and under what circumstances the factory would be exempted from compliance with aforesaid provisions of Principal Act.
Section 65(3)(iv)/Power to Make Exempting Orders	The exemption granted under Section 65(2) was subject to certain conditions set out in Section 65(3). One of the conditions was that no worker could work overtime for more than 7 days at a stretch and the total overtime hours could not exceed 75 hours in any quarter.	The limit of overtime hours has been increased from 75 to 115 hours per quarter.	The overall exemption/relaxation with respect to overtime hours that a factory can avail for dealing with exceptional requirement of work cannot exceed 115 hours per quarter.

Section/Particular	*Prior to Amendment*	*Post Amendment*	*Effect of Change*
Section 66(1)(b) **Proviso/Further Restrictions on Employment of Women**	Section 66(1) among others restricted women employees to work in any factory except between the hours of 6 AM and 7 PM. However, the state government could, by a notification in the Official Gazette, vary these limits to the extent that no woman shall be employed in factory between the hours of 10 AM and 5 PM.	The **women workers are now allowed to work even between 7:00 PM and 6:00 AM** in any provided prescribed adequate safety and security measures or safeguards are provided.	Women workers are now allowed to work in night shift subject to the condition that prescribed rules as to their safety and safeguards are adequately provided. Note: At present the rules for adequate safety and safeguard of women employees have not been provided in the Maharashtra Factories Rules 1963.
Section 79(1)/Annual Leave with Wages	In order to be eligible for leave with wages, every worker had to work in a factory for 240 days or more during a calendar year.	The requirement of working 240 days has **now been reduced to 90 days.** A corresponding change has been incorporated in Explanation *1* which deals with computation of the period of 240 days.	Now workers will be entitled for leaves with wages in the subsequent year if they work for 90 or more days in a calendar year.
Section 85(1)(i)/Power to Apply the Act to Certain Premises	Pursuant to this Section, the state government could notify applicability of any or all provisions of the Principal Act on any premises where manufacturing process is carried on: i. with aid of power and employing less than 10 workers; ii. without the aid of power and employing less than 20 workers.	The state government is empowered to notify applicability of any or all provisions of the Principal Act on any premises where manufacturing process is carried on: i. with aid of power and employing less than 10 workers **or such number of workers as may be specified by the state government under Section 2(m)(i);** ii. without the aid of power and employing less than 20 workers **or such number of workers as may be specified by the state government under Section 2(m)(ii).**	This amendment is in line with the amendment carried out in the definition of the term 'factory' under Section 2(m) of the Principal Act.

Section/Particular	*Prior to Amendment*	*Post Amendment*	*Effect of Change*
Section 92A/ Compounding of Certain Offences and Fourth Schedule	-	A new Section has been introduced pursuant to which offences set out in the Fourth Schedule (new schedule) may be compounded before the institution of prosecution. The offences shall be compounded by an officer not below the rank of Deputy Chief Inspector. The amount of fine shall not be more than ₹100,000 as mentioned in Section 92 of the Principal Act. Once the offence set out in the Fourth Schedule is compounded, no further proceedings shall be taken against the offender in respect of the offence.	The Fourth Schedule lays down 33 non-compliances under the Principal Act which can be compounded prior to initiation of the prosecution.
Section 105 (1)/ Cognizance of Offences)	Court could take cognizance of any offence upon complaint by or written sanction of an inspector.	Court will take cognizance of any offence upon complaint by or written sanction of a Chief Inspector.	The process of investigation into any offence under the Principal Act and subsequent prosecution for the same can now start only upon complaint made/sanction given by Chief Inspector of Factories.

Source: http://www.mondaq.com/india/x/462712/employee+rights+labour+relations/Note+On+Changes+In+The+Factories+Maharashtra+Amendment+Act+2015, accessed on 8 February 2017.

ANNEXURE B

S. No.	*Sections*	*State*	*Amendments*
1	Section 6	West Bengal	**Application of Section 6** Excepting clauses (aa), (b) and (c) of Subsection (1) of Section 6 in Chapter I, Sections 43, 46, 47, 48, 49 and 50 in Chapter V and Chapters VI and VIII of the Act shall apply to any place in the state of West Bengal wherein the manufacturing processes specified in the Schedule below are carried on with or without the aid of power or is ordinarily so carried on, notwithstanding that: The number of persons employed therein is less than 10, if working with the aid of power and less than 20 if working without the aid of power, or, The persons working therein are not employed by the owner thereof but are working with the permission of, or under agreement with, such owner: provided that the said manufacturing processes are not being carried on by the owner only with the aid of his family. Schedule (1) Manufacture of rubber and plastic products, (2) Manufacturing process involving repair of motor vehicles and motor cycles, (3) Manufacturing process using or producing explosive or highly inflammable articles or substances, (4) Fireworks manufacturing and its packaging units, (5) Manufacturing of leather goods, (6) Manufacturing of ice using ammonia as refrigerant, (7) Pesticides formulation unit, (8) Manufacturing, handling and processing of asbestos and its products.[6]
2	Section 106	Uttar Pradesh	**Insertion of Section 106A—Compounding in offences** The inspector may, subject to any general or special order of the state government in this behalf, compound any offences punishable under this Act with fine only, and committed for the first time, either before or after the institution of the prosecution, on realization of such amount of composition fee as he thinks fit not exceeding the maximum amount of fine fixed for the offence; and where the offence is so compounded, before the institution of the prosecution, the offender shall not be liable to prosecution, for such offence and shall, if in custody, be set at liberty; after the institution of the prosecution, the composition shall amount to acquittal of the offender.[7]

[6] Vide Notification No. 781-LW/IF-11/06, dated 3 October 2007, published in the Kolkata Gazette, Extra., Pt. I, dated 23 October 2007.

[7] Vide Uttar Pradesh Act, 35 of 1979, sec. 4 (w.e.f. 21-12-1979).

4

CHAPTER

Contract Labour (Regulation and Abolition) Act, 1970

LEARNING OBJECTIVES

Upon completing this chapter, the reader would be able to:

LO1. Understand the objectives, scope and important definitions of the Act.
LO2. Describe the process of registration of establishments employing contract labour.
LO3. Know about the constitution of the advisory boards.
LO4. Explain the process of prohibition of employment of contract labour.
LO5. Explore the process of licensing of contractors.
LO6. Get the insights of the provisions for the welfare and health of contract labour.
LO7. Understand the offences by companies and penalty provisions.

Introduction

Contract labour is a significant and growing form of employment. It is prevalent in almost all industries and allied operations, and also in the service sector. It generally refers to workers engaged by a contractor for user enterprise. Contract labour has very little bargaining power, has little or no social security and is often engaged in hazardous occupations, endangering their health and safety. The exploitation of workers under the contract labour system has been a matter of deep concern for the government.

The government enacted the Contract Labour (Regulation and Abolition) Act in 1970, and it came into force on 10 February 1971. The Act applies to every establishment/contractor in which 20 or more workmen are employed or were employed on any day of the preceding 12 months as contract labour. Every establishment and contractor, to whom the act applies, have to register themselves or obtain a licence for execution of the contract work. Under the Act, interests of contract workers are protected in terms of wages, hours of work, welfare, health and social security. The amenities to be provided to contract labour include a canteen, rest rooms, first aid facilities and other basic necessities at the work place like drinking water and so on. The liability to ensure payment of wages and other benefits is primarily that of the contractor and, in case of default, that of the principal employer. In this chapter, students will be acclimatized to the legal framework stipulated under the Contract Labour (Regulation and Abolition) Act, 1970.

LO1: Objectives, Scope and Important Definitions

Objectives

The Contract Labour (Regulation and Abolition) Act, 1970 (the Act), was enacted to regulate the employment of contract labour in certain establishments and to provide for its abolition in certain circumstances, and for matters connected therewith. Thus, the prime objective of the Act is to protect the interest of contract labour employed in the industrial establishment and also to abolish the practice of employing contract labour in certain cases. The employment relationship of contract labour is different from that of direct labour as they are hired by the employer through a contractor. The method of wage payment to contract labour also is not the same as followed for direct labour. The contract labour is hired, supervised and remunerated by the contractor, who, in turn, is remunerated by the establishment hiring the services of the contractor. This type of employment relationship leaves a gap for exploitation of contract labour. The Act provides specific provisions to prevent the exploitation of contract labour and also to introduce better conditions of work for them.

Scope and Application

The Act extends to the whole of India. According to Section 1(4), it applies:

1. To every establishment in which 20 or more workmen are employed or were employed on any day of the preceding 12 months as contract labour.
2. To every contractor who employs or who employed 20 or more workmen on any day of the preceding 12 months. The appropriate government may, after giving not less than 2 months' notice of its intention to do so, by notification in the Official Gazette, apply the provisions of this Act to any establishment or contractor employing such number of workmen less than 20 as may be specified in the notification.

An act not to apply to certain establishments: According to Section 1(5), certain establishments are beyond the application of this Act. The Act provides that the provisions of this Act are not applicable to establishments in which work only of an intermittent or casual nature is performed. If a question arises whether work performed in an establishment is of an intermittent or casual nature, the appropriate government shall decide that question after consultation with the Central Board or, as the case may be, the State Board, and its decision shall be final.

Important Definitions

1. **Appropriate government (Sec 2(1)(a)):** 'Appropriate government' under the Act means,
   a. In relation to an establishment in respect of which the appropriate government under the Industrial Disputes Act, 1947, is the central government.
   b. In relation to any other establishment, the government of the State in which that other establishment is situated.
2. **Contract labour (Section 2(1)(b)):** According to the Act, a workman is deemed to be employed as contract labour in or in connection with the work of an establishment if he is hired on or in

connection with such work by or through a contractor, with or without the knowledge of the principal employer.

3. **Contractor section (2(1)(c)):** 'Contractor' in relation to an establishment means a person who undertakes to produce a given result in the establishment, other than a mere supply of goods or articles of manufacture to such establishment, through contract labour, or who supplies contract labour for any work of the establishment and includes a subcontractor.
4. **Controlled industry (Section 2(1)(d)):** 'Controlled industry' is any industry, the control of which by the union has been declared by any Central Act to be expedient in the public interest.
5. **Establishment (Section 2(1)(e)):** The Act defines 'establishment' as:
   a. Any office or department of the government or local authority, or
   b. Any place where any industry, trade, business, manufacture or occupation is carried on.
6. **Principal employer (Section 2(1)(g)):** 'Principal employer' means:
   a. In relation to any office or department of the government or a local authority, the head of that office or department or such other officer as the government or the local authority, as the case may be, may specify in this behalf.
   b. In a factory, the owner or occupier of the factory, and where a person has been named as the manager of the factory under the Factories Act, 1948, the person so named.
   c. In a mine, the owner or agent of the mine and where a person has been named as the manager of the mine, the person so named.
   d. In any other establishment, any person responsible for the supervision and control of the establishment.
7. **Workman (Section 2(1)(i)):** 'Workman' means any person employed in or in connection with the work of any establishment to do any skilled, semi-skilled or unskilled, manual, supervisory, technical or clerical work for hire or reward, whether the terms of employment be expressed or implied, but does not include any such person:
   a. Who is employed mainly in a managerial or administrative capacity; or
   b. Who, being employed in a supervisory capacity, draws wages exceeding ₹500 per mensem or exercises, either by the nature of the duties attached to the office or by reason of the powers vested in him, functions mainly of a managerial nature; or
   c. Who is an outworker, that is to say, a person to whom any articles or materials are given out by or on behalf of the principal employer to be made up, cleaned, washed, altered, ornamented, finished, repaired, adapted or otherwise processed for sale for the purposes of the trade or business of the principal employer, and the process is to be carried out either in the home of the out worker or in some other premises not being premises under the control and management of the principal employer.

LO2: Registration of Establishments Employing Contract Labour

As discussed before, the Act applies to the principal employer of an establishment and the contractor wherein 20 or more workmen are employed or were employed even for one day during the preceding 12 months as contract labour. For the purpose of calculating the number, contract labour employed for different purposes through different contractors has to be taken into consideration. In order to secure its objectives and purposes, the Act contains provisions for registration of establishments employing contract labour.

Appointment of registering officer (Section 6): The Act empowers the appropriate government to appoint, by notification in the Official Gazette, persons being Gazetted Officers of the government to be registering officers, and define the limits within which a registering officer shall exercise the powers conferred on him by or under the Act.

Registration of certain establishments (Section 7): Section 7 of the Act lays down that every principal employer of an establishment to which the Act applies is required to make an application to the registering officer in the prescribed manner for registration of the establishment within the prescribed time limit. A registration fee varying from ₹20 to ₹500, which is related to the number of workmen employed as contract labour, is payable. If the application is complete in all respects, the registering officer shall register the establishment and issue to the principal employer of the establishment a certificate of registration in the prescribed form.

Revocation of registration in certain cases (Section 8): The registration can be revoked in the following circumstances:

1. If the registering officer is satisfied, either on a reference made to him in his behalf or otherwise, that the registration has been obtained by misrepresentation or suppression of any material fact.
2. That the registration has become useless and ineffective for any other reason and, therefore, requires to be revoked. In both the cases, the registering officer shall give an opportunity to the principal employer of the establishment to be heard. He will also obtain previous approval of the appropriate government in case the registration is to be revoked.

Effect of non-registration (Section 9): The Act mandates the registration under the Act of all those establishments which are covered under this Act. It is provided under Section 9 of the Act that no principal employer of an establishment to which the Act applies can employ contract labour, if :

1. He has not obtained the certification of registration; or
2. A certificate has been revoked after being issued.

LO3: The Advisory Boards

Central Advisory Board (Section 3)

The Act directs the central government to constitute a Central Advisory Contract Labour Board to advise the central government on such matters arising out of the administration of the Act as may be referred to it and to carry out other functions assigned to it under the Act. The Central Board is constituted of following members:

1. A chairman to be appointed by the central government.
2. The Chief Labour Commissioner (Central), ex officio.

3. Such number of members, not exceeding 17 but not less than 11, as the central government may nominate to represent that government, the Railways, the coal industry, the mining industry, the contractors, the workmen and any other interests which, in the opinion of the central government, ought to be represented on the Central Board.

The Act further provides that the number of members representing the workmen cannot be less than the number of members representing the principal employers and the contractors.

State Advisory Board (Section 4)

As the central government constitutes a board at the central level, similarly, the Act directs the state government to constitute the State Advisory Contract Labour Board to advise the state governments on such matters arising out of the administration of the Act as may be referred to it and to carry out other functions assigned to it under the Act. The following members constitute the State Board:

1. A chairman to be appointed by the state government.
2. The Labour Commissioner, ex officio, or in his absence any other officer nominated by the state government in that behalf.
3. Such number of members, not exceeding 11 but not less than 9, as the state government may nominate to represent that government, the industry, the contractors, the workmen and any other interests which, in the opinion of the state government, ought to be represented on the State Board.

Like the Central Board, in State Board too, the number of members representing the workmen is required to be not less than the number of members representing the principal employers and the contractor.

Constitution of Committee (Section 5)

Both the Central Board and State Board are empowered to constitute such committees and for such purpose or purposes as it may think fit. Such constituted committees meet at such times and places and observe such rules of procedure in regard to the transaction of business at its meetings as prescribed by the Central Board or the State Board in respective cases. Committee members are paid fees and allowances for attending its meetings as decided by the respective boards. However, no fees are payable to a member who is an officer of the government or of any corporation established by any law for the time being in force.

LO4: Prohibition of Employment of Contract Labour

Process of Prohibition of Employment of Contract Labour (Section 10)

The most significant provision of the Act is the prohibition of employment of contract labour in certain establishments. It empowers the appropriate government to prohibit employment of contract labour in any process, operation or other work in any establishment by issuing a notification in the Official Gazette. The following steps are, however, required to be taken before such a notification is issued:

1. The appropriate government must consult the Central Board or, as the case may be, the State Board, to prohibit, by notification in the Official Gazette, employment of contract labour in any process, operation or other work in any establishment.
2. The appropriate government must give due consideration to the conditions of work and benefits provided for the contract labour in that establishment and other relevant factors such as:
   a. Whether the process, operation or other work incidental to, or necessary for the industry, trade, business, manufacture or occupation that is carried on in the establishment.
   b. Whether it is of perennial nature, that is to say, it is of sufficient duration having regard to the nature of industry, trade, business, manufacture or occupation carried on in that establishment.
   c. Whether it is done ordinarily through regular workmen in that establishment similar thereto.
   d. Whether it is sufficient to employ a considerable number of whole-time workmen.

Jurisdiction of Industrial Tribunals to Abolish Contract Labour

It was held by the Supreme Court in a landmark case (*Vegoils Private Ltd. v. The Workmen*) that after enforcement of the Contract Labour (Regulation and Abolition) Act, 1970, the sole jurisdiction for abolition of contract labour in any particular operation is vested with the appropriate Government and thereafter the Industrial Tribunals have no jurisdiction to abolish contract labour. It is also worth noting here that not even the Supreme Court under Article 32 of the Constitution can order for abolition of contract labour system in any establishment (1985 1 SCC 630). Let us discuss a case to get the insights of Section 10 of the Act (Case 4.1).

Case 4.1: *Vegoils Private Limited v. The Workmen*[1]

Vegoils Private Limited (the company), a private limited company, carried on the business of manufacturing edible oils, soaps and certain by-products. In connection with its business, the appellant employed about 700 permanent workmen. However, for loading and unloading seed and oil cake bags and for feeding the hoppers in the solvent extraction plant, the appellant employed labour through a contractor. The workmen in an industrial dispute claimed, inter alia, that the work of loading and unloading seed bags as well as that of feeding the hoppers was of a perennial nature and therefore in respect of these contract labour should be abolished. The stand taken by the union in its statement of claim dated 30 May 1967 was briefly as follows:

The company had work in this section which was on a regular and continuous nature. The work in that section was not intermittent or accidental type. The work required to be performed is of loading and unloading seed bags and also to feed the hoppers for the requirements of solvent extraction plants. The product left after the process of solvent extraction also is to be filled in gunny bags. All these items of work are of a permanent nature and were being regularly carried out by the contractor's workmen by employing on an average more than 200 workmen. The work being of a continuous nature is being carried out throughout the year. Further, this type of work is an essential part of the solvent extraction unit. As the jobs were essentially connected with the day-to-day work of the company, and as they were continuous, the employment of a contractor for getting these types of work done is nothing but an unfair labour practice adopted by the appellant.

The company argued that wherever the work was of a perennial nature, the company had been having that work done only by its permanent employees. But where certain items of work were of intermittent and

[1] *Vegoils Private Ltd. v. The Workmen*, (1971) II-LLJ, p. 567.

sporadic nature and irregular in its working, to ensure efficiency, economy and proper working, the appellant had to engage contract labour. In respect of the seeds godown and solvent extraction plants, the company classified the type of work into four parts: (a) unloading of seeds and cake bags from railway wagons and motor trucks and stacking the same in the godown for easy identification in separate lots, (b) loading of de-oiled cake meal bags into motor lorries and wagons whenever they had to be despatched from the factory, (c) feeding of cake in the hopper which in turn feeds the solvent extraction plants through a system of long screw conveyors and other necessary equipment; and (d) filling, weighing and stacking of small bags.

As argued by the company, all these items of work were of an intermittent and irregular nature. In view of these circumstances, it was not possible to employ permanent workmen to carry out the said items of work. Further, in particular, the company led evidence to show that the work of loading and unloading in the wagons and lorries was not of a continuous nature. The arrival of wagons on any particular day was uncertain. Nevertheless, the contractor has to be ready to clear the wagons as and when it arrives within the time allowed by the railway authorities, otherwise heavy demurrage had to be paid. While on certain days no wagon at all would arrive, on certain other days suddenly a large number of wagons would arrive, necessitating the clearance of the goods promptly and immediately for which purpose the contractor was always having workmen ready to meet the situation. This type of work, according to the appellant company, could be done efficiently and promptly only by a contractor.

It was also placed on record that the items of work had been carried out by the contract labour by three other concerns, namely, M/s Godrej Soap Works, M/s Tata Oil Mills and M/s Hindustan Lever. The feeding of cakes in the hoppers was done by contract labour in the appellant company and M/s Godrej Soap Works. That work was done by the departmental workmen in M/s Tata Oil Mills, and M/s Hindustan Lever did not have any solvent extraction plant but the work of feeding the seeds. In the hoppers, filling of cakes in the bags and stitching cake bags and stacking those bags were done by departmental workmen.

Discussion Points

1. Whether the contract system of employing the labour under the circumstances mentioned in the case should be abolished.
2. Whether the workmen employed by the contractor should be treated as the appellant's regular employees with all the benefits of service conditions that are available to the regular employees of the company.

Judgement and Explanation

One of the relevant factors taken into account by the Supreme Court was when contract labour regarding any particular type of work is proposed to be abolished, whether that type of work is done ordinarily through regular workmen in that establishment or an establishment similar thereto. When it was shown that in similar establishments, this type of work was not ordinarily done through regular workmen, but by contract labour, that was a circumstance which operated in favour of the company. The evidence on the side of the appellant was to the effect that the work of loading and unloading of trucks and wagons was not of a perennial and permanent nature. On the other hand, this type of work was of an intermittent and temporary nature and so little that it would not be possible and profitable to employ full-time workmen for the purpose and that that type of work was being done in the other concerns in the area through contract labour.

Discontinuation of contract labour: In Gujarat Electricity Board case, AIR 1995 SC 2942, the Supreme Court held that:

1. All undertakings on their own discontinue the contract labour who satisfy the factors mentioned in clauses (a) to (d) of Section 10(2) of the Act and abolish as many of the labour as is feasible as their direct employees.

2. Both the central and state governments should appoint a committee to investigate the establishments in which the contract labour is engaged on the basis of criteria laid down in clauses (a) to (d) of Section 10(2) of the Act. The investigation shall aim at concluding whether the contract labour system can be abolished and direct employment can be given to the contract labour. The appropriate government on its own should take initiative to abolish the labour contracts in the establishments concerned by following the procedure laid down under the Act.
3. The central government should amend the Act by incorporating a suitable provision to refer to industrial adjudicator the question of the direct employment of the contract workers of the ex-contractor in principal establishments, when the appropriate government abolishes the contract labour.

Absorption of contract labour: The Act does not have any provision for absorption of contract labour in the event of prohibition of employment of contract labour in any category of work/jobs under Section 10 of the Act. There have been complaints that contract workers are being thrown out of employment in the jobs covered by the relevant notification. In *Steel Authority of India v. National Union of Water Front Workers and others,*[2] the Supreme Court held that neither Section 10 of the Act nor any other provision in the Act, whether expressly or by necessary implication, provides for automatic absorption of contract labour on issuing a notification by the appropriate government under Section 10(1) prohibiting employment of contract labour in any process or operation or other work in any establishment. Consequently, the principal employer cannot be required to order absorption of contract labour working in the concerned establishment.

However, in a landmark case, the Supreme Court held that though there exists no express provision in the Act for absorption of employees in establishments where contract labour system is abolished by publication of notification under Section 10(1) of the Act, if the linkage between the contractor and employee stands snapped and direct relationship stands restored between the principal employer and contract labour as its employees, then the principal employer is under obligation to absorb the contract labour. Where the contract labour through a contractor engaged in keeping industrial premises clean and hygiene, but no licence was obtained by principal employer nor contractor and the contract itself stipulating number of employees to be engaged by contractor and overall control of working of contract labour including administrative control remaining with principal employer, it was held by the Court that the contract is a camouflage which could be easily pierced and the employee and the employer relationship could be directly visualized.[3]

LO5: Appointment of Licensing Officer and Licensing of Contractors

Licensing of Contractors (Section 11)

Apart from registration of establishments employing contract labour, the Act contains provisions for licensing of contractors. Section 11 empowers the appropriate government to appoint Gazetted Officers to be licensing officers and define the limits of their jurisdiction. Orders regarding appointment of

[2] *Steel Authority of India v. National Union of Water Front Workers and others,* AIR 2001 SC 3527.

[3] 1999 LAB IC SC 1323 *HSEB v. Suresh.*

licensing officers and the limits of their jurisdiction are to be notified in the Official Gazette. The Act provides under Section 12 that no contractor to whom the Act applies can undertake or execute any work through contract labour except under and in accordance with the licence issued in that behalf by the licensing officer. The licence may contain such conditions including, in particular, conditions as to hours of work, fixation of wages and other essential amenities in respect of contract labour as the appropriate government may deem fit to impose in accordance with the rules framed under the Act.

The licence is issued on the payment of the prescribed fee and on the deposit of security, if any, for the due performance of the conditions prescribed in the licence. The licensee fee ranges from ₹5 to ₹125 depending on the number of workmen employed by the contractor. It must be noted here that the licence is non-transferable.

Grant of Licence (Section 13)

An application for the grant of licence has to be made in the prescribed form. It should contain particulars regarding the location of the establishment, the nature of the process, operation or work for which contract labour is to be employed and such other particulars as may be prescribed. The licence is issued after necessary investigation by the licensing officer. It is valid for the period specified therein (12 months under the Central Rules) and may be renewed from time to time for such period and on payment of such fees and on such conditions as may be prescribed.

Revocation, Suspension and Amendment of Licence (Section 14)

If the licensing officer is satisfied, either on a reference made to him in this behalf or otherwise, that:

1. The licence has been obtained by misrepresentation or suppression of any material fact, or
2. The holder of licence has, without reasonable cause, failed to comply with the conditions subject to which the licence has been granted or has contravened any of the provisions of the Act or the rules made thereunder, the licensing officer may revoke or suspend the licence. He also has the powers to forfeit the sum, if any, or any portion thereof deposited as security for the due performance of the conditions subject to which the licence was granted.

However, before revoking or suspending the licence or ordering forfeiture of the security deposit by the contractor, the licensing officer has to give the holder of the licence an opportunity of showing cause. The licensing officer may vary or amend a licence subject to the rules that be made in this behalf.

Appeal Against the Orders Relating to Grant of Registration to Establishments (Section 15)

The Act makes provision for appeals against orders relating to grant of registration to establishments, revocation of registration and revocation/suspension of licences. The aggrieved person may, within 30 days from the date on which the order is communicated to him, prefer an appeal to an appellate officer who shall be a person nominated in this behalf by the appropriate government. The appellant officer may entertain an appeal even after the expiry of 30 days, if he is satisfied that there was sufficient cause for the delay. The appellant officer must, after giving the appellant an opportunity of being heard, dispose of the appeal as expeditiously as possible.

LO6: Welfare and Health of Contract Labour

The contractors are required to take certain specific measures for the welfare and health of contract labour. This, of course, arises in those employments in which the system of contract labour has not been abolished. The relevant provisions are as follows:

1. **Canteens (Section 16):** As per Section 16, the appropriate government is empowered to make rules requiring that every establishment to which the Act applies and wherein contract labour numbering 100 or more is ordinarily employed by a contractor and the employment of the contract labour is likely to continue for such period as may be prescribed, one or more canteens shall be provided and maintained by the contractor for the use of such contract labour. The rules may provide for the date by which the canteen shall be provided, the number of canteens and the standards in respect of construction, accommodation, furniture and other equipment of the canteens, the foodstuffs which may be served therein and the charges which may be made therefor.
2. **Rest rooms (Section 17):** In every place where contract labour is required to halt at night in connection with the work of an establishment to which the Act applies and in which work requiring employment of contract labour is likely to continue for such period as may be prescribed, there must be provided and maintained by the contractor for the use of the contract labour such number of rest rooms or such of the suitable alternative accommodation within such time as may be prescribed. The Act further provides that the rest room or alternative accommodation to be provided under Subsection (1) must be sufficiently lighted and ventilated and shall be maintained in a clean and comfortable condition.
3. **Other facilities (Section 18):** It is the duty of every contractor employing contract labour in connection with the work of an establishment to which the Act applies, to provide and maintain:
   a. A sufficient supply of wholesome drinking water for the contract labour in convenient places;
   b. A sufficient number of latrines and urinals of the prescribed types conveniently situated and accessible to the contract labour; and
   c. Washing facilities.

First aid facilities (Section 19): The contractor is required to provide and maintain a first aid box equipped with the prescribed contents at every place, where contract labour is employed by him. The first aid box should be readily accessible during working hours.

The liability of the principal employer in certain cases (Section 17): If the prescribed amenities (canteens, rest rooms and other facilities, first aid box) are not provided by the contractor within the prescribed time, then such amenities shall be provided by the principal employer within such time as may be specified. According to Section 20(2), all expenses incurred by the principal employer in providing the amenity may be recovered by him from the contractor either by deduction from any amount payable to the contractor under any contract or as a debt payable by the contractor.

Responsibility for payment of wages (Section 20): A common complaint against the contractors has been that some of them do not pay proper wages to the contract labourers or that payments are not made in time or that arbitrary deductions are made from wages. To take care of such malpractices, Section 21 of the Act lays down that the contractor shall pay wages in the presence of the authorized representative of the principal employer. An obligation is also cast on the principal employer to nominate a representative duly authorized by him to be present at the time of disbursement of wages.

LO7: Offences by Companies

Company Liable for Non-compliance (Section 25)

The Act states that if the company commits an offence under the Act, then the company as well as every person in charge of, and responsible to, the company for the conduct of its business at the time of the commission of the offence shall be deemed to be guilty of the offence and shall be liable to be proceeded against any punished accordingly. However, such a person is not laible to get punishment if he proves that the offence was committed without his knowledge or that he exercised all due diligence to prevent the commission of such offence.

Similarly, where an offence under this Act has been committed by a company and it is proved that the offence was committed with the consent or connivance of, or that the commission of the offence was attributable to any neglect on the part of, any director, manager, managing agent or any other officer of the company, such director, manager, managing agent or such other officer shall also be deemed to be guilty of that offence and shall be liable to be proceeded against and punished accordingly.

Cognizance of Offence (Section 26)

No court is permitted to take cognizance of any offence under this Act except on a complaint made by, or with the previous sanction in writing about, the inspector and no court inferior to that of a Presidency Magistrate or a magistrate of the first class shall try any offence punishable under this Act.

Limitation of Prosecutions (Section 27)

The Act stipulates that a court can take cognizance of an offence punishable under this Act only if the complaint thereof is made within 3 months from the date on which the alleged commission of the offence came to the knowledge of an inspector: Provided that where the offence consists of disobeying a written order made by an inspector, complaint thereof may be made within 6 months of the date on which the offence is alleged to have been committed.

Summary

1. The Contract Labour (Regulation and Abolition) Act, 1970, was enacted to regulate the employment of contract labour in certain establishments and to provide for its abolition in certain circumstances and for matters connected therewith.

2. Under the Act, a workman is deemed to be employed as contract labour in or in connection with the work of an establishment if he is hired on or in connection with such work by or through a contractor, with or without the knowledge of the principal employer.
3. 'Contractor' in relation to an establishment means a person who undertakes to produce a given result in the establishment, other than a mere supply of goods or articles of manufacture to such establishment, through contract labour or who supplies contract labour for any work of the establishment and includes a subcontractor.
4. Every principal employer of an establishment to which the Act applies is required to make an application to the registering officer in the prescribed manner for registration of the establishment within the prescribed time limit.
5. The Act empowers the appropriate government to prohibit employment of contract labour in any process, operation or other work in any establishment by issuing a notification in the Official Gazette.
6. The sole jurisdiction for abolition of contract labour in any particular operation is vested with the appropriate government and thereafter the Industrial Tribunals have no jurisdiction to abolish contract labour.
7. Section 11 empowers the appropriate government to appoint Gazetted Officers to be licensing officers and define the limits of their jurisdiction.
8. In the welfare and health of contract labour, the contractors are required to take certain specific measures for the welfare and health of contract labour.
9. In the Act Cognizance of Offence (Section 26), no court is permitted to take cognizance of any offence under this Act except on a complaint made by, or with the previous sanction in writing about, the inspector and no court inferior to that of a Presidency Magistrate or a magistrate of the first class shall try any offence punishable under this Act.

Multiple Choice Questions

1. The Contract Labour (Regulation and Abolition) Act, 1970 (the Act), was enacted to
   a. Regulate the employment of contract labour in certain establishments.
   b. Provide for its abolition in certain circumstances and for matters connected therewith.
   c. Both (a) and (b).
   d. None of the above.
2. The Act is applicable to every establishment in which ____________ are employed or were employed on any day of the preceding 12 months as contract labour.
   a. 10 or more workmen
   c. 25 or more workmen
   b. 20 or more workmen
   d. 5 or more workmen
3. Under the Act, ____________ is any industry the control of which by the union has been declared by any Central Act to be expedient in the public interest.
   a. 'Controlled industry'
   c. 'Industrial establishment'
   b. 'Establishment'
   d. None of the above

4. The licence issued to the contractor by the licensing officer remains valid for the period ______________ as specified under the Central Rules.
   a. 6 months
   b. 12 months
   c. 24 months
   d. 36 months
5. The jurisdiction for abolition of contract labour in any particular operation is vested with
   a. The appropriate government.
   b. The Industrial Tribunals.
   c. The Supreme Court.
   d. All of the above.

True/False Questions

1. The Act has the provision for absorption of contract labour in the event of prohibition of employment of contract labour in any category of work/jobs under Section 10 of the Act.
2. The provisions of this Act are not applicable to establishments in which work only of an intermittent or casual nature is performed.
3. If the linkage between the contractor and employee stands snapped and direct relationship stands restored between the principal employer and contract labour as its employees, then also the principal employer is under no obligation to absorb the contract labour.
4. No contractor to whom the Act applies can undertake or execute any work though contract labour except under and in accordance with the license issued in that behalf by the licensing officer.
5. The contractor shall pay wages in the presence of the authorized representative of the principal employer.

Descriptive Questions

1. Write short notes on the following:
   a. Workmen
   b. Contractor
   c. Principal employer
2. Discuss the importance of Section 10 of the Child Labour (Abolition and Regulation Act), 1970.
3. What are the functions of Central Advisory Board and State Advisory Board? How are they constituted?
4. Throw light on the provisions of the Act for ensuring health and work conditions of the contract labour.
5. Explain the process of obtaining the licence for the supply of contract labour. Also state the conditions under which the licence can be revoked.

ANNEXURE A

Sl.No	*Section*	*State*	*Amendment*
1.	Section 1	Maharashtra	**Insertion of Subsection (5), after clause (b) in Section 1** (c) Notwithstanding anything contained in clause (b) or any other provisions of this Act, the work performed or carried out in the area of Special Economic Zone (declared as such by the Government of India), which is of ancillary nature such as canteen, gardening, cleaning, security, courier services, transport of raw material and finished products, or loading and unloading of goods within the premises of a factory or establishments which are declared 100% export units by government, required to achieve the objective of a principal establishment in the said area, shall be deemed to be of temporary and intermittent nature irrespective of the period of performance of the work by the workers in such ancillary establishments.[4]
2.	Section 1	Andhra Pradesh	**Insertion of Subsection (1), after clause (d), in Section 1** (dd) 'core activity of an establishment' means any activity for which the establishment is set up and includes any activity which is essential or necessary to the core activity, but does not include: (1) sanitation works, including sweeping, cleaning, dusting and collection and disposal of all kinds of waste; (2) watch and ward services including security service; (3) canteen and catering services; (4) loading and unloading operations; (5) running of hospitals, educational and training institutions, guest houses, clubs and the like where they are in the nature of support services of an establishment; (6) courier services which are in nature of support services of an establishment; (7) civil and other constructional works, including maintenance; (8) gardening and maintenance of lawns, etc.; (9) housekeeping and laundry services, and so on, where they are in nature support services of an establishment; (10) transport services including ambulance services; (11) any activity that is intermittent in nature even if that constitutes a core activity of an establishment; and (12) any other activity which is incidental to the core activity: provided that the above activities by themselves are not the 'core activities' of such establishment.[5]

[4] Vide The Contract Labour (Regulation and Abolition) (Maharashtra Amendment) Act, 2005 (Maharashtra Act 13 of 2006), sec. 2 (w.e.f. 2 May 2006).

[5] Vide Contract Labour (Regulation and Abolition) (Andhra Pradesh) (Amendment) Act, 2003 (Andhra Pradesh Act 10 of 2003), sec. 2.

Sl.No	Section	State	Amendment
	Section 10		**Prohibition of employment of contract labour** (1) Notwithstanding anything contained in this Act, employment of contract labour in core activities of any establishment if prohibited: provided that the principal employer may engage contract labour or a contractor to any core activity, if: (a) the normal functioning of the establishments is such that the activity is ordinarily done through contractors; or (b) the activities are such that they do not require full-time workers for the major portion of the working hours in a day or for longer periods, as the case may be; (c) any sudden increase of volume of work in the core activity which needs to be accomplished in a specified time.[6]
3.	Section 31	Andhra Pradesh	**The power to exempt in special cases** (1) The appropriate government may, in public interest, direct, by notification in the Official Gazette, that subject to such conditions and restrictions, if any, and for such period or periods, as may be specified in the notification, all or any of the provisions of this Act or the rules made thereunder shall not apply to any establishment or class of establishment or any class of contractors, as the case may be. (2) Where the operation of any of the provisions of this Act, under Section 31(1) has been excluded, such exclusion may at any time be revoked by the appropriate government by subsequent notification in the Official Gazette.[7]

[6] Vide Contract Labour (Regulation and Abolition) (Andhra Pradesh) (Amendment) Act, 2003 (Andhra Pradesh Act 10 of 2003), sec. 4.

[7] Vide Contract Labour (Regulation and Abolition) (Andhra Pradesh) (Amendment) Act, 2003 (Andhra Pradesh Act 10 of 2003), sec. 5.

5 CHAPTER

The Child and Adolescent Labour (Prohibition and Regulation) Act, 1986

LEARNING OBJECTIVES

Upon completing this chapter, the reader would be able to:

LO1. Understand the objectives, scope and important definitions of the Act.
LO2. Get the insights of prohibition of employment of children in certain occupations and Processes.
LO3. Know about the regulation of conditions of work of children.
LO4. Explain about the provisions for penalty under the Act.

Introduction

Society must provide to children such an environment to grow that enables them to lead a life of freedom and dignity. Every child deserves an opportunity of education and training so that they grow into responsible and responsive citizens. Unfortunately, a large proportion of children in our country are deprived of their basic rights. At a very early age, they start working in various sectors of the economy, particularly in the unorganized sector. Most often the child labourers are exploited, exposed to hazardous work conditions and paid a pittance for their long hours of work. They are forced to forego education, shouldering responsibilities far beyond their years, becoming worldly-wise when their peers have yet to leave the cocoons of parental protection—these children never know what childhood is.

Although the problem of child labour is a global phenomenon, it is more acute in the developing countries than in the developed ones where stringent laws governing the employment of children exist and are implemented effectively. In India, the Child Labour (Prohibition and Regulation) Act, 1986, is in place to fight against the problem of child labour in our country. With the changing times, it was realized that the Act needs to undergo considerable changes, and the government decided to amend the Act. The amendments were first introduced in 2012, thereupon in 2015 and on 29 July 2016. The Child Labour (Prohibition and Regulation) Amendment Bill, 2016, received the assent of the President and was made effective from 30 July 2016. Pursuant to the Child Labour (Prohibition and Regulation) Amendment Act, 2016, of India, the name of the Act has been changed to 'Child and Adolescent Labour (Prohibition and Regulation) Act, 1986' (the Act).

LO1: Objectives, Scope and Important Definitions

Objectives

The Act was the culmination of ideas, deliberations and recommendations of various committees on child labour. Some important ones among them are the NCL (1966–1969), Gurupadaswamy Committee on Child Labour (1979), Sanat Mehta Committee (1984) and others.

The preamble of the Act indicates that it has the following twin objectives:

1. To prohibit the engagement of children in certain employments.
2. To regulate the conditions of work of children in certain other employments where children are allowed to work.

There are a number of other Acts that prohibit the employment of children below 14 years and 15 years in some specific employments, for example, Section 67 of the Factories Act, 1948, Section 45 of the Mines Act, 1952, and so on. However, there was no procedure in any of the law to decide that in which employments or processes the children must not be employed. Also, there was specific law regulating the working conditions of children in the employments where they could be employed.

Thus, the Act aims to:

1. Prohibit the employment of children who have not completed their 14th year of age, in specified occupations and processes.
2. Provide a procedure to decide modifications to the Schedule of prohibited occupations and processes.
3. Regulate the conditions of work of children employed in the occupations not prohibited from working.
4. Lay down enhanced penalties for the violation of the provisions of the Act, and other Acts dealing with the employment of children.
5. Ensure uniformity in the definition of 'child' in all the related laws.
6. Empower the central government to constitute Child Labour Technical Advisory (CLTA) Committee to advise the central government for the purpose of addition of occupation and processes to the Schedule appended to the Act.

Scope and Application

The Act received the President's assent on 23 December 1986. The Act extends to the whole of India. The Act provides under Section 1(3) that the provisions of this Act, other than Part III, shall come into force at once and Part III shall come into force on such dates as the central government may by notification in the Official Gazette appoint, and different dates may be appointed for different states and different class of establishments.

Important Definitions

1. **Adolescent (Section 2(a)):** Adolescent means a person who has completed his 14th year of age but has not completed his 18th year.
2. **Adult (Section 2(aa)):** Adult means a person who has completed his 18th year of age.
3. **Appropriate government (Section 2(i)):** In relation to an establishment under the control of the central government or a railway administration or a major port or a mine or oilfield, the central government is the appropriate government whole in all other cases, and the state government is the appropriate government.
4. **Child (Section 2(ii)):** Child is a person who has not completed his 14th year of age or such age as may be specified in the Right of Children to Free and Compulsory Education Act, 2009, whichever is more.
5. **Day (Section 2(iii)):** Day is a period of 24 hours beginning at midnight.
6. **Establishment (Section 2(iv)):** Establishment under the Act includes a shop, commercial establishment, workshop, farm, residential hotel, restaurant, eating house, theatre or other place of public amusement or entertainment.
7. **Family (Section 2(v)):** Family in relation to an occupier, the individual, wife or husband, as the case may be, of such individual, and the children, brother or sister of such individual.
8. **Occupier (Section 2(vi)):** In relation to an establishment or a workshop, occupier is the person who has the ultimate control over the affairs of the establishment or the workshop.
9. **Week (Section 2(viii)):** Week is a period of 7 days beginning at midnight on Saturday night or such other night as may be approved in writing for a particular area by the inspector.
10. **Workshop (Section 2(ix)):** Workshop under the Act is any premises (including the precincts thereof) wherein any industrial process is carried on. But it does not include any premises to which the provisions of Section 67 of the Factories Act, 1948, for the time being apply.

LO2: Prohibition of Employment of Children in Certain Occupations and Processes

Prohibition of Employment of Children in Any Occupation and Process with Exceptions (Section 3)

Pursuant to the said Child Labour (Prohibition and Regulation) Amendment Act, 2016, of India, Section 3 of the Act has undergone a significant change. According to the amended provisions, no child shall be employed or permitted to work in any occupation or process.

However, nothing in Subsection (1) shall apply in the following conditions:

1. Where the child helps his family or family enterprise, which is other than any hazardous occupations or processes set forth in the Schedule, after his school hours or during vacations.

2. Works as an artist in an audio-visual entertainment industry, including advertisement, films, television serials or any such other entertainment or sports activities except the circus, subject to such conditions and safety measures, as may be prescribed.

It is further provided that no such work as mentioned above shall affect the school education of the child.

For the purposes of this section, the expressions 'family', 'family enterprise' and 'artist' are defined as under:

1. 'Family' in relation to a child includes his mother, father, brother, sister and father's sister and brother, and mother's sister and brother.
2. 'Family enterprise' stands for any work, profession, manufacture or business which is performed by the members of the family with the engagement of other persons.
3. 'Artist' is a child who performs or practises any work as a hobby or profession directly involving him as an actor, singer, sportsperson or in such other activity as may be prescribed relating to the entertainment or sports activities falling under clause (b) of Subsection (2).

Prohibition of Employment of Adolescents in Certain Hazardous Occupations and Processes (Section 3A)

The Act directs that no adolescent shall be employed or permitted to work in any of the hazardous occupations or processes set forth in the Schedule provided under Section 3 of the Act. It is further provided that the central government may, by notification, specify the nature of the non-hazardous work to which an adolescent may be permitted to work under this Act.

Occupation set forth in Part A of the Schedule (18 entries): There are some occupations listed in Part A of the Schedule under Section 3. These occupations include transport, construction, railways, ports, crackers and firework industries, slaughter houses, automobile workshops and garages, explosives, handloom, mines, plastic units. The Amendment Act, 2008, added diving, and the Amendment Act, 2010, added circus and caring for elephants to the list. The Child Labour (Prohibition and Regulation) Amendment Act, 2016, of India also added mines, inflammable substances or explosives and hazardous process to the Schedule. For the purposes of this Schedule, 'hazardous process' has the meaning assigned to it in Clause (cb) of the Factories Act, 1948.

Processes set forth in part B of the Schedule (65 entries): Part B of the Schedule provides the list of workshops in which the employment of children is prohibited. It includes bidi making, carpet weaving, mica cutting, lead factory, oil expelling, brick kilns, manufacturing of glass, zari, electroplating and so on. In Amendment Act, 2008, eight processes were added to the list, for example, processes involving exposure to excessive heat (like working near furnaces) and cold, food processing and beverage industry and so on.

Exemption: Section 3 further provides the exemption of occupation and workshop engaging the child on the following two grounds:

1. Children can be engaged in the work in the workshop where in any of the processes set forth in Part B is carried out by the occupier with the aid of his family.

2. Children can also be engaged in the work in a school established by or receiving assistance or recognition from the government.

Power of Inclusion to Schedule under Section 3 (Section 4)

The Act empowers the central government to add any occupation or process in the schedule mentioned in Section 3. But this addition is done by the central government after giving not less than 3 months' notice of its intention to do so.

The Technical Advisory Committee of Child Labour found some of the employments to be hazardous in nature since mostly it results in physical, psychological and sexual abuse. The matter is of great concern, and it goes unnoticed because the offence on such children is advanced within the four walls of employment institution. On the advice of the Technical Advisory Committee, the central government in the Amendment Act of 2006 included two more entries to Part A of the Schedule namely:

1. (14) Employment of child as domestic worker or servant.
2. (15) Employment of child in *dhabas* (roadside eateries, tea stall, restaurants, etc.).

Let us discuss a case to understand the application of Section 3 of the Act (Case 5.1).

Case 5.1: *Hemendra Bhai v. State of Chhattisgarh*[1]

M/s Dayalal Meghji & Co. (hereinafter referred to as 'the firm') was a firm registered under the Partnership Act, 1932, having its principal place of business at Malviya Road, Raipur. The firm carried on business of manufacturing and selling of Badshahi Farmaish Bidi, popularly known as 345 Bidi since last several decades. The Supreme Court while deciding a Writ Petition issued certain directions. As per the said directions of the Supreme Court in that case, on 4 July 1997 a survey had been conducted by the Labour Department of the State. A surveyor named S. S. Shukla conducted the inspection of the house of one Santosh Sahu, resident of Village Datrangi, Bhatapara, District Raipur and found that Ku. Kevra, aged about 11 years, was making bidis. On being asked, she told him that the bidis were made for the firm. Thereafter, he filled up the prescribed form and submitted a report to the Assistant Labour Commissioner, Raipur.

On receiving the information, the Assistant Labour Commissioner, Raipur issued a show-cause notice to the firm directing it to deposit ₹20,000 as per the directions of the Supreme Court and further to provide education to the children engaged in the bidi manufacturing activities in the premises of the firm. The firm challenged the said demand notice before the High Court of Judicature, Madhya Pradesh at Jabalpur, and the High Court passed an order directing the firm to appear before the officer concerned and the said officer was directed to provide opportunity of hearing to the applicant. The Court further directed that the notice of demand shall not be given effect till the disposal of the representation made by the firm. The Court also directed the officer to consider the representation of the firm before initiating any criminal proceedings if the same had not been already initiated.

Following the instructions of the High Court, a show-cause notice was issued to the firm calling upon the firm to show cause to why an amount of ₹20,000 be not recovered from the firm as per the directions of the Apex Court. The firm submitted a detailed representation on 13 May 1998 before the concerned

[1] *Hemendra Bhai v. State of Chhattisgarh* 2003 (97) FLR 402, (2003) IILLJ 645 CG, 2003 (2) MPHT 1 CG.

officer. The inspector appointed under the Child Labour (Prohibition and Regulation) Act, 1986 (hereinafter referred to as 'the Act'), filed the charge sheet before the Chief Judicial Magistrate, Raipur, for the commission of the offence under Section 14 of the Act against partners of the firm showing them to be as the employer.

The firm raised the preliminary objections before the Court stating that the charge sheet was filed on the basis of the report submitted by the survey team appointed by the Collector. It did not appear from the charge sheet that the survey team had inspected the firm of the applicant. Application of section 14(1) of the Act is attracted only if the child labourer is employed in the firm.. Without inspecting the premises of the firm, it was not possible to hold that the firm had employed child labourer. The case related to scheme of supplying raw material to the worker employed by the firm for making bidis at his house where he made bidis at his convenience and thereafter handing over the same to the firm. If the worker employed by the firm took the help of anybody at his home for making bidis, there was no supervision or control of the firm over such persons or job, nor such persons could be said to be the employees of the firm.

Discussion Point

Is there a merit in the arguments presented by the firm?

Judgement and Explanation

It was held that the firm was not liable for the contravention of the provisions of Section 3 of the Act. The court observed that as per the bidi industry practice, the workers who were supplied raw materials for making bidis took the raw materials from the firm after giving the undertaking that they themselves would make bidis and if they rolled bidis in their respective houses taking the assistance of their children, the firm could not be held responsible since the firm had no control or supervision over the work of those workers who took raw material to their houses for making bidis. Hence, it could not be said that the firm is the employer of the child labourer and Section 3 of the Act has not been contravened by the firm.

Child Labour Technical Advisory Committee (Section 5)

The central government is empowered to notify in the Official Gazette, for the constitution of an advisory committee called the CLTA Committee. The Committee advises the central government for the purpose of addition of occupations and processes to the Schedule.

Constitution: The CLTA Committee consists of a chairman and such other members not exceeding 10, as may be appointed by the central government.

Meetings and power: The CLTA Committee is required to meet as often as it may consider necessary and is empowered to regulate its own procedure. This committee can also constitute a subcommittee.

Other committees: In addition, a Central Advisory Board on Child Labour was also constituted to review the implementation of the existing legislations and suggest measures for welfare of working children. In order to monitor the functioning of the National Child Labour Projects (NCLPs), a Central Monitoring Committee has also been formed. This Committee supervises, monitors and evaluates the National Child Labour Projects.

LO3: Regulation of Conditions of Work of Children

Part III of the Act consists of Sections 6 to 13. These sections lay down the provisions regarding the regulation of conditions of work of children.

Application of Part (Section 6)

Section 6 directs that a child can be employed in any of the establishments other than those specified in Part A & B of the schedule. However, it further defines the application within the ambit of some regulations provided under further sections. The provisions of this Part shall apply to an establishment or a class of establishments in which none of the occupations or processes referred to in Section 3 is carried on.

Regulation of Conditions of Work (Sections 7–9)

To regulate the conditions of work, the following grounds are provided under the Act:

Hours and period of work (Section 7): Section 7 mentions the following six conditions for the employment of the children in an establishment or a workshop:

1. No child must be made to work in any establishment in excess of such number of hours as may be prescribed for such establishment or class of establishments.
2. The period of work on each day has to be so fixed that in one stretch no period exceeds 3 hours followed by an interval of 1 hour before he resumes his work.
3. The period of work of a child has to be so arranged that it concludes his interval of rest. The work period cannot be spread over for more than 6 hours, including the time spent in waiting for work.
4. No child can be made to work between 7 PM and 8 AM.
5. Overtime work is not permitted to an employed child.
6. Dual engagement of a child in two establishments is not allowed. In simple words, no child is to work on any day on which he has already been working in another establishment.

Weekly holidays (Section 8): Section 8 makes it mandatory to allow one whole day in a week as holiday to a child. Such declared holidays are required to be specified in a notice permanently exhibited on a conspicuous place in the establishment. No occupier can alter this holiday more than once in 3 months.

Health and safety (Section 13): The appropriate government is empowered to notify the rules for the health and safety of the children employed. Such rules will cover the heads provided under clause (2) of Section 13 under 24 different heads, such as, cleanliness in the place of work and its freedom from nuisance, disposal of wastes and effluents, ventilation and temperature, lighting, drinking water, latrines and urinals, spittoons, fencing of machinery, employment of children on dangerous machines, excessive weights, protection of eyes, explosive or inflammable gases, and so on.

Duties of occupier (Sections 9–12): The Act under Part III imposes certain duties upon the occupier of the establishment to ensure that a healthy and safe work environment is provided by the occupier to the employed children. Following is the discussion on the provisions laying down duties of the occupier.

Notice to inspector (Section 9): Every occupier is directed to inform in writing to the inspector with respect to the employment of children in his establishment. The inspector is a public servant under Section 21 of IPC. This notice to the inspector carries the following particulars:

1. The name and situation of the establishment.
2. The name of the person in actual management of the establishment.
3. The address to which communications relating to the establishment should be sent.
4. The nature of the occupation or process carried on in the establishment.

Verification of age of child (Section 10): If there arises a dispute with respect to the age of the child, the dispute must be referred to a medical practitioner by the inspector (in the absence of certificate of age).

Maintenance of register (Section 11): The Act requires the occupier to maintain the register in respect of children employed. The register is to be kept open for inspection at all times during working hours. The register must present the following information:

1. The name and date of birth of every child employed.
2. Working hours and period of work and intervals of rest.
3. Nature of work of any such child.
4. Other particulars as may be prescribed.

Display of notice (Section 12): It is compulsory for every railway administration port authority and every occupier to display a notice containing abstract of Section 3 and Section 14 (penalties) at a conspicuous and accessible place. The notice must be displayed in both English and local language.

LO4: Provisions for Penalty

Penalties under the Act (Sections 14 and 15)

The Act provides for penalties in Sections 14 and 15. Section 14 gives the penalties for contravention with the provisions of this Act, whereas Section 15 gives the penalties for the contraventions given in other Acts.

Penalties for the Violation of the Provisions of the Act (Section 14)

The Act states that contravention of the provisions of Section 3 of this Act will attract a punishment of imprisonment for a term not less than 6 months and may extend to 2 years or with fine not less than ₹20,000 but may extend to ₹50,000 or with both. In cases of subsequent contravention of Section 3, the term of imprisonment shall not be less than 1 year, but may extend to 3 years. The contravention of the provisions of Section 3A will attract the imprisonment of not less than 6 months which may extend to 2 years or a fine of ₹20,000 to 50,000, or both.

The Act further provides that any person who fails to comply with or contravenes with Sections 9, 11, 12 or any other provision of the Act shall be punishable with simple imprisonment extending to 1 month or with fine which may extend to ₹10,000 or with both.

Modified Application of Certain Laws in Relation to Penalties (Section 15)

If any person is found guilty and convicted of contravention of any of the provisions mentioned in Subsection (2), he shall be liable to penalties as provided in Subsections (1) and (2) of Section 14 of this Act and not under the Acts in which those provisions are contained:

1. Section 67 of the Factories Act, 1948.
2. Section 40 of the Mines Act, 1952.

3. Section 109 of the Merchant Shipping Act, 1958.
4. Section 21 of the Motor Transport Workers Act, 1961.

Procedure to file complaint against the offences committed under the Act (Section 16): Any person, police officer or inspector may file a complaint of the commission of the offence under this Act in any court of competent jurisdiction. Offences under this Act can be tried by a Metropolitan Magistrate or a magistrate of the first class, and not below this rank.

The word 'complaint' has been used in a wide sense since it includes even an oral allegation. Although no particular form of complaint is prescribed, a complaint must be an allegation prima facie disclosing the necessary facts that are necessary to constitute the offence alleged. For the purposes of this Act, the certificate as to the age of the child, granted by a prescribed medical authority, is considered to be conclusive evidence as to the age of the child.

Power to Make Rules (Sections 18 and 19)

The appropriate government has power to make rules through notification with respect to:

1. Appointment, allowances, conditions, restrictions upon CLTA Committee and subcommittees.
2. Fixation of working hours of the child.
3. Medical authority which shall grant the certificate of age of child seeking employment.
4. Particulars of Register to be maintained.

Every rule made under this Act by the central government and every notification issued under Section 4 are required to be (as soon as may be after it is made or issued) laid down before each House of Parliament for its approval. However, such approval shall be without prejudice to the validity of anything previously done under the rule or notification. Similarly, every rule made by a state government under this Act must be laid (as soon as may be after it is made) before the legislature of the State for its approval.

Summary

1. The preamble of the Act (The Child and Adolescent Labour (Prohibition and Regulation) Act, 1986) indicates the following twin objectives:
   a. It intends to prohibit the engagement of children in certain employments.
   b. It regulates the conditions of work of children in certain other employments where children are allowed to work.
2. The Act aims to prohibit the employment of children who have not completed their 14th year of age, in specified occupations and processes.
3. It lays down enhanced penalties for the violation of the provisions of the Act, and other Acts dealing with the employment of children.
4. As per Section 2(ii), child is a person who has not completed his 14th year of age or such age as may be specified in the Right of Children to Free and Compulsory Education Act, 2009, whichever is more.

5. Prohibition of employment of children in any occupation and process is not applicable where the child helps his family or family enterprise, which is other than any hazardous occupations or processes set forth in the Schedule, after his school hours or during vacations.
6. Prohibition of employment of children in any occupation and process is not applicable where the child works as an artist in an audio-visual entertainment industry, including advertisement, films, television serials or any such other entertainment or sports activities except circus, subject to such conditions and safety measures, as may be prescribed.
7. No child can be made to work between 7 PM and 8 AM.
8. Overtime work is not permitted to an employed child.
9. Dual engagement of a child in two establishments is not allowed.
10. It is mandatory to allow one whole day in a week as holiday to a child.
11. No occupier can alter this holiday more than once in 3 months.
12. Every occupier is directed to inform in writing to the inspector with respect to the employment of children in his establishment.
13. Contravention of the provisions of Section 3 of this Act will attract a punishment of imprisonment for a term not less than 6 months and may extend to 2 years or with a fine of not less than ₹20,000 but may extend to ₹50,000 or with both.
14. Offences under this Act can be tried by a Metropolitan Magistrate or a magistrate of the first class, and not below this rank.

Multiple Choice Questions

1. Day is a period of 24 hours beginning ____________.
   a. Early morning at 6 AM
   b. Evening at 6 PM
   c. At midnight
   d. At noon 12 PM

2. Week is a period of 7 days beginning at midnight on ____________ or such other night as may be approved in writing for a particular area by the inspector.
   a. Saturday night
   b. Sunday night
   c. Monday night
   d. Friday night

3. No ____________ shall be employed or permitted to work in any of the hazardous occupations or processes set forth in the Schedule provided under Section 3, of the Act.
   a. Child
   b. Adolescent
   c. Adult
   d. None of the above

4. Children can be engaged in the work in the ____________ where in any of the processes set forth in Part B is carried out by the occupier with the aid of his family.
   a. Factory
   b. Industrial establishment
   c. Workshop
   d. All of the above

5. No child can be made to work between ____________.
   a. 9 PM and 8 AM
   b. 8 PM and 8 AM
   c. 6 PM and 6 AM
   d. 7 PM and 8 AM

True/False Questions

1. The CLTA Committee consists of a chairman and such other members not exceeding 105.
2. The Act ensures uniformity in the definition of 'child' in all the related laws.
3. Overtime work is permitted to an employed child provided the overtime wages are paid by the occupier.
4. Dual engagement of a child in two establishments is not allowed.
5. 'Family' in relation to a child includes his mother, father, brother, sister and father's sister and brother and mother's sister and brother.

Annexure A: The Schedule

Part A—Occupations

Any occupation connected with:

1. Transport of passengers, goods or mails by railway.
2. Cinder picking, clearing of an ash pit or building operation in the railway premises.
3. Work in a catering establishment at a railway station, involving the movement of a vendor or any other employee of the establishment from one platform to another or into or out of a moving train.
4. Work relating to the construction of a railway station or with any other work where such work is done in close proximity to or between the railway lines.
5. A port authority within the limits of any port.
6. Work relating to selling of crackers and fireworks in shops with temporary licences.
7. Abattoirs/slaughter houses.

Part B—Processes

1. Bidi making.
2. Carpet weaving.
3. Cement manufacture, including bagging of cement.
4. Cloth printing, dyeing and weaving.
5. Manufacture of matches, explosives and fireworks.
6. Mica cutting and splitting.
7. Shellac manufacture.
8. Soap manufacture.
9. Tanning.
10. Wool cleaning.
11. Building and construction industry.
12. Manufacture of slate pencils (including packing).

13. Manufacture of products from agate.
14. Manufacturing processes using toxic metals and substances such as lead, mercury, manganese, chromium, cadmium, benzene, pesticides and asbestos.
15. 'Hazardous processes' as defined in Section 2(cb) and 'dangerous operations' as notified in rules made under Section 87 of the Factories Act, 1948 (63 of 1948).
16. Priming as defined in Section 2(k)(iv) of the Factories Act, 1948 (63 of 1948).
17. Cashew and cashew nut descaling and processing.
18. Soldering processes in electronic industries.

Source: https://www.ilo.org/dyn/natlex/docs/WEBTEXT/27803/64848/E86IND01.htm

6

CHAPTER

The Employees' Compensation Act, 1923

LEARNING OBJECTIVES

Upon completing this chapter, the reader would be able to:

LO1. Understand the objectives, scope and important definitions of the Act.
LO2. Explain the eligibility criteria for availing the benefits offered by the Act.
LO3. Know the rules for workmen's compensation.
LO4. Gain insights into amount and distribution of compensation.
LO5. Understand the provisions for notice and claims and also some other important provisions of the Act.
LO6. Gain insights into enforcement of the Act and provisions of penalty for the contravention of the Act.

Introduction

The growing complexity of industry, increasing use of machinery and consequent danger to workmen, along with the comparative poverty, render it necessary to protect the health and life of a workman so far as possible from hardship arising on account of accidents. The Workmen's Compensation Act, 1923, provided for the payment of compensation to the employee who suffered any injury by an accident while working for his employer.

The Workmen's Compensation Act, 1923, was the first piece of legislation towards social security of the employees. It deals with compensation for employees who are injured in the course of duty. The point to be noted is that the scheme of the Workmen's Compensation Act is not to compensate the employee in lieu of wages, rather it is to compensate for the loss of health incurred by an employee during the course of duty. The general principle is that an employee who suffers an injury in the course of his employment, resulting in a disablement, should be entitled to compensation. If the injury was fatal in nature, then the dependants of the deceased must be compensated. The meaning of compensation in this Act is limited to compensation granted under the Act for employment injuries sustained during the course of work. It is also limited to specifically monetary compensation other than a salary, travel allowance and any other form of remuneration that could be paid under normal circumstances of employment. Unlike the Employees' State Insurance Act (ESI Act), the Workmen's Compensation Act renders the employer responsible to pay compensation.

LO1: Objectives, Scope and Important Definitions of the Act

Objectives of the Act

The Workmen's Compensation Act was the first measure of social security to the workmen introduced in 1923. This Act came into force on 1 July 1924 and it provided for the payment by certain classes of employers to their workmen of compensation for injury by accident. The workmen or their dependants are at liberty to file a suit for damage against the employer and run the risk of employer's escape from his liability. The Workmen's Compensation Act was intended to promote the welfare of public community and it did not concern itself with the measure of preventive nature.

The Workmen's Compensation Act, 1923, was renamed as Employee's Compensation Act, 1923 (the Act), with effect from 31 May 2010. The Act aims at providing financial protection to the workmen and/or their dependants in case of accidents arising out of and in the course of employment and causing either death or disablement of workmen. Besides, the Act has a provision of paying compensation to the workmen for some occupational diseases contracted by them during the course of their employment.

Scope of the Act

To which establishments does the Act apply: The Act extends to the whole of India and applies to employees employed in any capacity specified in Schedule II of the Act which includes factories, mines, plantations, mechanically propelled vehicles, construction work, and certain other hazardous occupations and specified categories of railway servants.

As we know that the establishments hiring 20 employees and above must compulsorily register themselves under the ESI Act. This Act is only applicable to those establishments which employ a lesser number of employees and therefore do not come within the purview of the ESI Act. Thus, the Act does not apply to factories covered by the ESI Act. It is also to be noted that if employers fail to register themselves under the ESI Act, then they will be responsible to pay compensation under the Employee's Compensation Act.

The Act will only apply to those persons considered 'employees' and those employers who are considered 'employers', as defined under the Act. Although there is no wage limit for coverage of employees under the Act, yet it does not apply to:

1. Persons serving in the Armed Forces.
2. Employees covered by the ESI Act, 1948.

Important Definitions

1. **Dependant (Section 2(d)):** A 'dependant' is defined in the Act under Section 2(d). This definition plays a key role in determining who will be eligible to receive the compensation, in case the employee dies in course of his employment. The section states that all the people listed below fall under one category as being dependants of the deceased employee:
   a. A widower.
   b. A parent other than a widowed mother.
   c. A minor illegitimate son, an unmarried illegitimate daughter or a daughter legitimate or illegitimate or adopted if married and a minor or if widowed and a minor.
   d. A minor brother or an unmarried sister or a widowed sister if a minor.
   e. A widowed daughter-in-law.
   f. A minor child of a pre-deceased son.
   g. A minor child of a pre-deceased daughter where no parent of the child is alive.
   h. A paternal grandparent if no parent of the [employee] is alive.

   A careful examination of the above definition clarifies that the law does not intend to benefit all the legal heirs of a deceased employee, but only those relations who to some extent depend upon the employee's earnings for their daily necessities. However, all persons mentioned in Sub-clause (i) above are the beneficiaries who only have to prove their relationship with the deceased employee but do not have to prove that they were dependent on the earnings of the employee.
2. **Minor (Section 2(ff)):** As laid down under Section 2(ff), minor means a person who has not attained the age of 18 years.
3. **Employer (Section 2(e)):** Definition of employer in the Act is provided as under:

   > Employer includes any body of persons, whether incorporated or not and any managing agent of an employer and the legal representative of a deceased employer, and, when the services of an employee are temporarily lent or let on hire to another person by the person with whom the employee has entered into a contract of service or apprenticeship, means such other person while the employee is working for him.

   Thus the term 'employer' includes the following people:
   a. Any body of persons, whether incorporated or not.
   b. Any managing agent of an employer.
   c. The legal representatives of a deceased employer.
   d. Any person to whom the services of a workman are temporarily lent or let out while the workman is working for him.

   It is clear from the above discussion that the employer under the Act is defined as a body of person/s who the employee has entered into a contract of apprenticeship or service with; the term 'employer' also extends to his agent, legal representative of a dead employer or a temporary employer on to whom the employee has been lent to hire basis. However, it must be noted that the above list is not exhaustive.
4. **Disablement:** The definition of 'disablement' in the Act is of vital value as it determines the extent of compensation that can be claimed by the employee injured in the course of his employment. Disablement, in ordinary language, means loss of capacity to work or move. Such incapacity may be partial or total and accordingly there are two types of disablement, partial and total.

a. **Total disablement (Section 2(l)):** Following is the definition of total disablement as provided under the Act:

> "Total disablement" means such disablement, whether of a temporary or permanent nature, as incapacitates an employee for all work which he was capable of performing at the time of the accident resulting in such disablement: Provided that permanent total disablement shall be deemed to result from every injury specified in Part I of Schedule I or from any combination of injuries specified in Part II thereof where the aggregate percentage of the loss of earning capacity, as specified in the said Part II against those injuries, amounts to one hundred% or more.

Thus, it is clear that total disablement is a type of disablement that incapacitates an employee from all kinds of work. Here, permanent total disability has a different meaning under the Act from its meaning in normal language. The Act clarifies that disability is determined with reference to the work that the employee was doing immediately before accident took place and if the resulting injury leaves him incapable of performing any work of a similar nature than his disability is considered as permanent total disablement.

b. **Partial disablement (Section 2(g)):** The Act defines partial disablement as under:

> "Partial disablement" means, where the disablement is of a temporary nature, such disablement as reduces the earning capacity of a employee in any employment in which he was engaged at the time of the accident resulting in the disablement, and, where the disablement is of a permanent nature, such disablement as reduces his earning capacity in every employment which he was capable of undertaking at that time: provided that every injury specified in Part II of Schedule I shall be deemed to result in permanent partial disablement.

A disablement that reduces the capacity to work in any employment similar to that the employee was performing at the time of the accident is named as partial disablement. In a case of partial disablement, it is necessary that:

i. There should be an accident.
ii. As a result of the accident, the workman should suffer injury.
iii. Which should result in permanent disablement.
iv. As a result whereof, his earning capacity must have decreased permanently.

c. **Temporary disablement:** This may be total or partial disablement, which is of temporary nature, which reduces the earning capacity of the employee in any similar employment for the period of disablement.

5. **Wages (Section 2(m)):** As defined under Section 2(m) of the Act,

> Wages include any privilege or benefit which is capable of being estimated in money, other than a travelling allowance or the value of any travelling concession or a contribution paid by the employer of an employee towards any pension or provident fund or a sum paid to an employee to cover any special expenses entailed on him by the nature of his employment.

Wages, the basis for the amount of compensation paid, is defined as the privilege or benefit which is measurable in terms of money other than any travel allowance, or PF or any other special benefit claimable by the employee, during the course of his employment.

The definition of wages is important because an employee whose monthly wages exceed ₹1,000 is not considered as an employee for the purpose of this Act. As discussed above, that compensation payable under this Act is calculated on the basis of the monthly wage received by the employee.

Thus, two employees earning different salaries, therefore, will get different amounts of compensation even though the injury they suffered might be identical.

6. **Monthly Wages (Section 5):** The Act defines 'monthly wages' and provides the methods of calculating it. 'Monthly' wages here means the amount of wages deemed to be payable for a month's service (whether the wages are payable by the month or by whatever other period or at piece rate). Monthly wages are calculated by following the rules explained below:
   a. In the cases where the workman was in service for a continuous period of 12 months immediately preceding the accident, monthly wages shall be one-twelfth of the total wages due for the last 12 months of the period.
   b. If the whole period of continuous service was less than 1 month, monthly wages shall be the average monthly amount which during the 12 months immediately preceding the accident was being earned by a workman employed on the same work by the same employer, or if there was no workman so employed, by a workman employed on similar work in the same locality.
   c. In all other cases, including those cases in which it is not possible for want of necessary information to calculate the monthly wages under clause (b), the monthly wages shall be 30 times the total wages earned in respect of the last continuous period or service immediately preceding the accident from the employer who is liable to pay compensation divided by the number of days comprising such period.

Here, a period of service is deemed to be continuous which has not been interrupted by a period of absence exceeding 14 days.

LO2: Eligibility

Employees Eligible to Receive the Benefits under the Act

Every employee who is engaged for the purposes of employer's business and who suffers an injury in any accident arising out of and in the course of his employment, including the employee who is employed through a contractor but excluding casual employees, is entitled for compensation under the Act. Therefore, only a person covered under the definition of employee under the Act is entitled to the reliefs provided by the Act.

Employee (Section 2(dd)): Clause (dd) of the Act was inserted by Workmen's Compensation (Amendment) Act, 2009. According to this subsection, 'employee' means a person, who is:

1. A railway servant as defined in clause (34) of Section 2 of the Railways Act, 1989 (24 of 1989), not permanently employed in any administrative district or subdivisional office of a railway and not employed in any such capacity as is specified in Schedule II; or
2. a. A master, seaman or other members of the crew of a ship,
   b. A captain or other member of the crew of an aircraft,
   c. A person recruited as a driver, helper, mechanic, cleaner or in any other capacity in connection with a motor vehicle,

d. A person recruited to work abroad by a company, and who is employed outside India in any such capacity as is specified in Schedule II and the ship, aircraft or motor vehicle, or company, as the case may be, is registered in India; or

3. Employed in any such capacity as is specified in Schedule II, whether the contract of employment was made before or after the passing of this Act and whether such contract is expressed or implied, oral or in writing, but does not include any person working in the capacity of a member of the Armed Forces of the Union, and any reference to any employee who has been injured shall, where the employee is dead, include a reference to his dependants or any of them.

The above-stated definition of 'employee' must be read with Schedule II to the Act. In Schedule II, a list (consisting of 32 items) is given by persons who fall in the category of employee. The provisions of the Act have been extended to cooks employed in hotels, restaurants using power, liquefied petroleum gas or any other mechanical device in the process of cooking.

Employees covered under the Act: Subject to the exceptions noted below, the term employee covers:

1. A railway servant as defined in Section 3 of the Indian Railways Act of 1890 who is not permanently employed in any administrative, district or subdivisional office of a railway, and not employed in any capacity as is specified in Schedule II or
2. A person employed on monthly wages not exceeding ₹1,000 in any such capacity as is mentioned in Schedule II. The contract of employment may be expressed or implied, oral or in writing.

Employees not covered under the Act: The Act provides that the following categories of persons are not to be deemed as an employee for the purposes of this Act:

1. Persons working in the capacity of a member of the Armed Forces of the Union.
2. A person whose employment is of a casual nature and who is employed otherwise than for the purposes of the employer's trade or business.

Regarding the question who is an employee under the Act, the general rule is that there must be the relationship of master and servant between the employer and the employee. Employee is a person whom the employer can command and control in the manner of performing the work. Following points are to be taken into consideration in determining the question whether a person is an employee:

1. The term of engagement.
2. The payment of wages.
3. The power of control over the work.
4. The power of dismiss.

Some Important Rules for Deciding the Entitlement of Benefits under the Act

With the amendment of the Workmen's Compensation Act in 2000, now it is not necessary that the employee in question is engaged in the employer's trade or business. By the effect of the Amendment of 2000, now even casual employees are covered by this law. The only requirement is that the employee should be employed in an activity, which has to be either listed in schedule II of the Act or any duty having connection with the specified activity mentioned in the schedule.

Employment of a casual nature: Employees of a casual nature, if not employed in the employer's trade or business, are not covered within the definition of the term employee as used in the Act. Generally, casual work is defined as one which is not regular or continuous. Whether the employment is for the purpose of the employer's trade or business depends on whether the contract of service entered into by the employer was of his capacity as businessman or in a private capacity.

Example:

If a coal mine employs employees to dig for coal, it is for his trade or business. But if the same mine owner engaging employees for building his residence is not engaging them for his trade or business.

This should also be kept in mind that a person who does service which is illegal and void cannot be an employee and cannot claim compensation.

Eligibility of contract labour to receive benefits (Section 12): The Act lays down the rule for deciding the eligibility of the contract labour to receive the compensation under the Act in the cases where a part of the work of an establishment is contracted out to a contractor and an employee who is employed by the contractor for this purpose gets injured. In such cases, the principal employer, and not the contractor (who is the employee's immediate employer), is responsible for paying compensation as though the employee was directly employed by him. However, this principal employer holds the right to be indemnified by the person who would normally pay for the compensation of an injured/deceased employee, that is, the contractor. But nothing shall prevent the employee from claiming his compensation from the principal employer.

LO3: Rules for Workmen's Compensation

Employer's Liability to Pay Compensation (Section 3(i))

As provided by the Act, if personal injury is caused to an employee by accident arising out of and in the course of employment, his employer shall be liable to pay compensation. In light of the provision stated above, the employer is liable to pay compensation only when:

1. Injury is caused to an employee by accident.
2. The accident arises out of and in the course of employment.

To decide whether an employee is entitled to compensation under the Act or not, the following terms/ phrases need to be discussed in detail:

An accident: Lord Macnaghten defined an accident as 'an unlocked for mishap or untoward event which is not expected or designed'. In simple words, a self-inflicted injury is not an accident ordinarily. In one case, a person became insane as a result of the accident and then committed suicide. It was held that death was the result of the accident, and compensation was awarded. But where insanity is not the direct result of the accident, then compensation cannot be awarded. However, a series of tiny accidents, each producing some unidentifiable result and operating cumulatively to produce the final condition of injury, would constitute together an accident to furnish a proper foundation for a claim under the Act.

Personal injury: A personal injury under the Act is not necessarily confined to the physical or bodily injury. It also includes psychological and physiological injury such as nervous shock and insanity. Here, the injury must be personal. An injury to the belonging of an employee does not come within the Act. In one case, an employee had to go into a heating room and from there to cooling plant. The changes of temperature caused pneumonia, and the employee died. It was held that the death was due to personal injury and the employee was entitled to compensation.

In the course of employment: This part of the phrase covers the period of time during which the employment continues. According to the provisions of the Act in this regard, the compensation is payable only if the accident occurs within the period of employment. The employment is deemed to commence when the employee reaches his place of work and ceases when he leaves the place. But there are following exceptions to this rule:

a. **Usage of transport by the employee:** If the employee uses transport provided by the employer for the purpose of going to and from the place of work, the time during which he uses the transport is also included in the course of his employment.
b. **Employee on the premise of the employer:** The time during which the workman is upon the premises of the employer has to be included in the period of employment. In a case where an employee of the railways was knocked down and killed by a train while returning from duty by crossing the platform area, the accident was held to arise out of and in the course of employment.
c. **Early reporting by the employee:** If the workman reaches the place of employment before the time when the employment begins when it was necessary and not too early, or if at the time of accident, he was doing something to equip himself for the work, he is in course of employment.
d. **In the course of proceeding:** If the employee with the knowledge and permission of the employer lives at some distance from the place where he is called upon to work and if in the course of proceeding at a reasonable time and in a reasonable manner from this place to the place of work, he meets with fatal accident, then his accident must be held to arise out of and in course of employment.
e. **Rest period:** The period of rest during the period of employment is also included in the course of employment. But if the employee goes outside the employer's premises during the rest period and meets with an accident, it is not included in the course of employment.

Notional Extension

As a general rule, the employment of an employee does not commence until he has reached the place of employment and ends when he has left the place of employment. Here, the journey to and from the place of employment is excluded from the course of employment. However, it is now well settled and accepted that the above-stated rule is subject to the theory or notional extension of the employer's premises so as to include an area which an employee passes and re-passes in going to and in leaving the actual place of work.

Case 6.1 will provide the insights into the entitlement of compensation for the injuries or accidents occurred in the course of employment.

Case 6.1: *Bai Shakri w/o Naraindas Maganlal v. New Manekchowk Mills Company Limited*[1]

On 14 August 1955, Mr Naraindas Maganlal who was employed in the weaving department of New Manekchowk Mills Company Limited (the respondent company) had gone to work in the second shift which was to commence at 3:30 PM. At 3:20 PM, while he was sitting in the grey folding department, where he had gone to meet a friend, he had a serious heart attack and was moved from the mills to the Civil Hospital. He remained as an indoor patient in the Civil Hospital for about a month and a half and was then discharged. Later on, he died on 16 March 1956.

Wife of the deceased (the appellant's) filed an application for the compensation from the respondent company under the Workmen's Compensation Act, 1923. She argued that although the deceased was discharged from the hospital, he was not completely cured; after he was brought home, he was again taken to the hospital where he remained for 8 or 10 days as an indoor patient and was brought home again. Dr Gupta of the Civil Hospital treated the deceased from 14 August 1955 to 10 September 1955. Dr Desai of the Civil Hospital stated in his evidence that the deceased was a patient who could have continued with a bad heart all his life. He has also stated that when the appellant's husband left the hospital, he had survived the attack, thereby meaning that he had survived the heart attack which the appellant's husband had on 14 August 1955. Dr Desai was of the opinion that a subsequent heart attack was not caused by a previous heart attack and that the appellant's husband might have died on 16 March 1956 because he might have had a further attack after he left the hospital.

The respondent company argued that the deceased had an attack at 3:20 PM on 14 August 1955 before the second shift commenced, while he was sitting in the grey folding department where he had gone, not for the mill's work but for his personal work. Hence, the deceased died due to a subsequent heart attack while he was not in the mill's employment and, therefore, he could not be said to have died of an injury which occurred as a result of and in the course of his employment.

Discussion Point

In light of the facts stated above, can it be concluded that the deceased had suffered personal injury by an accident arising out of and in the course of his employment with the respondent mills even though he died on 16 March 1956, long after his employment with the respondent's mill had ceased?

Judgement and Explanation

It was held that the wife of the deceased (the appellant) failed to establish that her husband died as a result of injury caused by accident arising out of and in the course of his employment. The appeal, therefore, failed and was dismissed. The court stated in its order that there was no evidence whatsoever which showed that the work the deceased had been doing until 14 August 1955 had contributed to the causing of his death. There was no evidence also to show as to what was the condition of the deceased during all these months while he was living at Bhayala. The burden was upon the appellant to establish that the heart of the workman which was already in a diseased condition after the first attack had, by the strain of the work he was doing, become weaker and which ultimately collapsed causing his death on 16 March 1956. The appellant failed to establish any such fact.

The above discussion clarifies that although an accident must be a particular occurrence which happens at a particular time, in order that it may constitute an accident within the meaning of Section 3, it is not necessary that the employee should be able to locate it in order to succeed in the claim. There are cases where a series of tiny accidents, each producing some unidentifiable result and operating cumulatively to produce the final condition of injury, would constitute together an accident for the purposes of the Act.

---

[1] *Bai Shakri w/o Naraindas Maganlal v. New Manekchowk Mills Company Limited*, (1961) ILLJ 585 Guj.

Occupational Disease (Section 3(2))

Occupational disease is defined under Section 3(2) of the Act as under:

> If an employed in any employment specified in Part A of Schedule III contracts any disease specified therein as an occupational disease peculiar to that employment, or if an employee, whilst in the service of an employer in whose service he has been employed for a continuous period of not less than six months (which period shall not include a period of service under any other employer in the same kind of employment) in any employment specified in Part B of Schedule III, contracts any disease specified therein as an occupational disease peculiar to that employment, or if an employee whilst in the service of one or more employers in any employment specified in Part C of Schedule III for such continuous period as the Central Government may specify in respect of each such employment, contracts any disease specified therein as an occupational disease peculiar to that employment, the contracting of the disease shall be deemed to be an injury by accident within the meaning of this section and, unless the contrary is proved, the accident shall be deemed to have arisen out of, and in the course of, the employment: Provided that if it is proved,
>
> (a) That an employee whilst in the service of one or more employers in any employment specified in Part C of Schedule III has contracted a disease specified therein as an occupational disease peculiar to that employment during a continuous period which is less than the period specified under this subsection for that employment; and
>
> (b) That the disease has arisen out of and in the course of the employment, the contracting of such disease shall be deemed to be an injury by accident within the meaning of this section.

Meaning of occupational disease: A careful examination of the above-stated definition reveals that under the Act, an 'Occupational Disease' while in service is a disease that inflicts employees in that particular occupation in which s/he was employed in and resulting from exposure to a hazardous working atmosphere, particular to that employment. An occupational disease that is contracted in the course of employment falls within the meaning of an 'accident' for the purposes of this Act.

Conditions for qualification: As provided by the definition stated above, an occupational disease is deemed to be an injury by accident within the meaning of this section. Unless the contrary is proved, the accident is deemed to have arisen out of, and in the course of, the employment subject to the condition that the employee was employed by the employer for a continuous period of 6 months.

Section 3(4) further lays down that save as provided above, no compensation needs to be paid to a workman in respect of any disease unless the disease is directly attributable to a specific injury by accident arising out of and in the course of his employment.

Let us go through a case discussion to understand the application of this section (Case 6.2).

Case 6.2: *Laxmibai v. Chairman and Trustees, Bombay Port Trust*[2]

The deceased workman was a watchman employed by the Port Trust at its pumping station at Carnac Bunder, Bombay. He was on night duty on the night of 20 August 1951, and the hours of his duty were 7 PM to 7 AM. At 1 AM, on 2 August 1951, the deceased complained of pain in his chest and was asked to lie down. His condition deteriorated, and at about 6 AM, he died. The medical evidence showed that he was suffering from

[2] *Laxmibai v. Chairman and Trustees*, Bombay Port Trust (1954) ILLJ 614.

heart disease and that the death was brought about by the strain caused to the deceased being on his legs for a certain period of time. Wife of the deceased filed an application for compensation from the Port Trust and presented the medical evidence in the support with her claim. She argued that her husband died of injury by an accident arising out of and in the course of his employment.

Port Trust denied the liability and argued that the deceased did not die of injury by an accident arising out of and in the course of his employment, but he died of his bad health.

Discussion Point

Did the deceased die of injury by an accident arising out of and in the course of his employment?

Judgement and Explanation

It was held that Port Trust was liable to pay compensation to the deceased's wife as the workman died of an injury by an accident, falling within the scope of Section 3 of the Workmen's Compensation Act, 1923. It was further stated that the employment of the deceased accelerated his death and the death was due to not only the disease but also the disease coupled with the employment. Hence, the employer would not be free from the liability and it could then be said that death arose out of the employment of the deceased.

The case discussion makes it clear that if an employee suffers from a particular disease and as a result of wear and tear of his health he dies of that disease, no liability would be fixed upon the employers. If, however, the employment is a contributory cause, then the employer will not be free from the liability and it could then be said that death arose out of the employment of the deceased.

Joint liability of all employers (Section 3(2A)): The Act further provides that if an employee who is employed in any employment specified in Part C of Schedule III contracts any occupational disease peculiar to that employment, the contracting whereof is deemed to be an injury by accident within the meaning of this section. If such employment was under more than one employer, all such employers are liable for the payment of the compensation in such proportion as the Commissioner may, in the circumstances, deem just.

Addition to Schedule III by the Government (Section 3(3)): After giving, by notification in the Official Gazette, not less than 3 months' notice of its intention so to do so, the central government or the state government is empowered to add any description of employment to the employments specified in Schedule III and to specify in the case of employments so added the diseases which shall be deemed for the purposes of this section to be occupational diseases peculiar to those employments, respectively, and thereupon the provisions of Subsection (2) shall apply.

When Is Employer Not Liable to Pay Compensation?

Section 3 of the Act states that the employer is not liable to pay compensation in the following cases:

1. If any injury which does not result in the total or partial disablement of the employee for a period exceeding 3 days.
2. If any injury not resulting in death, caused by an accident which is directly attributable to
   a. The employee having been at the time thereof under the influence of drink or drugs.
   b. The wilful disobedience of the employee to an order expressly given, or to a rule expressly framed, for the purpose of securing the safety of employees.

c. The wilful removal or disregard by the employee of any safety guard or other device which he knew to have been provided for the purpose of securing the safety of employees.

In relation to the exception clause (b), an employee would not lose his right to compensation only by reason of the fact that he had acted thoughtlessly or foolishly. From Section 3, it follows that the cases in which the employer is free from paying compensation under the Act can be summarized as under:

1. When the accident did not arise out of or in the course of the employment.
2. When the workmen filed a suit for damages in the civil court.
3. When disablement lasted 3 days or less and the injuries were not significant.

Case 6.3 will throw more light on employer's liability to compensate the injured employee in case of injury.

Case 6.3: *Harris v. Associated Portland Cement Manufacturers Limited*[3]

A was an employee who used to work at a furnace in a factory. She had a history of previous eye disorders, but despite knowing that she continued to work in an employment, which by the very nature of work might cause further strain on her eyes and might thereby suffer a permanent injury to her eyes. Subsequently, her eyes got permanently damaged and she claimed compensation from her employer. She argued that she suffered from injury arising out of an accident in the course of her employment, and thus she was covered under Section 3 of the Workmen's Compensation Act.

The employer denied the liability and argued that despite knowing that the work would cause strain on her eyes, the injured employee continued working and precipitated the permanent injury. Thus, it was an act of pure negligence on the part of the employee, in the opinion of the employer.

Discussion Point

Could the employer avoid the liability to compensate the injured employee on the grounds of negligence at employee's end?

Judgement and Explanation

It was held that the employee suffered from injury arising out of an accident. The fact that she continued in employment against the advice of a doctor and also knowing that her work would cause strain on her eyes and precipitated the permanent injury is irrelevant. Once it was found that the work which she had been doing was to be within the scope of her employment, the question of negligence, great or small on her part, was thus irrelevant.

Liability of Employer in Case of Insolvency (Section 14)

If the employer of the employee has entered into an agreement with insurers, to pay compensation and subsequently the employer becomes bankrupt, then in the event of any accident happening, the employer's liabilities get transferred to the insurers, and they would be treated as the employers of the

[3] *Harris v. Associated Portland Cement Manufacturers Limited* (1939 A.C. 71).

aggrieved employee for the purpose of paying compensation. The insurer is liable to pay compensation irrespective of whether the employer is bankrupt or not. If he has taken insurance to cover claims arising out of employees' accidents, the insurance company will be responsible to pay compensation. However, the insurance company will be no more liable to the employee than the original employer. If the liability of the insurers is to be less than that of the original employers, then the employee can claim the balance amount only from the insolvency proceedings.

Void or voidable contract of insurance: Under the provisions of this Act, if the insurer is liable to pay compensation to the workman, and the contract of the employer with the insurers is void or voidable by reason of non-compliance on the part of the employer with any terms or conditions of the contract (other than a stipulation for the payment of premia), the rights of the workman to claim compensation from the insurer will remain unaffected as if the contract were not void or voidable. Thus, in such case, the insurer will have to pay compensation to the workman, but insurers shall be entitled to prove in the insolvency proceedings or liquidation for the amount paid to the workman. However, the protection of right of workman to claim the compensation from the insurer under this section will not be available if the workman fails to give notice to the insurers of the happening of the accident and of any resulting disablement as soon as practicable after he becomes aware of the institution of the insolvency or liquidation proceedings.

Let us discuss a case to gain insights into the circumstances when an employer is liable to compensate the workman and also the situation when he can avoid this liability (Case 6.4).

Case 6.4: *S. S. Manufacturing Co. v. B. V. Raja*[4]

Saurashtra Salt Manufacturing Co. (the appellant) employed workmen both temporary and permanent. The salt works of the company were situated near a creek, opposite to the town of Porbandar. There were at least two ways to go to the salt works from the said town, one an overland route nearly 6 to 7 miles long and the other via the creek which had to be crossed by a boat. At the Porbandar end of the creek was the Asmavati Ghat and the creek could be crossed from there at point A to the other side at point B which was on a sandy piece of land. Those crossing the creek from point A alight from the boat at point B. From point B, after traversing the sandy area, one could reach the salt jetty of the salt works and the salt works itself. On the sandy area near point B, there was also a public foot path which ran to the salt works at point D, the distance being 11/4 mile.

In the evening of 12 May 1952, a boat carrying certain workmen, who were employed that day by the company, while crossing the creek from point B to point A capsized due to bad weather and overloading. The accident took place when the boat had practically reached point A. As mentioned above, from the town of Porbandar, there were two ways of going to and returning from the salt works of the appellant, and it was not disputed by the parties that the usual and the ordinary way to go to and return from the salt works was via the creek to be crossed at points A and B.

The deceased workmen were not regular workmen employed by the appellant; however, the company had provided the quarters to the deceased near the salt works. The Commissioner for Workmen's Compensation found that the accident arose out of and in the course of the employment of the workmen. Accordingly, he awarded compensation.

Dissatisfied with the decision of the Commissioner, the company appealed against the decision in the competent court. The Commissioner contended that there was an arrangement between the company and

[4] *S. S. Manufacturing Co. v. B. V. Raja*, 1958 II LLJ 249.

the ferrywalas or Kharvas for its workmen to be ferried to and from the salt works thereof, and therefore the company was liable to compensate the dependants of the deceased workmen as the accident arose out of and in the course of the employment while they were returning crossing the creek between points A and B. The company denied any such arrangement and the liability arising out of the accident.

Discussion Point

Whether the deceased workmen were in the course of employment while crossing the creek between points A and B and thus the employer was liable to pay compensation under the Act.

Judgement and Explanation

It was held that the Commissioner for Workmen's Compensation was in error in supposing that the deceased workmen in that case were still in the course of their employment when they were crossing the creek between points A and B. The accident which took place when the boat was almost at point A resulting in the death of so many workmen was unfortunate, but for that accident the company (the appellant) could not be held liable. In the above case, even if it was assumed that the theory of notional extension extended up to point D, the theory could not be extended beyond it. The moment the workmen left point B in the boat or left point A but had not yet reached point B, they could not be said to be in the course of their employment and any accident happening to them on the journey between these two points could not be said to have arisen out of and in the course of their employment. The appeal was accordingly allowed and the order of the Commissioner for Workmen's Compensation directing the appellants to pay compensation was set aside.

It is clear from the above discussion that a workman is not in the course of his employment from the moment he leaves his home and is on his way to his work. The workman certainly is in the course of his employment if he reaches the place of work or a point or an area which comes within the theory of notional extension, outside of which the employer is not liable to pay compensation for any accident happening to him. Thus, under the doctrine of notional extension, where an obligation is present on a workman to discharge his duty, and he meets with an accident, then only it is an accident in the course of employment.

LO4: Amount and Distribution of Compensation

The Amount of Compensation

The amount of compensation to be paid by the employer for injuries caused depends on the extent of the disablement suffered by the workman. Therefore, more severe disablements naturally receive higher compensation. There are different categories of disablements caused in the course of employment for which a workman can claim compensation from the employer. Following is the categorization:

Compensation payable in case of:

1. Death.
2. Disablement:
    a. Permanent total disablement.
    b. Permanent partial disablement.
    c. Temporary disablement:
        i. Temporary total disablement.
        ii. Temporary partial disablement.

In addition, the guiding principle for determining the amount of compensation is that higher the age of the injured workman, the lower the compensation. Thus, a younger workman suffering any disablement in the course of employment would receive higher compensation than that of an elder workman suffering from the same disablement. In determining the amount of compensation payable under the Act, Section 4 has to be read with Schedule IV to the Act. Table 6.1 presents Schedule IV of the Act.

TABLE 6.1 Factors for Working Out Lump Sum Equivalent of Compensation Amount in Case of Permanent Disablement and Death (Schedule IV)[5]

Completed Years of Age on the Last Birthday of the Workman Immediately Preceding the Date on Which the Compensation Fell Due	*Factors*	*Completed Years of Age on the Last Birthday of the Workman Immediately Preceding the Date on Which the Compensation Fell Due*	*Factors*
1	*2*	*1*	*2*
Not more than 16	228.54	41	181.37
17	227.49	42	178.49
18	226.38	43	175.54
19	225.22	44	172.52
20	224	45	169.44
21	222.71	46	166.29
22	221.37	47	163.07
23	219.95	48	159.8
24	218.47	49	156.47
25	216.91	50	153.09
26	215.28	51	149.67
27	213.57	52	146.2
28	211.79	53	142.68
29	209.92	54	139.13
30	207.98	55	135.56
31	205.95	56	131.95
32	203.85	57	128.33
33	201.66	58	124.7
34	199.4	59	121.05
35	197.06	60	117.41
36	194.64	61	113.77
37	192.14	62	110.14
38	189.56	63	106.52
39	186.9	64	102.93
40	184.17	65 or more	99.37

[5] Workmen's Compensation Act, 1923.

Rules Regarding the Amount of Compensation

Section 4 of the Act states that save as provided by Subsections (2), (2A) and (3), a workman can claim compensation in respect of a disease only when the disease is directly attributable to a specific injury by accident arising out of and in the course of his employment. Following are the rules to be followed while deciding the amount of compensation:

1. **For death:** The employer must pay the amount mentioned in the column 2 of Schedule IV (refer Table 6.1 for details).
2. **For permanent total disablement:** In the case of total permanent disablement, the employer has to pay the amount mentioned in column 3 of Schedule IV. Where there is total permanent disablement resulting from the injury suffered, the workman is entitled to be paid 60% of his monthly salary, multiplied by the relevant factor, or an amount of ₹90,000, whichever is more. The minimum compensation in such cases, in no circumstances, can be less than ₹90,000.
3. **For permanent partial disablement:** In the case of partial disablement of the workman, the amount he is entitled to is the percentage of that for total permanent disablement, the percentage being given in the schedule of the Act. Schedule I of the Act contains a list of injuries deemed to result in permanent partial disablement together with the percentage loss of earning capacity which is presumed to occur in each case. When permanent partial disablement occurs from an injury specified in Schedule I, the amount of compensation is to be calculated by finding out from Schedule IV the compensation payable for permanent total disablement to the workman concerned and multiplying it with the percentage loss of earning capacity as stated in Schedule I.

   If an injury is not specified in Schedule I, the percentage loss of earning capacity permanently caused must be found out. This figure multiplied by the amount of compensation for permanent total disablement is the amount of compensation payable for the partial disablement. Where more injuries than one are caused by the same accident, the amount of compensation payable under this head is to be aggregated but the aggregated amount must not exceed the amount which would have been payable if permanent total disablement had resulted from the injuries.
4. **For temporary disablement (Section 4(2) to 4(4)):** Where as a result of the injury there is a temporary disablement, total or partial, the employer is required to make payments equal to 25% of the workman's wages at half-monthly intervals. The rate of half-monthly payment is given in column 4 of Schedule IV. In case of temporary disablement, payments equal to 25% of the workman's wages are to be made at half-monthly intervals. In case the disablement lasts for more than 28 days, then the employer should make the payment on the 16th day from the day of the disablement. This wait for 3 days is to ascertain whether temporary disablement is likely to get over before 28 days or take longer. In case the employer makes any payment to the workman before the payment of this half-monthly or lump sum amount, it shall be deducted from this.
5. **Compensation for non-scheduled injury resulting in permanent partial disablement:** If the partial disablement resulting from the injury is not listed in the schedule, then a reasonable percentage is to be given, as decided by the commissioner. In such cases, the procedure to be followed is to obtain a certificate from a medical practitioner who will certify the percentage of disability suffered. The certificate forms the basis for determining the loss of earning capacity, by the labour commissioner. Hence, the percentage loss of earning capacity may not be equal

to the percentage of disability suffered. In some cases, it could be more, which the commissioner is to decide. Once the percentage of permanent disability is ascertained by the doctor, the amount of compensation due to the injured workman can be arrived at using the calculation mentioned above.

Distribution of Compensation (Section 8)

Section 8 lays down the following rules for the distribution of compensation:

1. **Compensation payable to a woman:** Compensation for death and a lump sum payment due to a woman or to a person under a legal disability must be deposited with the commissioner.
2. **Advance on account of compensation:** In case of a deceased workman, an employer may make to any dependant advances on account of compensation not exceeding an aggregate of ₹100. So much of such aggregate as does not exceed the compensation payable to that dependant must be deducted by the commissioner from such compensation and repaid to the employer.
3. **Deposit with the commissioner:** Any other amount not less than ₹10 which is payable as compensation may be deposited with the commissioner on behalf of the person entitled thereto.
4. **Receipt:** The receipt of the commissioner is a sufficient proof discharging the employer from his liability in respect of any compensation deposited with him.
5. **Funeral expenses:** After the compensation has been deposited, the commissioner must deduct there from the actual cost of the workman's funeral expenses to an amount not exceeding ₹50 and pay the same to the person by whom the expenses were incurred.
6. **Calling the dependants:** The commissioner may serve notices to call upon the dependants to appear before him for the purpose of determining the distribution of the compensation. If the commissioner is satisfied that the deceased workman is not survived with any dependant, he shall repay the balance of the money to the employer.
7. **Disbursement details:** On application by the employer, the commissioner must furnish a statement showing in detail all disbursements made.
8. **Distribution among dependants:** The compensation amount is to be distributed among the dependants in such proportions as the commissioner thinks fit. The whole of the compensation amount may be given to one person. Except in the case of a woman or a person under a legal disability, the compensation money is to be paid to the person entitled thereto.
9. **Money payable to a legal disable person:** Money payable to a workman or a person under a legal disability may be invested or otherwise dealt with as the commissioner thinks fit. Half-monthly payments payable to a person under a legal disability may be paid to a dependant of the workman or to any other person whom the commissioner thinks well fitted to provide for the welfare of the workman.
10. **Variation in the order of the commissioner:** The orders of the commissioner regarding the distribution of compensation may be varied later if necessary. However, a notice must be given to all the parties affected. Where the commissioner varies an order on the grounds that the payment of compensation to any person has been obtained by fraud, impersonation or other improper means, any amount so paid may be recovered by the procedure laid down for the recovery of arrears of land revenue.

Payment of Compensation (Section 4A)

The Act states that compensation must be paid as soon as it falls due. Where the employer does not accept the liability to the extent claimed, he must make provisional payment based on the extent of liability which he accepts. This in any case will not affect the right of the workman to make any further claim. If an employer does not pay the compensation within 1 month of the date on which it fell due, the commissioner may direct the payment of simple interest thereon at 6%. If the commissioner thinks that there is no justification for the delay, he may direct the payment of a further sum, not exceeding 50% of the sum due, by way of penalty.

As provided by this Act, no lump sum or half-monthly payment payable under the Act is in any way capable of being assigned or charged or be liable to attachment or pass to any person other than the workman by operation of law, nor can any claim be set off against the same.

LO5: Notice, Claims and Other Important Provisions

Notice and Claims (Section 10)

According to Section 10 of the Act, the commissioner cannot entertain any claim or compensation unless notice of the accident has been given in the manner provided as soon as practicable. The required notice is to be served upon the employer or upon any of several employers or upon any person responsible to the employer for the management of any branch of the trade or business in which the injured workman was employed. A workman is bound to give notice of any accident which is not merely trivial, and it is not for him to decide whether it is likely to give rise to a claim for compensation. The notice may be served by the injured workman or by anybody on his behalf. It may be served by delivering it or sending it by registered post and an entry in the notice book is sufficient notice.

Exceptions: Despite being a mandatory requirement of serving notice of claim upon the employer, there are some cases in which the want of notice or any defect or irregularity does not affect the entitlement of claim. Following are such cases:

1. In the cases where a workman dies or an accident occurring on the premises of the employer or while working under the control of the employer or of any person employed by him and the workman died on the premises or without leaving the vicinity of the premises, no notice is required to be served upon the employer.
2. Where the employer or anyone of several employers or any person responsible to the employer for the management of any branch of the trade or business in which the injured workman was employed had knowledge of the accident from any other source at or about the time when it occurred, it is not required to serve a notice in relation to the claim.
3. In the cases where the commissioner is satisfied that the failure to give notice was due to sufficient cause, a notice may not be served.

Notice book: The state government may direct a prescribed class of employers to maintain at their premises at which workmen are employed a notice book, in the prescribed form, which is readily accessible at all reasonable times to any injured workman employed on the premises and to any person acting bona fide on his behalf.

Modes of serving of notice: A notice under this section may be served by delivering it at, or sending it by registered post addressed to, the residence or any office or place of business of the person on whom it is to be served, or, where a notice book is maintained, by an entry in the notice book.

Time Frame for Notice

Section 10 also instructs that a claim for compensation has to be preferred before the commissioner within 2 years of the occurrence of the accident or the date of death as the case may be. In case the accident is the contracting of a disease, the date of its occurrence is the first of the days during which the workman was continuously absent from work in consequence of the disablement caused by the disease. However, the commissioner may entertain a claim filed after the prescribed time, if he is of opinion that the failure to file it within time was due to a genuine reason.

Fatal accident (Section 10A): The Act provides that when a commissioner receives information that a workman has died as a result of an accident arising out of and in the course of his employment, he may send by registered post a notice to the workman's employer instructing him to submit, within 30 days of the service of the notice, a statement in the prescribed form.

The statement should state the circumstances attending the death of the workman and indicate whether in the opinion of the employer he is or is not liable to deposit compensation on account of the death. If the employer agrees that he is liable, he is required to deposit the compensation payable within 30 days of the service of the notice. But if he is of opinion that he is not liable, he must state his grounds in the statement. The commissioner, after such enquiry as he may think fit inform any of the dependants of the deceased workman that it is open to them to prefer a claim and may give them such further information as he may think fit.

Medical Examination (Section 11)

After a workman gives notice of an accident, the employer may, within 3 days of the service of the notice, offer to have him examined free of charge by a qualified medical practitioner. Any workman in receipt of half-monthly payments may also be required to submit for examination from time to time. It must be ensured by the employer that the examination is done in accordance with the rules framed for the purpose under the Act.

Absence of workman from examination: If the workman refuses, without sufficient cause, to submit to the examination or if he leaves the vicinity of the place in which he was employed, his right to receive compensation gets suspended during the continuance of the refusal or until his return to the vicinity and undergoes the examination. In case the workman who refused medical examination subsequently dies, the commissioner is empowered to make direct payment of compensation to the dependants of the deceased workman.

If the condition of an injured workman is aggravated by refusal to submit to medical examination or refusal to follow the instructions of the medical examiner or failure to be attended by or follow the instructions of a qualified medical practitioner, then he would get compensation, not for the aggravated injury, but for what the injury would have been had he been properly treated.

Compensation to the Workmen Employed by Contractors (Section 12)

When an employer engages contractors who engage workmen and any such workman gets injured, he may recover compensation from the employer only if the following conditions are satisfied:

1. The contractor is engaged to do a work, which is part of the trade or business of the principal.
2. The engagement is in the course of or for the purposes of his trade or business.
3. The accident occurred in or about the vicinity of the employer's premises.

The workman may also proceed against the contractor, if he decides so. Thus, he has alternative remedies available to him to either proceed against the principal employer or contractor. However, when the employer pays compensation to a workman engaged by a contractor, he is entitled to be indemnified by the contractor.

Remedies of Employer Against Stranger (Section 13)

Where a workman has recovered compensation in respect of any injury caused under circumstances which creates a legal liability of some person over than the person by whom the compensation was paid and any person who has been called on to pay an indemnity under Section 12 is to be indemnified by the person so liable to pay damages as aforesaid.

Contracting Out (Section 17)

The Act provides that any contract by which a workman relinquishes or surrenders his right to receive compensation for injury is null and void. Thus, an employer cannot enter into a contract with his workman, enforcement of which will take away the right of such workman to claim compensation under the Act. This is so because it purports to remove or reduce the liability of any person to pay compensation under this Act.

Information to employee (Section 17A): The Employee's Compensation (Amendment) Act, 2017, inserted Section 17A which provides that every employer must immediately, at the time of employment of an employee, inform the employee of his rights to compensation under this Act, in writing as well as through electronic means, in English or Hindi or in the official language of the area of employment, as may be understood by the employee.

LO6: Enforcement of Act and Provisions for Penalty

Enforcement of Act

Commissioner of workman's compensation: The Act provides for appointment of officers to determine the liability of any person to pay compensation (including the question whether a person is or is not a workman) and the amount or duration of compensation (including any question as to the nature or extent of disablement). These appointed officers are known as Commissioners of Workman's

Compensation and the commissioner who is vested with the powers of a civil court. As discussed above, no civil court has jurisdiction to deal with matters which are required to be dealt by a commissioner appointed under the provisions of this Act.

Process to claim the compensation: No technical procedure is followed in workman compensation cases. However, as the employer must be heard, and the matter may need to be investigated, there is some minimum procedure followed. If the employer does not pay compensation after notice has been issued and after the lapse of 30 days from the date of the accident or where the workman and employer fail to arrive at an agreement, an application can be made to the Labour Officer by the workman. The proceedings before the Labour Officer are quasi-judicial in nature. It is the duty of the government to dispose of workman's claims, in a speedy way in case of workman's injuries.

Form of Application (Section 22)

The Act states it clearly that no application for settlement of any matter by a commissioner is required to be made, if the parties have been able to settle it by agreement. In the other cases, an application to the commissioner must be made in the prescribed form according to the rules and accompanied by a prescribed fee. If the applicant is illiterate or for any reason is unable to furnish the required information, on the desire of the applicant, the application is to be prepared under the direction of the commissioner. Following particulars must be given along with the application namely:

1. Concise statement of the circumstances and the relief claimed.
2. In case of claim for compensation against an employer, the date of service of notice of accident, with its due time of notice and the reason why notice was not given.
3. The names and addresses of the parties.
4. Except in case of application by a dependant for compensation a concise statement of the matter on which agreement has and of those on which agreement has not been coming to.

Appearance of Parties (Sections 24 and 25)

The concerned parties must make their appearance before the commissioner. A registered legal practitioner/trade union member/inspector or other person appointed by the government for this purpose can also represent the workman or can represent the parties if necessary.

Appeals and References (Section 27)

For proceedings under the Act, the High Court of the state is the appellate court. The commissioner can refer a question of law to the High Court for decision and he must decide the matter according to such decision. An appeal lies to the High Court from the following orders of a commissioner:

1. An order awarding as compensation a lump sum whether by way of redemption of a half-monthly payment or otherwise or an order awarding interest or penalty under Section 4A.
2. An order rejecting to allow redemption of a half-monthly payment.
3. An order providing for the distribution of compensation among the dependants of a deceased workman, or disallowing the claim of the person alleging himself to be such dependant.

4. An order allowing or disallowing any claim for the amount of an indemnity under the provisions of Section 12(2).
5. An order refusing to register a memorandum of agreement or registering the same or providing for the registration of the same subject to conditions.

Other Provisions Regarding Appeal

Following are some other important provisions related to appeal:

1. No appeal can be made against any order unless a substantial question of law is involved in the appeal and, in the case of an order other than an order such as is referred to in clause (b), unless the amount in dispute in the appeal is not less than ₹300.
2. The parties cannot appeal against the order if they have agreed to abide by the decision of the commissioner, or in which the order of the commissioner gives effect to an agreement made by the parties.
3. The employer cannot file an appeal unless the memorandum of appeal is accompanied by a certificate by the commissioner to the effect that the applicant has deposited with him the amount payable under the order appealed against.
4. The period of limitation for an appeal under this section is 60 days and the provisions of Section 5 of the Indian Limitation Act, 1908, are applicable to appeals under this section.

Penalty (Section 18A)

Section 18A of the Act provides for penalties for failure to perform the duties prescribed under the Act. If an employer does not send the commissioner a statement, or report as required in case of fatal accidents fails to do so, or maintain a notice book s/he is liable to pay a fine, which may extend to ₹5,000. However, such a proceeding cannot be made without the previous permission of the commissioner. The court does not take cognizance of any offence, if such matter is not brought before the court at least within 6 months from the time that the commissioner becomes aware of such offence.

Bar to Civil Suits (Section 19(2))

Section 19(2) of the Act states that a civil court has no jurisdiction to settle, decide or deal with any question which, because of the provisions of the Act, is required to be decided or dealt with by the commissioner or to enforce any liability under this Act. Section 31 mentions that recovery of the compensation amount awarded, amount payable under the Act, whether under an agreement or otherwise has to be recovered as an arrear of land revenue.

Summary

1. The Workmen's Compensation Act, 1923, provides for payment of compensation to the workmen suffered injury by accident.

2. The meaning of compensation in this Act is limited to compensation granted under the Act for employment injuries sustained during the course of work.
3. The Workmen's Compensation Act aims to provide workmen and/or their dependants some relief in case of accidents arising out of and in the course of employment and causing either death or disablement of workmen.
4. The Act extends to the whole of India and applies to workmen employed in any capacity specified in Schedule II of the Act.
5. The Workmen's compensation Act will only apply to those persons considered 'workmen' and those who are considered as 'employers', as defined under the Act.
6. With the amendment of the Workmen's Compensation Act in 2000, now it is not necessary that the workman in question is engaged in the employer's trade or business. Further with the amendment of 2000, now even casual workmen are covered by this law.
7. Workmen of a casual nature, if not employed in the employer trade or business, are not covered within the definition of the term workman as used in the Act.
8. If personal injury is caused to a workman by accident arising out of and in course of employment, his employer shall be liable to pay compensation.
9. A self-inflicted injury is not an accident ordinarily.
10. A personal injury under the Act is not necessarily confined to physical or bodily injury.
11. Compensation under the Act is payable only if the accident occurs within the period of employment.
12. The employment of a workman does not commence until he has reached the place of employment and ends when he has left the place of employment.
13. An occupational disease that is contracted in the course of employment falls within the meaning of an 'accident' for the purposes of this Act.
14. The amount of compensation to be paid by the employer for injuries caused depends on extent of the disablement suffered by the workman; more severe disablements naturally receive higher compensation.
15. Compensation for death and lump sum payment due to a woman or to a person under a legal disability must be deposited with the commissioner.
16. Compensation must be paid as soon as it falls due. Where the employer does not accept the liability to the extent claimed, he must make provisional payment based on the extent of liability which he accepts.
17. A claim for compensation has to be preferred before the commissioner within 2 years of the occurrence of the accident or the date of death as the case may be.
18. Any contract by which a workman relinquishes his right to receive compensation for injury is null and void.
19. A civil court has no jurisdiction to settle, decide or deal with any question which, because of the provisions of the Act, is required to be decided or dealt with by the commissioner or to enforce any liability under this Act.
20. The Act provides for appointment of officers to determine the liability of any person to pay compensation and the amount or duration of compensation.
21. The commissioner can refer a question of law to the High Court for decision and he must decide the matter according to such decision.

Multiple Choice Questions

1. ______________ is the first measure of social security introduced in 1923 came into force from 1 July 1924.
   a. The Factories Act
   b. The Workmen's Compensation Act
   c. The Workman's Provident Funds and Miscellaneous Provisions Act
   d. The Payment of Wages Act
2. The establishments hiring ______________ and above must compulsorily register themselves under the Workman's State Insurance Act (ESI Act).
   a. 20 workmen
   b. 30 workmen
   c. 50 workmen
   d. 100 workmen
3. The Workmen's Compensation Act does not apply to ______________.
   a. Persons serving in Armed Forces
   b. Workmen covered by the Workman's State Insurance Act, 1948
   c. Both (a) and (b)
   d. Neither (a) nor (b)
4. A workman whose monthly wages exceed ______________ is not considered as a workman for the purpose of this Act.
   a. ₹100
   b. ₹500
   c. ₹750
   d. ₹1,000
5. Period of service is deemed to be continuous which has not been interrupted by a period of absence exceeding ______________.
   a. 14 days
   b. 7 days
   c. 5 days
   d. 2 days
6. The employer is liable to pay compensation only when ______________.
   a. Injury is caused to a workman by accident
   b. The accident arises out of and in course of employment
   c. Both (a) and (b)
   d. Neither (a) nor (b)
7. ______________ is not necessarily confined to physical or bodily injury. It also includes psychological at physiological injury such as nervous shock and insanity.
   a. A personal injury
   b. An occupational disease
   c. Both (a) and (b)
   d. Neither (a) nor (b)
8. ______________ while in service is a disease that inflicts workmen in that particular occupation in which s/he was employed in and resulting from exposure to a hazardous working atmosphere, particular to that employment.
   a. A personal injury
   b. An occupational disease
   c. Both (a) and (b)
   d. Neither (a) nor (b)

9. The minimum compensation in case of ____________ in no circumstances can be less than ₹90,000.
   a. Permanent total disablement
   b. Permanent partial disablement
   c. Temporary disablement
   d. Non-scheduled injury resulting in permanent partial disablement
10. In case of contract labour, ____________ is responsible for paying compensation as though the workman was directly employed by him.
   a. The principle employer
   b. The contractor
   c. Both (a) and (b)
   d. Decided on a case-to-case basis

True/False Questions

1. The Act applies to all the factories covered by the Workman's State Insurance Act.
2. To answer the question who is a workman, it is not required that there is a relationship of master and servant between the employer and the workman.
3. Workmen of a casual nature, if not employed in the employer trade or business, are not covered within the definition of the term workman as used in the Act.
4. Compensation is payable even if the accident occurs after the expiry of the period of employment.
5. The employment of a workman does not commence until he has reached the place of employment and ends when he has left the place of employment. Here the journey to and from the place of employment is included in the course of employment.
6. Under the doctrine of notional extension, where an obligation is present on a workman to discharge her duty, and she meets with an accident, it is an accident in the course of employment.
7. The principal employer holds the right to be indemnified by the person who would normally pay for the compensation of an injured/deceased workman, that is, the contractor.
8. If a workman suffers from a particular disease and as a result of wear and tear of his employment he dies of that disease, the employers are held liable.
9. The amount of compensation to be paid by the employer for injuries caused depends on the extent of the disablement suffered by the workman.
10. Where as a result of the injury there is a temporary disablement, total or partial, the employer is required to make payments equal to 50% of the workman's wages at half-monthly intervals.

Descriptive Questions

1. What are the salient features of Workmen's Compensation Act, 1923?
2. State the circumstances under which the employer is liable to pay compensation to a workman under the Workmen's Compensation Act, 1923?
3. Are the daily rated casual labour, apprentices or the substitutes covered by the provisions of Workmen's Compensation Act, 1923? What are the relevant provisions of the Act?

4. How are monthly wages determined for the purpose of calculation of compensation under the provisions of Workmen's Compensation Act, 1923?
5. What are the different kinds of disablements and compensation payable for each under the Act?
6. Define and explain following:
   a. Permanent partial disablement.
   b. Temporary partial disablement.
   c. Workman under the Act.
   d. Wages under the Act.
   e. Total disablement.

Annexure A

Schedule II

List of Persons Who Subject to the provisions of Section 2(1)(n) Are Included in the Definition of Workman

The following persons are workmen within the meaning of Section 2(1)(n) and subject to the provisions of that section that is to say any person who is:

1. Employed otherwise than in a clerical capacity or on a railway in connection with the operation repair or maintenance of a lift or a vehicle propelled by steam; or other mechanical power or by electricity or in connection with the loading or unloading of any such vehicle; or
2. Employed otherwise than in clerical capacity in any premises wherein or within the precincts whereof a manufacturing process as defined in clause (k) of Section 2 of the Factories Act, 1948 (63 of 1948), is being carried on or in any kind of work whatsoever incident to or connected with any such manufacturing process or with the article made whether or not employment in any such work is within such premises or precincts and steam water or other mechanical power or electrical power is used; or
3. Employed for the purpose of making, altering, repairing, ornamenting, finishing or otherwise adapting for use transport or sale any article or part of an article in any premises. However, this provision is attracted only if twenty or more persons are so employed; or
   Explanation: For the purposes of this clause, persons employed outside such premises or precincts but in any work incidental to or connected with the work relating to making, altering, repairing, ornamenting, finishing or otherwise adapting for use, transport or sale of any article or part of an article shall be deemed to be employed within such premises or precincts; or
4. Employed in the manufacture or handling of explosives in connection with the employer's trade or business; or
5. Employed in any mine as defined in clause (j) of Section 2 of the Mines Act, 1952 (35 of 1952), in any mining operation or in any kind of work other than clerical work incidental to or connected with any mining operation or with the mineral obtained or in any kind or work whatsoever below ground; or

6. Employed as the master or as a seaman of:
   (a) Any ship which is propelled wholly or in part by steam or other mechanical power of by electricity or which is towed or intended to be towed by a ship so propelled; or
   (b) Any ship not included in Sub-clause (a) of 25 tonnes net tonnage or over; or
   (c) Any seagoing ship not included in Sub-clause (a) or Sub-clause (b) provided with sufficient area for navigation under sails alone; or
7. Employed for the purpose of:
   (a) Loading, unloading, fuelling, constructing, repairing, demolishing, cleaning or painting any ship of which he is not the master or a member of the crew or handling or transport within the limits of any post subject to the Indian Ports Act, 1908 (15 of 1908), or the Major Port Trusts Act, 1963 (18 of 1963), of goods which have been discharged from or are to be loaded into any vessel; or
   (b) Warping a ship through the lock; or
   (c) Mooring and unmooring ships at harbour wall berths or in pier; or
   (d) Removing or replacing dry dock caissons when vessels are entering or leaving dry docks; or
   (e) The docking or undocking of any vessel during an emergency; or
   (f) Preparing splicing chir springs and check wires painting depth marks on locksides removing or replacing fenders whenever necessary landing of gangways maintaining lifebuoys up to standard or any other maintenance work of a like nature; or
   (g) Any work on jolly boats for bringing a ship's line to the wharf; or
8. Employed in the construction maintenance repair or demolition of:
   (a) Any building which is designed to be or is or has been more than one storey in height above the ground or 12 feet or more from the ground level to the apex of the roof; or
   (b) Any dam or embankment which is 12 feet or more in height from its lowest to its highest point; or
   (c) Any road bridge tunnel or canal; or
   (d) Any wharf quay sea wall or other marine work including any moorings of ships; or
9. Employed in setting up, maintaining, repairing or taking down any telegraph or telephone line or post or any overhead electric line or cable or standard or fittings and fixtures for the same; or
10. Employed otherwise than in a clerical capacity in the construction working repair or demolition of any aerial ropeway canal pipeline or sewer; or
11. Employed in the service of any fire brigade; or
12. Employed on a railway as defined in clause (31) of Section 2 and Subsection (1) of Section 197 of the Indian Railway Act, 1989 (24 of 1989), either directly or through a subcontractor by a person fulfilling a contract with the railway administration; or
13. Employed as an inspector mail guard sorter or van peon in the Railway Mail Service or as a telegraphist or as a postal or railway signaller or employed in any occupation ordinarily involving outdoor work in the Indian Posts and Telegraphs Department; or
14. Employed otherwise than in a clerical capacity in connection with operations for winning natural petroleum or natural gas; or
15. Employed in any occupation involving blasting operations; or
16. Employed in the making of any excavation in which on any one day of the preceding 12 months more than 25 persons have been employed or explosives have been used or whose depth from its highest to its lowest point exceeds 12 feet; or

17. Employed in the operation of any ferry boat capable of carrying more than 10 persons; or
18. Employed otherwise than in a clerical capacity on any estate which is maintained for the purpose of growing cardamom, cinchona, coffee, rubber or tea and on which on any one day in the preceding 12 months 25 or more persons have been so employed; or
19. Employed otherwise than in a clerical capacity in the generating, transforming, transmitting or distribution of electrical energy or in generation or supply of gas; or
20. Employed in a lighthouse as defined in clause (d) of Section 2 of the Indian Lighthouse Act, 1927 (17 of 1927); or
21. Employed in producing cinematograph pictures intended for public exhibition or in exhibiting such pictures; or
22. Employed in the training, keeping or working of elephants or wild animals; or
23. Employed in the tapping of palm trees or the felling or logging of trees or the transport of timber by inland waters or the control or extinguishing or forests fires; or
24. Employed in operations for the catching or hunting of elephants or other wild animals; or
25. Employed as a diver; or
26. Employed in the handling or transport of goods in or within the precincts of:
    (a) Any warehouse or other place in which goods are stored and in which on any one day of the preceding 12 months 10 or more persons have been so employed; or
    (b) Any market in which on any one day of the preceding 12 months 50 or more persons have been so employed; or
27. Employed in any occupation involving the handling and manipulation of radium or X-ray apparatus or contract with radioactive substances; or
28. Employed in or in connection with the construction, erection, dismantling operation or maintenance of an aircraft as defined in Section 2 of the Indian Aircraft Act, 1934 (22 of 1934); or
29. Employed in horticultural operations, forestry, beekeeping or framing by tractors or other contrivances driven by steam or other mechanical power or by electricity; or
30. Employed otherwise than in a clerical capacity in the construction working repair or maintenance of a tube well; or
31. Employed in the maintenance repair or renewal of electric fittings in any building; or
32. Employed in a circus; or
33. Employed as watchman in any factory or establishment; or
34. Employed in any operation in the sea for catching fish; or
35. Employed in any employment which requires handling of snakes for the purpose of extraction of venom or for the purpose of looking after snakes or handling any other poisonous animal or insects; or
36. Employed in handling animals such as horses, mules and bulls; or
37. Employed for the purpose of loading or unloading any mechanically propelled vehicle or in the handling or transport of goods which have been loaded in such vehicles; or
38. Employed in cleaning of sewer lines or septic tanks within the limits of a local authority; or
39. Employed on surveys and investigation, exploration, or garage or discharge observation of rivers including drilling operations, hydrological observations and flood forecasting activities, groundwater surveys and exploration; or
40. Employed in cleaning of jungles or reclaiming land or ponds in which on any one day of the preceding 12 months more than 25 persons have been employed; or

41. Employed in cultivation of land or rearing and maintenance of livestock or forest operations or fishing in which on any one day of the preceding 12 months more than 25 persons have been employed; or
42. Employed in installation maintenance or repair of pumping equipment used for lifting of water from wells, tube wells, ponds, lakes, streams and the like; or
43. Employed in the construction boring or deepening of an open well bore well, bore-cum-dug well filter point and the like; or
44. Employed in spraying and dusting of insecticides or pesticides in agricultural operations or plantations; or
45. Employed in mechanized harvesting and threshing operations; or
46. Employed in working or repair or maintenance of bulldozers, tractors, power tillers and the like; or
47. Employed as artists for drawing pictures on advertisement boards at a height of 3.66 meters or more from the ground level; or
48. Employed in any newspaper establishment as defined in the Working Journalists and Other Newspaper Workman's (Conditions of Services) and Miscellaneous Provisions Act 1955 (45 of 1955) and engaged in outdoor work.

Explanation: In this Schedule, the preceding 12 months relate in any particular case to the 12 months ending with the day on which the accident in such case occurred.

Source: http://labour.gov.in/sites/default/files/TheWorkmenAct1923(1).pdf, accessed on 24 May 2017.

ANNEXURE B

Sl. No.	*Sections*	*State*	*Amendments*
1.	Section 8	Andhra Pradesh	**Addition of a provision to Subsection (4)** In respect of a workman belonging to an establishment to which the Andhra Pradesh Labour Welfare Fund Act, 1987, applies, the Commissioner shall pay the said balance of the money into the fund constituted under that Act in lieu of repaying to the employer.[6]
		Goa	**Addition of a provision to Subsection (4)** In respect of a workman belonging to an establishment to which Goa, Daman and Diu Labour Welfare Fund Act, 1986, applies, the Commissioner shall pay the said balance of the money into the fund constituted under that Act in lieu of repaying to the employer.[7]
2.	Sections 24A and 24B	West Bengal	**Insertion of Section 24A: Reference of disputed medical questions to a medical referee.** (1) If any question arises in any proceedings under this Act pending before the Commissioner as to: (a) the nature and extent of the permanent disablement of a workman, or (b) the duration of his temporary disablement, or

[6] Vide Andhra Pradesh Act 34 of 1987, sec. 40 (w.e.f. 1 May 1988).
[7] Vide Goa Act 4 of 1987, sec. 40 (w.e.f. 26 January 1990).

Sl. No.	Sections	State	Amendments
			(c) whether the incapacity of a workman is due to personal injury by accident, or (d) whether a workman has contracted any occupational disease specified in Schedule III, the question shall, in default of agreement, on the joint application of both parties or on the application of either party in the prescribed manner, and on payment in the prescribed manner by the parties, or the party making the application, as the case may be, of the prescribed fees and expenses be referred by the commissioner to a medical referee appointed by him in his discretion from among the medical practitioners included in the list prepared under Section 24B: provided that where an application is made by only one of the parties, if the commissioner is of the opinion that the question is one which ought not on account of the exceptional difficulty of the case or of any other sufficient reason be referred to a medical referee, he may after recording his reasons in writing reject the application: provided further that if the parties themselves jointly select any medical practitioner included in the said list for appointment as the medical referee, the commissioner shall, on payment of the prescribed fees and expenses in the prescribed manner, appoint that medical practitioner: provided further that a medical practitioner whose services have been used for the medical treatment of an injury by accident to a workman, or of an occupational disease specified in Schedule III contracted by such workman, by or on behalf of such workman or his employer or by or on behalf of any insurers interested in any proceeding under this Act arising out of such injury or disease, shall not act as a medical referee in any proceedings under this Act in respect of such injury or disease.

7

CHAPTER

The Employees' State Insurance Act, 1948

LEARNING OBJECTIVES

Upon completing this chapter, the reader would be able to:

LO1. Understand the objectives, scope and important definitions of the Act.
LO2. Gain insights into administration of the Act.
LO3. Explain the provisions for finance and audit laid down by the Act.
LO4. Examine provisions and rules for contribution.
LO5. Get the details of various benefits provided by the Act and related rules.
LO6. Describe the obligations of the employers.
LO7. Know about the adjudication of disputes, claims and provisions for the penalty under the Act.
LO8. Understand various possible exemptions from the operation of the ESI Act as provided by the Act.

Introduction

The ESI Act, 1948 (the Act), is a social welfare legislation which was enacted to extend certain benefits to employees in specific circumstances, such as illness, maternity and employment injury. The Act also provides for some other matters incidental thereto and covers a wider spectrum of employees than that of the Factories Act, 1948. While the Factories Act deals with the issues related to their health, safety, welfare, leave and so on of only those workers who are employed in the factory premises only, the benefits of this Act are extended to the employees whether they work inside the factory or establishment or elsewhere. The benefits provided under this Act are even available to those employees who are directly employed by the principal employee or through an intermediate agency, if the employment is incidental or in connection with the factory or establishment.

LO1: Objectives, Scope and Important Definitions

Objectives

The ESI Act was promulgated by the Parliament of India in the year 1948. It was the year 1952 when the Employees' State Insurance Corporation (ESIC) scheme was first launched in just two industrial centres in the country, namely Kanpur and Delhi. The scheme covered a total of about 1.20 lakh workers. Thereafter, with active involvement of the respective state governments, the scheme was implemented in a phased manner across the country.

As discussed above, the ESI Act is a social welfare act and hence it aims at attaining socio-economic justice enshrined in the Directive Principles of State Policy under Part IV of our Constitution. The Act specifically focuses on Articles 41, 42 and 43 which direct the state to make necessary and effective provision for securing the right to work, to education and public assistance in cases of unemployment, old age, sickness and disablement.

Applicability and Scope of the Act

Factory: The ESI Act extends to whole of India, including all the government factories, but excluding seasonal factories, employing 10 or more employees and carrying on a manufacturing process with the aid of power and 20 employees where the manufacturing process is carried out without the aid of power. It must be noted that a factory or establishment, to which this Act applies, continues to be governed by its provisions even if the number of workers employed falls below the specified limit or the manufacturing process therein ceases to be carried on with the aid of power subsequently.

Shops and establishments: The shops and establishments employing more than 20 employees are also covered under the Act. Here 'shop' according to the Delhi Shops and Establishment Act, 1954, means any premises where goods are sold by either retail or wholesale or where services are rendered to customers and includes an office, storeroom, godown, and warehouse or workhouse or workplace, whether in the same premises or otherwise, used in or in connection with such trade or business, but does not include a factory or a commercial establishment. However, 'establishment' is defined as a shop, a commercial establishment, residential hotel, restaurant, eating house, theatre or other place of public amusement or entertainment to which this Act applies and it includes such other establishments that the government may, by notification in the Official Gazette, declare to be an establishment for the purpose of this Act.

Employees: An employee, including the one who is a casual, temporary or contract employee, drawing wages less than ₹15,000 per month is covered under the Act. The ceiling limit was raised from ₹1,000 to ₹15,000 with effect from 1 May 2010. However, the ESI Act does not apply to any member of Indian Naval, Military or Air Forces. Where an employee is covered under the ESI scheme, compensation under the Employee's Compensation Act cannot be claimed in respect of employment injury and also no benefits can be claimed under the Maternity Benefits Act.

Apprentices not covered: Apprentices covered under the Apprenticeship Act are not entitled to the benefits provided under the ESI Act as those are covered under this Act. Here apprentice means a person who is undergoing apprenticeship training in pursuance of a contract of apprenticeship. Thus, an apprentice comes to learn the tricks of the trade and may not count much so far as the output of the factory is concerned; therefore, the apprentices are exempted from the operation of laws relating to labour. However, the state government is empowered to make specific provisions to include apprentices in a particular Act dealing with labour.

Exemptions from Applicability of the Act

As provided under the Act, the ESI Act does not apply to the following factories or establishments:

1. Factories working with the aid of power employing less than 10 persons.
2. Factories working without the aid of power employing less than 20 persons.
3. Seasonal factories engaged exclusively in any of the activities, namely, cotton ginning, cotton or jute pressing, decortication of groundnuts, the manufacture of coffee, indigo, lac, rubber, sugar (including *gur*) or tea or any manufacturing process incidental to or connected with any of the aforesaid activities, and factories engaged for a period not exceeding 7 months in a year in blending, packing or repackaging of tea or coffee or in such other process as may be specified by the central government.
4. A factory which was exempted from the provisions of the Act as being a 'seasonal factory' will carry the benefit of the exemption on account of the amendment of the definition of 'seasonal factory'.
5. Mines subject to the Mines Act, 1952.
6. Railway running sheds.
7. Government factories or establishments, whose employees receive the benefits similar or superior to the benefits provided under the Act and Indian Naval, Military or Air Forces.

The appropriate government is empowered to exempt any factory or establishments or class of factories or establishments or any employee or class of employees from the provisions of this Act.

Important Definitions

1. **Confinement (Section 2(3)):** Confinement means labour resulting in the issue of a living child or labour after 26 weeks of pregnancy resulting in the issue of a child whether alive or dead.
2. **Contribution (Section 2(4)):** Contribution under the Act means the sum of money payable to the Corporation by the principal employer in respect of an employee and includes any amount payable by or on behalf of the employee in accordance with the provisions of this Act.
3. **Contribution period (Section 2(5)):** Contribution period means any such period as may be specified in the regulations. The contribution period must not exceed 6 consecutive months. But in case of the first contribution period, a longer period may be specified by or under the regulations.
4. **Dependant (Section 2(6A)):** Dependant under the Act means any of the following relatives of a deceased or insured person, namely:
    a. A widow, a legitimate or adopted son who has not attained the age of 25; an unmarried legitimate or adopted daughter; a widowed mother.
    b. If wholly dependent on the earnings of the insured person at the time of his death, a legitimate or adopted son or daughter who has attained the age of 25 and who is infirm.

c. If wholly or in part dependent on the earnings of the insured person at the time of his death:
   i. A parent other than a widowed mother,
   ii. A minor illegitimate son, an unmarried illegitimate daughter or a daughter legitimate or adopted or illegitimate if married and a minor or if widowed and a minor,
   iii. A minor brother or an unmarried sister or a widowed sister if a minor,
   iv. A widowed daughter-in-law,
   v. A minor child of a pre-deceased son,
   vi. A minor child of a pre-deceased daughter if no parent of the child is alive or
   vii. A paternal grandparent if no parent of the insured person is alive.

5. **Employment injury (Section 2(8)):** Employment injury under the Act is explained as a personal injury to an employee caused by an accident or occupational disease arising out of and in the course of his employment, being an insurable employment, whether the accident occurs or the occupational disease is contracted within or outside the territorial limits of India.

Case 7.1 throws light on the application of this Section.

Case 7.1: *General Manager, B.E.S.T. Undertaking, Bombay v. Mrs Agnes*[1]

Mr P. Nanu Raman was a bus driver of the B.E.S.T. Undertaking, Bombay (the appellant corporation). One day after finishing the work, he left the bus in the depot and boarded another bus to go to his residence. Before he could reach his home, the bus met with an accident. He was seriously injured in the accident and as a result of the injuries he died. His widow, the respondent, claimed compensation from the employing company by referring to Section 3(1) of the Workmen's Compensation Act, 1923, that states, 'If personal injury is caused to a workman by accident arising out of and in the course of his employment, his employer shall be liable to pay compensation in accordance with the provision of this chapter'.

The appellant corporation did not agree with the argument that the deceased employee died out of and in the course of his employment and argued that the right of a bus driver to travel in the bus is merely an added facility and cannot be claimed as a right. Thus, travelling in the appellant corporation's bus was not a part of the deceased employee's duty. Hence, the respondent was not entitled to receive any compensation on the ground stated above.

Thereafter she, through an application in the Court of the Commissioner for Workmen's Compensation, claimed compensation by arguing that the death of her husband in an accident is alleged to have arisen 'out of and in the course of his employment'. Later, the High Court allowed the compensation and the appellant corporation appealed in the Supreme Court against the order of the High Court.

Discussion Point

Under the light of the facts shared above, was the respondent entitled to receive compensation on the grounds that her husband died out of and in the course of his employment?

Judgement and Explanation

It was held that the respondent was entitled to receive compensation as her husband died out of and in the course of his employment. It was explained in the judgement that under the rules of the Act, a bus driver is given the facility in his capacity as a driver to travel on any bus belonging to the undertaking, presumably, to ensure punctuality and to discharge his onerous obligations. This facility was given to him not as grace but

[1] *General Manager, B. E. S. T. Undertaking, Bombay v. Mrs Agnes*, AIR 1964 SC 193.

as a right because efficiency of the service demanded that. Therefore, the right of a bus driver to travel in the bus in order to discharge his duties punctually and efficiently was a condition of his service. There was an implied obligation on his part to travel in the said buses as a part of his duty.

Thus, the important condition for constituting an employment injury for claiming compensation under the ESI Act, in respect of the injury caused, is that the injury must arise only out of and in the course of employment, must be personal to the employee and must be caused by an accident resulting in his/her disablement, whether temporarily or permanently, or fully or partially, to attend his/her work.

6. **Employee (Section 2(9)):** Under the Act, employee is any person employed for wages in or in connection with the work of a factory or establishment to which this Act applies and:
   a. Who is directly employed by the principal employer on any work of, or incidental or preliminary to or connected with the work of, the factory or establishment, whether such work is done by the employee in the factory or establishment or elsewhere.
   b. Who is employed by or through an immediate employer in the premises of the factory or establishment or under the supervision of the principal employer or his agent on work which is ordinarily part of the work of the factory or establishment or which is preliminary to the work carried out in or incidental to the purpose of the factory or establishment.
   c. Whose services are temporarily lent or let on hire to the principal employer by the person with whom the person whose services are so lent or let on hire has entered into a contract of service.

   Other persons covered under the definition of employee: Following persons are also covered under the definition of employee provided by the Act and hence are entitled to benefits extended by the Act:
   a. Any person employed for wages on any work connected with the administration of the factory or establishment or any part, department or branch thereof or with the purchase of raw materials for, or the distribution or sale of the products of, the factory or establishment or
   b. Any person engaged as an apprentice, not being an apprentice engaged under the Apprentices Act, 1961 (52 of 1961) and includes such a person engaged as an apprentice whose training period is extended to any length of time.

   Persons not covered under the definition of employee: The Act does not include following persons in the category of employees:
   a. Any member of Indian Naval, Military or Air Forces or
   b. Any person so employed whose wages (excluding remuneration for overtime work) exceed such wages as may be prescribed by the central government.

   It must be noted here that if an employee starts earning the wages exceeding the wages (excluding remuneration for overtime work) prescribed by the central government at any time after (and not before) the beginning of the contribution period, then he continues to be an employee under the Act until the end of that period.
7. **Exempted employee (Section 2(10)):** The Act exempts those employees who are not liable under this Act to pay the employee contribution.
8. **Family (Section 2(11)):** As provided under the Act, family includes all or any of the following relatives of an insured person, namely:
   a. A spouse.
   b. A minor legitimate or adopted child dependent upon the insured person.

c. A child who is wholly dependent on the earnings of the insured person and who is:
   i. Receiving education, till he or she attains the age of 21 or
   ii. An unmarried daughter.
d. A child who is infirm by reason of any physical or mental abnormality or injury and is wholly dependent on the earnings of the insured person, so long as the infirmity continues.
e. Dependant parents, whose income from all sources does not exceed such income as may be prescribed by the central government.
f. A minor brother or sister wholly dependent upon the earnings of the insured person in case the insured person is unmarried and his or her parents are not alive.

9. **Factory (Section 2(12)):** The Act defines factory as any premises, including the precincts thereof, whereon 10 or more persons are employed or were employed on any day of the preceding 12 months and in any part of which a manufacturing process is being carried on or is ordinarily so carried on, but it does not include a mine subject to the operation of the Mines Act, 1952 (35 of 1952), or a railway running shed.
10. **Seasonal factory (Section 2(19A)):** The Act explains seasonal factory as a factory which is exclusively engaged in one or more of the following manufacturing processes, namely, cotton ginning, cotton or jute pressing, decortication of groundnuts, the manufacture of coffee, indigo, lac, rubber, sugar (including *gur*) or tea or any manufacturing process which is incidental to or connected with any of the aforesaid processes, and includes a factory which is engaged for a period not exceeding 7 months in a year.
    a. In any process of blending, packing or repacking of tea or coffee or
    b. In other such manufacturing processes as the central government may, by notification in the Official Gazette, specify.
11. **Immediate employer (Section 2(13)):** According to the ESI Act, immediate employer in relation to employees employed by or through him is a person who has undertaken the execution on the premises of a factory or an establishment to which this Act applies or is under the supervision of the principal employer or his agent, of the whole or any part of any work, which is ordinarily part of the work of the factory or establishment of the principal employer or is preliminary to the work carried on in, or incidental to the purpose of, any such factory or establishment and includes a person by whom the services of an employee who has entered into a contract of service with him are temporarily lent or let on hire to the principal employer and includes a contractor also.
12. **Insurable employment (Section 2(13A)):** Every employment in a factory or establishment to which this Act applies is covered under the definition of insurable employment under the Act.
13. **Disablement:** The Act covers the following two types of disablement:
    a. **Permanent disablement:** There are further two types of permanent disablements defined under the Act:
       i. **Permanent partial disablement (Section 2(15A)):** The Act considers a disablement as permanent partial disablement if such disablement is of a permanent nature reducing the earning capacity of an employee in every employment which he was capable of undertaking at the time of the accident resulting in the disablement.

          It must be noted here that every injury specified in Part II of Schedule II is deemed to result in permanent partial disablement.
       ii. **Permanent total disablement (Section 2(15B)):** Permanent total disablement is a disablement of a permanent nature incapacitating an employee for all work which he was capable of performing at the time of the accident resulting in such disablement.

Here permanent total disablement is deemed to result from every injury specified in Part I of Schedule II. A disablement will be considered as permanent total disablement under the Act if any combination of injuries specified in Part II thereof where the aggregate percentage of the loss of earning capacity, as specified in Part II against those injuries, amounts to 100% or more.

b. **Temporary disablement (Section 2(2a)):** Temporary disablement refers to a condition of an employee resulting from an employment injury requiring medical treatment and rendering that employee, as a result of such injury, temporarily incapable of doing the work which he was doing prior to or at the time of the injury.

14. **Principal employer (Section 2(17)):** The definition of a principal employer is very clearly defined under the Act for various establishments and factories. A principal employer in the Act means:
    a. In a factory, the owner or occupier of the factory and includes the managing agent of such an owner or occupier, the legal representative of a deceased owner or occupier, and where a person has been named as the manager of the factory in the Factories Act the person so named.
    b. In any establishment under the control of any department of any government in India, the authority appointed by such government in this behalf or where no authority is so appointed, the head of the department.
    c. In any other establishment, any person responsible for the supervision and control of the establishment.

Let us discuss a case to understand the coverage of the term 'principal employer' under the Act (Case 7.2).

Case 7.2: *Royal Talkies Hyderabad and Others v. Employees' State Insurance Corporation*[2]

In this case, the appellants were the owners of theatres in the twin cities of Hyderabad and Secunderabad, where films were exhibited. Within the same premises as the theatres, in every case, there was a canteen and a cycle stand, leased out to contractors under instruments of the lease. The contractors used to employ their own servants to run the canteen and the cycle stand. In regard to persons so employed by the contractors, the owners of the theatres were treated as 'principal employers' and notices of demands were issued to them calling upon them to pay contribution under the ESI Act. Thereupon the appellant filed an application under Section 75 of the Act before the Employees Insurance (EI) Court and declared that the provisions of the Act were not applied to their theatres and that they were not liable to any contributions in respect of the persons employed in the canteen and the cycle stands attached to their theatres.

The EI Court during the review of the declaration of the appellants found that the canteens were meant primarily for the convenience and comfort of those visiting the cinema theatres, though in a few cases the persons in charge of the canteens seemed to be allowing the general public also to have access to the canteens, and that the cycle stands were meant exclusively for the convenience of the persons visiting the theatres. The EI Court rejected the application of the appellants and held that the owners of the theatres were principal employers with reference to the persons employed by the contractors in the canteens and the cycle stands attached to the theatres and therefore were liable to contribute towards the funds.

The appellants appealed in the higher court against the order.

[2] *Royal Talkies Hyderabad and Others v. Employees' State Insurance Corporation*, AIR 1978 SC 1478.

Discussion Point

Can a cinema theatre manager who had no statutory obligation to run a canteen or private cycle stand but for better amenities of his customers and improvement of his business enter into an arrangement with another to maintain a canteen and a cycle stand and for the employees in connection with such canteens and the cycle stands be held liable for contribution as the 'principal employer' of the employees although they were engaged independently by the owner of the canteen or the cycle stand?

Judgement and Explanation

The appeals were dismissed. The court stated that under Section 2(9), the definition has been cast deliberately in the widest terms and the draftsman has endeavoured to cover every possibility so as not to exclude even distant categories of men employed either in the primary work or in cognate activities. It was further stated in the judgement that any exemption would defeat the object of the statute to truncate its semantic sweep and throw out of its ambit those who obviously were within the benign contemplation of the Act.

We must note that law is essentially the formal expression of the regulation of economic relations in society. Keeping in view the complexities of modern business organizations, the principal employer is made primarily liable for payment of contribution in respect of every employee, whether directly employed by him or through an immediate employer under the ESI Act. The main purpose here is to insure all employees in factories or establishments against sickness and allied disabilities, but the funding to implement the policy of insurance is by contribution from the employers and the employees.

15. **Wages (Section 2(22)):** Under the definition of wages, the Act covers all remunerations paid or payable in cash to an employee, if the terms of the contract of employment, express or implied, are fulfilled, and includes any payment to an employee in respect of any period of authorized leave, lockout, strike which is not illegal or layoff and other additional remuneration, if any, paid at intervals not exceeding 2 months.

    Remunerations not covered under wages: However, the definition of wages does not cover the following:

    a. Any contribution paid by the employer to any pension fund or PF or under this Act.
    b. Any travelling allowance or the value of any travelling concession.
    c. Any sum paid to the person employed to defray special expenses entailed on him by the nature of his employment.
    d. Any gratuity payable on discharge.

16. **Wage period (Section 2(23)):** Under the Act, wage period in relation to an employee means the period in respect of which wages are ordinarily payable to him whether in terms of the contract of employment, express or implied, or otherwise.

Employees Entitled for Benefits under the Act

An employee including casual and temporary employees, whether employed directly or through a contractor, is entitled to be insured under the Act who receives wages up to ₹15,000 per month (with effect from 1 May 2010). However, as mentioned before, the apprentices engaged under the Apprentices

Act are not covered under the definition of employee and hence are not entitled to the benefits extended by the ESI Act. Coverage of part-time employees under the ESI Act also depends on whether they have contract of service or contract for service with the employer as both have different implications. The former that is contract of service is entitled for benefits but an employee contracting for service is not entitled for the benefits of the Act.

Besides the employees mentioned above, in the following cases, the employees have been held to be covered under the Act; however, the following list should not be considered as an exhaustive list:

1. Persons employed in a canteen of a club.
2. Employees of cycle stands and canteens run in cinema theatres by contractors.
3. Medical representative.
4. Drivers employed by the transport organization.
5. Persons carrying administrative work of processing the orders and executing sales.
6. Hawkers employed for sale of products.
7. Book binders engaged by a contractor.
8. Part-time doctor employed for ambulance rooms.
9. Members of editorial and administrative staff of a printing press publishing newspapers.
10. Persons engaged in distribution and sale of products.
11. A homeworker rolling bidis at home.
12. Persons employed in a hospital attached to and maintained by the factory.
13. Sales clerks working in a factory.

LO2: Administration of the Act

The Employees' State Insurance Corporation

The provisions of the Act are administered by the ESIC. The ESIC (the Corporation) is a premier social security organization in the country. It is the highest policy-making and decision-taking authority under the ESI Act, which oversees the functioning of the ESI scheme under the Act. The Corporation comprises members representing employees, employers, the central and state government. Besides these, the representatives of Parliament and the medical profession are also the members of the ESIC. Union Minister of Labour functions as the Chairman of the Corporation. A standing committee is constituted by members of the Corporation which acts as an executive body for the administration of the scheme.

The Medical Benefit Council, constituted by the central government, is another statutory body that advises the ESIC on matters regarding administration of medical benefit, the certification for purposes of the grant of benefits and other related matters. The Corporation primarily promotes the scheme of benefits provided by the Act, but the functions of the ESIC are not limited to the primary function only. It promotes measures for the improvement of the health and welfare of insured persons and for the rehabilitation and re-employment of insured persons who have been disabled or injured and may incur in respect of such measures expenditure from the funds of the Corporation within the limits prescribed by the central government in this regard.

The role of ESIC: The Corporation strives to ensure the following:

1. Developing a responsive, purposive and productive relationship with employers.
2. Seeking the active role of employers in the improvement of the scheme as a confidence-building measure.
3. Providing them necessary guidance to meet their lawful obligations under the ESI Act.
4. Enabling them to access the requisite forms and pro forma as may be required by them from time to time.
5. Ensuring that no lax medical certification on part of the ESIC is issued that brings down the productivity of a factory or establishment.
6. In case of any difficulty, doubt or misunderstanding, providing the employer a chance to be heard at an appropriate level.
7. Responding to all correspondence emanating from the employer in a faster and objective manner.
8. ESIC ensures that no employer is harassed by any official of the Corporation authorized to inspect the premises or the records.
9. Promptly addressing to any grievances received from employers and ensuring speedy redressal.

Constitution of Corporation (Section 4): The Corporation consists of the following members, namely:

1. A chairman to be appointed by the central government.
2. A vice chairman to be appointed by the central government.
3. Not more than five persons to be appointed by the central government.
4. One person each representing each of the states in which this Act is in force to be appointed by the state government concerned.
5. One person to be appointed by the central government to represent the union territories.
6. Ten persons representing employers to be appointed by the central government in consultation with such organizations of employers as may be recognized for the purpose by the central government.
7. Ten persons representing employees (three appointed by the central government) to be in consultation with such organizations of employees as may be recognized for the purpose by the central government.
8. Two persons representing the medical profession (three appointed by the central government) to be in consultation with such organizations of medical practitioners as may be recognized for the purpose by the central government.
9. Three members of Parliament of whom two shall be members of the House of the People (Lok Sabha) and one shall be a member of the Council of States (Rajya Sabha) elected, respectively, by the members of the House of the People and the members of the Council of States.
10. The Director General of the Corporation, ex officio. The EI Court is constituted by the state government for such local areas as may be specified and consists of the number of judges as the government may think fit.

Term of office of the members of the Corporation (Section 5): The term of office of members of the Corporation, other than the members referred to in clauses (a), (b), (c), (d) and (e) of Section 4 and the ex-officio member, is 4 years commencing from the date on which their appointment or election is notified, if not otherwise expressly provided in this Act. However, a member of the Corporation, notwithstanding the expiry of the said period of 4 years, continues to hold office until the appointment or election of his successor is notified. Subsection (2) further provides that the member of the Corporation referred to in clauses (a), (b), (c), (d) and (e) of Section 4 holds office during the pleasure of the government appointing them.

The powers of the Corporation (Section 19): The Corporation has the power to promote measures for health and so on of insured persons. The Corporation may, in addition to the benefit schemes specified in this Act, promote measures for the improvement of the health and welfare of insured persons and for the rehabilitation and re-employment of insured persons who have been disabled or injured and may incur in respect of such measures expenditure from the funds of the Corporation within such limits as may be prescribed by the central government.

Standing Committee

Constitution of the standing committee (Section 8): The members of the Corporation constitute the standing committee. The following is the composition of the standing committee:

1. A chairman, who is appointed by the central government.
2. Three members of the Corporation are appointed by the central government.
3. Three members of the Corporation represent three such state governments thereon as the central government may, by notification in the Official Gazette, specify from time to time.
4. Eight members are elected by the Corporation in the following manner:
   a. Three members from among the members of the Corporation are chosen to represent the employers;
   b. Employees are represented by three members chosen from among the members of the Corporation;
   c. Medical profession is represented by one member from among the members of the Corporation; and
   d. One member from among the members of the Corporation is elected by Parliament.
5. The Director General of the Corporation is an ex officio.

Term of office of members of the standing committee (Section 9): The term of office of the members of the standing committee other than a member referred to in clause (a) or clause (b) or clause (bb) of Section 8 is 2 years from the date of the notification of their election, unless otherwise expressly provided in this Act. It must be noted that a member of the standing committee, however, cannot, notwithstanding the expiry of the aforesaid period of 2 years, leave the office until the election of his successor is notified. Since the members of standing committee are chosen from among the members of the Corporation, a member of the standing committee ceases to hold office when he ceases to be a member of the Corporation. So far as the term of office of a member of the standing committee referred to in clause (a) or (b) or clause (bb) of Section 8 is concerned, such a member continues to hold office during the pleasure of the central government.

Powers of the standing committee (Section 18): The main function of the standing committee is to administer the affairs of the Corporation. However, the committee functions under the general superintendence and control of the Corporation. The committee is empowered to perform any of the functions of the Corporation. The standing committee must submit for the consideration and decision of the Corporation all such cases and matters as may be specified in the regulations made in this behalf.

However, the committee is free to submit some matters or cases also for the decision of the Corporation which it thinks appropriate to be forwarded to the Corporation.

Medical Benefit Council

Constitution of the Medical Benefit Council (Section 10): The central government constitutes a Medical Benefit Council consisting of the following members:

1. The director general of the ESIC is appointed as the ex-officio chairman.
2. The ex-officio co-chairman of the Medical Benefit Council is the director general, health services.
3. The medical commissioner of the Corporation, ex officio.
4. In the states where the ESIC Act is in force, each concerned state government (other than union territories) appoints one to represent itself.
5. Three members representing employers are appointed by the central government in consultation with organizations of employers as may be recognized for the purpose by the central government.
6. Central government in consultation with such organizations of employees as may be recognized for this purpose appoints three members representing employees.
7. Three members who represent the medical profession, of whom not less than one has to be a woman, are appointed by the central government in consultation with such organizations of medical practitioners as may be recognized for the purpose by the central government.

Term of office of members of the Medical Benefit Council (Section 10(2)): The term of office of the members of the Medical Benefit Council other than a member referred to in clause (a) or from clause (a) to (d) of Subsection (1) is 4 years from the date of the notification of their election, unless otherwise expressly provided in this Act. However, a member of this council is not permitted to vacate his office before the expiry of the aforesaid period of 4 years until the appointment of his successor is notified. As provided by Section 10(3), a member of the council referred to in clauses (b) and (d) of Subsection (1) continues to hold office during the pleasure of the government appointing him.

Duties of the Medical Benefit Council (Section 22): Duties of the Medical Benefit Council are listed as follows:

1. The council advises the Corporation and the standing committee on specific issues which are related to the administration of medical benefits, the certification for purposes of the grant of benefits and other connected matters.
2. If prescribed, the council also conducts investigation in relation to complaints against medical practitioners in connection with medical treatment and attendance.
3. The council performs all other duties as may be specified in the regulations in connection with medical treatment and attendance.

Cessation of Membership (Section 12)

If a member of the Corporation, the standing committee or the Medical Benefit Council fails in attending three consecutive meetings of the respective body, then such a member ceases to be a member of that body. Subject to rules made by the central government in this behalf, all the three aforementioned bodies are empowered to restore the ceased membership of a member. In the cases where in the opinion of the central government any person who was representing employers, employees or the medical profession on any of the aforesaid bodies (the Corporation, the standing committee or the Medical Benefit Council) has ceased to represent such employers, employees or the medical profession, the central government may notify in the Official Gazette that with effect from such date as may be specified therein such person shall cease to be a member of the concerned body. It must also be noted that a person referred to in clause (i) of Section 4 will no longer be a member of the Corporation when he ceases to be a member of Parliament.

Disqualification (Section 13)

The following persons stand disqualified from holding the position of a member or being considered to be chosen for the membership of the Corporation, the standing committee or the Medical Benefit Council:

1. A person with an unsound mind as declared by a competent court; or
2. An undischarged insolvent; or
3. A person having directly or indirectly by himself or by his partner any interest in a subsisting contract with, or any work being done for, the Corporation except in the cases where such a person is a medical practitioner or a shareholder (not being a director) of a company; or
4. A person convicted for an offence involving moral turpitude (before or after the commencement of this Act).

Registration of Factories and Establishments

The Act demands every employer to get his factory or establishment registered with the ESIC within 15 days after the Act is applicable to it. The employer is also required to obtain the employer's code number. For this purpose, the employer has to make an application in Form 01 to the regional office of the Corporation. After being satisfied with the completeness and correctness of the application form, the regional office allots a code number to the employer. The allotted code number must be quoted by the employer in all documents and correspondence in the future with the Corporation.

Identity card: After registration, with the regional office, a 'temporary identification certificate' is issued to every insured person which remains valid ordinarily for a period of 3 months, but the validity period may be extended, if necessary, for a further period of 3 months. The identity card bearing the signature/thumb impression of the insured person serves as a means of identification of the insured person. Within this period, a permanent 'family photo identity card' in exchange for the certificate is issued to the insured person. The identity card has to be produced by the insured person while he claims medical care at the dispensary/clinic and cash benefit at the local office of the Corporation. The medical benefits provided by the Corporation are not only available to the insured person but are also available to the families of the insured persons. Therefore the particulars of family members entitled to medical benefit are also given in the identity card affixed with a postcard-size family photo. If the insured person changes the employment, the identity card has to be produced before the new employer which serves the purpose of an evidence of registration under the scheme, thus preventing any duplicate registration. In case the identity card is lost by the insured person, a duplicate card is issued on the payment of the prescribed amount.

Case 7.3 will provide the insight into the liabilities of the ESIC towards the employees.

Case 7.3: *Allied Industries v. Mool Chand and Another*[3]

As stated by Mr Mool Chand, he was employed at the factory owned by Allied Industries (the appellant). On 3 June 1999, when he was working on the lathe machine, his left hand was caught in the machine. Consequently, he lost two fingers and sustained a fracture in this thumb and the smallest finger. Mr Mool Chand filed an application for compensation under Section 3 of the Workmen's Compensation Act and claimed that the injury to him was caused by an accident arising out of and in the course of his employment. Despite the notice sent by Mool Chand to the appellant on 21 August 1999, the compensation under the Workmen's Compensation Act, 1923 ('the Act of 1923', for short), was not paid to him.

The appellant filed their reply and denied that Mool Chand had ever worked for them. They also denied the factum of the accident arid the factum of their receiving the notice dated 21 August 1999. The appellant also claimed that they were covered under the ESI Act, 1948 ('the Act of 1948', for short). Therefore, the application filed under the Act of 1923 was not maintainable. The ESIC ('the Corporation', for short) also confirmed that Allied Industries had sent a list of labourers working in their factory. However, the said list did not have the name of Mr Mool Chand. Moreover, on the date of the accident, the employee was not insured. Therefore, the Corporation was not liable to pay any compensation to Mool Chand. On the other hand, Mr Mool Chand contended that since the factory for which he worked was registered with the Corporation, the Corporation was liable to extend medical benefits to him.

Discussion Points

1. Would the Corporation be liable to pay compensation under the ESI Act on the ground that the employer was registered with the Corporation?
2. Was the Corporation legally bound to pay compensation even if the employer did not contribute any money to the Corporation?

Judgement and Explanation

It was held that merely because a factory or an establishment is registered with the ESIC, it would not ipso facto impose a duty on the Corporation to grant medical benefits to the employee. Unless the employer fills its part of the legal duties imposed by the ESI Act, the ESIC cannot be held liable to pay the benefits under the ESI Act.

Thus, it is essential for an employer to make the contributions in order for the employees to obtain benefits from the ESIC. However, in the above case, the facts were quite different. The factory was registered prior to the accident and the employee singularly failed to pay the employees' contribution. Thus, he failed in fulfilling the requirements of the ESI Act. The second discussion point was addressed by the court by stating that the prohibition contained in Section 53 could not be invoked by the employer who has blatantly violated the provisions of the Act of 1948, Section 53 was not maintained as an escape route for an employer.

[3] *Allied Industries v. Mool Chand and Another*, RLW 2007 (4) Raj 2937.

Inspector: Their Duties and Powers

The ESIC may appoint Inspectors to meet the objectives of the Act, within the local limits assigned to each of them.

Duties: The duties of an Inspector are to:

1. Conduct enquiry to verify the correctness of the particulars stated in any Return of Contribution.
2. Ascertain the fact that the provisions of the Act have been complied with.
3. Perform all such duties as may be authorized by the Corporation or specified in the regulations.

Powers: The Inspectors are entrusted with the following powers to carry out their duties and functions as mentioned above:

1. The Inspector is empowered to collect necessary information from any employer or contractor.
2. The Inspector appointed under the Act can enter, at any reasonable time, any office, establishment, factory or other premises of the employer or contractor. He may require the person in change thereof to produce for examination accounts, books and documents relating to the employment of persons and payment of wages or to furnish to him necessary information.
3. The Inspector is empowered to examine the employer or contractor, his agent or servant, any person found in the factory, establishment, office or other premises or any employee.
4. He can make copies of, or take extracts from, any register, account books or other documents maintained in such factories, establishments and offices.

LO3: Finance and Audit

Employees' State Insurance Fund (Section 26)

All contributions paid under this Act and all other moneys received on behalf of the Corporation are to be paid into a fund called the ESI Fund. For all or any of the purposes of this Act, the Corporation is allowed to accept grants, donations and gifts from the central or any state government, local authority or any individual or body whether incorporated or not. All money collected in this fund is paid to the Reserve Bank of India (RBI) or an approved bank by the central government to be credited to the account of the ESI Fund. Such an account is to be operated on by such officers as may be authorized by the standing committee with the approval of the Corporation.

Purposes for Which the Employees' State Insurance Fund May Be Expended (Section 28)

The Act provides under Section 28 the purposes for which the ESI Fund can be used. The Section states that subject to the provisions of this Act and of any rules made by the central government in that behalf, the ESI Fund can be used only for the following purposes, namely:

1. Payment of benefits and provision of medical treatment and attendance to insured persons and, where the medical benefit is extended to their families, the provision of such medical benefit to

their families, in accordance with the provisions of this Act and defraying the charges and costs in connection therewith.

2. Payment of fees and allowances to members of the Corporation, the standing committee and the Medical Benefit Council, the regional boards, local committees and regional and local Medical Benefit Councils.
3. Payment of salaries, leave and joining time allowances, travelling and compensatory allowances, gratuities and compassionate allowances, pensions, contributions to provident or other benefit funds of officers and servants of the Corporation and meeting the expenditure in respect of offices and other services set up for the purpose of giving effect to the provisions of this Act.
4. Establishment and maintenance of hospitals, dispensaries and other institutions and the provision of medical and other ancillary services for the benefit of insured persons and where the medical benefit is extended to their families.
5. Payment of contributions to any state government, local authority or any private body or individual towards the cost of medical treatment and attendance provided to insured persons and, where the medical benefit is extended to their families, including the cost of any building and equipment, in accordance with any agreement entered into by the Corporation.
6. Defraying the cost (including all expenses) of auditing the accounts of the Corporation and of the valuation of its assets and liabilities.
7. Defraying the cost (including all expenses) of the EI Courts set up under this Act.
8. Payment of any sums under any contract entered into for the purposes of this Act by the Corporation or the standing committee or by any officer duly authorized by the Corporation or the standing committee in that behalf.
9. Payment of sums under any decree, order or award of any court or Tribunal against the Corporation or any of its officers or servants for any act done in the execution of his duty or under a compromise or settlement of any suit or other legal proceeding or claim instituted or made against the Corporation.
10. Defraying the cost and other charges of instituting or defending any civil or criminal proceedings arising out of any action taken under this Act.
11. Defraying expenditure, within the limits prescribed, on measures for the improvement of the health, welfare of insured persons and for the rehabilitation and re-employment of insured persons who have been disabled or injured.
12. Such other purposes may be authorized by the Corporation with the previous approval of the central government.

Holding of Property (Section 29)

As provided under Section 29 of the Act, ESIC may, subject to such conditions as may be prescribed by the central government, hold both movable property and immovable property. The Corporation is also free to invest any moneys which are not immediately required for expenses properly defrayable under this Act and may also re-invest or realize such investments on a time-to-time basis. With the previous sanction of the central government and on such terms as may be prescribed by it, ESIC can sell or transfer both movable property and immovable property for the purposes for which the Corporation is established and can also raise loans and take measures for discharging such loans. The

Corporation is also empowered to constitute, for the benefit of its staff or any class of them, provident or other benefit funds as it may think fit. Section 30 further provides in this relation that all the above details or properties, income derived and expenditure incurred, must be maintained in the books of the Corporation.

Accounts Audit and Valuation of Assets and Liabilities (Sections 33–37)

1. **Accounts:** Section 30 of the Act directs the Corporation to maintain correct accounts of its income and expenditure in such form and in such manner as may be prescribed by the central government.
2. **Audit:** Section 34 of the Act deals with the audit of accounts maintained by the Corporation. It provides that the accounts of the Corporation must be audited every year by the Comptroller and Auditor General (CAG) of India. Any expenditure incurred by the CAG in connection with such an audit is to be paid by the Corporation to him (the auditor). The auditor while performing his duty may demand to produce the books, account, connected vouchers and other documents and papers and inspect any of the offices of the Corporation. An audit report prepared by the auditor must be forwarded to the Corporation which has to forward the same to the central government along with its comments on the report of the auditor.
3. **Annual report:** Section 35 provides that the Corporation must submit to the central government an annual report of its work and activities.
4. **Valuation of assets and liabilities:** As amended in the year 2010, Section 37 of the Act directs the Corporation to make valuation of its assets and liabilities for every 3 years of the period (2010 amendment).

LO4: Contribution

Like most of the social security schemes, the world over, the ESI scheme also is a self-financing health insurance scheme. The contributions paid under this Act and all other moneys received on behalf of the ESIC are transferred to a fund called the ESI Fund This fund is held and administered by the Corporation (ESIC) for the purposes of this Act. Contributions are raised from the employers and covered employees as a fixed percentage of wages.

Contribution (Section 38)

According to Section 2(4) of the Act, the contribution is the sum of money payable to the Corporation by the principal employer in respect of an employee and includes any amount payable by or on behalf of the employee in accordance with the provisions of the Act. Section 38 of the Act mandates every factory or establishment having more than 10 employees to be insured under the ESI Act. Section 39 provides that the employer and employee both are required to contribute to the ESIC. Thus, the ESI Fund is contributory in nature. The contribution paid by the employer is called as employer's contribution and the contribution paid by the employee is termed 'employee's contribution'. The rate of contribution paid by employer and employee is decided by the central government. However, the rates so prescribed must not be more than the rates which were in force immediately before the commencement of the ESI (Amendment) Act, 1989.

Rate of Contribution (Section 39)

As discussed above, the rate of contribution by employer and employee to the ESI Fund is revised from time to time. Currently (with effect from 1 January 1997), the employer is required to contribute at the rate of 4.75% of the wages paid/payable in respect of every wage period while the employees contribute at the rate of 1.75% of their wages, except when the 'average daily wages in a wage period' are equal to or less than ₹100. Thus, the employees earning less than and up to ₹100 per day are not required to make any contribution to the ESI Fund and the employer of such employees will pay his contribution to the ESI Fund for all of them at the specified rate. The contribution is deposited by the employer in cash or by cheque at the designated branches of some nationalized banks. The employer is responsible for payment of all contributions made by him and his employees and hence he is entrusted with a right to deduct the employees' share of contribution from employees' wages relating to the period in respect of which the contribution is payable.

Method of calculating contribution: The following items are taken into account for computation of wages/salary for payment of contribution:

1. Basic salary.
2. Dearness allowance, house rent allowance, overtime allowance, night shift allowance, efficiency allowance, heat/gas allowance, education allowance, food and tea allowance, conveyance allowance.
3. Wages/salary/pay for weekly off and public holidays.
4. Commission paid to sales staff.
5. Substance allowance paid to an employee during the period of suspension.
6. Attendance bonus or incentive.
7. Regular honorarium or salary or remuneration paid to director.
8. Collection Bhatta paid to running staff, actual payment made towards leave salary, layoff compensation or wages for strike period.
9. Any other remuneration paid to an employee if the terms of contract of employment are fulfilled.

Contribution period: The Act provides two contribution periods each of 6 months' duration and two corresponding benefit periods. It must be noted that the cash benefits under the scheme are generally linked with contribution paid.

Delay or Default in the Payment of Contribution

As mentioned above, the employer is responsible to deposit his own as well as the employee's contributions in respect of all employees including the contract labour, into the ESI Account. If the wage is received every month by the employee, the contribution to the ESIC should be made by the employer and employee every month without any delay or default. In case of any delay or default, the employee will not be held responsible, but it is the employer who will have to pay interest at 12% per year to the ESIC for any delay or default in depositing the contribution to the Corporation.

Principal Employer's Responsibility to Pay Contributions in the First Instance (Section 40)

As discussed above, the employer pays the contribution to the ESIC on behalf of his employee. The employer is permitted to deduct the employee contribution from the employee wage for payment of contribution to the ESIC. However, the employer can recover the employee contribution paid from the wage of the employee which does not exceed the amount equivalent to employer contribution. Thereafter (after deduction of the employee contribution from the employee wage), the employer becomes responsible for the payment to the ESI contribution. The employer has to bear the expenses occurred in the payment of contributions to the Corporation.

General Provisions as to Payment of Contributions (Section 42)

Section 42 of the Act lays down some general provisions in relation to payment of contributions. The Section states that if an employee is earning average daily wages during a wage period below such wages as may be prescribed by the central government, then he is not required to contribute towards the ESI Funds. In such a case, the employer of such an employee only will make a contribution towards the ESI fund. Here, the average daily wages of an employee are calculated in such a manner as may be prescribed by the central government. It is to be kept in mind that in all such cases, the employer will keep paying his contribution to ESI Fund and all such employees are entitled to all the benefits under the Act despite the fact they do not contribute to the Fund.

Method of Payments of Contribution (Section 43)

Section 43 empowers the ESIC to frame the following rules and regulations in payments and collection of contributions payable under this Act.

1. The manner of payment of contribution.
2. The time of payment of contribution.
3. Fixation of stamps for payment of contribution.
4. Benefits distributed in the case of the insured persons by the Corporation.
5. Maintenance of books and cards of contribution of the insured person by the ESIC.
6. The issuance, sale, custody, production, inspection and delivery of books or cards and the replacement of books or cards which have been lost, destroyed or defaced.

Returns and Registers (Section 44)

According to Section 44 of the Act, the Corporation or such an officer of the Corporation as it may direct is empowered to demand from a principal and immediate employer such returns in such form and containing such particulars relating to persons employed by him. Every principal and immediate employer is required to maintain such registers or records in respect of his factory or establishment.

Recovery of Contribution (Section 45A) (2010 Amendment)

If the employer does not maintain the records or particulars of employed persons as required under this Act, the social security officer by order determines the amount of contributions payable in respect of the employees of that factory or establishment. No order can be passed by the Corporation in respect of the period beyond 5 years from the date on which the contribution becomes payable.

Social Security Officers, Their Functions, and Duties (Section 45) (2010 Amendment)

The Act empowers the Corporation to appoint such persons as social security officers, as it thinks fit, for the purposes of this Act. As a part of his functions and duties, the social security officer is empowered to:

1. Enquire into the correctness of any of the particulars stated in any return referred to in Section 44.
2. Demand any principal or immediate employer to furnish to him such information as he may consider necessary for the purposes of this Act.
3. Enter at any reasonable time any office, establishment, factory or other premises for inspection and examine such accounts, books and other documents relating to the employment of persons and payment of wages or to furnish to him such information as he may consider necessary.
4. Examine the employer, his agent or servant or any person found in such a factory, establishment and office.
5. Make copies of, or take extracts from, any register, account book or other documents maintained in such a factory, establishment, office or other premises.
6. Do reinspection on whether the records and returns submitted under Section 44 are correct or not.

Certification of Return of Contribution by the auditor: The ESI (General) Regulations, 1950, amended Regulation 26 of the Act and directs the employers to include certain details to be mentioned in the Return of Contribution to be submitted by employers. The employers employing less than 40 individuals have to provide self-certification without any certification from the chartered accountants in Return of Contribution. The chartered accountant should certify that he has verified the return from the records and registers of the company.

LO5: Benefits

Provisions for Benefits (Sections 46–73)

Employees covered under the scheme of the Act are entitled to avail medical facilities for self and dependants. They are also entitled to cash benefits in the event of specified contingencies resulting in loss of wages or earning capacity. The insured women are also entitled to maternity benefit for confinement. In case, the death of an insured employee occurs due to employment injury or occupational disease, the dependants are entitled to family pension.

1. Medical benefits.
2. Sickness benefits.
3. Extended sickness benefit.
4. Enhanced sickness benefit.
5. Maternity benefit.
6. Disablement benefit.
7. Dependants' benefit.
8. Other benefits such as funeral expenses, vocational rehabilitation, free supply of physical aids and appliances, preventive healthcare and medical bonus.

Various benefits mentioned above that the insured employees and their dependants are entitled to, the duration of benefits and contributory conditions thereof are discussed below.

1. Sickness Benefits (Section 46(1)(a), 49 and Rule 55)

Entitlement: Sickness signifies a state of health requiring medical treatment and attendance and abstention from work on medical grounds. Financial support extended by the Corporation on such a contingency is called sickness benefit. Sickness benefit includes periodical payments made to an insured person for the period of certified sickness after completing 9 months in insurable employment. Thus, every insured employee is entitled to the cash benefit for the period of sickness occurring during any benefit period and certified by a duly appointed medical practitioner if the contributions in respect of him were payable for not less than 78 days in the corresponding contribution period (Rule 55).

Newly appointed employee: However, if an employee is newly appointed, eligible for the first time who has got a shorter contribution period of less than 156 days, he is entitled to claim sickness benefit if he pays contribution for not less than half the number of days available for working in such a contribution period. The benefit is payable at the standard benefit rate, corresponding to his daily average wages. The benefit is, however, not available for any day on which the employee works, remains on leave, on holiday or strike, in respect of which he receives wages.

Conditions to be observed: The employee has to meet the following conditions to avail the sickness benefit. Any person in receipt of sickness benefit:

a. Must remain under medical treatment at the ESI dispensary or hospital and carry out the instructions of the medical officer.
b. Must not do anything which retards or reduces his chances of recovery.
c. Must not leave the area where medical treatment is provided without the medical officer's permission.
d. Must get himself examined by the medical officer.

Sickness benefit to an employee on strike: Sickness benefit is allowed to an employee for any day on which he remains on strike, if:

a. He is receiving medical treatment and attendance as an indoor patient in any ESI hospital or a hospital recognized by the ESIC for such treatment; or

b. He is entitled to receive extended sickness benefit for any of the diseases for which such benefit is admissible; or
c. He is in receipt of sickness benefit immediately preceding the date of commencement of notice of the strike given by the employees' union to the management of the factory/establishment.

Standard benefit rate: The benefit rate corresponds to the average daily wage of an insured employee during the corresponding contribution period and is roughly half of the daily wage rate. With effect from 1 December 2007, the standard benefit rate has increased by 20% resulting in the benefit rate of about 60% of the wages. The maximum duration for availing sickness benefit is 91 days in two consecutive benefit periods. However, no sickness benefit is payable for the first 2 days of sickness following, at an interval of not more than 15 days, after the sickness in respect of which sickness benefits were last paid.

Extended sickness benefit (Section 99): It is a cash benefit paid for prolonged illness (tuberculosis/leprosy, mental and malignant diseases) due to any of the 34 specified diseases. This is an additional sickness benefit provided by the Corporation in exercise of its powers under Section 99 of the Act. To avail the befit of this category, the insured person should have been in continuous employment for a period of 2 years and should have contributed for at least 156 days in four preceding contributions. Daily rate of extended sickness benefit is 40% more than the standard sickness benefit rate admissible. After exhausting sickness benefit payable for 91 days, the extended sickness benefit is payable up to a further period of 124/309 days that can be extended up to 2 years in special circumstances.

Enhanced sickness benefit: To promote the norms of small family, this cash benefit is paid to the insured person for undergoing vasectomy/tubectomy operation. This benefit is paid at double the standard benefit rate. Thus, it amounts to full wages, for a period of 7 days for vasectomy operation and for 14 days for tubectomy operation. This period can be extended in case of any postoperative complications.

2. Maternity Benefit (Section 46(1)(b), 50 and Rule 56)

Entitlement: Maternity benefit is cash payable to insured women for the specified period of abstention from work for confinement or miscarriage or for sickness arising out of pregnancy, 'confinement' and 'premature birth of child or miscarriage'. Here 'confinement' connotes labour after 26 weeks of pregnancy, whether the result issue is alive or dead and 'miscarriage' means expulsion of the contents of a pregnant uterus at any period prior to or during the 26th week of pregnancy. Criminal abortion or miscarriage is not, however, entitled to maternity benefit. This cash payable benefit is payable if the contributions, in respect of insured woman, were payable for at least 70 days in the two immediately preceding contribution periods (Rule 56).

Conditions to be observed: Maternity benefit is payable to insured women in case of confinement or miscarriage or sickness related thereto.

a. For claiming this benefit, an insured woman should have paid for at least 70 days in two consecutive contribution periods, that is, 1 year.
b. The benefit is normally payable for 12 weeks, which can be further extended up to 16 weeks on medical grounds.

c. The rate of payment of the benefit is equal to the wage or double the standard sickness benefit rate.
d. The benefit is payable within 14 days of duly authenticated claim papers.

Standard benefit rate and amount (Section 50): The qualification of an insured woman to claim maternity benefit, the conditions subject to which such benefits may be given, the rates and the period thereof shall be such as may be prescribed by the central government. The contribution condition is the same as for sickness benefit but daily benefit rate is double the sickness benefit rate and is thus roughly equivalent to the full wages. The maternity benefit is paid for Sundays also. The benefit is payable at twice the standard benefit rate or ₹20, whichever is higher, for all days on which she does not work for remuneration during the period prescribed as below.

Claim before confinement: An insured woman who is pregnant may obtain a certificate of pregnancy (new Form 17) and submit it along with a notice of pregnancy. The notice of pregnancy, to be valid, has to be submitted, by post or otherwise, to the branch office within 7 days of the date on which the certificate of pregnancy is obtained (Regulation 87). However, it is not mandatory for the insured woman to give any notice of the pregnancy, but it is advisable for her to give notice because:

a. It helps to determine whether the birth of a dead child may be deemed as 'confinement' entitling her to maternity benefit for 12 weeks or 'miscarriage' which entitles her to maternity benefit for just 6 weeks; and
b. If she decides to move to her village for her confinement, it helps establish her bona fides for acceptance of birth certificates issued in her village.

Duration of benefit: The payments to be made in respect of maternity benefit are periodical, but the periods at which they are to be made are not fixed. Further, payments relating to this benefit cannot be commuted into a lump sum.

a. **For confinement:** The benefit is available for a total period of 12 weeks, beginning not more than 6 weeks before the expected date of child birth; if the insured woman dies during confinement or within 6 weeks thereafter, leaving behind the living child, the benefit continues to be payable for the whole of the period. But if the child also dies during that period, the benefit is paid up to and including the day of the death of the child.
b. **For miscarriage:** In case of miscarriage, the benefit is available for the period of 6 weeks following the date of miscarriage.
c. **For sickness arising out of pregnancy, confinement, premature birth of a child or miscarriage:** In all such cases, the benefit can be availed for an additional period or up to four weeks. Here, the benefit is paid only if the insured woman does not work for remuneration during the period for which benefit is claimed. There is no waiting period.

Benefits not to be combined: An insured woman is not entitled to receive for the same period:

a. Both sickness benefit and maternity benefit.
b. Both maternity benefit and disablement benefit for temporary disablement.

Section 65 provides that where an insured woman is entitled to more than one of the benefits mentioned above, she is entitled to choose which benefit she wishes to receive.

Disqualification for maternity benefit: An insured woman may be disqualified from receiving maternity benefit if she fails without good reason to attend or to submit herself to medical examination when so required. She may, however, refuse to be examined by one other than a female doctor or a midwife. If an insured woman is disqualified for the above-stated reason, the disqualification is to be for such number of days as may be decided by the authority authorized by the Corporation, which is the appropriate regional office (Regulation 93).

Repayment of benefit improperly received: If any insured woman has received maternity benefit when not lawfully entitled thereto, she is liable to repay to the Corporation the amount of such payment. In case of her death, her legal representative has to repay the same from the assets of the deceased, if any, in his hands. The amount can be recovered as arrears of land revenue as laid down by Section 70 or Sections 45C–45I.

Medical bonus: Medical Bonus is lump sum payment made to an insured woman or an insured person in respect of his wife per each confinement to meet the confinement expenses, if the confinement occurs at a place where necessary facilities under the ESI scheme are not available. Currently, the confinement expense paid is ₹2,500 per each confinement.

3. Disablement Benefit (Section 46(1)(c), 51, 51A–51D, 52A, 53–55 and 57)

Disablement is a condition resulting from employment injury, which may render the insured person temporarily incapable of doing his work and requiring medical treatment (temporary disablement). It may reduce his earning capacity (permanent partial disability) or it may totally deprive him from the capacity of doing any work (permanent total disability).

Entitlement: Section 46(1)(c) of the Act provides for periodical payments to an insured person suffering from disablement as a result of employment injury sustained as an employee under the Act and certified to be eligible for such payments by an authority specified in this behalf by the regulations. Disablement benefit is paid in the form of cash instalments, to an employee who is injured in the course of his employment and is, permanently or temporarily, disabled or contacts any occupational disease. To avail this benefit, it is sufficient if it is proved that the injury was caused by an accident arising out of, and in the course of, employment, no matter when it occurred and where it occurred.

Presumption as to accident arising in the course of employment (Section 51A): The accident is deemed to have arisen out of and in the course of employment unless there is evidence to the contrary,

Accidents happening while acting in breach of regulations and so on (Section 51B): An accident is deemed to arise out of and in the course of employment notwithstanding that the employee is at the time of the accident acting in contravention of the provisions of any law applicable to him, or of any orders given by or on behalf of his employer or that he is acting without instructions from his employer, if:

a. The accident would have been deemed so to have arisen had the act not been done in contravention as aforesaid on or without instructions from his employer, as the case may be.
b. The act is done for the purpose of and in connection with the employer's trade or business.

Accidents happening while travelling in employer's transport (Section 51C): This subsection states that when an accident happens while an employee is, with the express or implied permission of his employer, travelling as a passenger by any vehicle to or from his place of work, the accident shall, notwithstanding that he is under no obligation to his employer to travel by that vehicle, be deemed to arise out of and in the course of his employment, if:

a. The accident would have been deemed so to have arisen had he been under such obligation.
b. At the time of the accident, the vehicle:
   i. Is being operated by or on behalf of his employer or some other person by whom it is provided in pursuance of arrangements made with his employer.
   ii. Is not being operated in the ordinary course of public transport service.

Here, vehicle includes vessel and an aircraft.

Accidents happening while meeting emergency (Section 51D): Section 51 under Subsection D further provides for accidents occurring while meeting emergency. As laid down by this Section, an accident happening to an insured person in or about any premises at which he is for the time being employed for the purpose of his employer's trade or business is deemed to arise out of and in the course of his employment, if it happens while he is taking steps, on an actual or supposed emergency at those premises, to rescue, succour or protect persons who are, or are thought to be or possibly to be, injured or imperilled or to avert or minimize serious damage to property.

Accidents happening while commuting to the place of work and vice versa (Section 51E): Section 51E deals with the accidents happening while commuting to the place of work and vice versa. It states that accidents occurring to an employee while commuting from his residence to the place of employment for duty or from the place of employment to his residence after performing duty are deemed to have arisen out of and in the course of employment if nexus between the circumstances, time and place in which the accident occurred and the employment is established.

Occupational disease (Section 52A): As laid down under Section 52A, contracting of any occupational disease specified in Schedule III to the Act is, unless contrary, proved deemed to be an 'employment injury' arising out of and in the course of employment:

a. If an employee employed in any employment specified in Part A of Schedule III contracts any disease specified therein as an occupational disease peculiar to that employment; or
b. If an employee employed in the employment specified in Part B of that Schedule for a continuous period of not less than 6 months contracts any disease specified therein as an occupational disease peculiar to that employment; or
c. If an employee employed in any employment specified in Part C of that Schedule for such a continuous period as the Corporation may specify in respect of every such employment.

The Section further specifies that the central government or a state government, as the case may be, is empowered to add any description of employment to the employments specified in Schedule III to the Workmen's Compensation Act, 1923 (8 of 1923), by virtue of the powers vested in it under Subsection (3) of Section 3 of the said Act. The said description of employment and the occupational diseases specified under that subsection as peculiar to that description of employment forms part of Schedule III. Without prejudice to the provisions of the above-mentioned, the Corporation after giving, by notification in the Official Gazette, not less than 3 months of notice of its intention so to do may, by a similar notification, add any description of employment to the employments specified in Schedule III and specify in the case of employments so added the diseases which are for the purposes of this Section to be occupational diseases peculiar to those employments, respectively, and thereupon the provisions of this Act apply as if such diseases had been declared by this Act to be occupational diseases peculiar to those employments.

It is to be noted here that no benefit is payable to an employee in respect of any disease unless the disease is directly attributable to a specific injury by an accident arising out of and in the course of his employment. The provisions of Section 51A shall not apply to the cases to which this Section applies.

Standard benefit rate: The benefit rate for disablement benefit can be discussed under the following heads:

a. **Temporary disablement benefit**: In case of temporary disability arising out of an employment injury or occupational disease, disablement benefit is admissible to the insured person for the entire period so certified by an insurance medical officer/practitioner for which the insured employee does not work for wages. The benefit is not subject to any contributory condition and is payable at a rate which is not less than 70% of daily average wages. However, the benefit is not payable if the incapacity lasts for less than 3 days excluding the date of accident.
b. **Permanent disablement benefit**: If an employment injury or occupational disease results in permanent, partial or total loss of earning capacity, periodical payments are made to the insured employee for life at a rate depending on the actual loss of earning capacity as may be determined and certified by a duly constituted medical board. The rates of disablement benefits are determined in accordance with the provisions of Rule 57 of the ESI (Central) Rules, 1991. In order to product erosion in real value of the periodical payments of permanent disablement benefits, against rise in the cost of living index, periodical increases are granted, based on actuarial calculation of permanent disablement benefit.

   It is to be noted here that commutation of periodical payments into lump sum (one-time payment) is permissible where the permanent disablement stands assessed as final and daily rate of benefit does not exceed ₹1.50 per day. Here, the total commuted value must not exceed ₹30,000.

Reference to medical boards: The employee claiming any disablement benefit has to furnish a medical certificate as prescribed under the regulations. The employee is also required to observe certain conditions as to medical examination and so on, as prescribed for sickness benefit. The benefit for temporary disablement is, however, not payable for any day on which the employee works, remains on lease, on holiday or strike, in respect of which he receives wages.

Disablement benefit for temporary disablement to an employee on strike: The disablement benefit for temporary disablement is allowed to an employee for any day on which he remains on strike, if:

a. The insured employee is receiving medical treatment and attendance as an indoor patient in any ESI hospital or a hospital recognized by the ESIC, for such treatment; or
b. The insured employee is in receipt of such disablement benefit immediately preceding the date of commencement of notice of the strike given by the employees' union to the management of the factory/establishment.

Notice of injury: The insured employee who sustains an employment injury should give a notice of the same to the employer or manager or supervisor or foreman, and so on, by means of entry in the accident book or otherwise in writing or even orally. This notice is very important for claiming the disablement benefit.

Accident report by the employer: In case of an accident in the establishment, the employer is required to prepare an 'accident report' in Form 16 (in triplicate) and submit to the local office and the insurance medical officer. The third copy is to be kept by the employer as the office copy. These reports are to be submitted within 48 hours in ordinary cases and immediately in death cases.

Employer should arrange first aid: It is the responsibility of the employer to make arrangements for first aid and medical treatment and transport as an insured person may require, in case of an accident.

Let us discuss a case to understand the provisions of disablement compensation benefits extended to the employees under the Act (Case 7.4).

Case 7.4: *Rajappa v. Employees State Insurance Corporation*[4]

Mr A was employed as a helper in a factory for over 16 years covered by the ESI, 1948. Mr A had been paying regularly the ESI contribution. He was working in the first shift on 6 March 1980. He was residing in the village Chikkondugula, about 6 km away from the factory. On the day while he was returning home directly from the factory, when he was about 1 km away from his house, three persons attacked him with scythes and knives. His left hand was cut off. The bones of his left leg were also cut. He was then taken to a government hospital. Mr A was treated there for 3.5 months and thereafter taken to ESI hospital, Bangalore. There also he was treated for a further period of 3.5 months. The ESIC met all the medical expenses of the claimant, when he was under treatment. Thereafter, Mr A made representation to the ESIC to give him the disablement benefit.

The ESIC in a written letter intimated that he was not entitled to the disablement benefit. The claimant filed an application before the ESI Court claiming the benefit. The claim was contested by the ESIC. The ESIC admitted that Mr A was an employee and he was attacked by the unknown assailants while he was returning from the factory. It was, however, denied that the injury was in the course of employment, much less caused by accident arising out of and in the course of employment. The Corporation further asserted that there was no nexus between the injury and the employment. He was attacked by the persons with whom he has personal enmity.

The ESI Court dismissed the claim of the claimant/applicant holding that there was no material to link the incident with his employment. It was established that the said assailants had no grouse or enmity against the workman in connection with the factory work or some other activities of the workman connected with his employment and there was no material on record which helps the claimant to claim that the injuries sustained arose out of and in the course of employment.

Mr A filed an appeal in the Supreme Court to claim the disablement benefit from the Corporation.

Discussion Point

Was Mr A entitled to claim the disablement benefits from the ESIC?

Judgement and Explanation

It was held that Mr A was not entitled for disablement benefit from the Corporation. The court stated in the decision that there must be a casual relationship between the accident and the employment. For the same reason, the appeal failed and was dismissed. As it is clear from the facts, the above case does not establish any intimate relationship between the assault-causing injury to the appellant employee and the employment. Thus, the expression 'arising out of employment' is again not confined to the mere nature of the employment. The expression applies to employment as such to its nature, its conditions, its obligations and its incidents.

[4] *Rajappa v. Employees State Insurance Corporation*, ILR 1992 KAR 284.

4. Dependants' Benefits (Section 46(1)(d), 52, 55A and Rule 58)

Entitlement

Section 46(d) provides for the periodical payments to dependants of an insured person who dies as a result of an employment injury sustained as an employee under this Act as are entitled to compensation under this Act (hereinafter referred to as dependants' benefit). Dependants' benefit is a monthly pension payable to the eligible dependants of an insured person who dies as a result of an employment injury or occupational disease. Thus, the dependants of only those insured employees who die of employment injury and not otherwise are entitled for this benefit.

Beneficiaries and duration of benefit: The Act recognizes the following beneficiaries for the purpose of disablement benefit:

a. A widow, a minor legitimate or adopted son or an unmarried daughter.
b. A widowed mother.
c. If wholly dependent on the earnings of the insured person at the time of his death, a legitimate or adopted son or daughter who has attained the age of 18 and is infirm.
d. If wholly or in part dependent on the earnings of the insured person at the time of his death.
e. A parent other than a widowed mother.
f. A minor illegitimate son, an unmarried illegitimate daughter or a daughter legitimate or adopted or illegitimate, if unmarried, and a minor or if widowed and a minor.
g. A minor brother or unmarried sister or a widowed sister if minor.
h. A widowed daughter-in-law.
i. A minor child of a predeceased son.
j. A minor child of a predeceased daughter where no parent of the child is alive.
k. A paternal grandparent if no parent of the insured person is alive.
l. In the absence of any widow or legitimate child, the benefit is paid to a parent or grandparent for life, to any other male dependant until age 18 or to an unmarried or widowed female dependant until age 18.

Standard rate and distribution of benefit: Rule 58 makes a mention of the rate of dependant benefit payable to the dependant of the deceased insured employee. The total divisible benefit is equivalent to the temporary disablement benefit rate (roughly 70% of the wage rate). In case of death of insured employee, the amount of benefit is distributed among the dependants as follows:

a. Widow till death or remarriage at three-fifth of the full rate.
b. Widowed mother till death at two-fifth of the full rate.
c. Sons at two-fifth of the full rate each till he attains the age of 25.
d. Unmarried daughters at two-fifth of the full rate till they get married.
e. If the son or daughter is infirm and wholly dependent on the earnings of the insured person at the time of his death, they continue to receive the benefit even after attaining the age of 25/marriage as the case may be.

If the total benefit so divided exceeds the full rate, there is a proportionate reduction in the respective shares of the beneficiaries. The amount of pension paid to the dependants of a deceased insured person is reviewed vis-à-vis the cost of living index and increases are granted from time to time to compensate for erosion in its real value. The benefit is not payable to married major daughters.

As per Rule 58 of the ESI (Central) Rule, 1950, when the deceased insured person does not leave behind any widow or child, the benefit is payable to other dependants. In such cases also, the amount of cash benefit paid to the dependants of deceased insured person is linked with the cost of living index and periodical increases are sanctioned from time to time.

Review of dependants' benefit (Section 55A): The Act states that any decision awarding dependants' benefit under this Act may be reviewed at any time by the Corporation if it is satisfied by fresh evidence that:

a. The decision was given in consequence of non-discloser or misrepresentation by the claim at or any other person of a material part or that the decision is no longer in accordance with this Act due to any birth or death or due to the marriage, remarriage or cessation of infirmity of, or attainment of the age of 18 by a claimant.
b. Subject to the provisions of the Act, the Corporation may on such review as aforesaid direct that the dependants' benefit be continued, increased, reduced or discontinued.

After reviewing the case, the ESIC may direct the dependants' benefit to be continued, increased, decreased or discontinued.

5. Medical Benefit (Section 46(1)(e), 46 (2), 56–59 and Rules 60 and 61)

Section 46(1)(e) of the Act extends medical benefit to the insured employee and his family member. Medical benefit is the medical attendance and treatment to the insured persons covered under the Act and their families as and when needed. Thus, it means medical care of insured persons and their families, wherever covered for medical benefit. This is the only benefit provided in kind through the state governments (except in Delhi) and uniform to all as per their requirement without linking it to their wages and contributions.

The standard medical care includes outdoor treatment, in-patient treatment, all necessary drugs and dressing, pathological and radiological specialist consultation and care, antenatal and postnatal care, emergency treatment and so on. Outdoor medical care is provided at the state insurance dispensaries or mobile dispensaries manned by full-time doctors (service systems) or at the private clinics of insurance medical practitioners (panel system).

Entitlement (Section 56): An employee who is covered under the scheme for the first time is eligible for medical care for the period of 3 months. If he/she contributes at least for 78 days in a contribution period, the eligibility is there up to the end of the corresponding benefit period. An employee is also eligible for extended sickness benefit when he/she is suffering from any one of the long-term 34 diseases listed in the Act. This is admissible after the worker has been under ESI and has successfully met all the laid down conditions. The medical benefit is admissible for a maximum period of 730 days for the insured person and his/her family.

Scale of benefit (Section 57): The scale of medical benefit under Section 57 of Act to be provided to the insured employee and members of their families is prescribed by the state government in consultation with the Corporation under Section 58(1 and 3) of Act under State Medical Benefit Rules. The insured employee and members of his family do not have the right to claim medical services over and above those which have been so prescribed. The beneficiaries are entitled to reasonable medical, surgical and obstetric treatment.

a. **Medical facilities to insured persons:** He is entitled to avail treatment in ESI dispensary/ hospital/diagnostic centre and recognized institutions, to which he is attached such as the following:
    i. Outpatient treatment.
    ii. Domiciliary treatment by visits at their residences.
    iii. Specialists' consultation.
    iv. In-patient treatment (Hospitalization).
    v. Free supply of drugs, dressings and artificial limbs, aids and appliances.
    vi. Imaging and laboratory services.
    vii. Integrated family welfare, immunization and maternal and child health (MCH) programme and other national health programmes and so on.
    viii. Ambulance service or reimbursement of conveyance charges for going to hospitals, diagnostic centres and so on.
    ix. Medical certification.
    x. Special provisions.
b. **Medical facilities to family members of insured persons**: While in all implemented areas the insured person is entitled to medical care as detailed above, his family members are entitled to one or other of the following scales of medical benefits:
    i. 'FULL' Medical Care, that is, all facilities as for IPs including hospitalization.
    ii. 'EXPANDED' Medical Care, that is, all facilities as for IPs except hospitalization. A small number of insured persons in the states of Gujarat and Bihar fall under this category.

6. Funeral Expenses (Section 46(1)(f) and Rule 59) Entitlement

Section 46(1)(f) of the Act provides for payment to the eldest surviving member of the family of an insured person who has died, towards the expenditure for the funeral of the deceased insured person, or where insured person did not have a family or was not living with his family at the time of his death, to the person who actually incurs the expenditure on the funeral of the deceased insured person (to be known as 'funeral expenses'). The payment under this Section is subject to the condition that the amount of such payment does not exceed such amount as may be prescribed by the central government and the claim for such payment has to be made within 3 months of the death of the insured person or within such extended period as the Corporation or any officer or authority authorized by it in this behalf may allow.

Amount and distribution of benefit: Funeral expenses are payable in the nature of lump sum payment up to a maximum of ₹2,500 made to defray the expenditure on the funeral of a deceased insured employee. The amount is paid either to the eldest surviving member of the family or, in his absence, to the person who actually incurs the expenditure on the funeral.

Rehabilitation Allowance: The ESIC, vide its Resolution dated 22 December 1979, resolved to grant rehabilitation allowance to the insured persons, for each day, on which they remain admitted in an artificial limb centre. On the rates, which generally confirm to double the standard sickness benefit rate, the above benefit was introduced with effect from 1 January 1980.

General Provisions Regarding Benefits

Benefit not assignable or attachable (Section 60): The right to receive any payment of any benefit under this Act is not transferable or assignable. The Section further clarifies that no cash benefit payable under this Act is liable to attachment or sale in execution of any decree or order of any court.

Bar of benefits under other enactments (Section 61): Section 61 states, if a person is entitled to any of the benefits provided by this Act, he will not be entitled to receive any similar benefit admissible under the provisions of any other enactment.

Benefits not available in certain cases (Section 62): The Act denies the access to the benefits in certain circumstances and states that no person is entitled to sickness benefit or disablement benefit for temporary disablement on any day on which he works or remains on leave or on a holiday in respect of which he receives wages or on any day on which he remains on strike.

Recipients of sickness or disablement benefit to observe conditions (Section 64): A person who is in receipt of sickness benefit or disablement benefit excluding the benefit granted on permanent disablement has to meet following conditions:

1. He should remain under medical treatment at a dispensary, hospital, clinic or another institution provided under this Act and must carry out the instructions given by the medical officer or medical attendant in charge thereof.
2. He should not while under treatment do anything and have chances of recovery.
3. He must not leave the area in which medical treatment provided by this Act is being given, without the permission of the medical officer, medical attendant or another such authority as may be specified in this behalf by the regulations.
4. He should allow himself to be examined by any duly appointed medical officer or another person authorized by the Corporation in this behalf.

Benefits not to be combined (Section 65): Section 65 states that an insured person is not entitled to receive for the same period:

1. Both sickness benefit and maternity benefit;
2. Both sickness benefit and disablement benefit for temporary disablement; or
3. Both maternity benefit and disablement benefit for temporary disablement.

The Section further mentions, if a person is entitled to more than one of the benefits mentioned in Subsection (1), he is entitled to choose which benefit he wishes to receive.

Negligence of employer to pay any contribution (Section 68): In case of default by the principal employer to pay any contribution under the Act, the principal employer is held liable to pay in respect of any employee and by reason thereof such person becomes disentitled to any benefit or entitled to a benefit on a lower scale. In such cases, the Corporation may, on being satisfied that the contribution should have been paid by the principal employer, pay to the person the benefit at the rate to which he would have been entitled if the failure or neglect had not occurred. Here, the Corporation is entitled to recover from the principal employer either where:

1. The difference between the amount of benefit which is paid by the Corporation to the said person and the amount of the benefit which would have been payable on the basis of the contributions which were in fact paid by the employer; or

2. Twice the amount of the contribution which the employer failed or neglected to pay, whichever is greater.

Section further mentions that the amount recoverable under this Section may be recovered as if it were an arrear of land revenue or under Section 45C–45I.

Excessive sickness benefit (Section 69): Section 69 of the Act deals with liability of the owner or occupiers of the factories in case of excessive sickness benefits. The Act provides the case where the Corporation considers that the incidence of sickness among insured persons is excessive by reason of:

1. Insanitary working conditions in a factory or establishment or the neglect of the owner or occupier of the factory or establishment to observe any health regulations enjoined on him by or under any enactment; or
2. Insanitary condition of any tenements or lodgings occupied by insured persons and such insanitary conditions are attributable to the neglect of the owner of the tenements or lodgings to observe any health regulations enjoined on him by or under any enactment.

The Corporation is empowered to send to the owner or occupier of the factory or establishment or to the owner of the tenements or lodgings, as the case may be, a claim for the payment of the amount of the extra expenditure incurred by the Corporation as sickness benefits. If the claim is not settled by agreement, the Corporation may refer the matter, with a statement in support of its claim, to the appropriate government.

Inquire by a competent person: After receiving such statements from the Corporation, if the appropriate government is of opinion that a prima facie case for inquiry is disclosed, it may appoint a competent person or persons to hold an inquiry into the matter, where, upon such inquiry, it is proved to the satisfaction of the person or persons holding the inquiry that the excess in incidence of sickness among the insured persons is due to the default or neglect of the owner or occupier of the factory or establishment or the owner of the tenements or lodgings; as the case may be, the said person or persons is required to determine the amount of the extra expenditure incurred as sickness benefit and the person or persons by whom the whole or any part of such amount is to be paid to the Corporation.

Repayment of benefit improperly received (Section 70): If any person receives any benefit or payment under this Act when he is not lawfully entitled thereto, such a person is liable to repay to the Corporation the value of the benefit or the amount of such payment, or in the case of his death his representative has to repay the same from the assets of the deceased if any, in his hands. The Section further states that the value of any benefits received other than cash payments is to be determined by such authority as may be specified in the regulations made in this behalf and the decision of such authority is considered to be final.

Benefit payable up to and including day of death (Section 71): In case an insured person dies during any period for which he is entitled to a cash benefit under this Act, the amount of such benefit up to and including the day of his death is to be paid to any person nominated by the deceased person in writing in such form as may be specified in the regulations or, if there is no such nomination, to the heir or legal representative of the deceased person.

Employer not to reduce wages and so on (Section 72): As laid down by Section 72 of the Act, no employer by reason only of his liability for any contributions payable under this Act should, directly or indirectly, reduce the wages of any employee or, except as provided by the regulations, discontinue or reduce benefits payable to him under the conditions of his service which are similar to the benefits conferred by this Act.

Employer not to dismiss or punish employee during period of sickness and so on (Section 73): The act directs the employer not to dismiss, discharge, reduce or otherwise punish an employee during the following circumstances:

1. Sickness.
2. Maternity leave.
3. Pregnancy or confinement.
4. Under treatment in the hospital.
5. Temporary disablement.

LO6: Obligations of Employers under the Act

The obligations of employers under the Act are as follows:

1. The employer must get his factory or establishments registered with the ESIC within 15 days after the Act becomes applicable to it and obtain the employers' code number.
2. The employer must obtain the declaration form from the employees covered under the Act and submit the same along with the return of declaration forms to the ESI office. He should also arrange for the allotment of insurance numbers to the employees and their identity cards.
3. The employer is responsible to deposit the employees' and his own contributions to the ESI Account in the prescribed manner. Employer's liability under the Act cannot be disputed on the ground that he has no sufficient resources. He cannot avoid the ESI contribution for non-availability of finance.
4. The employer has to furnish a Return of Contribution along with the challans of monthly payment, within 30 days of the end of each contribution period.
5. The employer must not reduce the wages of an employee on account of the contribution payable by him (employer).
6. The employer must maintain the prescribed records/registers properly for the purpose of inspection. Such records/registers include the following:
    a. Attendance registers/muster rolls (in respect of all employees including those employed through contractors).
    b. Wage register.
    c. Cash book/bank book.
    d. Account books including ledgers and vouchers, balance sheets.
    e. Employees' register.
    f. Accident book.
    g. Returns of Contribution.
    h. Return of declaration forms.
    i. Copies of challans.
    j. Inspection book.
7. It is the duty of the employer to inform the ESI authorities of any accident in the place of employment within 24 hours or immediately in case of serious or fatal accidents. He also has to furnish to the

authorities such further information and particulars of an accident as may be required. The employer should make arrangements for first aid and transportation of the employee to the hospital.

8. In case of death of any employee, the employer must inform the local office and the nearest ESI dispensary/hospital, immediately.
9. The employer must ensure not to put to work any sick employee and grant him leave, if he has been issued the prescribed certificate.
10. The employer must not dismiss or discharge any employee during the period he/she is in receipt of sickness/maternity/temporary disablement benefit, or is under medical treatment, or is absent from work as a result of illness duly certified or due to pregnancy or confinement.

LO7: Adjudication of Disputes, Claims and Penalties

Employees' Insurance Court (Sections 74 and 75)

Section 75 of the Act provides for the adjudication under the ESI Act. Any dispute arising under the ESI Act will be decided by the EI Court and not by a Civil Court. The covered employees and their employers have a forum in the form of an EI Court to settle their disputes or grievances subject to the condition that a deposit of 50% dues is made unless this deposit is waived for reasons at the discretion of the court.

Constitution of Employees' Insurance Court (Section 74)

The Act empowers the state government to, by notification in the Official Gazette, constitute an EI Court for such local areas as may be specified in the notification. The state government decides to its wisdom the number of judges in the court. Any person who is or has been a judicial officer or is a legal practitioner of 5 years' standing is qualified to be a judge of the EI Court. The state government may appoint the same court for two or more local areas or two or more courts for the same local area. If more than one court has been appointed for the same local area, the state government by general or special order regulates the distribution of business between them.

Role and power of the state government: The power of the state government to constitute an ESI Court also includes the power to reconstitute it. Thus, the power of reconstitution of an ESI Court is to be exercised in the same manner as the power of constitution, namely by notification in the Official Gazette. Neither constitution nor reconstitution of an ESI Court becomes effective before the date of the publication of the notification under Subsection (1) of Section 74 of the Act in the Official Gazette.

Matters to Be Decided by Employees' Insurance Court (Section 75)

Adjudication of Question or Dispute (Section 75)

The ESI Court decides the questions or disputes that arise as to:

1. Whether any person is an employee within the meaning of this Act or whether he is liable to pay the employee's contribution.
2. The rate of wages or average daily wages of an employee for the purposes of this Act.

3. The rate of contribution payable by a principal employer in respect of any employee.
4. The person who is or was the principal employer in respect of any employee.
5. The right of any person to any benefit and as to the amount and duration thereof.
6. Any direction issued by the Corporation under Section 55A on a review of any payment of the dependant's benefits.
7. Any other matter which is in dispute between:
   a. A principal employer and the Corporation,
   b. Between a principal employer and an immediate employer,
   c. Between a person and the Corporation,
   d. Between an employee and a principal or immediate employer, in respect of any contribution or benefit or other dues payable or recoverable under this Act, or
   e. Any other matter required to be or which may be decided by the EI Court under this Act.

Above-mentioned questions or disputes subject to the provisions of Subsection (2A) are decided by the EI Court in accordance with the provisions of this Act.

Adjudication of Claims (Section 75(2A))

The following claims are decided by the EI Court, namely:

1. Recovery of contributions from the principle employer.
2. Recovery of contributions from a contractor.
3. Recovery for short payment or non-payment of any contribution under Section 68.
4. Recovery of the value or amount of benefits received improperly under Section 70.
5. Recovery of any benefit admissible under the Act.

It is to be noted here that no dispute is admitted unless the employer deposits with the Court 50% of the amount due from him as claimed by the Corporation.

Powers of Employees' Insurance Court (Section 78)

The position of the ESI Court is as that of a Domestic Tribunal. As discussed above, the court decides the questions in regard to entitlement of disablement benefit and the claims for recovery of benefit and while deciding the court acts in the capacity of exercising original jurisdiction and not as a court of appeal or a civil court reviewing a decision of the Domestic Tribunal.

According to Section 78 of the Act, the EI Court has all the powers of a Civil Court for the following purposes:

1. Summoning and enforcing the attendance of witnesses.
2. Compelling the discovery and production of documents and material objects.
3. Administering oath and recording evidence.

The ESI Court is deemed to be a Civil Court within the meaning of Section 195 and Chapter XXVI of the Code of Criminal Procedure, 1973. The court follows the procedure as prescribed by rules made by the state government. All costs incidental to any proceeding before an EI Court are subject to the rules made in this behalf by the state government.

It must be noted that an order of the EI Court is enforceable as if it were a decree passed in a suit by a Civil Court.

Appeal (Section 82)

Presentation of an appeal before the High Court from an order of the ESI Court solely depends upon the involvement of substantial question of law. The question whether a particular person is an employee or not is a question of fact and has to be decided on the assessment of facts.

Section 82 directs that no appeal must be attended from an order of EI Court. The Section further clarifies that the High Court will attend to an appeal from an order of an EI Court only if it involves substantial question of law. The period of limitation for an appeal under this Section is 60 days and the provisions of Sections 5 and 12 of the Limitation Act, 1963, are applicable to appeals under this Section.

Stay of Payment Pending Appeal (Section 83)

If the Corporation has presented an appeal against an order of the EI Court, that court, may, and, if so directed by the High Court, is allowed to keep the decision of the appeal pending and withhold the payment of any sum directed to be paid by the order appealed against.

Penalty (Sections 84–86)

The Act provides for penalty for specific offences under Sections 84, 85 and 86. Table 7.1 provides the detail of such offences and respective penalty or punishment decided by the Act under respective Sections.

Offences by the Companies (Section 86A)

Any person who for the purpose of causing any increase in payment or benefit under this Act, or for the purpose of causing any payment or benefit to be made where no payment or benefit is authorized by or under this Act, or for the purpose of avoiding any payment to be made by himself under this Act or enabling any other person to avoid any such payment, knowingly makes or causes to be made any false statement or false representation is punishable with imprisonment or with fine or with both.

If the offender under this Act is a company, every person, who at the time the offence was committed was in charge of, and was responsible to, the company for the conduct of the business of the company, as well as the company, is deemed to be guilty of the offence and is liable to be proceeded against and punished accordingly.

Criminal breach of trust: Non-payment of employees' contribution which is deducted from the wages of the employees but not paid attracts an action under Section 405/406/409 of the Indian Penal Code (IPC). In such cases, the offender is liable for an imprisonment which may extend to 3 years or with fine or both.

TABLE 7.1 Penalties under ESI Act

Section	Offence	Act	Penalty
84	Punishment for false statement	• Whoever, for the purpose of causing any increase in payment • Whoever, for the purpose of causing any payment or benefit to be made where no payment • Whoever, for the purpose of avoiding any payment to be made by himself under this Act • Whoever, enabling any other person to avoid any such payment, knowingly makes • Whoever, made any false statement or false representation	Punishable with imprisonment for a term which may extend to 6 months, or with a fine not exceeding ₹2,000 or with both Provided that where an insured person is convicted under this Section, he shall not be entitled for any cash benefit under this Act for such a period as may be prescribed by the central government
85	Punishment for failure to pay contributions and so on	Fails to pay any contribution which under this Act he is liable to pay	Imprisonment for a term which may extend to 3 years but which shall not be less than 1 year
		In case of failure to pay the employee's contribution which has been deducted by him from the employee's wages	A fine of ₹10,000 and imprisonment which shall not be less than 6 months
		• fails or refuses to submit any return required by the regulations or makes a false return • deducts or attempts to deduct from the wages of an employee the whole or any part of the employer's contribution • obstructs any Inspector or other official of the Corporation in the discharge of his duties	Imprisonment for a term which may extend to 1 year or with fine which may extend to ₹4,000, or with both
85A	Enhanced punishment after previous conviction	Repeated failure by the employer to pay any contribution which under this Act he is liable to pay	Imprisonment for a term which may extend to 5 years but which shall not be less than 2 years and shall also be liable to fine of ₹25,000

Source: Employees' State Insurance Act, 1948.

LO8: Exemptions

- **Exemption of a factory or establishment or class of factories or establishments (Section 87):** The Act empowers the appropriate government to, by notification in the Official Gazette and subject to such conditions as may be specified in the notification, exempt any factory or establishment or class of factories or establishments in any specified area from the operation of this Act for a period not exceeding 1 year and may from time to time by like notification renew any such exemption for periods not exceeding 1 year at a time.

  The above-stated exemption can be granted only if the employees in such factories or establishments are otherwise in receipt of benefits substantially similar or superior to the benefits provided under this Act. The Act further provides that an application for renewal is required to be made 3 months before the date of expiry of the exemption period and a decision on the same is to be taken by the appropriate governments within 2 months of receipt of such application.

- **Exemption of persons or class of persons (Section 88):** The appropriate government can, by notification in the Official Gazette and subject to such conditions as it may deem fit to impose, exempt any person or class of persons employed in any factory or establishment or class of factories or establishments to which this Act applies from the operation of the Act.
- **Corporation to make representation (Section 89):** Section 89 of the Act directs not to exempt or renew under Section 87 or Section 88, unless a reasonable opportunity has been given to the Corporation to make any representation it may wish to make in regard to the proposal and such representation has been considered by the appropriate government. An application in the prescribed format for exemption is to be made to the appropriate government which in turn forwards the same to the Corporation for its comments/representation. The application should be accompanied by documents having the details of various benefits provided by the employer to his employees. On receipt of the exemption application, the regional office/sub-regional office (RO/SRO) examines the benefits provided by the employer to its employees with that provided under the Act and thereafter sends its justification for the same.
- **Exemption of factories or establishments belonging to the government or any local authority (Section 90):** As per Section 90, the appropriate government may, after consultation with the Corporation by notification in the Official Gazette and subject to such conditions as may be specified in the notification, exempt any factory or establishment belonging to any local authority, from the operation of the Act, if the employees in any such factory or establishments otherwise receive benefits substantially similar or superior to the benefits provided under this Act.
- **Exemption from one or more provisions of the Act (Section 91):** The appropriate government may, with the consent of the Corporation, by notification in the Official Gazette, exempt any employees or class of employees in any factory or establishment or class of factories or establishment from one or more of the provisions dealing with the benefits provided under this Act.
- **Exemption to be either prospective or retrospective (Section 91A):** Any notification granting exemption under above-discussed Sections (u/s 87, u/s 88, u/s90 or u/s91) can be issued so as to take effect prospectively (with effect from 1 June 2010) on such dates as may be specified therein.
- **Central government to be appropriate government (Section 91AA):** Notwithstanding anything contained in this Act, in respect of establishments located in the states where medical benefit is provided by the Corporation, the central government is the appropriate government.

Power of State Government to Make Rules (Section 96)

The state government is authorized, after consultation with the Corporation, subject to the condition of previous publication, to make rules not inconsistent with this Act in regard to all or any of the following matters:

1. The constitution of EI Courts, the qualifications of persons who may be appointed judges thereof and the conditions of service of such judges;
2. The procedure to be followed in proceedings before such courts and the execution of orders made by such courts;

3. The fee payable in respect of applications made to the EI Court, the costs incidental to the proceedings in such courts, the form in which applications should be made to it and the particulars to be specified in such applications;
4. The establishment of hospitals, dispensaries and other institutions and the allotment of insured persons or their families to any such hospital, dispensary or other institutions;
5. The scale of medical benefit which shall be provided at any hospital, clinic, dispensary or institution, the keeping of medical records and the furnishing of statistical returns and the nature and extent of the staff, equipment and medicines that shall be provided at such hospitals, dispensaries and institutions;
6. The conditions of service of the staff employed at such hospitals, dispensaries and institutions; and
7. Any other matter which is required or allowed by this Act to be prescribed by the state government.

Summary

1. The ESI Act, 1948, is a social welfare legislation enacted primarily to provide certain benefits to employees in case of sickness, maternity and employment injury and also to make provisions for certain others matters incidental thereto.
2. The ESIC scheme was implemented in a phased manner across the country with the active involvement of respective state governments.
3. The Act in fact aims to attain socio-economic justice enshrined in the Directive Principles of State Policy.
4. The shops and establishments employing more than 20 employees are covered by the Act. All employees including casual, temporary or contract employees drawing wages less than ₹10,000 per month are covered under the Act.
5. All employees including casual, temporary or contract employees drawing wages less than ₹10,000 per month are covered under the Act.
6. Where a workman is covered under the ESI scheme, compensation under the Workmen's Compensation Act cannot be claimed in respect of employment injury.
7. The provisions of the Act are administered by the ESIC.
8. The Corporation comprises of members representing employees, employers, the central and state governments, besides representatives of Parliament and medical professions.
9. Subject to the general superintendence and control of the Corporation, the standing committee administers the affairs of the Corporation.
10. The central government constitutes a Medical Benefit Council advising the Corporation and the standing committee on matters relating to the administration of medical benefit.
11. The employer should get his factory or establishment registered with the Corporation (ESIC) within 15 days after the Act becomes applicable to it and also obtain the employer's code number.
12. After registration with the regional office, a 'temporary identification certificate' is issued to every insured person. It remains valid ordinarily for a period of 3 months.
13. The ESI Corporation may appoint Inspectors to meet the objectives of the Act, within the local limits assigned to each of them.
14. Like most of the social security schemes, the world over, ESI scheme also is a self-financing health insurance scheme.
15. All contributions paid under this Act and all other moneys received on behalf of the Corporation are to be paid into a fund called the ESI Fund.

16. As provided under Section 29 of the Act, the ESIC may subject to such conditions as may be prescribed by the central government, and can hold both movable property and immovable property.
17. The accounts of the Corporation have to be audited annually by the CAG of India and any expenditure incurred by him in connection with such audits is to be paid by the Corporation to the CAG of India (the auditor).
18. Every factory or establishment having more than 10 employees has to be insured under the ESI Act.
19. Currently (with effect from 1 January 1997), the employer is required to contribute at the rate of 4.75% of the wages paid/payable in respect of every wage period.
20. The employees are also required to contribute at the rate of 1.75% of their wages, except when the 'average daily wages in a wage period' are equal to or less than ₹100.
21. There are two contribution periods each of 6 months' duration and two corresponding benefit periods.
22. The employers employing less than 40 employees have to provide self-certification without any certification from the chartered accountants in Return of Contribution.
23. Employees covered under the scheme of the Act are entitled to avail medical facilities for self and dependants.
24. Sickness benefit includes periodical payments made to an insured persons for the period of certified sickness after completing 9 months in insurable employment.
25. Maternity benefit is cash payable to insured women for the specified period of abstention from work for confinement or miscarriage or for sickness arising out of pregnancy, 'confinement', 'premature birth of child or miscarriage'.
26. Disablement benefit is paid in the form of cash instalments, to an employee who is injured in the course of his employment and is, permanently or temporarily, disabled or contacts any occupational disease.
27. Dependants' benefit is a monthly pension payable to the eligible dependants of an insured person who dies as a result of an employment injury or occupational disease.
28. Medical benefit is the medical attendance and treatment to the insured persons covered under the Act and their families as and when needed.
29. The employer must get his factory or establishments registered with the Corporation (ESIC) within 15 days after the Act becomes applicable to it and obtain the employer's code number.
30. The employer must not reduce the wages of an employee on account of the contribution payable by him (employer).
31. The Act empowers the state government to, by notification in the Official Gazette, constitute an ESI Court for such local areas as may be specified in the notification.
32. Any dispute arising under the ESI Act will be decided by the EI Court and not by a Civil Court.
33. The power of reconstitution of an ESI Court is to be exercised in the same manner as the power of constitution, namely by notification in the Official Gazette.
34. Presentation of an appeal before the High Court from an order of the ESI Court solely depends upon the involvement of substantial question of law.
35. The Act provides for penalty for specific offences under Sections 84, 85 and 86.
36. The Act empowers the appropriate government to exempt any factory or establishment or class of factories or establishments in any specified area from the operation of this Act for a period not exceeding 1 year.
37. The appropriate government can exempt any person or class of persons employed in any factory or establishment, or class of factories or establishments, to which this Act applies.

Multiple Choice Questions

1. The ESI Act extends to the whole of India including all the government factories (excluding seasonal factories), which employ ____________ and carry on a manufacturing process with the aid of power.
   a. 10 or more employees
   b. 50 or more employees
   c. 70 or more employees
   d. 100 or more employees
2. The ESI Act extends to the whole of India including all the government factories (excluding seasonal factories), which employ ____________ where manufacturing process is carried out without the aid of power.
   a. 10 or more employees
   b. 20 or more employees
   c. 50 or more employees
   d. 100 or more employees
3. Every employee including casual and temporary employees who is in receipt of wages up to ____________. (with effect from 1 May 10) is entitled to be insured under the Act.
   a. ₹5,000 p.m.
   b. ₹10,000 p.m.
   c. ₹12,000 p.m.
   d. ₹15,000 p.m.
4. ____________ is the highest policy-making and decision-taking authority under the ESI Act which oversees the functioning of the ESI scheme under the Act.
   a. Employees' State Insurance Corporation
   b. Labour Commission
   c. Central government
   d. State government
5. All contributions paid under this Act and all other moneys received on behalf of the Corporation are to be paid into a fund called the
   a. Employers' State Insurance Fund.
   b. Employees' contribution Fund.
   c. Employees' State Insurance Fund.
   d. None of the above.
6. Employees' State Insurance Corporation can hold ____________.
   a. Movable property
   b. Immovable property
   c. Both movable property and immovable property
   d. None of the above
7. Every insured person is entitled to sickness benefit if the contributions in respect of him were payable for not less than ____________ in the corresponding contribution period.
   a. 70 days
   b. 78 days
   c. 730 days
   d. 91 days
8. Maternity benefit is payable if the contributions, in respect of insured woman, were payable for at least ____________ in the two immediately preceding contribution periods.
   a. 70 days
   b. 78 days
   c. 730 days
   d. 91 days

9. For availing the _____________, it is sufficient if it is proved that the injury was caused by an accident arising out of, and in the course of, employment, no matter when it occurred and where it occurred.
   a. Disablement benefit
   b. Dependants' benefit
   c. Sickness benefit
   d. None of the above

10. _____________ is a monthly pension payable to the eligible dependants of an insured person who dies as a result of an employment injury or occupational disease.
   a. Disablement benefit
   b. Dependants' benefit
   c. Sickness benefit
   d. None of the above

11. Medical benefits are admissible for a maximum period of _____________ for the insured person and his/her family.
   a. 70 days
   b. 78 days
   c. 730 days
   d. 91 days

12. The employer must get his factory or establishments registered with the Corporation (ESIC) within _____________ after the Act becomes applicable to it.
   a. 30 days
   b. 15 days
   c. 7 days
   d. 2 days

True/False Questions

1. The principal employer is not primarily liable for payment of contribution in respect of the employee, employed by him through an immediate employer under the Insurance Act.
2. Under the definition of wages, the Act covers all remuneration paid or payable in cash to an employee.
3. The employees earning less than and up to ₹100 per day are exempted from payment of contribution to the ESI Fund.
4. The right to receive any payment of any benefit under this Act is freely transferable or assignable.

Descriptive Questions

1. Discuss the objective and scope of the Employees' State Insurance (ESI) Act, 1948.
2. Write short notes on the following:
   a. Employees under the ESI Act.
   b. Seasonal factory.
   c. Insured person under ESI Act.
3. Throw light on administrative bodies constituted under the ESI Act to enforce different provisions of the Act. Also write their roles and constitution of boards.

4. What is the purpose of the ESI Fund? Discuss various provisions for audit laid down by the ESI Act.
5. What do you understand by Contribution as defined under the ESI Act? Explain general provisions for payment of contribution under the ESI Act.
6. Write short notes on entitlement and standard rates of benefit in relation to the following benefits:
   a. Maternity benefit.
   b. Sickness benefit.
   c. Disablement benefit.
7. Explain in detail general provisions for benefits offered to insured person under the ESI Act, 1948.
8. List the obligations of the employer under the ESI Act, 1948.
9. What are the penalties provided under the ESI Act, 1948, for the contravention of the provisions of the Act?
10. Which are the provisions under the ESI Act, dealing with various exemptions possible from the operation of the ESI Act? Discuss in detail.

8
CHAPTER

The Employees' Provident Funds and Miscellaneous Provisions Act, 1952

LEARNING OBJECTIVES

Upon completing this chapter, the reader would be able to:

LO1. Understand the objectives, scope and important definitions of the Act.
LO2. Gain insights into administration of different schemes provided by the Act.
LO3. Understand the functioning of different boards constituted for the administration of the Act.
LO4. Understand the method of calculation of money due from employers, their recovery and employees' provident funds (EPF) appellate tribunal.
LO5. Know the provisions for the enforcement of the Act.
LO6. Get the details of rules dealing with penalties for offences recognized under the Act.
LO7. Explore various miscellaneous provisions of the Act.

Introduction

The umbrella legislation dealing with provident fund is the Employees' Provident Funds & Miscellaneous Provisions Act, 1952. The main objective of the Act was to make some provisions for the future of industrial workers after their retirement and for their dependants in case of death. The Act provides insurance to workers and their dependants against risks of old age, retirement, discharge, retrenchment or death of the workers. The provisions of the Act are applicable to every establishment which is engaged in any one or more of the industries specified in Schedule I of the Act or any activity notified by central government in the Official Gazette and employing 20 or more persons.

LO1: Objectives, Scope and Important Definitions

Objectives

The Employees Provident Funds and Miscellaneous Provisions Act, 1952, is a beneficial piece of social welfare legislation aimed at promoting and securing the well-being of the employees. Usually, the court does not adopt a narrow interpretation which will have the effect of defeating the very object and purpose the Act. The preamble to the Act states that this is an Act for the employees in factories and other establishments, to provide for the institution of:

1. Provident funds.
2. Pension fund.
3. Deposit-linked insurance fund.

It is with this background that one must interpret the various provisions of the Act and the Scheme related to it.

As mentioned above, the Act aims at providing institution of provident funds, pension funds and deposit-linked insurance funds for the employees in the factories and other establishments. Accordingly, three schemes are in operation under the Act. These schemes taken together extend to the employees the benefits of an old age and survivorship, a long-term protection and security to the employee and after his death to his family members, and timely advances including advances, during sickness and for the purchase/construction of a dwelling house during the period of membership. The three schemes provided by the Act are as follows:

1. Employees' Provident Fund Scheme, 1952.
2. Employees' Deposit-Linked Insurance Scheme, 1976.
3. Employees' Pension Scheme (EPS), 1995 (replacing the Employees' Family Pension Scheme, 1971).

These three schemes aim to provide social security and to inculcate among the employees a spirit of savings while they are gainfully employed and to make provision for their benefit after they retire from service and for their family members after their unfortunate death.

Scope and Applicability

The Employees' Provident Fund and Miscellaneous Provisions Act, 1952, applies to the whole India except Jammu and Kashmir. It is an important social security legislation and is applicable to certain kind of industries/classes of establishments, as notified in the Gazette by the central government, Ministry of Labour from time to time. This Act was made applicable to educational institutions in the year 1982. According to Section 3 of the Act, the Act applies to:

1. Every establishment which is a factory engaged in any industry specified in Schedule I and in which 20 or more persons are employed.
2. Any establishment employing 20 or more persons or class of such establishments which the central government may, by notification in the Official Gazette, specify.

Let us discuss a case to understand the applicability of the Act in a detailed manner (Case 8.1).

Case 8.1: *M/s Tin Printers Pvt. Ltd v. Regional Provident Fund*[1]

M/s Tin Printers Pvt. Ltd (the petitioners) had started a partnership business under a deed of partnership and was engaged in printing and composing work since 1984. At the beginning, there were only five employees with two partners. As the time passed, the number of partners was increased from 2 to 5 and later on 11 employees were engaged. Subsequently, in March 1996, the partnership business was dissolved and the business was converted into a private limited company under the name and style as S.G. Tin Printers Pvt. Ltd, incorporated under the provisions of the Companies' Act.

The Inspector of the Provident Fund Commissioner (the respondent) inspected the establishment, and at such time it was noticed that the establishment engaged 16 employees and 5 directors were shown to be also the employees of the company. The respondent in his letter dated 30 December 1994 communicated to the petitioners that the provisions of the Employees' Provident Fund and Miscellaneous Provisions Act, 1952 (the Act), were applicable since it had engaged more than 20 employees. In response to the said letter, the petitioners denied the applicability of the Act. The matter was then enquired into under Section 7(A) of the Act and the respondents were of the view that since the petitioners' establishment covered under the Act, therefore, they could not disown their liability to make contribution towards the provident fund. The respondents demanded ₹232,196 (Rupees two lakhs thirty-two thousand one hundred and ninety-six only) to be remitted by petitioners latest by October 1998 as their contribution.

The petitioners argued that they constituted a partnership firm and the partners agreed to share profit and loss of the business carried on by all of them, even as they received their salary/pay for the works rendered to the firm, notwithstanding such receipt of salary, the firm would not be liable to pay any contribution. If the directors who had been working as workers in the establishment were excluded from computing the number of persons engaged in the establishment, then the establishment was not covered under the Act. They further contended that in view of the existence of the relationship between the partnership and the firm, it was not open to the authority to treat the partners as an employee so that to make the firm liable to pay the contribution.

Discussion Point

Was the establishment covered under the Act on the basis of number of employees and the appellants could be held liable for the contribution towards the scheme of the Act?

Judgement and Explanation

It was held that an appeal against the order of the respondents could not be accepted and the applicability of the Act is well established. It was further explained that M/s S. G. Tin Printers Pvt. Ltd started their work as a partnership firm in the year 1984 but after the firm was merged into a private limited company, all the characteristics of the partnership firm in existence got merged into a private limited company. Therefore, it has lost all characteristics of the partnership firm after the company was incorporated. Those five directors had been receiving a salary as stated in the balance sheet of the company. There has been master and servant relationship between the company and the working partners. The declaration has been submitted by one of the partners that they are the employees of the company. Therefore, those partners could not be treated as the employees of the company. Accordingly, those 5 directors who have been working as the working partners were to be included in the category of the employees, thus increasing the number of employees to 21 and attracting the coverage of the Act.

---

[1] *M/s Tin Printers Pvt. Ltd. v. Regional Provident Fund* (2000) 2 CALLT 570 HC, 2001 (88) FLR 187.

Non-applicability of the Act to Certain Establishments (as Amended by the Amendment Act, 1988)

Section 16 of the Act mentions that the Act shall not apply to any of the following establishments:

1. The establishments registered under the Co-operative Societies Act, 1912, or under any other law for the time being in force in any state relating to cooperative societies employing less than 50 persons and working without the aid of power; or
2. The establishments belonging to or under the control of the central government or a state government and whose employees are entitled to the benefits of contributory provident fund or old age person in accordance with any scheme or rule framed by the central government or the state government governing such benefits; or
3. The establishments set up under any Central Provincial or State Act and whose employees are entitled to the benefits of contributory provident fund or old age person in accordance with any scheme or rule framed under that Act governing such benefits; or
4. The establishments newly set up until the expiry of a period of 3 years from the date on which such establishment has been set up.

Important Definitions

1. **Appropriate government (Section 2(a)):** 'Appropriate government' means the central government in relation to following:
   a. An establishment belonging to, or under the control of, the central government; or
   b. An establishment connected with a railway company, a major port, a mine or an oilfield or a controlled industry; or
   c. An establishment having departments or branches in more than one state and in relation to any other establishment, the appropriate government is the state government.
2. **Authorized officer (Section 2(aa)):** Authorized officer under the Act is the Central Provident Fund Commissioner, Additional Central Provident Fund Commissioner, Deputy Provident Fund Commissioner, Regional Provident Fund Commissioner or such other officer as may be authorized by the central government, by notification in the Official Gazette.
3. **Basic wages (Section 2(b)):** Basic wages are defined in the act to mean all emoluments which are earned by an employee while on duty or on leave or holiday with wages in either case in accordance with the terms of the contract of employment and which are paid or payable in cash. But, it does not include the following:
   a. The cash value of any food concession.
   b. Any dearness allowance (that is to say, all cash payment by whatever name called paid to an employee on account of a rise in the cost of living), house rent allowance, overtime allowance, bonus, commission or any other allowance payable to the employee in respect of employment or of work done in such employment.
   c. Any present made by the employer.
4. **Contribution (Section 2(c)):** Contribution in the Act stands for a contribution payable in respect of a member under a scheme or the contribution payable in respect of an employee to whom the Insurance Scheme applies.

5. **Controlled industry (Section 2(d)):** The Act declares that any industry is the controlled industry, the control of which by the union has been declared by a Central Act to be expedient in the public interest.
6. **Employer (Section 2(e)):** Employer means:
   a. In relation to an establishment which is a factory, the owner or occupier of the factory, including the agent of such owner or occupier, the legal representative of a deceased owner or occupier and, where a person has been named as a manager of the factory under clause (f) of Subsection (1) of Section 7 of the Factories Act, 1948, the person so named; and
   b. In relation to any other establishment, the person who, or the authority which, has the ultimate control over the affairs of the establishment, and where the said affairs are entrusted to a manager, managing director or managing agent, such manager, managing director or managing agent.
7. **Employee (Section 2(f)):** An employee here means one who is employed for wages in any kind of work, manual or, otherwise, on or in connection with the work of an establishment, and who gets wages directly or indirectly from the employer and includes any person:
   a. Employed by or through a contractor in or in connection with the work of an establishment.
   b. Engaged as an apprentice, not being an apprentice engaged under the Apprentices Act, 1961, or under the standing orders of the establishment.

Here, an apprentice is a person who, according to the certified standing orders applicable to a factory or establishment, is an apprentice or who is declared to be an apprentice by the authority specified by the appropriate government. Thus, personal or domestic servants are not covered under the definition of employees in the Act. It is also to be noted that a person doing work of the principal employer, even though employed by a contractor, is also an employee covered by the definition. It has also been decided by the courts that trainees are not employees and are not covered by the EPF Act.

Case 8.2 will provide the insights into the definition of employee under the act.

Case 8.2: *Sri Rama Vilas Service Ltd v. Regional Provident Fund*[2]

Sri Rama Vilas Service Ltd (the petitioner company) had its goods transport services and also workshop. Besides the permanent employees, the petitioner had been engaging trainees for the purpose of training in accordance with the training scheme, the rules and regulations as well as the standing orders of the company in force. Some trainees were trained on the technical side and some trainees were trained on the nontechnical side. Minimum qualifications and the training period were prescribed. The person who was considered to be trained as a trainee was required to be physically fit and free from any disease or disability. He was required to undergo medical examination either in the company's medical centre or by a medical practitioner authorized by the company. The trainees were paid a consolidated stipend, which used to increase year after year, during the period of training. The management also reserved its right to determine the period of training, if they find that there was no proper response from the trainees.

Thus, it could be seen that a comprehensive training scheme has been prescribed by the petitioner, and persons were recruited as trainees and trained in their respective departments.

[2] *Sri Rama Vilas Service Ltd. v. Regional Provident Fund*, 1999 (2000) ILLJ 709 Mad.

On 11 June 1988, a communication was received from the enforcement officer of the respondent stating that a number of persons were employed in the various departments and they were not enrolled as provident fund members from the date of eligibility. He also directed certain particulars with regard to the trainees to be furnished and the provident fund dues to be paid. The petitioner company replied to the same by their letter dated 3 October 1988, stating that in terms of the provisions of the standing orders applicable to the petitioner company, they had classified the trainees as learners, who might be paid or unpaid during the period of such training and it was also not obligatory on the part of the petitioner company to provide an apprentice with work, in the company after his training period got over. The petitioner company further clarified that the engagement of a trainee was in accordance with the training scheme and that the training was given to the individuals who possessed the requisite qualifications. The petitioner company also pointed out that the trainees were paid a stipend and were not eligible for any other benefits, monetary or otherwise, which were extended to the permanent category of workmen. The company explained that the trainees were recruited for a specified period under the scheme and there was no guarantee for their employment in the company after the completion of the training period.

The respondent did not accept the contention of the petitioner company and sent a notice on 16 December 1989, stating that the Regional Provident Fund Commissioner would be holding an enquiry in accordance with Section 7A of the EPF & MP Act. After hearing the petitioner company and going through the written submissions of the petitioner, the respondent by his order dated 11 October 1990, holding that the trainees were all employees under the Employees' Provident Funds (EPF) Act and directed that a total sum of ₹63,700.85 which comprised contribution to the tune of ₹51,310 and other charges to be remitted within 15 days from the receipt of the impugned order.

The petitioner company appealed in the Supreme Court against the order of the respondent.

Discussion Point

Whether the apprentice or trainees could be treated as a regular employee and were covered under the definition of employee in the Employees' Provident Funds and Miscellaneous Provisions Act, 1952.

Judgement and Explanation

In the Supreme Court case, it was held that the respondent could not consider the persons in question therein as employees of the petitioner company and claim contribution from the petitioner for the payments made to them. It was further stated that certain payments were made during the apprenticeship, by whatever name called, and that the apprentice had to be under certain rules of discipline did not convert the apprentice as a regular employee under the employer. Such a person remained a learner and was not an employee. Thus, the Supreme Court set the order of the respondent aside.

8. **Excluded employee (Section 2(ff))**: Excluded employee has been defined in Section 2(ff) to mean an employee:
    a. Who having been a member of the fund, withdrew the full amount of his accumulations on retirement or emigration or
    b. Whose pay at the time he is otherwise entitled to become a member of the fund exceeds ₹15,000 per month.
9. **Exempted establishment (Section 2(fff))**: The exempted establishment is an establishment in respect of which an exemption has been granted under Section 17 from the operation of all or any of the provisions of any Scheme or the Insurance Scheme, as the case may be, whether such exemption has been granted to the establishment as such or to any person or class of persons employed therein.

The central government may, by notification in the Official Gazette and subject to such conditions, exempt any establishment prospectively or retrospectively, from operation of all or any of the provisions of the EPF Scheme, if:

a. The rules relating to its provident fund are not less favourable that of Section 6 of the EPF Act; or
b. Its employees are in enjoyment of benefits in the nature of PF, pension or gratuity, which are not less favourable to employees covered by the Act or the Scheme.

If an establishment is exempted from any of the provisions of the Act, then such an institution must have its own trust and fulfil following requirements:

i. It must have a Board of Trustees for the trust.
ii. It must maintain detailed accounts.
iii. It should submit such returns to the Regional PF Commissioner.
iv. The establishment must invest monies in accordance with the directions of the central government issued from time to time.
v. It must transfer the account of any employee, where necessary.
vi. It must perform such other duties as may be specified.

10. **Factory (Section 2(g)):** In the Act, factory is any premises, including the precincts thereof, in any part of which a manufacturing process is being carried on or is ordinarily so carried on, whether with the aid of power or without the aid of power.

Let us discuss a case to better understand the concept of factory and exempted establishments under the Act (Case 8.3).

Case 8.3: *Hotel Mahaveer and Ors. v. Regional Provident Fund*[3]

Hotel Mahaveer (the appellants) ran two businesses, namely, Hotel New Abiruchi Restaurant and Mahaveer Lodge, from the same premises in Hassan. Provident Fund Commissioner (the respondent) took into consideration the combined employee strength of these two businesses called upon the appellants to comply with the provisions of the Employees' Provident Funds and Miscellaneous Provisions Act, 1952 (the Act). The appellants disputed the applicability of the Act on the grounds that the two businesses were two distinct and separate establishments and the employee strength of each unit, separately, never exceeded 19 and, therefore, the Act was not applicable to either of the establishments.

The respondent did not accept the argument and then enquired the matter under Section 7A of the Act and reached to the conclusion that the Act was applicable to the two businesses as they were, for the purposes of the Act, one and the same establishment. Thus, having the commissioner held on the question of applicability of the Act called upon the appellants to comply with the Act and also quantified the total dues to be paid by the appellants.

Aggrieved, the appellants moved the higher court against the order of the commissioner (the respondent) and contended on a number of factors such as the businesses being carried on by two different partnership firms, they being assessed separately for tax, the maintenance of two different accounts which were being audited separately too and the fact that the businesses were operated under two different licences, no functional integrity and therefore, the establishments could not be treated as one entity for the

[3] *Hotel Mahaveer and Ors. v. Regional Provident Fund*, 2002 (92) FLR 1131.

purposes of the Act. On the other hand, the respondent submitted that there was functional or financial dependence between the two businesses and, therefore, they had to be treated as 'one establishment' for the purposes of the Act.

Discussion Point

Could the two establishments be treated as one and therefore attracting the applicability of the Employees' Provident Funds and Miscellaneous Provisions Act, 1952?

Judgement and Explanation

It was held that the respondent made no mistake in concluding that the two units to be treated as one establishment. It was further stated that from deeper probe into the functional aspects of these two units, the functional or financial dependence between the two businesses was well established. There was no bar on the authorities to lift the veil of a company, whether a manufacturer or a buyer, to see it was not wearing the mask of not being treated as related person when, in fact, both the manufacturer and the buyer were in fact the same persons. Thus, the order passed by the first respondent treating the two units as one establishment was well founded.

11. **Fund (Section 2(h)):** The Act declares that 'Fund' means the provident fund established under a Scheme.
12. **Industry (Section 2(i)):** 'Industry' stands for any industry specified in Schedule I and includes any other industry added to the Schedule by notification under Section 4.
13. **Manufacturer or manufacturing process (Section 2(i-c)):** The Act declares that 'manufacture' or 'manufacturing process' means any process for making, altering, repairing, ornamenting, finishing, packing, oiling, washing, cleaning, breaking up, demolishing or otherwise treating or adapting any article or substance with a view to its use, sale, transport, delivery or disposal.
14. **Member (Section 2(j)):** 'Member' under the Act means a member of the fund.
15. **Occupier of a factory (Section 2(k)):** 'Occupier of a factory' is the person who has ultimate control over the affairs of the factory, and, where the said affairs are entrusted to a managing agent, such agent shall be deemed to be the occupier of the factory.
16. **Pension fund (Section 2(ka)):** 'Pension fund' stands for the Employees' Pension Fund established under Subsection (2) of Section 6A.
17. **Pension scheme (Section 2(kb)):** 'Pension scheme' under the Act is the Employees' Pension Scheme framed under Subsection (1) of Section 6A.
18. **Retaining allowances** are the allowances payable for the time being to an employee of any factory or other establishment during any period in which the establishment is not working, for retaining his services.

LO2: Administration of the Schemes under the Act

Since its enactment in 1952, the Act has been amended several times. The Act is administered by the Government of India through the Employees' Provident Fund Organisation (EPFO) which is one of the largest provident fund institutions in the world in terms of members and volume of financial transactions that it has been carrying on. This organization is an autonomous tripartite body under the control of the Ministry of Labour. Its head office is in New Delhi. The main aim of EPFO is to extend the reach and quality of publicly managed old-age income security programmes through its consistent efforts and ever-improving standards of compliance and benefit delivery system to its members. This way it seeks to contribute to the economic and social well-being of the country.

Constitution and Functions of EPFO

The Act and Schemes framed are administered by a tripartite board known as the Central Board of Trustees. EPFO functions under the overall superintendence of the policies framed by this board. This board is headed by Union Minister for Labour as Chairman. It administers a contributory provident fund, pension scheme and an insurance scheme for the workforce engaged in the organized sector in India. The board consists of representatives of

1. Government (both central and state).
2. Employers.
3. Employees.

The board functions to

1. Administer the funds created and vested in the Board and performing other works incidental thereto.
2. Maintain accounts of income and expenditure in the prescribed form and manner.
3. Delegate the powers for administration of the schemes.
4. Submit audited accounts with comments and annual report on performance of the organization to government.

Employees' Provident Fund Scheme, 1952

Establishment of the Fund (Section 5)

Section 5 of the Act provides the EPF Scheme 1952 which is a contributory Provident Fund. This fund is created with a purpose of providing financial security and stability to elderly people. Generally, one contributes in these funds when one starts as employee and the contributions are generally made on monthly basis. The main purpose of this fund is to help employees save a fraction of their salary every month which can be used in an event that the employee is temporarily or no longer fit to work or at retirement. The investments made by a number of people/employees are pooled together and invested by a trust. The fund is vested in and administered by the Central Board constituted under Section 5A.

Employees Required to Join the Fund and Registration

The EPF Scheme lists following employees who are required to join the fund:

1. Every employee employed in or in connection with the work of the factory or other establishment to which the EPF Scheme applies except an employee who is drawing a salary exceeding ₹15,000 in a month (excluded employee).

2. Every employee is required to join the fund from the date of joining the factory or establishment.
3. Every excluded employee on his ceasing to be excluded employee has to make an application jointly with the employer.

When an organization finds that the Employees' Provident Fund and Miscellaneous Provisions Act, 1952, is applicable to it, it is required to fill in a pro forma for registration. The duly filled-in pro forma along with one or more of the documents mentioned in the pro forma is to be submitted to the respective provident fund offices for getting the registration. It should be noted here that employees who are drawing basic salary above ₹6,500 and are enrolled under PF and intends to continue contributing towards PF need to submit a joint undertaking.

Contribution (Section 6)

The contribution to be paid by the employer to the fund is 8.33% of the basic wages, dearness allowances and retaining allowance (if any) for the time being payable to each of the employees, while employees' contribution is equal to the contribution payable by the employer in respect of him. If any employee so desires and if the Scheme makes provision therefore, the employee may contribute an amount not exceeding 8.33% of his basic wages, dearness allowances and retaining allowance (if any), subject to the condition that the employer shall not be under an obligation to pay any contribution over and above his contribution payable under the Act.

Dearness and retaining allowance: For this section, 'dearness allowance' includes the cash value of any food concession allowed to the employee. The 'retaining allowance' here means an allowance payable for the time being to an employee for retaining his services, when the establishment is not working. Basic wage means as defined under Section 2(b) of the Act and explained above. However, the encashment of leave does not fall under dearness allowance or retaining allowance or basic wages and is not to be considered while computing the amount to be deposited under the EPF Act.

Upper limit: There is no upper limit for contribution by an employee towards the EPF.

Calculation of contribution (contribution by employer and employee): The contribution paid by the employer is 12% of basic wages plus dearness allowance plus retaining allowance. An equal contribution is payable by the employee also. In the case of establishments which employ less than 20 employees or meet certain other conditions, as per the EPFO rules, the contribution rate for both employee and the employer is limited to 10%.

Payment of contribution: The employer, in the first instance, has to pay both the contribution payable by himself towards employer's contribution and also, on behalf of the member employed by him directly or by/through a contractor, the contribution payable by such member. So far as the employees employed by or through a contractor are concerned, the contractor has to recover the contribution payable by such employee pay to the principal employer the amount of member's contribution so deducted together with an equal amount of contribution and inspection charges too.

Thus, it is the responsibility of the principal employer to pay both the contributions payable by himself in respect of the employees directly employed by him and also in respect of the employees employed by or through a contractor and also inspection charges.

Recovery of a Member's Share of Contribution

The amount of a member's contribution paid by the employer (or a contractor) is to be recoverable by means of deduction from the wages of the member and not otherwise, provided it does not violate the provisions of any law for the time being in force or there is no contract to the contrary.

It is to be kept in mind that such deduction can be made only from the wages which is paid in respect of the period or part of the period in respect of which the contribution is payable. However, the employer (or a contractor) is entitled to recover the employees' share from a wage other than that which is paid in respect of the period for which the contribution has been paid or is payable where the employee has in writing given a false declaration at the time of joining service with the employer (or a contractor) that he was not already a member of the fund. In case where no such deductions were made on account of an accidental mistake or a clerical error, such deductions may, with the consent in writing of the Regional Provident Fund Commissioner, be made from the subsequent wages.

Investment

It is the constant endeavour of the EPFO to find ways and means of providing the members of Employees' Provident Fund with best return of the contributions and in the process to adopt the basic parameters of investment, namely, safety and yield. To achieve this, timely and judicious investment of funds is made.

The monies of the fund not immediately required by the Board of Trustees are to be invested by the Board within 2 weeks from the date of receipt of contribution from the employer, in the pattern prescribed by the central government from time to time. The securities are obtained in the name of trust. These securities are in dematerialized (DEMAT) form and in case the required facility is not available in the areas where the trust operates, the Board of Trustees is required to inform the Regional Provident Fund Commissioner, concerned about the same.

Advances and Withdrawals from the Fund

The members can withdraw monies as advances from their PF Account for purposes such as marriage, education and medical treatment, subject to the prescribed conditions as mentioned here below.

So far as final withdrawal is concerned, a member is eligible to apply for withdrawing his provident fund and pension fund only after 2 months from the date of resignation, subject to the condition that he/she is not employed during the said 2 months. The Board of Trustees may on an application from such member in a form as may be prescribed and subject to the conditions mentioned above sanction from the standing to the credit of the member in the Fund a withdrawal. Normally, it takes about 40 days to have the monies credited to the bank account of the member after applying for withdrawal.

Taxation: The withdrawn advance money is totally tax-free and interest-free, while the withdrawals are exempt from tax only if the concerned employee has rendered continuous service of more than 5 years. Otherwise, it would be taxable at the applicable slab rates.

Employees' Pension Scheme, 1995

Establishment of Employees' Pension Fund (Section 6A)

The Government framed the EPS, 1995, and Employees' Family Pension Scheme got merged under the new scheme. The pension scheme is financed by diverting 8.33% of employer's monthly contribution from the EPF (restricted to 8.33% of 15,000 or ₹1,250) and government's contribution of 1.17% of the worker's monthly wages. The purpose of the scheme is to provide for:

1. **Superannuation pension** to the member who has rendered eligible service of 20 years and retires on attaining the age of 58 years.

2. **Retiring pension** to the member who has rendered eligible service of 20 years and retires or otherwise ceases to be in employment before attaining the age of 58 years.
3. **Permanent total disablement pension** to the member who is permanently totally disabled as a result of the work-related injury or occupational disease (an illness or condition caused by your employment). Here, 'permanent total disablement' means such disablement of permanent nature that incapacitates an employee for all work which he/she was capable of performing at the time of disablement, regardless whether such disablement is sustained in the course of employment or otherwise.
4. **Short service pension** to the member has to render eligible service of 10 years and more but less than 20 years.

Eligibility for the scheme: The EPS was compulsory for all the existing members of the Family Pension Scheme and those who became members of the Employees' Provident Fund Scheme on or after 16 November 1995, besides the following employees who had an option to join the new Scheme:

1. Employees who ceased to be members of the pension fund between 1 April 1993 and 15 November 1995.
2. Employees who were the members of the Provident Fund as on 16 November 1995 and not members of the pension fund.
3. Members who died between 1 April 1993 and 15 November 1995 were deemed to have exercised the option of joining the scheme on the date of the death.

New joiners: New joiners drawing basic salary above ₹15,000 at the time of joining will not be eligible for EPS, 1995. However, if he/she is already a member of pension with his/her previous employer and wishes to transfer his/her PF/EPS, he/she would continue to be a member of pension scheme subject to the condition that his/her pension contribution will be restricted to salary of ₹15,000 only.

Existing employees: In case of existing employees, who are contributing towards pension scheme beyond the statutory limit and intend to continue contributing towards the pension scheme beyond the statutory limit, they need to exercise the fresh option of contributing towards pension scheme beyond ₹1,500, within a period of 6 months from 1 September 2014. The employees who opt for the aforesaid option will have to contribute towards the government share of contribution at 1.16% on the salary exceeding ₹15,000 per month from his/her share of contribution.

Term of scheme: Every member of the Employees' Pension Fund Scheme continues to remain the member till the earliest happening of any of the following events:

1. He attains the age of 58 years; or
2. He avails the withdrawal benefit to which he is entitled vide paragraph 14 of the scheme; or
3. He dies; or
4. The pension is vested in him.

The EPS, 1995, provides that all monies accruing to Employees' Pension Fund except the contributions of the central government are to be invested in accordance with the provisions of the Employees' Provident Fund Scheme, 1952.

Minimum amount of pension payable: According to the Act, the minimum pension or relief payable under the Act to any existing or future member or in case of the member's death to his widow/widower shall not be less than ₹1,000 per month. The minimum children pension for each child is ₹250, while the minimum monthly orphan pension which is payable where a deceased member is out survived by any widow or where the pension is not payable to the widow (in case of remarriage) is ₹750.

Computation of pensionable salary: For all the cases of exit and death, the pensionable salary (i.e., the salary based on which pension is to be computed) will be the average monthly pay drawn during the contributory period of service in the span of 60 months preceding the date of the exit from membership of the pension fund or death of the employee. However, in case of exit/death up to 31 August 2014, average monthly pay drawn during the contributory period of service shall be 12 months only.

It should also be noted here that the pensionable salary is determined on a pro-rata basis for the pensionable service up to 31 August 2014, subject to a maximum of ₹6,500 per month and for the period with effect from 1 September 2014, subject to the maximum of ₹15,000 per month. The same rule will be applicable for withdrawal benefit.

Special Grant by Central Government

Section 17(1C) of the Act provides for grant of exemption from the operation of EPS, 1995. It is granted by the appropriate government through a notification in the Official Gazette. Exemption may be granted to an establishment as a whole or to a class of establishments. The grant of exemption is subject to the conditions specified by the appropriate government. The exemption is granted where the establishment or the class of establishments are in enjoyment of benefits in a nature of pensionary benefits which are at par, or are more favourable than the benefits provided under this Scheme.

Employees' Deposit-linked Insurance Scheme and Fund (EDLI), 1976

Employees' Deposit-linked Insurance Scheme (EDLI) (Section 6C)

The EDLI scheme was launched in 1976. All employers who provide Employee's Provident Fund (EPF) provisions to their employees are covered under this scheme. The purpose of the scheme is to provide life insurance coverage to all their employees. This benefit under the Act is termed as 'assurance benefit'.

'Assurance benefit' under the Act means a payment linked to the average balance in the Provident Fund Account of an employee, payable to a person belonging to his family or otherwise entitled to it in the event of death of the employee while being a member of the Fund.

Subscription to EDLI: The EDLI Scheme is clubbed and linked to the EPF scheme and EPS scheme. All employees who subscribe to the EPF scheme get automatically enrolled in the EDLI scheme. If the employee is not able to choose which of these three schemes (EPF, EPS and EDLI) he or she wishes to subscribe to, the schemes are transferrable when the employee shifts jobs. In such cases, the contributions will continue in the same account from the new employer.

Contribution under the Scheme

The contribution payable by the employer and the central government under Subsection (2) and Subsection (3) of Section 6C of the Act is calculated on the basis of the basic wages, dearness allowance (including the cash value of any food concession) and retaining allowance, if any, actually drawn during the whole month whether paid on daily, weekly, fortnightly or monthly basis. It is further provided that where the monthly pay of an employee exceeds ₹5,000, the contribution payable in respect of him

BOX 8.1: Formula to Calculate the Contribution under the EDLI Scheme

Employee's Provident Fund (EPF) contribution by Employee: 12%.
Employee's Provident Fund (EPF) contribution by Employer: 12% minus EPS contribution.
Employees' Pension Scheme (EPS) contribution by Employee: none.
Employees' Pension Scheme (EPS) contribution by Employer: 8.33% (subject to a maximum of ₹1,250).
EDLI contribution by Employee: none.
EDLI contribution by Employer: 0.50% (subject to a maximum of ₹75).

by the employer and the central government shall be limited to the amounts payable on a monthly pay of ₹5,000 including dearness allowance, retaining allowance if any and cash value of food concession.

Contributions to the scheme are calculated by using a formula of a fixed percentage of dearness allowance and salary. The formula is given in Box 8.1.

Employer's contribution not to be deducted from the wages of the employees: The point to be noted here is that the employee does not contribute to EDLI Scheme and the amount due under this scheme cannot be attached by any decree or order of any court, nor can it be assigned or charged.

Deposit-linked Insurance Fund Account: The amount received as the employer's contribution and also the central government's contribution to the Insurance Fund under Subsections 2 and 3 of Section 6C is credited to an account called the 'Deposit-Linked Insurance Fund Account'. All expenses towards the cost of any benefits provided by or under the Scheme are to be met out of this account.

Scales of Assurance Benefit and the Minimum Average Balance to Be Maintained by an Employee

Assurance benefit to full-time employee: In case of death of an employee, who was a member of the Fund or of a provident fund exempted under Section 17 of the Act, as the case may be, the persons entitled to receive the provident fund accumulations of the deceased must, in addition to such accumulations be paid an amount, equal to the average balance in the account of the deceased in the fund or of a provident fund exempted under Section 17 of the Act, as the case may be, during preceding 12 months or during the period of his membership, whichever is less, except where the average balance exceeds ₹25,000. When the amount payable exceeds ₹25,000, the payable amount shall be ₹25,000 plus 25% of the amount in excess of ₹25,000 up to maximum ₹35,000.

Assurance benefit to part-time employee: In the case of a part-time employee who was a member of the Fund or of a provident fund exempted under Section 17 of the Act, as the case may be, while serving in more than one factory or establishment, the quantum of benefit under this Scheme is determined with reference to the average of the aggregate balance in all his accounts in the Fund or of a provident fund exempted under Section 17 of the Act, as the case may be, during the preceding 12 months (Box 8.2).

Procedure to Claim the 'Assured Benefit' under EDLI Scheme

Claimants under the scheme: The amount payable can be claimed by the nominee of the deceased employee. If there has been no nominee named, the surviving family members of the deceased employee

BOX 8.2: Features and Benefits of EDLI Scheme

1. Claim amount under the EDLI Scheme turns out to be 30 times the salary.
2. Salary for the calculation of contribution under the EDLI Scheme is calculated as (dearness allowance + basic salary).
3. The quantum of coverage is directly linked to the salary of the employee.
4. Premium payable is similar for all employees, and factors like age and so on are not considered for this purpose.
5. Similarly, age and other individual factors do not affect any employee's eligibility to be covered under this scheme.
6. The contribution towards this scheme is 0.50% of the employee's salary and is payable only by the employer.
7. Payments are made by the employer to the Provident Fund Authorities and the employee is not required to contribute under this scheme.
8. Under Section 17(2A) of the Act, the employer can opt out of contributing to this scheme if the employer has already opted for a better insurance policy for its employees under a different scheme.
9. The employer has an option to choose the schemes like the LIC Group Insurance Scheme over EDLI scheme.

can claim the amount. If no nomination subsists or if the nomination relates only to part of the amount standing to his credit in the Fund or of a provident fund exempted under Section 17 of the Act, as the case may be, the whole amount or the part thereof to which the nomination does not relate, as the case may be, shall become payable to the members of his family in equal shares. However, no share shall be payable to:

1. Sons who have attained majority.
2. Sons of a deceased son who have attained majority.
3. Married daughters whose husbands are alive.
4. Married daughters of a deceased son whose husbands are alive.

In case there is no nominee or eligible surviving family member, the claim can be made by the legal heir. While none of the above category of claimants are surviving, then the claim can be made by the legal guardian.

Procedure to claim: While filling out the claim, it should be kept in mind that the claim under the EDLI is only admissible if the deceased person was actively employed at the time of death. In order to initiate the claims process, the nominee or nominees or other claimants are required to send a written application to the commissioner through the employer in such form as the commissioner may specify, to claim payment under this Scheme. In case the employer is no longer able/available to attest the claim application, attestation can also be done with the official seal of either of the following authorities:

1. Gazetted officer.
2. Magistrate.
3. President of village panchayat.
4. Chairman/Secretary/Member of Municipal or District Local Board.

5. Postmaster or sub-postmaster.
6. MP or MLA.
7. Member of CBT or Regional Committee of EPF.
8. Bank manager (of the bank in which the account was maintained).

If the person to whom any amount is to be paid under this Scheme is a minor or a lunatic, the payment is made in accordance with the provisions in the EPF Scheme, 1952, relating to payment to such persons. The payment may be made, at the option of the person to whom payment is to be made:

1. By postal money order, or
2. By deposit in the payee's bank account in any Scheduled Bank or any Co-operative Bank (including the Urban Co-operative Bank) or any post office, or
3. By deposit in the payee's name (the whole or part of the amount) in the form of annuity term deposits scheme in any Nationalized Bank, or
4. Through the employer.

The claims complete in all respects along with the requisite documents must be submitted to the commissioner. The benefit amount payable to the beneficiaries must be paid within 30 days from the date of its receipt by the commissioner. If he finds any deficiency in the claim, the same is required to be recorded in writing and communicated to the applicant within 30 days from the date of receipt of such application. If the commissioner fails in doing so without sufficient cause to settle a claim complete in all respect within 30 days, the commissioner is held liable for the delay beyond the set period and penal interest 12% per annum may be charged on the benefit amount and the same may be deducted from the salary of the commissioner.

Recovery of Damages for Default in Payment of Any Contribution: Where an employer defaults in the payment of any contribution to the Insurance Fund, or in the payment of any charges payable under any other provision of the Act or of the Scheme, the Central Provident Fund Commissioner or such officer as may be authorized by the central government, by notification in the Official Gazette, in this behalf, may recover from the employer, by way of penalty, damages at the rates given in Table 8.1.

The damages are calculated to the nearest rupee, ₹0.50 or more to be counted as the nearest higher rupee and fraction of a rupee less than ₹0.50 must be ignored.

TABLE 8.1 Recovery of Damages from Employer

Period of Default Rate of Damages	*Percentage of Arrears Per Annum*
Less than 2 months	17
Two months and above but less than 4 months	22
Four months and above but less than 6 months	27
Six months and above	37

Source: https://taxguru.in/corporate-law/rates-contribution-epf-eps-edli-admin-charges-india.html?amp

TABLE 8.2 Rates of Contribution of EPF, EPS, EDLI, Admin Charges in India

Scheme	*Employee's Contribution (%)*	*Employer's Contribution (%)*
Employee Provident Fund	12	3.67
Employees' Pension Scheme	0	8.33
Employees Deposit-linked Insurance	0	0.5
EPF Administrative Charges	0	1.1
EDLIS Administrative Charges	0	0.01

Source: https://taxguru.in/corporate-law/rates-contribution-epf-eps-edli-admin-charges-india.html?amp
Note: In industries like beedi, jute, guar gum factories, coir industry (other than spinning sector), the employee's contribution is 10% and employer's contribution is 1.67%.

Summary of employer's contribution towards EPF and pension fund: The employer is required to contribute the following amounts towards EPF and pension fund (Table 8.2):

1. **In case of establishments having less than 20 employees or a sick industrial Board of Industrial and Financial Reconstruction (BIFR) company or 'sick establishments' or any establishment in the jute, beedi, brick, coir or gaur gum industry**—the employer contributes 10% of the basic wages, dearness allowance and retaining allowance, if any.
2. **In case of all other establishments' employing 20 or more employees**—the employer contributes 12% of basic wages, dearness allowance and retaining allowance, if any.
   a. A part of the contribution is remitted to the pension fund and the remaining balance continues to remain in Provident Fund Account.
   b. Where the pay of an employee exceeds ₹15,000 per month, the contribution payable to pension fund is limited to the amount payable on his pay of ₹15,000 only.
   c. 'Basic wages' includes all emoluments as defined under Section 2(b) of the Act and explained in the previous section of the chapter.
   d. The employer is also required to pay administrative charges at 1.10% of emoluments towards provident fund charges and 0.01% towards EDLI Scheme 1976.

LO3: Administration of the Act

Central Board (Section 5A)

Constitution of the board: The central government is authorized to issue a notification in the Official Gazette with effect from such date as may be specified therein to constitute a Board of Trustees for the territories to which this Act extends. The Board consists of following persons as members namely:

1. A Chairman and a Vice Chairman to be appointed by the central government;
   a. the Central Provident Fund Commissioner, ex officio.

2. Not more than five persons appointed by the central government from among its officials.
3. Not more than 15 persons representing governments of such states as the central government may specify in this behalf, appointed by the central government.
4. Ten persons representing employers of the establishments to which the Scheme applies, appointed by the central government after consultation with such organizations of employers as may be recognized by the central government in this behalf.
5. Ten persons representing employees in the establishments to which the Scheme applies, appointed by the central government after consultation with such organizations of employees as may be recognized by the central government in this behalf.

Functions of the board: The Central Board administers the fund vested in it in such a manner as may be specified in the Scheme. The Central Board also performs such other functions as it may be required to perform by or under any provisions of the Scheme (Family Pension Scheme and the Insurance Scheme). The Central Board maintains proper accounts of its income and expenditure in such form and in such manner as the central government, after consultation with the CAG of India, specifies in the Scheme.

Audit of the accounts of the board: The accounts of the Central Board are audited annually by the CAG of India and any expenditure incurred by him in connection with such audit is payable by the Central Board to the CAG of India. The accounts of the Central Board as certified by the CAG of India or any other person appointed by him in this behalf together with the audit report thereon are forwarded to the Central Board. Thereafter, the Central Board forwards the same to the central government along with its comments on the report of the CAG.

Executive Committee (Section 5AA)

Constitution and functions of the board: The central government is empowered to constitute an Executive Committee by issuing a notification in the Official Gazette with effect from such date as may be specified therein. The Executive Board functions to assist the Central Board in the performance of its functions.

The Executive Committee consists of the following persons as members, namely:

1. A chairman appointed by the central government from among the members of the Central Board.
2. Two persons appointed by the central government from among the persons referred to in clause (b) of Subsection (1) of Section 5A.
3. Three persons appointed by the central government from among the persons referred to in clause (c) of Subsection (1) of Section 5A.
4. Three persons representing the employers elected by the Central Board from among the persons referred to in clause (d) of Subsection (1) of Section 5A.
5. The Central Provident Fund Commissioner, ex officio.

Membership of the executive committee: The Scheme provides for the terms and conditions subject to which a member of the Central Board is appointed or elected to the Executive Committee and the time, place and procedure of the meetings of the Executive Committee.

State Board (Section 5B)

Constitution and functions of the board: The Scheme provides the manner in which the central government, after consultation with the government of any state, by notification in the Official Gazette, constitutes for that state a Board of Trustees. The State Board exercises such powers and performs such duties as the central government assigns to it from time to time. The Scheme also provides the terms and conditions subject to which a member of a State Board is appointed and the time, place and procedure of the meetings of a State Board.

State Board to be a body corporate: Every Board of Trustees constituted under Section 5A or Section 5B is a body corporate under the name specified in the notification constituting it, having perpetual succession and a common seal and shall by the said name sue and be sued.

Appointment of officers: The following officers are appointed to discharge various duties for the State Board:

1. **Central Provident Fund commissioner:** The central government appoints a Central Provident Fund Commissioner who is the chief executive officer of the Central Board who functions under the general control and superintendence of that Board.
2. **Financial adviser and chief accounts officer:** The central government also appoints a Financial Adviser and Chief Accounts Officer to assist the Central Provident Fund Commissioner in the discharge of his duties.
3. **Other officers:** The Central Board appoints Deputy Provident Fund Commissioners, Regional Provident Fund Commissioners, Assistant Provident Fund Commissioners and such other officers and employees as it may consider necessary for the efficient administration of the Scheme.

It is to be noticed here that the appointment to the post of the Central Provident Fund Commissioner or a Financial Advisor and Chief Accounts Officer or any other post under the Central Board carrying a scale of pay equivalent to the scale of pay of any Group 'A' or Group 'B' post under the Central Government can be done only in consultation with the Union Public Service Commission.

Delegation (Section 5E)

For the efficient administration of the Scheme, the Central Board can delegate its functions and powers to the Executive Committee or to the Chairman of the Board or to any of its officers. While a State Board can delegate to its Chairman or to any of its officers, subject to such conditions and limitations, if any, as it may specify, such of its powers and functions under this Act as it may deem necessary for the efficient administration of the Scheme.

LO4: Calculation of Money Due from Employers, Their Recovery and Employees' Provident Funds Appellate Tribunal

Determination of Money Due from the Employers (Section 7A)

If there arises a dispute, regarding the applicability of this Act to an establishment or regarding the determining the amount due from any employer under any provision of this Act, the Scheme or the Insurance Scheme, the following officers are empowered to decide such dispute:

1. The Central Provident Fund Commissioner.
2. Additional Central Provident Fund Commissioner.
3. Deputy Provident Fund Commissioner.
4. Regional Provident Fund Commissioner.
5. Assistant Provident Fund Commissioner.

For any of the aforesaid purposes, any of the above-mentioned officers may conduct such inquiry as he may deem necessary.

Powers of the inquiry officer: The officer conducting the inquiry as mentioned above (under Subsection (1)) is entrusted with the same powers as are vested in a court under the Code of Civil Procedure, 1908, for trying a suit in respect of the following matters:

1. Enforcing the attendance of any person or examining him on oath.
2. Requiring the discovery and production of documents.
3. Receiving evidence on affidavit.
4. Issuing commissions for the examination of witnesses.

Any such inquiry is deemed to be judicial proceeding within the meaning of Sections 193 and 228, and for the purpose of Section 196 of the IPC.

Review of the Orders Passed under Section 7A (Section 7B)

The review of the order (under Subsection (1) of Section 7A) passed by an officer appointed under the provisions of the Act from which no appeal has been preferred under this Act is possible when the aggrieved person applies for the review in any of the following circumstances:

1. The aggrieved person discovers new and important matter or evidence which, after the exercise of due diligence, was not within his knowledge or could not be produced by him at the time when the order was made.
2. There was some mistake or error apparent on the face of the record.
3. There are some other sufficient reasons to review the decision or order.

An officer may also on his own motion review his order if he is satisfied that it is necessary so to do on any such ground which is mentioned above.

Every application for review is to be filed in such form and manner and within such time as may be specified in the Scheme. The officers can reject the application for review if it appears to him that there is no sufficient ground for review. But, if the officer is of the opinion that the application for review should be granted, he grants the same.

Determination of the Escaped Amount (Section 7C)

Where an order determining the amount due from an employer under Section 7A or Section 7B has been passed, the officer who passed the order is empowered to reopen the case and pass appropriate orders redetermining the amount due from the employer in accordance with the provisions of this Act.

However, the reopening or redetermining the amount can be done within a period of 5 years from the date of communication of the order passed only if the officer who passed the order:

1. Has reason to believe that by reason of the omission or failure on the part of the employer to make any document or report available, or to disclose, fully and truly, all material facts necessary for determining the correct amount due from the employer, any amount so due from such employer for any period has escaped his notice.
2. Has in consequence of information in his possession, reason to believe that any amount to be determined under Section 7A or Section 7B has escaped from his determination for any period notwithstanding that there has been no omission or failure as mentioned in clause (a) on the part of the employer.

It is further provided that where an officer has reason to believe that an amount due from the employer has escaped determination, he is empowered to reopen such case within 5 years and redetermine the amount due from the employer. The employer is liable to pay simple interest at 12% per annum on any amount due from him under the Act, from the date on which it becomes due till the date of its actual payment.

Opportunity to be heard: Before making any order, the officer must conduct necessary inquiry and must offer a reasonable opportunity to the employer for representing his case.

Employees' Provident Funds Appellate Tribunal (Section 7D–P)

Tribunal and its constitution (Section 7D–N): The central government is authorized by issuing a notification in the Official Gazette, to constitute one or more Appellate Tribunals to be known as the Employees' Provident Funds Appellate Tribunal. The Tribunal exercises the powers and discharges the functions conferred on it by this Act. Every such Tribunal has the jurisdiction in respect of establishments situated in such area as may be specified in the notification constituting the Tribunal.

Membership and qualification: A Tribunal consists of one person only to be appointed by the central government. A person is not qualified for appointment as a Presiding Officer of a Tribunal unless he is or has been, or is qualified to be

1. A judge of a high court; or
2. A district judge.

Term of office (Section 7E): The Presiding Officer of a Tribunal holds office for a term of 5 years from the date on which he enters upon his office or until he attains the age of 62 years, whichever is earlier.

Appeal to tribunal (Section 7I): Any person aggrieved by a notification issued by the central government, or an order passed by the central government or any authority (under the proviso to Subsection (3), or Subsection (4), of Section 1, or Section 3, or Subsection (1) of Section 7A, or Section 7B), except an order rejecting an application for review referred to in Subsection (5) thereof, or Section 7C, or Section 14B, is free to tender an appeal to a Tribunal against such notification or order. However, every appeal under Subsection (1) must be filed in such form and manner, within such time and be accompanied by such fees, as prescribed under the Scheme.

Orders and rectification of mistakes (Section 7L): The Tribunal gives the parties to the appeal an opportunity of being heard and thereafter passes such orders thereon as it thinks fit. The order may confirm, modify or annul the original order appealed against. The Tribunal after taking additional evidence, if necessary, may also refer the case back to the authority which passed such order with some directions, for a fresh adjudication or order.

A Tribunal is empowered to amend any order passed by it under Subsection (1) at any time within 5 years from thc date of its order, with a view to rectifying any mistake apparent from the record. It can make such amendment in the order if the mistake is brought to its notice by the parties to the appeal.

Filling up of vacancies (Section 7M): If there occurs any vacancy in the office of the Presiding Officer, the central government appoints another person in accordance with the provisions of this Act, to fill the vacancy, and the proceedings are continued before a Tribunal from the stage at which the vacancy is filled.

Process of Filing an Appeal (Section 7O–Q)

A Tribunal does not entertain any appeal by the employer unless he has deposited with it 75% of the amount due from him as determined by an officer referred to in Section 7A. All applications which are pending before the central government under Section 19A before its repeal stand transferred to a Tribunal exercising jurisdiction in respect of establishments in relation to which such applications had been made as if such applications were appeals preferred to the Tribunal.

The employer is liable to pay simple interest at the rate of 12% per annum or at such higher rate as may be specified in the Scheme on any amount due from him under this Act from the date on which the amount has become so due till the date of its actual payment. However, the higher rate of interest specified in the Scheme cannot exceed the lending rate of interest charged by any scheduled bank.

Recovery of Money Due from the Employer (Section 8)

Section 8 provides for any amount due:

1. **From the employer in relation to an establishment covered under any scheme:** In respect of any contribution payable to, damages recoverable under Section 14B, accumulations required to be transferred under Subsection (2) of Section 15 or under Subsection (5) of Section 17 or any charges payable by him under any other provision of this Act or of any provision of the scheme.
2. **From the employer in relation to an exempted establishment:** In respect of any damages recoverable under Section 14B or any charges payable by him to the appropriate government under any provision of this Act under any of the conditions specified or in respect of the contribution payable by him towards the Scheme or the Insurance Scheme.

Above-mentioned amount along with the amount in arrears can be recovered in the manner specified in Sections 8B–8G of the Act.

Recovery of Money by Employers and Contractors (Section 8A)

The amount of contribution (the employer's contribution as well as the employee's contribution in pursuance of any Scheme and the employer's contribution in pursuance of the Insurance Scheme) and any charges for meeting the cost of administering the fund paid or payable by an employer in respect of an employee employed by or through a contractor are recoverable by such employer from the contractor, either by deduction from any amount payable to the contractor under any contract or as a debt payable by the contractor.

The section further provides that a contractor from whom the above-mentioned amounts are payable can recover such amounts in respect of any employee employed by or through him by deduction from the basic wages, dearness allowance and retaining allowance (if any) payable to such employee. Notwithstanding any contract to the contrary, no contractor is entitled to deduct the employer's contribution or the charges referred to in Subsection (1) from the basic wages, dearness allowance and retaining allowance (if any) payable to an employee employed by or through him or otherwise to recover such contribution or charges from such employee.

Modes of Recovery (Sections 8B–8G)

Certificate by recovery officer (Section 8B): If any amount is in arrears under Section 8, the authorized officer will issue, to the Recovery Officer, a certificate under his signature specifying the amount of arrears. On the receipt of this certificate, the Recovery Officer proceeds to recover the amount specified therein from the establishment or the employer. The Act provides the following modes to recover from an employer any amount of contribution, damages, accumulations required to be transferred or administrative charges, due from him:

1. Attachment and sale of the movable or immovable property of the establishment/employer.
2. Arrest of the employer and his detention in prison.
3. Appointment of a receiver for the management of the movable or immovable properties of the establishment/employer.

Recovery officer to whom certificate is to be forwarded (Section 8C): The authorized officer forwards the certificate referred above (Section 8B) to the Recovery Officer within whose jurisdiction the employer:

1. Carries on his business or profession or within whose jurisdiction the principal place of his establishment is situated.
2. Resides or any movable or immovable property of the establishment or the employer is situated.

If an establishment or the employer has property within the jurisdiction of more than one Recovery Officer and the Recovery Officer to whom a certificate is sent by the authorized officer:

1. Is not able to recover the entire amount by the sale of the property, movable or immovable, within his jurisdiction; or
2. Is of the opinion that, for the purpose of expediting or securing the recovery of the whole or any part of the amount, it is necessary so to do, he may send the certificate or, where only a part of the amount is to be recovered, a copy of the certificate certified in the prescribed manner and specifying the amount to be recovered to the Recovery Officer within whose

jurisdiction the establishment or the employer has property or the employer resides. After receiving the certificate, such Recovery Officer must proceed to recover the amount due under this section as if the certificate or the copy thereof had been the certificate sent to him by the authorized officer.

Validity of certificate (Section 8D): When the authorized officer issues a certificate to the Recovery Officer under Section 8B, the Act does not permit the employer to dispute before the Recovery Officer the correctness of the amount. No objection to the certificate on any other ground is entertained by the Recovery Officer. The authorized officer has the power to withdraw the certificate or correct any clerical or arithmetical mistake in the certificate by sending intimation to the Recovery Officer. The Section further mentions that it is the duty of the authorized officer to intimate the Recovery Officer any order withdrawing or cancelling a certificate or any correction made by him or any amendment made.

Stay of proceedings (Section 8E): The authorized officer may grant time for the payment of the amount, and thereupon the Recovery Officer has to stay the proceedings until the expiry of the time so granted.

Other Modes of Recovery (Section 8F)

Besides the modes mentioned above, the Central Provident Fund Commissioner or any other officer authorized by the Central Board may recover the amount by any one or more of the following modes provided in this section:

1. **Recovery from any person of amount due from him to the employee who is in arrears:** Where any amount is due from any person to any employer who is in arrears, the Central Provident Fund Commissioner or any other officer authorized by the Central Board in this behalf is empowered to instruct such person to deduct from the said amount the arrears due from such employer under this Act. Such person has to comply with any such requisition and pay the deducted sum to the credit of the Central Provident Fund Commissioner or the officer so authorized.
2. **Application for release of money to the Court in whose custody there is money belonging to the employer:** By issuing a written notice, an authorized officer by the Central Board in this behalf is empowered to, at any time or from time to time, instruct any person from whom money is due or may become due to the employer or, the establishment or any person who holds or may subsequently hold money for or on account of the employer, the establishment to pay to the Central Provident Fund Commissioner either forthwith upon the money:
    a. Becoming due; or
    b. Being held or at; or
    c. Within the time specified in the so much of the money as is sufficient to pay the amount due from the employer in respect of arrears; or
    d. The whole of the money when it is equal to or less than that amount.
3. **Recovery by distrait and sale of movable property:** The Central Provident Fund Commissioner or any officer not below the rank of Assistant Provident Fund Commissioner may, if so authorized

by the central government by general or special order, recover any arrears of amount due from an employer or from the establishment by distraint and sale of his or its movable property in the manner laid down in the Third Schedule to the Income Tax Act, 1961 (43 of 1961).

Recognized Funds under Indian Income Tax Act, 1961 (Section 9): For the purposes of the Indian Income Tax Act, 1922, the Fund is deemed to be a recognized provident fund within the meaning of Chapter IX-A of that Act.

Protection of the Amount Standing to the Credit of an Employee in Provident Fund Against Attachment (Section 10)

According to Section 10 of the Act, the amount standing to the credit of any member in the fund or of any exempted employee in a provident fund cannot in any way be assigned or charged and is not liable to attachment under any decree or order of any court in respect of any debt or liability incurred by the member or exempted employee, and neither the official assignee appointed under the Presidency Town Insolvency Act, 1909, nor any receiver appointed under the Provincial Insolvency Act, 1920, is entitled to or have any claim on any such amount.

This protection also applies to provident fund, pension and insurance amount receivable by employee under the scheme. If such person dies, the money will be payable to nominees and the amount will be free from any debt or other liability incurred by the deceased or the nominee before the death of the member or of the exempted.

Priority of Payment of Contribution over Other Debts (Section 11)

If any employer is adjudicated insolvent or, being a company, an order for winding up is made:

1. **In relation to an establishment to which any Scheme or the insurance Scheme applies:** Any contribution payable to the Fund or the Insurance Fund, damages recoverable under Section 14B, accumulations required to be transferred under Subsection (2) of Section 15 or any charges payable by him under any other provision of this Act or of any provision of the Scheme or the Insurance Scheme; or
2. **In relation to an exempted establishment:** Any contribution to the provident fund or any insurance fund (insofar as it relates to exempted employees), any contribution payable by him towards the pension fund damages recoverable or any charges payable by him to the appropriate government under any provision of this Act (under any of the conditions specified under Section 17).

Where the liability has accrued before the order of adjudication or winding up is made, the amount due from the employer in the above two mentioned cases is deemed to be included among the debts which under Section 49 of the Presidency Towns Insolvency Act, 1909, or under Section 61 of the Provincial Insolvency Act, 1920, or under Section 530 of the Companies Act, 1956, are to be paid in priority to all other debts in the distribution of the property of the insolvent or the assets of the company being wound up.

Without prejudice to the provisions discussed above, if any amount is due from an employer, the amount so due is deemed to be the first charge on the assets of the establishment and notwithstanding anything contained in any other law for the time being in force is paid in priority to all other debts.

Employer Not to Reduce Wages (Section 12)

In relation to an establishment to which any Scheme or the Insurance Scheme is applicable, no employer can, just to avoid his liability for the payment of any contribution to the Fund or the Insurance Fund or any charges under this Act or the Scheme or the Insurance Scheme, reduce directly or indirectly the wages of any employee to whom the Scheme or the Insurance Scheme is applicable or the total quantum of benefits in the nature of old age pension, gratuity provident fund or life insurance to which the employee is entitled under the terms of his employment, whether express or implied.

LO5: Enforcement of the Act

Appointment of the Inspector (Section 13)

By issuing a notification in the Official Gazette, the appropriate government appoints such persons as it thinks fit to be Inspectors for the purposes of this Act and defines their jurisdiction.

Powers of the Inspector

The appointed Inspector under the Act is empowered to:

1. Require an employer to furnish such information as he may consider necessary.
2. At any reasonable time and with such assistance, if any, as he may think fit, enter and search any establishment, or any premises connected therewith and require any one found in charge thereof to produce before him for examination any accounts, books, registers and other documents relating to the employment of persons or the payment of wages in the establishment.
3. Examine, with respect to any matter relevant to any of the aforementioned purposes, the employer or any contractor from whom any amount is recoverable under Section 8A, his agent or servant or any other person found in charge of the establishment, or any premises connected there with or whom the Inspector has reasonable cause to believe to be or to have been an employee in the establishment.
4. Make copies of, or take extracts from, any book, register or other document maintained in relation to the establishment and, where he has reason to believe that any offence under this Act has been committed by an employer, seize with such assistance as he may think fit, such book, register or other document or portions thereof as he may consider relevant in respect of that offence.
5. Exercise such other powers provided by the scheme.

LO6: Penalties and Offences

Penalties (Section 14)

The Act strictly restricts an employer in relation to an establishment to which any scheme of the Act applies, by reason only of his liability for the payment of any contribution to the fund, or any charges under this Act or the scheme, from reducing whether directly or indirectly the wages of any employee to whom the scheme applies or the total quantum of benefits in the nature of old age pension gratuity provident fund or life insurance to which the employee is entitled.

The Act provides penalty for the person who for the purpose of avoiding any payment to be made by himself under this Act or of enabling any other person to avoid such payment, knowingly makes or causes to be made any false statement or false representation, is liable to be punished with imprisonment or with fine or with both.

If an employer who contravenes, or makes default in (the provisions of Section 6 or clause (a) of Subsection (3) of Section 17) making the payment of inspection charges, or of administrative charges, shall be punishable with imprisonment for a term which may extend to 3 years. The imprisonment is not more than 1 year and fine of ₹10,000 in case of default in payment of employees' contribution which has been deducted by the employer from the employees' wages, while in other cases the imprisonment is not less than 6 months and fine of ₹5,000. However, the court may, for any adequate and special reasons to be recorded in the judgement, impose a sentence of imprisonment for a lesser term.

Offences by the Companies (Section 14A)

Where the person committing offence under this Act, the scheme, the pension scheme or the insurance scheme is a company, every person, who at the time the offence was committed was in charge of, and was responsible to, the company for the conduct of the business of the company, as well as the company, is deemed to be guilty of the offence and is liable to be proceeded against and punished accordingly. However, any of the persons mentioned above is not liable to any punishment, if he proves that the offence was committed without his knowledge or that he exercised all due diligence to prevent the commission of such offence.

Here, 'Company' means any corporate body and includes a firm and other association of individuals, and 'director', in relation to a firm, means a partner in the firm.

Cognizance and Trial of Offences (Section 14AB)

No court takes cognizance of any offence punishable under the Act except on a report in writing of the facts constituting such offence made with the previous sanction of the Central Provident Fund Commissioner or such other officer authorized by the central government, by notification in the Official Gazette, in this behalf, by an Inspector appointed under Section 13 of the Act.

The central government may by notification in the Official Gazette constitute one or more Employees' Provident Funds Appellate Tribunal to exercise the powers and discharge the duties conferred on such

Tribunal by this Act. Every such Tribunal has the jurisdiction in respect of establishments situated in such area as specified in the notification constituting the Tribunal.

Power to Recover Damages (Section 14B)

Where an employer makes default in the payment of any contribution to the Fund or in the transfer of accumulations required to be transferred by him or in the payment of any charges payable under any other provision of this Act or of any Scheme or Insurance Scheme or under any of the conditions specified under Section 17, an authorized officer by the central government issues a notification in the Official Gazette, in this behalf to recover from the employer by way of penalty such damages, not exceeding the amount of arrears, as may be specified in the Scheme. It is to be noted here that before levying and recovering such damages, the authorized officer has to ensure that the employer is given a reasonable opportunity of being heard.

It is further provided that the Central Board can reduce or waive the damages levied under this section in relation to an establishment which is a sick industrial company and in respect of which Scheme for rehabilitation has been sanctioned by the Board for industrial and financial reconstruction established under Section 4 of the Sick Industrial Companies (Special Provisions) Act, 1985 (1 of 1986). Such reduction or waiver is subject to the terms and conditions as specified in the Scheme.

Power of a Court to Make an Order (Section 14C)

Where an employer is convicted of an offence of making default in the payment of any contribution to the Fund or in the transfer of accumulations required to be transferred by him, the court may, in addition to awarding any punishment, by order in writing instruct the defaulted employer to pay the amount of contribution or transfer the accumulations, as the case may be, within a period specified in the order.

Where any such order is passed, the employer is not be liable under this Act in respect of the continuation of the offence during the period or extended period, if any, allowed by the court. But if, on the expiry of such period or extended period, the order of the court has not been fully complied with, the employer is deemed to have committed a further offence and is punished with imprisonment in respect thereof under Section 14. Such an employer is also liable to pay fine which may extend to ₹100 for every day after such expiry on which the order has not been complied with.

LO7: Miscellaneous Provisions of the Act

Special Provisions for Existing Provident Funds (Section 15)

Subject to the provisions of Section 17, every employee, who is a subscriber to any provident fund of an establishment to which this Act applies, continues to be entitled to the benefits accruing to him under the provident fund, and the provident fund continues to be maintained in the same manner and subject to the same conditions as it would have been if this Act had not been passed.

On the application of any Scheme, the accumulations in any provident fund of the establishment, standing to the credit of the employees who become members of the fund established under the Scheme, notwithstanding anything to the contrary contained in any law for the time being in force or in any deed or other instrument establishing the provident fund but subject to the provisions, if any, contained in the Scheme, are to be transferred to the Fund established under the Scheme, and are to be credited to the accounts of the employees entitled thereto in the Fund.

Power to Exempt (Section 17)

By notification in the Official Gazette, and subject to such conditions as may be specified in the notification, the appropriate government is authorized to exempt from the operation of all or any of the provisions of any Scheme:

1. Any establishment to which this Act applies if, in the opinion of the appropriate government, the rules of its provident fund with respect to the rates of contribution are not less favourable than those specified in Section 6 and the employees are also enjoying other provident fund benefits which on the whole are not less favourable to the employees than the benefits provided under this Act or any Scheme in relation to the employees in any other establishment of similar character; or
2. Any establishment if the employees of such establishment are in enjoyment of benefits in the nature of provident fund, pension or gratuity and the appropriate government is of opinion that such benefits, separately or jointly, are on the whole not less favourable to such employees than the benefits provided under this Act or any Scheme in relation the employees in any other establishment of a similar character.

Such an exemption from the operation of all or any of the provisions of any Scheme can be either prospective or retrospective. It is to be noted here that no such exemption can be made without consultation with the Central Board which, on such consultation, forwards its views on exemption to the appropriate government within such time limit as may be specified in the Scheme.

Transfer of Balance of Provident Fund (Section 17A)

When an employee of an establishment to which this Act applies leaves his employment and obtains re-employment in another establishment to which this Act does not apply, the amount of accumulations to the credit of such employee in the Fund or, as the case may be, in the provident fund in the establishment left by him has to be transferred to the credit of his account in the provident fund of the establishment in which he is re-employed, if the employee so desires and such transfer is not contrary to the rules in relation to the provident fund.

On the other hand, when such an employee obtains re-employment in an establishment to which this Act applies, the amount of accumulations to the credit of such an employee in the provident fund of the establishment, if the employee so desires and the rules in relation to such provident fund permit, may be transferred to the credit of his account in the fund or, as the case may be, in the provident fund of the establishment in which he is re-employed.

Protection of Action Taken in Good Faith (Section 18)

The Act provides protection from any suit, prosecution of other legal proceeding against the central government, a state government, to the Presiding Officer of a Tribunal, any authority referred to in Section 7A, an Inspector or any other person for anything which is in good faith done or intended to be done in pursuance of this Act, the Scheme, the Pension or the Insurance Scheme.

Delegation of Powers (Section 19)

The appropriate government is empowered to issue directions and lay down conditions in relation to any power or authority or jurisdiction exercisable by it (under this Act, the scheme, the pension scheme or the insurance scheme). Such powers are exercisable also:

1. Where the appropriate government is the central government, by such officer or authority subordinate to the central Government or by the state government or by such officer or authority subordinate to the government, as specified in the notification.
2. Where the appropriate government is a state government, by such officer or authority subordinate to the state government as specified in the notification.

Powers to Make Rule (Section 21)

The central government (by notification in the Official Gazette) makes rules to carry out the provisions of this Act. Without prejudice to the generality of the foregoing power, such rules may provide for all or any of the following matters:

1. The salary and allowances and other terms and conditions of service of the Presiding Officer and the employees of a Tribunal.
2. The form and the manner in which, and the time within which, an appeal is to be filed before a Tribunal and the fees payable for filing such an appeal.
3. The manner of certifying the copy of the certificate, to be forwarded to the Recovery Officer under Subsection (2) of Section 8C.
4. Any other matter, which has to be, or are prescribed by rules under this Act.

Every rule made under this Act is required to be approved by each House of the Parliament, while it is in session. Both Houses may either agree in making any modification in the rule or both Houses agree that the rule should not be made. The rule thereafter has effect only in such modified form or be of no effect, as the case may be. However, any such modification or annulment has to be without prejudice to the validity of anything previously done under that rule.

Power to Remove Difficulties (Section 22)

As amended by the Employees' Provident Funds and Miscellaneous Provisions (Amendment) Act, 1988, if there arises any difficulty in giving effect to the provisions of this Act, the Central Government is empowered to make some provisions for the removal of such difficulty. These provisions must not be inconsistent with the provisions of this Act and every order made under this section is to be laid before each House of the Parliament. It is to be noted that no such order can be made after the expiry of a period of 3 years from the date on which the said Amendment Act receives the assent of the President.

Duties of Employers

1. It is the duty of every employer to send to the commissioner within 15 days of the close of each month a return:
   a. In Form 5 of the employees qualifying to become members of the Fund for the first time during the preceding month together with the declarations in Form 2 furnished by such qualifying employees; and
   b. In the prescribed form of the employees leaving service of the employer during the preceding month.
2. Every employer must maintain an inspection notebook in the prescribed form for an Inspector to record his observation on his visit to the establishment.
3. Every employer must maintain all accounts of the amounts contributed to the Fund by him and by his employees as directed by the Central Board from time to time. It is the duty of every employer to assist the Central Board in making such payments from the Fund to his employees as are sanctioned by or under the authority of the Central Board.
4. Every employer in relation to a factory or other establishment to which the Act applies must furnish in duplicate to the Regional Commissioner the particulars of all the branches and departments, owners, occupiers, directors, partners, manager or any other person or persons who have the ultimate control over the affairs of such factory or establishment. He must also send intimation of any change in such particulars, within 15 days of such change, to the Regional Commissioner by registered post.

Duties of Contractors

Every contractor is required to, within 7 days of the close of the month, submit to the principal employer a statement showing the recoveries of contributions for employees employed by or through him and such other information to the principal employer as is required to be filed with the Regional PF Commissioner.

Summary

1. The Employees Provident Funds and Miscellaneous Provisions Act, 1952, is a beneficent piece of social welfare legislation aimed at promoting and securing the well-being of the employees.
2. The Act aims to provide for institution of provident funds, pension funds and deposit-linked insurance funds for the employees in the factories and other establishments.
3. The Act applies to every establishment which is a factory engaged in any industry specified in Schedule I and in which 20 or more persons are employed and any establishment employing 20 or more persons or class of such establishments which the central government may, by notification in the Official Gazette, specify.
4. A person doing work of the principal employer, even though employed by a contractor, is also an employee covered by the definition.

5. The Act is administered by the Government of India through the EPFO.
6. EPFO functions under the overall superintendence of the policies framed by this Central Board of Trustees.
7. The main purpose of EPF is to help employees save a fraction of their salary every month which can be used in an event that the employee is temporarily or no longer fit to work or at retirement.
8. The contribution to be paid by the employer to the Provident Fund is 8.33% of the basic wages, dearness allowances and retaining allowance (if any) for the time being payable to each of the employees.
9. The pension scheme is financed by diverting 8.33% of employer's monthly contribution from the EPF (restricted to 8.33% of 15,000 or ₹1,520) and government's contribution of 1.17% of the worker's monthly wages.
10. EDLI is a scheme to provide life insurance benefits to the members of Provident Fund. The cost of the scheme is to be borne by the employer.
11. The Central Board maintains proper accounts of its income and expenditure in such form and in such manner as the central government, after consultation with the CAG of India, specifies in the Scheme.
12. The Executive Board functions to assist the Central Board in the performance of its functions.
13. The State Board exercises such powers and performs such duties as the central government assigns to it from time to time.
14. An authorized officer settles the dispute in relation to the determination of the amount due from the employer.
15. Every application for review is to be filed in such form and manner and within such time as may be specified in the Scheme.
16. Where an officer has reason to believe that an amount due from the employer has escaped determination, he is empowered to reopen such case within 5 years and redetermine the amount due from the employer.
17. If any amount is in arrears under Section 8, the authorized officer will issue, to the Recovery Officer, a certificate under his signature specifying the amount of arrears.
18. By issuing a notification in the Official Gazette, the appropriate government appoints such persons as it thinks fit to be Inspectors for the purposes of this Act and defines their jurisdiction.
19. No employer can reduce, whether directly or indirectly, the wages of any employee to whom the scheme applies or the total quantum of benefits in the nature of old age pension gratuity provident fund or life insurance to which the employee is entitled.
20. The central government may, by notification in the Official Gazette, constitute one or more Employees' Provident Funds Appellate Tribunal to exercise the powers and discharge the duties conferred on such Tribunal by this Act.
21. Every employee who is a subscriber to any provident fund of an establishment to which this Act applies continues to be entitled to the benefits accruing to him under the provident fund.
22. The appropriate government is authorized to exempt some specific establishments from the operation of all or any of the provisions of any Scheme.
23. The Act provides protection from any suit, prosecution of other legal proceedings against the central government, a state government, to all authorized officers for anything which is in good faith done.
24. If there arises any difficulty in giving effect to the provisions of this Act, the central government is empowered to make some provisions for the removal of such difficulty.

Multiple Choice Questions

1. The Act aims at providing institution of ____________ for the employees in the factories and other establishments.
   a. Provident funds
   b. Pension funds
   c. Deposit-linked insurance funds
   d. All of the above
2. Basic wages includes all emoluments which are earned by employee while ____________ with wages in either case in accordance with the terms of the contract of employment and which is paid or payable in cash.
   a. On duty only
   b. On leave also
   c. On holiday also
   d. All of the above
3. The appropriate government can exempt any establishment, prospectively or retrospectively, from operation of all or any of the provisions of the EPF Scheme, if ____________.
   a. The rules relating to its provident fund are not less favourable than that of Section 6 of the EPF Act
   b. Its employees are in enjoyment of benefits in the nature of PF, pension or gratuity. which are not less favourable to employees covered by the Act or the Scheme
   c. Both (a) and (b)
   d. Neither (a) nor (b)
4. Excluded employee means an employee ____________.
   a. Who, having been a member of the fund, withdrew the full amount of his accumulations on retirement or emigration
   b. Whose pay at the time he is otherwise entitled to become a member of the fund exceeds ₹15,000.00 per month
   c. Both (a) and (b)
   d. Neither (a) nor (b)
5. Employee gets wages directly or indirectly from the employer and includes any person:
   a. Employed by or through a contractor in or in connection with the work of an establishment.
   b. Employed by contractor only.
   c. Employed through a contractor in or in connection with the work of an establishment.
   d. None of the above.
6. Every employee is required to join EPF scheme who is employed in or in connection with the work of the factory or other establishment to which the EPF Scheme applies, except an employee who is drawing a salary exceeding ____________ in a month.
   a. ₹5,000
   b. ₹15,000
   c. ₹25,000
   d. ₹50,000
7. The contribution to be paid by the employer to the fund is ____________ of the basic wages, dearness allowances and retaining allowance (if any) for the time being payable to each of the employees.
   a. 8.33%
   b. 5.33%
   c. 8.25%
   d. 10.33%

8. The ______________ for the provisions of Section 6 means an allowance payable for the time being to an employee for retaining his services, when the establishment is not working.
   a. Retaining allowance
   b. Dearness allowance
   c. Basic wages
   d. None of the above
9. The pension scheme is financed by diverting______________of employer's monthly contribution from the EPF and government's contribution of 1.17% of the worker's monthly wages.
   a. 10.33%
   b. 8.50%
   c. 8.33%
   d. 6.33%
10. Superannuation pension is payable to the member who has rendered eligible service of ______________ and retires on attaining the age of 58 years.
    a. 10 years
    b. 20 years
    c. 30 years
    d. 35 years

True/False Questions

1. Wages under the Act includes the cash value of any food concession.
2. Personal or domestic servants are covered under the definition of employees in the Act.
3. Employees' contribution is equal to the contribution payable by the employer in respect of him.
4. The employer, in the first instance, has to pay both the contribution payable by himself towards employer's contribution and on behalf of the member employed by him.
5. The amount of a member's contribution paid by the employer or a contractor cannot be recovered by means of deduction from the wages of the member and not otherwise.

Descriptive Questions

1. Write a note on applicability and non-applicability of Employees Provident Funds and Miscellaneous Provisions Act, 1952, on establishments and employees.
2. Write short notes on the following:
   a. Employee under the Act
   b. Wages under the Act
3. Explain the scope and objectives of Employees Provident Funds and Miscellaneous Provisions Act, 1952.
4. Explain different schemes provided under Employees Provident Funds and Miscellaneous Provisions Act, 1952.
5. Provide a summary of contribution by the employer in different schemes of Employees Provident Funds and Miscellaneous Provisions Act, 1952.

6. Throw light on constitution and functioning of different boards provided by the Act.
7. Discuss the method of calculation of amount due to the employer under various schemes of the Act.
8. What are the provisions for the enforcement of various provisions of the Act?
9. How are the offences by the companies dealt by the Act? Discuss in detail.
10. Write short notes on the following:
    a. Power of appropriate government to exempt the establishments from the operations of the Act
    b. Transfer of balance of Provident Fund under Section 17A

ANNEXURE A

S. No.	Area of Amendment	Amendment
1.	**EPF contribution rate**[4]	In the Union Budget 2018, the EPF contribution rate for the newly recruited female employees has been reduced from 12% to 8%. The contribution from the employer's end towards EPF, however, will continue to be at the rate of 12%. Additionally, the government has proposed to contribute 12% of the wages of new employees towards EPF; this is applicable to all the sectors of the economy for the next 3 years.
2.	**The assurance benefits**[5]	The assurance benefits shall not be less than ₹250,000 and further that the assurance benefit shall not exceed ₹600,000 under paragraph 22 (3) of EDU Scheme, 1976.
3.	**Employees' Deposit-Linked Insurance (Amendment) Scheme 2018**[6]	The central government further amended the Employees' Deposit-Linked Insurance Scheme, 1976. 1. **Renaming and enforcement of the scheme** a. This Scheme may be called the Employees' Deposit-Linked Insurance (Amendment) Scheme, 2018. b. It shall come into force from the date of its publication in the Official Gazette. 2. In the Employees' Deposit-Linked Insurance Scheme, 1976, in paragraph 22. 2. **Ceiling on provident fund** a. The average monthly wages drawn (subject to a maximum of ₹50,000), during the 12 months preceding the month in which he died, multiplied by 30 times plus 50% of the average balance in the account of the deceased in the Fund or of a provident fund exempted under Section 17 of the Act or under paragraph 27 or 27A of the Employees' Provident Funds Scheme, 1952, as the case may be, during the preceding 12 months or during the preceding 12 months or during the period of his membership, whichever is less subject to a ceiling of ₹150,000. Provided that the assurance benefit shall not be less than ₹250,000, and provided further that the assurance benefit shall not exceed ₹600,000.

[4] https://cleartax.in/s/epf-act-amendments-2018

[5] The Gazette notification G. S. R. No. 170 (E) on assurance benefits shall not be less than ₹200,000 and ₹50,000 under paragraph 22 (3) of EDU Scheme, 1976, dated 15 February 2018.

[6] file:///C:/Users/Admin/Downloads/EDLI_Amendment_GSR_AssuranceBenefits_26694.pdf

9
CHAPTER

The Payment of Gratuity Act, 1972

LEARNING OBJECTIVES

Upon completing this chapter, the reader would be able to:

LO1. Understand the objectives, scope and important definitions of the Act.
LO2. Get the insights into the provisions regulating the payment and forfeiture of gratuity.
LO3. Understand the provisions for the compulsory insurance and protection of gratuity under the Act.
LO4. Get the details of provisions for the determination and recovery of gratuity.
LO5. Know the provisions for the enforcement of the Act.
LO6. Get the details of rules dealing with penalties and offences against the Act.

Introduction

The meaning of gratuity is a sort of retiring benefit of the workmen who have rendered long and unblemished service to the employer. The expression 'gratuity' means 'a gift or present', often in return for services. Often a lump sum amount is paid by an employer to an employee in consideration of his past service when an employee's service is terminated. In case of retirement or superannuation, gratuity enables the affected employee to meet the new situation which quite often means a reduction in earnings or even a total stoppage of earnings, and in the case of death of an employee, it provides much-needed financial assistance to the dependants of the deceased employee. Gratuity schemes, therefore, are an instrument of social security.

In the earlier days, in some establishments, gratuity schemes were voluntarily introduced by the employers or sometimes under agreements between employers and workers. These schemes were, however, limited to particular establishments and, even within those establishments, to certain categories of staff. There was no general legislation requiring payment of gratuity to industrial workers.

In the year 1972, a Central Act, namely, the Payment of Gratuity Act, 1972 (the Act), was enacted, which came into force on 16 September 1972.

LO1: Objectives, Scope and Important Definitions

Objectives

The main objective of this Act is to provide a scheme for the payment of gratuity to employees engaged in factories, mines, oilfield plantations, ports, railway companies, shops or other establishments and to lay down provisions to address the issues related to payment of gratuity. The Act extends to the whole of India. However, so far as it relates to plantations or ports, the Act does not extend to the state of Jammu and Kashmir. The objectives of the Act are summarized below:

1. To provide for a scheme for the payment of gratuity to employees.
2. To provide for matters related or incidental to the scheme for payment of gratuity.
3. To provide retiring benefits to employees who have rendered continuous services to his employer and thereby contributed to his prosperity.
4. To define the principles of payment of gratuity according to the prescribed formula.
5. To provide machinery for the employment of liability for payment of gratuity.

Applicability and Scope (Section 1(3))

The Act is applicable to the persons employed in an establishment to which the Act applies and establishments to which the Act applies covers:

1. Every factory, mine, oilfield, plantation, port and railway company.
2. Every shop or establishment within the meaning of any law for the time being in force in relation to shops and establishments in a state, in which 10 or more persons are employed, or were employed, on any day of the preceding 12 months.
3. Such other establishment, or class of establishment in which 10 or more employees are employed, or were employed on any day of the preceding 12 months.

Section 1(3A) of the Act further provides that a shop or establishment to which the Act has become applicable once continues to be governed by it, even if the number of persons employed therein at any time after it had become so applicable falls below 10. Out of the above provisions, it is clear that the Act is wide enough to bring within its scope the whole organized sector of industry as well as commerce.

Non-applicability: This Act, however, is not applicable on:

1. Apprentices.
2. (Section 2(e)) Persons who hold civil posts under the central government or a state government and are governed by any other Act or rules providing for the payment of gratuity.

Section 5 of this Act empowers the central government to exempt any shop or establishment covered by this Act from the provisions of the Act, if its employees are in receipt of gratuity or pensionary benefits not less favourable than the benefits provided under this Act.

Important Definitions

1. **Appropriate government (Section 2(a)):** According to the Act, 'appropriate government' means:
   a. In relation to an establishment:
      i. Belonging to, or under the control of, the central government,
      ii. Having branches in more than one state,
      iii. Of a factory belonging to, or under the control of, the central government,
      iv. Of a major port, mine, oilfield or railway company belonging to, or under the control of, the central government.
   b. In any other case, the state government.
2. **Completed year of service (Section 2(b)):** The Act states that completed year of service means continuous service for 1 year.
3. **Continuous service (Section 2(A)):** An employee is said to be in continuous service for a period if he has for that period been in uninterrupted service, including service which may be interrupted because of sickness, accident, leave, absence for duty without leave (not being absent in respect of which an order treating the absence as break in service has been passed in accordance with the standing orders, rules or regulations governing the employees of the establishment), layoff, strike or a lockout or cessation of work not due to any fault of the employee, whether such uninterrupted or interrupted service was rendered before or after the commencement of the Gratuity Act.
4. **Deemed continuous service:** Where an employee (not being an employee employed in a seasonal establishment) is not in continuous service within the meaning of clause (1), for any period of 1 year or 6 months, he is deemed to be in continuous service under the employer:
   a. For the said period of 1 year, if the employee during the period of 12 calendar months preceding the date with reference to which calculation is to be made has actually worked under the employer for not less than:
      i. One hundred and ninety days, in the case of an employee employed below the ground in a mine or in an establishment which works for less than 6 days in a week; and
      ii. Two hundred and forty days, in any other case.
   b. For the said period of 6 months, if the employee during the period of 6 calendar months preceding the date with reference to which the calculation is to be made has actually worked under the employer for not less than:
      i. Ninety-five days, in the case of an employee employed below the ground in a mine or in an establishment which works for less than 6 days in a week; and
      ii. One hundred and twenty days, in any other case.

Let us discuss a case to get the insights of the term 'continuous service' (Case 9.1).

Case 9.1: *M. C. Chamaraju v. Hind Nippon Rural Industrial (P) Ltd.*[1]

In September 1984, Mr Chamaraju, the appellant, was appointed as Supervisor by Mr V. K. Poddar, Managing Director of Aggarwal Investments, Poddar Granites and Hind Nippon Co. Ltd. (the respondent company). Mr V. K. Poddar used to run the establishments that included Aggarwal Investments, Poddar Granites and Hind Nippon. He worked as a Supervisor in Poddar Mines in Sira till 1990. Thereafter, he was transferred to another quarry of Mr Poddar. He worked at various places like Bellary, Sira and Chamaraya Nagar. The appellant worked during the period from 1984 onwards with Poddar Granites and Aggarwal Investments. He worked with the respondent company till February 1993. From March 1993, however, the respondent company neither paid his salary nor was he served with any order of termination or dismissal. On 27 September 1993, the appellant addressed a letter asking the management to settle his dues and also to pay gratuity under the Act. But the gratuity was not paid. He, therefore, approached the Controlling Authority (CA) and Assistant Labour Commissioner, Bangalore, for the same by making an application under Subsection (4) of Section 7 of the Act read with Sub-rule (1) of Rule 10 of the Payment of Gratuity (Central) Rules, 1972.

The appellant contended that he had worked in different units during his tenure of service with the respondent company. Thus he did not complete the tenure of 5 years of continuous service to get the entitlement for gratuity. The CA, however, reached a different conclusion after hearing both the parties and examining the material placed before him. The authority concluded that different units where the appellant had worked were 'one' as there was 'functional unity', and thus the appellant was entitled to gratuity. Accordingly, an order was passed on 26 May 2003 that the appellant was entitled to a sum of ₹16,875 towards gratuity. Since the respondent company had not paid the amount of gratuity within 30 days of leaving of services by the appellant workman, the payment was ordered to be made with interest at 10% p.a. from 12 June 1993 till the date of payment.

Being dissatisfied by the order of the CA, the respondent company filed an appeal in the higher court.

Discussion Point

Whether the appellant had completed 5 years of continuous service so as to be eligible to claim gratuity under the Act.

Judgement and Explanation

The court was in full agreement with the findings of the CA. The court added that Shri V. K. Poddar used to run the establishments of Aggarwal Investments, Poddar Granites and Hind Nippon, and that there was just interchangeability in the services of the respondent. Thus, the three companies including the appellant company were run by Shri V. K. Poddar and, hence, there was functional integrally among these three establishments and the services of the respondent had been merely transferred to the appellant company without his knowledge. It appeared that the appellant had been changing the employership of the respondent solely to deprive him of the statutory benefits. The court further stated that the Act has been enacted with a view to grant benefit of workers, a 'weaker section' in the industrial adjudicatory process. A benefit had been extended by the Authorities under the Act to the workman by recording a finding that the applicant (appellant herein) had completed requisite service of 5 years to be eligible to get gratuity.

Thus, it is clear that in interpreting the provisions of such beneficial legislation, a liberal view should be taken.

5. **Controlling authority (Section 2(d)):** According to the Act, CA means an authority appointed by the appropriate government under Section 3.
6. **Employee (Section 2(e)):** An 'employee' under this Act means any person (other than the one who is an apprentice) employed on wages, in any establishment, factory, mine, oilfield, plantation, port, railway company or shop, to do any skilled, semi-skilled or unskilled, manual, supervisory, technical

[1] *M. C. Chamaraju v. Hind Nippon Rural Industrial (P) Ltd.*, 2007 LLR 1129.

or clerical work, whether the terms of such employment are expressed or implied, and whether or not such person is employed in a managerial or administrative capacity. But the definition of an employee does not include any such person who holds a post under the central government or a state government and is governed by any other Act or by any rules providing for payment of gratuity.

7. **Employer (Section 2(f)):** In the Act, an employer means, in relation to any establishment, factory, mine, oilfield, plantation, port, railway company or shop:
   a. Belonging to, or under the control of, the central government or a state government, a person or authority appointed by government to supervise and control the employees, or where no person or authority has been so appointed, the head of the Ministry or Department concerned.
   b. Belonging to, or under the control of, any local authority, the person appointed by such authority to supervise and control the employees, or where no person has been so appointed, the chief executive officer of the local authority.
   c. In any other case, the person, who, or the authority which, has the ultimate control over the affairs of the establishment, factory, mine, oilfield, plantation, port, railway company or shop, and where the said affairs are entrusted to any other person, whether called a manager, managing director or by any other name, such person.
8. **Factory (Section 2 (g)):** In the Act, 'factory' has the same meaning as assigned to it in clause (m) of Section 2 of the Factories Act, 1948 (63 of 1948).
9. **Family (Section 2(h)):** The Act defines family in relation to an employee to be consisting of:
   a. In the case of a male employee, himself, his wife, his children, whether married or unmarried, his dependent parents and the dependent parents of his wife, and the widow and children of his predeceased son, if any.
   b. In the case of a female employee, herself, her husband, her children, whether married or unmarried, her dependent parents and the dependent parents of her husband, and the widow and children of her predeceased son, if any.
10. **Retirement (Section 2(q)):** Retirement under the Act means termination of the service of an employee otherwise than on superannuation.
11. **Superannuation (Section 2(r)):** According to the Act, superannuation in relation to an employee means the attainment by the employee of such age as is fixed in the contract or conditions of service as the age on the attainment of which the employer shall vacate the employment.
12. **Wages (Section 2(s)):** As defined under the Act, wages means all emoluments which are earned by an employee while on duty or on leave in accordance with the terms and conditions of his employments and which are paid or are payable to him in cash and includes dearness allowance. It must be noted that wages does not include any bonus, commission, house rent allowance, overtime wages and any other allowance.

LO2: Payment and Forfeiture of Gratuity and Exemption

Payment of Gratuity (Section 4(1))

The Act states that gratuity is payable to an employee on the termination of his employment after he has rendered continuous service for not less than 5 years:

1. On his superannuation, or
2. On his retirement or resignation, or
3. On his death or disablement due to accident or disease.

Completion of continuous service of 5 years is not necessary where the termination is due to death or disablement. According to Section 4(1), disablement here means a disablement that incapacitates an employee for the work, which he was capable of performing before the accident resulting in such disablement.

In case of death of the employee, gratuity payable to him is to be paid to his nominee or, if no nomination has been made, to his heirs, and where any such nominee or heir is a minor, the shares of such minor has to be deposited with the CA who shall invest the same for the benefit of such minor in such bank or other financial institution, as may be prescribed, until such minor attains majority. Employee not resigning but being treated as having voluntarily abandoned the services of his own accord is also entitled to payment.

Rate of Gratuity (Section 4(2))

The provisions relating to calculation of gratuity amount specify that for every completed year service or part thereof in excess of 6 months, the employer is required to pay gratuity to an employee at the rate of 15-day wages based on rate of wages last drawn by the employee concerned. But the rate of wages paid for any overtime is not to be taken into account while calculating the gratuity amount.

Payment of gratuity to piece-rated employees: In the case where employees are paid for each piece (piece-rated employee), daily wages are computed on the average of the total wages received by him for a period of 3 months immediately preceding the termination of his employment. For this purpose, the wage paid for any overtime work is taken into account.

Payment of gratuity to the employees of seasonal establishments: The Act classifies the employees into two categories on the basis of the type of establishment they work for and provides different method for calculation of gratuity amount for both categories. These employees are grouped in following two categories:

1. Those who work throughout the year.
2. Those who work only during the season.

The former category employees are entitled to gratuity at the rate of 15 days wages for every completed year of service or part thereof in excess of 6 months. The latter (those who work for seasonal establishments) are, however, entitled to receive gratuity at the rate of 7 days for each season.

The formula for calculating the gratuity can be read as under:

$$\text{Gratuity} = \frac{\text{Monthly salary} \times 15 \times \text{Number of years of service}}{26}$$

where

Monthly salary = last month drawn salary by the employee.
26 = total number of working days in a month.
15 = number of days in half of the month.

In the case of a monthly rated employee, the 15 days wages is to be calculated by dividing the monthly rate of wages last drawn by him by 26 and multiplying the quotient by 15.

Maximum gratuity (Section 4(3)): As laid down by the Act, the maximum amount of gratuity payable to an employee must not exceed ₹10 lakhs. However, with implementation of Seventh Central Pay Commission, in case of government servants, the ceiling has now been raised to ₹20 lakhs. The employer may be pleased to offer better terms of gratuity. However, any amount exceeding the maximum prescribed limit of gratuity becomes taxable in the hands of the recipient. The Act further provides that the amount of gratuity payable to an employee must not exceed 20 months wages (Section 4(3)).

The Payment of Gratuity (Amendment) Bill, 2018—Major implications

The Payment of Gratuity (Amendment) Bill, 2018, was passed by the Rajya Sabha on 22 March 2018 and the Lok Sabha on 15 March 2018. The Bill aims at ensuring harmony among employees in the private sector and public sector undertakings/autonomous organizations under government who are not covered under CCS (Pension) Rules.

The present upper ceiling on gratuity amount under the Act is ₹10 lakh. The provisions for central government employees under Central Civil Services (Pension) Rules, 1972, with regard to gratuity are also similar. Before implementation of Seventh Central Pay Commission, the ceiling under CCS (Pension) Rules, 1972, was ₹10 lakh. However, with implementation of Seventh Central Pay Commission, in case of government servants, the ceiling has now been raised to ₹20 lakhs. Considering the inflation and wage increase even in case of employees engaged in private sector, this government decided to increase the entitlement of gratuity in respect of employees who are covered under the Payment of Gratuity Act, 1972. Accordingly, the government initiated the process for amendment to Payment of Gratuity Act, 1972, to increase the maximum limit of gratuity to such amount as may be notified by the central government from time to time. Another important change proposed under the Act is the delegation of the power to notify the ceiling of the amount of gratuity under the Payment of Gratuity Act, 1972, shall stand delegated to the central government so that the limit can be revised from time to time keeping in view the increase in wage and inflation and future pay commissions.

Besides, the Bill also envisages to amend the provisions relating to calculation of continuous service for the purpose of gratuity in case of female employees who are on maternity leave from '12 weeks' to such period as may be notified by the central government from time to time.

Better terms of gratuity (Section 4(5)): The Act provides that the provisions of Section 4 do not affect the right of an employee to receive better terms of gratuity under any award or agreement or contract with the employer.

Rules for the Payment of Gratuity

Employees who have completed 5 years of continuous service with the employer are eligible for gratuity. It is paid to them at the time of termination of employment due to retirement, resignation, superannuation, disablement or death.

If an employee works below the ground (e.g., mine), every year in which the employee works for more than 190 days in a year is considered as 1 year. If the employee works above the ground, 240 working days in a year is taken as 1 year for gratuity calculation.

If the number of days the employee has worked in a year is less than prescribed above, it is ignored for gratuity payment calculation. For example, if an employee has worked for 4 years and 10 months, the duration is considered as 5 years and the employee will be eligible for gratuity. On the other hand, if the employee has worked for 4 years and 5 months, it is treated as less than 5 years and no gratuity will be paid.

If an employee expires, gratuity is paid to him for the number of years he worked with the company irrespective of his tenure with the company.

If the employee becomes disabled due to an accident or illness, gratuity is paid to him for the number of years he worked with the company, irrespective of his tenure with the company.

If a person has been terminated from his job due to illegal activities like riot or violence or due to acts that are morally wrong, gratuity is not payable to him.

Power to Exempt under Section 5 (Section 21)

The Act empowers the appropriate government, by notification, and subject to such conditions as may be specified in the notification, to exempt any establishment, factory, mine, oilfield, plantation, port, railway company or shop to which this Act applies from the operation of the provisions of this Act. The appropriate government shall exercise the aforementioned power only if, in its opinion, the employees in such establishment, factory, mine, oilfield, plantation, port, railway company or shop are in receipt of gratuity or pensionary benefits not less favourable than the benefits conferred under this Act.

The section further provides that power to exempt from the application of this Act may also be exercised by giving a due notification and subject to the conditions as specified, in relation to any employee or class of employees employed in any establishment, factory, mine, oilfield, plantation, port, railway company or shop to which this Act applies, if, in the opinion of the appropriate government, such employee or class of employees are in receipt of gratuity or pensionary benefits not less favourable than the benefits conferred under this Act.

Forfeiture of Gratuity (Section 4(6))

If the services of an employee are terminated for any of wilful omission or negligence causing any damage or loss to, or destruction of, property belonging to the employer, then gratuity is forfeited to the extent of the damage or loss so caused. Following are the cases which attract the application of this section:

a. Termination for riotous and disorderly conduct or any other act of violence on his part.
b. Termination for any act which constitutes an offence involving moral turpitude, if such offence is committed by him in the course of his employment.

In such cases, the gratuity payable to the employee may be wholly or partially forfeited.

Payment of Gratuity to a Disabled Employee

If an employee becomes disabled due to any accident or disease and cannot do the same work with the same efficiency, the employer may re-employ such employee only on reduced wages. The gratuity of these disabled workmen will be computed in two parts:

1. For the period preceding the disablement, gratuity is calculated on the basis of wages last drawn by him at the time of the termination of his service.
2. For the period subsequent to the disablement, gratuity is computed on the basis of the reduced wages as drawn by him at the time of the termination of his service.

The total of the gratuity of these two periods will be the amount of gratuity payable to the disabled employed.

LO3: Compulsory Insurance and Protection of Gratuity

Compulsory Insurance (Section 4(A))

The Act mandates that with effect from such date as may be notified by the appropriate government in this behalf, the establishment belonging to or under the control of, the central government or a state government to obtain an insurance in a manner prescribed by the Act, for his liability for payment towards the gratuity, from the Life Insurance Corporation of India or any other prescribed insurer. It is further provided that different dates may be appointed for different establishments or class of establishments or for different areas.

Exemptions (Section 4A(2)): The Act empowers the appropriate government subject to such conditions as may be prescribed, to exempt every employer who had already established an approved gratuity fund in respect of his employees and who desires to continue such arrangement, and every employer employing 500 or more persons who establishes an approved gratuity fund in the manner prescribed from the provisions of Subsection (1).

Registration with CA: Every employer must get his establishment registered with the CA in the prescribed manner within such time as prescribed. No employer is registered under the provisions of this section unless he has taken insurance or has established an approved gratuity fund.

Case 9.2 will provide further insights into payment of gratuity to the employees.

Case 9.2: *E. I. D. Parry (I) Ltd. v. G. Omkar Murthy & Ors.*[2]

The respondents' employees were in the employment of E.I.D. Parry (I) Ltd., the appellant between the years 1958 and 1984. On 1 October 1984, voluntary retirement scheme was introduced by the appellant company and the respondents availed of that benefit and left the services after obtaining the terminal benefits as provided under the Payment of Gratuity Act, 1972 (The Central Act). Thereafter, the respondent employees filed the petitions under Section 44 of the Andhra Pradesh Shops and Establishments Act, 1966 (The State Act) claiming the difference between the gratuity received by them and the gratuity payable under Section 40 of the State Act.

The appellant company did not agree to pay the difference. Before the CA under the State Act, some objections were raised by the appellant company against the claims of the respondent employees. Those were as follows:

1. There had been inordinate delay in preferring the claim.
2. For payment of gratuity, the Central Act prevailed over the State Act, by virtue of Article 254 of the Constitution and Section 40(3) was invalid and the claims were unsustainable.

[2] *E.I.D. Parry (I) Ltd. v. G. Omkar Murthy & Ors.*, 2001 LLLR 497.

The respondent employees argued that at the relevant time when they voluntarily retired from service, the definition of employee under the definition of employee under Section 2(e) of the Central Act read as not to include employee whose wages exceeded ₹1,000 per mensem while all of them were getting wages more than ₹1,600 per mensem and, therefore, the Central Act could not be applied.

The authority dismissed all the appeals. Thereafter, the appellant company filed a revision petitions filed before the higher court.

Discussion Point

Whether the Central Act or the State Act would apply for payment of gratuity.

Judgement and Explanation

It was held that there was no substance in the contentions of the appellant company. The appeals, therefore, were dismissed. The court stated that at the time of the voluntary retirement of respondent employees, the definition of employee under the Central Act did not cover them. If that is so, it was certainly permissible for the respondents to make an application for payment of gratuity under Section 40(3) of the State Act. Further, the scheme of the Central Act would indicate that it would not be applicable in cases where the State Act is more beneficial than the Central Act. In this case, the finding was that the State Act was more beneficial than the Central Act. Therefore, the contentions sought to be advanced on behalf of the appellant as to repugnancy or otherwise of the State Act would not arise at all.

The above discussion clarifies that the State Act can prevail over the Central Act when the former is found more beneficial for the employees than the latter one.

Failure to Pay Insurance Premium or Contribution

If an employer fails to make any payment by way of premium to the insurance or by way of contribution to an approved gratuity fund, such an employer is liable to pay the amount of gratuity due under this Act (including interest, if any, for delayed payments) forthwith to the CA. It is further provided that such a defaulter employer is punishable with fine which may extend to ₹10,000 and in the case of a continuing offence with a further fine which may extend to ₹1,000 for each day during which the offence continues.

Nominations (Section 6)

Every employee covered under the Act is required to make a nomination within a specified time and manner. Following are the rules in this regard:

1. **Nomination within prescribed time:** Section 6 of the Act instructs every employee who has completed 1 year of service to nominate a person or persons for the purpose of payment of gratuity in the event of his death within prescribed time, form manner.
2. **Distribution of gratuity amount:** An employee may, in his nomination, distribute the amount of gratuity payable to him among more than one nominee.

3. **Nomination in favour of family members:** If at the time of making a nomination, the employee does not have a family, the nomination may be made in favour of any person or persons. But if such an employee subsequently acquires a family, such nomination forthwith becomes invalid and the employee is required to make a fresh nomination in favour of one or more members of his family, within the prescribed time.
4. **Modification in nomination:** An employee can modify nomination at any time, after giving to his employer a written notice in the prescribed form and in the prescribed manner.
5. **Death of the nominee:** If a nominee predeceases the employee, the interest of nominee is reverted to the employee who will make a fresh nomination, in the prescribed form, in respect of such interest.
6. **Safe custody of nomination:** Every nomination, fresh nomination or modification of nomination is to be sent by the employee to his employer and employer has to keep the same in his safe custody.

LO4: Determination and Recovery of Gratuity

Determination of the Amount of Gratuity (Section 7)

It is the duty of the employer to determine the amount of gratuity as soon as it becomes payable and also to give notice of the same to the person to whom gratuity is payable and to the CA too. The Act provides in this regard that a person eligible for payment of gratuity under this Act or any person authorized by him, in writing, to act on his behalf must send a written application to the employer, within such time and in such form, as may be prescribed, for payment of such gratuity. Soon after the gratuity becomes payable, the employer must determine the amount of gratuity and give notice in writing to the person to whom the gratuity is payable and also to the CA specifying the amount of gratuity so determined. It is immaterial here whether an application referred above has been made or not.. The payable amount has to be arranged by the employer within 30 days from the date it becomes payable to the person to whom the gratuity is payable.

The Act provides penalty provisions for the employer who fails to arrange the amount of gratuity payable under this section within the specified period. In such case, the employer has to pay, from the date on which the gratuity becomes payable to the date on which it is paid, simple interest at such rate, not exceeding the rate notified by the central government from time to time for repayment of long-term deposits, as that government may, by notification, specify.

Mode of payment of gratuity: The gratuity payable under the Act is paid in cash or, if so desired by the payee, in demand draft or bank cheque to the eligible employee, nominee or legal heir, as the case may be. If the eligible employee, nominee or legal heir so desires and the amount of gratuity payable is less than ₹1,000, payment may be made by postal money order after deducting the postal money order commission, therefore, from the total gratuity amount payable.

It is provided further that the employer must intimate about the details of payment to the CA of the area. In the case of nominee, or an heir, who is minor, the CA will invest the gratuity amount deposited with him for the benefit of such minor in term deposit with the State Bank of India or any of its subsidiaries or any nationalized bank.

Payment of interest: The employer is required to arrange to pay the amount of gratuity within 30 days from the date it becomes payable to the person eligible for getting the payment of gratuity. Failure to do so shall render him liable to pay the interest at the prevailing rate from time taken. In simple words, if the amount of gratuity payable is not paid by the employer within the 30 days, the employer has to pay, from the date on which the gratuity becomes payable to the date on which it is paid, simple interest at such rate, not exceeding the rate notified by the central government. However, no such interest is payable if the delay in the payment is due to the fault of the employee and the employer has obtained permission in writing from the CA for the delayed payment on this ground.

Dispute as to gratuity (Section 7(4)): If there arises any dispute related to the amount of gratuity payable to an employee under this Act or as to the admissibility of any claim of, or in relation to, an employee for payment of gratuity, or as to the person entitled to receive the gratuity, the employer is required deposit with the CA such amount as he admits to be payable by him as gratuity. In case of such dispute, the employer or employee or any other person raising the dispute is free to make an application to the CA for deciding the dispute.

The CA after due inquiry and after giving the parties to the dispute a reasonable opportunity of being heard determines the matter or matters in dispute. If, after such enquiry, the CA fixes any amount to be payable to the employee, the employer must pay such amount as reduced by the amount already deposited by the employer. The amount payable under this section is paid:

1. To the applicant where he is the employee.
2. Where the applicant is not the employee, to the (nominee or, as the case may be, the guardian of such nominee) heir of the employee if the CA is satisfied that there is no dispute as to the right of the applicant to receive the amount of gratuity.

Appeal: Any person in dispute not satisfied with decision order by the CA can make, within 60 days from the date of order, appeal to the appropriate government or the appellate authority. For admitting the appeal by the employer to the appellate authority, employer should deposit the amount equal to the amount of gratuity with the appellate authority.

Recovery of Gratuity (Section 8)

If the employee is not paid the due amount of gratuity, he should apply, within 30 days, to the employer. Even after receiving the notice, if the employer does not pay due gratuity, the claimant employee or his nominee or legal heir, within 90 days of the occurrence of the case for the application, should apply to the CA for issuing direction to the employer. After conducting the required enquiry, the CA will determine the amount payable and direct the employer to make the payment.

If the employer does not comply with the direction, the CA is authorized to issue a certificate to the collector to recover the amount and pay to the applicant. The amount will carry compound interest at such rate as the central government specifies, from the date of expiry of prescribed time. However, the amount of interest payable in any case cannot exceed the amount of the gratuity payable under the Act.

Case 9.3 will further clarify the application of this section.

Case 9.3: *Charan Singh v. Birla Textiles & Anr*[3]

Mr Charan Singh, the appellant, was in the service of Birla Textiles, the respondent firm from April 1944 till he resigned on 25 May 1983. The employer did not determine the amount of gratuity payable to the appellant. Appellant furnished the necessary application for payment of gratuity, but still no action was initiated by the respondent employer. Thereafter, the appellant approached the statutory CA for gratuity payment and also the due interest thereon to be paid for delay in the payment of gratuity amount.

The employer contested. After hearing from both the parties and examining the material placed before him, the CA determined the amount of gratuity at ₹16,380 and directed the employer to pay the same along with compound interest at 9 per cent. The respondent employer contested the payment of interest on the gratuity amount and appealed against the order of the CA.

Discussion Point

Whether the employee is entitled to interest on the gratuity amount.

Judgement and Explanation

It was held that in the above case, the appellant was not entitled to interest on the amount of gratuity found due to him. It was only when the collector issued a certificate for recovery of the dues as a public demand that interest as provided under Section 8 was admissible. The CA had directed interest as provided in Section 8 to be paid, which the Appellate Authority had vacated. It was further held that from the facts of the case, it was clear that the stage for action under Section 8 had not been reached in as much the appellant had not applied for recovery of gratuity to the collector.

Protection of gratuity: Gratuity payable under this Act cannot be attached in the execution of any decree or order of any civil, revenue or criminal court.

LO5: Enforcement of the Act

Appointment of Inspector (Section 7A)

The Act provides for the appointment of inspector for the smooth administration of the Act. The Act states that the appropriate government may, by notification, appoint as many inspectors, as it deems fit, for the purposes of this Act. The appropriate government is empowered to define the area to which the authority of an inspector or inspectors appointed shall extend. The appropriate government also distributes or allocates the work to be performed by them under this Act. It should also be noted here that every inspector is deemed to be a public servant within the meaning of Section 21 of the Indian Penal Code (45 of 1860).

[3] *Charan Singh v. Birla Textiles & Anr* on 31 August 1988 AIR 2022, 1988 SCR Suppl. (2) 742.

Powers of Inspectors (Section 7B)

Subject to any rules made by the appropriate government in this behalf, an Inspector under the Act is empowered to all or any of the following powers, namely:

1. Require an employer to furnish such information as he may consider necessary.
2. Enter and inspect, at all reasonable hours, with such assistants (if any), being persons in the service of the government or local or any public authority, as he thinks fit, any premises of or place in any factory, mine, oilfield, plantation, port, railway company, shop or other establishment to which this Act applies, for the purpose of examining any register, record or notice or other document required to be kept or exhibited under this Act or the rules made thereunder, or otherwise kept or exhibited in relation to the employment of any person or the payment of gratuity to the employees, and require the production thereof for inspection.
3. Examine with respect to any matter relevant to any of the purposes aforesaid, the employer or any person whom he finds in such premises or place and who, he has reasonable cause to believe, is an employee employed therein.
4. Make copies of, or take extracts from, any register, record, notice or other document, as he may consider relevant, and where he has reason to believe that any offence under this Act has been committed by an employer search and seize with such assistance as he may think fit, such register, record, notice or other document as he may consider relevant in respect of that offence.
5. Exercise such other powers as may be prescribed.

LO6: Penalties and Offences

Penalties (Section 9)

Section 9 of the Act provides any employer who contravenes any of the provisions of the Act can be punished with imprisonment for a term of not less than 3 months but which may extend to 1 year or with fine which is not less than ₹10,000 but which may extend to ₹20,000 or with both. Where the offence relates to non-payment of gratuity, the employer can be punished with imprisonment for a term which is not less than 6 months.

The following is the summary of penalties provided under the Act:

1. If the employer knowingly makes false statement/representation to avoid payment, he is liable to punished with imprisonment up to 6 months, or with fine which may extend to ₹10,000 or with both.
2. If the employer breaches or makes default in complying with any of the provisions of this Act, he is liable to be punished with imprisonment for three months to one year, or with fine which shall not be less than ₹10,000 but which may extend to ₹20,000 or with both.
3. For non-payment of any gratuity, the employer shall be punished with imprisonment of 6 months to 2 years and a fine.

Cognizance of Offences (Section 11)

Section 11 states that unless the complaint to court is made by the CA under the authorization of the government regarding the non-payment of gratuity and recovery of gratuity, court will not institute any judicial action against the employer. The complaint has to be made by CA to magistrate (court) within 15 days from the date of the authorization by government to the CA. It is to be noted here that no court inferior to that of a Metropolitan Magistrate or a Judicial Magistrate of the first class is allowed to try any offence punishable under this Act.

Protection of action taken in good faith: The Act protects the CA or any other person in respect of an act done in good faith or intended to be done under this Act or any rule or order made thereunder. No suit or other legal proceeding can be instituted against such authority or person.

Power to Make Rules

The Act empowers the appropriate government by notification to make rules for the purpose of carrying out the provisions of this Act. It is further provided that central government after framing the rules under this Act must lay down these rules before each House of Parliament while it is in session, for a total period of 30 days which may be comprised in one session or in two or more successive sessions. If both Houses agree in making any modification in the rule or both Houses agree that the rule should not be made, the rule shall, thereafter, have effect only in such modified form or be of no effect, as the case may be. However, any such modification or annulment shall be without prejudice to the validity of anything previously done.

Summary

1. Gratuity is a lump sum amount that is paid by an employer to an employee in consideration of his past service when employee's service is terminated.
2. In the year 1972, a Central Act, namely, the Payment of Gratuity Act, 1972, was enacted, which came into force on 16 September 1972.
3. The main objective of this Act is to provide a scheme for the payment of gratuity to employees engaged in factories, mines, oil fields plantations, ports, railway companies, shops or other establishments.
4. The Act is applicable on the persons employed in an 'establishment' to which the Act applies and establishments to which the Act applies covers.
5. The Act states that gratuity is payable to an employee on the termination of his employment after he has rendered continuous service for not less than 5 years; on his superannuation, or on his retirement or resignation, or on his death or disablement due to accident or disease.
6. Completion of continuous service of 5 years is not necessary where the termination is due to death or disablement.
7. The provisions relating to calculation of gratuity amount specify that for every completed year service or part thereof in excess of 6 months, the employer is required to pay gratuity to an employee at the rate of 15 days' wages based on rate of wages last drawn by the employee concerned.
8. The maximum amount of gratuity payable to an employee must not exceed ₹10 lakh.

9. The gratuity payable under the Act is paid in cash or, if so desired by the payee, in demand draft or bank cheque to the eligible employee, nominee or legal heir, as the case may be.
10. If the services of an employee are terminated for any of wilful omission or negligence causing any damage or loss to, or destruction of, property belonging to the employer, then gratuity is forfeited to the extent of the damage or loss so caused.
11. Every employee, who has completed 1 year of service, has to nominate a person or persons for the purpose of payment of gratuity in the event of his death within prescribed time, form manner.
12. It is the duty of the employer to determine the amount of gratuity as soon as it becomes payable and also to give notice of the same to the person to whom gratuity is payable and to the CA too.
13. If the employee is not paid the due amount of gratuity, he should apply, within 30 days, to the employer.
14. If the employer does not comply with the direction, the CA is authorized to issue a certificate to the collector to recover the amount and pay to the applicant.
15. If there arises any dispute in payment of the gratuity, the employer should deposit the gratuity payable amount with CA until the dispute is settled by the authority.

Multiple Choice Questions

1. The payment of Gratuity Act, 1972, is not applicable on ____________.
   a. Apprentices
   b. Persons who hold civil posts under central government or a state government
   c. Governed by any other Act or rules providing for the payment of gratuity
   d. All of the above

2. The Act states that completed year of service means continuous service for ____________.
   a. 6 months
   b. 1 year
   c. 2 years
   d. 3 years

3. Wage includes dearness allowance but does not include ____________.
   a. Any bonus
   b. Commission
   c. Overtime wages
   d. All of the above

4. The gratuity is payable to an employee on the termination of his employment after he has rendered continuous service for not less than ____________.
   a. 2 years
   b. 4 years
   c. 5 years
   d. 6 years

5. The employees who work for the whole year are entitled to gratuity at the rate of ____________ wages for every completed year of service or part thereof in excess of 6 months.
   a. 7 days
   b. 15 days
   c. 20 days
   d. 30 days

6. The maximum amount of gratuity payable to an employee must not exceed ____________.
   a. ₹1,000,000
   b. ₹700,000
   c. ₹500,000
   d. ₹300,000

7. The Act provides that the amount of gratuity payable to an employee must not exceed ____________ wages.
   a. 20 months
   b. 25 months
   c. 30 months
   d. 35 months

8. In the case where employees are paid for each piece (piece-rated employee), daily wages are computed on the average of the total wages received by him for a period of ____________ immediately preceding the termination of his employment.
   a. 8 months
   b. 5 months
   c. 3 months
   d. 2 months

9. Those who work only during the season are entitled to gratuity at the rate of ____________ wages for every completed year of service or part thereof in excess of 6 months.
   a. 7 days
   b. 15 days
   c. 20 days
   d. 30 days

10. ____________ is not to be taken into account while calculating the gratuity amount.
    a. Dearness allowance
    b. Basic wages
    c. The rate of wages paid for any overtime
    d. All of the above

Descriptive Questions

1. State the objects and scope of the Payment of Gratuity Act, 1972.
2. Define the following terms:
   a. Employee
   b. Continuous service.
3. When is the gratuity payable? Also discuss to whom gratuity is payable?
4. Discuss who is eligible for the payment of gratuity?
5. Can gratuity be forfeited? If yes, state the circumstance under which gratuity is forfeited.

ANNEXURE A

S. No.	*Amendment Act*	*Amendment*
1.	**The Payment of Gratuity (Amendment) Act, 2018**[4]	**Substitution of words in Section 2A** In explanation clause (iv), for the words 'twelve weeks', the words 'such period as may be notified by the central government from time to time' shall be substituted.
		Substitution of words in Section 4 In Subsection (3), for the words 'ten lakh rupees', the words 'such amount as may be notified by the central government from time to time' shall be substituted.

[4] http://www.prsindia.org/uploads/media/Payment%20of%20Gratuity%20Bill,%202017/Payment%20of%20Gratuity%20Act,%202018.pdf

S. No.	Amendment Act	Amendment
2.	**The Payment of Gratuity (Amendment) Bill, 2017**[5]	**Wider coverage of employees under the Act** The Payment of Gratuity Act, 1972, allows for the payment of gratuity to employees in any establishment, factory, mine, oilfield, plantation, port, railways, company or shop employing 10 or more workers. Employees are paid gratuity if they have provided at least 5 years of continuous service at the time of termination. **Empowerment of central government** The 2017 Bill empowers the central government to (i) notify the period of maternity leave eligible for qualifying as continuous service; and (ii) determine the amount of gratuity available to employees. **The period of maternity leave eligible for qualifying as continuous service under the Act** The maximum maternity leave, for the purpose of calculating continuous service under the Act, was based on the maternity leave provided under the Maternity Benefit Act, 1961. The maximum maternity leave under the 1961 Act was changed from 12 weeks to 26 weeks by the Maternity Benefit (Amendment) Act, 2017. The Bill removes the reference to 12 weeks in the 1972 Act and empowers the central government to notify the maximum maternity leave. **Ceiling on gratuity amount to be notified by central government** Under the Act, the maximum amount of gratuity payable to an employee cannot exceed ₹10 lakh. The Bill removes the existing ceiling and states that the ceiling may be notified by the central government.

[5] http://www.prsindia.org/billtrack/the-payment-of-gratuity-amendment-bill-2017-5002/

10
CHAPTER

The Maternity Benefit Act, 1961

LEARNING OBJECTIVES

Upon completing this chapter, the reader would be able to:

LO1. Understand the objectives, scope and important definitions of the Act.
LO2. Gain insights into provisions related to maternity benefits under the Act.
LO3. Understand the enforcement of the Act.
LO4. Know the provisions for penalty for the offences identified under the Act.
LO5. Find out the details of important miscellaneous provisions of the Act.

Introduction

Maternity benefits were first recognized and discussed in the Maternity Protection Conference organized by the ILO in 1919. Article 42 of Indian Constitution contains the directive that the state shall make provision for securing just and humane conditions of work and maternity benefits. In order to regulate the employment of women in certain establishments for certain periods before and after childbirth, and to provide for maternity benefits and certain other benefits, the Indian Parliament enacted the Maternity Benefit Act, 1961. The Act was enacted keeping in view not only all those legislations related to maternity that existed from the pre-Constitution days but also ILO's mandate regarding maternity protection. The Maternity Benefit Act of 1961 is not the only piece of legislation in the country that provides for maternity protection or benefit. The ESI Act, 1948, and the Central Civil Services (CCS) Rules, 1972, also cover maternity protection.

LO1: Objectives, Scope and Important Definitions

Objectives

The Maternity Benefit Act, 1961, provides directions to regulate the employment of women in certain establishments for a certain period before and after childbirth, and provides for maternity and other benefits. These benefits are aimed to protect the dignity of motherhood by providing for the full and healthy maintenance of women and her child when she is not working. With the object of providing maternity leave and benefit to women employees, the Maternity Benefit Bill was passed by both the Houses of Parliament and, subsequently, it received the assent of President in the year 1961 to become an Act under the short title and numbers 'The Maternity Benefit Act, 1961 (53 of 1961)'.

The Maternity Benefit Act, 1961, was brought into force with a view to reduce disparities under the existing Maternity Benefit Acts and to bring uniformity with regard to rates, qualifying conditions and duration of maternity benefits for the women employees. The Act repealed the Mines Maternity Benefit Act, 1941; the Bombay Maternity Benefit Act, 1929; the provisions of maternity protection under the Plantations Labour Act, 1951; and all other provincial enactments covering the same field.

Applicability and Scope

The Act extends to the whole of India. It applies, in the first instance, to every establishment be it a factory, a mine or plantation including any such establishment belonging to government and to every establishment wherein persons are employed for the exhibition of equestrian, acrobatic and other performances, and to every shop or establishment within the meaning of any law for the time being in force in relation to shops and establishments in a state, in which 10 or more persons are employed, or were employed, on any day of the preceding 12 months. The Act can be further extended to other establishments by the state governments.

Non-applicability: The Act is not applicable to any factory or other establishment to which the provisions of the ESI Act, 1948, apply except as otherwise provided in Sections 5A and 5B of the Act.

Important Definitions

1. **Child (Section 3(b)):** The Act includes a stillborn child under the definition of child.
2. **Delivery (Section 3(c)):** 'Delivery' means the birth of a child.
3. **Employer (Section 3(d)):** Under the Act, 'employer':
   a. In relation to an establishment which is under the control of the government, is a person or authority appointed by the government for the supervision and control of employees or, where no person or authority is so appointed, the head of the department.
   b. In relation to an establishment under any local authority, is the person appointed by such authority for the supervision and control of employees or, where no person is so appointed, the chief executive officer of the local authority.
   c. In any other case, is the person who, or the authority which, has the ultimate control over the affairs of the establishment and where the said affairs are entrusted to any other person, whether called a manager, managing director, managing agent or by any other name, such person.
4. **Establishment (Section 3(e)):** According to Section 3(e) of the Act, 'establishment' means:
   a. A factory.
   b. A mine.
   c. A plantation.
   d. An establishment wherein persons are employed for the exhibition of equestrian, acrobatic and other performances.
   e. A shop or establishment.

   f. An establishment to which the provisions of this Act have been declared under Subsection (1) of Section 2 to be applicable.
5. **Maternity benefit (Section 3(h)):** Under the Act, maternity benefit is defined as the payment referred to in Subsection (1) of Section 5.
6. **Mine (Section 3(i)):** The Act defines mine as defined in clause (j) of Section 2 of the Mines Act, 1952.
7. **Miscarriage (Subsection (14B) of Section 2):** Miscarriage means expulsion of the contents of a pregnant uterus at any period prior to or during the 26th week of pregnancy but does not include any miscarriage the causing of which is punishable under the Indian Penal Code (IPC).
8. **Wages (Section 3(n)):** Under the Act, the term 'wages' stands for all remuneration paid or payable in cash to a woman, if the terms of the contract of employment, express or implied, were fulfilled and include:
   a. Such cash allowances (including dearness allowance and house rent allowance) as a woman is for the time being entitled to;
   b. Incentive bonus; and
   c. The money value of the concessional supply of food grains and other articles but does not include the following:
      i. Any bonus other than incentive bonus.
      ii. Overtime earnings and any deduction or payment made on the account of fines.
      iii. Any contribution paid or payable by the employer to any pension fund or provident fund or for the benefit of the woman under any law for the time being in force.
      iv. Any gratuity payable on the termination of service.
9. **Woman (Section 3(o)):** Here, the term 'woman' refers to a woman employed, whether directly or through any agency, for wages in any establishment.

Insured Woman

The term 'insured woman' is not defined in the Act. However, Subsection (14) of Section 2 of the Act defines an 'insured person' as a person who is or was an employee in respect of whom contributions are or were payable under the Act and who is, by reason thereof, entitled to any of the benefits provided by this Act. The term 'insured person' also covers an 'insured woman'. By virtue of the definition of the term 'insured person', a woman continues to be an 'insured woman' even after she has left insurable employment. Thus, an insured woman is entitled to maternity benefit during a benefit period during which she may no longer be in insurable employment, subject to the condition that she satisfies the contributory condition relevant to the said benefit period.

LO2: Provisions Related to Maternity Benefits

Employment of, or Work with, Women Prohibited during Certain Periods (Section 4)

Section 4 of this Act directs that no employer should knowingly employ a woman in any establishment during the 6 weeks immediately following the day of her delivery, or miscarriage, nor shall any woman work during this period. The section further provides that no pregnant woman shall, on a request made by her in this behalf, be required by her employer to do any work of arduous nature, or that which involves long hours of standing, or which in any way is likely to interfere with her pregnancy or the normal development of the foetus, or is likely to cause her miscarriage or otherwise to adversely affect her health, during the 1 month immediately preceding the 6 weeks before the date of her expected delivery.

Entitlement for Maternity Benefit (Section 5)

Under Section 5 of the Act, women get entitlements to gain benefits under the Act only if the woman employee, whether employed directly or through a contractor, has actually worked in the establishment for a period of at least 80 days during the 12 months immediately preceding the date of her expected delivery. The qualifying period of 80 days, however, is not applicable to a woman who may have immigrated into the state of Assam and was pregnant at the time of immigration. It is also to be noted that there is no wage ceiling for coverage under the Act nor is there any restriction so far as to the type of work a woman is engaged in is concerned.

Payment of maternity benefits: Section 5 elaborates on the payment of maternity benefits and states in this regard that every woman employee is entitled to, and her employer is liable for, the payment of maternity benefit at the rate of the average daily wage for the period of her actual absence immediately preceding and including the day of her delivery and for the 6 weeks immediately following that day. The 'average daily wage' means the average of the woman's wages payable to her for the days on which she has worked during the period of 3 calendar months immediately preceding the date from which she was absent on account of maternity, or ₹1 a day, whichever amount is higher.

Case 10.1 will throw light on some important aspects to be kept in mind while calculating the payment for maternity benefits for a woman employee.

Case 10.1: *B. Shah v. Presiding Officer, Labour Court*[1]

Ms B. Shah, the respondent working in Mount Stuart Estate belonging to the appellant was allowed leave of absence on maternity leave. After her delivery, the appellant paid the respondent on account of maternity benefit an amount equivalent to what she would have earned on the basis of her average daily wages in 72 working days falling within 12 weeks of the maternity period, excluding 12 Sundays being wageless holidays which fell during the period of the respondent's actual absence immediately preceding and including the day of her delivery and the 6 weeks immediately following that day.

The respondent was not happy with the amount paid to her on account of maternity benefit. She claimed the maternity benefit for the entire period of 12 weeks, that is, for 84 days on the plea that a week consisted of 7 days including Sundays. Her request was refused by the appellant. The appellant contended that 12 weeks for which maternity benefit was provided for in Subsection (3) of Section 5 of the Act must be taken to mean 12 weeks of work and the computation of the benefit had to be made with reference to the actual days on which the woman would have worked but for her inability.

Aggrieved by this, the respondent moved to the court.

[1] *B. Shah v. Presiding Officer, Labour Court, ...* on 12 October 1977, AIR 12, 1978 SCR (1) 701.

Discussion Point

In calculating the maternity benefit for the period covered by Section 5, should Sundays being wageless holiday be excluded?

Judgement and Explanation

It was held that in calculating the maternity benefit for the period covered by Section 5, Sundays must also be included. The court applied the beneficial rule of construction in favour of the woman worker and observed that the benefit conferred by the Act read in the light of Article 42 of the Constitution was intended to enable the woman worker not only to subsist but also to make up her dissipated energy, nurse her child, preserve her efficiency as a worker and maintain the level of her previous efficiency and output.

Condition for claiming benefits: The following are the conditions to be met by a woman employee to claim the maternity benefit under the Act:

1. Ten weeks before the date of her expected delivery, the woman employee may ask the employer to give her light work for a month. At that time, she had to produce a certificate that she is pregnant.
2. She should give written notice to the employer about 7 weeks before the date of her delivery that she will be absent from the workplace for 6 weeks before and after her delivery. She should also name the person to whom payment will be made in case she cannot take it herself.
3. She should take the payment for the first 6 weeks before she proceeds on leave.
4. For the rest 6 weeks, she will get the after childbirth payment within 48 hours of giving proof that she has had a child.
5. She is entitled to two nursing breaks of 15 minutes each in the course of her daily work till her child is 15 months old.
6. The employer is not allowed by the Act to discharge a woman employee or change her conditions of service while she is on maternity leave.

Maximum period of maternity benefit: The maximum period for which any woman is entitled to maternity benefit is 26 weeks, of which not more than 8 weeks must precede the date of her expected delivery. The Maternity Benefit (Amendment) Act, 2017, has increased the duration of paid maternity leave available for women employees from the existing 12 weeks to 26 weeks. Under the Maternity Benefit (Amendment) Act, 2017, this benefit could be availed by women for a period extending up to a maximum of 8 weeks before the expected delivery date and the remaining time can be availed post-childbirth. For women who are expecting after having 2 children, the duration of paid maternity leave shall be 12 weeks out which 6 weeks are pre- and 6 weeks are post-expected date of delivery.

Maternity leave for adoptive and commissioning mothers: The Maternity Benefit (Amendment) Act, 2017, extends certain benefits to adoptive mothers as well and provides that every woman who adopts a child shall be entitled to 12 weeks of maternity leave, from the date of adoption.

Continuance of payment of maternity benefit in certain cases: Section 5A guarantees women the security of tenure during such period of leave. Their employer will continue to pay her wages even though she is unable to attend work. The Section states that every woman who is entitled to the payment of maternity benefit under this Act, notwithstanding the application of the ESI Act, 1948 (34 of 1948), to

BOX 10.1: Maternity Benefit (Amendment) Act, 2017—Major Amendments

The Maternity (Amendment) Bill, 2017, an amendment to the Maternity Benefit Act, 1961, was passed in Lok Sabha on 09 March 2017, in Rajya Sabha on 11 August 2016 and received an assent from President of India on 27 March 2017. The Maternity Benefit Amendment Act makes it mandatory for employers to educate women about the maternity benefits available to them at the time of their appointment.

The provisions of the Maternity Benefit (Amendment) Act, 2017, were made effective from 01 April 2017. However, provision on crèche facility (Section 11A) came into effect from 01 July 2017.

Key Amendments

Increased paid maternity leave: The duration of paid maternity is leave available for women employees from the existing 12 weeks to 26 weeks. Out of the total 26 weeks, a maximum of 8 weeks paid maternity leave can be availed before the expected delivery date and the remaining time can be availed post-childbirth. For women who are expecting after having two children, the duration of paid maternity leave shall be 12 weeks (i.e., 6 weeks pre- and 6 weeks post-expected date of delivery).

Maternity leave for adoptive and commissioning mothers: Every woman who adopts a child is now entitled to 12 weeks of maternity leave, from the date of adoption.

Work from home option: The Amendment Act, 2017, has introduced the work from home option for women employees that may be exercised after the expiry of the 26 weeks of leave period. Depending upon the nature of work, women employees may be able to avail this benefit on terms that are mutually agreed with the employer.

Crèche facility: Every establishment employing 50 or more employees is required to provide the crèche facility in the establishment. Women employees would be permitted to visit the crèche four times during the day.

the factory or other establishment in which she is employed, continues to be so entitled until she becomes qualified to claim maternity benefit under Section 50 of that Act.

Work from home option: The Maternity Benefit (Amendment) Act, 2017, has also introduced an enabling provision relating to 'work from home' for women. The option of work from home may be exercised after the expiry of the 26 weeks of leave period. However, depending upon the nature of work, women employees may be able to avail this benefit on terms that are mutually agreed with the employer (Box 10.1).

Notice of Claim for Maternity Benefits (Section 6)

Section 6 directs that a notice of claim for maternity benefit has to be provided to the employer. A woman employee entitled to maternity benefit may give a notice in writing following the prescribed form to her employer, stating that:

1. Her maternity benefit may be paid to her or her nominee, specified in the notice.
2. She will not work in any establishment during the period for which she receives the maternity benefit.
3. She will be absent from work from such date (to be specified by her), which cannot be earlier than 6 weeks before the date of her expected delivery.

It is to be noted here that the amount of maternity benefit for the period preceding the date of her expected delivery is required to be paid in advance by the employer to the woman on production of prescribed proof that the woman is pregnant. The amount due for the subsequent period has to be paid by the employer to the woman within 48 hours of production of prescribed proof that the woman has delivered a child.

The above-discussed notice may be given during the pregnancy or as soon as possible, after the delivery. On receipt of the notice, the employer has to permit such a woman to absent herself from work after the day of her delivery. The point to be noted here is that the failure to give notice, however, does not disentitle the woman to the benefit of the Act.

Payment of Maternity Benefit in Case of Death of a Woman (Section 7)

In case a woman dies during this period, the maternity benefit is to be paid only for the days up to and including the day of her death. Similarly, if the woman employee dies during her delivery, or during the period of 6 weeks immediately following the date of delivery, leaving behind in either case the child, the employer shall extend the maternity benefits for the entire period of 6 weeks immediately following the day of her delivery. But, if the child also dies during the above-mentioned period, then the days up to and, including, the day of the death of the child are considered for the payment of maternity benefit in case of death of a woman employee.

In the event of a woman employee's death, the employer has to pay the maternity benefits or amount to the person nominated by the deceased in the notice given as directed by Section 6 and if no notice has been given, then to her legal representatives. Any woman who has not given the notice when she was pregnant may give such notice as soon as possible after delivery. The provision under Section 6(5) says that the amount of maternity benefits for a period preceding the date of her expected delivery is to be paid in advance by the employer. Miscarriage has also been given the same importance in the Act and is treated in the same manner as delivery is treated.

Payment of Medical Bonus (Section 8)

As discussed above, the Act has a provision of maternity leave with average pay for 6 weeks before the delivery and leave with average pay for 6 weeks after the delivery. Section 8 further extends the benefit in terms of medical bonus to a pregnant woman employee. The act states that the woman employee is entitled to a medical bonus of ₹25 if the employer does not provide free medical care to the woman and in case of miscarriage, 6-week leave with average pay from the date of miscarriage.

Leave for Miscarriage and Tubectomy Operation (Section 9)

Section 9 of the Act provides that in case of miscarriage, a woman employee is entitled to leave with wages at the rate of maternal benefit for a period of 6 weeks immediately following the day of her miscarriage. The women employees are also entitled to leave with wages at the rate of maternity benefit for a period of 2 weeks immediately following the day of her tubectomy operation.

Leave for Illness Arising out of Pregnancy and so on (Section 10)

A woman employee suffering from illness arising out of pregnancy, delivery or the premature birth of child (miscarriage, medical termination of pregnancy or tubectomy operation) is entitled, in addition to the period of absence allowed, to her leave with wages at the rate of maternity benefit for a maximum period of 1 month.

Let us discuss a case to gain the insights of provision of leave under the Act and its extension in certain cases (Case 10.2).

Case 10.2: *Seema Gupta v. Guru Nanak Institute of Management*[2]

On 28 March 2001, Ms Seema Gupta, the petitioner, was appointed by Guru Nanak Institute of Management, the respondent college. She joined the college on 1 May 2001. According to the terms of appointment, the appointment was on probation for 1 year, which could be extended for another 1 year and the appointment could be terminated without any notice and without assigning reason during the first year and by 1 month's notice on either side.

The petitioner claimed that though entitled, she was not granted summer vacation leave for 2 years. The petitioner was blessed with a child on 28 December 2003 and was sanctioned maternity leave for 135 days with effect from 29 December 2003. She had requested for maternity leave of 180 days as per the Guru Nanak Dev University Rules (GNDU Rules) which, it is averred, allowed maternity leave for that period. In response to her application, the petitioner was informed that as the CCS Rules were applicable to her services, the provisions of GNDU Rules were inapplicable.

Meanwhile, as per the pleadings, she was applying for extension of leave, initially sanctioned up to May 2004, on medical grounds. Her requests were granted by the college, for 31 days, later for another 14 days. The college used to send her show-cause notices to report back to duty. Subsequently, the respondent college informed her that the petitioner was governed by the CCS Rules and not by the GNDU Rules and that as per the CCS rules she was not entitled for the maternity leave beyond 135 days. The college also directed her to rejoin forthwith, threatening disciplinary action against her.

The petitioner, by a letter referred to Rule 43(4) (b) of CCS Leave Rules whereby she was entitled to continuation of maternity leave up to a maximum period of 1 year, requested for extension of maternity leave. The petitioner was terminated on the basis of unauthorized leave/absence, on 14 October 2004, that is, within 2 months of the extended maternity leave.

The petitioner contended that the CCS Leave Rules were applicable to the petitioner and those Rules clearly stipulated that maternity leave could be extended up to 1 year. In case of maternity leave, even the requirement of producing medical certificates has been waived off. Based on this, the petitioner alleged that the termination was impugned as arbitrary, illegal and contrary to the provisions of the CCS Rules which are violative of Articles 14 and 16 of the Constitution of India, as well as provisions of the Maternity Benefits Act.

The respondent college in its return disclaimed any liability and stated that the petitioner could not claim to continue in its services on the basis of any entitlement, since she was not a regular employee but merely engaged in ad hoc service. It was also averred that repeated show-cause notices were issued to the petitioner for overstaying the leave; the college was within its right to terminate her, in the larger interests of the

[2] *Seema Gupta v. Guru Nanak Institute of Management*, 135 (2006) DLT 404.

students. It was submitted that the petitioner enjoyed a full 6 months, or 180 days leave; the college's refusal to grant any further extension, and in issuing an ultimatum to her, to rejoin the services, was justified. These circumstances established that the action impugned was justified.

Discussion Point

Was the termination of the petitioner impugned as arbitrary, illegal and contrary to the provisions of the Maternity Benefits Act?

Judgement and Explanation

It was held that the impugned termination letter could not be sustained; it was illegal and was thereby quashed. The respondent college was directed to reinstate the petitioner to her post; the petitioner was also declared to be entitled to full arrears of salary. The court stated that the respondent treated the request for extension of leave by 5 months, as a normal request.

Exigencies of service bound all employers, that reason would be available in all cases where a request for extended maternity leave was sought. If such reasons given in a routine manner were to be upheld, the right for extended maternity leave of up to 1 year would be meaningless, as every employer could cite that as a ground for denial. The special nature of the right then would exist only on paper, in negation.

Nursing Breaks (Section 11)

Regarding nursing breaks, Section 11 states that every woman employee who delivered a child and returns to duty after such delivery is, in addition to the interval for rest allowed to her, allowed in the course of her daily work two breaks of the prescribed duration for nursing the child until the child attains the age of 15 months.

Crèche facility (Section 11A): The Maternity Benefit (Amendment) Act, 2017, provides that every establishment employing 50 or more employees is required to provide the crèche facility in the establishment. Women employees would be permitted to visit the crèche 4 times during the day.

Prohibition of Dismissal during Absence of Pregnancy (Section 12)

A woman cannot be discharged or dismissed by the employer when she absents herself from work in accordance with the provisions of this Act. Section 12 of the Act restricts an employer from dismissing a woman employee for absence who is availing maternity benefit. Such a dismissal by the employer cannot deprive such a woman employee from claiming maternity benefits. However, an employer can deprive a female employee of the maternity benefit if she was dismissed for gross misconduct. Notice of dismissal or discharge is also prohibited. The Section also states that conditions of service cannot be altered to her disadvantage, during such absence. As mentioned above, maternity benefit or medical bonus or both can be deprived only for dismissal for any prescribed gross misconduct. On dismissal and deprivation of benefit, the woman can appeal to the prescribed authority whose decision is final.

Case 10.3 provides an understanding of the application of this Section.

Case 10.3: *Dr Vishakha Kapoor v. National Board of Examination and Anr.*[3]

Dr Vishakha Kapoor, the appellant, was a qualified ophthalmic surgeon with MBBS, DO and MS degrees from Gujarat University. National Board of Examination, the respondent, was a registered society under the administrative control of the Ministry of Health and Family Welfare, Government of India. The society used to conduct postgraduate examination in modern medicine and allied sciences at the national level. The appellant was appointed as an Assistant Controller of Examination in the respondent society, which was later redesignated as Deputy Director (Medical). The appointment was made on 9 October 2006 and was on probation for a period of 2 years.

On 4 May 2007, the appellant suffered miscarriage and was advised to take bed rest. The appellant claimed to be pregnant in April 2007 after 5 years of her marriage. As stated by the appellant, she became pregnant once again while on leave and she was advised to remain on bed rest in view of the 'high-risk' pregnancy due to pregnancy-induced hypertension and gestational diabetes mellitus. Accordingly, she submitted repeated leave applications to the respondent society along with medical certificates from the gynaecologist/doctors.

The respondent did not dispute applications for leave and the medical certificates, enclosed with the applications. The respondent accepted that no response or reply was written into the repeated applications made by the appellant asking for leave due to medical reasons. The respondent stated that leave was granted and extended from time to time up to 3 October 2007 and not thereafter. The respondent claimed that the appellant was on unauthorized absence after 4 October 1997. The respondent further claimed that they wrote two letters informing the appellant that no leave was due to her and directed her to resume duties with immediate effect. It was also stated in the letter that in case no reply was received from the appellant's side within 3 days of receipt of this letter, it would be presumed that she had nothing to state in the matter and her leave would be treated as unauthorized absence, as stated by the respondent.

On 16 January 2008, the appellant gave birth to a child and immediately thereupon wrote an application seeking maternity leave. On 8 February 2008, the appellant received a letter from the respondent terminating her services. The appellant approached the court and instituted a case for striking down the termination order issued by the respondent.

Discussion Point

Under the light of the facts shared above, was the termination order liable to be struck down?

Judgement and Explanation

It was held that termination order was liable to be struck down under the provisions of Section 12 of the Act. The court referred to Section 12 of the Act and stated that in the above case, it was clear that the appellant was entitled to 12 weeks of leave including up to 6 weeks before delivery and the rest after the birth of the child on 16 January 2008. The entitlement to leave up to the maximum period of 12 weeks is statutory and mandatory. The termination order ignored that and treated this period of 12 weeks as unauthorized leave and was therefore contrary to law. Second, the notice of discharge/dismissal could not have been issued during this period of statutory leave/absence.

Now it is clear that where a woman absents herself from work in accordance with the provisions of the Act, her employer cannot discharge or dismiss her on account of such absence. The second part of said Subsection further stipulates that any notice of discharge or dismissal that would expire during such absence or which would vary to her disadvantage any of the conditions of her service is also unlawful.

[3] *Dr Vishakha Kapoor v. National Board of Examination and Anr.*, MANU/DE/0971/2009.

No Deductions in Wages in Certain Cases (Section 13)

Section 13 of this Act stops any deduction from the normal and usual daily wages of a woman entitled to maternity benefits under the provisions of this Act to be made by reasons that:

1. The nature of work assigned to her by virtue of the provisions contained in Section 4(3) concerning prohibition of assignment of work of arduous nature; or
2. Breaks for nursing the child allowed to her under the provisions of Section 11.

LO3: Enforcement of the Act

Inspector (Section 14)

Section 14 of the Act empowers the appropriate government to (by notification in the Official Gazette) appoint such officers as it thinks fit to be Inspectors for the purposes of this Act. The government also defines the local limits of the jurisdiction within which the Inspector exercises his functions under this Act.

Powers and Duties of Inspectors (Sections 15 and 16)

Subject to such restrictions or conditions as may be prescribed, an Inspector exercises all or any of the following powers. The Inspector can:

1. Enter at all reasonable times with such assistants, if any, being person in the service of the government or any local or other public authority, as he thinks fit, any premises or place where women are employed or work is given to them in an establishment, for the purposes of examining any register, records and notices required to be kept or exhibited by or under this Act and require their production for inspection.
2. Examine any person whom he finds in any premises or place and who, he has reasonable cause to believe, is employed in the establishment. However, no person can be compelled under this Section to answer any question or give any evidence tending to incriminate himself.
3. Require the employer to give information regarding the names and addresses of women employed, payments made to them and applications or notices received from them under this Act.
4. Take copies of any registers and records or notices or any portions thereof.

Inspector to be a public servant: Section 16 declares that every Inspector appointed under this Act is deemed to be a public servant within the meaning of Section 21 of the IPC (45 of 1860).

Power of Inspector of Direct Payments to Be Made (Section 17)

A woman can make a complaint to the Inspector if she claims that:

1. Maternity benefit or any other amount to which she is entitled under this Act and any person claiming that payment due under Section 7 has been improperly withheld.

2. Her employer has discharged or dismissed her during or on account of her absence from work in accordance with the provisions of this Act.

The Act further empowers the Inspector of his own motion or on receipt of a complaint as discussed above to make an inquiry or cause an inquiry to be made in this regard. Upon enquiry, if the Inspector is satisfied that the payment has been wrongfully withheld, he can direct the payment to be made in accordance with his orders. If the Inspector discovers that the complainant (the woman) has been discharged or dismissed during or on account of her absence from work in accordance with the provisions of this Act, the Inspector can pass such orders as are just and proper according to the circumstances of the case.

Appeal (Section 17(3))

Any person aggrieved by the decision of the Inspector can appeal to the prescribed authority against the decision of the Inspector. Such appeal is to be filed within 30 days from the date on which such decision is communicated to such a person. The decision of the prescribed authority stands final and binding on the parties, where an appeal has been preferred or of the Inspector where no such appeal has been preferred. The amount payable under this Section is recoverable by the Collector on a certificate issued for that amount by the Inspector as an arrear of land revenue.

Forfeiture of Maternity Benefit (Section 18)

If a woman employee, permitted by her employer to absent herself under the provisions of Section 6, works in any other establishment for any period during such authorized absence, her claim for the maternity benefit for such period is forfeited. In simple words, a woman employee cannot work in any other establishment during the period for which she has been permitted by her employer to remain absent from work under Section 6 of the Act. If she does so, she cannot claim the maternity benefit under the Act.

LO4: Penalties and Offences

Penalty for the Contravention of the Act by Employer (Section 21)

If any employer contravenes the provisions of this Act or the rules made thereunder, he/she is punishable with imprisonment or with fine or with both. Where the contravention is of any provision regarding maternity benefit or regarding payment of any other amount and such maternity benefit or amount has not already been recovered, the court is empowered in addition to recover such maternity benefit or the amount as if it were a fine and pay the same to the person entitled thereto.

Section 21 of the Act provides a penalty for non-payment of maternity benefits, discharging or dismissing a woman employee during or on account of her absence from work under Section 6 of the Act. The defaulting employer is liable to be punished with imprisonment which shall not be less than 3 months, but it will extend to 1 year and with a fine, not exceeding ₹5,000. Other provisions of the Act include imprisonment which may extend up to 1 year or fine which may extend up to ₹5,000.

The Penalty for Obstructing the Inspector (Section 22)

Section 22 states that contravening the provisions of this Act and obstructing the Inspector from viewing registers and documents result in imprisonment of 1 year and fine of ₹5,000.

Cognizance of Offence (Section 23)

Following persons can file a complaint regarding the commission of an offence under this Act in any court of competent jurisdiction:

1. Any aggrieved woman.
2. An office bearer of a trade union registered under the Trade Unions Act, 1926 (16 of 1926), of which such a woman is a member.
3. A voluntary organization registered under the Societies Registration Act, 1860 (21 of 1860).
4. An Inspector.

Any complaint under the Act is to be filed before the expiry of 1 year from the date on which the offence is alleged to have been committed. No court inferior to that of a Metropolitan Magistrate or a Magistrate of the first class can try any offence under this Act.

Protection of Action Taken in Good Faith (Section 24)

Section 24 of the Act provides protection to any person for anything which is done in good faith or intended to be done in pursuance of this Act or of any rule or order made thereunder from any suit, prosecution or other legal proceedings.

LO5: Miscellaneous Provisions of the Act

Abstract of the Act and Rules to Be Exhibited (Section 19)

Every employer is required to exhibit an abstract of the provisions of this Act and the rules made thereunder in the language or languages of the locality in a conspicuous place in every part of the establishment in which women are employed.

Maintenance of Registers and so on (Section 20)

The Act directs every employer to prepare and maintain such registers, records and muster rolls and in such manner as may be prescribed.

Effect of Laws and Agreements Inconsistent with the Act (Section 27)

The provisions of this Act are effective only when anything in the Act is not inconsistent with something contained in any other law or in the terms of any award, agreement or contract of service, whether made before or after the coming into force of this Act. The Act further states, if under any award, agreement, contract of service or otherwise a woman is entitled to benefits in respect of any matter which are more favourable to her than those to which she would be entitled to under this Act, the woman continues to be entitled to the more favourable benefits in respect of that matter. Here, such woman is entitled to receive benefits in respect of other matters under this Act.

The Act clearly precludes a woman from entering into an agreement with her employer for granting her rights or privileges in respect of any matter which are more favourable to her than those to which she would be entitled to under this Act.

Power to Make Rules (Section 28)

Subject to the condition of previous publication and by notification in the Official Gazette, the appropriate government is allowed to make rules for carrying out the purpose of this Act. Such rules may provide for:

1. The preparation and maintenance of registers, records and muster rolls.
2. The exercise of powers (including the inspection of establishments) and the performance of duties by Inspectors for the purposes of this Act.
3. The method of payment of maternity benefit and other benefits under this Act insofar as provision has not been made in this Act.
4. The form of notices under Section 6.
5. The nature of proof required under the provisions of this Act.
6. The duration of nursing breaks referred to in Section 11.
7. Acts which may constitute gross misconduct for purposes of Section 12.
8. The authority to which an appeal under clause (b) of Subsection (2) of Section 12 shall lie, the form and manner in which such appeal may be made and the procedure to be followed in disposal thereof.
9. The authority to which an appeal shall lie against the decision of the Inspector under Section 17, the form and manner in which such appeal may be made and the procedure to be followed in disposal thereof.
10. The form and manner in which complaints may be made to Inspectors under Subsection (1) of Section 17 and the procedure be followed by them when making inquiries or causing inquiries to be made under Subsection (2) of that Section.
11. Any other matter which is to be or may be prescribed.

It is to be noted that every rule made by the central government under this Section is to be approved by both Houses of the Parliament. If the houses suggest any modification, the rule shall thereafter have effect only in such modified form. However, any such modification or annulment must be made without prejudice to the validity of anything previously done under that rule.

Summary

1. Article 42 of Indian Constitution contains the directive that the state shall make provision for securing just and humane conditions of work and maternity benefits.

2. The Maternity Benefit Act, 1961, provides directions to regulate the employment of women in certain establishments for a certain period before and after childbirth and provides for maternity and other benefits.
3. The Act is not applicable to any factory or other establishment to which the provisions of the ESI Act, 1948, apply except as otherwise provided in Sections 5A and 5B of the Act.
4. No employer shall knowingly employ a woman in any establishment during the 6 weeks immediately following the day of her delivery, or miscarriage, nor shall any woman work during this period.
5. Every woman employee is entitled to, and her employer is liable for, the payment of maternity benefit at the rate of the average daily wage for the period of her actual absence immediately preceding and including the day of her delivery and for the 6 weeks immediately following that day.
6. The maximum period for which any woman is entitled to maternity benefit is 26 weeks of which not more than 8 weeks must precede the date of her expected delivery.
7. A woman cannot be discharged or dismissed by the employer when she absents herself from work in accordance with the provisions of this Act.
8. A woman employee cannot work in any other establishment during the period for which she has been permitted by her employer to remain absent from work under Section 6 of the Act.
9. The Act empowers the appropriate government to appoint such officers as it thinks fit to be Inspectors for the purposes of this Act.
10. Every Inspector appointed under this Act is deemed to be a public servant within the meaning of Section 21 of the IPC (45 of 1860).
11. Any person aggrieved by the decision of the Inspector can appeal to the prescribed authority against the decision of the Inspector.
12. If any employer contravenes the provisions of this Act or the rules made thereunder, he/she is punishable with imprisonment or with fine or with both.
13. Contravening the provisions of this Act and obstructing the Inspector from viewing registers and documents result in imprisonment of 1 year and fine of ₹5,000.
14. The provisions of this Act are effective only when anything in the Act is not inconsistent with something contained in any other law or in the terms of any award, agreement or contract of service, whether made before or after the coming into force of this Act.
15. Subject to the condition of previous publication and by notification in the Official Gazette, the appropriate government is allowed to make rules for carrying out the purpose of this Act.

Multiple Choice Questions

1. Under the Maternity Benefit Act, the term 'woman' refers to a ________, for wages in any establishment.
   a. Woman employed directly
   b. Woman employed through any agency
   c. Both (a) and (b)
   d. Neither (a) nor (b)

2. No employer should knowingly employ a woman in any establishment during the ________ immediately following the day of her delivery, or miscarriage, nor shall any woman work during this period.
   a. 6 weeks
   b. 8 weeks
   c. 10 weeks
   d. 12 weeks

3. Women get entitlement to gain benefits under the Act only if the woman employee has actually worked in the establishment for a period of at least ____________ immediately preceding the date of her expected delivery.
   a. 40 days during the 12 months
   b. 80 days during the 12 months
   c. 40 days during the 06 months
   d. 80 days during the 06 months
4. There is ____________ for coverage under the Maternity Act for a woman who is covered under the Act.
   a. A wage ceiling of ₹1,000
   b. A wage ceiling of ₹2,000
   c. A wage ceiling of ₹2,500
   d. No wage ceiling
5. ____________ before the date of her expected delivery, the woman employee may ask the employer to give her light work for a month.
   a. Two weeks
   b. Four weeks
   c. Eight weeks
   d. Ten weeks
6. Maximum period for which any woman is entitled to maternity benefit is ____________ of which not more than 6 weeks must precede the date of her expected delivery.
   a. 12 weeks
   b. 14 weeks
   c. 16 weeks
   d. 26 weeks
7. A woman employee is entitled to ____________ in the course of her daily work till her child is 15 months old.
   a. Four nursing breaks of 15 minutes each
   b. Six nursing breaks of 15 minutes each
   c. Two nursing breaks of 15 minutes each
   d. Two nursing breaks of 30 minutes each
8. In case of miscarriage, ____________ with average pay from the date of miscarriage.
   a. 4-week leave
   b. 6-week leave
   c. 8-week leave
   d. 10-week leave
9. ____________ can be deprived only for dismissal for any prescribed gross misconduct.
   a. Maternity benefit
   b. Medical bonus
   c. Both (a) and (b)
   d. Neither (a) nor (b)

True/False Questions

1. The Act is not applicable to any factory or other establishment to which the provisions of the ESI Act, 1948, apply.
2. An employer cannot deprive a female employee of the maternity benefit even if she was dismissed for gross misconduct.
3. A woman continues to be 'insured woman' even after she has left insurable employment.
4. If a woman absents herself from work in accordance with the provisions of the Act, her employer cannot discharge or dismiss her on account of such absence.
5. The amount of maternal benefits for a period preceding the date of female employee's expected delivery is not required to be paid in advance by the employer.
6. The failure to give notice disentitles the woman employee to the benefit of the Act.

Descriptive Questions

1. Write a note on objects, scope and applications of the Maternity Benefit Act, 1962.
2. What are the conditions to obtain the entitlement for the maternity benefits under the Act?
3. What do you understand by maternity benefits? Discuss important provisions of the Act for maternity benefits.
4. State the provisions regarding nursing benefits to woman employees.
5. Is it necessary for a woman employee to serve a notice to her employer for maternity benefits? Discuss related provisions.
6. What are the duties and powers of the Inspector appointed under the Maternity Act, 1961?
7. Discuss various provisions for the penalties for the contravention of the Maternity Act, 1961.
8. Throw light on the powers of the state government to frame rules for carrying out the purpose of the Maternity Act, 1961.

11 CHAPTER

The Payment of Wages Act, 1936

LEARNING OBJECTIVES

Upon completing this chapter, the reader would be able to:

LO1. Understand the objectives, scope and important definitions of the Act.
LO2. Gain insights into provisions for the payment of wages under the Act.
LO3. Get the details of permitted deductions and their treatment.
LO4. Understand the enforcement of the Act.
LO5. Know the provisions for penalty for the offences identified under the Act.
LO6. Find out the details of important miscellaneous provisions of the Act.

Introduction

With the industrial growth in India, problems relating to payment of wages to persons employed in the industry started increasing with a rapid pace. The industrial units used to delay the payment of wages to their workers at regular intervals, and wages were not uniform.

In 1926, the Government of India instructed local governments to ascertain the position with regard to the delays which occurred in the payment of wages to the persons employed in the industry. The investigations revealed the existence of abuses in both directions, and the material collected from this exercise was placed before the Royal Commission on the Labour which was appointed in 1929. The Government of India reexamined the subject in the light of the report submitted by the commission, and in February 1933, the Payment of Wages Bill, 1933, was introduced in the Legislative Assembly and circulated for the purpose of eliciting opinions. But the motion could not be passed and the Bill lapsed.

A thoroughly revised Payment of Wages Bill, based upon the same principles as the earlier Bill of 1933, was introduced in the Legislative Assembly on 15 February 1935. The Bill was referred to the Select Committee, and incorporating the recommendations of the Select Committee, the Payment of Wages Bill, 1935, was again introduced in the Legislative Assembly. It was passed in 1936 and came into force on 21 March 1936. The Payment of Wages (Amendment) Act, 1976, extends the Act to the whole of India.

LO1: Objectives, Scope and Important Definitions

Objectives

The preamble of the Act states that the object of the Act is to regulate the payment of wages to certain classes of employed persons. The regulation contemplated by the Act is twofold:

1. The date of payment of wages.
2. The deductions from wages, as fine or otherwise.

Certain provisions have been made in this Act to ensure payment of wages to persons covered by the Act. The Bombay High Court in one case observed that the general purpose of the Act is to provide that employed persons shall be paid wages in a particular form and at regular intervals without any unauthorized deductions. The use of the expression 'certain classes of persons' in the preamble refers to persons drawing on an average wage less than ₹1,600 per month.

Applicability and Scope

This Act is applicable to the payment of wages to persons employed in any factory and to persons employed (otherwise than in a factory) on any railway by a railway administration or, either directly or through a subcontractor, by a person fulfilling a contract with a railway administration for coal mines and plantations. The application of the Act also extends to the establishments in which work relating to the construction, development or maintenance of buildings, roads, bridges, canals or relating to operations connected with navigation, irrigation or the supply of water, or relating to generation, transmission and distribution of electricity or any other form of power is carried on. The state governments are empowered to extend all or any of the provisions of the Act to any industrial establishment. The state government, however, cannot do so in relation to any industrial establishment owned by the central government having the objects not confined to one state, without consulting the central government.

Important Definitions

1. **Employed person (Section 2(ia)):** Under the Act, an employed person includes the legal representative of a deceased employed person.
2. **Employer (Section 2(ib)):** The Act defines an employer as the legal representative of a deceased employer.
3. **Factory (Section 2(ic)):** 'Factory' under the Payment of Wages Act has the meaning assigned to it in clause (m) of Section 2 of the Factories Act, 1948 (63 of 1948).
4. **Industrial or other establishment (Section 2(ii)):** Industrial establishment is defined as any tramway or motor omnibus service; air transport service; dock, wharf or jetty, inland vessel mechanically propelled; mine, quarry or oilfield; plantation; workshop or other establishment in which articles are produced, adapted or manufactured with a view to their use, transport or sale; establishment in which any work relating to the construction, development or maintenance of buildings, roads, bridges or canals, or relating to operations connected with navigation, irrigation

or the supply of water, or relating to the generation, transmission and distribution of electricity or any other form of power is being carried on.

5. **Mine (Section 2(iia)):** 'Mine' carries the same meaning as it is assigned to it in clause (j) of Subsection (1) of Section 2 of the Mines Act, 1952 (35 of 1952).
6. **Plantation (Section 2(iii)):** 'Plantation' has the meaning assigned to it in clause (f) of Section 2 of the Plantations Labour Act, 1951 (69 of 1951).
7. **Wages (Section 2(vi)):** In the Act, wages covers all remunerations (whether by way of salary, allowance or otherwise) expressed in terms of money or capable of being so expressed which would, if the terms of employment, express or implied, were fulfilled, be payable to a person employed in respect of his employment or of work done in such employment.

   Wages include the following:

   a. Any remuneration payable under any award or settlement between the parties or order of a Court.
   b. Any remuneration to which the person employed is entitled, related to overtime work or holidays or any leave period.
   c. Any additional remuneration payable under the terms of employment, whether called a bonus or by any other name.
   d. Any sum because of the termination of employment of the person employed is payable under any law, contract or instrument which provides for the payment of such sum, which is with or without deductions, but does not provide for the time within which the payment is to be made.
   e. Any sum the person employed is entitled to, under any scheme framed under any law for the time being in force.

   Wages do not include the following:

   a. Any bonus (whether under a scheme of profit sharing or otherwise) which is not a part of the remuneration payable under terms of employment or which is not payable under any award or settlement between the parties or order of a Court.
   b. The value of any housing accommodation, or of the supply of light, water, medical attendance or other amenity, or of any service excluded from the computation of wages by a general or special order of the state government.
   c. Any contribution paid by the employer to any pension or provident fund, and the interest which may have accrued on such contribution.
   d. Any travelling allowance or the value of any travelling concession.
   e. Any sum paid to the employed person to defray special expenses entailed on him by the nature of his employment.
   f. Any gratuity amount payable on the determination of employment in cases other than those specified in subclause (d).

LO2: Provisions for Payment of Wages

Responsibility for Payment of Wages (Section 3)

According to Section 3 of the Act, the employer is primarily responsible for the payment of wages to workmen. In the case of factories, it is the manager of the industrial establishments, the person answerable to employer for supervising and control of the establishment, and in railways, the person nominated by the railway administration on this behalf for the local area is responsible for the payment of wages to workmen. In respect of contractors, the Act specifies that the contractor is held responsible for such payment where he undertakes actual work for the principal employer and is in charge of the labour. In case where the contractor merely contracts for the supply of labour to the employer, the principal employer or his manager is responsible for the payment of wages.

Wage Periods (Section 4)

Every person who is responsible for the payment of wages as provided by Section 3 of the Act must fix wage periods in respect of which wages are payable and ensure that no wage period exceeds 1 month in any case. The penalty for contravention of this provision is fine extending to ₹200.

Time of payment of wages (Sections 5 and 6): The Act instructs to follow the following rules in regard to the time of payment of wages:

1. Where an undertaking employs less than 1,000 persons, the wages must be paid before the expiry of the 7th day and in other cases before the expiry of the 10th day, after the last day of the wage period in respect of which the wages are to be paid. In the case of persons employed on a dock, wharf or jetty or in mine, the balance of wages found due on completion of the final tonnage account of the ship or wagons loaded or unloaded, as the case may be, are payable before the expiry of the 7th day from the day of such completion.
2. A discharged worker has to be paid his wages before the expiry of the second working day from the day on which his employment is terminated.
3. Section 5 of the Act states that all payments of wages must be made on a working day only.

Section 6 provides that all wages are required to be paid in current coin or currency notes or in both or with the written authorization of the employed person; wages may be paid by cheque or by crediting the wages in his bank account.

Medium of Payment of Wages (Section 6)

The Act directs that the wages have to be paid in current coin or currency note only. However, the employer may, after obtaining the written authorization of the employed person, pay him the wages either by cheque or by crediting the wages in his bank account.

LO3: Deductions from Wages

Deduction Allowed from the Wages (Section 7)

Every payment made by the employed person to the employer or his agent is deemed to be a deduction from wages. It is laid down in Section 7 of the Act that, notwithstanding the provisions of Section 47(2) of the Indian Railways Act, 1890, the wages of employed person are payable to him without deductions of any kind except those authorized by or under this Act. Section 47(2) of the Indian Railways Act provides for fine or forfeiture of 1-month pay for breach of rules made under that Section. Section 7 of the present Act, however, specifies that no such deduction can be made in respect of any railway worker whose monthly wages is more than or is equal to ₹1,600 or more.

Any loss of wages resulting from the imposition, for good and sufficient cause, upon a person employed by any of the following penalties, namely:

1. The withholding of increment or promotion that includes the stoppage of increment of an efficiency bar.
2. The reduction to a lower post or time scale or to a lower stage in a time scale.
3. Suspension is not deemed to be a deduction from wages in any case where the rules framed by the employer for the imposition of such penalty meet the requirements as specified by the state government in this regard.

Deductions from the wages of an employed person can be made only in accordance with the provisions of this Act and may be of the following kinds only:

1. Fines.
2. For absence from duty.
3. For damages or loss.
4. For house accommodation.
5. For amenities and services.
6. For the advances which the employer is compelled to make, including advances for travelling allowance or conveyance allowance, or for adjustment of overpayment of wages.
7. For the payments to certain provident funds, to cooperative societies, or premium for life insurance.
8. For recovery of loans made from any fund constituted for the welfare of labour; for recovery of loans granted for house building.
9. For income tax payable by the employed person.
10. Under an order of a Court.
11. For payment to cooperative societies.
12. Made with the written Authority of the worker in furtherance of any war savings scheme approved by the state government for the purchase of securities of the Government of India.
13. For payment of insurance premium.
14. For recovery of losses sustained by a railway administration for acceptance by the employed person of counterfeit or base coins, mutilated or forged currency notes.
15. Other losses sustained by a railway administration on account of the negligence of an employed person.

Kinds of Deductions

Let us have a discussion in detail on important provisions of the Act dealing with the kinds of deductions and their treatment.

1. **Deductions for fines (Sections 7(2)(a) and 8):** This lays down following rules for the deductions by way of fines:
   a. The acts and omissions for which fine can be imposed are required to be specified in notices approved by the state government, or the Chief Inspector of Factories in the case of factories, or the supervisor in other cases.

b. No fine can be imposed on any employed person without giving him an opportunity of showing cause against the fine.
c. No fine can be imposed on any employed person who is under the age of 15 years.
d. The Act further provides that the total amount of deductions which may be made in any wage period from the wages of any employed person must not exceed 75% of such wages in cases where such deductions are wholly or partly made for payment to cooperative societies and 50% of such wages in any other case.
e. The fine is deemed to have been imposed on the day of the act or omission in respect of which it is imposed and cannot be recovered from the person by instalments or after the expiry of 60 days front the day on which it was imposed.
f. All the fines so collected by the employer have to be recorded in a prescribed register and must be credited to a fine fund.
g. The proceeds of the fine fund are to be utilized only for such purposes beneficial to the workers of the factory or the establishment as being approved by the prescribed Authority.

2. **Deductions for the absence from duty (Sections 7(2)(b) and 9):** Deductions for absence from duty are permitted under the Act, but the amount of such deductions cannot exceed the sum which the person would have been entitled to if he had worked the same number of days for which the deduction is made. Application of this section is subject to any rules made in this behalf by the state government. If 10 or more employed persons acting in concert absent themselves, without due notice and without reasonable cause, such deduction from any such person may include such amount not exceeding his wages for 8 days as may by any such terms be due to the employer in lieu of the due notice. The amending Act of 1937 permitted the employers to withhold wages in die case of 'stay-in' strikes.
3. **Deductions for damage or loss (Sections 7(2)(c), (m), (n), (o) and 10):** The Act provides for the deduction for damage to or loss of good expressly entrusted to the employed person for custody, or for the loss of money for which he is required to account. But such deductions are permitted only where such damage or loss is directly attributable to his neglect or default and only after he has been given an opportunity of showing cause against the deduction. Such deductions must not exceed the amount of the damage or loss to the employer and must be recorded in a prescribed register.
4. **Deductions for services rendered (Section 7(2)(d), (e) and 11):** Under the Act, deductions for housing accommodation and for amenities and services rendered by the employer are permitted only when an employed person has accepted the house accommodation, amenity or service as a term of employment or otherwise, and such deduction must not exceed an amount equivalent to their value. Furthermore, the deductions in respect of amenities and services can be made subject only to the following conditions:
   a. The approval of the Chief Inspector of Factories has to be obtained in writing to compulsory or general deductions from waves for any amenities or services provided by the employer.
   b. The kind and standard of services and amenities provided are subject to the approval of the Chief Inspector of Factories.
   c. The maximum deduction must not exceed half the wages at that period.
   d. The house accommodation, for which deductions are allowed, may be supplied by the employer or by government or by any housing board set up under the law, for example, under the Subsidised Industrial Housing Scheme (whether the government or the board is

the employer or not) or any other Authority engaged in the business of subsidizing housing accommodation.

5. **Deductions for recovery of advances (Section 7(2)(f) and 12):** According to Section 12 of the Act, deductions for the recovery of advances or for adjustment of overpayments of wages are subject to the following conditions:
   a. An advance of money made before employment has to be recovered from the first payment of wages, but advances given for travelling expenses can in no case be recovered.
   b. Advances of wages not already earned are subject to rules made by state governments in this regard.
   c. Recovery of advances of wages not already earned shall be subject to any rules made by the appropriate government regulating the extent to which such advances may be given and the instalments by which they may be recovered.
6. **Deductions for the recovery of loans (Sections 7(2)(fff) and 12A):** The Act permits the deductions for recovery of loans made from any fund constituted for the welfare of labour in accordance with the rules approved by the state government, and the interest due in respect thereof.
7. **Deductions for the payment to cooperative societies and insurance schemes (Section 7(2)(i), (k) and 13):** Following deductions are covered under this section:
   The appropriate government or any officer specified by it in this behalf or to a scheme of insurance maintained by the Indian Post Office:
   a. Deductions for the payment to cooperative societies approved by the state government and insurance schemes maintained by the Indian Post Offices; and
   b. Deductions made with the written authorization of the person employed for payment of any premium on his life insurance policy to the Life Insurance Corporation of India established under the Life Insurance Corporation Act, 1956 (31 of 1956), or for the purchase of securities of the Government of India or of any state government or for being deposited in any Post Office Savings Bank in furtherance of any savings scheme of any such government.

The above-mentioned deductions are subject to such conditions as the appropriate government may think fit.

Other deductions permitted by the Act (Sections 12A and 13): The Act also permits the following deductions from the wages of an employee:

1. Deductions or income tax payable by the employed person.
2. Deductions required to be made by order of a Court or other competent Authority.
3. Deductions for contribution to and repayment of advance from any recognized or approved fund.
4. Deductions made with the written authorization of the employee for payment of any premium of his life insurance policy to the Life Insurance Corporation of India, or for the purchase of securities of the Government of India or of any state government or for being deposited in any Post Office Savings Bank in furtherance of any savings scheme of any such government.
5. Deductions made with the written authorization of the employed person, for a contribution to a fund like Prime Minister's National Relief Fund or to such other Fund as the central government may, by notification in the Official Gazette, specify.

Limit on deductions (Section 7(3)): The total amount of deductions made under Subsection (2) of the Act in any wage period from the wages of any employed person cannot exceed:

1. In cases where such deductions are wholly or partly made for payments to cooperative societies under clause (j) of Subsection (2), 75% of such wages, and
2. In any other case, 50% of such wages.

If the total deductions authorized under Subsection (2) exceed 75% or, as the case may be, 50% of the wages, the excess amount can be recovered in a prescribed manner.

Maintenance of registers and records (Section 13A): Section 13A states that every employer must maintain such registers and records in the prescribed manner containing the following particulars:

1. Particulars of persons employed by him.
2. The work performed by the persons employed.
3. The wages paid to the persons employed.
4. The deductions made from the wages of the persons employed.
5. Receipts given by the persons employed.
6. Such other particulars, if any.

LO4: Enforcement of the Act

Inspector (Section 14)

The Act entrusts the responsibility of administration and enforcement of the Act with the State Inspectors of Factories in the case of factories within their local limit, and that of the Chief Labour Commissioner (Central) in the case of persons employed on the railway (other than in railway factories). The Inspector or the Labour Commissioner may, at any reasonable hours, visit any premises and make such examination of register or document relating to the calculation and payment of wages, and take on the spot otherwise, such evidence of any person, and exercise such other powers of inspection, as he may deem necessary for carrying out the purpose of this Act. Section 14A further provides that every employer has to afford for an Inspector all reasonable facilities for making an entry, inspection, supervision or inquiry under the Act.

Claims for Wrongful Deductions (Section 15)

The state government is empowered to either appoint a Presiding Officer of any Labour Court or Industrial Tribunal or a Commissioner for Workmen's Compensation or other officer with judicial experience (Civil Judge or Magistrate) to hear and decide all claims made against the deductions from the wage and for the delay in payment of wages. Where any wrongful deductions have been made from the wages of a person, or any payment of wages has been delayed, such person himself within 12 months of the date of deduction or the date on which the payment of wages was due apply to the concerned Authority for a direction. Other persons who can act on behalf of the aggrieved employee include a legal practitioner or any official of a registered trade union authorized in writing to act on his behalf, or any

Inspector under this Act, or any other person acting with the permission or the Authority. If the application is presented after the expiry of 12 months, it can still be admitted by the Authority for sufficient cause.

Let us discuss a case to gain insights into the authority and jurisdiction of the Authority to adjudicate the claims under the Act (Case 11.1).

Case 11.1: *Administrator, Krishi Upaj Mandi ... v. Gauri Shanker*[1]

Mr Gauri Shanker, the respondent, was appointed by the Office of the Krishi Upaj Mandi Samiti, Dongargarh, on 6 May 1980 on a daily wage basis at the wages of ₹240 per month. On 30 June 1981, his services were terminated. The respondent challenged this order of termination of his services before the Labour Court. The Labour Court, while adjudicating the dispute, held that the action of the Administrator cum Secretary, Krishi Upaj Mandi Samiti, Dongargarh (the petitioner), terminating the services of Gauri Shanker with effect from 30 June 1981 was illegal. The Labour Court declared the order of termination void. It was quashed and set aside. While setting aside the termination order of the respondent, the Tribunal directed the respondents to reinstate the workman with full wages and to grant him the consequential benefits.

Dissatisfied petitioner challenged the Award of the Labour Court and also reinstated the respondent on 19 December 1984. The respondent, on 18 September 1984, moved an application under Section 15(2) of the Payment of Wages Act (the Act) before the Authority for the payment of Wages relating to the period between 1 July 1981 and 31 August 1984, the period for which the respondent was terminated from the service by the petitioner. He also moved another application under Section 15(2) of the Act before the same Authority on 18 September 1984 for the payment of wages relating to the period from 1 September 1984 to 18 December 1984. It was stated in these applications that the applicant has not been paid the wages in the regular pay scale of ₹350-5-430 and the petitioners have, thus, illegally deducted the amount of ₹18,552 (for the period from 1 July 1981 to 31 August 1984) and ₹2,160 for the period from 1 September 1984 to 1 April 1985, which should be paid to him along with the compensation.

The claim petitions were contested by the petitioner on the grounds that the applications under Section 15(2) of the Act were not maintainable as the applicant had prayed for the payment of wages in accordance with the regular pay scale and for the fixation of regular pay, which claim fell within the purview of potential wages and this question could not be determined by the Authority under the Act under Section 15(2) of the Act.

The Authority under the Payment of Wages Act, Bikaner, accepted the objections raised by the petitioner and held that the dispute raised could not be adjudicated by the Authority under Section 15(2) of the Act in the absence of any order passed by the competent Court in favour of the applicant for the grant of wages in the regular pay scale.

Dissatisfied with the orders passed by the Authority under the Payment of Wages Act, Bikaner, the workman respondent filed two appeals before the District Judge, who allowed both the appeals and, also, both the applications filed by him under Section 15(2) of the Act. The petitioner approached the higher court for the revision of the order.

The petitioner contended that the Authority, under Section 15(2) of the Act, was not authorized to adjudicate any dispute relating to the fixation of the applicant in the regular pay scale. The determination and computation of the workman's claim for computation of wages at a certain rate to the principle of equal pay for equal work were beyond the scope of Section 15(2). On the other hand, the respondent submitted that the Authority under Section 15(2) of the Act had jurisdiction to entertain such claim and could adjudicate the matter applying the doctrine of equal pay for equal work.

[1] *Administrator, Krishi Upaj Mandi ... v. Gauri Shanker*, (1998) IIILLJ 1272 Raj, 1996 (2) WLN 181.

Discussion Point

Is the Authority under 15(2) of the Act authorized to adjudicate the dispute relating to the fixation of the applicant in the regular pay scale?

Judgement and Explanation

It was held that the Authority, under this Section, had only limited jurisdiction. The entitlement of the applicant (respondent Gauri Shanker) on the basis of the doctrine of 'equal pay for equal work' had to be determined by the competent forum and this enquiry was beyond the scope of the Authority acting under Section 15(2) of the Act. Failure to pay according to the doctrine of 'equal pay for equal work' by the employer could not be considered to be either a deduction, which was unauthorized under the Act, or a failure under the class of delayed wages as envisaged under Sections 4 and 5 of the Act.

Now it is clear that the Authority under Section 15(2) of the Act has the jurisdiction to entertain the applications only in the cases where any unauthorized deduction has been made from the wages or any payment has been delayed beyond the period prescribed under Sections 4 and 5 of the Act. Therefore, no other claim under Section 15(2) of the Act on any other footing other than the two mentioned above can be grounds for attracting the application of this section and empowering the Authority to decide the dispute.

Procedure (Section 15(3)): After admitting the application, the Authority will give an opportunity to the applicant and the employer or any person responsible for the payment of wages to be heard and present his case. On being satisfied, the Authority will direct the employer or the other person responsible for the payment of wages to pay to the claimant the amount wrongfully withheld and also the compensation up to 10 times that sum in the case of deduction, and not exceeding ₹25 per head in the case of delay. But the payment of compensation for delayed wages will not be ordered if the delay was due to any of the following reasons:

1. Bona fide error or bona fide dispute as to the amount payable to the employee.
2. The occurrence of an emergency or the existence of exceptional circumstances, in a manner that the person responsible for the payment of the wages was unable, although exercising reasonable diligence, to make prompt payment.
3. The failure of the employed person to apply for or accept the payment of an amount directed to be paid by the employer to the employed person may be recovered as if it was a fine imposed by a magistrate.

The Authority is empowered to refuse to entertain the application, if after giving the applicant an opportunity to be heard, the Authority is satisfied that:

1. The applicant is not entitled to present an application.
2. The delay in payment of wages was excusable, on account of any of the reasons provided above.
3. The applicant shows no sufficient cause for making a direction for payment.
4. The application is insufficiently stamped or is otherwise incomplete.

Malicious or vexatious application (Section 15(4)(a)): If the Authority after hearing the applicant is satisfied that it was made either malicious or vexatious, the Authority may direct the applicant to pay a penalty not exceeding ₹50 to the employer.

Let us discuss a case to examine the scope of the Authority and also the circumstances under which it can reject the application for claims under the Act (case 11.2).

Case 11.2: *Maruti Mahipati Mullick v. Polson Limited*[2]

Mr Maruti Mahipati Mullick, the petitioner, was an employee of Polson Limited, the respondent. He was working in the coffee factory run by the respondent. In June 1959, a trade union representing the workmen in the coffee factory raised certain demands, including demands for pay scales and dearness allowance. The demands were admitted in conciliation under Section 12 of the Industrial Disputes Act, 1917. In the course of conciliation proceedings, a settlement the respondent and the Union reached to a settlement on 14 March 1960. Under the settlement, the lowest wage scale was ₹36-2-60 for mazdoors of different categories. As regards dearness allowance, the settlement provided that all workmen would be paid dearness allowance on the revised scale as was then available to the operatives in the cotton textile industry in Bombay City. It was provided that the settlement was to remain in force till 31 December 1962.

On 31 October 1964, the first petitioner, who was then working as a mazdoor in the coffee factory and was receiving basic wages of ₹40 per month and dearness allowance under the settlement, was retrenched by the respondent along with 14 other workmen. Thereafter, on 26 November 1964, the petitioner and the other 14 retrenched workmen were re-employed as casual workers in the coffee factory of the respondent. After re-employment, they were paid wages at a consolidated rate of ₹2.75 per day, which was much less than the amount of basic wage and dearness allowance which a mazdoor was entitled to receive under the aforementioned settlement. The petitioner and the 14 other workmen filed applications on 11 January 1965 before the Authority under the Payment of Wages Act alleging that the petitioner had made illegal deductions from their wages for the period between 26 November 1964 and 5 December 1964. They claimed that they were entitled to the wages drawn from them at the time of retrenchment or, in the alternative, to the lowest wage with dearness allowance which a mazdoor was entitled to receive under the aforementioned settlement.

The respondent raised two contentions in their defence. The first contention stated that the Authority did not have any jurisdiction to deal with the applications as the parties were at variance in regard to the contract of employment which determined the workmen's conditions of service. It was pointed out that while the workmen relied on the said settlement, the respondent relied on an oral contract, entered into at the time of the re-employment of the workmen, under which the re-employed workmen were to receive a consolidated daily wage of ₹2.75. The second contention of the respondent mentioned that the workmen were engaged as daily-rated casual workers and they could not ask the Authority to put them in the class of monthly rated workers. The Authority, therefore, had no jurisdiction to allow them wages which were available to monthly rated mazdoors under the settlement.

The Authority consolidated the 15 applications and heard the parties on the preliminary issue whether the Authority had jurisdiction to entertain the applications. The Authority concluded that he had no such jurisdiction and dismissed the 15 applications.

The disappointed petitioner along with other applicants challenged the legality of this order under Articles 226 and 227 of the Constitution.

Discussion Point

Under the circumstances mentioned in the case facts, was the Authority entitled to exercise its jurisdiction in the case?

[2] *Maruti Mahipati Mullick v. Polson Limited* (1969) 71 BOMLR 655.

Judgement and Explanation

It was held that the applications filed by the petitioner and the 14 other workmen had to be restored and the Authority was directed to hear and dispose of the applications in accordance with law. It was stated in the judgement that under the Act, an employee was entitled to claim actual as distinguished from potential wages. Where an employee applied to the recovery of actual wages, all matters incidental to his claim, however complicated, had to be heard and decided by the Authority.

Thus, it is clear that the Authority has no jurisdiction to upgrade an employee from one category into another and an employee cannot, therefore, approach the Authority for the recovery of wages which would be a clue to him if he were placed in a higher category. In a similar manner, an employee if dismissed from service, and who is not entitled to wages till the order of dismissal is set aside, cannot approach the Authority for the recovery of wages which would be due to him if he was reinstated in service. However, if the employee claims the actual wages, the Authority has to hear the parties and settle the dispute.

Single Application in Respect of Claims (Section 16)

A single application can be presented under Section 15 on behalf, or in respect of any number of employed persons belonging to the same unpaid group. In such case, every person on whose behalf such application is presented may be awarded maximum compensation to the extent specified in Subsection (3) of Section 15. Here, the employed persons are said to belong to the same unpaid group:

1. If they are borne on the same establishment and deductions have been made from their wages in contravention of this Act for the same cause and during the same wage period or periods, or
2. If their wages for the same wage period or periods have remained unpaid after the day fixed by Section 5.

The Authority is permitted to deal with any number of separate pending applications, presented under Section 15 in respect of persons belonging to the same unpaid group, as a single application presented under Subsection (2) of this section and the provisions of that subsection apply accordingly.

Appeal (Section 17)

This section allows an appeal by the unsatisfied party from the following orders or directions of the Authority:

1. An order directing the employer or the persons responsible for payment of wages to refund the delayed wages.
2. An order directing payment of compensation to the employee under Section 5(3).
3. An order imposing penalty whether on the employee or the employer under Section 5(4).

An appeal under this section has to be made within 30 days of the date on which the order or direction was made in presidency town before the Court of small causes and elsewhere before the District Court within whose jurisdiction the industrial establishment is situated.

The employer or other person responsible for the payment of wages under Section 3 may file an appeal, if

1. The total sum directed to be paid by way of wages and compensation is more than ₹300.
2. Such direction has the effect of imposing on the employer or the other person a financial liability exceeding ₹1,000.

Who may appeal: An employed person himself can file an appeal or any legal practitioner or any official of a registered trade union authorized in writing to act on his behalf or any inspector under this Act, or any other person permitted by the Authority to make an application under Section 15(2) can file an appeal on his behalf; if the total amount of wages claimed to have been withheld:

1. From the employed person is more than ₹20.
2. From the unpaid group to which the employed person belongs or belonged exceeds ₹50.

Conditional attachment of property of an employer or other person who is responsible for payment of wages (Section 17A): This section states that as much property of the employer or other person responsible for the payment of wages can be attached as is, in the opinion of the Authority or the Court, sufficient to satisfy the amount which may be payable under the direction. The conditional attachment may be made under the following circumstances:

1. When the application under Section 15(2) or appeal under Section 17 the employed person or any official of a registered trade union authorized in writing to act on his behalf, or any legal practitioner or any Inspector files an application under Section 15(2) of the Act.
2. When the Authority or the Court is satisfied that the employer or other person responsible for the payment of wages under Section 3 is likely to evade payment of any amount that may be directed to be paid under Section 15 or Section 17.
3. When the Authority or the Court has the opinion that the ends of justice would be defeated by the delay.

However, under the circumstances mentioned above, an order of attachment passed to the payment of wages, the employer or the person responsible for payment is to be given an opportunity to be heard.

LO5: Penalties and Offences

The Penalty for Delaying Payment of Wages within the Prescribed Period or Making Unauthorized Deductions (Section 20(1))

A person who is responsible for the payment of wages to an employed person delays the payment of wages, and such a person is liable to be punished with fine which is not being less than ₹1,500 but which may extend to ₹7,500.

Penalty for Not Paying Wages on a Working Day or in Current Coin or Not Recording Fines or Not Displaying the Abstract of the Act (Section 20(2))

Anybody who does not pay wages on a working day or in current coin or does not record fines or does not display the abstract of the Act, every such person is liable to be punished with fine which may extend to ₹3,750.

Penalty for Not Maintaining the Registers and Records (Section 20(3))

Any person responsible for contravention of the following provisions of the Act, for the payment of wages to an employed person is punishable with fine extending to not less than ₹200 but not exceeding of ₹1000:

1. Failure to maintain such register or records as specified by this Act.
2. Wilful refusal or neglect without lawful cause to furnish such information or return.
3. Wilfully furnishing or causing to be furnished any information or return which the employer knows to be false.
4. Refusal to answer or wilfully giving a false answer to any question necessary for obtaining any information required to be furnished under this Act.

Penalty for Stopping the Inspector Performing His Duty (Section 20(4))

Section 20(4) provides the fine for the following offences which are punishable with a minimum fine of ₹200 but not exceeding ₹1,000.

1. Wilfully obstructing an Inspector in the discharge of his duties under the Act.
2. Refusal or wilful neglect to afford an Inspector any reasonable facility for making any entry, inspection, examination, supervision or inquiry authorized by or under this Act in relation to any railway, factory or industrial or other establishment.
3. Wilful refusal to produce, on demand by an inspector, any register or other document kept in pursuance of this Act.
4. Preventing or attempting to prevent or doing anything which he has any reason to believe is likely to prevent any person from appearing before or being examined by an Inspector acting in pursuance of his duties under this Act.

Subsequent Offences (Section 20(5))

Section 20(5) lays down that if any person who has been convicted of any offence punishable under this Act gets involved again in contravention of the same provision, he is liable to be punished on subsequent conviction with imprisonment for a term which is not being less than 1 month, but which may extend to 6 months with fine, which is not being less than ₹500, but may extend to ₹3,000. For the purposes of this subsection, no cognizance is to be taken of any conviction made more than 2 years.

Additional Fine for Failure to Pay Wages by the Fixed Date (Section 20(6))

According to Section 20(6), if any person fails or wilfully neglects to pay the wages of any employed person by the date fixed by the Authority in this behalf, he is without prejudice to any other action that may be taken against him, to be punished with additional fine, which may extend to ₹100 for each day for which such failure or neglect continues.

LO6: Miscellaneous Provisions of the Act

Bar of Suits (Section 22)

Section 22 of the Act does not permit any court to entertain any suit for the recovery of wages or of any deduction from wages insofar as the sum so claimed:

1. Forms the subject of an application under Section 15 which has been presented by the plaintiff and which is pending before the Authority appointed under that section or of an appeal under Section 17.
2. Has formed the subject of a direction under Section 15 in favour of the plaintiff.
3. Has been adjudged, in any proceeding under Section 15, not to be owed to the plaintiff.
4. Could have been recovered by an application under Section 15.

Protection of action taken in good faith (Section 22A): The Act disallows any suit, prosecution or other legal proceeding against the government or any officer of the government for anything which is in good faith done or intended to be done under this Act.

Display by Notice of Abstract of the Act (Section 25)

The person responsible for the payment of wages to persons employed in a factory or an industrial or other establishment is responsible for displaying in such factory or industrial or other establishment a notice containing such abstracts of this Act and of the rules made thereunder in English and in the language of the majority of the persons employed in the factory, or industrial or other establishment as may be prescribed.

Payment of undisturbed wages in case of death of an employed person (Section 25A): If any amount payable to an employed person as wages could not or cannot be paid on account of death before payment of an account of his whereabouts not being known (subject to the other provisions of the Act), then every such amount has to:

1. Be paid to the person nominated by him in this behalf in accordance with the rules made under this Act.

2. Where no such nomination has been made or where for any reasons such amounts cannot be paid to the person so nominated, be deposited with the prescribed Authority who deals with the amounts so deposited in such a manner as may be prescribed.

The prescribed Authority deals with the amounts deposited in a prescribed manner.

Rule-making Power (Section 26)

The state government may make the rules to regulate the procedure to be followed by the Authorities and Courts referred to in Sections 15 and 17. Section 26 of the act empowers the state government to frame the rules:

1. Requiring the maintenance of such registers, records, returns, notices and so on.
2. Requiring the display in a conspicuous place on premises where the employment is carried on.
3. Providing for the regular inspection of the weights, measures and so on.
4. Prescribing the Authority competent to approve the omission in respect of which fines may be imposed.
5. Prescribing the procedure for the imposition of fines.
6. Prescribing the extent to which advances may be made and the instalments by which they may be recovered, including the rate of interest payable thereon.
7. Prescribing the powers of inspectors.
8. Prescribing the amount of Court fees payable in respect of any proceedings under the Act.

Every rule made by the central government under this section shall be laid before each House of Parliament.

Summary

1. In 1926, Government of India instructed to local governments to ascertain the position with regard to the delays which occurred in the payment of wages to the persons employed in the industry.
2. The Payment of Wages Bill, 1935, was passed in 1936 and came into force on 21 March 1936.
3. The general purpose of the Act is to provide that employed persons shall be paid wages in a particular form and at regular intervals without any unauthorized deductions.
4. The employer is primarily responsible for the payment of wages to workmen.
5. Every person who is responsible for the payment of wages as provided by Section 3 of the Act must fix wage periods in respect of which wages are payable and ensure that no wage period exceeds 1 month in any case.
6. All payments of wages must be made on a working day only.
7. Every payment made by the employed person to the employer or his agent is deemed to be a deduction from wages.
8. Deductions for absence from duty are permitted under the Act, but the amount of such deductions cannot exceed the sum which the person would have been entitled to if he had worked the same number of days for which the deduction is made.

9. Deductions for damage or loss must not exceed the amount of the damage or loss to the employer and must be recorded in a prescribed register.
10. Deductions for services rendered must not exceed an amount equivalent to their value.
11. Every employer must maintain such registers and records in the prescribed manner.
12. The state government is empowered to either appoint a Presiding Officer of any Labour Court or Industrial Tribunal or a Commissioner for Workmen's Compensation or other officer with judicial experience to hear and decide all claims made against the deductions from the wage and for the delay in payment of wages.
13. The Inspector or the Labour Commissioner may, at any reasonable hours, visit any premises and make such examination of registers or documents relating to the calculation and payment of wages.
14. The Authority under Section 15(2) of the Act has the jurisdiction to entertain the applications only in the cases where any unauthorized deduction has been made from the wages.
15. A single application can be presented under Section 15 on behalf or in respect of any number of employed persons belonging to the same unpaid group.
16. An appeal under this section has to be made within 30 days of the date on which the order or direction is issued.
17. This section states that as much property of the employer or other person responsible for the payment of wages can be attached as is, in the opinion of the Authority or the Court, sufficient to satisfy the amount which may be payable under the direction.
18. If a person who is responsible for the payment of wages to an employed person delays the payment of wages, such a person is liable to be punished under the Act.
19. If any person who has been convicted of any offence punishable under this Act gets involved again in contravention of the same provision, he is liable to be punished under the Act.
20. Section 22 of the Act does not permit any court to entertain any suit for the recovery of wages or of any deduction from wages.
21. The state government may make the rules to regulate the procedure to be followed by the Authorities and Courts referred to in Sections 15 and 17.
22. Every rule made by the central government under this section shall be laid before each House of Parliament.

Multiple Choice Questions

1. The regulation contemplated by the Payment of Wages Act regulates ____________.
   a. The date of payment of wages
   b. The deductions from wages, as fine or otherwise
   c. Both (a) and (b)
   d. Neither (a) nor (b)

2. ____________ is primarily responsible for the payment of wages to workmen.
   a. The employer
   b. The employee
   c. The contractor
   d. The state government

3. All payments of wages must be made on ____________.
   a. Any day
   b. A working day only
   c. Last day of every month
   d. First day of every month

4. All wages are required to be paid ____________.
   a. In current coin
   b. In currency notes
   c. By cheque or by crediting the wages in his bank account
   d. All of the above

5. Every payment made by the employed person to the employer or his agent is deemed to be a ____________ from wages.
   a. Deduction
   b. Fine
   c. Contribution
   d. None of the above

6. No fine can be imposed on any employed person who is below the age of ____________.
   a. 25 years
   b. 20 years
   c. 15 years
   d. 45 years

7. Deductions for house accommodation and for amenities and services rendered by the employer are permitted only when an employed person has accepted the house accommodation, amenity or service as a term of employment or otherwise, and such deduction must not exceed an amount ____________.
   a. Twice to their value
   b. Equivalent to their value
   c. Equivalent to wages of the employee
   d. The market value of the house accommodation

8. The Authority has the jurisdiction to entertain the applications only in the cases ____________.
   a. Where any unauthorized deduction has been made from the wages
   b. Any payment has been delayed beyond the period prescribed under Sections 4 and 5 of the Act
   c. Both (a) and (b)
   d. Neither (a) nor (b)

9. ____________ can make an application under Section 15(2) who can file an appeal on his behalf.
   a. An employed person himself or any legal practitioner
   b. Any official of a registered trade union authorized in writing to act on his behalf or any inspector under this Act
   c. Any person permitted by the Authority to the employed persons are said to belong to the same unpaid group
   d. All of the above

10. ____________ has to afford for an Inspector all reasonable facilities for making an entry, inspection, supervision or inquiry under the Act.
    a. Employer
    b. Employee
    c. Both (a) and (b)
    d. Neither (a) nor (b)

True/False Questions

1. In case where the contractor merely contracts for the supply of labour to the employer, the principal employer or his manager is responsible for the payment of wages.
2. The proceeds of the fine fund can be freely utilized by the employer and no approval from any Authority is required to utilize this fund.
3. Before an order of attachment is passed for the payment of wages, the employer or the person responsible for payment has to be given an opportunity to be heard.
4. The act allows any suit, prosecution or other legal proceedings against the government or any officer of the government for anything which is in good faith done or intended to be done under this Act.
5. No fine can be imposed on any employed person without giving him an opportunity of showing cause against the fine.

Descriptive Questions

1. Describe the salient features of the Payment of Wages Act, 1936.
2. Write about the applicability of the Payment of Wages Act, 1936.
3. What do you mean by 'wages' under the Payment of Wages Act? Throw light on major provisions dealing with the payment of wages under the Payment of Wages Act, 1936.
4. What do you mean by wage period? Also discuss the provisions regarding wage periods under the Act.
5. What are permissible deductions from the wages of the employee governed under Payment of wages Act, 1936?
6. Discuss in detail the appointment, rights and duties of the Inspector appointed under the Act.
7. List out different Acts and omissions suggested under Payment of Wages Act? What are the penalties prescribed under the Payment of Wages Act for the breach of acts?
8. Write short notes on the following:
   a. Bar of suits under Section 22.
   b. Rule-making power of the state government under Section 26.

12

CHAPTER

The Minimum Wages Act, 1948

LEARNING OBJECTIVES

Upon completing this chapter, the reader would be able to:

LO1. Understand the objectives, scope and important definitions of the Act.
LO2. Gain insights into the process of fixation and revision of wages.
LO3. Understand the step-by-step process of determining the bonus amount.
LO4. Examine the provisions for the enforcement of the Act.
LO5. Get the details of provisions relating to disputes, penalties and offences under the Act.
LO6. Know the special and miscellaneous provisions of the Act dealing with various matters related to payment of bonus to employees.

Introduction

The need to have the concept of minimum wages first emerged with reference to the remuneration of workers in those industries where the level of wages was substantially low as compared to the wages for similar types of labour in other industries. In 1928, the International Labour Conference of ILO at Geneva adopted a draft convention on minimum wages. The draft convention required the member countries to bring a machinery in force to fix minimum rates of wages for workers employed in such industries in which no arrangements existed for the effective regulation of wages and where wages were exceptionally low. The need of a legal framework for fixation of minimum wages in India received an impetus after Second World War, to protect the interest of demobilized persons seeking employment in industries. To provide for machinery for fixing and revision of minimum wages, a draft Bill was prepared and discussed at the Seventh Session of the Indian Labour Conference in November 1945, and the Minimum Wages Bill was introduced in the Central Legislative Assembly on 11 April 1946.

LO1: Objectives, Scope and Important Definitions

Objectives

The objectives of the Minimum Wages Act, 1948, are to ensure a minimum subsistence wage for workers and to prevent sweating or exploitation of labour through payment of low wages. The Act was enacted to safeguard the interests of workers who were employed by the unorganized sector by providing for the fixation of minimum wages in certain specified employments. The Act binds the employers to pay their workers the minimum wages fixed under the Act from time to time. The Bill provides for fixation by the Provincial Governments of minimum wages for employments covered by the Schedule to the Bill, and review and revise these rates at intervals not exceeding 5 years. The Schedule contains those items where sweated labour is more prevalent or where there is a big chance of exploitation of labour. Once a minimum wage is fixed according to the provisions of the Act, it is not open to the employer to plead his inability to pay the said wages to his employees. The minimum wage rate may be fixed at time rate, piece rate, guaranteed time rate and overtime rate.

Scope and Applicability

The Act extends to the whole of India and is applicable to the schedule employments for which minimum wages are fixed/revised. The Act applies to persons engaged in scheduled employments or in a specified class of work in respect of which minimum wages have been fixed. The Act does not permit any employee to give up by contract or agreement his rights insofar as it purports to reduce the minimum rates of wages fixed under the Act. Thus, any contract or agreement made for less than the minimum rates of wages fixed is null and void in the eyes of law.

Important Definitions

1. **Adolescent (Section 2(a)):** The Act defines 'adolescent' as a person who has completed his 14th year of age but has not completed his 18th year.
2. **Adult (Section 2(aa)):** Under the Act, adult is a person who has completed his 18th year of age.
3. **Appropriate government (Section 2(b)):** 'Appropriate government' is defined as follows:
   a. In relation to any scheduled employment carried on by or under the authority of the central government or a railway administration or in relation to a mine, oil field or major port, or any corporation established by Central Act, the central government.
   b. In relation to any other scheduled employment, the state government.
4. **Child (Section 2(bb)):** Under the Act, every person who has not completed his 14th year of age is considered as a child.
5. **Competent authority (Section 2(c)):** The Act describes the competent authority as an authority appointed by the appropriate government by notification in its Official Gazette to ascertain from time to time the cost of living index number applicable to the employees employed in the scheduled employments specified in such notification.
6. **Cost of living index number (Section 2(d)):** Cost of living index number in relation to employees in any scheduled employment for which minimum rates of wages have been fixed

means the index number ascertained and declared by the competent authority by notification in the Official Gazette to be the cost of living index number applicable to employees in such employment.

7. **Employer (Section 2(e)):** The Act states that an employer is any person who employs whether directly or through another person or whether on behalf of himself or any other person, one or more employees in any scheduled employment in respect of which minimum rates of wages have been fixed under this Act, and includes the following, except in Subsection (3) of Section 26:
   a. In a factory where any scheduled employment is carried on in respect of which minimum rates of wages have been fixed under this Act, any person named under clause (f) of Subsection (1) of Section 7 of the Factories Act, 1948 (63 of 1948), as manager of the factory.
   b. In any scheduled employment under the control of any government in India in respect of which minimum rates of wages have been fixed under this Act, the person or authority appointed by such government to supervise and control employees or, where no person or authority is so appointed, the head of the department.
   c. In any scheduled employment under any local authority in respect of which minimum rates of wages have been fixed under this Act, the persons appointed by such authority to supervise and control employees or, where no person is so appointed, the chief executive officer of the local authority.
   d. In any other case where any scheduled employment is carried on, in respect of which minimum rates of wages have been fixed under this Act, any person responsible to the owner for the supervision and control of the employees or for the payment of wages.
8. **Schedule employment (Section 2(f)):** Schedule employment stands for an employment specified in the Schedule or any process or branch of work forming part of such employment.
9. **Wages (Section 2(h)):** Under the Act, wages means all remuneration capable of being expressed in terms of money, which would, in the terms of money, be payable to a person employed in respect of his employment or of work done in such employment and includes a house rent allowance, but does not include the following:
   a. The value of:
      i. Any house accommodation, supply of light water, medical attendance.
      ii. Any other amenity or any service excluded by general or special order of the appropriate government.
   b. Any contribution paid by the employer to any person, fund or provident fund or under any scheme of social insurance.
   c. Any traveling allowance given to the employer or the value of any travelling concession.
   d. Any sum paid to the person employed to defray special expenses entailed on him by the nature of his employment.
   e. Any gratuity payable on discharge.
10. **Employee (Section 2(i)):** The Act states that employee is any person who is employed for hire or reward to do any work, skilled or unskilled, or manual or clerical, in a scheduled employment in respect of which minimum rates of wages have been fixed, and includes an outworker to whom any articles or materials are given out by another person to be made up cleaned, washed, altered, ornamented, finished, repaired, adapted or otherwise processed for sale for the purposes of the trade or business of that other person, where the process is to be carried out either in the home of the outworker or in some other premises not being premises under the control and

management of that other person, and also includes an employee declared to be an employee by the appropriate government, but does not include any member of the Armed Forces of the Union.

LO2: Fixation and Revision of Wages

The Act empowers both the central government and the state governments to fix, revise, review and enforce the payment of minimum wages to workers in respect of 'scheduled employments' under their respective jurisdictions. There are 45 scheduled employments in the central sphere and as many as 1,530 in state sphere mentioned in the Act.

Fixing of Minimum Rates of Wages (Section 3)

Fixation of minimum rate of wages depends on a number of factors such as level of income and paying capacity, prices of essential commodities, and productivity and local conditions. Since these factors vary from state to state, the wages fixed under this Act accordingly differ throughout the country. In the absence of a uniform national minimum wage, the central government introduced a 'national floor-level minimum wage'.

Fixation of minimum rate of wages (Section 3(a)): Section 3(a) of the Act states that the appropriate government is empowered to fix the minimum rates of wages payable to employees employed in an employment specified in Part I or Part II of the Schedule and in an employment subsequently added to the Schedule. The government may review the minimum rates of wages and revise the minimum rates from time to time but not exceeding 5 years. The Act further provides that any scheduled employment in which there are in the whole state less than 1,000 employees engaged, the appropriate government may not fix the minimum wages in respect of such employment.

Review and revision of minimum rate of wages (Section 3(b)): Section 3(b) adds that the minimum rate of wages is to be reviewed and revised if necessary at such intervals as the appropriate government may think fit. However, such intervals cannot exceed 5 years. The section further adds that where for any reason the appropriate government has not reviewed the minimum rates of wages fixed by it in respect of any scheduled employment within any interval of 5 years, the appropriate government can review the minimum rates even after the expiry of the period of 5 years and revise them, if necessary. Until the minimum rate of wages is so revised, the minimum rates in force immediately before the expiry of the period of 5 years remain in force.

Minimum number of employees (Section 3(1A)): Section 3(1A) states that the appropriate government may refrain from fixing minimum rates of wages in respect of any scheduled employment in which there are in the whole state less than 1,000 employees engaged in such employment. But if, at any time, the appropriate government discovers after such inquiry as it may make or cause to be made in this behalf that the number of employees in any scheduled employment in respect of which it has refrained from fixing minimum rates of wages has increased to 1,000 or more, it must fix minimum rates of wages payable to employees in such employment as soon as may be after such finding.

Minimum rate (Section 3(2)): The appropriate government is permitted to fix separate minimum rates of wages for time rate and for piece rate. Different wage rates may be fixed for different scheduled employments, different classes of work in the same scheduled employment, for adults, adolescents, children and apprentices, and for different localities and for any one or more of the wage periods, namely, by the hour or by the day or by the month or by such larger wage period as may be prescribed by the appropriate government. Thus, the Act provides for the fixation of:

1. A minimum rate of wages for time work (hereinafter, referred to as 'a minimum time rate').
2. A minimum rate of wages for piecework (hereinafter, referred to as 'a minimum piece rate').
3. A minimum rate of remuneration to apply in the case of employees employed on piecework for the purpose of securing to such employees a minimum rate of wages on a time work basis (hereinafter referred to as 'a guaranteed time rate').
4. A minimum rate (whether a time rate or a piece rate) to apply in substitution for the minimum rate, which would otherwise be applicable in respect of overtime work done by employees (hereinafter referred to as 'overtime rate').

Application of Section 3 during pendency of a case (Section 3(2)(2A)): As provided by Section 3 (2) (2A) where in respect of an industrial dispute relating to the rate of wages payable to any of the employees employed in a scheduled employment, any proceeding is pending before a Tribunal or National Tribunal under the Industrial Disputes Act, 1947, or before any like authority under any other law for the time being in force or an award made by any Tribunal, National Tribunal or such authority is in operation, and a notification fixing or revising the minimum rates of wages in respect of the scheduled employment is issued during the pendency of such proceeding or the operation of the award. Then the minimum rates of wages so fixed or so revised do not apply to those employees during the period in which the proceeding is pending and the award made therein is in operation or as the case may be. If the notification is issued during the period of operation of any award, during that period, and where such proceeding or award relates to the rates of wages payable to all the employees in the scheduled employment, no minimum rates of wages can be fixed or revised in respect of that employment during the said period.

Different minimum rate (Section 3(3)(a)): The appropriate government, while fixing or revising minimum rates of wages under this section can fix different minimum rates of wages for:

1. Different scheduled employment.
2. Different classes of work in the same scheduled.
3. Employments.
4. Adults, adolescents, children and apprentices.
5. Different localities.

Section 3(3)(b) further empowers the appropriate government to fix minimum rates of wages, by any one or more of the following wage periods, namely:

1. By the hour,
2. By the day,
3. By the month or
4. By such other larger wage period as may be prescribed.

When such rates are fixed by the day or by the month, the manner of calculating wages for a month or for a day, as the case may be, indicated. However, in the cases where any wage periods have been fixed under Section 4 of the Payment of Wages Act, 1936 (4 of 1936), minimum wages have to be fixed in accordance therewith.

Minimum Rate of Wages (Section 4)

As provided by Section 4 of the Act, the minimum wage fixed or revised by the appropriate government includes the following:

1. A basic rate of wages and a special allowance which are adjusted at a rate at regular intervals in such manner as directed by the appropriate government, to accord as nearly as practicable with the variation in the cost of living index number applicable to such workers.
2. A basic rate of wages with or without the cost of living allowance and the cash value of the concessions in respect of suppliers of essential commodities at concession rates, where the employee so authorized.
3. An all-inclusive rate, allowing for the basic rate, the cost of living allowance and the cash value of the concessions, if any.
4. The cost of living allowance and the cash value of the concessions in respect of supplies of essential commodities at concession rate to be computed by the competent authority at such intervals and in accordance with such directions as may be specified or given by the appropriate government.

Procedure for Fixing and Revising Minimum Wages (Section 5)

To fix minimum wages in respect of any scheduled employment for the first time or to revise minimum wages so fixed, the appropriate government has to follow either of the two methods provided under Section 5 of the Act:

1. **Committee method (Section 5(1)(a)):** Under this method, committees and subcommittees are set up by the appropriate governments to hold enquiries and make recommendations to fix and revise the minimum wages, as the case may be; or
2. **Notification method (Section 5(1)(b)):** Under this method, government proposals are published in the Official Gazette to inform all those persons who are likely to be affected thereby and specify a date not less than 2 months from the date of the notification on which the proposals will be taken into consideration.

The appropriate government considers the advice of the committee or committees appointed under clause (a) of Subsection (1), or, as the case may be and also considers all representations received by it before the date specified in the notification under clause (b) of that subsection. Thereafter, the appropriate government notifies in the Official Gazette the minimum rate of wages fixed or revised in respect of each scheduled employment. Unless such notification otherwise provides, the fixed or revised rates come into force on the expiry of 3 months from the date of its issue. It is to be noticed that where the appropriate government proposes to revise the minimum rates of wages by the mode specified in clause (b) of Subsection (1), the appropriate government has to also consult the Advisory Board, Before fixing or revising the minimum rate of wages.

Consultation with advisory board: If the appropriate government proposes to revise the minimum rate of wages under Section 5(1)(b), then it is required to consult with the advisory committee.

Government not bound to accept the recommendations of the committee appointed under Section 5(1)(a): The advisory committee constituted under Section 5(1)(a) is just an advisory committee and the appropriate government is not bound to accept the recommendations of the committee in every case. It is also to be noted that any irregularity in the constitution of the advisory committee or a procedure adopted by the committee will not affect the validity of the notification issued by the appropriate government under Section 5(1)(b). In a situation where the advisory committee fails in giving any advice or provides inadequate advice, the appropriate government is empowered and duty bound to fix the minimum rate of wages.

We will now examine a case (Case 12.1) to understand the applicability of the Act and powers extended to the state government for fixing minimum wages to achieve the objective of this Act.

Case 12.1: *Smt Krishna Devi-Devi Prasad v. State of Bihar and Ors*[1]

On 6 September 1990, a notification was issued by the State of Bihar in the exercise of its power conferred by clause (a) of Subsection (i) of Section 3 of the Minimum Wages Act (the Act) fixing the minimum rates of wages as specified in clause (iii) of the Schedule for each category of employees employed in the 'private hospitals, nursing homes and clinics' in the whole of the State of Bihar. Krishna Devi-Devi Prasad Kejariwal Matri Sadan, Muzaffarpur, the petitioner, was a charitable institution established under a trust deed duly registered under the Indian Registration Act. The petitioner did not agree to accept the application of the aforementioned notification on its employees.

The petitioner was of the opinion that since it was a charitable institution established under a trust deed duly registered under the Indian Registration Act, therefore the impugned notification fixing the minimum wages with respect to different categories of employees in the specified schedule was not applicable to the employees of the instant hospital. The petitioner further shared that the hospital in question was being run for charitable purposes without any profit motive and was not utilized for the benefit of a private individual. Hence, keeping this aspect under consideration, even the Income Tax Department had granted exemption under Section 22A of the Income Tax Act. A similar exemption was also granted by the Labour Court, Muzaffarpur, with regard to the applicability of Bihar Shops and Establishments Act. The Labour Court held that from a bare reference to the trust deed, it would be apparent that the object of the trust was purely charitable to grant relief to the poor as well as medical relief. Therefore, in view of the provisions of Section 4 of the said Act, a charitable institution was entitled to full exemption.

Apart from all above-stated contentions, it was further contended by the petitioner that the provisions of Section 3 of the Act state that rates of minimum wages can be fixed by the appropriate government only with respect to the employees of which establishment has been specified in Part II or Part III of the Schedule, and are in an employment added by notification under Section 27, while the respective Schedule of Part II includes only those employees who are employed in private hospitals, nursing homes and clinics. Thus, unless and until charitable hospitals, which were run for public purposes, were included in the schedule, the provisions of the Act were not applicable to the employees working under such institution.

The state government contended that the object of the Income Tax Act and Bihar Shops and Establishments Act to such institution was quite different to that of the applicability and implementation of the provisions of the Minimum Wages Act. Simply because the institution in question was granted exemption under the Income Tax Act, or with regard to the applicability of the Bihar Shops and Establishments Act, it would not be proper to take a plea that similar exemption is required to be granted under the Minimum Wages Act. The state further argued that just because the employees of this hospital were working purely for the purpose of charity, they could not be denied for their remuneration.

The petitioner filed a petition to quash the order of implementation of the aforementioned notification for its implementation.

[1] *Smt Krishna Devi-Devi Prasad v. State of Bihar and Ors.*, 2001 (90) FLR 1, (2001) IILLJ 15 Pat.

Discussion Point

Could the petitioner avoid the implementation of the notification of the state government, fixing the minimum rates of wages?

Judgement and Explanation

The court stated in its judgement under the provisions of the Minimum Wages Act, no exemption has been prescribed from the applicability of the provisions of the Act for the establishment working for treatment or for the care of the infirm, sick, destitute or mentally. Thus, the petitioner could not avoid the implementation of the notification of the state government, fixing the minimum rates of wages for its employees. It was further stated by the court that there might be cases where hospitals are run without any income or profit motive. Naturally, the provisions of the Income Tax Act could not be enforced unless there was ascertained income to the private individual. Similarly, the decision of the Labour Court with respect to a case under the provisions of Bihar Shops and Establishments Act would also not add any force to the contention of the petitioner because clause (2) of Section 4 of the Bihar Shops and Establishments Act clearly states that the provisions of the Act specified in the third column of the Schedule shall not apply to the employees and other persons referred to in the corresponding entry of the second column. Thus, the Bihar Shops and Establishments Act was also not applicable to the establishment in question. However, no such exemption is provided under the Minimum Wages Act, 1948, to the establishment in question.

Correction of errors (Section 10): The act empowers the appropriate government to correct clerical or arithmetical mistakes in and order fixing or revising minimum rates of wages under this Act, or errors arising therein from any accidental slip or omission. Such correction may be done anytime by issuing a notification in the Official Gazette. Every such notification is to be placed before the Advisory Board for information as soon as may be after it is issued.

Advisory Boards and Central Advisory Boards

1. **Advisory boards (Section 7):** The Act authorizes the appropriate government to appoint an Advisory Board to coordinate the work of committees and subcommittees appointed under Section 5. The Board also advises the appropriate government, generally in the matter of fixing and revising minimum rates of wages.
2. **Central Advisory Board (Section 8):** The Act under Section 8 provides for appointing a Central Advisory Board to advise the central and state governments in the matters of the fixation and revision of minimum rates of wages and other matters and also to coordinate the work of the Advisory Board. The Section further specifies that the Central Advisory Board consists of persons to be nominated by the central government representing employers and employees in the scheduled employments, who are equal in number, and independent persons not exceeding one-third of its total number of members; one of such independent persons is to be appointed the Chairman of the Board by the central government.
3. **Composition of committees and so on (Section 9):** Section 9 of the Act provides the composition of committees, subcommittees and boards. Each of the committees, subcommittees and the Advisory Board consists of persons to be nominated by the appropriate government who represent employers and employees in the scheduled employments. Such persons are equal in number, with independent persons not exceeding one-third of its total number of members, and one of such independent persons shall be appointed the Chairman by the appropriate government.

4. **Power of the central government to make rules (Section 29):** The central government is empowered, subject to the conditions of previous publication, by notification in the Official Gazette, to make rules prescribing the term of office of the members, the procedure to be followed in the conduct of business, the method of voting, the manner of filling up casual vacancies in membership and the quorum necessary for the transaction of business of the Central Advisory Board.

LO3: Payment of Minimum Wages

Wages in Kind (Section 11)

Section 11 of the Act specifies that minimum wages payable under the Act are to be paid in cash. However, the payment of minimum wages can be made wholly or partly in kind, by notifying in the Official Gazette, where it is customary to pay wages either wholly or partly in kind. The Act further provides that if the appropriate government finds it appropriate to have a provision for the supply of essential commodities at concessional rates, the appropriate government is empowered to authorize the provision of such supplies at concessional rates. The cash value of wages in kind and of concessions in respect of supplies of essential commodities at concessional rates must be estimated in a manner prescribed under the Act.

Payment of Minimum Rate of Wages (Section 12)

Under the Act, every employer is required to pay for every employee who is engaged in a scheduled employment under him, wages at a rate not less than the minimum rate of wages notified of that class of employees without any deduction except as may be authorized.

Let us examine a case (Case 12.2) to understand the application of the Act and the duty of the employer to pay minimum wages to employees covered under the Act.

Case 12.2: *Multipurpose Training Centre For ... v. Govt. of NCT of Delhi and Ors*[2]

The All India Federation of Deaf, the petitioner, was a society registered under the Societies Registration Act, 1860, and was affiliated to the World Federation of the Deaf, Helsinki, Finland. The Federation was engaged in providing vocational training to adult deaf boys and girls from all parts of the country in the trades such as computer DTP, tailoring, photography, offset printing, fitter and turner including welding at its institute known as a Multipurpose Training Centre for the Deaf. It had separate hostel blocks for boys and girls. The federation also used to organize sign language classes.

The petitioner employed workers on different posts that included, proof reader, peon, MC man, ink man, winder, instructor, sweeper and accountant. The petitioner establishment was paying the salary at the rate of minimum wages to its workers till 31 July 2002 and thereafter the management stopped paying minimum wages to the workers on the grounds that the Minimum Wages Act, 1948, was not applicable to their establishment.

The workers of the petitioner establishment through Delhi Mazdoor Union (Regd.) filed a claim application on 17 March 2005 under Section 20 of the Minimum Wages Act, 1948, to claim arrears of ₹90,759.60

[2] *Multipurpose Training Centre For ... v. Govt. of NCT of Delhi and Ors.*, 2010.

with interest at 12% per annum on account of difference of minimum wages admissible to them for the period for which they were not paid the minimum wages. The Authority under the Act ordered the petitioner to pay ₹24,924 on account of difference of minimum wages for the said period to 17 workmen named in the order along with ₹500 as penalty for each of these workmen.

The petitioner establishment filed a writ petition under Article 226 of the Constitution of India for quashing of the order of the Deputy Labour Commissioner, Authority under the Minimum Wages Act, 1948. The petitioner contended that the order must be set aside mainly on the grounds that the petitioner establishment was not included in the list of scheduled employment either in Part I or Part II of the Schedule. On the other hand, the workmen argued that the said order did not suffer from any jurisdictional error and, therefore, could not be interfered with this Court in exercise of its jurisdiction under Article 226 of the Constitution of India. According to the workmen, they were covered under the Minimum Wages Act and were entitled to the benefits of the said Act because the petitioner's establishment where they were working was covered by the definition of 'scheduled employment' within four corners of the Minimum Wages Act, 1948.

Discussion Point

Whether the establishment of the petitioner was covered by the provisions of the Minimum Wages Act, 1948, and if so, whether its workers were entitled to get minimum wages as fixed by the government from time to time.

Judgement and Explanation

It was held that the writ petition filed for quashing the order of the Authority under the Act was dismissed without any cost. The court found that in the above case, the petitioner's establishment where the respondent workers were working was covered by the definition of 'scheduled employment' within four corners of the Minimum Wages Act, 1948. Therefore, they could not be denied minimum wages ordered to be paid to them vide impugned order. This fact was admitted by the management of the petitioner itself that it was paying salary at the rate of minimum wages to its workers till July 2002. The court further stated that once it was proved that the establishment where the workmen were working was covered by the Minimum Wages Act, 1948, the management could not deprive them the benefit of minimum wages revised by the government from time to time.

Thus, it is clear that the object and policy of the Legislature in enacting the Minimum Wages Act are to prevent exploitation of the workers and, for that purpose, it aims at fixation of minimum wages which the employer must pay. The Act undoubtedly intended to cover those industries or localities in which by reason of causes such as unorganized labour or absence of machinery for regulation of wages, the wages paid to workers were, in the light of the general level of wages, and subsistence level, inadequate. Conditions of labour may vary in different industries and from locality to locality, and the expediency of fixing minimum wages and the rates thereof depend largely upon diverse factors. These diverse factors can properly be ascertained by the government, which is in charge of the administration of the state.

Fixing Hours for Normal Working Day (Section 13)

For any scheduled employment, minimum rates of wages in respect of which have been fixed under this Act, the appropriate government has the power to:

1. Fix the number of hours of work which constitute a normal working day, inclusive of one or more specified intervals.

2. Provide for a day of rest in every period of 7 days, which has been allowed to all employees or to any specified class of employees and also for the payment of remuneration in respect of such days of rest.
3. Provide for payment for work on a day of rest at a rate which is not less than the overtime rate.

Application of the provisions of Section 13(1): The provisions of Subsection (1), in relation to the following classes of employees, are applicable only to such extent and subject to such conditions as may be prescribed:

1. Employees engaged on urgent work or in any emergency which could not have been foreseen or prevented.
2. Employees engaged in work in the nature of preparatory or complementary work which must necessarily be carried on outside the limits laid down for the general working in the employment concerned.
3. Employees whose employment is essentially intermittent.
4. Employees engaged in any work which for technical reasons has to be completed before the duty is over.
5. Employees engaged in a work which could not be carried on except at times dependent on the irregular action of natural forces.

Intermittent employment: For the purposes of clause (c) of Subsection (2), the employment of an employee is essentially intermittent when the appropriate government declares it to be so on the grounds that the daily hours of duty of the employee, or if there be no daily hours of duty as such for the employee, the hours of duty, normally include periods of inaction during which the employee may be on duty but is not called upon to display either physical activity or sustained attention.

Overtime (Section 14)

Section 14 of the Act specifies that if any employee whose minimum rate of wages is fixed under the Act works on any day in excess of the number of hours constituting a normal working day, the employer will have to pay him for such excess hours at the overtime rate fixed under this Act or under any law of the appropriate government for the time being in force, whichever is higher.

Case 12.3 provides insights into Section 14 of the Act and its applicability.

Case 12.3: *Municipal Council Hatta v. Bhagat Singh and Ors*[3]

Bhagat Singh and Ors, the respondents, were the employees of the Municipal Council, the appellant. The respondents were governed by the provisions of the Madhya Pradesh Municipalities Act, 1961. Under Section 95 of the Madhya Pradesh Municipalities Act, the state government was entitled to frame rules in respect of

[3] *Municipal Council Hatta v. Bhagat Singh and Ors.*, AIR 1998 SC 1201, 1998 (79) FLR 338, RLW 1998 (2) SC 196, 1998 (1) SCALE 494, (1998) 2 SCC 443.

scale of pay and all allowances by whatever name called. The state government was also authorized to lay down service conditions of municipal employees. Pursuant to the power so vested, the Madhya Pradesh Municipal Services (Scales of Pay and Allowances) Rules, 1967, were framed. As per the framed rules, the pay scale of Moharrirs was fixed at ₹70-2-80-2 1/2-100-EB-4-120 and there was no provision under these rules for payment of any overtime allowance.

The respondents were not happy with the aforementioned rule of not having any provision of overtime for them. They contended that they would be entitled to overtime under the Minimum Wages Act, 1948, by virtue of Section 14 of the said Act. According to them, service with Local Authority was one of the employments covered by the Minimum Wages Act, 1948. The Municipal Council argued that the minimum wages which were prescribed under the Minimum Wages Act, 1948, which would be applicable to the respondents, were ₹50 per month. Admittedly, the respondents were getting ₹70 per month, which was above the minimum wages prescribed under the Minimum Wages Act, 1948.

The unsatisfied respondents knocked the door of the court for getting the entitlement of overtime under Section 14 of the Minimum Wages Act, 1948.

Discussion Point

Whether Section 14 of the Minimum Wages Act, 1948, would apply to such persons.

Judgement and Explanation

It was held that in the above case, the respondents could not be described as employees who were getting a minimum rate of wages fixed under the Minimum Wages Act, 1948. They were getting much more and that too under the Madhya Pradesh Municipal Service (Scales of Pay and Allowances) Rules, 1967. Therefore, Section 14 had no application to the respondents and there is no other provision in the Act under which they could claim overtime.

After the above discussion, it is clear that to claim overtime under Section 14 of the Act, the following conditions must be fulfilled by an employee:

1. The minimum rate of wages should be fixed under the Minimum Wages Act, 1948.
2. Such an employee should work on any day in excess of the number of hours constituting a normal working day.

Therefore, overtime under Section 14 is payable to those employees who are getting a minimum rate of wage as prescribed under the Minimum Wages Act, 1948, and these are the only employees to whom overtime under Section 14 would become payable.

The wages of workers who work for less than a normal working day (Section 15): An employee whose minimum rates of wages have been fixed under this Act by the day works on any day on which he was employed for a period less than the requisite number of hours constituting a normal working day, unless otherwise provided, such an employee is entitled to receive wages in respect of work done by him on that day as if he had worked for a full normal working day. It is, however, further provided that such an employee is not entitled to receive wages for a full normal working day:

1. In any case where his failure to work is caused by his unwillingness to work and not by the omission of the employer to provide him with work.
2. In such other cases and circumstances as may be prescribed.

Wages for Two or More Classes of Work (Section 16)

If an employee performs two or more classes of work, for each of which a different rate of wage is applicable, the employer is required to pay for such an employee in respect of the time, respectively, occupied in each such class of work, wages at not less than the minimum rate in force in respect of each such class.

Minimum Rate of Wages for the Piece of Work (Section 17)

In the cases where an employee is employed on piecework for which minimum time rate and not minimum piece rate has been fixed under this Act, the employer must pay to such employee wages at not less than the minimum time rate.

Maintenance of Registers and Records (Section 18)

Section 18 of the Act expects every employer to maintain registers and records giving particulars of employees, the work performed by them, the wages paid to them, the receipts given by them and any other required particulars. The Act provides following instructions in this regard to the employers:

1. Every employer has to maintain such registers and records giving such particulars of employees employed by him, the work performed by them, the wages paid to them, the receipts given by them and such other particulars and in such forms as may be prescribed.
2. Every employer must keep exhibited, in such manner, as may be prescribed in the factory, workshop or place where the employees in the scheduled employment may be employed, or in the case of outworkers, in such factory, workshop or place as may be used for giving out work to them, notices in the prescribed form containing prescribed particulars.
3. The appropriate government may, by rules made under this Act, provide for the issue of wage books or wage slips to employees employed in any scheduled employment in respect of which minimum rates of wages have been fixed and prescribe the manner in which entries are required to be made and authenticated in such wage books or wage slips by the employer or his agent.

LO4: Enforcement of the Act

Inspector (Section 19)

The Act empowers the appropriate government to correct clerical or arithmetical mistakes made while fixing or revising minimum rates of wages under this Act, or errors arising therein from any accidental slip or omission.

The powers of the inspector: Subject to any rules made in this behalf, an Inspector can exercise the following powers, within the local limits for which he is appointed. He can:

1. Enter at all reasonable hours, with an assistant (if any), being persons in the service of the government or any local or other public authority, as he thinks fit, any premises or place where

employees are employed or work is given out to outworkers in any scheduled employment in respect of which minimum rates of wages have been fixed under this Act, to examine any register, record of wages or notices required to be kept or exhibited. He may also require the production of any documents thereof for inspection.

2. Examine any person whom he finds in any such premises or place and who, he has reasonable cause to believe, is an employee employed therein or an employee to whom work is given out therein.
3. Require any person giving outwork and any outworkers to give any information, which is in his power to give, with respect to the names and addresses of the persons, to, for and from whom the work is given out or received, and with respect to the payment to be made for the work.
4. Seize or take copies of such register, record of wages or notices or portions thereof as he may consider relevant, in respect of an offence under this Act which he has reason to believe has been committed by an employer.
5. Exercise such other powers as may be prescribed.

Every Inspector is deemed to be a public servant within the meaning of the IPC (45 of 1860). Any person who is required to produce any document or thing or to give any information by an Inspector under Subsection (2) would be bound to do so within the meaning of Section 175 and Section 176 of the IPC (45 of 1860).

Claims (Section 20)

Section 20 of the Act states that the appropriate government may, by notification in the Official Gazette, appoint Labour Commissioner or Commissioner for Workmen's Compensation or any officer not below the rank of Labour Commissioner or any other officer with experience as a judge of a civil court or as a Stipendiary Magistrate to hear and decide for any specified area all claims arising out of the payment of less than the minimum rates of wages or in respect of:

1. The payment of remuneration for days of rest for work done on such days under clause (b) or
2. Clause (c) of Subsection (1) of Section 13 or
3. Of wages at the overtime rate under Section 14, to employees employed or paid in that area.

Who may apply: When an employee has any claim, covered under the Act, the following persons can apply to the authority for direction:

1. The employee himself, or
2. Any legal practitioner, or
3. Any official of a registered trade union authorized in writing to act on his behalf, or
4. Any Inspector, or
5. Any person acting with the permission of the Authority appointed under Subsection (1).

Every such application is to be presented within 6 months from the date on which the minimum wages or other amount became payable. However, any application may be admitted even after the expiry of 6 months when the applicant satisfies the Authority that he had sufficient cause for not making the application within such period.

The amount of compensation: Subsection 20(3) further states after receiving every application under Subsection 2, the Authority must hear the applicant and the employer, or give them an opportunity of being heard. After such further inquiry, if any, as it may consider necessary, the Authority may, without prejudice to any other penalty to which the employer may be liable under this Act, direct:

1. If a claim arising out of payment of less than the minimum rates of wages, the payment to the employee of the amount by which the minimum wages payable to him exceed the amount actually paid, together with the payment of such compensation as the Authority may think fit, not exceeding 10 times the amount of such excess.
2. In any other case, the payment of the amount due to the employee together with the payment of such compensation as the Authority may think fit, not exceeding ₹10.

The Authority may also direct payment of such compensation in cases where the excess or the amount due is paid by the employer to the employee before the disposal of the application.

Malicious or vexatious application: If the authority after hearing the case is satisfied that it was either malicious or vexatious, the Authority may direct that a penalty not exceeding ₹50 be paid to the employer by the person presenting the application. Such an amount may be recovered:

1. If the Authority is a Magistrate, by the Authority as if it were a fine imposed by the Authority as a Magistrate.
2. If the Authority is not a Magistrate, by any Magistrate, to whom the Authority makes application in this behalf, as if it were a fine imposed by such Magistrate.

Powers of the authority: Every direction of the Authority under this section is final and every Authority appointed under Subsection (1) is entitled to exercise all the powers of a Civil Court under the Code of Civil Procedure, 1908 (5 of 1908). By exercising these powers, the appointed authority can take evidence and compel the attendance of witnesses and production of documents. Every such Authority is deemed to be a Civil Court for all the purposes of Section 195 and Chapter XXXV of the Code of Criminal Procedure, 1898 (5 of 1898).

Single application in respect of a number of employees (Section 21): Only a single application is required to be presented under Section 20 on behalf or in respect of any number of employees employed in the scheduled employment in respect of which minimum rates of wages have been fixed. In such cases, the maximum compensation which may be awarded under Subsection (3) of Section 20 must not exceed 10 times the aggregate amount of such excess or ₹10 per head as the case may be.

Duties of Employer

Duties of an employer under the act can be summarized as follows:

1. Wages are to be paid in cash after obtaining the authorization. It can even be paid either by cheque or by crediting the wages in the employee's bank account.
2. For the fixation of minimum wages, the employment must appear in Schedule originally or added to the Schedule by a notification under Section 27 of the Act.

3. The employer can take actual work on any day only up to 9 hours in a 12-hour shift, but he is required to pay double the rate for any hour or part of an hour of actual work in excess of 9 hours or for more than 48 hours in any week.
4. Once a minimum wage is fixed according to the provisions of the Act, it is the duty of the employer to pay for every employee engaged in a Scheduled employment, minimum wages notification for that class of employees.
5. The employer should fix wage period for the payment of wages at intervals not exceeding 1 month or such other larger period as may be prescribed by the appropriate government.
6. If an employer employs less than 1,000 persons, the wages would be paid before the expiry of the seventh day of the following month. And in the other cases where more than 1,000 workers, the wages would be paid before the expiry of the 10th day of the following month.
7. The wages of a person discharged must be paid not later than the second working day after his discharge.
8. Every employer has to maintain a register of wages at workplace specifying the following particulars for each wage period in respect of each employed person:
   a. Minimum rate of wages payable.
   b. The number of days in which overtime was worked.
   c. The gross wages.
   d. The wages actually paid and the date of payment.
9. Every employer must get the signature or the thumb impression of every person employed on the wage book and the wage slips.
10. The employer has to exhibit at main entrance to the establishment and its offices a notice in respect of the following in English and local language:
    a. Minimum rate of wages.
    b. Abstracts of the Acts and rules made there under.
    c. Name and address of the Labour Inspector/Asst. Commissioner of Labour and so on.

LO5: Penalties and Offences

Penalties for Certain Offences (Section 22)

The Act provides for the penalties for the contravention of the provisions of this Act under Section 22. The section imposes penalty on each employer who:

1. Pays to any employee less than the minimum rates of wages fixed for that employee's class of work, by less than the amount due to him under the provisions of this Act 19.
2. Fails to pay the wages within the time prescribed under Subsection (1) of Section 12.
3. Contravenes any rule or order made under Section 13.

Every such employer is punishable with imprisonment for a term which may extend to 6 months or with fine which may extend to ₹500 or with both. The penalty is imposed subject to the condition that in imposing any fine for an offence under this section the Court has taken into consideration the amount of any compensation already awarded against the accused in any proceedings taken under Section 20.

Penalty for Obstructing Inspector

The Act has a provision of penalty for obstructing the Inspector in discharging his duties under the Act. According to this provision, any person who wilfully obstructs an Inspector in the exercise of any power conferred on him by or under this Act, or fails to produce on demand by an Inspector any registers, records or other documents in his custody, kept in pursuance of this act, and which he is required to produce by or under this Act shall, on conviction, be punished with fine which may extend to ₹500.

General Provision for Punishment of Other Offences (Section 22A)

Section 22A of the Act lays down general provisions for the punishment of other offences under the Act. This section states that if any employer contravenes any provision of this Act or of any rule or of an order made thereunder, and if no other penalty is provided for such contravention by this Act, such a person is to be punished with fine which may extend to ₹500.

Cognizance of Offences (Section 22B)

No Court is authorized to take cognizance of a complaint against any person for an offence:

1. Under clause (a) of Section 22 unless an application in respect of the facts constituting such offence has been presented under Section 20 and has been granted wholly or in part, and the appropriate government or an officer authorized by it in this behalf has approved the making of the complaint.
2. Under clause (b) of Section 22 or under Section 22A, unless a complaint is made by, or with the sanction of, an Inspector.

Section 22B further states that no Court shall take cognizance of an offence:

1. Under clause (a) or clause (b) of Section 22, except on a complaint thereof is made within 1 month of the grant of sanction under this section.
2. Under Section 22A, except for the complaint thereof is made within 6 months of the date on which the offence becomes known to the Inspector.

Offences by Companies (Section 22C)

The Act provides a separate provision of penalty for the offences committed by companies. Section 22C of the Act provides in this regard that if the person committing any offence under this Act is a company, every person who at the time the offence was committed was in charge of, and was responsible to, the company for the conduct of the business of the company as well as the company is deemed to be guilty of the offence and is liable to be proceeded against and punished accordingly. However, nothing contained in this subsection renders any such person liable to any punishment provided in this Act if he proves that the offence was committed without his knowledge or that he exercised all due diligence to prevent the commission of such offence.

The section further lays down that notwithstanding anything contained in Subsection (1), where an offence under this Act has been committed by a company and it is proved that the offence was committed with the consent or connivance of, or is attributable to any neglect on the part of any director, manager, secretary or other officer of the company, such director, manager, secretary or other officer of the company is also be deemed to be guilty of that offence and is liable to be proceeded against and punished accordingly.

LO6: Miscellaneous Provisions of the Act

Payment of Undisbursed Amounts due to Employees (Section 22D)

If all amounts payable by an employer to an employee as the amount of minimum wages of the employee under this Act or otherwise due to the employee under this Act or any rule or order made thereunder could not or cannot be paid to the employee on account of his death before payment or on account of his whereabouts not being known, then all such amounts are required to be deposited with the prescribed authority who would deal with the money so deposited in such manner as may be prescribed.

Any employer who contravenes any provision of this section is punishable with imprisonment for a term, which may extend to 6 months or with fine, which may extend to ₹500 or with both.

Protection Against Attachment of Assets of Employer (Section 22E)

Any amount deposited with the appropriate government by an employer to secure the due performance of a contract with that government and any other amount due to such employer from that government in respect of such contract is not liable to attachment under any decree or order of any Court in respect of any debt or liability incurred by the employer other than any debt or liability incurred by the employer towards any employee employed in connection with the aforesaid contract.

Application of Payment of Wages Act, 1936 (Section 22F)

The appropriate government is empowered to direct that all or any of the provisions of the Act are applicable to such notifications, if any, as may be specified in the notification, to wages payable to employees in such scheduled employment as may be specified in the notification. Where all or any of the provisions of the said Act are applied, the Inspector appointed under this Act are deemed to be the Inspector for the purpose of enforcement of the provisions so applied within the local limits of his jurisdiction.

Exemption of Employer from Liability in Certain Cases (Section 23)

An employer who is charged with an offence against this Act is entitled to charge any other person as the actual offender and bring such person before the Court at the time appointed for hearing the charge. If after the commission of the offence has been proved, the employer proves to the satisfaction of the Court:

1. That he has used due diligence to enforce the execution of this act.
2. That the said other person committed the offence in question without his knowledge, consent or connivance.

In the above-mentioned conditions are met, that other person would be convicted of the offence. Such other person will be liable to the like punishment as if he was the employer and the employer is discharged. While seeking to prove, as aforesaid, the employer may be examined on oath, and the evidence of the employer or his witness, if any, is subject to cross examination by or on behalf of the person whom the employer charges as the actual offender and by the prosecution.

Bar of Suits (Section 24)

Section 24 prohibits any Court to entertain any suit for the recovery of wages insofar as the sum so claimed:

1. Forms the subject of an application under Section 20 which has been presented by or on behalf of the plaintiff.
2. Has formed the subject of a direction under that section in favour of the plaintiff.
3. Has been adjudged in any proceeding under that section not to be due to the plaintiff.
4. Could have been recovered by an application under that section.

Contracting Out (Section 25)

Any contract or agreement between an employer, an employee (either before or after the commencement of this Act) to relinquish or reduce the employee's right to a minimum rate of wages or any privilege or concession accruing to him under this Act is treated as null and void insofar as it purports to reduce the minimum rate of wages fixed under this Act.

Exemptions and Exceptions (Section 26)

The appropriate government is empowered to direct that the provisions of this Act shall not apply in relation to the wages payable to disabled employees. The appropriate government for special reasons may also direct that subject to such conditions and for such period as it may specify the provisions of this Act or any of them will not be applicable to all or any class of employees employed in any scheduled employment or to any locality where there is carried on a scheduled employment.

If in the opinion of the appropriate government, having regard to the terms and conditions of service applicable to any class of employees in a scheduled employment generally or in a scheduled employment in a local area or to any establishment or a part of any establishment in a scheduled employment, it is not necessary to fix minimum wages in respect of such employees of that class or in respect of employees in such establishment or part of any establishment as are in receipt of wages exceeding such limit as may be prescribed in this behalf, then the appropriate government may keep such employees out of the scope of the Act. However, this exemption is not applicable to the wages payable by an employer to a member of his family who is living with him and is dependent on him. Here, a member of the employer's family includes his or her spouse or child or parent or brother or sister.

Power of State Government to Add to Schedule (Section 27)

The appropriate government is empowered to add to either Part of the Schedule any employment in respect of which it is of opinion that the minimum rates of wages should be fixed under this Act. However, this can be done only after giving a notice of not less than 3 months of its intentions to do so. Thereafter, the Schedule in its application to the State is to be amended accordingly.

Power of Central Government to Give Directions (Section 28)

The central government is entrusted with the power to give directions to a state government as to the carrying into execution of this Act in the state.

Power of the Central Government to Make Rules (Sections 29, 30 and 30A)

By the virtue of the power given to the central government under Section 29, it can frame rules prescribing the terms of office of the members, the procedure to be followed in the conduct of business, the method of voting, the manner of filling up casual vacancies in membership and the quorum necessary for the transaction of business of the Central Advisory Board. Every rule made by the central government under this Act is laid as soon as may be after it is presented before each House of Parliament while it is in session for a total period of 30 days. This period may be comprised in one session or in two successive sessions. If, before the expiry of the session in which it is so laid or the session immediately following, both Houses agree to make any modification in the rule, or both Houses agree that the rule must not be made, such rule remains effective only in such modified form or is not effective at all, as the case may be. However, any such modification or annulment has to be without prejudice to the validity of anything previously done under that rule.

Summary

1. The objective of the Minimum Wages Act, 1948, is to ensure a minimum subsistence wage for workers and to prevent sweating or exploitation of labour through payment of low wages.
2. The Act extends to the whole of India and is applicable to the schedule employments for which minimum wages are fixed/revised.
3. The Act empowers both the central government and the state governments to fix, revise, review and enforce the payment of minimum wages to workers in respect of 'scheduled employments' under their respective jurisdictions.
4. The government may review the minimum rates of wages and revise the minimum rates from time to time, but not exceeding 5 years.
5. The appropriate government is permitted to fix separate minimum rates of wages for time rate and for piece rate.
6. Section 5 of the Act provides two methods for fixation/revision of minimum wages, namely, the committee method and the notification method.
7. Section 8 of the Act authorizes the appropriate government in appointing an Advisory Board to coordinate the work of committees and subcommittees appointed under Section 5.

8. Minimum wages payable under the Act are to be paid in cash.
9. Section 11 of the Act specifies that minimum wages are payable under the Act are to be paid in cash.
10. The appropriate government may fix the number of hours of work which constitute a normal working day, inclusive of one or more specified intervals.
11. Overtime is payable to those employees who are getting a minimum rate of wage as prescribed under the Minimum Wages Act, 1948, and these are the only employees to whom overtime under Section 14 would become payable.
12. Every employer should maintain registers and records giving particulars of employees, the work performed by them, the wages paid to them, the receipts given by them and any other required particulars.
13. The Act empowers the appropriate government by notification in the Official Gazette to appoint inspectors for the purpose of this Act and define the local limits for their functions.
14. Every Inspector is deemed to be a public servant within the meaning of the IPC (45 of 1860). Any person who is required to produce any document or thing or to give any information by an Inspector under Subsection (2) would be bound to do so.
15. After receiving every application under Subsection 2, the Authority must hear the applicant and the employer, or give them an opportunity of being heard.
16. Every direction of the Authority under this section is final, and every Authority appointed under Subsection (1) is entitled to exercise all the powers of a Civil Court under the Code of Civil Procedure, 1908 (5 of 1908).
17. The Act provides for the penalties for the contravention of the provisions of this Act under Section 22.
18. The Act provides a separate provision of penalty for the offences committed by companies under Section 22 C of the Act.
19. An employer who is charged with an offence against this Act is entitled to charge any other person as the actual offender and bring such person before the Court at the time appointed for hearing the charge.
20. Any contract or agreement between an employer and employee to relinquish or reduce the employee's right to a minimum rate of wages or any privilege or concession accruing to him under this Act is treated as null and void.
21. The appropriate government for special reasons may also direct that subject to such conditions and for such period as it may specify the provisions of this Act or any of them will not be applicable to all or any class of employees employed in any scheduled employment or to any locality where there is carried on a scheduled employment.

Multiple Choice Questions

1. The Minimum Wages Act, 1948, applies to persons engaged in ____________.
   a. Scheduled employments
   b. Specified class of work in respect of which minimum wages have been fixed
   c. Both (a) and (b)
   d. Neither (a) nor (b)

2. The minimum rate of wages is to be reviewed and revised if necessary at such intervals as the appropriate government may think fit. However, such intervals cannot exceed ________.
   a. 2 years
   b. 5 years
   c. 10 years
   d. 15 years

3. The appropriate government may refrain from fixing minimum rates of wages in respect of any scheduled employment in which there are in the whole state ________ engaged in such employment.
   a. Less than 1,000 employees
   b. More than 1,000 employees
   c. Less than 500 employees
   d. More than 500 employees

4. Under ________, committees and subcommittees are set up by the appropriate governments to hold enquiries and make recommendations to fix and revise the minimum wages, as the case may be.
   a. Notification method
   b. Committee method
   c. Both (a) and (b)
   d. Neither (a) nor (b)

5. Under ________, government proposals are published in the Official Gazette to inform all those persons who are likely to be affected thereby and specify a date not less than 2 months from the date of the notification on which the proposals will be taken into consideration.
   a. Notification method
   b. Committee method
   c. Both (a) and (b)
   d. Neither (a) nor (b)

6. The employee is not entitled to receive wages for a full normal working day ________.
   a. In any case where his failure to work is caused by his unwillingness to work and not by the omission of the employer to provide him with work
   b. In such other cases and circumstances as may be prescribed
   c. Both (a) and (b)
   d. Neither (a) nor (b)

7. When an employee has any claim, covered under the Act, ________ can apply to the authority for direction.
   a. The employee himself, or any legal practitioner
   b. Any official of a registered trade union authorized in writing to act on his behalf
   c. Any Inspector, or any person acting with the permission of the Authority appointed under Subsection (1)
   d. All of the above

8. The appropriate government is to fix minimum rates of wages ________.
   a. By the hour
   b. By the day
   c. By the month, or by such other larger wage period as may be prescribed
   d. All of the above

9. Fixation of minimum rate of wages depends on ________.
   a. Level of income and paying capacity
   b. Prices of essential commodities
   c. Productivity and local conditions
   d. All of the above

True/False Questions

1. A contract or agreement made to pay to the employee less than the minimum rates of wages fixed is null and void in the eye of law.
2. The advisory committee constituted under Section 5(1)(a) is not just an advisory committee, and the appropriate government is bound to accept the recommendations of the committee in every case.
3. Only a single application is required to be presented under Section 20 on behalf or in respect of any number of employees employed in the scheduled employment in respect of which minimum rates of wages have been fixed.
4. The appropriate government cannot correct clerical or arithmetical mistakes and order fixing or revising minimum rates of wages under this Act, or errors arising therein from any accidental slip or omission.
5. Employer is required to pay to every employee who is engaged in a scheduled employment under him wages at a rate not less than the minimum rate of wages notified for that class of employees without any deduction except as may be authorized.
6. Overtime is payable to those employees who are getting a minimum rate of wage as prescribed under the Minimum Wages Act, 1948, and these are the only employees to whom overtime under Section 14 would become payable.

Descriptive Questions

1. Write short notes on the following:
   a. Cost of living index number
   b. Employer under Minimum Wages Act
   c. Employee under the Minimum Wages Act
2. Who is authorized to fix the minimum wages and in what manner under the Minimum Wages Act, 1948?
3. Enumerate the procedure for fixing and revising the minimum wages under the Act.
4. Throw light on the powers and duties of the Inspector appointed under Section 19 of the Minimum Wages Act, 1948.
5. Discuss various provisions of penalty for offences committed under the Minimum Wages Act, 1948.
6. Write short notes on the provisions for following under the Minimum Wages Act, 1948:
   a. Payment of undisbursed amounts due to employees
   b. Protection against attachment of assets of employer
   c. Exemptions and exceptions under Section 26

ANNEXURE A

S. No.	Sections	State	Amendments
1.	Section 2	Madhya Pradesh	**Explanation added to the definition of employee**[4] An employee who has been dismissed, discharged or retrenched from employment or whose employment has been otherwise terminated shall, in respect of all claims arising out of payment of less than the minimum rates of wages or in respect of the payment of remuneration for days of rest or for work done on such days under clause (b) or clause (c) of Subsection (1) of Section 13 or wages at the overtime rate under Section 14 during the period of his employment, be deemed to be an employee for the purpose of this Act.
		Maharashtra	**Substitution of the words in the definition of employee**[5] For the words and management of that other person, substitute the words and management of that other person, and include for the purposes of Sections 20, 21, 22, 22A, 22B, 22C and 22D any person who has been an employee and who has ceased to be so by reason of superannuation, retirement, dismissal, removal, discharge, termination of his service or otherwise howsoever.
2.	Section 3	Gujarat	**Empowerment of state government under Subsection (1A) of Section 3**[6] Where the state government had for any reason not fixed the minimum rates of wages in respect of any scheduled employment within 1 year from the date on which it came to a finding as aforesaid in respect of such employment, nothing contained in this subsection shall, after the commencement of the Minimum Wages (Gujarat Amendment) Act, 1961, prevent the state government from fixing the minimum rates of wages in respect of such employment even after the expiry of the said period of 1 year.
		Madhya Pradesh	**Empowerment of state government under Subsection (1A) of Section 3** • Where for any reason the state government has not fixed the minimum rates of wages in respect of any scheduled employment within the period specified in this subsection, the state government may, by notification, extend from time to time, the said period by a further period not exceeding 1 year in the aggregate. • Provided further that the state government may, instead of fixing minimum rates of wages under this subsection for the whole state, fix such rates for a part of the state or for any specified class or classes of such employment or category or categories of employees in such employment in the whole state or part thereof.

[4] Vide Madhya Pradesh Act 23 of 1961, Section 2 (w.e.f. 23 June 1961).
[5] Vide Maharashtra Act 3 of 1963, Section 2 (w.e.f. 14 January 1963).
[6] Vide Gujarat Act 22 of 1961, Section 2 (w.e.f. 18 May 1961).

S. No.	Sections	State	Amendments
			Split of class or classes of such employment or category or categories of employees and fixation of minimum wages for such class/category • The state government is authorized to split up the class or classes of such employment or category or categories of employees in such employment or amalgamate the class or classes of such employment or category or categories of employees in such employment and revise the minimum rates of wages fixed in respect thereof under Subsection (1); • Fix the minimum rates of wages for the class or classes of such employment or category or categories of employees in such employment as were not in existence at the time of fixing the minimum rates under Subsection (1) or were in existence but were not covered by such fixation; • (c) Fix the minimum rates of wages, mentioned under clause (a) or clause (b), for the whole state or for any such part thereof for which they were not fixed under Subsection (1) or extend the minimum rates fixed under Subsection (1) for any part of the state, to the whole state or any other part thereof.
		Maharashtra	**Empowerment of state government under Subsection (1A) of Section 3**[7] • Where the state government has not for any reason fixed the minimum rates of wages in respect of any scheduled employment within 1 year from the date on which it came to a finding as aforesaid in respect of such employment, nothing contained in this subsection shall, after the commencement of the Minimum Wages (Maharashtra Amendment) Act, 1960, prevent the state government from fixing the minimum rates of wages in respect of such employment even after the expiry of the said period of 1 year. • The state government may, instead of fixing the minimum rates of wages under this clause for the whole state, fix such rates for a part of the state or for any specified class or classes of such employment in the whole of the state or any part thereof and in the case of an employment under any local authority, or class of local authorities.[8]
3.	Section 12	Bihar	**Payment of higher wages than the minimum wages—Insertion of Subsection, namely '(1A)'**[9] Where immediately before the issue of a notification under Section 5 fixing or revising the minimum rates of wages in respect of any scheduled employment, wages at a rate higher than the rate so fixed or revised were payable either by contract or agreement, or under any other law for the time being in force, then, notwithstanding anything contained in this Act, wages at such higher rate shall be payable to the employees in such scheduled employment and the wages so payable shall be deemed to be minimum wages for the purposes of this Act.

[7] Vide Maharashtra Act 10 of 1961, Section 2 (w.e.f. 15 February 1961).
[8] Vide Maharashtra Act 3 of 1963, Section 3 (w.e.f. 14 January 1963).
[9] Vide Bihar Act 5 of 1983, Section 3 (w.e.f. 30 January 1983).

S. No.	Sections	State	Amendments
		Madhya Pradesh	**Payment of higher wages than the minimum wages—Insertion of Subsection, namely '(1A)'**[10] • Where immediately before the issue of a notification under Section 5 fixing or revising the minimum rates of wages in respect of any scheduled employment, wages at a rate higher than the rate so fixed or revised were payable under this Act, or under any law or award or agreement or custom or usage for the time being in force, then, notwithstanding anything contained in this Act, wages at such higher rate shall be payable to the employees in such scheduled and the wages so payable shall be deemed to be the minimum wages for the purposes of this Act. • Provisions of this section shall apply to minimum rates of wages specified in Section 3.[11]
4.	Section 21A	Gujarat	**Liability for payment of court fee—insertion of Subsection 21A** In any proceedings under Section 20, the applicant shall not be liable to pay any court fees (other than fees payable for service of process) in respect of such proceedings: provided that, when the application is presented by an Inspector, he shall not be liable to pay the process fees also.
5.	Section 22CC	Madhya Pradesh	**Liability of principals in certain cases—insertion of Subsection 22CC**[12] (1) Subject to the provisions of Subsection (2), where in any scheduled employment in respect of which minimum rate of wages has been fixed under this Act, any person contracts with any other person for having any goods made for sale for the purposes of the trade or business of the principal either wholly or partly out of materials supplied to the contractor by the principal, then, notwithstanding that the employees for making such goods are employed by the contractor, the principal shall also in addition to the contractor be deemed for all purposes of this Act to be the employer in relation to the employees: provided that where by virtue of the provision of Subsection (1), a principal is convicted of an offence punishable under Section 22, he shall be punishable only with fine as provided for in that section.

[10] Vide Madhya Pradesh Act 23 of 1961, Section 6 (w.e.f. 23 June 1961).

[11] Vide Madhya Pradesh Act 16 of 1962, Section 4 (w.e.f. 5 August 1962).

[12] Vide Madhya Pradesh Act 11 of 1959, Section 2 (w.e.f. 12 June 1959) as amended by Madhya Pradesh Act 23 of 1961, Section 21(b) (w.e.f. 23 June 1961).

13 CHAPTER

The Industrial Disputes Act, 1947

LEARNING OBJECTIVES

Upon completing this chapter, the reader would be able to:

LO1. **Understand the objectives, scope and important definitions of the Act.**

LO2. **Know the procedure for the settlement of industrial disputes and authorities under the Act.**

LO3. **Understand the restrictions of the change in condition of service.**

LO4. **Get the details of the provisions for the references of disputes to boards, courts or tribunals.**

LO5. **Explain the provisions for the enforcement of award and settlements.**

LO6. **Know the treatment of strikes and lockouts provided by the Act.**

LO7. **Learn the provisions for layoff and retrenchment as provided by the Act.**

LO8. **Discuss the procedure and guidelines for transfer and closing down of an undertaking.**

LO9. **Gain insights into special provisions for layoff, retrenchment and closure.**

LO10. **Explore the treatment of unfair labour practices by the Act.**

LO11. **Discuss some important miscellaneous provisions of the Act.**

Introduction

The prosperity of an industry depends upon its growing production to a larger extent, and production is possible when the industry functions smoothly without any disturbances. The industrial disputes adversely affect the industrial production, efficiency, costs, quality, human satisfaction, discipline, technological and economic progress, and finally the welfare of the society. A discontent labour force, nursing in its heart mute grievances and resentments, cannot be efficient in its work and will not possess a required degree of industrial morale. Thus, industrial peace through harmonious relationship between labour and management is required to be ensured to bring industrial growth at a desired rate. Therefore, legal machinery must exist to ensure all necessary preventive and curative measures to settle the industrial disputes as and when they emerge.

The Industrial Disputes Act, 1947 (the Act), came into force to ensure specific justice to both employers and workmen, and to advance the progress of the industry by bringing about harmony and cordial relationship between the parties. It is an important social legislation enacted to provide for investigation and settlement of industrial disputes and for maintaining industrial harmony. The Act also enumerates the contingencies as to when a strike or lockout can be lawfully resorted to, when they can be declared illegal and conditions for laying-off retrenching, discharging or dismissing a workman. The Act also specifies circumstances under which an industrial establishment can be closed down and several other matters related to industrial employees and the employers.

LO1: Objectives, Scope and Important Definitions

Objectives

The principal objective of the Industrial Disputes Act is to secure industrial peace and harmony by providing machinery and procedure for the investigation and settlement of industrial disputes. The Act deals with the retrenchment process of the employees, procedure for layoff, procedure and rules for strikes and lockouts of the company.

The main objectives of Industrial Disputes Act as analysed and interpreted by the Supreme Court are to:

1. Promote the measures for securing and preserving amity and good relations between employers and workmen.
2. Investigate and settle the industrial disputes between employers and employers, employers and workmen, or between workmen and workmen, with a right of representation by a registered trade union or Federation of Trade Unions or Association of Employers or a Federation of Association of Employers.
3. Prevent the illegal strikes and lockouts.
4. Provide relief to workmen in the matter of layoff, retrenchment and closure of an undertaking.
5. Conduct collective bargaining.

Scope and Application of the Act

The Industrial Dispute Act, 1947, came into force on the 1 April 1947, with the principal objective of protecting the workmen against victimization by the employers, and to ensure social justice to both employers and employees. The Act extends to the whole of India and it replaced the Trade Disputes Act of 1929. The Trade Disputes Act imposed certain restraints on the right of strike and lockout in public utility services. On the other hand, there was no provision for the settlement of industrial disputes, either by reference to a board of conciliation or to a Court of Inquiry. In order to remove this deficiency, the Industrial Disputes Act, 1947, was passed to provide procedures for the settlement of industrial disputes.

Important Definitions

1. Appropriate government (Section 2(a)): As defined by the Act, appropriate government means the central government in relation to any industrial dispute concerning any industry carried on by or under the authority of the central government, any industry carried on by a railway company, any controlled industry specified by the central government, the Unit Trust of India. Corporations under the central statutes, banking company, insurance company, mines, oilfield, cantonment board, major ports, and so on. In relation to any other industrial dispute, the appropriate government is the state government.

2. Average pay (Section 2(aaa)): Average pay is the average of the wages payable to a workmen. Average pay in the case of workmen means:

a. **In the case of monthly paid workman:** The average of monthly wages payable in three complete calendar months.
b. **In the case of weekly paid workman:** The average of the weekly wages payable in 4 complete weeks.
c. **In the case of daily paid workman:** The average of the wages for 12 full working days.

3. Award (Section 2(b)): Award is an interim or a final determination of any industrial dispute or of any question relating thereto by any labour court, Industrial Tribunal or National Industrial Tribunal, and includes an arbitration award made under Section 10A.

An award is enforceable in the ways given below:

a. The aggrieved party has an option to apply to the appropriate government for prosecuting the defaulting party under Section 29 or 31 of this Act.
b. Where the workman is to claim money from the employer, the workman may move the appropriate government for recovery of the money due to him under the award.
c. The party in whose favour the award has been granted may file a suit and obtain a decree, which shall be enforced extension under provisions of the Civil Procedure Code.

Where the interim order did not determine any part of the industrial dispute or any other question relating there to, but only determined whether the Industrial Tribunal has been properly constituted to which the industrial dispute could be referred for adjudication, such order cannot be said to be an award as defined in Section 2(b)2.

4. Banking company (Section 2(bb)): As defined in Section 5 of the Banking Companies Act, 1949, a banking company is one that has branches or other establishments in more than one state. The definition of banking company also includes the Export-Import Bank of India, the Industrial Reconstruction Bank of India, the Industrial Development Bank of India, the Small Industries Development Bank of India established under Section 3 of the Small Industries Development Bank of India Act, 1989, the Reserve Bank of India, the State Bank of India, a corresponding new bank constituted under Section 3 of the Banking Companies (Acquisition and Transfer of Undertakings) Act, 1970, a corresponding new bank constituted under Section 3 of the Banking Companies as defined in the State Bank of India (Subsidiary Banks) Act, 1959.

5. Board (Section 2(c)): 'Board' means a board of conciliation constituted under this Act.

6. Closure (Section 2(cc)): The Act defines 'closure' as the permanent closing down of a place of employment or part thereof.

7. Conciliation officer (Section 2(d)): Conciliation officer is one who is appointed under the Act.

8. Conciliation proceeding (Section 2(e)): As defined by the Act, 'conciliation proceeding' means any proceeding held by a conciliation officer or board under the Act.

9. Controlled industry (Section 2(ee)): The Act defines the controlled industry as any industry whose control, by the Union, has been declared by any Central Act to the expedient in the public interest, that is, an industry which is controlled by the central government. But it must also be declared by the Central Act to be controlled by the Union.

10. Court (Section 2(f)): Court is a Court of Inquiry constituted under this Act.

11. Employer (Section 2(g)): 'Employer' means, in relation to industries carried on by or under the authority of Central Government, State Government, or Local Authorities, the authority prescribed in this behalf, or where no authority is prescribed, the head of the department; while in relation to an industry carried on by or on behalf of a local authority, the chief executive officer of that authority.

12. Executive (Section 2(h)): According to Section 2(h) of the Act, the 'Executive', in relation to a trade union, means the body by whatever name called, to which by management of the affairs of the trade union is entrusted.

13. Independent (Section 2(i)): A person must be 'Independent' for the purpose of appointment of a person as Chairman or other member of a Board, Court or Tribunal. He is deemed to be 'independent' only if he is unconnected with the industrial dispute referred to such Board, Court or Tribunal or with any industry directly affected by such dispute. It is further provided in the Act that no person shall cease to be independent by reason only of the fact that he is a shareholder of an incorporated company which is connected with, or likely to be affected by, such industrial dispute; but in such a case, he shall disclose to the appropriate Government the nature and extent of the shares held by him in such company. In order that a person may be eligible for his appointment to these bodies, he must possess the following qualifications:

a. He must be unconnected with industrial dispute in question, or
b. He must be unconnected with any industry directly affected by such dispute.

14. Industry (Section 2(j)): Under the Act, industry means any business, trade, undertaking, manufacture or calling of employers and includes any calling, service, employment, handicraft or industrial occupation or avocation of workmen.

In a landmark case,[1] the Supreme Court considered the scope of industry and provided a triple test which is practically reiterated as under:

'Where there is

a. Systematic activity,
b. Organized by cooperation between employer and employee,

[1] Bangalore Water *Supply v. A Rajappa.*

For the production and/or distribution of goods and services calculated to satisfy human wants and wishes, prima facie, this is an 'Industry' in that enterprise'.

The following points are to be emphasized while bringing an establishment under the definition of industry for the purpose of the Industrial Disputes Act:

a. Industry does not include spiritual or religious services or services geared to celestial bliss, for example, making on a large scale, 'parsed' or food.
b. The absence of profit motive or gainful objective is not relevant, be the venture in the public, joint, private or other sector.
c. The true focus is functional and the decisive test is the nature of the activity with special emphasis on the employer–employee relations.
d. If the organization is a trade or business, it does not cease to be one because of philanthropy animating the undertaking.

Thus clubs, educational institutions, cooperatives, research institutions, charitable projects and other kind of adventures, if they fulfil the triple test stated above, cannot be exempted from the scope of industry.

15. Industrial dispute (Section 2(k)): An 'industrial dispute' is any dispute or difference between employers and employers, or between employers and workmen, or between workmen and workmen, which is connected with the employment or non-employment or the terms of employment or with the conditions of labour, of any person.

16. Industrial establishment or undertaking (Section 2(ka)): According to this subsection, an industrial establishment or undertaking is one in which any industry is carried on. The Act further provides that where several activities are carried on in an establishment or undertaking and only one or some of such activities is/are an industry or industries, then:

a. If any unit of such establishment or undertaking carrying on any activity, being an industry, is severable from the other unit or units of such establishment or undertaking, such unit shall be deemed to be a separate industrial establishment or undertaking.
b. If the predominant activity or each of the predominant activities carried on in such establishment or undertaking or any unit thereof is an industry, and the other activity or each of the other activities carried on in such establishment or undertaking or unit thereof is not severable from and is, for the purpose of carrying on, or aiding the carrying on of such predominant activity or activities, the entire establishment or undertaking or, as the case may be, unit thereof shall be deemed to be an industrial establishment or undertaking.

17. Insurance company (Section 2(kk)): As defined by the Act, an insurance is one, which is defined in Section 2 of the Insurance Act, 1938, having branches or other establishments in more than one state.

18. Labour Court (Section 2(kkb)): Labour Court is a court constituted under Section 7 of the Industrial Disputes Act, 1947.

19. Layoff (Section 2(kkk)): Layoff is defined as the failure, refusal or inability of an employer on account of shortage of coal, power or raw materials, or the accumulation of stocks or the breakdown of machinery or for any other reason to give employment to a workman whose name is borne on the muster rolls of his industrial establishment and who has not been retrenched.

The duration of layoff cannot be for a period longer than the period of emergency. It must be noted that the employer–employee relationship does not come to an end during the period of layoff but is merely suspended during the period of emergency.

20. Lockout (Section 2(l)): The Act defines lockout as the temporary closing of a place of employment, or the suspension of work, or the refusal by an employer to continue to employ any number of persons employed by him. The Supreme Court defines lockout as the antithesis of strike. Just as a strike is a weapon in the hands of the workers for enforcing their industrial demands, lockout is a weapon available to the employer to force the employees to see his points of view and to accept his demands.

21. Major port (Section 2(la)): Major port means a port as defined in clause 8 of Section 3 of the Indian Port Act, 1903, which is defined as follows:

> Any port which the central government may by notification in official Gazette declare or may by any law for the time being in force, have declared to be a major port.

22. Mine (Section 2(lb)): Mine means a mine as defined in clause (j) of Subsection (1) of Section 2 of the Mines Act, 1952, which is explained as under:

> Mine means any excavation where any operation for the purpose of searching for or obtaining minerals has been, or is being carried on, and includes (unless exempted by the central government by notification in the official Gazette) any premises or part thereof, on which any process ancillary to the getting, dressing or preparation for sale of mineral or of coke is being carried on.

23. National Tribunal (Section 2(ll)): National Tribunal is a tribunal constituted under Section 78 of the Act.

24. Public utility service (Section 2(n)): Public utility service is explained by the Act as written below:

a. Any railway service or any transport service for the carriage of passengers or goods by air.
b. Any service in, or in connection with the working of, any major port or dock.
c. Any section of an industrial establishment, on the working of which the safety of the establishment or the workmen employed therein depends.
d. Any postal, telegraph or telephone service.
e. Any industry which supplies power, light or water to the public.
f. Any system of public conservancy or sanitation.
g. Any industry specified in the First Schedule which the appropriate government may, if satisfied that public emergency or public interest so requires, by notification in the Official Gazette, declare to be a public utility service for the purposes of this Act, for such period as may be specified in the notification.

25. Retrenchment (Section 2(oo)): Retrenchment under the Act means the termination by the employer of the service of a workman for any reason whatsoever otherwise than as a punishment indicated by way of disciplinary action. But it does not include:

a. Voluntary retirement of a workman; or
b. Retirement of a workman on reaching the age of superannuation if the contract of employment between the employer and the workman concerned contains a stipulation in that behalf; or
    i. Termination of the service of a workman as a result of the non-renewal of the contract of employment between the employer and the workman concerned on its expiry or of such contract being terminated; or
c. Termination of the service of a workman on the ground of continuous illness.

26. Settlement (Section 2(p)): The Act defines 'settlement' as a settlement arrived at in the course of conciliation proceeding and includes a written agreement between an employer and a workman arrived at otherwise than in the course of conciliation proceeding where such agreement has been signed by the parties thereto in such manner as may be prescribed and a copy thereof has been sent to an officer authorized by the appropriate government and the conciliation officer.

27. Strike (Section 2(q)): Under the Act, 'strike' means a cessation of work by a body of persons employed in any industry acting in combination or a concerted refusal under a common understanding of any number of persons who are or have been so employed, to continue to work or to accept employment.

Thus, it is clear from the above definition that mere stoppage of work does not come within the meaning of strike unless it can be shown that such stoppage of work was a concerted action for the enforcement of an industrial demand. Following are main features of strike:

a. Strike is the stoppage of work by a body of workmen acting in concert with a view to bring pressure upon the employer to concede to their demands.
b. The workmen must be employed in any industry.
c. Mere cessation of work does not come within the preview of strike, unless it can be shown that such cessation of work was a concerted action for the enforcement of an industrial demand.

28. Trade Union (Section 2(qq)): The Act defines 'Trade Union' as a trade union registered under the Trade Unions Act, 1926.

29. Tribunal (Section 2(r)): Under the Act, 'Tribunal' means an Industrial Tribunal constituted under Section 7A of the Act. It also includes an Industrial Tribunal constituted before 10 March 1957 under this Act.

30. Unfair labour practice (Section 2(ra)): Unfair labour practices mean any of the practices specified in the Fifth Schedule.

31. Wages (Section 2(rr))[2]: Wages are defined as all remuneration capable of being expressed in terms of money, which would, if the terms of employment, express or implied, were fulfilled, be payable to a workman in respect of his employment or of the work done in such an employment and includes:

---

[2] 1. Ins. by Act 35 of 1965, s. 2 (w. e. f. 1 December 1965). 2. Ins. and Subs. by Act 46 of 1982, s. 2 (w. e. f. 21 August 1984). 3. Subs. by Act 18 of 1957, s. 2, for cl. (r) (w. e. f. 10 – 3 March 1957). 4. Ins. by Act 43 of 1953, s. 2 (w. e. f. 24 October 1953). 5. Subs. by Act 46 of 1982, s. 2 (w. e. f. 21 August 1984).

a. Such allowances (including dearness allowance) as the workman is for the time being entitled to.
b. The value of any house accommodation, or of supply of light, water, medical attendance or other amenity or of any service or of any concessional supply of food grains or other articles.
c. Any travelling concession.

But the following are excluded:

i. Any bonus.
ii. Any contribution paid or payable to any pension fund or provident fund, or for the benefit of the workman under any law for the time being in force.
iii. Any gratuity payable on the termination of his service.

32. Workman (Section 2(s)): Workman is any person (including an apprentice) employed in any industry to do any manual, unskilled, skilled, technical, operational, clerical or supervisory work for hire or reward, whether the terms of employment be express or implied, and for the purpose of any proceeding under this Act.

But a 'workman' does not include any such person:

a. Who is subject to the Air Force Act, 1950, or the Army Act, 1950, or the Navy Act, 1957, or
b. Who is employed in the Police Service or as an officer or other employee of a prison, or
c. Who is employed mainly in a managerial or administrative capacity, or
d. Who, being employed in a supervisory capacity, draws wages exceeding ₹1,600 per mensem, or exercises functions mainly of management nature.

Let us discuss case (Case 13.1) to understand the definition of 'workman' laid down by the Act.

Case 13.1: *M. M. Wadia Charitable Hospital v. Dr Umakant Ramchandra Warerkar, 1997*[3]

M. M. Wadia Charitable Hospital (the petitioner hospital) was a charitable trust, running a charitable hospital at Solapur in Maharashtra. On 6 October 1980, Dr Umakant Ramchandra Warerkar was appointed as a full-time paediatric physician and was allowed private practice. Services of Dr Warerkar were terminated vide notice dated 27 February 1982 offering him salary in lieu of 1-month notice. The termination was a result of the strike resorted to by the doctors. Initially, there was a 1-day token strike. Prior to the said strike, the members of the medical staff formed an association known as M. M. Wadia Charitable Hospital Doctors Association. On 17 September 1981, the association passed a resolution urging better facilities and disputes started on this issue. The association claimed that facilities at the hospital were not good. In the above circumstances, the strike was resorted to. The staff proceeded on a 1-day token strike on 17 February 1982. On 23 February 1982, the management issued show-cause notice to many doctors for going on token strike. In reply, the doctors pointed out the background and the reason for resorting to token strike. On 26 February 1982, the management issued a circular which was received by the doctors on 27 February 1982. By the said circular, the management informed the doctors that they would take strict disciplinary action for resorting to strike. On 28 February 1982, services of the respondent doctors were terminated. After knowing about the

[3] *M.M. Wadia Charitable Hospital v. Dr Umakant Ramchandra Warerkar*, 1997 (75) FLR 814, (1997) IILLJ 549 Bom.

termination order, the medical staff held a meeting after midnight and they resolved to go on an indefinite strike to protest against termination orders.

Out of 22 doctors, 20 doctors in the said hospital went on strike from 1 March 1982. Subsequently, the management of the hospital terminated the services of all respondent doctors on 1 March 1982. Against the said termination orders, the respondent doctors knocked the doors of Labour Court and argued that the terminated doctors were the workmen under Section 2(s) of the Industrial Disputes Act and since retrenchment compensation as contemplated by Section 25(F) of the Industrial Disputes Act and procedure laid down prior to retrenchment was not followed, the doctors were entitled to be reinstated. The Labour Court accepted the argument of the respondent doctors; however, since the respondent doctors were allowed to have private practice, both in the course of the employment and even after their termination, 50% of the back wages came to be awarded to the doctors. Even continuity of service was granted by the Labour Court, Solapur in the above references.

Being aggrieved by the said award of the labour court, the writ petitions were filed by the petitioner hospital. The petitioner hospital submitted that the respondent doctors were performing the work of a supervisory nature and thus they cannot be treated as workmen under the Industrial Disputes Act. However, the respondent doctors argued that the respondent doctors were performing the work of a technical nature. For this purpose, they relied upon certain broad features regarding the duties performed by the respondent doctors. It was further argued by the respondent doctors that since the doctors were required to devote full-time work during fixed hours, it was one of the main features which indicated that they were 'workman' as defined under Section 2(s) of the Industrial Disputes Act, 1947.

Discussion Point

Could the respondent doctors in the above case claim the status of a 'workman' as defined under Section 2(s) of the Industrial Disputes Act, 1947?

Judgement and Explanation

It was held that none of the respondent doctors in the above writ petitions could claim the status of a 'workman' as defined under Section 2(s) of the Industrial Disputes Act, 1947. The court stated that the object of the Act was to set up a machinery to protect poor sections of the society. It was to see that employment, which was scarce in the country, was duly protected and it was never thought that highly qualified medical doctors, esteemed surgeons or paediatricians would ever claim the protection of a welfare legislation. It was further stated in the judgement the relationship between the patient and doctor was not created at the instance of the hospital. The patient kept immense faith and confidence in a particular doctor. The doctor had a fiduciary duty towards the patient which concept would be totally obliterated if the doctors were treated as 'workman' as defined under Section 2(s) of the Industrial Disputes Act, 1947.

References of Certain Individual Disputes to Grievance Settlement Authorities (Chapter II-B, Section 9C—Introduced by the Amendment Act, 1982): A new Chapter II-B was added to the Act by Industrial Disputes (Amendment) Act, 1982, whereby a new Section 9-C was introduced. Section 9C has following provisions:

Constitution of Grievance Settlement Authority (Section 9C(1)): The employer of every industrial establishment employing 50 or more workmen on any day in the preceding 12 months must provide for a grievance settlement authority for settlement of industrial disputes with an individual workman employed in the establishment in accordance with the rules made in this behalf under the Act.

Reference of individual disputes to Grievance Settlement Authority (Section 9C(2)): If an individual dispute connected with an individual workman arises in an establishment referred to in

Subsection (1), a workman or any trade union of workmen of which such workman is a member is free to refer in a prescribed manner such dispute to the Grievance Settlement Authority provided for by the employer for settlement. The Grievance Settlement Authority must follow such procedure and complete its proceedings within prescribed period (Section 9C(3)).

Further reference of dispute under Chapter III (Section 9C(4)): No reference can be made under Chapter III with respect to any dispute referred to in this section unless such dispute has been referred to the concerned Grievance Settlement Authorities and the decision of the Grievance Settlement Authority is not acceptable to any of the parities to the dispute.

LO2: Procedure for Settlement of Industrial Disputes and Authorities under the Act (Chapter II)

At the first instance, the adjudication of industrial disputes has been kept out of the jurisdiction of Municipal Courts so that efforts are made for settlement of such disputes through some other agencies. The Act provides various modes of settlement of industrial disputes and those may be classified under three heads:

1. Conciliation.
2. Adjudication.
3. Arbitration.

Besides the modes of settlement of industrial disputes mentioned above, Section 10A of the Act makes provision for voluntary reference of disputes to arbitration. Apart from this, provision has also been made for constitution of a Court of Inquiry, whose main function is inquire into any matter appearing to be connected with or relevant to an industrial dispute.

Conciliation Machinery

The authorities that make use of conciliation on the sole method of settlement of disputes are as discussed further.

Works Committees (Section 3)

The works committee is a powerful social institution not only to secure cooperation between workers and employers, but also to make the will of the employees effective on the management. It deals with the workers problem arising day to day in the industrial establishment.

Section 3 of the Act provides that in the case of an industrial establishment in which 100 or more workmen are employed, the appropriate government may require the employer to constitute a 'Work Committee'. It consists of equal number of representatives of employers and workmen engaged in the establishment. The representatives of the workmen are chosen from among the workmen engaged in the establishment and in consultation with the registered trade union, if any under Section 3(1) of the Trade Unions Act, 1926.

Powers and duties of the works committee: The duties of the works committee are as follows:

1. To promote measures for securing and preserving amity and good relations between the employers and workmen.
2. To comment upon matters of their interest or concern.
3. To endeavour to compose any material difference of opinion in respect of matters of common intents or concern of employers and workmen.

Conciliation Appointment, Duties and Powers of Conciliation Officer (Section 4)

The appropriate government by notifying in the Official Gazette appoints the conciliation officers for any specified area or for one or more specified industries, either permanently or for a limited period of time. The jurisdiction, powers and other matters in respect of the conciliation officer are published in the Gazette. Conciliation officers are charged with the duty to hold conciliatory proceedings for the purpose of bringing about a fair and amicable settlement of any industrial dispute.

Powers of conciliation officer (Section 11): Section 11 of the Act empowers the conciliation officer to exercise following powers:

1. **Power to enter the premise:** The conciliation officer is authorized to, for the purpose of inquiry into any existing or apprehended industrial dispute, after giving reasonable notice, enter the premises occupied by any establishment which the dispute relates.
2. **Power to demand and inspect the documents:** The conciliation officer may call for and inspect any document which he has ground for considering to be relevant to the industrial dispute or be necessary for the purpose of verifying the implementation of any award or carrying out any duty imposed on him under the Act and for the aforesaid purposes. He has the same powers as one vested in a Civil Court, in respect of compelling the production of documents.

Duties of conciliation officers (Section 12): To bring about fair and amicable settlement of an industrial dispute, the conciliation officer is required to discharge the following duties:

1. **Holding conciliation proceedings (Section 12(1)):** If there exists any industrial dispute or is apprehended, the conciliation officer must hold conciliation proceedings. He will interview both the workmen concerned with the dispute and endeavour to bring about a settlement.
2. **Investigating the dispute (Section 12(2)):** The conciliation officer, for the purpose of bringing about a settlement of the dispute, investigates the dispute and all matters affecting the merits and the right settlement thereof and may do all such things as he thinks fit for the purpose of inducing the parties to come to a fair and amicable settlement of the dispute.
3. **Sharing a copy of report or memorandum of settlement to appropriate government (Section 12(3)):** When a settlement of the dispute or of any of the matters in dispute arrives at in the course of the conciliation proceedings, the conciliation officer is required to send a report thereof to the settlement singed by the parties to dispute.
4. **Sharing full report with the appropriate government, if no settlement arrives (Section 12(4)):** In the cases where no such settlement arrives, the conciliation officer must, as soon as practicable

after the close of the investigation, send to the appropriate government a full report setting forth the steps taken by him for ascertaining the facts and circumstances relating to the dispute and for bringing about a settlement thereof. A full statement of such facts and circumstances, and the reasons on account of which, in his opinion, a settlement could not be arrived at is also required to be sent to the appropriate government, along with the full report.

Submission of the report (Section 12(6)): The report has to be submitted within 14 days of the commencement of the conciliation proceedings or within such shorter period as may be fixed by the appropriate government. It is further provided that subject to the approval of the conciliation officer, the time for the submission of the report can be extended by such period as may be agreed upon in writing by all the parties to the dispute.

Appropriate government to refer the unsettled case to the appropriate bodies: If, on a consideration of the report in respect of failure of settlement, the appropriate government is satisfied that there is a case for reference to Board, Labour Court, Tribunal or National Tribunal, it may make such reference. Where the government does not make such a reference, it has to record and communicate to the parties concerned its reasons thereof.

Board of Conciliation (Section 5)

According to Section 5 of the Act, as occasion arises, the appropriate government is also authorized to constitute a board of conciliation for promoting the settlement of an industrial dispute. The board consists of a chairman who shall be an independent person, and two or four other members (Section 5(2)). Appointed members have to be in equal numbers to represent the parties to the dispute. When the dispute is referred to the board, it is the duty of the board to do all things as it thinks fit for the purpose of inducing the parties to come to a fair and amicable settlement.

The quorum for a meeting of the board of conciliation is two where the total number of members is three and three where the number is five. A board, having a quorum, may act not in the absence of the chairman or any of its members, or any vacancy in its number. But if the government informs the board that the services of the chairman or any other member have ceased to be available, the board must not act until a new chairman or member has been appointed (Section 5(4)).

Duties of board (Section 13): The act expects the board of conciliation to discharge following duties:

1. **To settle the dispute (Section 13(1)):** It is the duty of the board to endeavour to bring about a settlement of dispute. The board must investigate the matters relating to the dispute between parties and induce the parties to come to a fair and amicable settlement of the dispute.
2. **Sharing a copy of report or memorandum of settlement to appropriate government (Section 13(2)):** When a settlement of the dispute or of any of the matters in dispute arrives at in the course of the conciliation proceedings, the conciliation officer is required to send a report thereof to the settlement signed by the parties to dispute.
3. **Sharing full report with the appropriate government, if no settlement arrives (Section 13(3)):** In case of failure of settlement of dispute in between parties, it is the duty of the board to send to the government the report of facts and circumstances relating to the disputes and board opinion

that a settlement could not be arrived at. A full statement of such facts and circumstances, and the reasons on account of which, in his opinion, a settlement could not be arrived at is also required to be sent to the appropriate government, along with the full report.

4. **Communication to the concerned parties if no reference is made (Section 13(4)):** On the receipt of a report in respect of an industrial dispute relating to a public utility service, if the appropriate government does not make a reference of the dispute to the board, Labour Court, Tribunal or National Tribunal under Section 10, then the same decision has to be recorded and communicated to the concerned parties.
5. **Submission of the report (Section 13(5)):** The board must submit its report under this section within 2 months of the date on which the dispute was referred to it or within such shorter period as may be fixed by the appropriate government.

Report of the board to be in writing, signed and published (Section 16(1)): The report of the board has to be a written report signed by all the members of the board. Any member of the board can record his dissent from the report or from any recommendation made in the report. The report together with the minutes of the dissent recorded therewith has to be published by the appropriate government within 30 days (Section 17(1)).

Courts of Enquiry (Section 6)

If there is a need, the appropriate government can initiate a Court of Inquiry. This Court of Inquiry finds out matters connected with or relevant to an industrial dispute. It looks into only matters which are referred to it by government and submits its report to the government ordinarily within certain period from the date of reference.

Appointment and constitution: Section 6 of the Act provides in this regard, and states the appropriate government may, as occasion arises, by notification in the Official Gazette, constitute a Court of Inquiry for inquiring into any matter appearing to be connected with or relevant to an industrial dispute. This Court consists of one or more independent persons, appointed by the government. Where it consists of more than one member, one of them has to be appointed as chairman.

The Court of Inquiry having the prescribed quorum may act even if the chairman or a member is absent, but not if the services of the chairman have ceased to be available and a new chairman has not been appointed (Section 6(3)). The Court must inquire into the matters referred to it and report thereon to the appropriate government within 6 months from the date of commencement of the inquiry.

Members of Court of Inquiry are deemed to be public servants within the meaning of Section 21 of IPC. The Court of Inquiry, if it so thinks fit, is authorized to appoint one or more persons having special knowledge of the matter under consideration as assessor or assessors to advise it in the proceeding before it.

On a perusal of the relevant Sections 22, 23 and 33 of the Act, relating to the Court during the pendency of a proceeding before a Court of Inquiry, the following rights remain unaffected, such as:

1. The right of a workman to go on strike.
2. The right of an employer to look out his business.
3. The right of the employer to dismiss or otherwise to punish the workman in certain cases under Section 33.

Powers of the Court of Inquiry: The Court of Inquiry is entrusted with following powers:

1. **Power to enter the premise (Section 11(2)):** The members of the Court are authorized to, for the purpose of inquiry into any existing or apprehended industrial dispute, after giving reasonable notice, enter the premises occupied by any establishment which the dispute relates.
2. **Powers of a civil court:** The members of the Court of Inquiry have the same powers as one vested in a Civil Court, while they are trying a suit in respect of following matters:
   a. Enforcing the attendance of any person and examining him on oath.
   b. Compelling the production of documents and material objects.
   c. Issuing commissions for the examination of witnesses.
   d. In respect of such other matters as prescribed.

It is to be noted here that every inquiry or investigation carried out by the Court of Inquiry is treated as a judicial proceeding within the meaning of Sections 193 and 228 of the IPC, 1860 (Section 11(3)).

Duties of courts of inquiry (Section 14): The Court of Inquiry must inquire into the matters referred to it and the report of inquiry thereon be presented before the appropriate government, ordinarily within a period of 6 months from the commencement of inquiry (Section 14). The report of the Court of Inquiry has to be in writing and be signed by all the members of the Court, provided that a member may record a minutes of dissent also (Section 16(1)). The report together with the minutes of the dissent recorded therewith has to be published by the appropriate government within 30 days (Section 17(1)).

Adjudication Machinery

Sections 7 to 9 of the Act deal with the constitution of Adjudication Authorities. Such authorities that decide any dispute under the Act are as follows:

1. The Labour Court
2. Industrial Tribunal
3. National Tribunal

Labour Courts (Section 7)

The appropriate government may, by notification in the Official Gazette, constitute one or more Labour Courts for the adjudication of industrial disputes relating to any of matter specified in the Second Schedule (reproduced below) or for performing such other function as may be assigned to them under the Act.

The Second Schedule (Section 7)—Matters Within the Jurisdiction of Labour Courts

1. The propriety or legality of an order passed by an employer under the standing orders.
2. The application and interpretation of standing orders.
3. Discharge or dismissal of workmen including reinstatement of, or grant of relief to, workmen wrongfully dismissed.

4. Withdrawal of any customary concession or privilege.
5. Illegality or otherwise of a strike or lockout.
6. All matters other than those specified in the Third Schedule.

Appointment and qualification: According to Section 7(2), a Labour Court must consist of one person only who is to be appointed by the appropriate government. As provided under Section 7(3) of the Act, no person can be appointed as presiding officer of a Labour Court, unless

1. He is, or has been, a judge of a High Court; or
2. He has, for a period of not less than 3 years, been a District Judge or an Additional District Judge; or
3. He has held any judicial office in India for not less than 7 years; or
4. He has been the presiding officer of a Labour Court constituted under any Provincial Act or State Act for not less than 5 years.

Disqualification (Section 7(3)): The Act directs that no person can be appointed to, or continue in, the office of the presiding officer of a Labour Court, Tribunal or National Tribunal, if:

1. He is not an independent person; or
2. He has attained the age of 65 years.

Duties of Labour Court (Section 15): The Act expects the Labour Court to discharge following duties:

1. **To adjudicate upon industrial disputes specified in Second Schedule (Section 7(1)):** It is the duty of the Labour Court to adjudicate upon the industrial disputes relating to any matter specified in the Second Schedule.
2. **To give award within the specified period (Section 15):** If an industrial dispute is referred to Labour Court, for adjudication, it must hold its adjudication expeditiously and must submit its award to the appropriate government within the specified time. The period may be extended under the proviso 2 of Section 10(2A).
3. **Award to be in writing, signed and published (Section 17A):** Every award of Labour Court must within a period of 30 days from the date of its receipt by the appropriate government be published by if in the Official Gazette. The award published by the appropriate government is final and binding on the parties to dispute.

Enforceability of award (Section 17-A): The Act further provides that an award (including arbitration award) becomes enforceable on the expiry of 30 days from the date of its publication under Section 17. The award does not become enforceable on the expiry of 30 days:

1. If the appropriate government is of opinion in any case where the award has been given by a Labour Court or Tribunal in relation to an industrial dispute to which it is a party that it will be in expedient to give effect to the whole or any part of the award on public grounds effecting
   a. Either national economy or
   b. Social justice.

2. If the Central Government, in any case where the award has been given by a National Tribunal, on similar grounds is of the opinion that it would be in expedient to give effect to the whole or part of the award.

For the purpose of stopping the enforcement of any award, a notification in the Official Gazette is necessary.

Powers of the Labour Court (Section 11): Powers extended to the Labour Court to give appropriate relief in case of discharge or dismissal of workman are discussed below:

1. **Power to follow the procedure of its choice (Section 11(1)):** Subject to any rule that may be made in this behalf, the Labour Court is free to follow such procedure that it may think fit.
2. **Power to enter the premise (Section 11(2)):** The presiding officer of the Court may, for the purpose of inquiry into any existing or apprehended dispute, enter into the premises occupied by any establishment to which the dispute relates.
3. **Powers of a civil court (Section 11(3)):** The members of the Court of Inquiry have the same powers as one vested in a Civil Court, while they are trying a suit in respect of following matters:
   a. Enforcing the attendance of any person and examining him on oath;
   b. Compelling the production of documents and material objects;
   c. Issuing commissions for the examination of witnesses; and
   d. In respect of such other matters as prescribed.

   It is to be noted here that every inquiry or investigation carried out by the Court of Inquiry is treated as a judicial proceeding within the meaning of Sections 193 and 228 of the IPC, 1860 (Section 11(3)).
4. **Power to appoint other persons:** If the Labour Court thinks fit, it may appoint one or more persons, having special knowledge of the matter under consideration, as an assessor to advise it in the proceedings before it.

Prohibition of strike or lockout (Section 10(3)): The Act states that when an industrial dispute has been referred to a Labour Court, under this section, the appropriate government is empowered to prohibit the continuance of any strike or lockout in connection with such dispute which may be in existence on the date of the reference.

Jurisdiction (Section 10(4)): Where in an order referring an industrial dispute to a Labour Court under this section or in a subsequent order, the appropriate government has specified the points of dispute for adjudication, the Labour Court must confine its adjudication to only those points and matters incidental thereto.

Section 11(6) of the Act declares that the Presiding Officer of Labour Court shall be deemed to be public servants within the meaning of Section 21 of IPC.

Inclusion of other parties (Section 10(5)): In the cases where a dispute concerning any establishment or establishments has been, or is to be, referred to a Labour Court under Section 10 and the appropriate government is of opinion, whether on an application made to it in this behalf or otherwise, that the dispute is of such a nature that any other establishment, group or class of establishments of a similar nature is likely to be interested in, or affected by, such dispute, the appropriate government may, at the time of making the reference or at any time thereafter but, before the submission of the award, include in that reference such establishment, group or class of establishments, whether or not at the time of such inclusion any dispute exists or is apprehended in that establishment, group or class of establishments.

Cost of proceedings (Section 11(7)): Section 11(7) of the Act deals with the determination of the cost of the proceedings. The section empowers the Labour Court, Tribunal or National Tribunal, and the Labour Court, Tribunal or National Tribunal, as the case may be, to determine by and to whom and to what extent and subject to what conditions, if any, such costs are to be paid, and to give all necessary directions for the above-mentioned purposes. Such costs may, on application made to the appropriate government by the person entitled, be recovered by that government in the same manner as an arrear of land revenue.

Labour Court deemed to be a Civil court (Section 11(8)): Every Labour Court, Tribunal or National Tribunal shall be deemed to be civil court for the purposes of Sections 345, 346 and 348 of the Code of Criminal Procedure, 1973 (2 of 1974).

Industrial Tribunals (Section 7A)

Tribunals were for the first time created in 1947 under the Industrial Disputes Act, 1947, as a 'Dispute Redressal Mechanism by Adjudication'. The purpose of creating Industrial Tribunal was to introduce compulsory adjudication where voluntary negotiation fails to settle the dispute and the 'appropriate government' believes that the matter is grave enough to be referred to a tribunal. Subsequently, it was felt by the legislature that in order to work properly, it was necessary to limit the jurisdiction of such tribunal or courts. As a result, two schedules were created: the Second Schedule referred to matters within jurisdiction of Labour Courts and the Third Schedule which referred to matters within the jurisdiction of Industrial Tribunal.

Constitution (Section 7A(1)): For the constitution of the Industrial Tribunal, the Act states that the appropriate government may, by notification in the Official Gazette, constitute one or more Industrial Tribunals for the adjudication of industrial disputes relating to any matter, whether specified in the Second Schedule or the Third Schedule and for performing such other functions as may be assigned to them under this Act. The Section further specifies that a Tribunal consists of one person only (Section 7A(2)).

The Third Schedule (Section 7A)—Matters within the Jurisdiction of Industrial Tribunal: An Industrial Tribunal is empowered to adjudicate upon the matters related to following issues:

1. Wages including the period and mode of payment.
2. Compensatory and other allowances.
3. Hours of work and rest intervals.
4. Leave with wages and holidays.
5. Bonus, profit sharing, provident fund and gratuity.
6. Shift working otherwise than in accordance with standing orders.
7. Classification by grades.
8. Rules of discipline.
9. Rationalization.
10. Retrenchment of workmen and closure of establishment.
11. Any other matter that may be prescribed.

Appointment and qualification: Section 7A(3) of the Act specifies that to be the presiding officer of the Industrial tribunal, a person must be or must have been:

1. A Judge of a High Court; or
   a. He has, for a period of not less than 3 years, been a District Judge or an Additional District Judge;

Only experienced persons of high integrity can be appointed as presiding officer of the Tribunal. It is provided by Section 7A(4) further that the appropriate government, if thinks fit, may appoint two persons as assessors to advise the Tribunal in the proceedings before it and the presiding officer of a Tribunal is deemed to be Public Servant within the meaning of Section 21 of the IPC, 1860 (Section 11(6)).

Disqualifications for the Presiding Officers of Labour Courts, Tribunals and National Tribunals (Section 7C): The Act prohibits the appointment and continuation of a person to be the presiding officer a Labour Court, Tribunal or National Tribunal, if:

1. He is not an independent person; or
2. He has attained the age of 65 years.

Duties of an Industrial Tribunal (Section 10(2A)): If an industrial dispute is referred to a Tribunal for adjudication, it is the duty of the Tribunal to hold its adjudication expeditiously and must submit its award to the appropriate government within the specified time. The period may be extended under the proviso 2 of Section 10(2A).

Powers of the Tribunal: Powers extended to the Industrial Tribunal to settle the disputes referred to it are discussed below:

1. **Power to enter the premise (Section 11(2)):** The presiding officer of the Tribunal may, for the purpose of inquiry into any existing or apprehended dispute, enter into the premises occupied by any establishment to which the dispute relates.
2. **Powers of a civil court (Section 11(3)):** The members of the Tribunal of Inquiry have the same powers as one vested in a Civil Court, while it is trying a suit in respect of following matters:
   a. Enforcing the attendance of any person and examining him on oath.
   b. Compelling the production of documents and material objects.
   c. Issuing commissions for the examination of witnesses.
   d. In respect of such other matters as prescribed.

   It is to be noted here that every inquiry or investigation carried out by the Court of Inquiry is treated as a judicial proceeding within the meaning of Sections 193 and 228 of the IPC, 1860 (Section 11(3)).
3. **Power to appoint assessors (Section 11(5)):** A Tribunal has a power to appoint one or more persons having special knowledge of the matter under consideration as an assessor or assessors to advise it in the proceeding before it.
4. **Power to determine the cost of proceedings (Section 11(7)):** Section 11(7) of the Act deals with the determination of the cost of the proceedings. The section empowers the Tribunal to determine by and to whom and to what extent and subject to what conditions, if any, such costs are to be paid, and to give all necessary directions for the above-mentioned purposes. Such costs may, on application made to the appropriate government by the person entitled, be recovered by that government in the same manner as an arrear of land revenue.

The Industrial Tribunal deemed to be a Civil court (Section 11(8)): Every Industrial Tribunal shall be deemed to be civil court for the purposes of Sections 345, 346 and 348 of the Code of Criminal Procedure, 1973 (2 of 1974).

Prohibition of strike or lockout (Section 10(3)): The Act states that when an industrial dispute has been referred to an Industrial Tribunal under this section, the appropriate government is empowered to prohibit the continuance of any strike or lockout in connection with such dispute which may be in existence on the date of the reference.

Jurisdiction (Section 10(4)): Where in an order referring an industrial dispute to an Industrial Tribunal under this section or in a subsequent order, the appropriate government has specified the points of dispute for adjudication, the Tribunal must confine its adjudication to only those points and matters incidental thereto.

Section 11(6) of the Act declares that the presiding officer of an Industrial Tribunal shall be deemed to be public servants within the meaning of Section 21 of IPC.

Inclusion of other parties (Section 10(5)): In the cases where a dispute concerning any establishment or establishments has been, or is to be, referred to an Industrial Tribunal under Section 10 and the appropriate government is of opinion, whether on an application made to it in this behalf or otherwise, that the dispute is of such a nature that any other establishment, group or class of establishments of a similar nature is likely to be interested in, or affected by, such dispute, the appropriate government may, at the time of making the reference or at any time thereafter but before the submission of the award, include in that reference such establishment, group or class of establishments, whether or not at the time of such inclusion any dispute exists or is apprehended in that establishment, group or class of establishments.

Award to be in writing, signed and published: Every award of the Tribunal has to be in writing and signed by its presiding officer (Section 16(2)). The award must be published in the Official Gazette by the appropriate government within a period of 30 days from the date of its receipt by the appropriate government, in a manner it may find fit (Section 17(1)).

National Tribunals (Section 7B)

National Tribunals are set up by the central government to adjudicate upon the industrial disputes involving questions of national importance industrial establishments situated in more than one state. The state governments are debarred from referring the matter under adjudication of National Tribunal to any Labour Court or Industrial Tribunal.

Constitution (Section 7B(1)): The Act empowers the central government to, by notification in the Official Gazette, constitute one or more National Industrial Tribunals for the adjudication of industrial disputes which, in the opinion of the central government, involve questions of national importance or are of such a nature that industrial establishments situated in more than one state are likely to be interested in, or affected by, such disputes. A National Tribunal consists of one person only to be appointed by the central government (Section 7B(2)).

Appointment and qualification (Section 7B(3)): As laid down by Section 7B(3), in order to be qualified as a presiding officer of a National Tribunal, a person must be or must have been a Judge of a High Court, or must have held the office of the chairman or any other member of the Labour Appellate Tribunal for at least 2 years.

The central government may also appoint two assessors to advise the National Tribunal, in proceeding before it (Section 7B(4)).

Disqualifications for the Presiding Officers of Labour Courts, Tribunals and National Tribunals (Section 7C): The Act prohibits the appointment and continuation of a person to be the presiding officer a Labour Court, Tribunal or National Tribunal, if:

1. He is not an independent person; or
2. He has attained the age of 65 years.

Duties of the National Tribunal (Section 15): If an industrial dispute is referred to Labour Court, for adjudication, it must hold its adjudication expeditiously and must submit its award to the appropriate government within the specified time. The period may be extended under the proviso 2 of Section 10(2A).

Powers of the Tribunal: Powers extended to the Industrial Tribunal to settle the disputes referred to it are discussed below:

1. **Power to enter the premise (Section 11(2)):** The presiding officer of the Tribunal may, for the purpose of inquiry into any existing or apprehended dispute, enter into the premises occupied by any establishment to which the dispute relates.
2. **Powers of a civil court (Section 11(3)):** The members of the Tribunal of Inquiry have the same powers as one vested in a Civil Court, while it is trying a suit in respect of following matters:
   a. Enforcing the attendance of any person and examining him on oath.
   b. Compelling the production of documents and material objects.
   c. Issuing commissions for the examination of witnesses.
   d. In respect of such other matters as prescribed.

   It is to be noted here that every inquiry or investigation carried out by the Court of Inquiry is treated as a judicial proceeding within the meaning of Sections 193 and 228 of the IPC, 1860 (Section 11(3)).
3. **Power to appoint assessors (Section 11(5)):** A Tribunal has a power to appoint one or more persons having special knowledge of the matter under consideration as an assessor or assessors to advise it in the proceeding before it.
4. **Power to determine the cost of proceedings (Section 11(7)):** Section 11(7) of the Act deals with the determination of the cost of the proceedings. The section empowers the Tribunal to determine by and to whom and to what extent and subject to what conditions, if any, such costs are to be paid, and to give all necessary directions for the above-mentioned purposes. Such costs may, on application made to the appropriate government by the person entitled, be recovered by that government in the same manner as an arrear of land revenue.

Jurisdiction of Labour Court and Industrial Tribunal to cease on a reference made to the National Tribunal (Sections 10(4) and 10(6)): Where the central government is of opinion that any industrial dispute exists or is apprehended and the dispute involves any question of national importance or is of such a nature that industrial establishments situated in more than one state are likely to be interested in, or affected by, such dispute and that the dispute should be adjudicated by a National Tribunal, then, the central government may, whether or not it is the appropriate government in relation to that dispute, at any time, by order in writing, refer the dispute or any matter appearing to be connected with, or relevant to, the dispute. Here, it does not matter whether it relates to any matter specified in the Second Schedule or the Third Schedule to a National Tribunal for adjudication.

Subsection 10(6) further provides that if any reference has been made under Subsection (1A) to a National Tribunal, then no Labour Court or Tribunal can have jurisdiction to adjudicate upon any matter which is under adjudication before the National Tribunal, and accordingly:

1. If the matter under adjudication before the National Tribunal is pending in a proceeding before a Labour Court or Tribunal, the proceeding before the Labour Court or the Tribunal, as the case may be, insofar as it relates to such matter, will be treated as quashed on such reference to the National Tribunal; and
2. The appropriate government cannot refer the matter under adjudication before the National Tribunal to any Labour Court or Tribunal for adjudication during the pendency of the proceeding in relation to such matter before the National Tribunal.

Prohibition of strike or lockout (Section 10(3)): The Act states that when an industrial dispute has been referred to a National Tribunal under this section, the appropriate government is empowered to prohibit the continuance of any strike or lockout in connection with such dispute which may be in existence on the date of the reference.

Jurisdiction (Section 10(4)): Where in an order referring an industrial dispute to a national Tribunal under this section or in a subsequent order, the appropriate government has specified the points of dispute for adjudication, the Tribunal must confine its adjudication to only those points and matters incidental thereto.

Section 11(6) of the Act declares that the presiding officer of a National Tribunal shall be deemed to be public servants within the meaning of Section 21 of IPC.

Inclusion of other parties (Section 10(5)): In the cases where a dispute concerning any establishment or establishments has been, or is to be, referred to a National Tribunal under Section 10 and the appropriate government is of opinion, whether on an application made to it in this behalf or otherwise, that the dispute is of such a nature that any other establishment, group or class of establishments of a similar nature is likely to be interested in, or affected by, such dispute, the appropriate government may, at the time of making the reference or at any time thereafter but before the submission of the award, include in that reference such establishment, group or class of establishments, whether or not at the time of such inclusion any dispute exists or is apprehended in that establishment, group or class of establishments.

Award to be in writing, signed and published: Every award of the Tribunal has to be in writing and signed by its presiding officer (Section 16(2)). The award must be published in the Official Gazette by the appropriate government within a period of 30 days from the date of its receipt by the appropriate government, in a manner it may find fit (Section 17(1)).

Filing of Vacancies (Section 8): If a vacancy occurs for any reason other than a temporary absence in the office of the presiding officer, in the office of the presiding officer of a Labour Court, Tribunal or National Tribunal or in the office of the chairman or any other member of a Board or court, then, the appropriate government appoints another person in accordance with the provisions of this Act to fill the vacancy. The proceedings are to be continued before the Labour Court, Tribunal, National Tribunal, Board or court, as the case may be, from the stage at which the vacancy is filled.

Finality of orders constituting boards (Section 9): Section 9 of the Industrial Disputes Act aims to make immune any order of the appointment made under Sections 5 to 7 of the Act from being called in question. Therefore, no question can be raised whether an appointment was legally and properly made or not. Section 9(1) of the Act clearly mentions that no order of the appropriate government or of the central government appointing any person as the chairman or any other member of the Board or Court, or as the presiding officer of a Labour Court, Tribunal or National Tribunal shall be called in question in any manner on the ground of merely of the existence of any vacancy in, or defect in, the constitution of such Board or Court.

Settlement arrived after the expiry of the due period: The Act provides that the settlement arrived at in the course of a conciliation proceeding shall not be invalid just because such settlement was arrived at after the expiry of the period referred to in Subsection (6) of Section 12 or Subsection (5) of Section 13, as the case may be.

The Act further elucidates that if the report of any settlement arrived at in the course of conciliation proceeding before a Board is signed by the chairman and all the other members of the Board, then no such settlement becomes invalid by reason only of the casual or unforeseen absence of any of the members (including the chairman) of the Board during any stage of the proceeding.

LO3: Notice of Change in Conditions of Service (Chapter II-A)

Notice of Change (Section 9A)

As laid down by Section 9A of the Act, an employer who proposes to effect any change in the conditions of service applicable to any workman in respect of any matter specified in the Fourth Schedule cannot effect such change:

1. Without giving to the workmen likely to be affected by such change a notice in the prescribed manner of the nature of the change proposed to be effected; or
2. Within 21 days of giving such notice.

No notice required: No notice of change in the condition of service is required:

1. Where the change is effected in pursuance of any settlement or award; or
2. Where the workmen likely to be affected by the change are persons to whom the Fundamental and Supplementary Rules, Civil Services (Classification, Control and Appeal) Rules, Civil Services (Temporary Service) Rules, Revised Leave Rules, Civil Services Regulations, Civilians in Defence Services (Classification, Control and Appeal) Rules or the Indian Railway Establishment Code or any other rules or regulations that may be notified in this behalf by the appropriate government in the Official Gazette, apply.

The Fourth Schedule: Conditions of Service for Change of Which Notice Is to Be Given (Section 9B)

Following are the matters specified by the Fourth Schedule for which the notice of change in the conditions of service is required to be given prior to bring such changes into effect:

1. Wages, including the period and mode of payment.
2. Contribution paid, or payable, by the employer to any provident fund or for the benefit of the workmen under any law for the time being in force.
3. Compensatory and other allowances.

4. Hours of work and rest intervals.
5. Leave with wages and holidays.
6. Starting alteration or discontinuance of shift working otherwise than in accordance with standing orders.
7. Classification by grades.
8. Withdrawal of any customary concession or privilege or change in usage.
9. Introduction of new rules of discipline, or alteration of existing rules except insofar as they are provided in standing orders.
10. Rationalization, standardization or improvement of plant or technique which is likely to lead to retrenchment of workmen.
11. Any increase or reduction (other than casual) in the number of persons employed or to be employed in any occupation or process or department of shift (not occasioned by circumstances over which the employer has no control).

Power of Government to Exempt (Section 9B)

If the appropriate government finds that the application of the provisions of Section 9A to any class of industrial establishments or to any class of workmen employed in any industrial establishment affect the employers in relation thereto so prejudicially that such application may cause serious repercussion on the industry concerned and that public interest so requires, the appropriate government is empowered to direct that the provisions of the Section 9A (discussed above) shall not apply or shall apply, subject to such conditions as may be specified in the notification, to that class of industrial establishments or to that class of workmen employed in any industrial establishment.

LO4: References of Disputes to Boards, Courts or Tribunals and Voluntary References (Chapter III)

References of Disputes to Boards, Courts or Tribunals (Section 10)

According to Section 10(1) of the Industrial Disputes Act, 1947, if the appropriate government is of the opinion that any industrial dispute exists or apprehended, it may, at any time:

1. Refer the dispute to a board of conciliation for promoting a settlement there of; or
2. Refer any matter appearing to be connected with or relevant to the dispute to a Court for Inquiry; or
3. Refer the dispute or any matter appearing to be connected with, or relevant to the dispute to a Labour Court for adjudication provided the dispute relates to any matter specified in the Second Schedule; or
4. Refer the dispute or any matter appearing to be connected with or relevant to the dispute to a Tribunal for adjudication, where it relates to any matter specified in the Second or Third Schedule.

Reference to Labour Court under proviso 2 of Section 10(1): If the dispute relates to any matter specified in the Third Schedule and is not likely to affect more than 100 workmen, the appropriate government is empowered to make a reference to a Labour Court.

Reference to Labour Court or Tribunal constituted by state government under proviso 3 of Section 10(1): If the dispute in relation to which the central government is the appropriate government, it shall be competent for the government to refer the dispute to a Labour Court/Tribunal constituted by the state government.

Disputes related to public utility service: In the cases where the dispute is related to a public utility service and a notice of strike or lockout under Section 22 has been given, the appropriate Government shall be competent to refer the dispute to a Labour Court or any Industrial Tribunal, constituted by the Government.

Reference to National Tribunal under Section 10(1A)

The central government may refer any dispute to a National Tribunal for adjudication, if it is the opinion that:

1. Any dispute exists or is appended; and
2. The dispute involves any question of national importance; or
3. The dispute is of such nature that industrial establishment situated in more than one state is likely to be interested in, or affected by such dispute; and
4. The dispute should be adjudicated by National Tribunal (the reference to National Tribunal shall be made by the central government only).

Persons Applying to Represent Majority (Section 10(2))

In the case where the parties to an industrial dispute apply in the prescribed manner, whether jointly or separately, for a reference of the dispute to a Board, court, Labour Court, Tribunal or National Tribunal, the appropriate government, after being satisfied that the persons applying represent the majority of each party, makes the reference accordingly.

1. **Period for pronouncing the award (Section (2A)):** An order referring an industrial dispute to a Labour Court, Tribunal or National Tribunal under this section must specify the period within which such Labour Court, Tribunal or National Tribunal has to submit its award on such dispute to the appropriate government. It is further provided that where such industrial dispute is connected with an individual workman, such period must not exceed 3 months.

   However, if the parties to an industrial dispute apply in the prescribed manner, whether jointly or separately, to the Labour Court, Tribunal or National Tribunal for extension of such period or for any other reason, and the presiding officer of such Labour Court, Tribunal or National Tribunal considers it necessary or expedient to extend such period, he may, for reasons to be recorded in writing, extend such period by such further period as he may think fit.
2. **Computation of period of pronouncement of award:** The subsection provides in this regard that while computing the period specified in this subsection, the period, if any, for which the proceedings before the Labour Court, Tribunal or National Tribunal had been stayed by any injunction or order of a civil court has to be excluded. However, it is to be noted here that no proceedings before a Labour Court, Tribunal or National Tribunal will lapse merely on the grounds that any period specified under this subsection had expired without such proceedings being completed.

Prohibition of Strike or Lockout (Section 10(3))

The Act states that when an industrial dispute has been referred to a National Tribunal under this section, the appropriate government is empowered to prohibit the continuance of any strike or lockout in connection with such dispute which may be in existence on the date of the reference.

Jurisdiction (Section 10(4))

Where in an order referring an industrial dispute to a Labour Court, Tribunal or National Tribunal under this section or in a subsequent order, the appropriate government has specified the points of dispute for adjudication, the Labour Court or the Tribunal or the National Tribunal, as the case may be, must confine its adjudication to only those points and matters incidental thereto. As discussed before, Section 10(6) of the Act provides that where any reference has been made under Subsection (1A) to a National Tribunal, then no Labour Court or Tribunal can have jurisdiction to adjudicate dicta upon any matter which is under adjudication before the National Tribunal.

Voluntary References of Disputes to Arbitration (Section 10A)

Reference: This section provides that where any industrial dispute exists or is apprehended and the employer and the workman agree to refer the dispute to arbitration, they may refer the dispute to arbitration. Such reference by agreement may be made at any time before the dispute has been referred under Section 10 to a Labour Court, Tribunal or National Tribunal. It should be noted here that the agreement between the employer and employee to make a reference must be in writing. An arbitrator functioning under Section 10A of the Act is a statutory Tribunal.

It is also to be noted that Sections 10 and 10A are the alternative remedies to settle industrial dispute. Once the parties have chosen the remedy under Section 10A, the government cannot refer the same dispute for adjudication under Section 10. If any such reference is made, it is invalid.

1. **Umpire (Section 10A(1A)):** In the cases where an arbitration agreement provides for reference of the dispute to an even number of arbitrators, the agreement must provide for appointment of another person as umpire. Such an umpire will enter upon the reference if the arbitrators are equally divided in their opinion.
2. **Form of agreement (Section 10A(2)):** The Act provides that an arbitration agreement referred to in Subsection (1) has to be in a prescribed form and must be signed by the parties thereto in such a number as may be prescribed. The act further directs that a copy of the arbitration agreement must be forwarded to appropriate government and the conciliation officer, and the appropriate government must within 1 month from the date of receipt of such copy, publish the same in the Official Gazette (Section 10A(3)).
3. **Award (Section 10A(4)):** It is the duty of the arbitrator or arbitrators to investigate the dispute and submit to the appropriate government the arbitration award signed by the arbitrator or all arbitrators as the case may be.
4. **Prohibition of Strike or Lockout (Section (4A)):** Where an industrial dispute has been referred to arbitration and a notification has been issued, the appropriate government is authorized to prohibit the continuance of any strike or lockout in connection with such dispute. The appropriate government can do so by issuing an order. Subsection (5) of this Section further provides that nothing in the Arbitration Act, 1940, applies to arbitration under this section.

LO5: Award and Settlements

Form of Report or Award (Section 16)

The Act states under Section 16(1) that the report of a Board or court has to be in writing and to be signed by all the members of the Board or court, as the case may be. It is further provided this section does not prevent any member of the Board or court from recording any minute of dissent from a report or from any recommendation made therein. The award pronounced by Labour Court or Tribunal or National Tribunal has to be in writing and must be signed by its presiding officer (Section 16(2)).

Publication of Report and Awards (Section 17)

It is directed by Section 17(1) that every report of a Board or Court together with any minute of dissent recorded therewith, every arbitration award and every award of a Labour Court, Tribunal or National Tribunal must, within a period of 30 days from the date of its receipt by the appropriate government, be published in a manner prescribed by the appropriate government. It is further clarified that the award published under Subsection (1) is final and cannot be called in question by any court in any manner whatsoever (Section 17(2)).

Commencement of Award (Section 17A)

An award (including an arbitration award) becomes enforceable on the expiry of 30 days from the date of its publication under Section 17. However, the central government may, by notification in the Official Gazette, declare that the award shall not become enforceable on the expiry of the said period of 30 days, if:

1. The appropriate government thinks in any case where the award has been given by a Labour Court or Tribunal in relation to an industrial dispute to which it is a party; or
2. The central government is of opinion, in any case where the award has been given by a National Tribunal, that it will be inexpedient on public grounds affecting national economy or social justice to give effect to the whole or any part of the award, the appropriate government, or as the case may be.

Rejection or modification of award (Section 17A(2)): If any declaration has been made in relation to an award as discussed above, the appropriate government or the central government is empowered to make an order rejecting or modifying the award within 90 days from the date of publication of the award under Section 17. The government must, on the first available opportunity, lay the award together with a copy of the order before the Legislature of the State, if the order has been made by a state government, or before Parliament, if the order has been made by the central government.

Enforceability of the award (Section 17A(3)): Where any award as rejected or modified by an order made under Subsection (2) is laid before the Legislature of a state or before Parliament, such award becomes enforceable on the expiry of 15 days from the date on which it is so laid. If no order under Subsection (2) is made in pursuance of a declaration under the proviso to Subsection (1), the award is enforceable on the expiry of the period of 90 days referred to in Subsection (2).

Under Subsection 17A(4), the Act provides regarding the enforceability of an award and mentions that subject to the provisions of Subsection (1) and Subsection (3), the award comes into operation with effect from such date as may be specified therein, but where no date is so specified, it shall come into operation on the date when the award becomes enforceable under Subsection (1) or Subsection (3), as the case may be.

Payment of Full Wages Pending Proceedings (Section 17B)

In the case where a Labour Court, Tribunal or National Tribunal by its award directs reinstatement of any workman and the employer prefers any proceedings against such award in a High Court or the Supreme Court, the employer is liable to pay such workman, during the period of pendency of such proceedings in the High Court or the Supreme Court, full wages last drawn by him, inclusive of any maintenance allowance admissible to him under any rule. But the wages are payable to the employee by the employer only if:

1. The workman had not been employed in any establishment during such period and
2. An affidavit by such workman had been filed to that effect in such court.

It is further provided by the Act that where it is proved to the satisfaction of the High Court or the Supreme Court that such workman had been employed and had been receiving adequate remuneration during any such period or part thereof, then no wages are payable under this section for such period or part, as the case may be.

Let us discuss a case (case 13.2) to understand the effect of the order of reinstatement of an employee.

Case 13.2: *Calcutta Chemical Co. Ltd. And ... v. D. K. Barman and Anr., 1969*[4]

The Calcutta Chemical Company Limited had its head office in Calcutta. Mr Barman was employed as a salesman in the Patna branch of the Company. He was employed on 28 August 1961. According to Mr Barman's statement, he fell ill and applied for 3 days sick leave from 8 September 1964 to 10 September 1964. He extended his leave up to 12 September 1964 supported by a medical certificate. The Governing Director of the Company wrote a letter dated 10 September 1964, refusing the prayer for leave made by Barman by his letter dated 8 September 1964. Explanation was also asked for, and he was prohibited from resuming his duties till the matter was decided. Barman's case was that he submitted his explanation on 12 September 1964, and prayed for resumption of his duties on the expiry of his leave. He received its reply on 16 September 1964 whereby his service was terminated from 8 September 1964. He was offered 1 month's pay in lieu of notice.

Mr Barman further stated that he had sent a letter on 26 September 1964 to the management enquiring the authority and the reasons for his dismissal, but he received no reply. Subsequently Mr Barman filed a petition under Section 26 of the Act.

The company, on receipt of the notice of the petition filed by the employee (Mr Barman), filed two written statements in the court. In the statements, the respondent company stated that the work of Barman was never satisfactory. He neglected to carry out the instructions of the management while on tour by not submitting daily business reports, weekly account, arrival and departure reports and stock returns. He retained heavy cash balances. He drew daily allowances from the 10 to the 14 January 1963 on false report, a fact that

[4] *Calcutta Chemical Co. Ltd. And ... v. D.K. Barman And Anr.*, AIR 1969 Pat 371, 1969 (17) BLJR 510.

he admitted in a written letter, at an enquiry. Reports of misappropriation were received against Barman in July 1964 and it was found that Barman had taken some stock to his home which was declared to be damaged but was not returned. After the enquiry Barman returned those articles and they were entered in the Stock Register. These facts were admitted by Barman in a written statement signed by him. The company further submitted that Mr Barman was to go on tour on 9 September 1964, but he absented himself and was found absent from his house. He sent his application for leave on the grounds of illness which was reported to be a pretending illness, as he was found moving in the town. The management, therefore, was justified in both its orders in terminating the service of Barman.

Mr Barman denied all the charges levelled against him. He pleaded that if he was really guilty of allegedly gross misconduct, he must have been charge-sheeted. On the contrary, he was given several special increments for his good service. He submitted that the statements talked about were written by him under coercion and intimidation and at dictation. He alleged that sometimes some articles were left in the van due to short delivery and those used to be returned to the purchaser in the next trip.

The Labour Court held that the Governing Director had no reasonable cause for terminating the service of or dismissing Barman from 8 September 1964. Hence, the Court directed his reinstatement from 8 September 1964 with all the benefits under the terms and conditions of his service, excepting his salary and any special emolument. The Court has also awarded him compensation in the shape of his 6 month's pay at the undisputed rate of ₹189 per month which he was drawing on 8 September 1964.

The company feeling aggrieved by the order of the Labour Court preferred Civil Revision and requested to reconsider the order of reinstatement pronounced by the Labour Court.

Discussion Point

Was the relief of reinstatement awarded by the Labour Court to Mr Barman justified and appropriate in the above-mentioned circumstances?

Judgement and Explanation

It was held that the relief of reinstatement given to the employee was to be set aside. The services of Mr Barman would be deemed to had been dispensed with not from 9 September 1964 but from 14 September 1964, on and from which date, in view of the finding of the Labour Court that the services were dispensed with without reasonable cause, the employee would get by way of compensation 6 months' pay at the undisputed rate of ₹189 per month which he was drawing at that time. The court clarified in its judgement that the order of reinstatement is not to follow in all cases mechanically. Mr Barman was not an employee, in whose case an order of reinstatement could be or should have been made. The past record of Mr Barman, the nature of his alleged stated lapse and the grounds on which the order of the management was set aside were also relevant factors for consideration.

Thus, it is clear that even in cases under the Industrial Disputes Act, they may not follow in certain cases. While so ordering, the tribunal is expected to be inspired by a sense of fair play towards the employee on the one hand and considerations of discipline in the concern on the other.

Persons on Whom Settlement and Awards Are Binding (Section 18)

Section 18 of the Act deals with the matters related to persons on whom the awards are binding. For this purpose, settlements are classified into two categories, namely:

1. Settlement arrived at otherwise than in the course of conciliation proceedings, that is, without the aid of statutory agency.
2. Settlement arrived at in the course of conciliation proceedings with the aid of statutory agency.

In the first case, the Section provides that a settlement arrived at by agreement between the employer and workman except that in the course of conciliation proceeding is binding on the parties to the agreement (Section 18(1)).

In the second case, the Section states that subject to the provisions of Subsection (3), an arbitration award which has become enforceable is binding on the parties to the agreement who referred the dispute to arbitration (Section 18(2)). The Section further clarifies that a settlement arrived at in the course of conciliation proceedings under this Act or an arbitration award in a case where a notification has been issued under Subsection (3A) of Section 10A (3A) or an award of a Labour Court, Tribunal or National Tribunal which has become enforceable is binding on following parties:

1. All parties to the industrial disputes.
2. All other parties summoned to appear in the proceedings as parties to the dispute, unless the board of conciliation, Arbitrator, Labour Court, Tribunal or National Tribunal, as the case may be, records the opinion that they were so summoned without proper cause.
3. Where a party referred to in clause (a) or clause (b) is an employer, his heirs, successors or assigns in respect of the establishment to which the dispute relates.
4. Where a party referred to in clause (a) or clause (b) is composed of workmen, all persons who were employed in the establishment or part of the establishment, as the case may be, to which the dispute relates on the date of the dispute and all persons who subsequently become employed in that establishment or part (Section 18(3)).

Period of Operation of Settlement and Awards (Section 19)

1. **Period of operation of settlement (Section 19(1)):** As laid down by the Act, a settlement comes into operation on such date as is agreed upon by the parties to the dispute. But if no date is agreed upon, the settlement will be operational on the date on which the memorandum of the settlement is signed by the parties to the dispute.
2. **Settlement binding for period agreed upon or 6 months (Section 19(2)):** A settlement is binding upon the parties for such period as is agreed upon by them. If no such period is agreed upon, the settlement is binding for a period of 6 months from the date on which the memorandum of settlement is signed by the parties to the dispute and remains binding on the parties after the expiry of the above-mentioned period, until the expiry of 2 months from the date on which a notice in writing of an intention to terminate the settlement is given by one of the parties to the other party or parties to the settlement.
3. **Period of operation of award (Section 19(3)):** An award remains in operation for a period of 1 year from the date on which the award becomes enforceable under Section 17A. However, the appropriate government may reduce this period and fix such period as it thinks fit. Before the expiry of the said period, the appropriate government can extend the period of operation by any period not exceeding 1 year at a time. Thus total period of operation of any award must not exceed 3 years from the date on which it came into operation.

Example

If the court orders the employer to reinstate a workman in case of unreasonable removal or discharge, the employer is bound over for 1 year or in some cases, the period specified by the courts.

It must be noted that Subsection 19(3) does not apply to any award which by its nature, terms or other circumstances does not impose, after it has been given effect to, any continuing obligation on the parties bound by the award.

1. **Effect of material change in the circumstances on the period of operation (Section 19(4)):** In a case where the appropriate government, whether of its own motion or on the application of any party bound by the award, is satisfied that since the award was made, there has been a material change in the circumstances on which it was based, the appropriate government may refer the award or a part of it to a Labour Court, if the award was that of a Labour Court or to a Tribunal, if the award was that of a Tribunal or of a National Tribunal to decide whether the period of operation should not, by reason of such change, be shortened. In such case, the decision of Labour Court or the Tribunal, as the case may be on such reference, is final and binding on the parties.
2. **Notice of termination of award by the parties (Sections 19(6) and 19(7)):** Even after the expiry of the period of operation under Subsection (3), the award continues to be binding on the parties until a period of 2 months has elapsed from the date on which notice is given by any party bound by the award to the other party or parties intimating its intention to terminate the award. It is to be noted that no notice given under Subsection (2) or Subsection (6) has an effect, unless it is given by a party representing the majority of persons bound by the settlement or award, as the case may be (Section 19(7)).

Commencement and Conclusion of Proceedings (Section 20)

The Act declares a conciliation proceeding to have commenced on the date on which a notice of strike or lockout under Section 22 is received by the conciliation officer or on the date of the order referring the dispute to a Board, as the case may be (Section 20(1)).

So far as conclusion of the proceeding is concerned, the Act provides the details under Subsection 20(2). There are three possible situations and the Section provides the rules to deal with all three in the following manner:

1. **A case where a settlement is arrived at:** The conciliation proceeding is deemed to have concluded when a memorandum of the settlement is signed by the parties to the dispute.
2. **A case where no settlement is arrived at:** The conciliation proceeding is deemed to have concluded when the report of the conciliation officer is received by the appropriate government or when the report of the Board is published under Section 17, as the case may be.
3. **A case when a reference is made to a court, Labour Court, Tribunal or National Tribunal under Section 10:** The conciliation proceeding is deemed to have concluded during the pendency of conciliation proceedings.

Commencement and conclusion of proceedings in Arbitration and adjudication proceedings (Section 20(3)): Proceedings before an arbitrator under Section 10A or before a Labour Court, Tribunal or National Tribunal commence on the date of the reference of the dispute for arbitration or adjudication, as the case may be. Such proceedings conclude on the date on which the award becomes enforceable under Section 17A.

Penalty for the Breach of Settlement or Awards (Section 29)

As laid down by Section 29 of the Act, any person who commits a breach of any term of any settlement or award, which is binding on him under this Act, is punishable with imprisonment for a term which may extend to 6 months, or with fine, or with both, and where the breach is a continuing one, with a further fine which may extend to ₹200 for every day during which the breach continues after the conviction for the first. If the Court trying the offender fines him, the Court may direct that the whole or any part of the fine realized from him to be paid, by way of compensation, to any person who has been injured by such breach.

LO6: Strikes and Lockouts (Chapter V)

The meaning of the terms 'strike' and 'lockouts' as defined under Section 2 of the Act has already been explained before.

Strike

As discussed before, a strike is collective stoppage of work by workmen undertaken to bring pressure upon the employer. It is a spontaneous and concerted withdrawal of workmen from production. A strike is usually organized by mutual agreement on the part of the workers with a view to obtaining or resisting change to their conditions of work.

Features of strike: If we analyse the meaning of 'strike' explained above, we find following salient futures of strike:

1. It is the stoppage of work by a body of workmen acting in concert with a view to exert pressure upon the employer to concede to their demands.
2. At the time of strike, the participant workmen must be employed in any industry.
3. Mere cessation of work does not come within the preview of strike, unless it can be shown that such cessation of work was a concerted action for the enforcement of an industrial demand.

Lockout

Lockout means the closing of a place of employment, or the suspension of work, or the refusal by an employer to continue to employ any number of persons employed by him. As discussed before, lockout is a weapon in the hands of the employer to be used to curb the militant spirit of the workers. In lockout, an employer shuts down his place of business as a result of reprisal, or as an instrument of coercion or as a mode of exerting pressure upon the employees with a view it dictate his own terms to them.

Prohibition of Strikes and Lockouts (Sections 22 to 23)

Procedure of strikes in a public utility service (Section 22(1)): According to Section 22(1), no worker employed in a public utility service can go on strike in breach of contract:

1. Without giving to the employer notice of strike, within 6 weeks before striking; or
2. Within 14 days of giving such notice; or
3. Before the expiry of the date of strike specified in any such notice as aforesaid; or
4. During the pendency of any conciliation proceedings before a conciliation officer and 7 days after the conclusion of such proceedings.

It is clear from the provisions of Section 22(1) that the intention of the law makers is to ensure that a prior warning is given to the employer before the workmen go on strike. It is to be noted that a notice for strike remains valid only for 6 weeks.

Procedure of lockouts in a public utility service (Section 22(2)): According to Section 22(2), an employer carrying on any public utility service cannot lockout any of his workmen:

1. Without giving to the employer notice of lockout, within 6 weeks before locking out; or
2. Within 14 days of giving such notice; or
3. Before the expiry of the date of lockout specified in any such notice as aforesaid; or
4. During the pendency of any conciliation proceedings before a conciliation officer and 7 days after the conclusion of such proceedings.

It is clear from the provisions of Section 22(2) that the intention of the law makers is to ensure that a prior warning is given to the workmen before the employer locks out. It is to be noted that a notice for lockout is to be given in a prescribed manner (Section 22(5)) and such notice remains valid only for 6 weeks.

Notice of lockout or strike not necessary (Section 22(3)): The notice of lockout or strike under this section is not necessary where there is already in existence a strike or, as the case may be, lockout in the public utility service. But in such cases, the employer must send intimation of such lockout or strike on the day on which it is declared, to such authority as may be specified by the appropriate government either generally or for a particular area or for a particular class of public utility services.

Intimation of notice of lockout or strike (Section 22(6)): If on any day an employer receives from any person employed by him any notice of strike or gives any notice of lockout to his workmen, he must within 5 days thereof report to the appropriate government or to such authority as prescribed by that government, the number of such notices received or given on that day.

Let us discuss a case to understand the circumstance under which the notice of lockout is to be issues essentially (Case 13.3).

Case 13.3: *Lakshmi Devi Sugar Mills Ltd v. Pt. Ram Sarup, 1957*[5]

Seventy-six workers of Lakshmi Devi Sugar Mills Ltd (the appellant company) resorted to a tools-down strike in sympathy with a dismissed co-worker. Repeated attempts to persuade them to resume work failed and the general manager suspended them until further orders. After midday recess the appellant company prevented the workers from entering the mills but they violently entered the mills and the police had to be called in by the company to keep the peace. Thereafter the charges of misconduct and insubordination were framed

[5] *Lakshmi Devi Sugar Mills Ltd v. Pt. Ram Sarup*, 1957 AIR 82, 1956 SCR 916.

against the workers and they were called upon to show cause in an open enquiry to be held by the general manager why disciplinary action should not be taken against them and the order of suspension was extended pending the enquiry. This resulted in a total non-cooperation by the workers and the atmosphere was tense. Therefore, the enquiry could not be held within 4 days and the appellant company decided to dismiss the workers as a result of the enquiry. Since an appeal was then pending before the Labour Appellate Tribunal, the company applied to it under Section 22 of the Industrial Disputes (Appellate Tribunal) Act, 1950, for permission to do so and extended the period of suspension pending receipt of such permission.

In response to the action of the company, the workmen filed an application to the Appellate Tribunal for requisite action to be taken against the company for having contravened Section 22(b) of the Act by resorting to an illegal lockout and hereby punishing them without its prior permission. The Appellate Tribunal held that the company did not conduct the enquiry within the specified time specified and on that grounds dismissed its application. The application of the workers was admitted, holding that the suspension of the workers and preventing them from continuing work after the midday recess amounted to a lockout and punishment by the company and contravened Section 22(b) of the Act and directed their reinstatement.

Disappointed with the decision of the Tribunal, the company appealed and contended on its behalf that there had been neither a breach of clause 12 of the Standing Orders nor a contravention of Section 22(b) of the Act. The company further argued that the conduct of the company did not come within the definition of a lockout and even if there was any lockout it was in consequence of the illegal strike resorted to by the workmen and as such could not be deemed to be illegal by virtue of Section 24(3) of the Industrial Disputes Act, 1947. Moreover, even assuming that the company declared an illegal lockout it was not required for it to obtain the permission of the Appellate Tribunal under Section 22 of the Act before it could do so. Since a lockout was neither an alteration of the conditions of service nor a discharge or punishment by dismissal or otherwise, no permission, therefore, was required for its declaration.

Discussion Point

Was the company guilty of violating the provisions of Section 22 of the Act and a permission required before taking action against the workmen who went on strike?

Judgement and Explanation

It was held that the company did not violate the provisions of Section 22 of the Act and the appellant company was granted permission under Section 22 of the Act to discharge the respondents from its employ and the appellant was entitled to recover the same back from them. The Court further stated that the appellant company succeeded in establishing that the workmen had resorted to an illegal strike from 7 AM on 27 May 1952, and a fair enquiry into the alleged misconduct and insubordination of the workmen had been held by the management without violating any principles of natural justice. After the enquiry, the management found that the workmen had been guilty of misconduct and insubordination with which they had been charged and that the management came to the bona fide conclusion that continuing the workmen in its employ was detrimental to discipline and dangerous in the interests of the appellant.

General Prohibltion of Strike and Lockouts (Section 23)

The Act prohibits the strike and lockout in certain circumstances provided under Section 23. The underlying reason for enforcement of Section 23 is that where a dispute has been referred to conciliation or adjudication, a strike or lockout in furtherance thereof is not necessary and also inexpedient.

The section states that no workman who is employed in any industrial establishment can go on strike in breach of contract and no employer of any such workman can declare a lockout in the following circumstances:

1. During the pendency of conciliation proceedings before a Board and 7 days after the conclusion of such proceedings.
2. During the pendency of proceedings before a Labour Court, Tribunal or National Tribunal and 2 months after the conclusion of such proceedings.
   (bb) During the pendency of arbitration proceedings before an arbitrator and 2 months after the conclusion of such proceedings, where a notification has been issued under Subsection (3A) of Section 10A; or
3. During the period of operation of a settlement or award in respect of any of the matters covered by the settlement or award.

Case 13.4 provides deeper insights into the application of Section 23.

Case 13.4: *Chemicals & Fibres of India Ltd v. D. G. Bhoir & Others*, 1975[6]

On 14 August 1972, the Government of Maharashtra made a reference to the Labour Court under Section 10(1)(c) of the Industrial Disputes Act of an industrial dispute in respect of the dismissal by the appellant of one of its employees N. S. Bobhate.

On 14 August 1972, Chemicals & Fibres of India Ltd. (the appellant company) dismissed one of its employees N. S. Bobhate and subsequently on 27 August 1972 three other workers, Dastoor, Shome and Soman after an enquiry, leading to a strike in the appellant's factory. Towards the end of October 1972, the company dismissed about 312 of its employees who participated in the strike. The company filed 12 applications before the Industrial Tribunal for approval of these dismissals. The appellant company pleaded before the Tribunal that the strike was illegal as a reference was pending in respect of Bobhate and therefore the discharge of its workers by the appellant was in order and approval should be granted.

On 30 August 1973, the Tribunal rejected all the applications for the approval of the dismissal of the employees. Dissatisfied with the decision of the Tribunal, the appellant company approached the Court for the grant of special leave. It was contended on behalf of the appellant's company that as stated under Section 23 of the Industrial Disputes Act, 1947, during the pendency of the proceeding, the strike will be considered illegal. Since the proceeding was pending in this case and employees went on strike, hence the dismissal of these employees was in order and approval must be granted. On the other hand, the employees contended that Section 23(b) could not be attracted because here a single workman's cause had been espoused by a labour union which was not comprised of all the employees of the concerned employer.

Discussion Point

Was Section 23 of the Industrial Disputes Act applicable in the above case?

Judgement and Explanation

It was held that Section 23 was very well applicable in the above-mentioned case. The court further stated that the provisions of the Industrial Disputes Act clearly bring out the elaborate nature of the proceedings relating to conciliation, arbitration, settlement, inquiry and award. The intention behind all these provisions is to avoid strikes and lockouts as far as possible not only by bringing the parties together but also by referring points of dispute between them, either voluntarily or otherwise for decision by Labour Courts, Tribunals and National Tribunals.

[6] *Chemicals & Fibres of India Ltd v. D. G. Bhoir & others*, 1975 AIR 1660, 1975 SCR 415.

Thus, Section 23 should be interpreted in the light of following important points:

1. The important words in Section 23(b) of the Act are 'during the pendency of proceedings'. Even though the dispute between the employer and the employees might relate to a case of a single workman, the provisions of Section 23(b) would apply if the single workman's cause has been espoused by a labour union which need not necessarily comprise of all the employees of the concerned employer. [418 A-B]
2. Even though the proceedings pending before the Labour Court, Tribunal or National Tribunal might relate to certain matters only, there cannot be a strike or lockout even in relation to matters other than those which are pending before the Labour Court, Tribunal or National Tribunal. [418 B-C]

Illegal Strikes and Lockouts (Section 24)

Section 24 of the Act provides that a strike or a lockout will be declared illegal if:

1. It is commenced or declared in contravention of Section 22 or Section 23; or
2. It is continued in contravention of an order made under Subsection (3) of Section 10 or Subsection (4A) of Section 10A.

If a strike or lockout in pursuance of an industrial dispute has already commenced and is in existence at the time of the reference of the dispute to a Board, an arbitrator, a Labour Court, Tribunal or National Tribunal, the continuance of such strike or lockout will not be considered illegal, subject to the condition that such strike or lockout was not at its commencement in contravention of the provisions of this Act or the continuance thereof was not prohibited under Subsection(3) of Section 10 or Subsection (4A) of Section 10A.

Case 13.5 throws more light on legal aspects of strike and its treatment under the Act.

Case 13.5: *Buckingham and Carnatic Co. Ltd v. Workers of The Buckingham*, 1953[7]

On 1 November 1948, 859 night shift operatives of the carding and spinning department of the Carnatic Mills stopped work, at 4 pm, some at 4.30 pm and some at 5 pm. The stoppage ended at 8 pm in both the departments. By 10 pm, the strike ended completely. The apparent cause for the strike was that the management of the Mills expressed its inability to comply with the request of the workers to declare the forenoon of the 1 November 1948, as a holiday for solar eclipse. On 3 November 1948, the management put up a notice declaring that the stoppage of work on the 1 November amounted to an illegal strike and a break in service within the meaning of the Factories Act (XXV of 1934). The notice further stated that the management had decided that the workers who had participated in aforementioned strike would not be entitled to holidays with pay as provided by the Act.

[7] *Buckingham And Carnatic Co. Ltd v. Workers of The Buckingham*, 1953 AIR 47, 1953 SCR 219.

On 11 July 1949, the Madras Government referred, under Section 10(1)(c) of the Industrial Disputes Act (XIV of 1947), this dispute along with certain other disputes to the Industrial Tribunal, Madras. The adjudicator stated in his order that there could be little doubt that the stoppage of work by the night shift workers on the night of the last November 1948, was a strike, that it was an illegal strike, since the textile industry was notified as a public utility industry and there could be no legal strike without a proper issue of notice in the terms prescribed by the Industrial Disputes Act and no such notice had been given. In view of this finding, he upheld the view of the management that the continuity of service of the workers was broken by the interruption caused by the illegal strike and that as a consequence the workers who participated in such strike were not entitled to annual holidays with pay under Section 49B(1) of the Factories Act.

Being dissatisfied with the order of the adjudicator, the Union appealed against the order of the adjudicator and contended that the stoppage of work did not fall in the category of 'strike' in Section 2(q) of the Industrial Act and thus the workers could not be deprived form claiming the holidays with pay under Section 49B(1) of the Indian Factories Act, 1934.

Discussion Points

1. Did the stoppage of the work fall within the definition of a 'strike' in Section 2(q) of the Industrial Disputes Act, 1947 and the strike was an illegal strike?
2. Were the workers entitled to claim holidays with pay under Section 49B(1) of the Indian Factories Act, 1934?

Judgement and Explanation

It was held that the stoppage of the work fell within the definition of a 'strike' in Section 2(q) of the Industrial Disputes Act, 1947 and the strike was an illegal strike as the textile mills was a public utility industry and no notice had been given to the management, even though the refusal to work continued only for a few hours. It was further stated by the court that since the continuity of service of the workers was interrupted by that illegal strike, hence they were not entitled to claim holidays with pay under Section 49B(1) of the Indian Factories Act, 1934.

Prohibition of financial aid to illegal strikes and lockouts (Section 25): This section of the Act prohibits financial aid to illegal strikes and lockouts. The section provides that no person must knowingly spend or apply any money in direct furtherance or support of any illegal strike or lockout. Thus this Section has the following two ingredients:

1. Spending or applying money.
2. Money spent or applied in direct furtherance or support of an illegal strike.

Penalties Concerning Strike and Lockout

1. **Penalty for illegal strikes (Section 26(1)):** A workman who commences, continues or otherwise acts in furtherance of, a strike which is illegal under this Act, is punishable with imprisonment for a term which may extend to 1 month, or with fine which may extend to ₹50, or with both.
2. **Penalty for illegal lockouts (Section 26(2)):** An employer who commences, continues, or otherwise acts in furtherance of a lockout which is illegal under this Act is punishable with

imprisonment for a term which may extend to 1 month, or with fine which may extend to ₹1,000, or with both.

3. **Penalty for instigation (Section 27):** A person instigating or inciting others to take part in, or otherwise acts in furtherance of, a strike or lockout which is illegal under this Act, is punishable with imprisonment for a term which may extend to 6 months, or with fine which may extend to ₹1,000, or with both.
4. **Penalty for giving financial aid to illegal strikes and lockouts (Section 28):** A person who knowingly expends or applies any money in direct furtherance or support of any illegal strike or lockout is punishable with imprisonment for a term which may extend to 6 months, or with fine which may extend to ₹1,000, or with both.

LO7: Layoff and Retrenchment (Chapters V-A and V-B)

The meaning of the terms 'layoff' and 'retrenchment' as defined under Section 2 of the Act has already been explained before.

Layoff

Layoff means refusal or failure to employ a workman temporarily. During the period of layoff, the employer–employee relationship does not come to an end but is merely suspended during the period of emergency. The duration of layoff cannot be for a period longer than the period of emergency. As provided by the Act, layoff can be on account of:

1. Shortage of coal, power or raw materials or
2. The accumulation of stock; or
3. The breakdown of machinery; or
4. Natural calamity; or
5. Any other connected reasons.

Retrenchment

Retrenchment is the discharge of surplus labour or staff by the employer for any reason whatsoever. The term 'retrenchment' as defined under the Section 2(00) brings following features of retrenchment in light:

1. Retrenchment means the termination by the employer of the services of a workman.
2. The termination may be for any reason whatsoever.
3. The termination should not be as a measure of punishment by way of disciplinary action.

As explained by the Act, following cases of termination of service are not considered to be retrenchment:

1. Voluntary retirement of a workman, or
2. Retirement of a workman on reaching the age of superannuation if the contract of employment between the employer and the workman concerned contains a stipulation in that behalf, or
   a. Termination of the service of a workman as a result of the non-renewal of the contract of employment between the employer and the workman concerned on its expiry or of such contract being terminated.

Case 13.6 provides deeper insights of the termination of employees covered under retrenchment.

Case 13.6: *Gammon India Limited v. Niranjan Dass*, 1983[8]

Mr Niranjan Dass, the respondent, was employed by the appellant company as a Senior Clerk till he received a notice terminating his services. The notice stated that on account of reduction in volume of the business of the appellant company as a result of recession, his services were being terminated. There arose an industrial dispute between the appellant company and the respondent.

The respondent contended that the retrenchment was illegal and unjustified as the conditions for a valid retrenchment have not been complied with. He pleaded to be continued in service. The government referred the dispute to the Industrial Tribunal to decide whether the retrenchment of the respondent was unjustified or illegal. On the other hand, the appellant company argued that since the termination of the services was consequent upon the closure of the Delhi office, the case would be governed by Section 25 FFF of the Industrial Disputes Act 1947 which does not prescribe payment of compensation as a condition precedent to a valid termination of service by way of retrenchment. Thus, the company did not accept the argument of the worker that the services terminated on account of recession in work amounted to retrenchment rather in its opinion it was a closure of business due to recession in the work and thus governed by Section 25FFF of the Act.

The Industrial Tribunal held that since the conditions for a valid retrenchment have not been complied with, the respondent continued to be in service. Being unhappy with the decision of the Industrial Court, the appellant company filed an appeal in the Civil Court.

Discussion Point

Do the services terminated on account of recession in work amount to retrenchment?

Judgement and Explanation

It was held that the award of the Tribunal was correct and unassailable. The appellant company had become surplus on account of reduction in volume of work and that constituted retrenchment even in the traditional sense of the term. The respondent (worker) would be entitled to all back wages including the benefit of revised wages or salary if during the period there was revision of pay scales with yearly increment, revised dearness allowance or variable dearness allowance and all terminal benefits if he had reached the age of superannuation such as provident fund and gratuity. Back wages had to be calculated as if the respondent continued in service uninterrupted. He was declared entitled to leave encashment and bonus if other workmen in the same category were paid the same along with the arrears as calculated according to the directions herein given with 12% interest from the date the amount became due and payable till realization.

[8] *Gammon India Limited v. Niranjan Dass*, 5 December 1983, AIR 500, 1984 SCR (1) 959.

Difference between lockout and layoff: Following are the differentiating points between lockout and layoff:

1. Lockout is an act on the part of the employer to pressurize the labour, while layoff is for business reasons.
2. Lockout is an intentional act at the end of the employer, while layoff is unintentional and beyond the control of the employer.
3. Lockout is exercised due to an industrial dispute emerged between the employer and workmen, while layoff is not necessarily concerned with dispute with workmen.
4. Lockout continues during the period of dispute, while layoff cannot continue beyond the period of emergency.

Difference between lockout and retrenchment: The points explained below differentiate lockout from retrenchment:

1. Lockout is a temporary measure, while retrenchment is permanent in nature.
2. In lockout, the relationship between employer and employee is only suspended; it does not come to an end, while in retrenchment such a relationship is severed at the instance of the employer.
3. Lockout aims to coerce the workmen, while the intention of retrenchment is to dispense with surplus labour.
4. Lockout is due to an industrial dispute, whereas in case of retrenchment, there is not necessarily such a dispute.

Difference between lockout and closure: Let us discuss some points to differentiate lockout from closure.

1. Lockout is a temporary measure, whereas closure is permanent in nature. .
2. Lockout is a weapon of coercion in the hands of employer, while closure is usually made for trade reasons.
3. Lockout is declared due to an industrial dispute, while in case of closure, there need not be any dispute.

Difference between retrenchment and closure: Retrenchment and closure are different from each other on the basis of following points:

1. Retrenchment affects only some of the workman, whereas closure affects all workmen employed in an establishment.
2. In retrenchment the trade or business remains uninterrupted as it continues, while in closure the business itself is discontinued.

Payment of 'Layoff' or 'Retrenchment' Compensation

The Industrial Disputes Act, 1947, as originally enacted, had provision for the payment of 'layoff' or 'retrenchment' compensation. Thus, there was no uniform rule that could be observed by the adjudicating bodies in the case of payment of compensation for 'layoff' or 'retrenchment'. In order to overcome the situation, the President of India promulgated the Industrial Disputes (Amendment) Ordinance in October 1953 to the effect from 24 October 1953. The said Ordinance was repealed and replaced by the Industrial Disputes (Amendment) Act, 1953 to add Section 25A to Section 25J to deal with the payment of 'layoff' or 'retrenchment' compensation.

Application of Sections 25C to 25E (Section 25A)

Section 25A of the Act directs that the provisions as to layoff or retrenchment of workmen as embodied in Sections 25C to 25E (both inclusive) shall not apply to an industrial establishment:

1. To which Chapter V-B applies; or
2. In which less than 50 workmen on an average per working day have been employed in the preceding calendar month; or
3. Which is of a seasonal character or in which work is performed only intermittently (Section 25A(1)).

In simple words, the workmen employed by an exempted establishment under Section 25A are not entitled to layoff or retrenchment compensation and the Tribunal has no right to grant relief on any fanciful notices of social justice.

The appropriate government's decision is final on the issue whether an industrial establishment is of a seasonal character or whether work is performed therein only intermittently (Section 25A(2)).

Industrial establishment: For this section and in Sections 25C, 25D and 25E, 'industrial establishment' is as follows:

1. A factory as defined in clause (m) of Section 2 of the Factories Act, 1948 (63 of 1948); or
2. A mine as defined in clause (j) of Section 2 of the Mines Act, 1952 (35 of 1952); or
3. A plantation as defined in clause (f) of Section 2 of the Plantations Labour Act, 1951.

Continuous Service (Section 25B)

As provided under Subsection 25B(1), a workman is said to be in continuous service for a period if he is, for that period, in uninterrupted service, including service which may be interrupted on account of:

1. Sickness, or
2. Authorized leave, or
3. An accident, or
4. A strike which is not illegal, or
5. A lockout, or
6. A cessation of work which is not due to any fault on the part of the workman.

It is further provided that if a workman is not in continuous service as defined above (Section 25B(1)) for a period of 1 year or 6 months, he is deemed to be in continuous service under an employer:

1. **For a period of 1 year:** if the workman, during a period of 12 calendar months preceding the date with reference to which calculation is to be made, has actually worked under the employer for not less than
   a. One hundred and ninety days in the case of a workman employed below ground in a mine; and
   b. Two hundred and forty days, in any other case.
2. **For a period of 6 months:** if the workman, during a period of 6 calendar months preceding the date with reference to which calculation is to be made, has actually worked under the employer for not less than:
   a. Ninety-five days, in the case of a workman employed below ground in a mine.
   b. One hundred and twenty days, in any other case (Section 25B(2)).

Calculation of working days: The number of days on which workman has actually worked under an employer includes the days on which:

1. He has been laid off under an agreement or as permitted by standing orders made under the Industrial Employment (Standing Orders) Act, 1946 (20 of 1946), or under this Act or under any other law applicable to the industrial establishment.
2. He has been on leave with full wages, earned in the previous year.
3. He has been absent due to temporary disablement caused by accident arising out of and in the course of his employment.
4. In the case of a female, she has been on maternity leave; so, however, that the total period of such maternity leave does not exceed 12 weeks.

Layoff

Rights of Workmen Laid Off for Compensation (Section 25C)

Section 25C of the Act entitles a workman to get compensation from the employer for the period for which he is laid off. When the employer is unable to provide work to his workmen for reasons beyond his control, he owns duty to pay layoff compensation to such workmen. For a workman to be eligible to claim layoff compensation, he must fulfil the following conditions:

1. The workman must not be a badli or a casual workman. Here, the 'badli workman' means a workman who is employed in an industrial establishment in the place of another workman whose name is borne on the muster rolls of the establishment.
2. His name must be borne on the muster rolls of the industrial establishment.
3. The workman must have completed at least 1 year of continuous service.
4. A workman is entitled to layoff compensation for the period of his layoff other than for weekly holidays which may intervene.
5. The rate of compensation must be equal to 50% of the total of the basic wage and dearness allowance that might have been payable to him.
6. If during any period of 12 months, a workman is laid off for more than compensation is payable only for 45 days.

7. Where a workman is laid off for a period of 45 days during 12 months, the employer has a right to retrench such workman at any time after the expiry of 45 days of layoff. When an employer decides to retrench a workman, he has to comply with the requirements laid down by Section 25F of the Act.

Duty of Employer to Maintain Muster Rolls of Workmen (Section 25D)

The act enjoins upon the employer a duty to maintain a muster roll of workmen notwithstanding that workmen have been laid off. The employer also has to provide for the making of entries therein by workmen who may present themselves for work at the establishment at the appointed time during normal working hours.

Workmen Not Entitled to Compensation in Certain Cases (Section 25E)

The Act demands certain conditions to be met by the workman before providing him the entitlement to claim compensation for layoff. Section 25E provides in this regard and states that no compensation shall be paid to a workman who has been laid off:

1. If he refuses to accept any alternative employment in the same or any other establishment belonging to the same employer situated in the same town or village or within a radius of 5 miles and it does not require any special skill or previous experience, provided the same wages are offered.
2. If he does not present himself for work at the appointed time during normal working hours at least once a day.
3. If lay off is in the consequence of strike or slowing down of production by the workers in another part of the establishment.

Retrenchment

Conditions Precedent to Retrenchment of Workmen (Section 25F)

Section 25F lays down the requirements for a valid retrenchment of a workman who has been in continuous service for not less than 1 year. According to this section, a workman employed in any industry who has been in continuous service for not less than 1 year under an employer cannot be retrenched by the employer until:

1. The workman has been given 1 month's notice in writing indicating the reasons for retrenchment, or the workman has been paid in lieu of such notice, wages for the period of notice (Section 25F(a)).
2. The workman has been paid, at the time of retrenchment, compensation which shall be equivalent to 15 days average pay for every completed year of continuous service or any part thereof, in excess of 6 months (Section 25F(b)).
3. Notice in the prescribed manner is served on the appropriate government or such authority as may be specified by the appropriate government by notification in the Official Gazette (Section 25-F(c)).

Procedure for Retrenchment (Section 25G)

Where a workman in an industrial establishment who is a citizen of India is to be retrenched and he belongs to a particular category of workmen in that establishment, in the absence of any agreement between the employer and the workman in this behalf, the employer must ordinarily retrench the workman who was the last person to be employed in that category, unless the employer has the reasons to be recorded for the retrenchment of any other workman.

Re-employment of Retrenched Workmen (Section 25H)

This Section provides priority for a retrenched workman in the case of reemployment. The section provides that in the cases where any workmen are retrenched, and the employer proposes to take into his employ any persons, he must, in a prescribed manner, give an opportunity to the retrenched workmen who are citizens of India to offer themselves for re-employment, and such retrenched workmen who offer themselves for re-employment must have preference over other persons.

In simple words, in case the employer proposes to re-employ any person, he is under an obligation to offer first priority to the persons who have been retrenched.

Let us discuss a case (Case 13.7) to gain insights into the definition of retrenchment under the Act.

Case 13.7: *Hindustan Steel Ltd v. The Presiding Officer, Labour,* 1977[9]

In this case, three respondents were employed as Head Time Keepers in the Rourkela Unit of Hindustan Steel Limited, (the appellant company) herein. Respondents no. 1 and 2 were appointed for a period of 3 years as Head Time Keeper. While the respondent no. 3 was also appointed for a period of 3 years but as Time Keeper, not Head Time Keeper. In his case, the period was extended after the expiry of 3 years from time to time till 15 October 1962. In the meantime, the respondent no. 3 was promoted from Time Keeper to Head Time Keeper with effect from 3 November 1960. Pursuant to an alleged policy to 'streamline the organisation and to effect economies wherever possible', the appellant company decided not to renew the contracts of service of the Head Time Keepers who were eight in number including the above three respondents. However, no order terminating their services was served.

Being unhappy with the decision of the appellant company, the aforesaid three respondents raised an industrial dispute through their Union, named Rourkela Mazdoor Sabha. According to the appellant company, the termination was automatic on the expiry of the contractual period of service. On the other hand, the terminated employees alleged that the termination was nothing but retrenchment and condition precedent to the retrenchment of workmen laid down in Section 25F of the Industrial Disputes Act had not been satisfied.

The matter was taken to the Labour Court and by its award date the orders of termination passed against these three respondents were set aside. The Labour Court held that they were entitled to 'reinstatement with continuity of service' and also to 'full wages for the period between the date of their release from service and the date or dates of their reinstatement'. The award is based on the following findings:

1. The three respondents were retrenched from employment and, the requirements of Section 25F of the Industrial Disputes Act not having been satisfied, the retrenchment was contrary to law.

[9] *Hindustan Steel Ltd v. The Presiding Officer, Labour,* 1977 AIR 31, 1977 SCR (1) 586.

2. In terminating the services of these employees, the management adopted unfair labour practice and the action of the employer was not bona fide.
3. It was not proved that they had any alternative employment after they were released from service.

The appellant company challenged the award by filing a writ petition in the High Court. The company contended that the services of these employees came to end by efflux of time and the management did not terminate their services and thus these were not the cases of retrenchment. Another submission made by the management was that since the employees did not prove that the employees had made efforts to minimize their losses during the period of unemployment, the award for payment of full back wages was erroneous. The High Court overruled both the contentions and dismissed the writ petition.

Finally, the appellant company filed an appeal in the Supreme Court and again argued that such termination of service did not fall within the definition of retrenchment in Section 2(00) of the Industrial Disputes Act, 1947.

Discussion Point

Whether the termination of the services of the three respondents was justified and, if not, to what relief were they entitled to.

Judgement and Explanation

The Court rejected the appeal and stated that Section 2(00) which defines retrenchment makes it clear that the retrenchment means the termination by the employer of service of a workman for any reasons whatsoever. As laid down by Section 25F(a), no workman who has been in continuous service for not less than 1 year under an employer can be retrenched unless he has been given 1-month notice or wages in lieu thereof and the proviso would be quite unnecessary if the retrenchment as defined by Section 2(00) was intended not to include termination of service by efflux of time in terms of an agreement between the parties.

LO8: Transfer and Closing Down of Undertakings

Compensation to Workmen in Case of Transfer of Undertaking (Section 25FF)

Section 25FFF of the act deals with a situation when the ownership or management of an undertaking is transferred. The Section provides that where the ownership or management of an undertaking is transferred, whether by agreement or by operation of law, from the employer in relation to that undertaking to a new employer, every workman who has been in continuous service for not less than 1 year in that undertaking immediately before such transfer is entitled to:

1. Notice.
2. Compensation for retrenchment in accordance with the provisions of Section 25F.

However, the workman is not entitled to notice or compensation where there has been a change of employers by reason of the transfer, if:

1. The service of the workman has not been interrupted by such transfer.
2. The terms and conditions of service applicable to the workman after such transfer are not in any way less favourable to the workman than those applicable to him immediately before the transfer.

3. The new employer is under the terms of such transfer or otherwise legally liable to pay to the workman, in the event of his retrenchment, compensation on the basis that his service has been continuous and has not been interrupted by the transfer.

Thus it is clear from the above discussion that in order to be entitled to compensation under this section, the following conditions must be simultaneously complied with:

1. The service of the workman has been interrupted by the transfer.
2. Terms and conditions of service to a workman, after such transfer, are in any way less favourable to the workman than those applicable immediately before the transfer.

Notice for the Closure of Any Undertaking (Section 25FFA)

An employer intending to close down an undertaking of an industrial establishment to which Chapter V-B is applicable must make an application to the appropriate government for prior permission. The notice is required to give to the appropriate government stating clearly the reasons for the intended closure of the undertaking (Section FFA(1)).

However, no such notice is required to be served by:

1. An undertaking in which less than 50 workmen are employed, or less than 50 workmen were employed on an average per working day in the preceding 12 months.
2. An undertaking set up for the construction of buildings, bridges, roads, canals, dams or for other construction work or project.

Exemption by appropriate government: If the appropriate government is satisfied that owing to such exceptional circumstances as accident in the undertaking or death of the employer or the like, it is necessary so to do, the government is authorized to direct to exempt such undertaking from the application of the provisions of Subsection (1) for a specific period (Section FFA(2)).

Compensation to Workmen in Case of Closing Down of Undertaking (Section 25FFF)

The Act has made the provisions for compensation to the workmen in case of closing down of an undertaking. Section 25 FFF provides in this relation that where an undertaking is closed down for any reason whatsoever, every workman who has been in continuous service for not less than 1 year in that undertaking immediately before such closure is entitled to

1. Notice.
2. Compensation for retrenchment in accordance with the provisions of Section 25F (Section 25 FFF(1)).

The application of this subsection is subject to Section 25 FFF(2).

It is further provided that if the undertaking is closed down on account of unavoidable circumstances beyond the control of the employer, the compensation to be paid to the workman under clause (b) of Section 25F must not exceed his average pay for 3 months.

Unavoidable circumstances beyond the control of the employer: An undertaking is not deemed to be closed down on account of unavoidable circumstances beyond the control of the employer within the meaning of the proviso to this subsection, if it is closed down by any of the following reasons:

1. Financial difficulties (including financial losses); or
2. Accumulation of undisputed off stocks; or
3. The expiry of the period of the lease or license granted to it; or
4. In case where the undertaking is engaged in mining operations, exhaustion of the minerals in the area in which operations are carried on.

Closing down of an undertaking set up for construction, buildings, bridges, roads, canals, dams or other construction work: When any undertaking set up for the construction of buildings, bridges, roads, canals, dams or other construction work is closed down on account of the completion of the work within 2 years from the date on which the undertaking had been set up, the workmen employed therein are not entitled to any compensation under clause (b) of Section 25F, but if the construction work continues beyond 2 years, the workmen employed by such undertaking are entitled to notice and compensation under that section for every completed year of continuous service or any part thereof in excess of 6 months (Section 25 FFF(2)).

Case 13.8 provides insights of the provisions of compensation in case of closing down of an establishment;

Case 13.8: *Prakash Cotton Mills Pvt. Ltd v. Rashtriya Mills Mazdoor Sangh,* 1986[10]

Certain goods which are essential for the manufacturing process in Prakash Cotton Mills Pvt. Ltd (the appellant's mill) were detained by the Excise Authorities for non-payment of central excise duty. This resulted in a disruption in the functioning of the appellant's mill compelling the appellant to stop the working of the mill for the period from 24 March 1964 to 10 June 1964. The respondent Sangh demanded that the employees who were affected by the said closure had to be paid their wages for the aforesaid period. The demand was rejected by the appellant mill and respondent Sangh filed an application before the First Labour Court, praying for the payment of full closure compensation to the affected employees.

The Labour Court held that the appellant mill was liable to pay closure compensation to the employees affected by the closure of the mill for the aforesaid period at the rate of 50% of the basic wages and dearness allowance. The appellant mill filed an appeal in the Industrial Court and the Industrial Court partly allowed the appeal of the appellant mills and directed the appellant to pay closure compensation to the employees affected by the closure for the aforementioned period and further directed that where the employees was sick and enjoyed sickness benefits for all the days or had been on privilege leave or enjoyed leave with wages for all the days or secured alternative employment for any period during the closure, such employees would not be entitled to any closure compensation for such days, but in respect of such days half of the wages payable to badli workmen in lieu of the said three categories of workmen would be paid to the badli workmen equitably.

[10] *Prakash Cotton Mills Pvt. Ltd v. Rashtriya Mills Mazdoor Sangh,* 1986 AIR 1514, 1986 SCR (3) 419.

The appellant mill knocked the doors of the court against the decision of the Industrial Court and contended on behalf of the appellant that as the closure had been made in accordance with the provisions of the Standing orders 16 and 17 due to circumstances beyond the control of the appellant, the appellant mill was not liable to pay any compensation to its employees for the period of closure including payment to the badli workmen.

Discussion Point

Whether the mill was liable to pay any compensation to its employees for the period of closure including payment to the badli workmen.

Judgement and Explanation

It was held that the appellant mill was liable to pay compensation to its employees for the period of closure. However, the order of the Industrial Court to direct the payment of compensation to the badli workmen was set aside. It was stated in the judgement that an employee was entitled to challenge the refusal by the company to pay compensation of the closure and claim such compensation before the Labour Court whether or not such closure was due to circumstances beyond the control of the company, as enumerated in Standing order 16.

LO9: Special Provisions Related to Layoff, Retrenchment and Closure (Chapter V-B)

The Industrial Disputes (Amendment) Act, 1976, brought the following two important changes in the act:

1. The provisions of Sections 25C to 25E became inapplicable on the establishments to which Chapter V is applied.
2. A new Chapter V-B was added, which deals with the following issues:
    a. Special provisions relating to prohibition of layoff,
    b. Conditions precedent to retrenchment of workmen and closure in certain establishments,
    c. Restarting of undertaking closed prior to the commencement of the Amendment Act,
    d. Penalty for layoff and retrenchment without prior permission and
    e. Penalty for closure.

Application of Chapter V-B (Section 25K)

The provisions of this Chapter are applicable to an industrial establishment (not being an establishment of a seasonal character or in which work is performed only intermittently) employing not less than 100 workmen on an average per working day for the preceding 12 months (Section 25K(1)).

It is further clarified that to decide whether an industrial establishment is of a seasonal character or whether work is performed therein only intermittently, the decision of the appropriate government thereon shall be final (Section 25K(2)).

Definitions (Section 25L)

Industrial establishment: For this section and in sections 25C, 25D and 25E, 'Industrial establishment' is defined as follows:

1. A factory as defined in clause (m) of Section 2 of the Factories Act, 1948 (63 of 1948); or
2. A mine as defined in clause (j) of Section 2 of the Mines Act, 1952 (35 of 1952); or
3. A plantation as defined in clause (f) of Section 2 of the Plantations Labour Act, 1951.

For the purpose of this Chapter, the appropriate government is the central government.

1. In relation to any company in which not less than 51% of the paid-up share capital is held by the central government, or
2. In relation to any corporation not being a corporation referred to in subclause (i) of clause (a) of Section 2 established by or under any law made by Parliament.

Prohibition of Layoff (Section 25M)

Section 25M of Chapter V prohibits the laying off of the workman and specifies some procedures and rules to be adhered by before laying off a workman.

1. **Permission from the appropriate government (Section 25M(1)):** A workman (other than a 'badli' workman or a casual workman) whose name is borne on the muster rolls of an industrial establishment to which this Chapter V-B applies cannot be laid off by employer except with the prior permission of the appropriate government or such authority as may be specified by the government by notification in the Official Gazette.
2. **Application to lay off a workman (Section 25M(2)):** An employer intending to lay off the workmen has to make an application in the prescribed manner under Subsection (1) stating clearly the reasons to seek permission for the intended layoff. A copy of such application is also to be served simultaneously on the workmen concerned in the prescribed manner.
3. **Permission to continue lay off in a mine (Section 25M(3)):** Where the workman of a mine have been laid off for reasons of fire, flood or excess of inflammable gas or explosion, the employer in relation to such establishment must within a period of 30 days from the date of such layoff apply in the presented manner to the appropriate government or the specified authority to seek permission to continue layoff.
4. **Communication of order to the employer and workmen (Section 25M(4)):** After receiving the application for permission under Subsection (1) or Subsection (3), the appropriate government or the specified authority must conduct an enquiry. The appropriate government or the specified authority must give a reasonable opportunity of being heard to the employer, the workmen concerned and the persons interested in such layoff. Having regard to the genuineness and adequacy of the reasons for such layoff, the interests of the workmen and all other relevant factors, the appropriate government may grant or refuse to grant such permission. The reasons for such order are to be recorded in writing, and a copy of such order is to be communicated to the employer and the workmen.

5. **Presumption of permission (Section 25M(5)):** If the employer after making an application for permission under Subsection (1) or Subsection (3) does not receive the order granting or refusing to grant permission within a period of 60 days from the date on which such application is made, the permission applied for is deemed to have been granted on the expiration of the said period of 60 days.
6. **Order binding on all the parties (Section 25M(6)):** Subject to the provisions of Subsection (7), an order of the appropriate government or the specified authority granting or refusing to grant permission is final and binding on all the parties concerned. It remains in force for 1 year from the date of such order.
7. **Review of order (Section 25M(7)):** The appropriate government or the specified authority may, either on its own motion or on the application made by the employer or any workman, review its order granting or refusing to grant permission under Subsection (4) or refer the matter or, as the case may be, cause it to be referred to a Tribunal for adjudication. On such reference, a Tribunal must pass an award within a period of 30 days from the date of such reference.
8. **Illegal layoff (Section 25M(8)):** A layoff is deemed to be illegal from the date on which the workmen had been laid off, where:
   a. No application for permission under Subsection (1) is made, or
   b. Where no application for permission under Subsection (3) is made within the period specified therein, or
   c. Where the permission for any layoff has been refused.

   In case of illegal layoff, the workmen are entitled to all the benefits under any law for the time being in force as if they had not been laid off.
9. **Exemption (Section 25M(9)):** If the appropriate government is satisfied that owing to such exceptional circumstances as accident in the establishment or death of the employer or the like, it is necessary so to do, it may exempt the employer of such establishment from the application of the provisions of Subsection (1) or Subsection (3) as the case may be, for a specified period.
10. **Section 25C to apply (Section 25M(10)):** The provisions of Section 25C (other than the second proviso thereto) are applicable to cases of layoff referred to in this section.

If alternative employment offered: For the purposes of this section, a workman is not treated to be laid off by an employer if the employer offers any alternative employment (which in the opinion of the employer does not call for any special skill or previous experience and can be done by the workman)

1. In the same establishment from which he has been laid off or
2. In any other establishment belonging to the same employer, situated in the same town or village, or situated within such distance from the establishment to which he belongs that the transfer will not involve undue hardship to the workman.

For the application of this provision, the wages which would normally have been paid to the workman, the same are required to be offered for the alternative appointment also.

Conditions Precedent to Retrenchment of Workmen (Section 25N)

1. **Three months' notice and prior permission of the appropriate government (Section 25N(1)):** A workman employed in any industrial establishment to which Chapter V-B applies and who has

been in continuous service for not less than 1 year under an employer cannot be retrenched by that employer until,

a. Three months' notice in writing is given to the employee, indicating the reasons for retrenchment and the period of notice has expired, or the workman has been paid in lieu of such notice, wages for the period of the notice; and
b. On an application made in this behalf, the employer has obtained prior permission of the appropriate government or such authority as may be specified by that government by notification in the Official Gazette.

2. **Application to retrench a workman (Section 25N(2)):** An employer intending to retrench the workmen has to make an application in the prescribed manner under Subsection (1) stating clearly the reasons to seek permission for the intended retrenchment. A copy of such application is also to be served simultaneously on the workmen concerned in the prescribed manner.
3. **Communication of order to the employer and workmen (Section 25N(3)):** After receiving the application for permission under Subsection (1) or Subsection (3), the appropriate government or the specified authority must conduct an enquiry. The appropriate government or the specified authority must give a reasonable opportunity of being heard to the employer, the workmen concerned and the persons interested in such retrenchment. Having regard to the genuineness and adequacy of the reasons for such retrenchment, the interests of the workmen and all other relevant factors, the appropriate government may grant or refuse to grant such permission. The reasons for such order are to be recorded in writing, and a copy of such order is to be communicated to the employer and the workmen.
4. **Presumption of permission (Section 25N(4)):** If the employer after making an application for permission under Subsection (1) or Subsection (3) does not receive the order granting or refusing to grant permission within a period of 60 days from the date on which such application is made, the permission applied for is deemed to have been granted on the expiration of the said period of 60 days.
5. **Order binding on all the parties (Section 25N(5)):** Subject to the provisions of Subsection (6), an order of the appropriate government or the specified authority granting or refusing to grant permission is final and binding on all the parties concerned. It remains in force for 1 year from the date of such order.
6. **Review of order (Section 25N(6)):** The appropriate government or the specified authority may, either on its own motion or on the application made by the employer or any workman, review its order granting or refusing to grant permission under Subsection (4) or refer the matter or, as the case may be, cause it to be referred to a Tribunal for adjudication. On such reference, a Tribunal must pass an award within a period of 30 days from the date of such reference.
7. **Illegal retrenchment (Section 25N(7)):** A retrenchment is deemed to be illegal from the date on which the workmen had been retrenched, where
   a. No application for permission under Subsection (1) is made, or
   b. Where no application for permission under Subsection (3) is made within the period specified therein, or
   c. Where the permission for any retrenchment has been refused.

   In case of illegal retrenchment, the workmen are entitled to all the benefits under any law for the time being in force as if they had not been retrenched.
8. **Exemption (Section 25N(8)):** If the appropriate government is satisfied that owing to such exceptional circumstances as accident in the establishment or death of the employer or the like, it

is necessary so to do, it may exempt the employer of such establishment from the application of the provisions of Subsection (1) or Subsection (3) as the case may be, for a specified period.

9. **Compensation in case of permission for retrenchment (Section 25N(9)):** If the permission for retrenchment has been granted under Subsection (3) or where permission for retrenchment is deemed to be granted under Subsection (4), every workman who is employed in that establishment immediately before the date of application for permission under this section is entitled to receive, at the time of retrenchment, compensation which is equivalent to 15 days' average pay for every completed year of continuous service or any part thereof in excess of 6 months.

Penalty for illegal layoff and retrenchment (Section 25Q): Any employer who contravenes the provisions of Section 25M or Section 25N is punishable with imprisonment for a term which may extend to 1 month, or with fine which may extend to ₹1,000, or with both.

Let us discuss a case (Case 13.9) to differentiate between a genuine closure of business and retrenchment.

Case 13.9: *Workmen of The Indian Leaf Tobacco ... v. Management of The Indian Leaf*, 1970[11]

The Indian Leaf Tobacco (the respondent company) was an associate of the Imperial Tobacco Company Ltd., and the main business carried on by the respondent company was that of purchasing tobacco of all varieties and qualities, stemming, grading and packing of tobacco and supplying it to the Imperial Tobacco Co. The respondent company also used to export the tobacco to various foreign countries in the world. It had been carrying on this business for about 40 years and handled almost 35% of the tobacco grown in the state of Andhra Pradesh. For the work of stemming, grading and packing tobacco, the respondent company had two factories, one at Anaparty in East Godavari District and the other at Chirala in Guntur District. In connection with this business, the respondent company, in the year 1962, was maintaining 21 depots where, according to the workmen (the appellants), it was carrying on the work of collecting tobacco. But the respondent company's case was that the principal work done at these depots was that of handling the tobacco purchased at other places and only included the work of purchasing tobacco on a small scale.

On 16 August 1963, the respondent company issued a notice to the Union of the appellant workmen that 8 out of 21 depots mentioned therein would be closed down with effect from 30 September 1963. Thereafter, an industrial dispute was raised by the workmen, which related to the closure of these eight depots, as well as to a number of other demands, including revision of basic wages and dearness allowance, additional discomfort allowance and so on.

Being unhappy with the action of the respondent company, the workmen pleaded for the relief and compensation granted for retrenchment. They argued that the terminated workmen must be re-employed. They also challenged the closure of business and termed the termination as illegal retrenchment. On the other hand, the respondent company argued that the closure is stoppage of the activity or business of the company and such stoppage is an act of management which is entirely in the discretion of the company. No Industrial Tribunal can interfere with the discretion exercised in such a matter, or can have the power to direct the company to continue a part of the business which it had decided to shut down or direct it to reopen a closed depot or branch.

[11] *Workmen of the Indian Leaf Tobacco ... v. Management of The Indian Leaf*, 1970 AIR 860, 1969 SCR (2) 282.

Discussion Point

Whether the closure of business was genuine or was it a retrenchment. What relief or compensation could be granted to the workmen?

Judgement and Explanation

It was held that in the above-stated circumstances all that the workmen could claim was compensation for loss of their service and, in that respect, the workmen had already received adequate compensation. The Industrial Tribunal came to the finding that the closure of these depots was real and genuine. If the same business had been continued, though under a different guise, the claim of the workmen not to be retrenched could possibly be considered by the Tribunal; but, on the finding that there was a genuine closure of the business that used to be carried on at the depots, no question could arise of the retrenchment being set aside by the Tribunal. It was further stated in that the Tribunal could not ask the company to re-employ or reinstate the workmen, because there was no business for which the workmen could be required.

Procedure for Closing Down an Undertaking (Section 25O)

Application for the permission to close down an undertaking (Section 25O(1)): An employer intending to close down an undertaking of an industrial establishment to which Chapter V-B, must make an application to the appropriate government for prior permission. The application is to be made at least 90 days before the date on which the intended closure is to become effective and it must clearly state the reasons for the intended closure of the undertaking. A copy of such application has also to be served simultaneously on the representatives of the workmen in the prescribed manner:

In is to be noted that this subsection does not apply to an undertaking set up for the construction of buildings, bridges, roads, canals, dams or for other construction work.

Communication of order to the employer and workmen (Section 25O(2)): After receiving the application for permission under Subsection (1), the appropriate government must conduct an enquiry and provide a reasonable opportunity of being heard to the employer, the workmen concerned and the persons interested in such closure. Having regard to

1. The genuineness and adequacy of the reasons for such closure,
2. The interests of the workmen and
3. All other relevant factors,

the appropriate government may grant or refuse to grant such permission for closing down the undertaking. The reasons for such order are to be recorded in writing, and a copy of such order is to be communicated to the employer and the workmen.

Presumption of permission (Section 25O(3)): If the employer after making an application for permission under Subsection (1) does not receive the order granting or refusing to grant permission within a period of 60 days from the date on which such application is made, the permission applied for is deemed to have been granted on the expiration of the said period of 60 days.

Order binding on all the parties (Section 25O(4)): An order of the appropriate government granting or refusing to grant permission is final and binding on all the parties concerned. It remains in force for 1 year from the date of such order.

Review of order (Section 25O(5)): The appropriate government, either on its own motion or on the application made by the employer or any workman, reviews its order granting or refusing to grant permission under Subsection (3) or refers the matter or, as the case may be, cause it to be referred to a Tribunal for adjudication. On such reference, a Tribunal must pass an award within a period of 30 days from the date of such reference.

Illegal closure (Section 25O(6)): A closure is deemed to be illegal from the date of closure, where

1. Where no application for permission under Subsection (3) is made within the period specified therein, or
2. Where the permission for any closure has been refused.

In case of illegal closure, the workmen are entitled to all the benefits under any law for the time being in force as if the undertaking had not been closed.

Exemption (Section 25O(7)): If the appropriate government is satisfied that owing to such exceptional circumstances as accident in the establishment or death of the employer or the like, it is necessary so to do, it may exempt the employer of such establishment from the application of the provisions of Subsection (1) or Subsection (3) as the case may be, for a specified period.

Compensation in case of permission for closing down an undertaking (Section 25O(8)): If the permission for closure has been granted under Subsection (2) or where permission for retrenchment is deemed to be granted under Subsection (3), every workman who is employed in that establishment immediately before the date of application for permission under this section is entitled to receive, at the time of closure, compensation which is equivalent to 15 days' average pay for every completed year of continuous service or any part thereof in excess of 6 months.

Penalty for closure (Section 25R): Any employer who contravenes the provision of Section 25M or Section 25N is punishable with imprisonment for a term which may extend to 1 month, or with fine which may extend to ₹1,000, or with both.

In a similar manner, any employer who contravenes an order refusing to grant permission to close down an undertaking under Subsection (2) of Section 25-0 or a direction given under Section 25P is punishable with imprisonment for a term which may extend to 1 year or fine which may extend to ₹5,000, or with both. Where the contravention continuous further, the fine may extend to ₹2,000 for every day till the contravention continues after the conviction.

Let us discuss a case (Case 3.10) to get further insights of penalty provisions and relief available under the Act.

Case 13.10: *Calcutta Chemical Co. Ltd. And ... v. D.K. Barman and Anr*, 1969[12]

The Calcutta Chemical Company Limited had its head office in Calcutta. Mr Barman was employed as a salesman in the Patna branch of the Company. He was employed on 28 August 1961. According to Mr Barman's statement he fell ill and applied for 3 days' sick leave from 8 September 1964 to 10 September

[12] *Calcutta Chemical Co. Ltd. And ... vs. D.K. Barman and Anr.*, AIR 1969 Pat 371, 1969 (17) BLJR 510.

1964. He extended his leave up to 12 September 1964 supported by a medical certificate. The Governing Director of the Company wrote a letter dated 10 September 1964, refusing the prayer for leave made by Barman by his letter dated 8 September 1964. Explanation was also asked for, and he was prohibited from resuming his duties till the matter was decided. Barman's case was that he submitted his explanation on 12 September 1964 and prayed for resumption of his duties on the expiry of his leave. He received its reply on 16 September 1964 whereby his service was terminated from 8 September 1964. He was offered 1 month's pay in lieu of notice.

Mr Barman further stated that he had sent a letter on 26 September 1964 to the management enquiring the authority and the reasons for his dismissal, but he received no reply. Subsequently Mr Barman filed a petition under Section 26 of the Act.

The company, on receipt of the notice of the petition filed by the employee (Mr Barman), filed two written statements in the court. In the statements, the respondent company stated that the work of Barman was never satisfactory. He neglected to carry out the instructions of the management while on tour by not submitting daily business reports, weekly account, arrival and departure reports and stock returns. He retained heavy cash balances. He drew daily allowances from the 10 to 14 January, 1963 on false report, a fact that he admitted in a written letter, at an enquiry. Reports of misappropriation were received against Barman in July 1964 and it was found that Barman had taken some stock to his home which was declared to be damaged but was not returned. After the enquiry Barman returned those articles and they were entered in the Stock Register. These facts were admitted by Barman in a written statement signed by him. The company further submitted that Mr Barman was to go on tour on 9 September 1964, but he absented himself and was found absent from his house. He sent his application for leave on the grounds of illness which was reported to be a pretending illness, as he was found moving in the town. The management, therefore, was justified in both its orders in terminating the service of Barman.

Mr Barman denied all the charges levelled against him. He pleaded that if he was really guilty of allegedly gross misconduct, he must have been charge-sheeted. On the contrary, he was given several special increments for his good service. He submitted that the statements talked about were written by him under coercion and intimidation and at dictation. He alleged that sometimes some articles were left in the van due to short delivery and those used to be returned to the purchaser in the next trip.

The Labour Court held that the Governing Director had no reasonable cause for terminating the service of or dismissing Barman from 8 September 1964. Hence, the Court directed his reinstatement from 8 September 1964 with all the benefits under the terms and conditions of his service, excepting his salary and any special emolument. The Court has also awarded him compensation in the shape of his 6 months' pay at the undisputed rate of ₹189 per month which he was drawing on 8 September 1964.

The company feeling aggrieved by the order of the Labour Court, preferred Civil Revision and requested to reconsider the order of reinstatement under Section 26(5) of the Act, pronounced by the Labour Court.

Discussion Point

Was the relief of reinstatement under Section 26(5) of the Act awarded by the Labour Court to Mr Barman justified and appropriate in the above-mentioned circumstances?

Judgement and Explanation

It was held that the relief of reinstatement given to the employee was to be set aside. The services of Mr Barman would be deemed to had been dispensed with not from 9 September 1964 but from 14 September 1964, on and from which date, in view of the finding of the Labour Court that the services were dispensed with without reasonable cause, the employee would get by way of compensation 6 months" pay at the undisputed rate of ₹189 per month which he was drawing at that time. The court clarified in its judgement that the order of reinstatement is not to follow in all cases mechanically. Mr Barman was not an employee, in whose case an order of reinstatement could be or should have been made. The past record of Mr Barman, the nature of his alleged stated lapse and the grounds on which the order of the management was set aside were also relevant factors for consideration.

Thus, it is clear that even in cases under the Industrial Disputes Act, they may not follow in certain cases. While, so ordering, the tribunal is expected to be inspired by a sense of fair play towards the employee on the one hand and considerations of discipline in the concern on the other.

LO10: Unfair Labour Practices (Chapter V-C)

The Amendment Act, 1982, introduced Chapter V-C and added two Sections 25T and 25U. These Sections restrict certain unfair trade practices at the end of employers and their union as well as employees and their union. The term 'unfair trade practice' has already been explained in the chapter. There is a provision of punishment for the violation of these Sections. Fifth Schedule lists the unfair labour practices at the end of employer and employee.

Fifth Schedule

Unfair Trade Practices (Section 2(ra))

1. **On the part of employers and trade unions of employers**
   a. To interfere with, restrain from, or coerce, workmen in the exercise of their right to organize, form, join or assist a trade union or to engage in concerted activities for the purposes of collective bargaining or other mutual aid or protection, that is to say:
      i. Threatening workmen with discharge or dismissal, if they join a trade union.
      ii. Threatening a lockout or closure, if a trade union is organized.
      iii. Granting wage increase to workmen at crucial periods of trade union organization, with a view to undermining the efforts of the trade union at organization.
   b. To dominate, interfere with or contribute support, financial or otherwise, to any trade union, that is to say:
      i. An employer taking an active interest in organizing a trade, union of his workmen.
      ii. An employer showing partiality or granting favour to one of several trade unions attempting to organize his workmen or to its members, where such a trade union is not a recognized trade union.
   c. To establish employer-sponsored trade unions of workmen.
   d. To encourage or discourage membership in any trade union by discriminating against any workman, that is to say:
      i. Discharging or punishing a workman, because he urged other workmen to join or organize a trade union.
      ii. Discharging or dismissing a workman for taking part in any strike (not being a strike which it deemed to be an illegal strike under this Act).
      iii. Changing seniority rating of workmen because of trade union activities.
      iv. Refusing to promote workmen to higher posts on account of their trade union activities.

v. Giving unmerited promotions to certain workmen with a view to creating discord among other workmen, or to undermine the strength of their trade union.
vi. Discharging office bearers or active members of the trade union on account of their trade union activities.

e. To discharge or dismiss workmen
i. By way of victimization.
ii. Not in good faith, but in the colourable exercise of the employer's rights.
iii. By falsely implicating a workman in a criminal case on false evidence or on concocted evidence.
iv. For patently false reasons.
v. On untrue or trumped up allegations of absence without leave.
vi. In utter disregard of the principles of natural justice in the conduct of domestic enquiry or with undue haste.
vii. For misconduct of a minor or technical character, without having any regard to the nature of the particular misconduct or the past record of service of the workman, thereby leading to a disproportionate punishment.

f. To abolish the work of a regular nature being done by workmen, and to give such work to contractors as a measure of breaking a strike.
g. To transfer a workman mala fide from one place to another, under the guise of following management policy.
h. To insist upon individual workmen, who are on a legal strike to sign a good conduct bond, as a precondition to allowing them to resume work.
i. To show favourites or partiality to one set of workers regardless of merit.
j. To employ workmen as 'badlis', casuals or temporaries and to continue them as such for years, with the object of depriving them of the status and privileges of permanent workmen.
k. To discharge or discriminate against any workman for filing charges or testifying against an employer in any enquiry or proceeding relating to any industrial dispute.
l. To recruit workmen during a strike which is not an illegal strike.
m. Failure to implement award, settlement or agreement.
n. To indulge in acts of force or violence.
o. To refuse to bargain collectively, in good faith with the recognized trade unions.
p. Proposing or continuing a lockout deemed to be illegal under this Act.

2. **On the part of workmen and trade unions of workmen**

a. To advise or actively support or instigate any strike deemed to be illegal under this Act.
b. To coerce workmen in the exercise of their right to self-organization or to join a trade union or refrain from joining any trade union, that is to say
i. For a trade union or its members to picketing in such a manner that non-striking workmen are physically debarred from entering the work places.
ii. To indulge in acts of force or violence or to hold out threats of intimidation in connection with a strike against non-striking workmen or against managerial staff.

c. For a recognized union to refuse to bargain collectively in good faith with the employer.
d. To indulge in coercive activities against certification of bargaining representative.
e. To stage, encourage or instigate such forms of coercive actions as wilful 'go slow', squatting on the work premises after working hours or 'gherao' of any of the members of the managerial or other staff.

f. To stage demonstrations at the residences of the employers or the managerial staff members.
g. To incite or indulge in wilful damage to employer's property connected with the industry.
h. To indulge in acts of force or violence or to hold out threats of intimidation against any workman with a view to prevent him from attending work.

Prohibition of Unfair Labour Practices (Section 25T)

Section 25T of the Act prohibits any employer or workmen or a trade union, whether registered under Trade Union's Act, 1926, or not, from committing any unfair labour practice.

Penalty for the Committing Unfair Labour Practices (Section 25U)

Any person who commits any unfair labour practice is punishable with imprisonment for a term which may extend to 6 months or with fine which may extend to ₹1,000 or with both.

Penalties (Chapter VI)

The act provides for the penalty for different offences under Sections 26 to 31. Sections 26 to 30 have already been discussed in the chapter at appropriate places.

Penalty for General Offences (Section 31(2)): Section 31(2) of the Act states that a person who contravenes any of the provisions of this Act or any rule made there under is punishable with fine which may extend to ₹1,000, if no other penalty is elsewhere provided by or under this Act for such contravention.

LO11: Miscellaneous Provisions of the Act (Chapter VII)

Offences by Companies (Section 32)

Section 32 of the Act deals with the offences by the companies and provides that where a person committing an offence under this Act is a company, or other body corporate, or an association of persons (whether incorporated or not), every director, manager, secretary, agent or other officer or person concerned with the management thereof is deemed to be guilty of such offence. However, the penalty under this section is not applicable if such person is able to prove that the offence was committed without his knowledge or consent.

Conditions of Service to Remain Unchanged during Pendency of Proceedings (Section 33)

No alteration of conditions for service during the pendency of the proceedings (Section 33(1)): During the pendency of any conciliation proceeding before a conciliation officer or a Board or of any proceeding before an arbitrator or a Labour Court or Tribunal or National Tribunal in respect of an industrial dispute, an employer must not

1. In regard to any matter connected with the dispute, alter, to the prejudice of the workmen concerned in such dispute, the conditions of service applicable to them immediately before the commencement of such proceeding; or
2. For any misconduct connected with the dispute, discharge or punish, whether by dismissal or otherwise, any workmen concerned in such dispute, save with the express permission in writing of the authority before which the proceeding is pending.

Standing Order (Section 33(2)): During the pendency of any such proceeding in respect of an industrial dispute, the employer may, in accordance with standing orders applicable to a workman concerned in such dispute or, where there are no such standing orders, in accordance with the terms of the contract, whether express or implied, between him and the workman:

1. Alter, in regard to any matter not connected with the dispute, the conditions of service applicable to that workman immediately before the commencement of such proceeding; or
2. For any misconduct not connected with the dispute, discharge or punish, whether by dismissal or otherwise, that workman.

It is further provided that an employer must not discharge or dismiss any such workman, unless he has been paid wages for 1 month and an application has been made by the employer to the authority before which the proceeding is pending for approval of the action taken by the employer.

Protection to protected workman (Section 33(33)): During the pendency of any such proceeding in respect of an industrial dispute, an employer must not take any action against any protected workman concerned in such dispute

1. By altering, to the prejudice of such protected workman, the conditions of service applicable to him immediately before the commencement of such proceeding; or
2. By discharging or punishing, whether by dismissal or otherwise, such protected workman, save with the express permission in writing of the authority before which the proceeding is pending.

Protected workman: Here 'Protected workman', in relation to an establishment, means a workman who, being a member of the executive or other office bearer of a registered trade union connected with the establishment, is recognized as such in accordance with rules made in this behalf.

Number of protected workman (Section 33(4)): So far as number of protected workman in an establishment is concerned, the Act directs that in every establishment, the number of workmen to be recognized as protected workmen for the purposes of Subsection (3) is limited to 1% of the total number of workmen employed therein subject to a minimum number of five protected workmen and a maximum number of 100 protected workmen. For the purpose of the Subsection, the appropriate government has the power to frame rules providing for:

1. The distribution of such protected workmen among various trade unions, if any, connected with the establishment and
2. The manner in which the workmen may be chosen and recognized as protected workmen.

Penalty for the contravention of Section 33 (Section 33(1)): An employer who contravenes the provisions of Section 33 of the act is punishable with imprisonment for a term which may extend to 6 months or with fine extendable to ₹100 or both.

Recovery of Money Due from the Employer (Section 33C)

In a case where any money is due to a workman from an employer under a settlement or an award or for layoff or retrenchment, the workman himself or any other person authorized by him in writing in this behalf, or in the case of the death of the workman, his assignee or heirs may, without prejudice to any other mode of recovery, make an application, within 1 year from the date on which the money became due to the workman, to appropriate government for the recovery of money due to him. If the appropriate government is satisfied that any money is due to him, it issues a certificate for that amount to the Collector who must proceed to recover the same in the same manner as an arrear of land revenue.

Computation of money dues to be paid by the employer: The Act directs that if a workman is entitled to receive from the employer any money or any benefit which is capable of being computed in terms of money and if any question arises as to the amount of money due or as to the amount at which such benefit should be computed, then the question must be decided by such Labour Court within a period not exceeding 3 months. However, where the presiding officer of a Labour Court considers it necessary or expedient so to do, he may, for reasons to be recorded in writing, extend such period by such further period as he may think fit.

Cognizance of Offences (Section 34)

It is provided under Section 34 of the Act that no court can take cognizance of any offence punishable under this Act or of the abetment of any such offence, save on complaint made by or under the authority of the appropriate government. It is further clarified that no court inferior to that of a Metropolitan Magistrate or a Judicial Magistrate of the first class is authorized to try any offence punishable under this Act (Section 34(2)).

Protection of Persons (Section 35)

Section 35 of the Act states that a person who refuses to take part or continues to take part in any strike or lockout which is illegal under this Act must not, by reason of such refusal or by reason of any action taken by him under this section, be subject:

1. To expulsion from any trade union or society, or
2. To any fine or penalty, or to deprivation of any right or benefit to which he or his legal representatives would otherwise be entitled, or
3. Be liable to be placed in any respect, either directly or indirectly, under any disability, or
4. At any disadvantage as compared with other members of the union or society, anything to the contrary in rules of a trade union or society notwithstanding.

Subsection 35(2) further provides that nothing in the rules of a trade union or society requiring the settlement of dispute in any manner applies to any proceeding for enforcing any right or exemption secured by this section, and in any such proceeding the Civil Court may, in lieu of ordering a person who has been expelled from membership of a trade union or society to be restored to membership, order that he be paid out of the funds of the trade union or society such sum by way of compensation or damages as that Court thinks just.

Representation of Parties (Section 36)

Representation of workman (Section 36(1)): As provided under this section, a workman who is a party to a dispute is entitled to be represented in any proceeding under this Act by:

1. Any member of the executive or other office bearer of a registered trade union of which he is a member.
2. Any member of the executive or other office bearer of a federation of trade unions to which the trade union referred to in clause (a) is affiliated.
3. Where the worker is not a member of any trade union by any member of the executive or other office bearer of any trade union connected with, or by any other workman employed in the industry in which the worker is employed and authorized in such manner as may be prescribed.

Representation of employer (Section 36(2)): An employer who is a party to a dispute is entitled to be represented in any proceeding under this Act by

1. An officer of an association of employer of which he is a member.
2. An officer of a federation of associations of employers to which the association referred to in clause (a) is, affiliated.
3. Where the employer is not a member of any association of employers, by an officer of any association of employers connected with, or by any other employer engaged in, the industry in which the employer is engaged and authorized in such manner as may be prescribed.

Restriction on representation by legal practitioner (Section 36(3)): The act restricts any party to a dispute from being represented by a legal practitioner in any conciliation proceedings under this Act or in any proceedings before a Court. However, the Act permits, with the consent of the other parties to the proceeding and with the leave of the Labour Court, Tribunal or National Tribunal, as the case may be, the representation of parties to the dispute by a legal practitioner in any proceeding before a Labour Court, Tribunal or National Tribunal.

Power to Remove Difficulties (Section 36A)

If, in the opinion of the appropriate government, any difficulty or doubt arises as to the interpretation of any provision of an award or settlement, the question may be referred to such Labour Court, Tribunal or National Tribunal as it may think fit (Section 36A(1)). The Labour Court, Tribunal or National Tribunal to which such question is referred must give the parties an opportunity of being heard before deciding such question. Here, the decision pronounced by The Labour Court, Tribunal or National Tribunal is final and binding on all such parties (Section 36A(2)).

Power to Exempt (Section 36B)

The appropriate government is empowered to exempt conditionally or unconditionally from all or any of the provisions of this Act, any industrial establishment or undertaking or any class of industrial establishments or undertakings carried on by a department of that government, if it is satisfied in relation to such establishment that adequate provisions exist for the investigation and settlement of industrial disputes in respect of workmen employed in such establishment or undertaking or class of establishments or undertakings. Such exemption is to be notified in the Official Gazette.

Protection of Action Taken in Good Faith (Section 37)

No suit, prosecution or other legal proceeding shall lie against any person for anything which is in good faith done or intended to be done in pursuance of this Act or any rules made there under.

Power to Make Rules (Section 38)

The appropriate government has power to, subject to the condition of previous publication, make rules for the purpose of giving effect to the provisions of this Act (Section 38(1)). The rules made under this section may provide that a contravention thereof shall be punishable with fine not exceeding ₹50 (Section 38(2)).

It is to be noted that every rule made by the appropriate government under this section is to be laid as soon as may be after it is made, before each House of Parliament while it is in session for a total period of 30 days. This period may be comprised in one session or in two or more successive sessions. If, before the expiry of the session, both Houses agree in making any modification in the rule or both Houses agree that the rule should not be made, the rule is effective only in such modified form or be of not effective at all, as the case may be. However, any such modification or annulment has to be without prejudice to the validity of anything previously done under that rule (Section 38(5)).

Summary

1. The principal objective of the Industrial Disputes Act is to secure industrial peace and harmony by providing machinery and procedure for the investigation and settlement of industrial disputes.
2. An 'industrial dispute' is any dispute or difference between employers and employers, or between employers and workmen, or between workmen and workmen, which is connected with the employment or non-employment or the terms of employment or with the conditions of labour, of any person.
3. Layoff means putting aside workmen temporarily, and the duration of layoff cannot be for a period longer than the period of emergency.
4. Mere stoppage of work does not come within the meaning of strike unless it can be shown that such stoppage of work was a concerted action for the enforcement of an industrial demand.
5. A new Chapter II-B was added to the Act by Industrial Disputes (Amendment) Act, 1982, whereby a new Section 9C was introduced dealing with the references of certain individual disputes to grievance settlement authorities.
6. The Act provides various modes of settlement of industrial disputes and those may be classified under three heads; Conciliation, Adjudication and Arbitration.

7. The authorities that make use of conciliation on the sole method of settlement of disputes are as follows: works committee, conciliation officer and board of conciliation.
8. The works committee deals with the workers problem arising day to day in the industrial establishment.
9. Conciliation officers are charged with the duty to hold conciliatory proceedings for the purpose of bringing about a fair and amicable settlement of any industrial dispute.
10. According to Section 5 of the Act, as occasion arises, the appropriate government is also authorized to constitute a board of conciliation for promoting the settlement of an industrial dispute.
11. The Court of Inquiry looks into only matters which are referred to it by the government and submits its report to the government ordinarily within certain period from the date of reference.
12. The appropriate government may, by notification in the Official Gazette, constitute one or more Labour Courts for the adjudication of industrial disputes relating to any of matter specified in the Second Schedule or for performing such other function as may be assigned to them under the Act.
13. The purpose of creating an Industrial Tribunal was to introduce compulsory adjudication where voluntary negotiation fails to settle the dispute and the 'appropriate government' believes that the matter is grave enough to be referred to a tribunal.
14. National Tribunals are set up by the central government to adjudicate upon the industrial disputes involving questions of national importance industrial establishments situated in more than one state.
15. Section 9 of the Industrial Disputes Act aims to make immune any order of the appointment made under Sections 5 to 7 of the Act, from being called in question.
16. An employer who proposes to effect any change in the conditions of service applicable to any workman in respect of any matter specified in the Fourth Schedule cannot effect such change without giving to the workmen likely to be affected by such change a notice in the prescribed manner.
17. The Act states that when an industrial dispute has been referred to a National Tribunal under this section, the appropriate government is empowered to prohibit the continuance of any strike or lockout in connection with such dispute which may be in existence on the date of the reference.
18. Where any industrial dispute exists or is apprehended and the employer and the workman agree to refer the dispute to arbitration, they may refer the dispute to arbitration.
19. Where an industrial dispute has been referred to arbitration and a notification has been issued, the appropriate government is authorized to prohibit the continuance of any strike or lockout in connection with such dispute.
20. If the appropriate government is of the opinion that any industrial dispute exists or apprehended, it may, at any time, refer the dispute to a board of conciliation, Court of Inquiry or a Tribunal.
21. In the case where the parties to an industrial dispute apply in the prescribed manner, whether jointly or separately, for a reference of the dispute to a Board, court, Labour Court, Tribunal or National Tribunal, the appropriate government, after being satisfied that the persons applying represent the majority of each party, makes the reference accordingly.
22. An order referring an industrial dispute to a Labour Court, Tribunal or National Tribunal under this section must specify the period within which such Labour Court, Tribunal or National Tribunal has to submit its award on such dispute to the appropriate government.

23. No proceedings before a Labour Court, Tribunal or National Tribunal will lapse merely on the grounds that any period specified under this subsection had expired without such proceedings being completed.
24. This section provides that where any industrial dispute exists or is apprehended and the employer and the workman agree to refer the dispute to arbitration, they may refer the dispute to arbitration.
25. The report of a Board or court has to be in writing and shall be signed by all the members of the Board or court, as the case may be.
26. An award (including an arbitration award) becomes enforceable on the expiry of 30 days from the date of its publication under Section 17.
27. In the case where a Labour Court, Tribunal or National Tribunal by its award directs reinstatement of any workman and the employer prefers any proceedings against such award in a High Court or the Supreme Court, the employer is liable to pay such workman, during the period of pendency of such proceedings, full wages last drawn by him.
28. A settlement arrived between employer and employee by agreement except that in the course of conciliation proceeding is binding on both the parties.
29. A settlement comes into operation on such date as is agreed upon by the parties to the dispute.
30. An award remains in operation for a period of 1 year from the date on which the award becomes enforceable under Section 17A.
31. A conciliation proceeding will commenced on the date on which a notice of strike or lock-out under Section 22 is received by the conciliation officer or on the date of the order referring the dispute to a Board, as the case may be.
32. Strike is collective stoppage of work by workmen undertaken to bring pressure upon the employer. It is a spontaneous and concerted withdrawal of workmen from production.
33. Lockout means the closing of a place of employment, or the suspension of work, or the refusal by an employer to continue to employ any number of persons employed by him.
34. A prior warning has to be given to the employer before the workmen go on strike. It is to be noted that a notice for strike remains valid only for 6 weeks.
35. The notice of lockout or strike under this section is not necessary where there is already in existence a strike or, as the case may be, lockout in the public utility service.
36. Where a dispute has been referred to conciliation or adjudication, a strike or lockout in furtherance thereof is not necessary and also inexpedient and thus not permitted.
37. A strike or a lockout will be declared illegal if it is commenced or declared in contravention of Section 22 or Section 23, or is continued in contravention of an order made under Subsection (3) of Section 10 or Subsection (4A) of Section 10A.
38. Layoff means refusal or failure to employ a workman temporarily. During the period of layoff, the employer–employee relationship does not come to an end but is merely suspended during the period of emergency.
39. Retrenchment is the discharge of surplus labour or staff by the employer for any reason whatsoever.
40. The workmen employed by an exempted establishment under Section 25A are not entitled to layoff or retrenchment compensation, and the Tribunal has no right to grant relief on any fanciful notices of social justice.
41. Section 25C of the Act entitles a workman to get compensation from the employer for the period for which he is laid off.

42. The act enjoins upon the employer a duty to maintain a muster roll of workmen notwithstanding that workmen have been laid off.
43. In case the employer proposes to re-employ any person, he is under an obligation to offer first priority to the persons who have been retrenched.
44. Section 25FFF of the act deals with a situation when the ownership or management of an undertaking is transferred.
45. An employer who intends to close down an undertaking has to serve, at least 60 days before the date on which the intended closure, on the appropriate government.
46. The Act has made the provisions for compensation to the workmen in case of closing down of an undertaking.
47. If the undertaking is closed down on account of unavoidable circumstances beyond the control of the employer, the compensation to be paid to the workman under clause (b) of Section 25F must not exceed his average pay for 3 months.
48. The provisions of this chapter are applicable to an industrial establishment (not being an establishment of a seasonal character or in which work is performed only intermittently) employing not less than 100 workmen on an average per working day for the preceding 12 months.
49. A workman (other than a 'badli' workman or a casual workman) whose name is borne on the muster rolls of an industrial establishment to which this Chapter V-B applies cannot be laid off by employer except with the prior permission of the appropriate government.
50. In case of illegal layoff, the workmen are entitled to all the benefits under any law for the time being in force as if they had not been laid off.
51. An employer intending to retrench the workmen has to make an application in the prescribed manner under Subsection (1) stating clearly the reasons to seek permission for the intended retrenchment.
52. Any employer who contravenes the provisions of Section 25M or Section 25N is punishable with imprisonment for a term which may extend to 1 month, or with fine which may extend to ₹1,000, or with both.
53. An employer intending to close down an undertaking of an industrial establishment to which Chapter V-B must make an application to the appropriate government for prior permission.
54. Any employer who contravenes the provision of Section 25M or Section 25N is punishable with imprisonment for a term which may extend to 1 month, or with fine which may extend to ₹1,000, or with both.
55. The Amendment Act, 1982, introduced Chapter V-C and added two Sections 25T and 25U. These Sections restrict certain unfair trade practices at the end of employers and their union as well as employees and their union.
56. Section 25T of the Act prohibits any employer or workmen or a trade union, whether registered under Trade Union's Act, 1926 or not, from committing any unfair labour practice.
57. Any person who commits any unfair labour practice is punishable with imprisonment for a term which may extend to 6 months or with fine which may extend to ₹1,000 or with both.
58. Where a person committing an offence under this Act is a company, or other body corporate, or an association of persons (whether incorporated or not), every director, manager, secretary, agent, or other officer or person concerned with the management thereof is deemed to be guilty of such offence.

59. During the pendency of any conciliation proceeding before a conciliation officer or a Board or of any proceeding before an arbitrator or a Labour Court or Tribunal or National Tribunal in respect of an industrial dispute, an employer must not alter the service conditions of a workman.
60. An employer who contravenes the provisions of Section 33 of the Act is punishable with imprisonment for a term which may extend to 6 months or with fine extendable to ₹100 or both.
61. No court can take cognizance of any offence punishable under this Act or of the abetment of any such offence, save on complaint made by or under the authority of the appropriate government.
62. The Act restricts any party to a dispute from being represented by a legal practitioner in any conciliation proceedings under this Act or in any proceedings before a Court.
63. If, in the opinion of the appropriate government, any difficulty or doubt arises as to the interpretation of any provision of an award or settlement, the question may be referred to such Labour Court, Tribunal or National Tribunal as it may think fit.
64. The appropriate government has power to, subject to the condition of previous publication, make rules for the purpose of giving effect to the provisions of this Act.

Multiple Choice Questions

1. Average pay in the case of workmen in the case of monthly paid workman is the average of monthly wages payable in ____________.
   a. Two complete calendar months
   b. Three complete calendar months
   c. Six complete calendar months
   d. Twelve complete calendar months

2. ____________ is an interim or a final determination of any industrial dispute or of any question relating thereto by any Labour Court, Industrial Tribunal or National Industrial Tribunal.
   a. Wages
   b. Compensation
   c. Award
   d. None of the above

3. ____________ is defined as the failure, refusal or inability of an employer on account of shortage of coal, power or raw materials or the accumulation of stocks or the breakdown of machinery.
   a. Layoff
   b. Lockout
   c. Retrenchment
   d. Closure of the undertaking

4. ____________ is the temporary closing of a place of employment, or the suspension of work, or the refusal by an employer to continue to employ any number of persons employed by him.
   a. Layoff
   b. Lockout
   c. Retrenchment
   d. Closure of the undertaking

5. ____________ under the Act means the termination by the employer of the service of a workman for any reason whatsoever otherwise than as a punishment indicated by way of disciplinary action.
   a. Layoff
   b. Lockout
   c. Retrenchment
   d. Closure of the undertaking

6. The employer of every industrial establishment employing ______ workmen/employees have been employed on any day in the preceding 12 months, must provide for a grievance settlement authority for settlement of industrial disputes.
   a. 500 or more
   b. 250 or more
   c. 100 or more
   d. 50 or more
7. ______ is/are set up by the central government to adjudicate upon the industrial disputes involving questions of national importance in industrial establishments situated in more than one state.
   a. National Tribunals
   b. Court of Inquiry
   c. Industrial Tribunals
   d. Board of conciliation
8. An award (including an arbitration award) becomes enforceable on the expiry of ______ from the date of its publication under Section 17.
   a. 100 days
   b. 60 days
   c. 45 days
   d. 30 days
9. If the dispute relates to any matter specified in the ______ and is not likely to affect more than 100 workmen, the appropriate government is empowered to make a reference to a Labour Court.
   a. Second Schedule
   b. Third Schedule
   c. Fifth Schedule
   d. Both (a) and (b)
10. A strike or a lockout will be declared illegal if ______.
    a. It is commenced or declared in contravention of Section 22 or Section 23; or
    b. It is continued in contravention of an order made under Subsection (3) of Section 10 or Subsection (4A) of Section 10A.
    c. Both (a) and (b)
    d. Neither (a) nor (b)

True/False Questions

1. To be an industry for the purpose of the Industrial Disputes Act, the presence of profit motive or gainful objective is quite relevant factor, be the venture in the public, joint, private or other sector.
2. Retrenchment includes termination of the service of a workman as a result of the non-renewal of the contract of employment between the employer and the workman concerned on its expiry or of such contract being terminated.
3. Mere stoppage of work does not come within the meaning of strike unless it can be shown that such stoppage of work was a concerted action for the enforcement of an industrial demand.
4. Court of Inquiry looks into only matters which are referred to it by government and submits its report to the government ordinarily within certain period from the date of reference.

5. Even if an industrial dispute has been referred to a Labour Court, the appropriate government cannot prohibit the continuance of any strike or lockout in connection with such dispute which may be in existence on the date of the reference.
6. An award (including arbitration award) becomes enforceable on the expiry of 30 days from the date of its publication under Section 17.
7. Once the parties have chosen the remedy under Section 10A, the government cannot refer the same dispute for adjudication under Section 10. If any such reference is made, it is invalid.
8. The notice of lockout or strike is necessary where there is already in existence a strike or lockout in the public utility service.
9. An employer who intends to close down an undertaking has to serve at least 60 days before the date on which the intended closure, on the appropriate government.
10. Termination of the service of a workman on the grounds of continuous illness is considered as retrenchment under the Industrial Disputes Act, 1947.

Descriptive Questions

1. What are the salient features of the Industrial Disputes Act?
2. Write short notes on the following:
   a. Award (Section 2(b))
   b. Industry (Section 2(j))
   c. Settlement (Section 2(p))
3. What is the procedure of making a reference of certain individual disputes to grievance settlement authorities laid down by Section 9C of the Act?
4. Discuss in detail the settlement mechanism followed by the Work Committees constituted under Section 3 of the Act.
5. How does the board of conciliation function to settle the industrial disputes? Discuss in detail.
6. Write in detail the dispute settlement mechanism adopted by Arbitration Machinery constituted under Sections 7 to 9 of the Act.
7. Throw light on the matters specified under Third Schedule where a notice of change in the conditions of service is required?
8. Write a note on the voluntary references of disputes to arbitration under Section 10A.
9. Write short notes on following:
   a. Commencement of Award (Section 17A)
   b. Rejection or modification of the award
   c. Penalty for the Breach of Settlement or Awards (Section 29)
10. What do you mean by a strike? What are the provisions of the Industrial Disputes Act regarding strikes?
11. What is lockout? What are the differences between strike and lockout?
12. What is meant by illegal strikes? What are the effects of illegal strikes?

13. What do you mean by layoff? What are the provisions of the Industrial Disputes Act regarding strikes?
14. How is the term 'retrenchment' defined under the Act? What are the provisions of the Industrial Disputes Act regarding retrenchment?
15. Discuss in detail the provisions dealing with the compensation to workmen in case of transfer of undertaking.
16. What were the two important changes brought by the Industrial Disputes (Amendment) Act, 1976, in the Act? Discuss the application and impact of the introduced sections.
17. Which are the conditions precedent to retrenchment of workmen laid down by Section 25N?
18. Explain the provisions restricting certain unfair trade practices at the end of employers and their union as well as employees and their union.
19. Write short notes on the following:
    a. Recovery of money due from the employer
    b. Protection of persons
    c. Representation of parties

14

CHAPTER

The Industrial Employment (Standing Orders) Act, 1946

LEARNING OBJECTIVES

Upon completing this chapter, the reader would be able to:

LO1. Understand the objectives, scope and important definitions of the Act.
LO2. Learn main provisions of the Act relating to the process of certification of standing orders.
LO3. Know the details of other important provisions relating to standing orders.
LO4. Gain insights of important miscellaneous provisions of the Act.
LO5. Examine the provisions for the offences and penalties under the Act.

Introduction

In the year 1946, the Labour Investigation Committee had observed in its report that an industrial worker had the right to know the terms and conditions under which he was employed and the rules of discipline which he was expected to follow. During that time, in Indian industry, the rules of service were not definitely set out and like all unwritten laws, where they existed, they had been very elastic to suit the convenience of employers. Several large-scale industrial establishments had adopted standing orders and rules to govern the day-to-day relations between the employers and workers, but such standing orders or rules were clearly one-sided. Neither workers' organizations nor the government was generally consulted before these orders were drawn up, and more often than not they had given the employers the upper hand in respect of all disputable points.

It was to abolish these evils that the Industrial Employment (Standing Orders) Act, 1946, was passed to require the employers in industrial establishment to define with sufficient precision the conditions of employment under them and to make the said conditions known to workmen employed by them. Before this Act, there was no legal framework to prevent the employer from having different contracts of employment with workmen that led to confusion and discriminatory treatment.

LO1: Objectives, Scope and Important Definitions of the Act

Objectives

The Industrial Employment (Standing Orders) Bill, 1946, was passed by the legislature, and it received the approval on 23 April 1946. It came on the statute book as the Industrial Employment (Standing Orders) Act, 1946.

The Act was brought into force mainly to standardize the service conditions of the workmen employed in any industrial establishment. The Act aims to ensure uniformity in the service conditions of the employees in industrial establishments so that the employer and the employees know in a clear manner their rights and obligations. The Act requires the employers in industrial establishments to formally define conditions of employment under them and to make the said conditions known to the workmen employed by them.

The main objectives of the Act, other than maintaining a harmonious relationship between the employers and the employees, are to regulate the conditions of recruitment, discharge, disciplinary action, leave, holidays and so on of the workers employed in industrial units/undertakings/establishments.

Scope of the Act

Establishments covered under the Act (Section 1(3)): The Act applies to every industrial establishment which employs 100 or more workmen or were employed on any day of preceding 12 months. The appropriate government, however, is authorized to include other establishments also.

In case of establishments operating from Maharashtra and Gujarat, the words 'one hundred' has been substituted with 'fifty' (see Annexure A).

Exempted establishments: This Act does not apply to an industrial establishment insofar as the workmen employed therein are persons to whom the following rules are applicable:

1. The fundamental and supplementary rules, civil services (classification, control and appeal) rules, civil services (temporary service) rules, revised leave rules, civil service regulations,
2. Civilians in defence services (classification, control and appeal) rules, or
3. Indian Railways Establishment Code or any other rules or regulation that may be notified in this behalf by the appropriate government in the Official Gazette (Section 13B).

Important Definitions

1. **Workers (Section 2(i)):** The Industrial Employment (Standing Orders) Amendment Act (Act 18 of 1982) states that the 'workman' has the meaning assigned to it in clause(s) of Section 2, of the Industrial Disputes Act, 1974.
2. **Certifying officer:** Certifying officer under the Act means a Labour Commissioner or a Regional Labour Commissioner and includes any other officer appointed by the appropriate government, by notification in the Official Gazette, to perform all or any of the functions of a certifying officer as defined under the Act.

3. **Employer:** The Act defines employer as the owner of an industrial establishment to which this Act for the time being applies, and it includes:
   a. In a factory, any person named as manager of the factory under 5[clause (t) of Subsection (1) of Section 7 of the Factories Act, 1948 (63 of 1948)].
   b. In any industrial establishment under the control of any department of any Government of India, the authority appointed by such government in this behalf or, where no authority is so appointed, the head of department.
   c. In any other industrial establishment, any person responsible to the owner for the supervision and control of the industrial establishment.
4. **Industrial establishment:** Under the Act, industrial establishment includes:
   a. An industrial establishment as defined in clause (ii) of Section 2 of the Payment of Wages Act, 1936 (4 of 1936), or
   b. A factory as defined in clause (m) of Section 2 of the Factories Act, 1948 (63 of 1948), or
   c. A railway as defined in clause (4) of Section 2 of the Indian Railways Act, 1890 (9 of 1890), or
   d. The establishment of a person who, for the purpose of fulfilling a contract with the owner of any industrial establishment, employs workmen.
5. **Standing orders (Section 2(g)):** Standing order includes the rules relating to matters set out in the Schedule. These are the rules of conduct for workmen employed in industrial establishments. The schedule to the Act requires that following should be specified in standing orders:
   a. Classification of workmen, that is, temporary, badli, casual, permanent, skilled and so on.
   b. Manner of intimating to workmen working hours, shift working, transfers and so on.
   c. Holidays.
   d. Attendance and late coming rules.
   e. Leave rules.
   f. Leave eligibility and leave conditions.
   g. Closing and reopening of sections of industrial establishment.
   h. Termination of employment, suspension, dismissal and so on for misconduct and acts or omissions which constitute misconduct.
   i. Retirement age.
   j. Means of redressal of workmen against unfair treatment or wrongful termination by employer.
   k. Any other matter that may be prescribed.
   l. Besides, the Act, as amended in 1982, also provides for payment of subsistence allowance to the workmen who are kept under suspension pending domestic enquiry.

Classification of Workmen (Section 2)

The Act classifies the workmen as under:

a. **A permanent workman** is a workman who has been engaged on a permanent basis. Any person who has satisfactorily completed a probationary period of 3 months in the same or another occupation in the industrial establishment, including breaks due to sickness, accident, leave, lockout, strike (not being an illegal strike) or involuntary closure of the establishment, is also treated as a permanent worker.

b. **A probationer** is a workman who is provisionally employed to occupy a permanent vacancy in a post and has not completed 3 months' service therein. In the cases where a permanent employee is employed as a probationer in a new post, he may, at any time during the probationary period of 3 months, be reverted to his old permanent post.
c. **A badli** is a workman who is appointed to the post of a permanent workman or probationer who is temporarily absent from the workplace.
d. **A temporary workman** is a workman who is engaged in work which is of an essentially temporary nature likely to be finished within a limited period.
e. **A casual workman** is a workman whose employment is of a casual nature.
f. **An apprentice** is a learner who is paid an allowance by the employer during the period of his training.

6. **Wages (Section 2(i)):** Wages has the meanings, respectively, assigned to them in clauses (rr) and (s) of Section 2 of the Industrial Disputes Act, 1947.
7. **Trade union (Section 2(h)):** Under the Act, trade union is a trade union for the time being registered under the Indian Trade Unions Act, 1926.

LO2: Procedure for Certification of Standing Orders

Procedure for Submitting the Draft Standing Orders (Section 3)

Section 3 of the Act deals with the procedure for submitting the draft standing orders. It provides that the employer is required to submit to the certifying officer, five copies of the draft standing orders proposed by him for adoption in his industrial establishment within 6 months from the date on which the Act becomes applicable to his industrial establishment. It further provides that there has to be a provision in such draft for every matter set out in the Schedule which may be applicable to the establishment, and where model standing orders have been prescribed, has to be, as far as practicable, in conformity with such model. Thus, the draft standing orders normally provide for the following matters:

1. Classification of workmen, that is, permanent, temporary, apprentices, probationers or badlis.
2. Manner of intimating to workmen the periods and hours of work, holidays, pay days and wage rates.
3. Shift working.
4. Attendance and late coming.
5. Conditions of procedure in applying for and the authority, which may grant leave and holidays.
6. Requirement to enter the premises by certain gates and liability to search.
7. Closing and reopening of sections of the industrial establishment and temporary stoppages of work, and the rights and liabilities of the employer and workmen arising there from.
8. Termination of employment and the notice thereof to be given by employer to the workmen.
9. Suspension or dismissal for misconduct and acts of omission which constitute misconduct;
10. Means of redressal for workmen against unfair treatment or wrongful action by the employer or his agents or servants.
11. Any other matter, which may be prescribed from time to time.
12. The payment of subsistence allowance to the workmen who are kept under suspension pending domestic enquiry (as amended in 1982).

Conditions for Certification (Section 5)

On receipt of the draft, the certifying officer initiates to certify the standing orders, following procedure is laid down in Section 5 of the Act which, inter alia, states that all the registered trade unions, and in the absence of the registered trade unions, five elected representatives of the workmen have to be given an opportunity to raise objections to the proposed draft standing orders.

1. **Matters to be set out in the Schedule:** Section 4 of the Act requires the certifying officer to ensure that there is a provision made in the standing orders for every matter set out in the Schedule applicable to the industrial establishment with the additional matter prescribed by the appropriate government in this regard.
2. **Conformity with the model standing orders:** Where model standing orders have been prescribed, the draft submitted by the employers has to be in conformity with the model standing orders provided under Section 15(2)(b) of the Act.
3. **Fairness and reasonableness of standing order**: Prior to 1956, the certifying officer had no power to go into the question of reasonableness or fairness of the draft standing orders submitted to him by the employers. His role was limited to see that the draft incorporated all matters contained in the Schedule and that it was otherwise certifiable under the Act. This provision did not provide adequate safeguards against unfair provisions, in the standing orders and, therefore, caused great hardship upon workmen. In 1956, the Parliament amended the Act and thereby not only considerably widened the scope of the Act, but also gave a clear expression for the change in legislative policy. The amended Section 4 of the Act imposes a duty upon the certifying officer and appellate authority to adjudicate upon the fairness and reasonableness of the standing orders. If they find some provisions unreasonable, they must refuse to certify the same.

Case 14.1 will provide the insights of the reasonableness of the standing orders drafted by an employer.

Case 14.1: *Western India Match Co. Ltd v. Their Workmen*[1]

Western India Match Co. Ltd, the appellant company, was engaged in the manufacturing and selling of matches in four places in India, including Bareilly, in which there were factories as well as sales offices. In the year 1945, as an incentive to larger production of matches, the company introduced a Production Bonus Scheme which was made applicable to workmen engaged in the factory in making matches as also to those working in the factory office. Subsequently, in the year 1947, the Production Bonus Scheme was withdrawn in its application to the sales office. The workmen of the sales office (clerical staff, salesmen and inspectors of salesmen) made a claim to production bonus pointing out that there should be no discrimination between the employees in the same company.

The workmen contended that there was interdependence of the two activities, namely, manufacture of matches in the factory and their sale by the sales office, inasmuch as the sales office could not exist without the factory. The other argument presented by the workmen was that the factory itself could not conveniently function without a sales organization and the factory used arranged its volume of production in accordance with the programme made from time to time by the sales manager. It was also pointed out that the sales office and the factory had the same banking account, though separate cheque books were maintained and operated upon.

[1] *Western India Match Co. Ltd v. Their Workmen,* 1964 AIR 472, 1964 SCR (3) 560.

The appellant company resisted the claim. It argued that the sales office was entirely independent of the factory and that the salesmen, retail salesmen and inspectors employed by the sales office were not workmen within the meaning of the U.P. Industrial Disputes Act, 1947. The company further argued that the rules and practice in connection with the recruitment, control and discipline of manpower, as also documents, including letters of appointment and standing orders and the muster rolls, were kept distinct and separate between the factory and the sales office. It was further contended that the sales office paid rent to the factory for the area occupied by it by means of book adjustments and the evidence also showed that 75% of the time of the workmen in the sales office was devoted to writing work.

Discussion Point

Were the workmen entitled for the Production Bonus Scheme introduced by the appellant company as there was functional integrity and interdependence between the manufacturing and sales department?

Judgement and Explanation

It was held that there was functional integrity and interdependence or community of financial control and management of the sales office and the factory in the appellant company. Thus, the two must be considered part of one and the same unit of industrial production. Keeping this in view, there could not be any discrimination between the employees of two units so far as the benefits of the scheme were concerned. The court further said that the inspectors, salesmen and retail salesmen were workmen as defined in the UP Industrial Disputes Act, 1947. Hence, there was no dispute on this question.

Since the aforesaid conditions form the nucleus of a valid standing order, it is necessary to examine them. Only after being satisfied, the certifying officer certifies the standing orders and sends the authenticated copies together with the orders referred to the above, to the parties within 7 days from the date of his orders.

Certifying Officers (Section 11)

The certifying officers under the Act is a Labour Commissioner or a Regional Labour Commissioner and includes any other officer appointed by the appropriate government, by notification in the Official Gazette, to perform all or any of the functions of certifying officer under the Act. Section 11(1) of the act empowers the certifying officer and appellate authority with all the power of a Civil Court for the purposes of the following:

1. Receiving evidence.
2. Enforcing the attendance of witnesses.
3. Compelling the discovery and production of documents.

He is also deemed to be the 'Civil Court' within the meaning of Sections 345 and 346 of the Code of Criminal Procedure, 1973.

Appeals Against Certification (Section 6)

Section 6 provides that any employer, trade union or other prescribed representatives, aggrieved by the order of certifying officer made under Section 5(2) may appeal to the appellate authority within 30 days of the service to the appellate authority. The appellate authority's decision in this regard is final and such authority must writing confirm the standing orders either in the form certified by the certifying officer or after amending the said standing orders. However, every such modification or addition to render the standing orders certifiable under this Act has to be notified.

The Act further provides that the appellate authority must, within 7 days of its order as stated above, send copies thereof of the certifying officer, to the employer and also to the trade union or other prescribed representatives of the workmen, accompanied. However, no such procedure is required to be followed if the appellate authority has confirmed the standing orders without any amendment in the standing orders certified by the certifying officer.

LO3: Other Provisions Relating to Standing Orders

Date of Operation (Section 7)

Section 7 of the Act provides that unless an appeal is preferred under Section 6, the standing orders must come into operation on the expiry of 30 days from the date on which authenticated copies thereof are sent under Subsection (3) of Section 5. If an appeal as aforesaid is preferred, the standing orders will be enforced on the expiry of 7 days from the date on which copies of the order of the appellate authority are sent under Subsection (2) of Section 6. Thereafter, the standing orders become mandatory provisions and must be followed if an industrial dispute arises.

Register of Standing Orders (Section 8)

Section 8 of the Act requires a copy of all standing orders as finally certified under this Act to be filed by the certifying officer in a register in the prescribed form maintained for the purpose. The certifying officer may furnish a copy thereof to any person applying therefore, on payment of the prescribed fee.

Posting of Standing Orders (Section 9)

Section 9 of the Act requires the text of standing orders as finally certified in accordance with the provisions of this Act to be permanently posted by the employer in English and in the language understood by the majority of his workmen on special boards maintained for this purpose. Such notice boards must be displayed at or near the entrance through which the majority of the workmen enter the industrial establishment and in all departments thereof where the workmen are employed.

Modification of Standing Orders (Section 10)

Section 10 of the Act provides for the modification of the certified standing orders. According to this section, the standing orders can be modified even before the expiry of the prescribed time limit of 30 days provided both the management and its workmen agree to it. The employer or the workmen desiring the change are required to make an application for modification to the certifying officer. The procedure for submission of application for modification is the same as for initial certification under the Act. Such application must be accompanied by five copies of the modification proposed to be made. When it is proposed to make modifications by agreement between the employer and workmen, a certified copy of that agreement is also required to be filed along with application for modification.

Let us discuss a case (Case 14.2) to understand the scope of standing orders and authority and duties of a certifying officer while approving the standing orders.

Case 14.2: *Air Gases Mazdoor Sangh v. Indian Air Gases Ltd. And Ors.*[2]

Indian Air Gases Limited, the respondent company, was a manufacturer of oxygen, and it engaged in dissolving acetylene gases at its factory at Mughalsarai in Varanasi district. It had its registered office at Kanpur. Air Gases Mazdoor Sangh, the appellant, was the union of the employees working in the factory at Mughalsarai. In September 1975, the management of the respondent company transferred 10 of its employees from its factory at Mughalsarai to its head office at Kanpur under clause 8(b) of the standing orders. These employees of the respondent company had been working in the factory at Mughalsarai ever since their employment. The standing orders proposed by the respondent company were certified by the certifying officer on 23 July 1975, under the Industrial Employment (Standing Orders) Act, 1946. Clause 8(b) as certified by the certifying officer was in the following words:

> *8(b) Shift may be alternated at the discretion of the employer or its manager and a workman may be transferred from one job to another or from one shift to another or from one factory to another of the employer by its manager or the employer.*

The workmen contended that the impugned transfers were made mala fide by the way of victimization. They alleged that there was no factory in Kanpur owned by the employers; instead, there was only a registered office where only five persons were employed. The workmen further asserted that in the past, some workmen were transferred from Mughalsarai factory to Kanpur office and later on their services were terminated on the ground that there was no work for them in the office; in the background of these facts, the petitioners asserted that the impugned transfers were made malfide to victimize them with an ulterior motive to terminate their services in Kanpur.

The respondent company did not agree and the aggrieved appellants filed a petition under Article 226 of the Constitution, challenging the validity of the order of the certifying officer to the transfer of 10 workmen to Kanpur. It was contended by the workmen and union that the certifying officer did not apply his mind to the reasonableness of the same before certifying clause 8(b) of the standing orders. He failed to consider the question that the matter of transfer was outside the Schedule to the Act, and he further failed to consider the fairness or reasonableness of clause 8(b).

The respondent company urged that after the amendment of the Act in 1936 the legal position of the certifying officer had considerably changed. Since the certifying officer was empowered to adjudicate upon the reasonableness and fairness of the draft standing orders, it was permissible to frame standing orders which were not specifically covered by any of the topics mentioned in the Schedule. If the standing orders made provision in respect of matters which the employers consider to be necessary for the purpose of maintaining efficiency in the industrial establishment and if the certifying officer and the appellate authority were satisfied about the fairness or reasonableness of the provisions and certifies the such standing orders would not be invalid merely because there was no specific provision in the Schedule relating to that matter.

[2] *Air Gases Mazdoor Sangh v. Indian Air Gases Ltd. and Ors.*, 1977, IILLJ 503 All.

Discussion Points

1. Was clause 8(b) of the standing orders invalid as it was outside the scope of the Act?
2. Could the workmen be transferred from Mughalsarai factory to Kanpur office based on clause 8(b) of the standing orders?

Judgement and Explanation

It was held that clause 8(b) of the standing orders was not invalid, however this clause did not empower the employer to transfer the petitioner-workmen from its factory in Mughalsarai to its office in Kanpur. Clause 8(b) conferred only power on the employers and its manager to change the shifts of workmen or transfer them from one job to another and transfer them from one shift to another and from one factory to another. Thus, even under clause 8(b), a workman employed in the factory at Mughalsarai was liable to be transferred to another factory of the employers. The aggrieved workmen, however, had not been transferred from Mughalsarai to any other factory of the employers; instead, they had been transferred to the head office in Kanpur. Ex facie clause 8(b) did not empower the employers to transfer any workman from the factory at Mughalsarai to its head office in Kanpur.

Thus, the impugned transfer made by the employers was outside the scope of clause 8(b) of the standing orders.

Payment of Subsistence Allowance (Section 10A)

In the year 1982, a new Section 10A was added to make a provision for subsistence allowance for the suspended workmen. The Section states that in the cases where any workman is suspended by the employer pending investigation or inquiry into complaints or charges of misconduct against him, the employer has to pay to such workman subsistence allowance

1. At the rate of 50% of the wages which the workman was entitled to immediately preceding the date of such suspension, for the first 90 days of suspension, and
2. At the rate of 75% of such wages for the remaining period of suspension if the delay in the completion of disciplinary proceedings against such workman is not directly attributable to the conduct of such workman.

If any dispute arises regarding the subsistence allowance payable to a workman under Subsection (1), the workman or the employer concerned may take the dispute to the Labour Court, constituted under the Industrial Disputes Act, 1947 (14 of 1947) within the local limits of whose jurisdiction the industrial establishment wherein such workman is employed is situated. The Labour Court to which such dispute is so referred decides the dispute after giving the parties an opportunity of being heard and such decision is final and binding on the parties.

LO4: Miscellaneous Provisions of the Act

Temporary Application of Model Standing Orders (Section 12A)

When this Act becomes applicable to an industrial establishment and ending with the date on which the standing orders as finally certified under this Act come into operation under Section 7 in that establishment, the prescribed model standing orders are deemed to be adopted in that establishment. The provisions of Section 9, Subsection (2) of Section 13 and Section 13A apply to such model standing orders as they apply to the standing orders so certified. The Act further directs under Section 12A(1) that nothing contained in Subsection (1) applies to an industrial establishment in respect of which the appropriate government is the government of the state of Gujarat or the government of the state of Maharashtra (Section 12A (2)).

Power to Exempt (Section 14)

The Act empowers the appropriate government to, by notification in the Official Gazette exempt, conditionally, or unconditionally, any industrial establishment or class of industrial establishments from all or any of the provisions of this Act.

Delegation of Powers (Section 14A)

The appropriate government is authorized, by notification in the Official Gazette, to direct that any power exercisable by it under this Act or any rules made there under to be, in relation to such matters and subject to such conditions, if any, as may be specified in the direction, exercised also

1. Where the appropriate government is the central government, by such officer or authority subordinate to the central government or by the state government or by such officer or authority subordinate to the state government, as may be specified in the notification.
2. Where the appropriate government is a state government, by such officer or authority subordinate to the state government as may be specified in the notification.

Power to Make Rules (Section 15)

After previous publication, by notification, in the Official Gazette, the appropriate government is empowered to make rules to carry out the purposes of this Act. In particular and without prejudice to the generality of the foregoing power, such rules may:

1. Prescribe additional matters to be included in the Schedule, and the procedure to be followed in modifying standing orders, certified under this Act in accordance with any such addition.
2. Set out model standing orders for the purposes of this Act.
3. Prescribe the procedure to be followed by certifying officers and appellate authorities.
4. Prescribe the fee, which may be charged for copies of standing orders entered in the register of standing orders.
5. Provide for any other matter, which is to be or may be prescribed.

Section 15 further provides that before any rules are made under clause (a) of Subsection 15(2), representatives of both employers and workmen have to be consulted by the appropriate government.

It is to be noted that every rule made by the central government under this section is to be laid as soon as may be after it is made, before each House of Parliament while it is in session for a total period of 30 days. This period may be comprised in one session or in two or more successive sessions. If, before the expiry of the session, both Houses agree in making any modification in the rule or both Houses agree that the rule should not be made, the rule is effective only in such modified form or be not effective at all, as the case may be. However, any such modification or annulment has to be without prejudice to the validity of anything previously done under that rule.

LO5: Penalties and Offences

There exist provisions under the Act for the appointment of inspectors for its strict enforcement. Following offences are punishable under Section 18 of the Act, and the Central Industrial Relations Machinery is empowered to take suitable action wherever infringements of the provisions come to their notice:

1. Failures on the part of an employer to submit draft standing orders as per the requirement under Section 3 of the Act.
2. Modification by employer of the certified standing orders otherwise than in accordance with the prescribed procedure under Section 10 of the Act.
3. Any action of the employer which contravenes the provisions of the certified standing orders.

Penalties (Section 13)

Section 13 of the Act prescribes the penalties and procedure in case of violation of the provisions of the Act. The Section provides that any employer who fails to submit draft standing orders as required by Section 3 or who modifies his standing orders otherwise than in accordance with Section 10 is punishable with fine which may extend to ₹5,000, and in the case of a continuing offence with a further fine which may extend to ₹200 for every day after the first during which the offence continues.

The Act further provides that an employer who does any act in contravention of the standing orders finally certified under this Act for his industrial establishment is punishable with fine which may extend to ₹100, and in the case of a continuing offence with a further fine which may extend to ₹25 for every day after the first during which such offence continues.

No prosecution for an offence punishable under this section can be instituted except with the previous sanction of the appropriate government and no court inferior to that of a Metropolitan Magistrate or Judicial Magistrate of the second class is authorized to try any offence under this section.

Interpretation of Standing Orders (Section 13A)

Section 13A of the Act deals with the procedure to be followed if the question of the interpretation of any standing order arises. It provides that if any question arises as to the application or interpretation of a standing order, certified under this Act, the employer or workman or a trade union or other representative body of the workmen may refer such question to any one of the Labour Courts constituted under the Industrial Disputes Act, 1947, and specified for the disposal of such proceeding by the appropriate government by notification in the Official Gazette. The Court to whom such question is so referred decides the question after giving the parties an opportunity of being heard. Such decision is final and binding on the parties.

Summary

1. The Act was brought into force mainly to standardize the service conditions of the workmen employed in any industrial establishment.
2. The main objectives of the Act, other than maintaining a harmonious relationship between the employers and the employees, are to regulate the conditions of recruitment, discharge, disciplinary action, leave, holidays and so on of the workers employed in industrial units/undertaking/establishments.
3. The Act applies to every industrial establishment which employs 100 or more workmen or had employed 100 workers on any day of the preceding 12 months.
4. Standing order includes the rules relating to matters set out in the Schedule.
5. Section 3 of the Act provides that the employer is required to submit to the certifying officer five copies of the draft standing orders proposed by him for adoption in his industrial establishment within 6 months from the date on which the Act becomes applicable to his industrial establishment.
6. All the registered trade unions, and in the absence of the registered trade unions, five elected representatives of the workmen have to be given an opportunity to raise objections to the proposed draft standing orders.
7. The certifying officer must ensure that there is a provision made in the standing orders for every matter set out in the Schedule applicable to the industrial establishment with the additional matter prescribed by the appropriate government in this regard.
8. The certifying officer and appellate authority have the duty to adjudicate upon the fairness and reasonableness of the standing orders.
9. The certifying officers under the Act is a Labour Commissioner or a Regional Labour Commissioner, and includes any other officer appointed by the appropriate government, by notification in the Official Gazette to perform all or any of the functions of certifying officer under the Act.
10. Unless an appeal is preferred under Section 6, the standing orders must come into operation on the expiry of 30 days from the date on which authenticated copies thereof are sent under Subsection (3) of Section 5.
11. The text of standing orders as finally certified in accordance with the provisions of this Act has to be permanently posted by the employer.
12. Section 10 of the Act provides for the modification of the certified standing orders.
13. In the cases where any workman is suspended by the employer pending investigation or inquiry into complaints or charges of misconduct against him, the employer has to pay to such workman subsistence allowance.
14. When the Act becomes applicable to an industrial establishment and ending with the date on which the standing orders as finally certified under this Act come into operation, the prescribed model standing orders are deemed to be adopted in that establishment.
15. The Act empowers the appropriate government to, by notification in the Official Gazette exempt, conditionally or unconditionally, any industrial establishment or class of industrial establishments from all or any of the provisions of this Act.
16. Section 13 of the Act prescribes the penalties and procedure in case of violation of the provisions of the Act.
17. No prosecution for an offence punishable under this section can be instituted except with the previous sanction of the appropriate government.
18. Section 13A of the Act deals with the procedure to be followed if the question of the interpretation of any standing order arises.

Multiple Choice Questions

1. The main objectives of the Industrial Employment (Standing Orders) Act, 1946, are ________ of the workers employed in industrial units/undertaking/establishments.
   a. Regulation of the conditions of recruitment and discharge
   b. Disciplinary action
   c. Leave and holidays
   d. All of the above
2. The Act applies to every industrial establishment which employs ____________ or were employed on any day of preceding 12 months.
   a. 50 or more workmen
   b. 100 or more workmen
   c. 500 or more workmen
   d. 1,000 or more workmen
3. ____________ is a workman who is provisionally employed to occupy a permanent vacancy in a post and has not completed 3 months' service therein.
   a. A probationer
   b. An apprentice
   c. A temporary workman
   d. A casual workman
4. ____________ is a workman who is appointed in the post of a permanent workman or probationer who is temporarily absent from the workplace.
   a. A probationer
   b. A badli
   c. A temporary workman
   d. A casual workman
5. ____________ is a workman who is engaged for work which is of an essentially temporary nature, likely to be finished within a limited period.
   a. A probationer
   b. A badli
   c. A temporary workman
   d. A casual workman
6. ____________ is a workman whose employment is of a casual nature.
   a. A probationer
   b. An apprentice
   c. A temporary workman
   d. A casual workman
7. ____________ is a learner who is paid an allowance by the employer during the period of his training.
   a. A probationer
   b. An apprentice
   c. A temporary workman
   d. A casual workman
8. The certifying officers under the Act can be ____________, and includes any other officer appointed by the appropriate government to perform all or any of the functions of certifying officer under the Act.
   a. A Labour Commissioner
   b. A Regional Labour Commissioner
   c. Any of (a) or (b)
   d. Neither (a) nor (b)
9. The standing orders can be modified even before expiry of the prescribed time limit of ________ provided both the management and its workmen agree for it.
   a. 30 days
   b. 60 days
   c. 75 days
   d. 90 days

10. If any dispute arises regarding the subsistence allowance payable to a workman under Subsection (1), the workman or the employer concerned may take the dispute to ____________.
    a. The High Court
    b. The Civil Court
    c. The Labour Court
    d. Any of the above

True/False Questions

1. The Industrial Employment (Standing Orders) Act, 1946, was brought into force mainly to standardize the service conditions of the workmen employed in any industrial establishment.
2. The amended Section 4 of the Act imposes a duty upon the certifying officer and appellate authority to adjudicate upon the fairness and reasonableness of the standing orders.
3. Thus, the impugned transfer made by the employers is covered in the scope of clause 8(b) of the standing orders.
4. Before any rules are made under clause (a) of Subsection 15(2), representatives of both employers and workmen have to be consulted by the appropriate government.
5. The appropriate government has no power to make rules to carry out the purposes of this Act. It is only the certifying officer or labour commissioner who can frame rules in this regard.

Descriptive Questions

1. Why was the requirement of the Industrial Employment (Standing Orders) Act, 1946, felt by the government?
2. Throw light on main objectives of the Industrial Employment (Standing Orders) Act, 1946.
3. Write a short note on the following as defined under the Industrial Employment (Standing Orders) Act, 1946:
    a. Classification of employees
    b. Industrial establishments
    c. Standing order
4. What is the procedure for submitting the draft standing orders under the Industrial Employment (Standing Orders) Act, 1946?
5. Write a short note on the appointment and powers of certifying officers.
6. What are the conditions for certification of standing orders laid down by the Industrial Employment (Standing Orders) Act, 1946?
7. How can the standing orders be modified under the Industrial Employment (Standing Orders) Act, 1946.
8. Write short notes on following:
    a. Interpretation of standing orders
    b. Power of appropriate government to make the rules
9. Which are the offences punishable under the Industrial Employment (Standing Orders) Act, 1946? Also discuss the penalties for such offences as provided by the Act.

ANNEXURE A

Sl. No.	*Sections*	*State*	*Amendments*
1.	Section 1	Karnataka, Maharashtra and Gujarat	**Change in the establishments covered under the Act** **Subsection (3)** • **Karnataka:** The words 'one hundred' substitute 'fifty'.[3] • **Maharashtra:** The words 'one hundred' substitute 'fifty'[4] • **Gujarat:** The words 'one hundred' substitute 'fifty'.
2.	Section 2A	Maharashtra	**Insertion of new Subsection (2)** Notwithstanding anything contained in the proviso to Subsection (1) model standing orders made in respect of additional matters included in the Schedule after coming into force of the Act referred to in that proviso (being additional) matters relating to probationers or badlis or temporary or casual workmen shall unless such model standing orders are in the opinion of certifying officer less advantageous to them than the corresponding standing orders applicable to them under the said proviso also apply in relation to such workmen in the establishments referred to in the said proviso from such date as the state government may, by notification in the Official Gazette, appoint in this behalf.[5]
3.	Subsection (2) of Section 6	Maharashtra and Gujarat	**Applicability of model standing orders** Any model standing orders in respect of any industrial establishment and in operation on the date of the coming into force of this Act shall be deemed to be the model standing orders prescribed under Section 15 of the said Act and applied to the industrial establishment under Section 2A, and the provisions of the said Act shall apply thereto as they apply to the model standing orders duly applied under the said Section 2A. Nothing in this Act shall be deemed to affect any industrial establishment in respect of which the appropriate government is the central government.[6]
4.	Section 2(g)	Maharashtra: Gujarat	**Additional matters are included in the Schedule** • **Maharashtra:** After item 10B, insert the following item, namely: • '10C. Employment or re-employment of probationers or badlis or temporary or casual workmen and their conditions of service'.[7] • **Uttar Pradesh:** In addition to the matters set out in the Schedule, the following additional matters are included in the Schedule: • 1A: Recruitment. 8A: Issue of service certificate. 9A: Censure and warning notice. 10A: Condition for promotion of workmen. 11A: Issue of wages slips. 11B: Introduction of welfare schemes such as provident fund, gratuities and so on. 11C: Age of superannuation or retirement, rate of pension or any other facility, which the employers may like to extend or may be agreed upon by the parties.[8]

[3] Vide Karnataka Act 37 of 1975, sec. 2 (w.e.f. 11 July 1977).
[4] Vide Bombay Act 21 of 1958, sec. 4 (w.e.f. 15-1-1959) and Act 11 of 1960.
[5] Vide Maharashtra Act 54 of 1974, sec. 2.
[6] Vide Bombay Act 21 of 1958, sec. 12 and 21 (w.e.f. 15 January 1959); Act 11 of 1960, sec. 87 (w.e.f. 1 May 1960).
[7] Vide Maharashtra Act 54 of 1974, sec. 4.
[8] Vide Uttar Pradesh Gazette, Extra., Pt. 4, p. 2, dated 10 February 1978.

15

CHAPTER

The Trade Unions Act, 1926

LEARNING OBJECTIVES

Upon completing this chapter, the reader would be able to:

LO1. Understand the objectives, scope and important definitions of the Act.
LO2. Gain insights into registration and cancellation of the trade unions.
LO3. Understand the rights and duties of the registered trade unions provided by the Act.
LO4. Know the provisions for amalgamation and dissolution under the Act.
LO5. Get the details of rules dealing with penalties for offences against the Act.

Introduction

Trade unions made their headway due to rapid industrial development. The workers come together to maintain and improve their bargaining power on wages and working conditions, and these voluntary groups or organizations of workers or employers are now known as trade unions. These organizations aim at balancing and improving the relations between the employer and the employees. Trade unionism asserts collectively the rights of the workers. In industrially advanced countries, trade unionism dropped a great impact on the social, political and economic lives.

In India, the trade union movement began after the end of the First World War. A decade after the end of First World War, the pressing need for the coordination of the activities of the individual unions was recognized. Trade union leaders realized that they were liable to prosecution and imprisonment for bona fide union activities, and it was felt that some legislation for the protection of trade union was necessary. Consequently, in March 1921, Shri N. M. Joshi, then general secretary of the All India Trade Union Congress, successfully moved a resolution in the Central Legislative Assembly. It was recommended that government should introduce legislation for the registration and protection of trade unions. The Indian Trade Unions Bill, 1925, was introduced in the Central Legislative Assembly to provide for the registration of trade unions and in certain respects to define the law relating to registered trade unions in provinces of India.

The earliest known trade unions in India were the Bombay Millhand's Association formed in 1890, the Amalgamated Society of Railway Servants of India and Burma formed in 1897, the Printers' Union formed in Calcutta in 1905, the Bombay Postal Union formed in 1907 and the Kamgar Hitwardhak Sabha Bombay formed in 1910.

LO1 : Objectives, Scope and Important Definitions

Objectives

This Act deals with all modalities pertaining to registration of trade union to decision of trade-related disputes. This Act sets guidelines for both the workers and the industrialists. The Act provides for the registration of trade unions, their rights, their liabilities and responsibilities as well as ensures that their funds are utilized properly. It gives legal and corporate status to the registered trade unions. It also seeks to protect them from civil or criminal prosecution so that they can carry on their legitimate activities for the benefit of the working class.

Scope and Applicability

The Act is applicable not only to the union of workers but also to the association of employers. It extends to whole of India and was extended to Jammu and Kashmir but in the form of the Central Labour Laws (extension to Jammu and Kashmir) Act, 1970.

Agreements Not Affected by the Act

The Act does not affect:

1. Any agreement between the parties as to their own business.
2. Any agreement between an employer and those employed by him to such employment.
3. Any agreement in consideration of sale of the goodwill of a business or of instruction in any profession, trade or handicraft (proviso to Section 2).

Certain Acts, namely, the Societies Registration Act, 1860, the Co-operative Societies Act, 1912, and the Companies Act, 1956, do not apply to any registered trade union, and that the registration of any such trade union under any such Act is void.

Important Definitions

1. **Appropriate government (Section 2):** The Act states in relation to appropriate government that in relation to a trade union whose objects are not confined to one state, the appropriate government is the central government; in relation to all other unions, the state government is the appropriate government.
2. **Executive (Section 2(a)):** Executive means the body to which the management of the affairs of a trade union is entrusted.
3. **Office-bearer (Section 2(b)):** In the case of a trade union, office-bearer includes any member of the executive thereof, but does not include an auditor.

4. **Registered office (Section 2(d)):** The Act defines a registered office of a trade union to be an office which is registered under this Act as the head office thereof.
5. **Registered trade union (Section 2(e)):** Registered trade union under the Act means a trade union registered under this Act.
6. **Trade union (Section 2(h)):** Trade union is defined as any combination, whether temporary or permanent, formed primarily for the purpose of regulating the relations between workmen and employers, between workmen and workmen or between employers and employers, or for imposing restrictive conditions on the conduct of any trade or business, and it includes any federation of two or more trade unions. In simple words, we can say that a trade union is an organization of employees formed on a continuous basis for the purpose of securing a diverse range of benefits. It is a continuous association of wage earners for the purpose of maintaining and improving the conditions of their working lives.

   The above definition is very exhaustive as it includes associations of both the workers and employers, and the federations of their associations. Here, the relationships that have been talked about are both temporary and permanent. This means it applies to temporary workers (or contractual employees) as well. This definition primarily focuses on three relationships. They are the relationships between the:

   a. Workmen and workmen,
   b. Workmen and employers and
   c. Employers and employers.

Thus, a trade union can be seen as a group of employees in a particular sector whose aim is to negotiate with employers over pay, job security, working hours and so on, using the collective power of its members. In general, a union functions to represent the interests of its members and may even engage in political activity where legislation affects their members. Trade unions are voluntary associations formed for the pursuit of protecting the common interests of its members and also promote welfare. The trade unions protect the economic, political and social interests of their members.

7. **Trade dispute (Section 2(g)):** Trade dispute under the Act covers any dispute, between employer and workmen, between workmen and workmen, and between employer and employer. Any such dispute must be connected with the employment or non-employment or the terms of employment or the conditions of labour of any person. The definition of trade dispute in this act is almost identical with the definition of industrial disputes.
8. **Registrar:** Registrar of trade union is the one who is appointed by the appropriate government under Section 3. He also includes an additional or deputy registrar of trade union and in relation to any trade union the registrar for that state in which the head or registered office of the trade union is situated.

LO2: Registration and Cancellation of Registration of Trade Unions

Appointment of Registrars

State government appoints a person to the registrar of the trade union for the state. It may also appoint as many additional and deputy registrars of the trade union for the state as it deems required. The state government also defines the local limits within which the appointed registrar, and additional and deputy registrars exercise and discharge the powers and functions so specified. If any such additional or deputy registrar is appointed, and he exercises and discharges the powers and functions, he is deemed to be registrar for the purposes of this act.

Mode of Registration (Section 4)

Any seven or more members of a trade union may subscribe their names to apply for registrations of trade union. After filing the application for registering the trade union but before the application is accepted, if more than half of the members who applied for registration cease to be members or disassociate themselves from the application by giving a notice in writing to the registrar, then the applications are deemed to have become invalid, whereas if only half or less than half of the members cease to be the members of the union or disassociate themselves from the application, the application for registration remains valid.

Application for the Registration (Section 5)

Application for the registration is required to be sent to registrar within 7 days. The application must carry the names, occupations and addresses of the members making the application. The application must also propose the name of the trade union and also write the address of its head office. The application must also covey to the registrar, the titles, names, ages, addresses and occupations of the office-bearers of the trade union.

Rules of Trade Union (Section 6)

A trade union is entitled to registration if its executive is constituted in accordance with the provisions of the act. The trade union and its members provide guidelines for the administration of the trade union and its rules provide the following matters:

1. The name of the trade union.
2. The whole of its objects.
3. The purpose for which the general funds of the trade union shall be applicable.
4. The maintenance of a list of members and adequate facilities for the inspection thereof by the office-bearers and members of the trade union.
5. The person to be admitted must be an employee in the industry with which the trade union is connected.
6. Admission ot the number of honorary or temporary office-bearers to form the executive of the trade union.
7. Payment of the subscription: The Act states that the payment for the subscription shall be less than ₹0.25 per month per member.
8. Conditions under which any member shall be entitled to any benefit assured by the rules and under which any fine may be imposed on the member.
9. The manner in which the members of the executive and other office-bearers of the trade union shall be appointed and removed.

10. Safe custody of funds, annual audit of accounts, adequate facilities for the inspection of account books by the office-bearer and members of the trade union, and the manner in which the trade union may be dissolved.

Power to Call for Further Particulars and to Require Alteration of Name (Section 7)

Besides the information provided at the time of registration, the registrar may call for further information to satisfy himself that the application complies with the provisions of Section 5, or that the trade union applying for registration is entitled to registration under Section 6. The registrar may refuse to register the trade union until such information is supplied.

It is further provided the registrar must require the persons applying for registration to alter the name of the trade union stated in the application if the name under which a trade union is proposed to be registered is:

1. Identical with that by which any other existing trade union has been registered.
2. In the opinion of the registrar, so nearly resembles such name as to be likely to deceive the public or the members of either trade union.

The registrar must refuse to register the union until such alteration has been made.

Registration (Section 8)

The Act provides for the registration of the trade unions with the 'Registrars of Trade Unions' set up in different states. For registration of a trade union, seven or more members of the union are required to submit their application in the prescribed form to the registrar of trade unions. The application is to be accompanied by a copy of the 'rules of the trade union' as stated under Section 6 of the Act and a statement giving the following particulars:

1. Names, occupations and addresses of the members making the application.
2. The name of the trade union and the address of its head office.
3. The titles, names, ages, addresses and occupations of the office-bearers of the trade union as per the format given in the Act.

The registrar, on being satisfied that the union has complied with all the requirements of this Act, registers the trade union.

Certificate of Registration (Section 9)

On receipt of the application for registration, the registrar registering a trade union, under Section 8, issues a certificate of registration in the prescribed form which is conclusive that the trade union has been duly registered under this Act. The registrar on being satisfied that the trade union has complied with all the requirements of this Act shall register the trade union by making necessary entries in the register.

Cancellation of Registration (Section 10)

The registrar is empowered to withdraw or cancel the Certificate of Registration to the trade union in any of the following circumstances:

1. After receiving an application from the trade union for the cancellation or withdrawal of registration; or
2. If the registrar is satisfied that the certificate is obtained by fraud of mistake; or
3. If the trade union has ceased to exist; or
4. The trade union wilfully contravenes any provisions of the Act; or
5. The trade union has rescinded any rule which ought to be there.

Before the withdrawal, the registrar must give at least 2 months' notice in written, specifying the grounds on which it is proposed to take action. It is to be noted that in the absence of previous notice, any proceeding for cancellation or withdrawal of registration is illegal.

Registered Office (Section 12)

All communications and notices to a registered trade union are addressed to its registered office. Notice of any change in the address of the head office is required to be given within 14 days of such change to the registrar in writing, and the changed address is recorded in the register referred to in Section 8.

Characteristics of Registered Trade Union on Incorporation (Section 13)

Every registered trade union is considered to be a body corporate by the name under which it is registered. Following are the characteristics of a trade union:

1. Registered trade union will have perpetual succession, which means it will survive even after the death of the members of the trade union.
2. Every registered trade union will have common seal.
3. Every registered trade union can acquire and hold both movable and immovable property.
4. Every registered trade union can sue others.
5. Every registered trade union can be sued by others also.

Change of Name (Sections 23, 25 and 26)

The name can be changed with consent of at least two-thirds of the total number of the members of the union. If a registered trade union wants to change its name, the notice of change of name is required to be in writing and signed by the seven members and the secretary of the union. On obtaining properly signed written notice, the registrar registers the change in name, if he is satisfied that the proposed name is not identical with the name of another existing union and all the requirements in respect of change of name have been complied with.

Membership (Section 21): The Act permits any person who has attained the age of 15 years to be a member of a registered trade union and enjoy all the rights of a member.

Disqualifications of Office-bearers of Trade Unions (Section 21A)

The Act disqualifies a person for being chosen as, and for being member of the executive or any other office-bearer of a registered trade union, if:

1. He has not attained the age of 18 years.
2. He has been convicted by a Court in India of any offence involving moral turpitude and sentenced to imprisonment, unless a period of 5 years has elapsed since his release.

Appeal (Section 11a)

If the registration of a trade union is denied or a certificate of registration is withdrawn or cancelled, any person aggrieved or the trade union may appeal to the court not inferior to the court of principal district judge in the civil court of original jurisdiction as the appropriate government may appoint in this behalf for that area.

Thus, the members of the trade union can appeal to Labour Court or an Industrial Tribunal, with in jurisdiction, if registrar of the trade union:

1. Denies registration of the trade union or
2. Withdraws the registration.

Court may dismiss the appeal, or pass an order directing the registrar to register the trade union and to issue a certificate of registration under the provisions of Section 9, or set aside the order for withdrawal.

For the purpose of an appeal under Subsection (1), an appellate court shall, so far as may be, follow the same procedure and have the same powers as it follows and has when trying a suit under the Code of Civil Procedure, 1908 (5 of 1908), and it may direct by whom the whole or any part of the costs of the appeal shall be paid, and such costs shall be recovered as if they had been awarded in a suit under the said Code.

Dismissal of appeal: In case of dismissal of an appeal by any court appointed under clause (b) of Subsection (1), the aggrieved person can exercise the right of appeal to the high court. For the purpose of such appeal, the high court is vested with all the powers of an appellate court under Subsections (2) and (3), and the provisions of those subsections are applicable accordingly.

LO3: Rights and Duties of Registered Trade Unions

Rights of a Registered Trade Union

Following are the rights of a registered trade union recognized under the Act:

1. **Constitution of a separate fund:** Registered trade union may constitute a separate fund from contributions separately levied for or made to that fund from which payments may be made for the promotion of the civil and political interests of its members.

2. **Registered trade union a body corporate (Section 13):** A registered trade union becomes a body corporate and carries all the rights of a body corporate. It has perpetual succession and common seal with the power to acquire and hold both movable and immovable property and to contract. A registered trade union can sue and can be sued under its registered name.
3. **Construction of separate fund for political purposes (Section 16):** Apart from the primary objects, a trade union has a right to have certain other political objects. As provided under Section 16 of the Act, a registered union may constitute a separate fund in addition to the general fund, and the payment of such a fund shall be utilized for serving civic and political interest of its members.
4. **Immunity from punishment for criminal conspiracy (Section 17):** No office-bearer or member of a registered trade union can be punished under the Section 120B punishment of criminal conspiracy of the IPC (conspiracy cases are defined as cases in which two or more persons agree to commit a crime or to commit an illegal act) regarding matters of spending the general funds for proper purpose.
5. **Immunity from civil suit to certain cases (Section 18):** No suit or other legal proceeding is maintainable in any Civil Court against any registered trade union in the following activities and circumstances:
    a. Delay in matters relating to the member of the trade union regarding the trade disputes like 'contract of employment' is an agreement between an employer and an employee which sets out their employment rights, responsibilities and duties.
    b. Trade union or its members showing interest or interfering in matters of the trade or business.
    c. Trade union or its members showing interest or interfering in matters of the employment of the persons.
    d. Trade union or its members showing interest or interfering in matters of the removal of labour.
    e. Trade union or its members showing interest or interfering in matters of compensating or remunerating the employees.
6. **Immunity from the civil proceedings for tortious act:** Registered trade union is not liable in any suit or other legal proceeding in any Civil Court for the tortious act (wrongful act) committed by the agent of the trade union.
7. **Immunity from the vicarious liability:** Registered trade union is not liable for the vicarious liability (if an agent commits a mistake intentionally without the knowledge of the trade union, the agent is liable but not the trade union).
8. **Enforceability of agreements (Section 19):** Under the Indian Contract Act, an agreement in restraint of trade is void as against public policy but under The Trade Unions Act any agreement between the members of a registered trade union is not void or voidable in the eye of law merely because any of the objectives of the agreement is in restraint of trade.
9. **Right to inspect books of Trade Union (Section 20):** The account books of a registered trade union and the list of members thereof have to be open to inspection by the office-bearer or member of the trade union at such times as may be provided for in the rules of the trade union.
10. **Rights of minors to membership of trade unions (Section 21):** Any person who has attained the age of 15 years is entitled to be a member of a registered trade union and enjoy all the rights of a member.

Let us discuss a case (Case 15.1) to understand the rights and duties of registered trade unions and immunity provided to them.

Case 15.1: *Indian Express Newspapers ... v. T. M. Nagarajan And Ors.*, 1987[1]

The Delhi establishment of the plaintiff company (Indian Express Newspapers) published Indian Express, Jansatta and Financial Express dailies from its premises situated at Bahadur Shah Zafar Marg, New Delhi. The printing units as well as the editorial and administrative offices were situated in the same establishment. According to the plaintiff company, a small number of employees led by an outsider Mr T. M. Nagarajan (the defendants) staged a strike and on many occasions physically prevented an overwhelming majority of employees from entering the premises and attending to their duties. The methods adopted by that group of employees to prevent the entry of other employees included making it physically impossible for the employees to get into the building by forming human walls, by abuses, by physical assaults, by stone-throwing and so on. It was further added that the defendants and their supporters indulged in various acts of violence and intimidation against individual employees of the plaintiff company. Many of them were beaten and some of whom have been hospitalized with head injuries. Despite such intimidation and physical threat, over 350 employees of the plaintiff company entered the building on 20 October 1987 and made efforts to bring out the edition. However, the defendants along with their supporters successfully thwarted food supplies to these 350 employees inside with the result that the plaintiff company had to call off the operation of bringing out the publication and pull out the employees under police escort. Subsequently, majority of the executive members of the Indian Express Employees Union (the Union) requisitioned a general body meeting of the members of the union, attended by 410 members and it was unanimously resolved to remove Mr Nagarajan from the presidentship, appointed a Negotiating Committee to carry on discussions with the management on their demands and called off the strike. After the strike had been called off, a small minority of 20 to 25 persons with the help of outsiders were successfully preventing the overwhelming majority of the employees of the plaintiff company from resuming their work. In the plaint, it is also alleged that on 23 November 1987, a comprehensive settlement was reached between the management and the union represented by the working President and General Secretary and five other members of the Negotiating Committee appointed by the General Body at its meeting held on 18th November 1987 whereby extensive benefits were conferred on the employees.

The plaintiff company filed a suit against the defendants. The grievance of the plaintiff company was that despite the fact that all grievances had been settled and the overwhelming majority of the employees had sacked the President of the Union and wanted to resume work, the defendants, by picketing at the entrance of the Express Building, were preventing ingress and egress of the employees, and thus prevented the publications from coming out in Delhi.

The defendants denied the allegations made by the plaintiff company and contended that the above-mentioned suit is not maintainable and the same was barred under the provisions as contained in the Trade Unions Act, 1926. The defendants further argued in their defence that it was the legitimate right of employees to go on strike and the employees went on strike after serving a legal notice as required under Section 22 of the Industrial Disputes Act, 1947, as the demands of the employees were not accepted. The strike was a remedy under the Labour Laws including the Industrial Disputes Act and the Trade Unions Act for getting the genuine demands of the workers fulfilled or redressed. It was contended by the defendants that Section 17 of the Act provided protection to a registered trade union that it could not be held liable in any suit or other legal proceeding in any Civil Court in respect of any tortious act done in contemplation or furtherance of a trade dispute by an agent of the Trade Union if it was proved that such person acted without the knowledge of, or contrary to express instructions given by, the executive of the trade union. Here the defendants claimed that there was no agreement among the defendants to do any violence and therefore they were entitled to the immunity provided by Section 17 of the Act.

[1] DRJ 212, 1988 LablC 1067, 1988 RLR 194.

Discussion Points

1. Whether the jurisdiction of Civil Courts is barred under the provisions as contained in Section 18 of the Trade Unions Act, 1926.
2. Whether there was such an agreement among the workers as to exclude them from the immunity afforded by Section 17.

Judgement and Explanation

It was held that the workers acted in a combination to achieve a common aim or object and thus there was an implied agreement among them for the purpose of achieving the common aim that was committing an offence under the IPC and in that view of the matter the immunity created by Section 17 of the Act was not available to the workers, assuming that all of them are members of a registered trade union.

Thus it is clear, when a group of workers large or small, combined to do an act for the purpose of one common aim or object, it must be held that there is an agreement among the workers to do the act and if the act committed is an offence, it must be similarly held that there is an agreement to commit an offence.

Duties of a Registered Trade Union

There are a number of duties to be discharged by a registered trade union as directed by different sections of the Act. These duties are summarized as under:

1. **Objects on which general funds may be spent (Section 15):** The Act directs the trade unions under Section 15 not to spend the general funds of a registered trade union on any other objects than those specified in the Act. Also, a registered trade union may constitute a separate fund, from contributions separately levied for or made to that fund, for the promotion of the civic and political interest of its members. However, no member can be compelled to contribute to such fund. It is also to be remembered that a member who does not contribute to the said fund cannot be excluded from any benefits of the trade union.

   The Act specifies the following purposes for which the general funds of the union may be spent:

   a. Payment of salaries, allowances and so on to the office-bearers of the union.
   b. Payment of expenses for the administration of the union including other expenses spent on defending any legal proceedings by or against the union.
   c. Settlement of trade disputes.
   d. Special allowances to the members (including dependants) of the trade union on account of death, sickness or accidents and so on.
   e. Compensation to members for loss arising out of trade disputes.
   f. Providing educational, social and religious benefits to the members.
   g. Issue of assurance policies on the lives of members and also against sickness, accidents, unemployment, insurance and so on.
   h. Providing for publication of periodicals for the use of which is intended for the members benefit.
   i. Any other object that may be notified by the appropriate government in the Official Gazette.

If funds are spent for any purposes other than the above-stated purposes, such expenditure is treated as unlawful in the eye of law and the trade union can be restrained by the court for applying its funds in any other purposes.

2. **Construction of separate fund for political purposes (Section 16):** Along with the primary objects, a trade union is permitted to have certain other political objects. As allowed by Section 16 of the Act, a registered union may constitute a separate fund in addition to the general fund and the payment of such a fund has to be utilized for serving civic and political interest of its members. This fund can be utilized for:
    a. Holding of any meeting or distribution of any literature or document in support of any candidate for election as a member of legislative body constituted under the constitution or of any local authority.
    b. For maintenance of any person who is a member of any legislative body constituted under the constitution.
    c. For convening of political meeting of any kind or distribution of political literature or documents of any kind.
    d. The registration of electors for selection of a candidate for legislative body.

    It is to be noted here that the funds collected for political purposes cannot be clubbed with the general fund. As discussed above, no workman is compelled to contribute in this fund and the non-payment in this fund cannot be made a condition for admission to the trade union.
3. **Submission of returns (Section 28):** It is the duty of the registered trade union to send to the registrar annually on or before the prescribed date a general audited statement of all receipts and expenditure, during the year ending on the 31st day of December next preceding such prescribed date, and also a general audited statement of the assets and liabilities of the trade union existing on such 31st day of December. The statement is required to be prepared in a prescribed form and must comprise prescribed particulars.

    Together, with the general statement, a statement showing changes of office-bearers made by the trade union during the year to which the general statement refers is also to be sent to the registrar. The statement is to be accompanied by a copy of the rules of the trade union corrected up to the date of the despatch thereof to the registrar.
4. **Proportion of office-bearers to be connected with the industry (Section 22):** Not less than one half of the total number of the office-bearers of every registered trade union in an unrecognized sector are required to be persons actually engaged or employed in an industry with which the trade union is connected. However, by special or general order, the appropriate government is empowered to exempt any trade union or class of trade unions specified in the order from the application of the provisions of this section. Here, 'unorganized sector' means any sector which the appropriate government may, by notification in the Official Gazette, specify.

LO4: Amalgamation and Dissolution of Trade Union

Amalgamation of Trade Union (Section 24)

Two or more trade unions may be amalgamated to form one trade union with or without dissolution or division of funds of the trade union. The Act permits the amalgamation of any registered trade union with any other trade union where at least 50 per cent of the members of each such union record their votes and at least 60 per cent of the votes so recorded vote in favour of amalgamation. A notice of amalgamation is required to be signed by at least seven members and the secretary of each amalgamating union. This signed notice is required to be sent to the registrar. If the registrar is satisfied that all necessary formalities have been complied with, he may register the trade union. After the registration of the notice of amalgamation, the amalgamated trade union comes in operation. The amalgamation is effective from the date of such registration. The amalgamation of two or more registered trade unions must not prejudice any right of any such trade union or any right of a creditor or any of them.

Dissolution of Trade Union (Section 27)

A trade union gets dissolved by a notice of dissolution signed by seven members and the secretary of the union. Within 14 days of such dissolution, the signed notice of dissolution is required to be sent to the registrar of trade unions. The registrar registers the same, if he is satisfied that the dissolution has been effected in accordance with the rules of the trade union. Dissolution takes effect only from the date of such registration.

Where the dissolution of a registered trade union has been registered and the rules of the trade union do not provide for the distribution of funds of the trade union on dissolution, the registrar divides the funds among the members in such manner as may be prescribed.

Effects of change of name and of amalgamation: It must be noted here that the change in the name of a registered trade union does not affect any rights or obligations of the trade union or render defective any legal proceeding by or against the trade union. Any legal proceeding which might have been continued or commenced by or against it by its former name may be continued or commenced by or against it by its new name.

In a similar way, an amalgamation of two or more registered trade unions does not prejudice any right of any of such trade unions or any right of a creditor of any of them. Thus the claims of the creditor remain tenable against the amalgamated trade union as those were there before the amalgamation.

Approved Unions

Deemed Approved Unions (Section 28B)

The Act provides that a union entered on the approved list maintained under the Bombay Industrial Relations Act, 1947, as adopted in Madhya Bharat by the Madhya Bharat Industrial Relations (Adaptation) Act, Samvat 2006 (Madhya Bharat Act 31 of 1949), before the commencement of the Indian Trade Unions (Madhya Pradesh Amendment) Act, 1960 (Madhya Pradesh Act 28 of 1960), shall be deemed to be an approved union under this Act.

The Act entrusts with the registrar the duty to maintain a list of approved unions in such form as may be prescribed (Section 28B).

Application for and Entry in the Approved List (Section 28C)

As discussed above, the registrar of trade union maintains a list of approved unions, and a registered union under the Act will try to get an entry in this list. Following is the process to get an entry in the approved list of unions maintained by the registrar:

1. Any representative union or where there is no representative union, any registered trade union in any industry other than an industry for which the central government is the appropriate government (within the meaning of subclause (i) of clause (a) of Section 2 of the Industrial Disputes Act, 1947 (14 of 1947)), is entitled to apply in the prescribed form for being entered in the approved list.
2. After receiving such application, the registrar conducts a prescribed enquiry to be satisfied that the applicant union fulfils the conditions necessary for its entry in the approved list. On being so satisfied, he shall enter the name of such union in the approved list followed by issuance of a certificate of its entry. The Act further provides that:
   a. If there are two or more unions fulfilling the conditions necessary for registration specified in Section 28D apply for their entry in the approved list, the union having the largest membership of the employees employed in the industry must get an entry alone in approved list;
   b. The registrar must not enter any union in the approved list, if he is satisfied for reasons to be recorded in writing that the application for entry is not made bona fide in the interests of employees but is made in the interests of the employer.

Conditions of Entry in the Approved List (Section 28D)

The Act provides certain conditions to be fulfilled by a trade union aspiring to get an entry in the approved list maintained by the registrar of trade unions. The Act states that no union shall be entered in the approved list under this Act, unless:

1. The union has for the whole of the period of three months next preceding the date of application under section 28C a membership of not less than 15% of the employees employed in the industry in that local area
2. The constitution of the union is such as may be provided by or under this Act, and in particular, must require that:
   a. The subscription payable for membership must not less than ₹0.25 a month or such other sum as may be fixed by the state government under Subsection (2) and that the accounts of the union must be audited at least once in each financial year by an auditor appointed or approved by the state government.
   b. The executive of the union must meet at least once in 3 months and that all resolutions passed by the executive or general body shall be recorded in a minute book.
   c. The union must not sanction a strike as long as conciliation and arbitration are available and must not declare a strike until a ballot is taken and the majority of the members of the union vote in favour of the strike.

Largest membership trade union to replace the trade union in the approved list: The Act under Subsection (3) directs that a registered trade union which complies with the conditions specified above, and has a larger membership in an industry in a local area than an approved union for such industry, is entitled to an application in that behalf be entered in the approved list in place of such approved union by the registrar after holding such enquiry as he deems fit.

Membership subscription may be less than ₹0.25 in certain cases: The Act under Subsection (2) empowers the state government to direct that in the case of any registered trade union of workmen or employees engaged in any employment specified in the Schedule to the Minimum Wages Act, 1948, the membership subscription may be less than ₹0.25 for a specified period.

Approved Union to Continue to be so far Altered Local Area for Some Time (Section 28E)

The Act states that in case of an alteration in the local area or areas:

1. An approved union in an industry in the altered local area or areas; or
2. Where two or more approved unions exist in an industry in the altered local area or areas,

the union having the largest membership, whether by agreement of the other approved unions or as determined by the registrar after such inquiry as he deems fit, shall be deemed to be the approved union for the altered local area or areas, as the case may be, for a period of 6 months from the date on which such alteration is effected or where such approved union or any other union in the altered local area or areas makes an application under Section 28C within such period until the disposal of such application by the registrar.

Removal from Approved List (Section 28F)

The Act empowers the registrar to remove a union from the approved list if its certificate of registration is cancelled under Section 10. He may also so remove a union if after holding such enquiry, as he deems fit, he is satisfied that it:

1. Was entered in the list under mistake, misrepresentation or fraud; or
2. Has, since being included in the approved list, ceased to fulfil the conditions specified in section 28D.

Appeal against the decision of the registrar (Section 28G): This provides an opportunity to any person aggrieved by the order of the registrar:

1. Refusing to enter any registered trade union in the approved list; or
2. Removing a registered trade union from the approved list,

to file an appeal to the Industrial Court, within 30 days from the communication of such order to the trade union concerned. In such a case, the decision of the Industrial Court shall be final.

Rights of Officer of Approved Unions (Section 28H)

The officers and members of an approved union as may be authorized by or under rules made in this behalf by the state government can exercise the following rights:

1. To collect sums payable by members to the union on the premises where wages are paid to them.
2. To put up or cause to be put up a notice board on the premises of the undertaking in which its members are employed and affix or caused to be affixed notices thereon;
3. For the purpose of the prevention or settlement of a trade dispute:
   a. To hold discussions on the premises of the undertaking with the employees concerned who are the members of the union.

b. To meet and discuss with an employer or any person appointed by him for the purpose of removing the grievances of its members employed in his undertaking.
c. To inspect, if necessary, in any undertaking, any place where any member of the union is employed.

Regulations

Power to Make Regulations (Section 29)

The appropriate government is empowered to make regulations to carry out into effect the provisions of this Act. In particular and without prejudice to the generality of the foregoing power, such regulations may provide for all or any of the following matters:

1. The manner in which trade unions and the rules of trade unions are to be registered and the fees payable on registration.
2. The transfer of registration in the case of any registered trade union which has changed its head office from one state to another.
3. The manner in which, and the qualifications by whom, the accounts of registered trade unions or of any class of such unions is to be audited.
4. The conditions subject to which inspection of documents kept by registrars are allowed and the fees which is chargeable in respect of such inspections.
5. Any matter which is to be or may be prescribed.

Publication of Regulations (Section 30)

The power to make regulations conferred by Section 29 is subject to the condition that such regulations are previously published. The date is to be specified in accordance with clause (3) of Section 23 of the General Clauses Act, 1927, as that after which a draft of regulations proposed to be made will be taken into consideration has to be not less than 3 months from the date on which the draft of the proposed regulations was published for general information.

Regulations so made are required to be published in the Official Gazette and on such publication shall have effect as if enacted in this Act.

LO5: Penalties

Following are the reasons for levying penalties under the Act:

1. Failure to submit returns.
2. Supplying false information regarding trade unions.
3. Cognizance of offences.

1. Failure to submit returns (Section 31)

If there is a default on the part of any registered trade union in giving any notice or sending any statement or other document as required by or under any provision of this Act, every office-bearer or other person bound by the rules of the trade union to give or send the same, or, if there is no such office-bearer or person, every member of the executive of the trade union is punishable with fine which may extend to ₹5. If the default continues, an additional fine may be imposed which may extend to ₹5 for each week after the first during which the default continues. However, the aggregate fine cannot exceed ₹50.

The Act further provides for the penalty of fine which may extend to ₹500 for a person who wilfully makes, or causes to be make, any false entry in, or any omission from, the general statement required by Section 28 or in or from any copy of rules or of alterations of rules sent to the registrar under that section shall be punishable with.

2. Supplying false information regarding trade unions (Section 32)

Any person who, with intent to deceive gives to any member of a registered trade union or to any person intending or applying to become a member of such trade union any document purporting to be a copy of the rules of the trade union or of any alterations to the same which he knows, or has reason to believe, is not a correct copy of such rules or alterations as are for the time being in force, or any person who, with the like intent, gives a copy of any rules of an unregistered trade union to any person on the pretence that such rules are the rules of a registered trade union is punishable with fine which may extend to ₹200.

3. Cognizance of offences (Section 33)

No Court inferior to that of a Presidency Magistrate or a Magistrate of the first class is permitted to try any offence under this Act. No Court takes cognizance of any offence under this Act, unless complaint thereof has been made by, or with the previous sanction of, the Registrar or, in the case of an offence under Section 32, by the person to whom the copy was given, within 6 months of the date on which the offence is alleged to have been committed.

Case 15.2 will provide further insights into the jurisdiction of Labour Court under section 32.

Case 15.2: *Blue Star Limited v. Blue Star Workers Union & Another*, 1997[2]

The petitioner Blue Star Limited (the company) was a company incorporated under the Indian Companies Act, 1956, and was engaged in business of air-conditioning products and projects, software exports, medical electronics and so on. The company had its factory at Pokhran Road, Thane and western regional office at Band Box House, Mumbai. Blue Star Workers Union (the union), the respondent, was a trade union registered under the Trade Unions Act, 1926.

According to the company, on 1 July 1988 from 10.50 AM to 11.15 AM, 29 employees who were members of the union entered the cabin of Mr Anil B. Sawant, Manager—Administration and Personnel and gheraoed him. The employees neither took prior permission from their superiors before leaving their respective places of work nor they took permission of Mr Sawant before entering his cabin. On 11 July

[2] Bom CR 277, 1999 (82) FLR 925.

1988, the company issued notice displaying it on notice board stating therein that the act of 29 employees whose names were shown in the notice gheraoing the Manager Personnel and Administration of its western regional office at Band Box House amounted to stoppage of work in a concerted manner, withdrawing their labour unilaterally and the employees absented themselves from work for 25 minutes from 10.50 AM to 11.15 AM and, therefore, the said employees would not be paid the wages for the said period as they failed in earning the same. It was further stated in the notice that the adjustment would be carried out in the salaries for the month of July 1988.

The union challenged the said notice as an unfair labour practice on the part of the company by filing complaint under Item 9, of Schedule IV, of the Maharashtra Recognition of Trade Unions and Prevention of Unfair Labour Practices Act, 1971 (for short, 'MRTU & PULP Act'). The union set out the case in the complaint and that the notice was factually not true and correct. The said notice was bad in law being violative of principles of natural justice and against the rules and regulations framed by the company. According to the union, the contract of employment could not be divided in minutes and hours as had been sought to be made out by the company and the directions were in fact punitive in nature amounting to unfair labour practice.

The company resisted the complaint by filing a written statement raising the plea that complaint did not disclose any unfair labour practice on its part nor the company committed any unfair labour practice under 'MRTU & PULP Act'. The company justified its action and submitted that the conduct of the concerned employees in gheraoing the Manager, Administration and Personnel was violative of clauses 26, 28, 35 and 79 of the rules and regulations framed by the company.

The Labour Court directed the company to return the deducted wages to the employees. Disappointed because of the decision of the Labour Court, the company filed a writ petition and challenged the jurisdiction of the Labour Court in this matter. The company contended that this was beyond the jurisdiction of the Labour Court to decide the issue; however, the employees submitted that Section 32 of the Trade Unions Act empowers the Labour Court to settle such issues as mentioned above.

Discussion Point

Does Section 32 of the Act extend the scope of jurisdiction of Labour Court?

Judgement and Explanation

The court stated in the judgement that Section 32 of the Act did not enlarge the scope or extent of the jurisdiction of the Industrial Court or Labour Court beyond what was conferred upon it by other provisions of MRTU & PULP Act. As it was the very scheme of the Act clearly spelt out that the entire exercise of power by the Industrial Court or Labour Court under MRTU & PULP Act was dependent upon its finding that the person named in the complaint had engaged in unfair labour practice or was engaging in any unfair labour practice and to curb that unfair labour practice, the appropriate order as contemplated under Section 30(1) or Section 32 of the Act could be passed.

Major Amendments under the Trade Unions (Amendment) Act, 2001

The Trade Unions Act, 1926, has been amended from time to time and the most important being the Trade Unions (Amendment) Act, 2001. This Act has been enacted in order to bring more transparency and to provide greater support to trade unionism in India. Some of the salient features of the Trade Unions (Amendment) Act, 2001 are as follows:

1. No trade union of workmen can be registered unless at least 10 per cent or 100, whichever is less, subject to a minimum of 7 workmen engaged or employed in the establishment or industry with which it is connected are the members of such trade union on the date of making of application for registration.
2. A registered trade union of workmen is required to have not less than 10 per cent or 100 of the workmen, whichever is less, subject to a minimum of 7 persons engaged or employed in the establishment or industry with which it is connected, as its members. A provision for filing an appeal before the Industrial Tribunal/Labour Court in case of non-registration or for restoration of registration has been provided.
3. All office-bearers of a registered trade union, except not more than one-third of the total number of office-bearers or five, whichever is less, are required to be persons actually engaged or employed in the establishment or industry with which the trade union is connected.
4. Minimum rate of subscription by members of the trade union is fixed at ₹1 per annum for rural workers, ₹3 per annum for workers in other unorganized sectors and ₹12 per annum in all other cases.
5. The employees who have been retired or have been retrenched cannot be construed as outsiders for the purpose of holding an office in the trade union concerned.
6. For the promotion of civic and political interest of its members, unions are authorized to set up separate political funds.

Summary

1. The Trade Unions Act deals with all modalities pertaining to registration of trade union and to decision of trade-related disputes.
2. A trade union can be seen as a group of employees in a particular sector, whose aim is to negotiate with employers over pay, job security, working hours and so on, using the collective power of its members.
3. The state government may also appoint as many additional and deputy registrars of the trade union for the state as it deems required.
4. Any seven or more members of a trade union may subscribe their names to apply for registrations of trade union.
5. Application for the registration is required to be sent to a registrar within 7 days.
6. The registrar on being satisfied that the trade union has complied with all the requirements of this act shall register the trade union by making necessary entries in the register.
7. The registrar is empowered to withdraw or cancel the Certificate of Registration to the trade union.
8. A registered trade union becomes a body corporate and carries all the rights of a body corporate.
9. Apart from the primary objects, a trade union has a right to have certain other political objects.
10. A registered trade union is not liable in any suit or other legal proceeding in any Civil Court for the tortious act (wrongful act) committed by the agent of the trade union.

11. Under Section 15, the Act directs not to spend the general funds of a registered trade union on any object other than those specified in the Act.
12. The funds collected for political purposes cannot be clubbed with the general fund.
13. It is the duty of the registered trade union to send to the registrar annually on or before the prescribed date a general audited statement of all receipts and expenditure.
14. Two or more trade unions may be amalgamated to form one trade union with or without dissolution or division of funds of the trade union.
15. A trade union gets dissolved by a notice of dissolution signed by seven members and the secretary of the union. Within 14 days of such dissolution, the signed notice of dissolution is required to be sent to the registrar of trade unions.
16. The appropriate government is empowered to make regulations to carry out into effect the provisions of this Act.
17. The reasons for levying penalties under the Act are failure to submit returns, supplying false information regarding trade unions and cognizance of offences.
18. The Trade Unions Act, 1926, has been amended from time to time, with the most important being the Trade Unions (Amendment) Act, 2001.

Multiple Choice Questions

1. The Act provides for the ______________.
   a. Registration of trade unions
   b. Their rights, their liabilities and responsibilities
   c. The proper utilization of their funds
   d. All of the above

2. Trade dispute under the Act covers any dispute ______________.
   a. Between employer and workmen
   b. Between workmen and workmen
   c. Between employer and employer
   d. All of the above

3. Trade unions include associations of ______________.
   a. Both the workers and employers and the federations of their associations
   b. Only the workers
   c. Only the employees
   d. Only c

4. ______________ are voluntary associations formed for the pursuit of protecting the common interests of its members and also for promoting welfare.
   a. Association of workers
   b. Association of employers

c. Trade unions
d. The federations of employer–employee associations

5. Any ______________ of a trade union may subscribe their names to apply for registrations of trade union.
   a. Five or more members
   b. Seven or more members
   c. Nine or more members
   d. Ten or more members
6. Before the withdrawal, the registrar must give at least ______________ in written, specifying the ground on which it is proposed to take action.
   a. 2 months' notice
   b. 5 months' notice
   c. 8 months' notice
   d. 1-year notice
7. The members of the trade union can appeal to ______________, within jurisdiction, if the registrar of the trade union denies registration of the trade union or withdraws the registration
   a. Labour Court
   b. Industrial Tribunal
   c. Either Labour Court or an Industrial Tribunal
   d. Neither Labour Court nor an Industrial Tribunal
8. The Act specifies the purposes for which the general funds of the union may be spent that includes ______________.
   a. Payment of salaries and payment allowances and so on, to the office-bearers of the union.
   b. Payment of expenses for the administration of the union
   c. Both (a) and (b)
   d. Neither (a) nor (b)
9. Not less than ______________ of the total number of the office-bearers of every registered trade union in an unrecognized sector are required to be persons actually engaged or employed in an industry with which the trade union is connected.
   a. One-half
   b. One-third
   c. One-fourth
   d. One-eighth
10. A notice of amalgamation is required to be signed by at least ______________.
    a. Seven members
    b. The secretary of each amalgamating union
    c. Both (a) and (b)
    d. Neither (a) nor (b)

True/False Questions

1. The Act is applicable only to the union of workers but not to the association of employers.
2. In the absence of previous notice, any proceeding for cancellation or withdrawal of registration is illegal.
3. Every registered trade union is considered to be a body corporate by the name under which it is registered.
4. Along with from the primary objects, no trade union has a right to have certain other political objects.
5. A registered trade union will have perpetual succession, which means it will survive even after the death of the members of the trade union.

Descriptive Questions

1. Define the following terms as defined under Trade Unions Act, 1926
   a. Trade dispute
   b. Trade union
2. Discuss in detail the process of registration of trade unions and also the procedure to cancel the same.
3. What are the rules to be met to change the name of a registered trade union?
4. What are the privileges enjoyed by a trade union? Discuss in detail.
5. For which purpose can the political fund created by a trade union be used?
6. Discuss the provisions dealing with the amalgamation of trade unions.
7. Write a short note on dissolution of trade union and related provisions under the Trade Unions Act, 1926.
8. What is the penalty for supplying false information under the Trade Unions Act, 1926?

ANNEXURE A

Sl. No.	*Sections*	*State*	*Amendments*
1.	Section 2	Gujarat	**Insertion of clause, namely '(aa)'** 'Industrial Court' means the Industrial Court constituted under the Bombay Industrial Relations Act, 1946, as in force in the state of Gujarat.[3]

[3] Vide Gujarat Act 7 of 1962, sec. 3 (w.e.f. 1 July 1962).

Sl. No.	*Sections*	*State*	*Amendments*
		Madhya Pradesh	**Insertion of the clauses, namely '(a)' defining 'approved list'** Approved list means the list of approved unions maintained by the registrar under Section 28A.[4]
2.	Section 6 (ee)	Madhya Pradesh	**Payment of subscription by members of the trade union** Payment of subscription by members of the trade union shall not be less than ₹0.25 per month per member: provided that the minimum rate of subscription in the case of members of a trade union of agricultural workers shall be 5 paise per month per member.[5]
3.	Section 10A	Gujarat	**Notice specifying the grounds for cancellation of registration of a trade union** If no provision as required by Subsection (1) is made in the rules of any existing trade union before the expiry of 6 months from the date mentioned in Subsection (1), the registrar may cancel the registration of such trade union: provided that not less than 2 months' notice in writing specifying the grounds on which it is proposed to cancel the certificate shall be given by the registrar to the trade union before the certificate is cancelled.[6]
4.	Section 281A	Maharashtra	**Power of Industrial Court to decide certain disputes** • Where there is a dispute as respects whether or not any person is an office-bearer or a member of a registered trade union (including any dispute relating to wrongful expulsion of any such office-bearer or member), or where there is any dispute relating to the property (including the account books) of any registered trade union, any member of such registered trade union for a period of not less than 6 months may, with the consent of the registrar, and in such manner as may be prescribed, refer the dispute to the Industrial Court constituted under the Bombay Industrial Relations Act, 1946, for decision. • The Industrial Court shall, after hearing the parties to the dispute, decide the dispute and may require an office-bearer or member of the registered trade union to be appointed whether by election or otherwise under the supervision of such person as the Industrial Court may appoint in this behalf or removed, in accordance with the rules of the trade union: provided that the Industrial Court may, pending the decision of the dispute, make an interim order specifying or appointing any person or appointing a Committee of Administration for any purpose under the Act including the purpose of taking possession or control of the property in dispute and managing it for the purposes of the union pending the decision.

[4] Vide Madhya Pradesh Act 28 of 1960, sec. 2 (w.e.f. 31 December 1960).

[5] Vide Madhya Pradesh Act 16 of 1968, sec. 2.

[6] Vide Gujarat Act 7 of 1962, sec. 5 (w.e.f. 1 April 1965).

Sl. No.	Sections	State	Amendments
			• The decision of the Industrial Court shall be final and binding on the parties and shall not be called in question in any Civil Court. • No Civil Court shall entertain any suit or other proceedings in relation to the dispute referred to the Industrial Court as aforesaid, and if any suit or proceeding is pending in any such Court, the Civil Court shall, on receipt of an intimation from the Industrial Court that it is seized of the question, cease to exercise jurisdiction in respect thereof. • Save as aforesaid, the Industrial Court may, in deciding disputes under this section, exercise the same powers and follow the same procedure as it exercises or follows for the purpose of deciding industrial disputes under the Bombay Industrial Relations Act, 1946.[7]

[7] Vide Maharashtra Act 3 of 1968, sec. 3 (w.e.f. 1 October 1968).

16

CHAPTER

The Payment of Bonus Act, 1965

LEARNING OBJECTIVES

Upon completing this chapter, the reader would be able to:

LO1. Understand the objectives, scope and important definitions of the Act.
LO2. Gain insights into eligibility for bonus payable under the Act and provisions related to minimum and maximum amount of bonus.
LO3. Understand the step-by-step process of determining the bonus amount.
LO4. Know the special and miscellaneous provisions of the Act dealing with various matters related to payment of bonus to employees.
LO5. Get the details of provisions relating to disputes, penalties and offences under the Act.

Introduction

It was the year 1917, during the First World War, when certain textile mills in India granted 10% of wages as a war bonus to their workers. There started a practice of giving bonus to the workers in the country. Subsequently, in certain cases of industrial disputes, demand for payment of bonus was also included, and in 1950, the full bench of the Labour Appellate evolved a formula for the determination of bonus. In March/April 1960, during second and third meetings of the Eighteenth Session of Standing Labour Committee held in New Delhi, it was agreed that a Commission be appointed to go into the question of bonus and evolve suitable norms. A Tripartite Commission was set up by the Government of India to consider in a comprehensive manner the question of payment of bonus based on profits to employees employed in establishments and to make recommendations to the government in this regard. On 24 January 1964, the report of the committee was submitted to the government and the Government of India accepted the recommendations of the Commission subject to certain modifications.

To implement these recommendations, the Payment of Bonus Bill was introduced in the Parliament. The Act provides for payment of bonus to persons employed in certain establishments on the basis of profits or on the basis of production or productivity and for matters connected therewith.

LO1: Objectives, Scope and Important Definitions of the Act

Objectives

The Payment of Bonus Act, 1965, is the principal Act dealing with the payment of bonus to the employees, which was formed with an objective for rewarding employees for their good work for the organization. It aims at sharing the prosperity of the establishment reflected by the profits earned by the contributions made by capital, management and labour with the employees. Thus, the main objective of the Payment of Bonus Act is to provide a statutory right to the employees of an establishment to share the profits of his employer. The objective of the Act is:

1. To improve statutory liability to pay bonus (reward for good work) in case of profits or losses.
2. To prescribe a formula for calculating bonus.
3. To prescribe minimum and maximum percentage bonus.
4. To provide of set off/set of on mechanism.
5. To provide redressal mechanism.

Scope and Applicability

The Act extends to the whole of India and is applicable to:

1. Every factory.
2. Every other establishment employing 20 or more persons.

The government can, however, apply the Act to any establishment employing even less than 20 but not less than 10 persons. Section 1 of the Act clearly mentions that an establishment to which the Act applies continues to be governed by the Act irrespective of any fall in the number of persons employed therein.

The establishments in the public sector: The Act is not applicable to all public sector establishments. As provided by Section 20(1), the applicability of the Act is limited to only those public sector establishments which sell the goods or renders services in competition with an establishment in the private sector, and the income from such sale or services or both is not less than 20% of the gross income of the establishment in the public sector for that year. In other cases, the provisions of this Act do not apply to the employees employed by any establishment in the public sector (Section 20(2)). The Act is also not applicable to any institution established not for purposes of profit.

An establishment comprising of a number of departments, undertakings or branches: Section 3 of the Act provides that if an establishment consists of different departments or undertakings or has branches, whether situated in the same place or in different places, all such departments of undertakings or branches should be treated as parts of the same establishment for the purpose of computation of bonus, unless a separate balance sheet and profit and loss account are prepared and maintained in respect of them. It should also be noted that once they are treated as parts of the same establishment, they continued to be treated as such.

Important Definitions

1. **Accounting year (Section 2(1)):** Under the Act, 'accounting year' means:
   a. In relation to a corporation, the year ending on the day on which the books and accounts of the corporation are to be closed and balances.
   b. In relation to a company, the period in respect of which any profit and loss account of the company laid before it in annual general meeting is made up.
   c. In any other case:
      i. The year commencing on the 1 April; or
      ii. If the accounts of an establishment maintained by the employer thereof are closed and balances on any day other than the 31 March, then, at the option of the employer, the year ending on the day on which its accounts are so closed and balanced.

   The Act further provides in Section 2(1) that an option once executed by the employer under paragraph (b) of this subclause cannot again be exercised except with the previous permission in writing of the prescribed authority and upon such conditions as that authority may think fit.
2. **Allocable surplus (Section 2(4)):** The Act explains 'allocable surplus' as follows:
   a. In relation to an employer, being a company which is not a banking company, and that has not made the arrangements prescribed under the Income Tax Act for the declaration and payment within India of the dividends payable out of its profits in accordance with the provisions of Section 194 of that Act, 67% of the available surplus in an accounting year.
   b. In any other case, 60% of such available surplus.
3. **Appropriate government:** 'Appropriate government' under the Act means in relation to an establishment in respect of which the appropriate government under the Industrial Disputes Act, 1947 (14 of 1947), is the central government. For any other establishment, the government of the state in which that other establishment is situated.
4. **Available surplus (Section 2(6)):** Available surplus means the available surplus under Section 5 of the Act.
5. **Award (Section 2(7)):** 'Award' under the Act stands for an interim or a final determination of any industrial dispute or of any question relating thereto by any Labour Court, Industrial Tribunal or National Tribunal constituted under the Industrial Disputes Act, 1947, or by any other authority constituted under any corresponding law relating to investigation and settlement of industrial disputes in force in a state and includes an arbitration award made under Section 10A of that Act or under that law.
6. **Corporation (Section 2(11)):** Under the Act, 'corporation' is any corporate body established by or under any Central Provincial or State Act excluding a company or a cooperative society.
7. **Employee:** According to the Act, the term 'employee' includes any person employed on a salary or wage not exceeding ₹3,500 per month in any industry to do any skilled or unskilled manual, supervisory, managerial, administrative, technical or clerical work for hire or reward, whether the terms of employment be express or implied.

8. **Employer (Section 2(14)):** According to the definition pronounced by Section 2(14) of the Act, employer for the purpose of this Act includes:
    a. In relation to an establishment which is a factory, the owner or occupier of the factory, including the agent of such owner or occupier, the legal representative of a deceased owner or occupier and where a person has been named as a manager of the factory under clause (f) of Subsection (1) of Section 7 of the Factories Act, 1948 (63 of 1948), the person so named.
    b. In relation to any other establishment, the person who, or the authority which, has the ultimate control over the affairs of the establishment and, where the said affairs are entrusted to a manager, managing director or managing agent, such manager, managing director or managing agent.
9. **Establishment:** The Act does not define the word 'establishment'. Normally, 'establishment' is a permanently fixed place for business. The term 'establishment' is much wider than 'factory' which covers any office or fixed place where business is carried out.
10. **Establishment in the public sector (Section 2(16)):** Establishment in the public sector includes an establishment owned, controlled or managed by:
    a. A government company as defined in Section 617 of the Companies Act, 1956 (1 of 1956).
    b. A corporation in which not less than 40% of its capital is held (whether singly or taken together) by the government; or the Reserve Bank of India, or a corporation owned by the government or the Reserve Bank of India.
11. **Establishment in the private sector (Section 2(15)):** The Act specifies that establishment which is not in the public sector is an 'establishment in private sector'.
12. **Factory (Section 2(17)):** Under the Act, the factory has the same meaning as in clause (m) of Section 2 of the Factories Act, 1948 (63 of 1948).
13. **Gross profit (Section 2(18)):** For the purpose of this Act, gross profit is nothing but the gross profits calculated under Section 4.
14. **'Salary' or 'wage':** The Act defines 'salary' or 'wage' as all remuneration (other than remuneration in respect of overtime work) that may be expressed in terms of money and includes dearness allowance. But salary or wages do not include the following:
    a. Any other allowance which the employee is, for the time being, entitled to.
    b. The value of any accommodation or supply of light, water, medical attendance or any other amenity or of any service or any concessional supply of food.
    c. Grains or other articles.
    d. Any travelling concession.
    e. Any bonus (including incentives, production and attendance bonus).
    f. Any contribution paid or payable by the employers to any pension fund or provident fund.
    g. Any retrenchment compensation or any gratuity or other retirement benefits, payable to the employee or any ex gratia payment made to him.
    h. Any commission payable to the employee.

The Act further provides an explanation that if an employee is given in lieu of the whole or part of the salary or wage payable to him, free food allowance or free food by his employer, such food allowance or the value of such food shall, for the purpose of this clause, be deemed to form part of the salary or wage of such employee.

LO2: Eligibility, Disqualification and Amount of Bonus

Meaning of Bonus

The term 'bonus' has not been defined in the Payment of Bonus Act, 1965. According to Webster's International Dictionary, bonus is something given in addition to what is ordinarily received by or strictly due to the recipient. Therefore, bonus is something for to the good into the bargain gratuity to workmen beyond their wages. In simple words, we can say that bonus is a reward that is paid to an employee for his good work towards the organization. The basic objective of the bonus is to share the profit earned by the organization among the employees and staff members.

Eligibility for Bonus (Section 8)

Section 8 relates to the eligibility for bonus. The Act entitles every employee (other than apprentice) receiving salary or wages up to ₹21,000 per month and engaged in any kind of work, whether skilled, unskilled, managerial, supervisory, etc., to bonus for every accounting year if he has worked for at least 30 working days in that year. Section 32 of the Act, however, mentions that employees of LIC, universities and educational institutions, hospitals, Chamber of Commerce, RBI, IFCI, UTI and social welfare institutions are not entitled to bonus under this Act.

1. **Eligibility of seasonal worker for bonus:** As discussed above, the only requirement of Section 8 related to the eligibility for bonus is that the employee should have worked in an establishment for not less than 30 working days in an accounting year. This rule applies to seasonal workers as well. Therefore, if a seasonal worker has worked in an establishment for more than 30 working days, he is entitled to get bonus.
2. **Eligibility of managerial employee for bonus:** An employee, irrespective of whether he is a managerial employee or not, so long as he is covered within the definition of employee by virtue of drawing a salary falling within the maximum prescribed under Section 2(13) of the Act, is eligible for payment of bonus under the Act.

Let us discuss a case (Case 16.1) to understand the eligibility of employees for bonus under special circumstances.

Case 16.1: *The Project Manager, Ahmedabad ... v. Sham Kumar Sehgal*[1]

Mr Sham Kumar Sehgal was employed as an Assistant Grade (I) (R) with the Oil and Natural Gas Commission (ONGC). It was the case of the ONGC that, while functioning as Junior Assistant, Technical and Purchase Section, ONGC, Cambay, Mr Sehgal committed misconduct. Therefore, ONGC initiated disciplinary action against him under Regulation 25 of the Oil and Natural Gas Commission (Conduct, Discipline and Appeal) Regulation, 1964. During the enquiry Mr Sehgal was placed under suspension in

---

[1] *The Project Manager, Ahmedabad ... v. Sham Kumar Sehgal (Since Decd.) ...*, 1995 (71) FLR 176, (1995) 1 GLR 116, (1995) ILLJ 863 Guj.

October 1963. The Inquiry Officer completed the inquiry and recorded in his findings that Mr Sehgal was guilty and awarded a penalty of stoppage of one increment with cumulative effect. It was also directed that the period of suspension would not be counted as on duty for any purpose except for continuity of service. The respondent was served with the order of reinstatement on 6 April 1978 and immediately, on the next day, that is, on 7 April 1978, he resumed his duties.

Thereafter, Mr Sehgal submitted an application under Section 33C(2) of the Industrial Disputes Act, 1947, for recovery of bonus amount due from the petitioner to him. In the said application, it was contended by Mr Sehgal that he was ready and willing to serve, but he was not allowed to do so by the petitioner and, therefore, he was entitled to receive bonus for the disputed period. The respondent claimed a total amount of ₹6,448.78 being the amount of bonus which he was entitled to receive for the years 1966–1967 to 1976–1977. On being served with the recovery application, the petitioner contested the application and contended that the deceased respondent was under suspension during the relevant period and had not rendered any service to the ONGC, and, therefore, he was not entitled to claim the amount of bonus from the petitioner. It was also pleaded by the petitioner that the employee had not worked in the establishment for 30 working days during the relevant period and as thus he was not eligible for bonus in view of the provisions of Section 8 of the Payment of Bonus Act, 1965.

Discussion Point

Could Mr Sehgal claim the bonus for the suspension period under the circumstances mentioned in the above case?

Judgement and Explanation

It was held that Mr Sehgal was prevented from rendering work in ONGC, the establishment by an overt Act of the company. The fact that Mr Sehgal was ready and willing to perform his work was apparent as he resumed duty on 7 April 1978 pursuant to the order dated 6 April 1978 issued by the petitioner. It could not therefore be said that though the deceased employee was deemed to have been in service pursuant to the reinstatement, he could not be deemed to have put in the attendance required by the relevant statutory provisions to claim the bonus.

Disqualification for Bonus

The Act further provides that if an employee is dismissed from service for fraud or riotous or violent behaviour while in the premises of the establishment or theft, misappropriation or sabotage of any property of the establishment, he is disqualified from receiving bonus.

Case 16.2 will throw more light on the circumstances under which an employee is disqualified from receiving bonus.

Case 16.2: *Pandiyan Roadways Corporation Ltd. v. Labour Court, 1996*[2]

Pandiyan Roadways Corporation Ltd., a Government of Tamil Nadu Undertaking and the petitioner, was engaged in passenger transport. The respondent was working as a conductor under the petitioner. While so, in the year 1984, he reissued two tickets already sold in the previous trip and thus misappropriated a sum of

[2] *Pandiyan Roadways Corporation Ltd. v. Labour Court,* 1996, LIC 2589: 1997 LLR 83: 1996-II LLj 1229 (Mad HC).

₹1.60. Hence, a charge memo was issued to him and he submitted his explanation. His explanation was found to be unsatisfactory and, therefore, a full-fledged enquiry was conducted. The Enquiry Officer found that the charge levelled against the respondent was proved. Hence the respondent was dismissed from service for the proved charge of fraud and misappropriation.

Aggrieved by the order of dismissal, the respondent raised a dispute and on failure of conciliation the matter was referred for adjudication. In the year 1987, during the pendency of the above case, by virtue of a settlement under Section 18(1) of the Industrial Disputes Act, the respondent was appointed as a fresh entrant by a settlement and, accordingly, he reported for duty with effect from 16 March 1989. As per clause 3 of the settlement, the respondent agreed that he will not claim any benefit or approved privileges, for the period of his service before dismissal, that is, for the period from 1 January 1977 to 21 October 1984.

Thereafter, the respondent claimed bonus for the period from 1983–1984 to 1984–1985 amounting to ₹1,842. The claim was based on Section 9 of the Payment of Bonus Act. According to the petitioner, in the case of a dismissal from service on grounds of fraud of theft or misappropriation, the employer forfeited his bonus and he was disqualified from receiving any bonus under the Payment of Bonus Act. The petitioner contended that respondent was disqualified from receiving bonus even if the bonus was in respect of a year other than the accounting year in which the respondent/employee was found guilty of misconduct causing financial loss to the petitioner/employer.

Discussion Point

Under the above-mentioned circumstances, was the respondent entitled to bonus?

Judgement and Explanation

It was held that the employer was entitled to disqualify the employee for bonus for the accounting year 1983–1984 as well as for the accounting year 1984–1985. The respondent had entered into a settlement under Section 18(1) of the Act by which he gave up his claim prior to his dismissal. Therefore, he could not at all claim any benefit for the period prior to that dismissal.

Thus, if an employee is dismissed from service, he stands disqualified from receiving any bonus under the said Act and not the bonus only for the accounting year.

Amount of Bonus

The bonus formula provided by the Act has the provisions for minimum and maximum bonus to the employees in an accounting year to ensure that the employees are not deprived of bonus in the accounting year. The bonus is to be paid to the employees, even in the accounting years in which company earns nothing but loss. This is how a regular, sustained income to employees is ensured in addition to their salary or wages.

Let us discuss the provisions under the Act for the computation of minimum and maximum bonus in an accounting year:

1. **Minimum bonus payable (Section 10):** According to Section 10 of the Act, every employer is bound to pay for every employee in respect of any accounting year, a minimum bonus which is to be 8.33% of the salary or wage earned by the employee during the accounting year or ₹100, whichever is higher, whether or not the employer has any allocable surplus in the accounting year. In a case where an employee has not completed 15 years of age at the beginning of the accounting year, the minimum bonus payable is 8.33% or ₹60 whichever is higher.

The Payment of Bonus (Amendment) Bill, 2015

The Payment of Bonus (Amendment) Bill, 2015, was passed by the Parliament in the just concluded Winter Session of the Parliament and it was published in the Gazette of India, Extraordinary on 1 January 2016 as Act No. 6 of 2016. The provisions of the Payment of Bonus (Amendment) Act, 2015, came into force on the 1 April 2014.

The Payment of Bonus (Amendment) Act, 2015, envisaged enhancement of eligibility limit under Section 2(13) from ₹10,000 per month to ₹21,000 per month and Calculation Ceiling under Section 12 from ₹3,500 to ₹7,000 or the minimum wage for the scheduled employment, as fixed by the appropriate government, whichever is higher.

Computation of working days: Section 14 of the Act states that while computing number of working days, an employee is deemed to have worked in an establishment even on the days on which

a. He was laid off.
b. He was on leave with salary/wages.
c. He was absent due to temporary disablement caused by accident arising out of and in the course of employment.
d. The employee was on maternity leave with salary/wages.

It must be noted here that any agreement or settlement whereby the employees relinquish their right to receive the minimum bonus under Section 10 is considered to be null and void insofar as it purports to deprive them of such right (Section 38).

2. **Maximum bonus payable (Section 11):** If in respect of any accounting year, the allocable surplus exceeds the amount of minimum bonus payable to the employees, the employer is, in lieu of such minimum bonus, bound to pay for every employee in respect of that accounting year bonus which is to be an amount in proportion to the salary or wage earned by the employee during the accounting year subject to a maximum of 20% of such salary or wage.

   Computation of allocable surplus: In computing the allocable surplus under this section, the amount set on or the amount set off under the provisions of Section 15 has to be taken into account in accordance with the provisions of that section (Section 11(2); setting on or setting off under Section 15 will be discussed in the following section of this chapter).

Calculation of Bonus with Respect to Certain Employees (Section 12)

As amended by the Payment of Bonus (Amendment) Bill, 2015, if the salary or wage of an employee exceeds ₹7,000 per month, the bonus payable to such employee under Section 10 or, as the case may be, under Section 11, is to be calculated as if his salary or wage were ₹7,000 per month.

Proportionate Reduction in Bonus in Certain Cases (Section 13)

If an employee does not work for all the working days in an accounting year, the minimum bonus of ₹100 or, as the case may be, ₹60, if such bonus is higher than 8.33% of his salary or wages for the days he has worked in that accounting year, is to be proportionately reduced.

Computation of Number of Working Days (Section 14)

For the computation of the number of working days for the purpose of this Act, an employee is deemed to have worked in an establishment in any accounting year also on the days on which:

1. He has been laid off.
2. He has been on leave with salary or wage.
3. He had been absent due to temporary disablement caused by accident arising out of and in the course of his employment.
4. The employee has been on maternity leave with salary or wage, during the accounting year.

LO3: Calculation of Bonus

Annual Bonus (Section 2(21))

As laid down by the Act, for the purpose of calculation of bonus, a salary or wage includes only basic salary or wage and dearness allowance excluding other allowances like overtime salary or wage, house rent allowance, traveling concessions, bonus, employer's contribution to provident fund, retrenchment compensation, gratuity or commission.

Bonus payable under the Act is linked to profits. The employer calculates the 'gross profits' of his establishment in the manner specified in Section 4 of the Act. Then from 'gross profits' so calculated, he had to deduct the sums referred to in Section 6 as prior charges. The balance is called 'available surplus'. After the calculation of available surplus, a percentage of it is calculated in accordance with the provisions of Subsection (4) of Section 2 to calculate 'allocable surplus'. As discussed above, if in respect of any year the allocable surplus is more than the amount of minimum bonus payable to the employees, the employer must pay for every employee in respect of that year bonus in proportion to the salary or wage earned by the employee during the year subject to a maximum of 20% of such salary or wage.

Determination of Bonus

Following are the steps for the determination of the bonus amount in an accounting year.

1. **Step One: Computation of Gross Profit (Section 4)**

The Act explains that the gross profits derived by an employer from an establishment in respect of the accounting year:

   a. In the case of a banking company, is to be calculated in the manner specified in the First Schedule.
   b. In any other case, is to be calculated in the manner specified in the Second Schedule.
      i. **Computation of gross profits for a banking company (Section 4(a)):** First Schedule of the Act explains the manner in which the gross profit for the banking companies is to be computed for the purpose of this Act. There are some items that are required either to be added or to be deducted from the net profit in the profit and loss account of last accounting year after making usual and necessary provisions (Table 16.1).

TABLE 16.1 Computation of Gross Profit for Banking Companies: First Schedule

Item No.	*Particulars*	*Amount of Sub-items*	*Amount of Main Items*	*Remarks*
1.	Net profit shown in the profit and loss account after making usual and necessary provisions. (Where the profit subject to taxation is shown in the profit and loss account and the provision made for taxes on income is shown, the actual provision for taxes on income shall be deducted from the profit.)	₹	₹	
	Items to be added back to net profit: Following are the items that are required to be added to the net profit in the profit and loss account of last accounting year after making usual and necessary provisions.			
2.	**Add back provision for:**			
	a. Bonus to employees.			See footnote (1)
	b. Depreciation			
	c. Any other Rebate Reserve			
	d. Any other reserves.			
	Total of Item No. 2	₹		See footnote (1)
3.	**Add back also:**			
	a. Bonus paid to employees in respect of previous accounting years.			See footnote (1)
	b. The amount debited in respect of gratuity paid or payable to employees in excess of the aggregate of:			
	i. the amount, if any, paid to, or provided for payment to, an approved gratuity fund; and			See footnote (1)
	ii. the amount actually paid to employees on their retirement or on termination of their employment for any reason.			
	c. Donation in excess of the amount admissible for income tax.			
	d. Capital expenditure (other than capital expenditure on scientific research which is allowed as a deduction under any law for the time being in force relating to direct taxes) and capital losses (other than losses on sale of capital assets on which depreciation has been allowed for income tax).			
	e. Any amount certified by the Reserve Bank of India in terms of Subsection (2) of Section 34A of the Banking Regulation Act, 1949 (10 of 1949).			
	f. Losses of, or expenditure relating to, any business situated outside India.			
	Total of Item No. 3	₹		

Item No.	*Particulars*	*Amount of Sub-items*	*Amount of Main Items*	*Remarks*
4.	Add also income, profits or gains (if any) credited directly to published or disclosed reserved, other than:			
	a. capital receipts and capital profits (including profits on the sale of capital assets on which depreciation has not been allowed for income tax);			
	b. profits of, and receipts relating to, any business situated outside India;			
	c. income of foreign banking companies from investment outside India.			
	Net Total of Item No. 4	₹		
5.	Total of Item Nos. 1, 2, 3 and 4	₹		

Items to be deducted from the net profit: Following are the items that are required to be deducted from aggregate of the items added back to the net profit as shown above in the table.

Item No.	*Particulars*	*Amount of Sub-items*	*Amount of Main Items*	*Remarks*
6.	**Deduct:**			
	a. Capital receipts and capital profits (other than profits on the sale of assets on which depreciation has been allowed for income tax).			See footnote (2)
	b. Profits of, receipts relating to, any business situation outside India.			See footnote (2)
	c. Income of foreign banking companies from investments outside India.			See footnote (2)
	d. Expenditure or losses (if any) debited directly to published or disclosed reserves, other than:			See footnote (2)
	i. capital expenditure and capital losses (other than losses on sale of capital assets on which depreciation has not been allowed for income tax);			See footnote (2)
	ii. losses of any business situated outside India.			See footnote (2)
	e. In the case of foreign banking companies, proportionate administrative (overhead) expenses of Head Office allocable to India business.			
	f. Refund of any excess direct tax paid for previous accounting years and excess provision, if any, of previous accounting years, relating to bonus, depreciation or development rebate, if written back.			
g.	Cash subsidy, if any given by the government or by any law for the time being in force or by any other agency through budgetary grants, whether given directly to through any agency for specified			

Item No.	Particulars	Amount of Sub-items	Amount of Main Items	Remarks
	purposes and the proceeds of which are reserved for such purpose.			
	Total of Item No. 6	₹		
7.	Gross profits for purpose of bonus (Item No. 5 minus Item No. 6)	₹		

Source: The Payment of Bonus Act, 1965.

Notes: 1. If, and to the extent, charged to profit and loss account.
2. If, and to the extent, credited to profit and loss account.
3. In the proportion of India gross profit (Item No. 7) to total world gross profit (as per consolidated profit and loss account adjusted as in Item No. 2 above only).

ii. **Computation of gross profits for other companies (Section 4(b)):** Second Schedule of the Act explains the manner in which the gross profit for companies other than banking companies is to be computed for the purpose of this Act. There are some items that are required to either to be added or deducted from the net profit in the profit and loss account of last accounting year after making usual and necessary provisions (Table 16.2).

TABLE 16.2 Computation of Gross Profit for Other Companies: Second Schedule

Item No.	Particulars	Amount of Sub-items	Amount of Main Items	Remarks
1.	Net profit as per profit and loss account	₹	₹	
	Items to be added back to net profit: Following are the items that are required to be added to the net profit in the profit and loss account of last accounting year after making usual and necessary provisions.			
2.	**Add back provision for:**			
	a. Bonus to employees			
	b. Depreciation			
	c. Direct taxes, including the provision (if any) for previous accounting years.			
	d. Development rebate/investment allowance/ development allowance reserve.	₹	₹	See footnote (1)
	e. Any other reserves.			
	Total of Item No. 2	₹		See footnote (1)
3.	**Add back also:**			
	a. Bonus paid to employees in respect of previous accounting years.			See footnote (1)

Item No.	*Particulars*	*Amount of Sub-items*	*Amount of Main Items*	*Remarks*
	2(aa) The amount debited in respect of gratuity paid or payable to employees in excess of the aggregate of:			
	i. the amount, if any, paid to, or provided for payment to, an approved gratuity fund; and			See footnote (1)
	ii. the amount actually paid to employees on their retirement or on termination of their employment for any reason.			
	b. Donation in excess of the amount admissible for income tax.			
	c. Any annuity due, or commuted value of any annuity paid, under the provisions of Section 280D of the Income Tax Act during the accounting year.			
	d. Capital expenditure (other than capital expenditure on scientific research which is allowed as a deduction under any law for the time being in force relating to direct taxes) and capital losses (other than losses on sale of capital assets on which depreciation has been allowed for income tax or agricultural income tax).			
	e. Losses of, or expenditure relating to, any business situated outside India.			See footnote (1)
	Total of Item No. 3	₹		
4.	**Add also income—profits or gains (if any) credited directly to reserves, other than:**			
	a. capital receipts and capital profits (including profits on the sale of capital assets on which depreciation has not been allowed for income tax or agricultural income tax);			
	b. profits of, and receipts relating to, any business situated outside India;			
	c. income of foreign concerns from investments outside India.			
	Net Total of Item No. 4	₹		
5.	Total of Item Nos. 1, 2, 3 and 4	₹		
	Items to be deducted from the net profit: Following are the items that are required to be deducted from aggregate of the items added back to the net profit as shown above in the table.			
6.	**Deduct:**			
	a. Capital receipts and capital profits (other than profits on the sale of assets on which depreciation has been allowed for income tax or agricultural income tax).			See footnote (2)

Item No.	Particulars	Amount of Sub-items	Amount of Main Items	Remarks
	b. Profits of, and receipts relating to, any business situated outside India.			See footnote (2)
	c. Income of foreign concerns from investment outside India.			See footnote (2)
	d. Expenditure or losses (if any) debited directly to reserves, other than:	₹	₹	
	i. capital expenditure and capital losses (other than losses on sale of capital assets on which depreciation has not been allowed for income tax or agricultural income tax);			See footnote (2)
	ii. Losses of any business situated outside India.			See footnote (2)
	e. In the case of foreign concerns proportionate administrative (overhead) expenses of Head Office allocable to India business.			
	f. Refund of any tax paid for previous accounting years and excess provision, if any, of previous accounting year relating to bonus, depreciation, taxation or development rebate or development allowance, if written back.			
	1g. Cash subsidy, if any, given by the government or by the body corporate established by any law for the time being in force or by any other agency through budgetary grants, whether given directly or through any agency for specified purpose and the proceeds of which are reserved for such purposes.			
	Total of Item No. 6	₹		
7.	Gross profits for purposes of bonus (Item No. 5 minus Item No. 6)	₹		

Source: The Payment of Bonus Act, 1965.

Explanation: In sub-item (aa) of Item 3, 'approved gratuity fund' has the same meaning assigned to it in clause (5) of Section 2 of the Income Tax Act.

Notes:
1. If, and to the extent, charged to profit and loss account.
2. If, and to the extent, credited to profit and loss account.
3. In the proportion of Indian gross profit (Item No. 7) to total world gross profit (as per consolidated profit and loss account, adjusted as in Item No. 2 above only).

2. **Step Two: Determination of Available Surplus (Section 5)**
   Next step, after determining gross profit by applying the method explained above, is to determine the available surplus.

   Sums deductible from gross profit (Section 6): To determine the available surplus following sums is to be deducted from the gross profits as prior charges, namely:

Determination of Bonus

1. **Gross profit:** The gross profits derived by an employer from an establishment in respect of the accounting year is as follows:
   a. In the case of a banking company, calculated in the manner specified in the First Schedule.
   b. In any other case, calculated in the manner specified in the Second Schedule.
2. **Available surplus:** ***Available Surplus = A+B***
   where:
   A = gross profit—depreciation admissible under Section 32 of the Income-tax Act—development allowance—direct taxes payable for the accounting year (calculated as per Section 7)—sums specified in the Third Schedule.
   B = direct taxes (calculated as per Section 7) in respect of gross profits for the immediately preceding accounting year—direct taxes in respect of such gross profits as reduced by the amount of bonus, for the immediately preceding accounting year.
3. **Calculate allocable surplus**: Allocable Surplus = 60% of Available Surplus, 67% in case of foreign companies.
4. **Make adjustments for set on or set off.**
5. **The allocable surplus so computed is distributed among the employees in proportion to salary or wages received by them during the relevant accounting year.**

a. Any amount by way of depreciation admissible in accordance with the provisions of Subsection (1) of Section 32 of the Income Tax Act, or in accordance with the provisions of the agricultural income-tax law, as the case may be. This deduction is to be done only in the cases where an employer has been paying bonus to his employees under a settlement or an award or agreement made before the 29 May 1965, and subsisting on that date after deducting from the gross profits notional normal depreciation. Then, the amount of depreciation to be deducted under this clause, at the option of such employer (such option to be exercised once and within one year from that date), continues to be such notional normal depreciation;
b. Any amount by way of (development rebate or investment allowance or development allowance) which the employer is entitled to deduct from his income under the Income Tax Act;
c. Subject to the provision of Section 7, any direct tax which the employer is liable to pay for the accounting year in respect of his income, profit and gain during that year.

The amount left after deducting above-mentioned sums from the gross profit is the 'available surplus' to be distributed as 'bonus'.

Calculation of Direct Tax Payable by the Employer (Section 7): Section 7 of the Act directs that any direct tax payable by the employer for any accounting year is to, subject to the following provisions, be calculated at the rates applicable to the income of the employer for that year, namely:

a. In calculating such tax, no account is to be taken of:
   i. Any loss incurred by the employer in respect of any previous accounting year and carried forward under any law for the time being in force relating to direct taxes.

ii. Any arrears of depreciation which the employer is entitled to add to the amount of the allowance for depreciation for any following accounting year or years under Subsection (2) of Section 32 of the Income-tax Act.

iii. Any exemption conferred on the employer under Section 84 of the Income Tax Act or of any deduction to which the employer is entitled under Subsection (1) of Section 101 of that Act, as in force immediately before the commencement of the Finance Act, 1965 (10 of 1965).

b. Where the employer is a religious or a charitable institution to which the provisions of Section 32 are not applicable and the whole or any part of its income is exempt from tax under the Income Tax Act, then, with respect to the income so exempted, such institution is to be treated as if it were a company in which the public are substantially interested within the meaning of that Act.

c. Where the employer is individual or a Hindu Undivided Family, the tax payable by such employer under the Income Tax Act is to be calculated on the basis that the income derived by him from the establishment is his only income.

d. Where the income of any employer includes any profits and gains derived from the export of any goods or merchandise out of India and any rebate on such income is permitted under any law for the time being in force relating to direct taxes, then no account is to be taken of such rebate.

e. No account is required to be taken of any rebate (other than development rebate or investment allowance or development allowance) or credit or relief or deduction (not hereinbefore mentioned in this section) in the payment of any direct tax allowed under any law for the time being in force relating to direct taxes or under the relevant annual Finance Act, for the development of any industry.

3. **Step Three: Allocable Surplus (Section 2(4))**
After determining the 'available surplus', the next step in the direction of calculating bonus amount is to determine employees' share known as 'allocable surplus'. According to Section 2(4) of the Act, for a company other than the banking which has not made the arrangements prescribed under the Income Tax Act for the declaration and payment within India of the dividends payable out of its profits in accordance with the provisions of Section 194 of that Act, 67% of the available surplus in an accounting year is treated as allocable surplus for the purpose of this Act. However, in any other case, 60% of such available surplus amounts to allocable surplus under this Act.

4. **Step Four: Set on and Set off of Allocable Surplus (Section 15)**
The principle behind fixing a minimum and maximum limit for payment of bonus is that the rate of bonus should not fluctuate widely from year to year.

a. **Set on:** Where for any year the allocable surplus exceeds the amount of maximum bonus payable to the employees, then the excess is, subject to a limit of 20% of the total salary or wages of the employees, carried forward for being set on in the succeeding year and so on. This carried forward surplus amount is to be utilized for the purpose of payment of bonus.

b. **Set off:** On the other hand, where for any year there is no available surplus, or the allocable surplus in respect of that year falls short of the amount of minimum bonus payable to the employees, and also there is no amount or sufficient amount carried forward and set on which could be utilized for the purpose of payment of the minimum bonus, then such minimum amount or the deficiency, as the case may be, is to be carried forward for being set off in the succeeding year and so on. This is called carry forward for being set off in succeeding years.

Thus, in every accounting year, 'allocable surplus' is calculated. To this amount, set on from previous years is added. Similarly, set off, if any, from previous years is deducted. This calculation results in the amount which is available for distribution as bonus. The amount set off is carried forward only up to and inclusive of the fourth accounting year. If the amount carried forward is not set off in that period, it lapses (Section 15(2)).

LO4: Special and Miscellaneous Provisions

Special Provisions for Certain Establishments (Section 16)

Following provisions have been made for the same;

1 **Newly setup establishment:** In case of an establishment which is newly set up whether before or after commencement of this Act, the employees of such establishment are entitled to be paid bonus under this Act in accordance with the provisions of Subsections (1A), (1B) and (1C).

a. **First 5 years:** According to Subsection (1A), in case of all new establishments, in the first 5 accounting years following the accounting year in which the employer sells the goods produced or manufactured by him or renders services as the case may be, bonus is to be paid only in respect of the accounting year in which the employer derives profit from such establishment. Such bonus is to be calculated in accordance with the provisions of this Act in relation to that year, but without applying the provisions of Section 15.

Here, the word 'profit' is construed according to its ordinary sense. A sense which is understood in trade and industry because the rationale behind Section 16(1A) is that it is only when the employer starts making profits in the commercial sense that he will become liable to pay bonus under the Act. Profit in the commercial sense is ascertained only after deducting depreciation. There are several methods of computing depreciation, and the one adopted by the employer, in the absence of any statutory provision to the contrary, would govern the calculation.

b. **For sixth and seventh years:** Subsection (1B) provides that for the sixth and seventh accounting year in which the employer sells the goods produced or manufactured by him or renders services as the case may be, from such establishment, the provisions of Section 15 are applied subject to the following modifications:

i. **For the sixth accounting year:** Set on or set off, as the case may be, is to be made in the manner illustrated in the Fourth Schedule taking into account the excess or deficiency, if any as the case may be, of the allocable surplus set on or set off in respect of the fifth and sixth accounting year.

ii. **For the seventh accounting year:** Set on or set off, as the case may be, is to be made in the manner illustrated in the Fourth Schedule taking into account the excess or deficiency, if any, as the case may be of the allocable surplus set on or set off in respect of the fifth, sixth and seventh accounting years.

c. **From 8 accounting years:** Subsection (1C) deals with the 8 accounting years and states that from the eighth accounting year following the accounting year in which the employer sells the goods produced or manufactured by him or renders services, as the case may be from such establishment, the provisions of Section 15 apply in relation to such establishment as they apply in relation to any other establishment.

Something that should be kept in mind in relation to above-explained subsections is that for the purpose of Subsection (1), an establishment cannot be deemed to be newly set up merely by reason of a change in its location, management or ownership. Also to be noted that an employer is not deemed to have derived profit in accounting year unless:

a. The provision for that year's depreciation has been made to which he is entitled under the Income Tax Act or, as the case may be, under the Agriculture Income tax law, and
b. The arrears of such depreciation and losses incurred by him in respect of the establishment for the previous accounting years have been fully set off against his profits.

For the purposes of above-mentioned Subsections [(1A), (1B) and (1C)], sale of the goods produced or manufactured during the course of the trial running of any factory or of the prospecting stage of any mine or an oil field is not included where any question arises with regard to such production or manufacture. The decision of the appropriate government, made after giving the parties a reasonable opportunity of representing the case, is final and cannot be called in question by any court or other authority.

2. **Applicability of Sections (1A), (1B) and (1C) to an existing establishment consisting of different departments or undertakings or branch:** If an employer of an existing establishment consisting of different departments or undertakings or branches (whether or not in the same industry) set up at different periods, before the Act came into force, has been paying bonus to the employees of all such departments or undertakings or branches on the basis of the consolidated profits computed in respect of all such departments or undertakings or branches, then such an employer is liable to pay bonus in accordance with the provisions of this Act to all such employees of all such departments or undertakings or branches (whether set up before or after that date) on the basis of the consolidated profits computed as aforesaid.

Adjustment of Customary or Interim Bonus (Section 17)

To understand the application of Section 17, first we need to understand the meaning of customary bonus. Customary bonus is the bonus which is being paid by way of tradition or custom at a uniform rate over a number of years and which has no link with profit. Where in any accounting year an employer has paid any puja bonus or other customary bonus to an employee, or he has paid a part of the bonus payable under this Act to an employee before the date on which such bonus becomes payable, then, the employer is entitled to deduct the amount of bonus so paid from the amount of bonus payable by him to the employee under this Act in respect of that accounting year. In such case, the employee is entitled to receive only the balance of the bonus left with the employer.

Deductions of Certain Amounts from Bonus (Section 18)

In any accounting year, if an employee is found guilty of misconduct causing financial loss to the employer, then it is lawful for the employer to deduct the amount of loss from the amount of bonus payable by him to the employee under this Act, in respect of that accounting year only. In such case, the employee is entitled to receive only the balance of the bonus left with the employer, if any.

Time Limit for Payment (Section 19)

The Act provides under Section 19, in relation to time limit for the payment of the bonus. It states that if there is no dispute about payment of bonus, bonus is to be paid within a period of 8 months from the close of the accounting year. But, if there is a dispute about the payment of bonus pending before any authority, bonus is to be paid within 1 month from the date on which the award in respect of such dispute becomes enforceable or the settlement in respect of such dispute comes into operation. However, if there is sufficient cause, extension may be applied for. In all cases, bonus must be paid in cash.

Rights of Employer

An employer has the following rights:

1. Right to forfeit bonus of an employee, who has been dismissed from service for fraud, riotous or violent behaviour, or theft, misappropriation or sabotage of any property of the establishment.
2. Right to make permissible deductions from the bonus payable to an employee, such as festival/interim bonus paid and financial loss caused by misconduct of the employee.
3. Right to refer any disputes relating to application or interpretation of any provision of the Act, to the Labour Court or Labour Tribunal.

Rights of Employees

Following are the rights of an employee against the employer:

1. Right to claim bonus payable under the Act and to make an application to the government, for the recovery of bonus due and unpaid. Such application has to move within 1 year of its becoming due.
2. Right to refer any dispute to the Labour Court/Tribunal Employees, to whom the Payment of Bonus Act does not apply, but cannot raise a dispute regarding bonus under the Industrial Disputes Act.
3. Right to seek clarification and obtain information, on any item in the accounts of the establishment.

Recovery of Bonus Due (Section 21)

Section 21 of the Act deals with the recovery of the bonus. It states that if any bonus is due to an employee under a settlement, award or agreement, then such an employee can make an application to the government for its recovery. On receiving such application and being satisfied that money is due to an employee by way of bonus, the government may issue a certificate to the Collector to recover the same as an arrear of land revenue. But such an application should be made within 1 year from the date on which bonus became due to the employee from the employer. However, the application may be entertained after a year also if the applicant shows that there was sufficient cause for not making the application within time.

Maintenance of Registers under the Act (Section 26 and Rules 4 and 5)

The Act requires every employer to maintain, in the prescribed form, the following three registers:

1. A register having the details of the computation of the allocable surplus.
2. A register showing the set on and set off of the allocable surplus.
3. A register carrying the details of the amount of bonus payable to each of employees. the amount of deductions if any and the amount actually paid.

The employer is also required to send, in the prescribed form, an annual return to the Inspector appointed under the Act within 30 days from the expiry of the time limit specified in Section 19 for payment of bonus.

Power of Exemption (Section 36)

The Act empowers the appropriate government to exempt for such period as may be notified in the Official Gazette and subject to such conditions as it may think fit to impose, an establishment or class of establishments from all or any of the provisions of this Act, if the appropriate government, having regard to the financial position and other relevant circumstances of any establishment or class of establishments, is of opinion that it will not be in public interest to apply all or any of the provisions of this Act thereto. The appropriate government should consider public interest, financial position and whether workers contributed to the loss, before grant of any such exemption under this section.

Let us discuss a case (Case 16.3) to gain insights into Section 36 of the Act and its application.

Case 16.3: *Phoenix Mills Ltd v. The State of Maharashtra*, 1993[3]

Phoenix Mills Ltd., the first petitioner mills, was engaged in the business of spinning yarn and weaving and processing of cloth. On 2 September 1977, a catastrophic fire engulfed the three-storey building which housed the first petitioner mills. The fire caused a lot of damage apart from the building, and only 14,500 out of the total of 96,000 spindles could be saved. In the year 1977, the petitioners filed their applications before the government under Section 36 of Payment of Bonus Act to claim exemption from payment of the bonus for the year ending 31 March 1977. The government passed an order granting exemption as prayed for. In the year 1978, the petitioners filed their second application for exemption for the year ended 31 March 1978 and the same was granted. In the year 1979, the petitioner mills was declared a relief undertaking. Subsequently in the year 1982, there was a general textile industries strike in the city of Bombay.

The strike continued for a period of 3 to 4 months and the first petitioner started limping back to work gradually thereafter. The financial condition of the first petitioner on account of the aforesaid factors suffered a severe setback for the financial year 1 April 1981 to 31 March 1982. The petitioners therefore filed an application under Section 36 for exemption from payment of minimum bonus for the financial year ending

[3] *Phoenix Mills Ltd. v. The State of Maharashtra*, 1993 (11I LL) (Supp) 844: 1993 LLR 783: 1993(67) FLR 231 (Born HC).

31 March 1982. After some months in the same year, the government issued notices to the petitioners as also several other cotton textile mills which had made similar applications for a meeting and it was informed by the government that the application for exemption was rejected. The petitioners requested the government to furnish them with the detailed order rejecting its prayer for exemption.

The government contended in the order that the exemption under Section 36 could not be sought by the management on any ground of natural calamity. It was further mentioned that mere losses suffered by the petitioners were not a sufficient consideration for grant of relief under Section 36. It was only when the financial condition had been hopeless for several years and losses were suffered continuously and the entire capital and the assets were wiped out that the exemption under Section 36 could be granted.

Discussion Point

Could the petitioner mill be granted an exemption under Section 36 of the Payment of Bonus Act in above-mentioned circumstances?

Judgement and Explanation

The court granted exemption under Section 36 of the Payment of Bonus Act, 1965, to the petitioner mill. The court order stated that the exemption sought by the management was not on any ground of natural calamity. The petitioner mill had sustained heavy losses in a devastating fire and was adversely affected by the general textile industries strike. In the opinion of court, there are two stages in Section 36.

The court clarified that the legislature did not contemplate arising of such liability to pay minimum bonus, when the reserves of the concern were wiped out and the capital itself was exposed to erosion and leaving no hope of any profits further exposing the concern to the danger of being closed or wiped out completely. However, mere losses in successive years might not create such danger as long as such losses do not expose the capital itself to danger.

Inspector (Section 27)

Under Section 17 of the Act, by notification in the Official Gazette, the government is authorized to appoint such persons as it thinks fit to be Inspectors for the purpose of this Act. The government also defines the limits within which they shall exercise jurisdiction.

Powers of the Inspector

To ensure that all the provisions of this Act are complied with, an Inspector appointed under Section 27 of this Act is empowered to:

1. Enquire an employer to furnish such information as he may consider necessary.
2. At any reasonable time and with such assistance, if any, as he thinks fit, enter any establishment or any premises connected therewith and require any one found in charge thereof to produce before him for examination any accounts, books, registers and other documents relating to the employment of persons or the payment of salary or wage or bonus in the establishment.
3. Examine with respect to any matter relevant to any of the purposes aforesaid, the employer, his agent or servant or any other person found in charge of the establishment or any premises connected therewith or any person whom the Inspector has reasonable cause to believe to be or to have been an employee in the establishment.

4. Make copies of, or take extracts from, any book, register or other documents maintained in relation to the establishment.
5. Exercise such other powers as may be prescribed.

Every Inspector is deemed to be a public servant within the meaning of the IPC (45 of 1860) and any person required to produce any accounts, book, register or other documents or to give information by an Inspector under Subsection (1) is legally bound to do so. The Act further directs the Inspector must not force a banking company to furnish or disclose any statement or information or to produce, or give inspection of, any of its books of account or other documents, which a banking company cannot be compelled to furnish, disclose, produce or give inspection of, under the provisions of Section 34A of the Banking Regulation Act, 1949 (10 of 1949).

LO5: Dispute, Penalties and Offences

Reference of Disputes under the Act (Sections 22 and 39)

If there is a dispute about bonus payable under the Act, it has to be raised by the employees concerned in accordance with the provisions of the Industrial Disputes Act, 1947, or any corresponding state law, as is applicable to them. A dispute is deemed to be an industrial dispute within the meaning of such laws.

Penalties (Section 28)

The Act mentions clearly under Section 28 that every person is punishable:

1. Who contravenes any of the provisions of this Act or any rule made thereunder; or
2. To whom a direction is given or a requisition is made under this Act and he fails to comply with the direction or requisition.

The Act imposes the penalty of imprisonment up to 6 months, or fine up to ₹1,000, or both for contravention of the provisions of the Act or rules. For failure to comply with the directions or requisitions made, the offender is liable to be imprisoned for up to 6 months, or fine up to ₹1,000, or both.

Offences by the Companies (Section 29)

In case of offences by companies, firms, body corporate or association of individuals, its director, partner or a principal officer responsible for the conduct of its business, as the case may be, are deemed to be guilty of that offence and punished accordingly, unless the person concerned proves that the offence was committed without his knowledge or that he exercised all due diligence to prevent the offence.

Cognizance of Offences (Section 30)

The Act does not allow any court to take cognizance of any offence punishable under this Act, save on complaint made by or under the authority of the appropriate government or an officer of that government (not below the rank of a Regional Labour Commissioner in the case of an officer of the central government, and not below the rank of a Labour Commissioner in the case of an officer of the state government) specially authorized in this behalf by that government. It is further provided that no court inferior to that of a presidency magistrate or a magistrate of the first class shall try any offence punishable under this Act.

Protection of Action (Section 31)

The Act directs under Section 31 that no one can file a suit, prosecution or other legal proceeding against the government or any officer of the government for anything which is in good faith done or intended to be done in pursuance of this Act or any rule made thereunder.

Payment of Bonus Linked with Production or Productivity (Section 31A)

The Act provides two situations in which special bonus is payable to the employees. Following are the situations:

1. If there is an agreement or a settlement entered into by the employees with their employer before the commencement of the Payment of Bonus (Amendment) Act, 1976 (23 of 1976); or
2. If the employees enter into any agreement or settlement with their employer after such commencement, for payment of an annual bonus linked with production or productivity in lieu of bonus based on profits payable under this Act.

In both the above-mentioned cases, such employees are entitled to receive bonus due to them under such agreement or settlement, as the case may be.

Power to Exempt (Section 36)

The Act empowers the appropriate government to exempt some establishment or class of establishments from all or any of the provisions of this Act, subject to some terms and conditions as it deems fit. However, while exercising the power under this section, the appropriate government must consider the financial position and other relevant circumstances of an establishment or class of establishments and also the public interest. Every such exemption is required to be published in an Official Gazette.

Summary

1. The Payment of Bonus Act provides for payment of bonus to persons employed in certain establishments on the basis of profits, or on the basis of production or productivity, and for matters connected therewith.
2. The main objective of the Payment of Bonus Act is to provide a statutory right to employees of an establishment to share the profits of his employer.

3. The Act extends to the whole of India and is applicable to every factory and every other establishment employing 20 or more persons.
4. Under the Act, 'corporation' is any corporate body established by or under any Central Provincial or State Act excluding a company or a cooperative society.
5. The term 'employee' includes any person employed on a salary or wage not exceeding ₹3,500 per month in any industry to do any skilled or unskilled manual, supervisory, managerial, administrative, technical or clerical work for hire or reward, whether the terms of employment be express or implied.
6. The Act defines 'salary' or 'wage' as all remuneration (other than remuneration in respect of overtime work) that may be expressed in terms of money and includes dearness allowance.
7. The only requirement of Section 8 related to the eligibility for bonus is that the employee should have worked in an establishment for not less than 30 working days in an accounting year.
8. If an employee is dismissed from service for fraud or riotous or violent behaviour while in the premises of the establishment or theft, misappropriation or sabotage of any property of the establishment, he is disqualified from receiving bonus.
9. A minimum bonus payable is to be 8.33% of the salary or wage earned by the employee during the accounting year or ₹100, whichever is higher, whether or not the employer has any allocable surplus in the accounting year.
10. Bonus payable under the Act is linked with profits.
11. In the case of a banking company, gross profit is to be calculated in the manner specified in the First Schedule, while in any other case, it is to be calculated in the manner specified in the Second Schedule.
12. The next step, after determining the gross profit by applying the method explained above, is to determine the available surplus.
13. After determining the 'available surplus', the next step in the direction of calculating bonus amount is to determine employees' share known as 'allocable surplus'.
14. In computing the allocable surplus under this section, the amount set on or the amount set off under the provisions of Section 15 has to be taken into account.
15. Section 16 of the Act deals with the payment of bonus in the case of newly set up establishments.
16. For the purposes Subsections [(1A), (1B) and (1C)], sale of the goods produced or manufactured during the course of the trial running of any factory or of the prospecting stage of any mine or an oil field is not included where any question arises with regard to such production or manufacture.
17. Customary bonus is the bonus which is being paid by way of tradition or custom at a uniform rate over a number of years and which has no link with profit.
18. Bonus is to be paid within a period of 8 months from the close of the accounting year.
19. If any bonus is due to an employee under a settlement, award or agreement, then such employee can make an application to the government for its recovery.
20. The Act empowers the appropriate government to exempt, an establishment or class of establishments from all or any of the provisions of this Act.
21. The government is authorized to appoint such persons as it thinks fit to be Inspectors for the purpose of this Act. The government also defines the limits within which they shall exercise jurisdiction.
22. In case of a dispute about bonus payable under the Act, it has to be raised by the employees concerned in accordance with the provisions of the Industrial Disputes Act, 1947, or any corresponding state law, as is applicable to them.

Multiple Choice Questions

1. The government can, however, apply the Act to any establishment employing __________.
   a. Less than 10 but not less than 05 persons
   b. Less than 20 but not less than 10 persons
   c. Less than 30 but not less than 10 persons
   d. Less than 50 but not less than 20 persons

2. The Payment of Bonus Act, 1976, entitles every employee receiving salary or wages up to ______ for the purpose of bonus.
   a. ₹3,500 per month
   b. ₹5,500 per month
   c. ₹7,500 per month
   d. ₹10,000 per month

3. The Payment of Bonus Act, 1965, entitles every employee engaged in __________ work to bonus for every accounting year if he has worked for at least 30 working days in that year.
   a. Skilled
   b. Unskilled
   c. Managerial or supervisory
   d. All of the above

4. In a case where an employee has not completed 15 years of age at the beginning of the accounting year, the minimum bonus payable is __________ whichever is higher.
   a. 6.33% or ₹60
   b. 8% or ₹60
   c. 8.33% or ₹60
   d. 10% or ₹60

5. If the salary or wage of an employee exceeds ₹3,500 per month, the bonus payable to such an employee is to be calculated __________.
   a. As if his salary or wage were ₹3,500 per month
   b. On the basis of his actual salary
   c. On a case-to-case basis
   d. Like other employees of the company

6. First Schedule of the Act explains the manner in which the gross profit for __________ is to be computed for the purpose of this Act.
   a. The banking companies
   b. The non-banking companies
   c. Both (2) and (b)
   d. Neither (a) nor (b)

7. __________ of the Act explains the manner in which the gross profit for companies other than banking companies is to be computed for the purpose of this Act.
   a. First Schedule
   b. Second Schedule
   c. Third Schedule
   d. Fourth Schedule

8. In the process of determining the bonus, after determining the gross profit, the next step is to determine __________.
   a. The allocable surplus
   b. The available surplus
   c. The customary bonus
   d. Set on or set off as applicable

9. After determining the 'available surplus', the next step in the direction of calculating bonus amount is to determine employees' share known as __________.
   a. The allocable surplus
   b. The gross profit
   c. The customary bonus
   d. Set on or set off as applicable

10. ______________ is the bonus which is being paid by way of tradition or custom at a uniform rate over a number of years and which has no link with profit.
    a. The allocable surplus
    b. The gross profit
    c. The customary bonus
    d. Set on or Set off as applicable

True/False Questions

1. An establishment to which the Act applies does not continue to be governed by the Act if there is any fall in the number of persons employed in subsequent years.
2. If an employee is dismissed from service, he stands disqualified from receiving any bonus under the said Act and not the bonus only for the accounting year.
3. For the purposes of above-mentioned Subsections [(1A), (1B) and (1C)] of Section 16, sale of the goods produced or manufactured during the course of the trial running of any factory or of the prospecting stage of any mine or an oil field is also included.
4. If there is no dispute about payment of bonus, bonus is to be paid within a period of 8 months from the close of the accounting year.
5. In case of customary bonus, the employee is entitled to receive only the balance of the bonus left with the employer.

Descriptive Questions

1. Throw light on the requirement of a legal framework to regulate the payment of bonus.
2. Write a note on major objectives and scope of the Payment of Bonus Act, 1976.
3. On which type of establishments, the Payment of Bonus Act, 1976, is applicable? Discuss in detail.
4. Write a short note on the following as defined in the Act:
    a. Award
    b. Allocable surplus
    c. Establishments in public sector
5. Who are entitled to receive bonus? Discuss in the light of provisions of Section 8 of the Act.
6. What are the rules regarding the payment of minimum and maximum bonus payable under the Act?
7. How is the bonus payable in an accounting year calculated? Discuss all the steps of computing the bonus amount in detail.
8. What is the procedure of set on and set off provided under the Payment of Bonus Act, 1976?
9. What is the provision under the Act, for the payment of bonus in the case of newly set up establishments?
10. How can a bonus be recovered? Discuss in the light of provisions of Payment of Bonus Act, 1976.
11. What are the provisions for the settlement of dispute and penalty in case of dispute for the payment of bonus?

17

CHAPTER

The Apprentices Act, 1961

LEARNING OBJECTIVES

Upon completing this chapter, the reader would be able to:

LO1. Understand the objectives, scope and important definitions of the Act.
LO2. Gain insights into provisions dealing with training of apprentices and their training.
LO3. Get the details of provisions dealing with health, safety and welfare of apprentices.
LO4. Discuss the obligations for employer and apprentices under the Act.
LO5. Know the authorities identified under the Act.
LO6. Understand the details of the provisions dealing with penalty and offences identified under the Act.

Introduction

Industrial development has been one of the prime needs of our country, and a lot of attention has been given to this factor in different development plans of the country. Trained personnel are required to perform the multifarious functions necessary for the development and sustenance of industry. However, there has been acute shortage of manpower in the skilled categories in many industries. To ensure the optimum supply of skilled, trained manpower to the industry, the Apprentices Act, 1961, was enacted. By enforcing the Apprentices Act, it was made obligatory for employers in specified industries to engage apprentices in designated trades to impart apprenticeship training on the job in industry to youth and persons having National Trade Certificates issued by NCVT to develop skilled manpower for the industry. The central/state apprenticeship adviser makes arrangement to locate the industries to be covered under the Apprentice Act with the assistance of various associations of industries such as Confederation of Indian Industries (CII), Chamber of Commerce and government departments such as industries, employment exchange and local body, and a list of such identified industries is prepared in the prescribed pro forma.

LO1: Objectives, Scope and Important Definitions

Objectives

It is generally observed that institutionally trained youths are not able to produce desired results because training imparted in institutions alone is not sufficient for acquisition of skills; it needs to be supplemented by training in the actual place of work. To facilitate training and enhancing the employability of job seekers in private/corporate sectors, the Apprentices Act, 1961, was enacted with the following objectives:

1. To regulate the programme of training of apprentices in the industry so as to conform to the prescribed syllabi, period of training and so on, as laid down by the Central Apprenticeship Council (CAC).
2. To fully utilize the facilities available in industry for imparting practical training with a view to meet the requirements of skilled manpower for industry.

Scope and Application of the Act

The National Apprenticeship Scheme was launched in 1959, initially on a voluntary basis. The Apprentices Act, 1961 (the Act), was enacted in the Parliament on 23 December 1961 and it came into force from 1 March 1962. The Act is applicable to the whole of India, and it was subsequently amended in 1973 and 1986.

Applicability of the Act

The Act extends to the whole of India. But the provisions of this Act do not apply to:

1. Any area or to any industry in any area unless the central government by notification in the Official Gazette specifies that area or industry as an area or industry to which the said provisions apply with effect from such date as may be mentioned in the notification.
2. Any such special apprenticeship scheme for imparting training to apprentices as any be notified by the central government in the Official Gazette. This Scheme covers all categories of apprentices except the graduate, technician and technician (vocational) apprentices which are covered by the Scheme administered by Ministry of HRD.

Eligible employers: The employers of any establishment where trade, occupation or subject field in engineering or technology is carried out in terms of the Apprentices Act, 1961, as amended from time to time, are covered under the Act. The following additional conditions are required to be fulfilled for being an eligible employer under the Scheme:

1. Keeping in view the recommendations of the CAC to permit apprentices within a range of 2.5% to 10% of the total strength of the establishment, the establishments eligible in the Scheme should have strength of at least six.
2. Not more than two apprentices are allowed in one establishment under this Scheme at a time.

3. Self-certification by the employer that the selected apprentice is not related to him, and this self-certification is to be displayed on the portal.

Eligible apprentices: The Act set the minimum age for being engaged as an apprentice at 14 years. The Apprentices (Amendment) Bill, 2014, added that the minimum age for apprenticeship in designated trades related to hazardous industries shall be 18 years.

The Apprentices (Amendment) Bill, 2014

The Apprentices (Amendment) Bill, 2014, was introduced in Lok Sabha on 7 August 2014 to amend the Apprentices Act, 1961. The Act regulates the training of apprentices in the industry, and an inter-ministerial group (IMG) recommended various changes to the Act to make apprenticeship more responsive to youth and industry. The Statement of Objects and Reasons of the Amendment Bill stated that the amendments proposed in the Bill were based on IMG's recommendations.

Following are the highlights of major amendments brought by the Amendment Bill in the Act:

1. **Definitions:** The Bill amended the definition of appropriate government to include an establishment operating in four or more states to be regulated by the central government. It also amends the definitions of: (a) designated trade, (b) graduate or technician apprentice, (c) trade apprentice, (d) industry and (e) worker. The Bill adds two definitions: (a) optional trade and (b) portal site.
2. **Minimum age for an apprentice:** The Act set the minimum age for being engaged as an apprentice at 14 years. The Bill added that the minimum age for apprenticeship in designated trades related to hazardous industries shall be 18 years.
3. **Number of apprentices:** The Act stated that the central government, after consulting the CAC established under the Act, is to determine the ratio of trade apprentices to workers (except unskilled workers) for each designated trade. The Bill stated that the central government must prescribe the number of apprentices to be engaged by an employer for designated trade and optional trade.
4. **Cooperation between employers for training:** The Bill permitted multiple employers to come together, either themselves or through an approved agency (vs. only themselves as per the Act), to provide apprenticeship training (vs. practical training as per the Act) to apprentices under them.
5. **Practical training to apprentices:** The Act stated that every employer had to make suitable arrangements in his workshop for imparting practical training to apprentices, as per the programme approved by the adviser, and the Bill removed the requirement for adviser's approval.
6. **Basic training to apprentices:** The Act expected that trade apprentices who had not received prior institutional training were required to be imparted basic training before admission in the workshop for practical training. But the Bill specified in this regard that such training can now be provided in any institute with adequate facilities.
7. **Syllabus and equipment for practical training:** The Act states that the syllabus and equipment for practical training shall be as approved by the central government (with CAC consultation). The Bill limits the provision for training in a designated trade only.
8. **Grant of certificate:** The Act specifies that every trade apprentice should appear for a proficiency test conducted by the NCVT, on completion of his training. On passing the test, NCVT shall grant him a certificate of proficiency. The Bill adds that such tests may be conducted and certificates may be granted by other authorized agencies as well.

9. **Hours of work, overtime, leave and holidays:** The Act states that the weekly and daily hours of work and leave entitlements of an apprentice shall be as prescribed by rules. The Bill states that the hours of work and leave will be as per the discretion or policy of the employer.
10. **Offences and penalties:** The Act specifies certain offences which are punishable with imprisonment up to 6 months or with a fine (quantum unspecified) or both. The Bill specifies the amount/ maximum amount of the fine and removes the provision for imprisonment for such offences.
11. **Power to make rules:** The Act permits the central government (after consulting with the CAC) to make rules for implementing the Act. The Bill states that these powers shall include the power to make rules retrospectively with effect from a date on or after the President grants his assent to the Bill. No rule shall have a retrospective effect if it prejudicially affects the interests of any person to whom such rule may be applicable.

Who Is an Apprentice

The word 'Apprentice' has originated from Old French Aprentis (from apprendre 'learn', from Latin apprehendere 'apprehend'). An apprentice is a person who is learning a trade from a skilled employer, having agreed to work for a fixed period at low wages. The apprentice provides help to a skilled worker in order to learn the trade himself. An example of an apprentice would be a person who works with an electrician to learn the skills necessary to become a skilled electrician. Thus, in simple words, we can say that an apprentice is a person who agrees to work for a specified time in order to learn a trade, craft or profession in which the employer, traditionally called the master, assents to instruct him or her.

Nature of Apprentice Contract

Apprentice contract: The apprentice contract is a contract entered into between a person who understands some art, trade or business, who is called the master, and another person, commonly a minor, during his or her minority, who is called the apprentice, with the consent of his or her parent or next friend by which the former undertakes to teach such minor his art, trade or business, and to fulfil such other covenants as may be agreed upon, and the latter agrees to serve the master during a definite period of time, in such art, trade or business.[1] The term during which the apprentice is to serve is also called his apprenticeship.[2]

Duties and rights of master: The principal duties of the master are as follows:

1. The employer (master) is bound to instruct the apprentice by teaching him, bona fide, the knowledge of the art of which he has undertaken to teach him the elements.
2. He ought to watch over the conduct of the apprentice, giving him prudent advice and showing him a good example, and fulfilling towards him the duties of a father, as in his character of master, he stands in loco parentis.
3. He is also required to fulfil all the covenants he has entered into by the indenture.
4. He must not abuse his authority, either by bad treatment or by employing his apprentice in menial employments that are wholly unconnected with the business he has to learn.
5. After the apprenticeship is at an end, he cannot retain the apprentice on the grounds that he has not fulfilled his contract, unless specially authorized by statute.

[1] Daug. 500.
[2] Pardessus, Dr. Com. n. 34.

Duties and rights of the apprentice: Following are the duties of an apprentice:

1. An apprentice is bound to obey his master in all his lawful commands, take care of his property, promote his interest, endeavour to learn his trade or business, and perform all the covenants in his indenture not contrary to law.
2. He must not leave his master's service during the term of the apprenticeship.
3. The apprentice is entitled to payment for extraordinary services when promised by the master and, even when no express promise has been made, under peculiar circumstances.
4. Apprenticeship is a relation which cannot be assigned at the common law, although the apprentice may work with a second master by order and consent of the first, which is a service to the first under the indenture.
5. Apprentice remains a learner after getting the entitled payment and in no case can be treated as an employee.

Section 18 of the Act makes a mention in this regard as follows:

1. Every apprentice undergoing apprenticeship training in a designated trade in an establishment shall be trainees and not an employee.
2. The provisions of any law with respect to labour shall not apply to or in relation to such apprentice.

Following are the important points in relation to the relationship shared between the master and apprentice:

1. An apprentice is merely a trainee and can never be treated as an employee.
2. The apprentice works for his master for a fixed payment.
3. The employer is not bound to employ the apprentice when the apprenticeship gets over.
4. The provisions of labour mentioned in any law are not applicable on an apprentice.

Let us discuss a case (Case 17.1) to understand the rights of an apprentice.

Case 17.1: *National Small Industries Corporation ... v. V. Lakshminarayanan*[3]

The case made out by V. Lakshminarayanan (hereinafter referred to as V. L.) before the Labour Court under Section 2(a) of the 1947 Act was that he had joined the appellant herein as a casual labourer on daily wages on 6 April 1987. It was further stated that V. L. had continued to work in the Marketing Development Centre of the appellant at Nungambakkam on daily wages at ₹15 per day continuously till 2 May 1990. While working with the appellant, he had been called for a direct interview on 13 April 1990 for the post of apprenticeship trainee (shop assistant) and he was selected as per the order dated 26 April 1990. V. L. also asserted that during the first year, he was paid a salary of ₹600 per month and during the second year he was paid ₹750 per month as salary, and after the training period was over, the appellant herein had agreed to appoint him as a peon. It is his case that on 8 July 1991, he was transferred to the Government Purchase Section of the Regional Office where he was made to perform dispatch work. Suddenly, on 1 May 1992,

[3] *National Small Industries Corporation ... v. V. Lakshminarayanan*, 10 November 2006.

without any reason or inquiry, he was removed from service, and that since he had served continuously for more than 240 days, his removal from service should be treated as retrenchment since the appellant herein had not followed the procedure indicated in Section 25F of the 1947 Act. He further argued that while juniors were allowed to continue in service, he was not reinstated, and his removal from service without any reason violates the provisions of Section 25F of 1947 Act.

On the other hand, National Small Industries Corporation (hereinafter referred as the employer) completely denied all the allegations framed by V. L. The employer stated that V. L. was interviewed on 13 April 1990, and in the orders of his selection passed in this regard on 26 April 1990, it was specifically mentioned that the training period would be for 2 years only. V. L. was directed to report for training before 3 May 1990, and the training period consequently came to an end on 2 May 1992. On 29 April 1992, V. L. requested the appellant to confirm him in service, and by subsequent letters dated 12 August 1992 and 7 December 1992, the respondent requested the appellant to make him permanent. The request was not entertained by the employer. The employer also contended that since the 2-year training period of the respondent as a trainee had come to an end, he was not entitled to any relief as prayed for.

Discussion Points

1. Whether it is correct to say that the petitioner V. L. was employed only as a trainee in the respondent/management, as contended by the employer.
2. Whether the removal of the petitioner from service is justifiable.

Judgement and Explanation

It was held by the Honourable Supreme Court that an apprentice cannot be treated as workman and thus is not entitled to claim any benefit available to a workman under the Industrial Disputes Act, 1947. It was clarified in the judgement that it must be noted that, on the one hand, while an apprentice is also treated to be a workman for the purposes of the 1947 Act, by virtue of Section 18 of the 1961 Act, it has been categorically provided that apprentices are not workers and the provisions of any law with respect to labour shall not apply to or in relation to such apprentice. Even if it is accepted that V. L. was a workman within the meaning of the 1947 Act, on account of his contractual tenure, his case would come within the exception of clause (bb) of Section 2(oo) thereof. In such a case also, the provisions of Section 25F of the said Act would have no application to the respondent's case. In the aforesaid circumstances, The Apex court was of the view that the V. L.'s case was covered by the provisions of Section 18 of the 1961 Act.

Important Definitions

1. **All Indian Council (Section 2(a))**: The Act defines 'All India Council' as the All India Council of Technical Education established by the resolution of the Government of India in the former Ministry of Education No. F. 16-10/44-E.III, dated 30 November 1945.
2. **Apprentice (Section 2(aa))**: Apprentice is a person who is undergoing apprenticeship training in pursuance of a contract of apprenticeship.
3. **Apprenticeship adviser (Section 2(b))**: Apprenticeship adviser is the central apprenticeship adviser appointed under Subsection (1) of Section 26, or the state apprenticeship adviser appointed under Subsection (2) of that section.
4. **Apprenticeship council (Section 2(c))**: Under the Act 'apprenticeship council' is the CAC or the State Apprenticeship Council established under Subsection (1) of Section 24.

5. **Apprenticeship training (Section 2(aaa)):** Apprenticeship training is a course of training in any industry or establishment undergone in pursuance of a contract of apprenticeship and under prescribed terms and conditions which may be different for different categories of apprentices.
6. **Appropriate government (Section 2(d)):** Under the Act, 'appropriate government' means:
   a. In relation to:
      i. The CAC, or
         - The Regional Boards, or
         - The practical training of graduate or technician apprentices or of technician (vocational) apprentices, or
      ii. Any establishment of any railway, major port, mine or oil field, or
      iii. Any establishment owned, controlled or managed by:
         - The central government or a department of the central government,
         - A company in which not less than 51% of the share capital is held by the central government or partly by that government and partly by one or more state governments,
         - A corporation (including a co-operative society) established by or under a Central Act which is owned, controlled or managed by the Central Government
   b. In relation to:
      i. A State Apprenticeship Council, or
      ii. Any establishment other than an establishment specified in subclause (1) of this clause, the state government.
7. **Board of state council of technical education (Section 2(dd)):** Under the Act, 'board or state council of technical education' is the board or state council of technical education established by the state government.
8. **Designated trade (Section 2(e)):** Designated trade means any trade or occupation or any subject field in engineering or technology or any vocational course which the central government, after consultation with the CAC, may, by notification in the Official Gazette, specify as a designated trade for the purposes of this Act.
9. **Employer (Section 2(f)):** According to Section 2(f) of the Act, employer is any person who employs one or more other persons to do any work in an establishment for remuneration, and includes any person entrusted with the supervision and control of employees in such establishment.
10. **Establishment (Section 2(g)):** As defined by the Act, establishment includes any place where any industry is carried on, and where an establishment consists of different departments or has branches, whether situated in the same place or at different places, all such departments or branches shall be treated as part of that establishment.
11. **Graduate or technical apprentice (Section 2(j)):** Graduate or technician apprentice is an apprentice who holds or is undergoing training in order that he may hold a degree or diploma in engineering or technology or an equivalent qualification granted by any institution recognized by the government and undergoes apprenticeship training in any such subject field in engineering or technology as may be prescribed.
12. **Industry (Section 2(h)):** Under the Act, 'industry' means any industry or business in which any trade, occupation or subject field in engineering or technology or any vocational course may be specified as a designated trade.

13. **National council (Section 2(l)):** The Act defines the 'national council' as the National Council for Training in Vocational Trades established by the resolution of the Government of India in the Ministry of Labour (Directorate General of Resettlement and Employment) No. TR/E.P-24/56, dated 21 August 1956 and renamed as the NCVT by the resolution of the Government of India in the Ministry of Labour (Directorate General of Employment and Training) No. DGET/12/21/80-TC, dated the 30 September 1981.
14. **Regional board (Section 2(mm)):** 'Regional Board' is defined as any Board of Apprenticeship Training registered under the Societies Registration Act, 1860 (21 of 1860) at Bombay, Calcutta, Madras or Kanpur.
15. **State (Section 2(n)):** 'State' includes a union territory.
16. **State council (Section 2(o)):** 'State council' is a state council for training in vocational trades established by the state government.
17. **State government in relation to a union territory (Section 2(p)):** 'State government' in relation to a union territory means the administrator thereof.
18. **Technical (vocational) apprentice (Section 2(pp)):** The Act defines 'technician (vocational) apprentice' as an apprentice who holds or is undergoing training in order that he may hold a certificate in vocational course involving 2 years of study after the completion of the secondary stage of school education recognized by the All India Council, and who undergoes apprenticeship training in any such subject field in any vocational course as may be prescribed.
19. **Trade apprentice (Section 2(q)):** Under the Act, 'trade apprentice' is an apprentice who undergoes apprenticeship training in any such trade or occupation as may be prescribed.

LO2: Apprentices and Their Training

Apprenticeship training course in each designated trade consists of following three types:

1. **Basic training:** Basic training is imparted to a learner for acquiring a reasonable ability to handle instruments/machineries/equipment independently before he is moved to shop floor/work area for furthering trade skills. This training is imparted either in a recognized industrial training institute or in a separate building set up by an employer. It is obligatory to set up basic training centre for the establishment employing 250 or more workers and engage fresher apprentices.
2. **On the job or shop floor training (in-plant training):** The basic training is followed by the shop floor training. It is imparted to an apprentice by the employer in the workshop for further enhancing his trade skills.
3. **Related instructions:** The trade apprentice who is undergoing apprenticeship training in an establishment is given, during the period of training, a course of related instructions appropriate to the trade. These instructions are required to be approved by the state government. Related training includes trade theory, workshop calculation and engineering drawing. This knowledge is essential for the apprentices to declare him a fully qualified skilled craftsman. Related instructions are imparted at the cost of the appropriate government but the employer has to, when so required, afford all facilities for imparting such instructions.

Qualification for Being Engaged as an Apprentice (Section 3)

Under Section 3, the Act lays down the qualification to be engaged as an apprentice. The section states that a person will not be qualified for being engaged as an apprentice to undergo apprenticeship training in any designated trade, unless he:

1. Is not less than 14 years of age, and
2. Satisfies such standards of education and physical fitness as may be prescribed.

It is to be noted here that different standards may be prescribed in relation to apprenticeship training in different designated trades and for different categories of apprentices.

Standard of education: A person is eligible for being engaged as a trade apprentice if he satisfies the minimum educational qualifications as specified in Schedule I. Schedule IA specifies the minimum educational qualifications for being engaged as a graduate technician or technician vocational apprentice and the apprentice has to meet any one of these laid down qualifications to be eligible for apprenticeship, provided that:

1. No engineering graduate or diploma holder or vocational certificate holder who had training or job experience for a period of 1 year or more, after the attainment of these qualifications he is eligible for being engaged as an apprentice under the Act.
2. No sandwich course student is eligible for being engaged as an apprentice under the Act after passing the final examination of the technical institution wherein such student is undergoing the course, unless so approved by the Regional Central Apprenticeship Advisers.
3. A person who has been a graduate or technician or technician (vocational) apprentice under the Act and in whose case the contract of apprenticeship was terminated for any reason whatsoever is not eligible for being engaged as an apprentice again under the Act without the prior approval of the apprenticeship adviser.

Training Places (Section 3A)

Section 3A provides in relation to training places that, in every designated trade, training places have to be reserved by the employer for the Scheduled Castes and the Scheduled Tribes and where there is more than one designated trade in an establishment, such training places have to be reserved also on the basis of the total number of apprentices in all the designated trades in such establishment. The number of training places to be reserved for the Scheduled Castes and the Scheduled Tribes has to be such as may be prescribed, having regard to the population of the Scheduled Castes and the Scheduled Tribes in the State concerned.

Contract of Apprentices (Section 4)

It is obligatory for the employer and the apprentice to enter into the contract of apprenticeship and no person can be engaged as an apprentice to undergo apprenticeship training in a designated trade without entering into a contract of apprenticeship with the employer. Section 4 of the Act provides in this regard that every person regarded as an apprentice or if he is a minor his guardian has to execute a contract of apprenticeship with the employer in the prescribed form, which is to be registered with the apprenticeship adviser. The apprenticeship training is imparted in pursuance of this contract. The apprentice and the employer are bound to carry out their obligation under this contract.

Every contract of apprenticeship is required to be sent by the employer within such period as may be prescribed to the apprenticeship adviser for registration. Most of the state government and union territories have exempted contracts of apprenticeship under the Act from the payment of stamp duty and hence these contracts can be executed only on a plain paper (Case 17.2).

Case 17.2: *Chairman-Cum-Managing ... v. Regional Labour Commissioner*[4]

Fertilizer Corporation of India Limited was a multi-unit public sector undertaking. Of its five units, one was situated at Gorakhpur. An advertisement No. 35/89 was published in newspaper by the petitioners—the Fertilizer Corporation of India Ltd., Gorakhpur Unit, Gorakhpur (hereinafter referred to as 'the Corporation'). The relevant extract of conditions for training, eligibility and so on relevant for the purpose of case discussion is quoted below for ready reference:

> *'(1) Qualifications: (a) Must have, passed:*
> *Essential (i) High School Examination with science and mathematics.*
> *Or*
>
> ....
>
> *(b) Candidates having qualifications as per above:*
> *Consolidated: First year : ₹110 p.m Second and third year: ₹120 p.m. General: In addition to stipend, the apprentices will be eligible for free hostel accommodation, water charges, electricity and medical aid to the extent available at Gorakhpur in accordance with the rules governing this.*
> *They will not be eligible for any other allowances during apprenticeship.*
> *Suitable reservation will be made in the case of Scheduled Caste/Tribe candidates.*
>
> *Selection of a candidate as an apprentice does not guarantee any employment under the corporation but subject to vacancies and successful completion of apprenticeship, the apprentices will be eligible for appointment as Operator/Technicians Gr. II in the scale of ₹150-205 plus the usual Dearness Allowance and benefit of contributory Provident fund as per rules of the Corporation.*
> *Selected candidates will have to execute a 'Bond' undertaking to serve the corporation for a minimum period of 5 years after appointment to regular post, besides the period of apprenticeship mentioned above.*
> *Candidates already in employment of the Government or any State Undertakings should apply through proper channel'.*

Mr X, Mr Y and Mr Z (the respondent employees) applied for 'craftsman training' in pursuance of the aforesaid advertisement and were selected. After completing their apprenticeship of 3 years with effect from 16 November 1970 to 15 November 1973, they were appointed by the Corporation and they joined their service on 16 November 1973.

All the units of the Corporation except Jodhpur Minding Organization suffered huge losses, and reference was made to the Board of Industrial and Financial Reconstruction (BIFR). The corporation was declared a sick company by the BIFR vide order dated 6 November 1992. The Government of India ultimately decided to close down all sick units of the Corporation except Jodhpur Mining Organization. It offered better terms for separation with golden handshake under Voluntary Separation Scheme to the employees of the

[4] *Chairman-Cum-Managing ... v. Regional Labour Commissioner ...* 2005 (2) ESC 1547.

Corporation. The eligibility clause of the amended Voluntary Retirement Scheme provides that the Scheme was operative in respect of all categories of permanent regular employees of the company. The general conditions provided that the calculation of compensation under the Voluntary Separation Scheme would be based on every completed year of service or part thereof.

The respondent employees opted for the Voluntary Separation Scheme offered by the petitioners and were paid gratuity amounting to ₹115,873 excluding the period of training on their retirement on 31 December 2002. However, the respondent employees claimed that they were entitled to a further sum of ₹11,987 towards gratuity. They claimed that period of their service during the training of 3 years as craftsman trainee had not been counted towards their total length of 32 years of service for the purposes of computation of gratuity.

The Corporation rejected the claim of the respondent employees and argued that the respondent was selected as 'Craftsman Trainee' for a period of 3 years stipulated therein on a consolidated monthly stipend. The training was to be imparted at the Training Centre and plants of Gorakhpur Unit or in any Unit/Division of the FCI; that on successful completion of training, he was appointed, as Operator on 16 November 1973 in the corporation. The respondent employee was relieved from employment on 31 December 2002 under the Voluntary Separation Scheme and was paid gratuity amounting to ₹115,873 and other dues/benefits for the period of his service. It was also stated in the objections that during the period of 3 years of apprenticeship, the concerned respondent employees were not in employment of the petitioners and did not work in their business or trade and also did not earn any wages as such their length of service was to be reckoned from their date of appointment in service of the Corporation, that is, 16 November 1973.

Discussion Points

1. Could the respondent employees be treated as apprentices appointed under the Apprentice Act, 1961?
2. Were the respondent employees eligible for gratuity benefits during the period of training?

Judgement and Explanation

It was held by the Apex court that the respondents were not employed as apprentice under the Apprentices Act, 1961, and, therefore, their entitlement to gratuity would not be ineffective in view of clause 4.2 of the Voluntary Separation Scheme even though apprentices are barred under the definition of employee under the Payment of Gratuity Act. It must be noted here that the Payment of Gratuity Act, 1972, does not prohibit the payment of gratuity to an employee on better terms than provided under the Gratuity Act, 1972. Voluntary Retirement Scheme is independent of the provisions of the payment of Gratuity Act. The argument that respondents are not entitled to the relief of 'service' for training period, therefore, cannot be sustained. The employees cannot be denied the relief on the grounds that apprentices are leaned under the said Act.

Novation of Contract of Apprentice (Section 5)

Novation of contract of apprenticeship stands for the termination of contract of apprenticeship with one employer and continuation of apprenticeship training for the remaining period with another employer. Section 5 of the Act deals with the novation of contracts of apprenticeship; however, to attract the application of Section 5, following conditions are required to be fulfilled:

1. Where an employer with whom a contract of apprenticeship has been entered into, is for any reason unable to fulfil his obligations under the contract.
2. With the approval of the apprenticeship adviser, it is agreed between the employer, the apprentice or his guardian, and any other employer that the apprentice will be engaged as apprentice under the other employer for the unexpired portion of the period of apprenticeship training.

3. The agreement is approved by the apprenticeship adviser.
4. The agreement is registered with the apprenticeship adviser.

On registration with the apprenticeship adviser, it is deemed to be the contract of apprenticeship between the apprentice or his guardian and other employer. From the date of such registration, the contract of apprenticeship with the first employer is terminated and no obligation under the contract is enforceable at the instance of any party to the contract against the other party thereto.

Period of Apprentice Training (Section 6)

On the basis of the allotted trades, the period of apprenticeship training in the case of trade apprentices varies from 6 months to 4 years. Section 6 of the Act mentions in this regard that the period of apprenticeship training specified in the contract of apprenticeship has to be decided as follows:

1. In the case of trade apprentices who, having undergone institutional training in a school or other institution recognized by the National Council, have passed the trade tests or examinations conducted by that Council or by an institution recognized by that Council, the period of apprenticeship training has to be such as may be determined by that Council or by an institution recognized by that Council:
   a. In the case of trade apprentices who, having undergone institutional training in a school or other institution affiliated to or recognized by a Board or State Council of Technical Education or any other authority which the central government may, by notification in the Official Gazette specify in this behalf, have passed the trade tests or examinations conducted by that Board or State Council or authority, the period of apprenticeship training must be such as may be prescribed.
2. In the case of other trade apprentices, the period of apprenticeship training has to be such as may be prescribed.
3. In the case of graduate or technician apprentices, technician (vocational) apprentices the period of apprenticeship training shall has to such as may be prescribed.

Number of Apprentices for a Designated Trade (Section 8)

The Act empowers the central government to determine for each designated trade the ratio of trade apprentices to workers other than unskilled workers in that trade, after consulting the CAC, by order notified in the Official Gazette. However, this does not prevent any employer from engaging a number of trade apprentices in excess of the ratio determined by the central government.

The section further provides under Section 8(2) that in determining the ratio, the central government has to give due regard to the facilities available for apprenticeship training under this Act in the concerned designated trade. Due attention is also given to the facilities that may have to be made available by an employer for the training of graduate or technician apprentices, technician (vocational) apprentices if any, in pursuance of any notice issued to him under Subsection (3A) by the central apprenticeship adviser or such other person as is referred to in that subsection.

It is further provided under Subsection 3 of Section 8 that the apprenticeship adviser is empowered to, by notice in writing, direct an employer to engage a specific number of trade apprentices within the ratio determined by the central government for any designated trade in his establishment. The employer is required to comply with such requisition provided that in making any requisition under this subsection, the apprenticeship adviser has had regard to the facilities actually available in the establishment concerned.

Section 8(3A) states that the central apprenticeship adviser or any other person not below the rank of an assistant apprenticeship adviser authorized by the central apprenticeship adviser in writing in this behalf must give regard to some specific points, before directing an employer to impart training to such number of graduate or technician apprentices, or technician (vocational) apprentices, as specified in a written notice issued to him. Following are the points to be considered in this regard:

1. The number of managerial persons (including technical and supervisory persons) employed in a designated trade.
2. The number of management trainees engaged in the establishment.
3. The totality of the training facilities available in a designated trade.
4. Such other factors as he may consider fit in the circumstances of the case.

'Management trainee' mentioned above means a person who is engaged by an employer for undergoing a course of training in the establishment of the employer (not being apprenticeship training under this Act) subject to the condition that, on successful completion of such training, such person shall be employed by the employer on a regular basis.

It is to be noted that several employers may join together for the purpose of providing practical training to the apprentices under them by moving them between their respective establishments.

If in the public interest, a number of apprentices in excess of the ratio determined by the central government or in excess of the number specified in a notice issued under Subsection (3A) should in the opinion of the appropriate government be trained, the appropriate government may require employers to train the additional number of apprentices (Section 8(5)). Every employer to whom above-mentioned requisition is made must comply with the requisition if the government concerned makes available such additional facilities and such additional financial assistance as are considered necessary by the apprenticeship adviser for the training of the additional number of apprentices (Section 8(6)).

Any employer not satisfied with the decision of the apprenticeship adviser under Subsection (6) is free to make a reference to the CAC and such reference is decided by a committee thereof appointed by that Council for the purpose. In such cases, the decision of that committee is final (Section 8(7)).

Termination of Apprenticeship Contract (Section 7)

The contract of the apprenticeship gets terminated under the following three circumstances:

1. **On the expiry of the contract of apprentices (Section 7(1)):** The contract of apprenticeship terminates on the expiry of the period of training.
2. **By the order of the Apprenticeship adviser (Section 7(3)):** Either party to a contract may make an application to the apprenticeship adviser for the termination of the contract. When such

application is made, a copy of the application is to be sent by post to the other party to the contract. After considering the contents of the application and the objections, if any, filed by the other party, the apprenticeship adviser, by order in writing terminates the contract, if he is satisfied that

a. The parties to the contract or any of them have or has failed to carry out the terms and conditions of the contract, and
b. It is desirable in the interests of the parties or any of them to terminate the same (Section 7(3)).

If the contract is terminated for failure on the part of the employer to carry out the terms and conditions of the contract, the employer has to pay to the apprenticeship such compensation as may be prescribed. On the other hand, when the contract is terminated for such failure on the part of the apprentice, the apprentice or his guardian is bound to refund to the employer as cost of training such amount as may be determined by the apprenticeship adviser.

3. **On the novation of the contract of apprentices (Section 5):** When a contract of apprenticeship is terminated by the apprenticeship adviser before the expiry of the period of apprenticeship training and a new contract of apprenticeship is being entered into with a new employer, the apprenticeship adviser may, if he is satisfied that the contract of apprenticeship with the previous employer could not be completed because of any lapse on the part of the previous employer, allow the period of apprenticeship training already undergone by the apprenticeship with the previous employer to be included in the period of apprenticeship training to be undertaken with the new employer.

Practical and Basic Training of Apprentices and Related Instructions (Sections 9 and 10)

Practical and basic training of apprentices (Section 9): Section 9 of the Act provides for the practical and basic training of apprentices. It states that every employer must make suitable arrangements in his workshop for imparting a course of practical training to every apprentice engaged by him in accordance with the programme approved by the apprenticeship adviser.

1. **Testing of the work of apprentices (Section 9(2)):** It is further provided that the central apprenticeship adviser or any other person not below the rank of an assistant apprenticeship adviser authorized by the central apprenticeship adviser in writing in this behalf is to be provided all reasonable facilities for access to each such apprentice to test his work and to ensure that the practical training is being imparted in accordance with the approved programme. Apprenticeship adviser authorized by the state apprenticeship adviser in writing in this behalf must also be given such facilities in respect of apprentices undergoing training in establishments in relation to which the appropriate government is the state government.
2. **An untrained a trade apprentice (Section 9(3)):** Before admission in the workshop for practical training, a trade apprentice who has not undergone institutional training in a school or other institution recognized by the National Council or any other institution affiliated to or recognized by a Board or State Council of Technical Education or any other authority which the central government notifies in the Official Gazette in this behalf has to undergo a course of basic training.
3. **Establishments with 500 or more workers (Section 9(4)):** In the cases where an employer employs in his establishment 500 or more workers, the basic training is to be imparted to the

trade apprentices either in separate parts of the workshop building or in a separate building which is set up by the employer himself. Here, the appropriate government may grant loans to the employer on easy terms and repayable by easy instalments to meet the cost of the land, construction and equipment for such separate building.

4. **Number of apprentices less than 12 (Section 9(4A)):** If the number of apprentices to be trained at any time in any establishment in which 500 or more workers are employed is less than 12, the employer of such establishment is permitted to depute all or any of such apprentices to any basic training centre or industrial training institute for basic training in any designated trade, in either case, run by the government. In these cases, the employer has to pay to the government the expenses incurred by the government on such training, at such rate as may be specified by the central government (Section 9(4B)).
5. **Establishments with less than 500 workers (Section 9(5)):** In the establishments employing less than 500 workers, the employer must impart the basic training to the trade apprentices in training institutes set up by the government.
6. **Joint training of apprentices engaged by two or more employers (Section 9(5)):** In any such training institute, which shall be located within the premises of the most suitable establishment in the locality or at any other convenient place, the trade apprentices engaged by two or more employers may be imparted basic training.
7. **Syllabus and equipment of the practical training (Section 9(7) and 9(7A)):** In the case of an apprentice other than a graduate or technician apprentice, or technician (vocational) apprentice, the syllabus of and the equipment to be utilized for practical training including basic training have to be such as may be approved by the central government in consultation with the CAC. In the case of graduate or technician apprentices, or technician (vocational) apprentices, the programme of apprenticeship training and the facilities required for such training in any subject field in engineering or technology or vocational course must be approved by the central government in consultation with the CAC.
8. **Bearing of recurring cost (Section 9(8)):** Recurring costs that include the cost of stipends incurred by an employer in connection with basic training, imparted to trade apprentices other than those referred to in clauses (a) and (aa) of Section 6 have to be borne by the employer alone, if:
    a. Such employer employs 250 workers or more, by the employer.
    b. Such employer employs less than 250 workers, by the employer and the government in equal shares up to such limit as may be laid down by the central government and beyond that limit, borne by the employer alone.
9. **Recurring cost including the cost of stipend (Section 9(b)):** It further provided that recurring costs including the cost of stipends, if any, incurred by an employer in connection with practical training, including basic training, imparted to trade apprentices referred to in clauses (a) and (aa) of Section 6, in every case, is borne by the employer.
10. **Recurring costs excluding the cost of stipends (Section 9(c)):** Recurring costs excluding the cost of stipends incurred by an employer in connection with the practical training imparted to graduate or technician apprentices, or technician (vocational) apprentices is to be borne by the employer and the cost of stipends is borne by the central government and the employer in equal shares up to such limit as may be laid down by the central government and beyond that limit, by the employer alone.

LO3: Health, Safety and Welfare of Apprentices

Health, Safety and Welfare of Apprentices (Section 14)

When the apprentices undergo the training in factory, the provisions of Chapters III, IV and of the Factories Act, 1948, are applicable in relation to the health safety and welfare of apprentices as if they were workers within the meaning of that Act. Where the apprentices are undergoing training in a mine that provision of Chapter V of the Mines Act, 1952, are applicable in relation to the health and safety of the apprentices as if they were persons employed in the mine too.

Hours of Work, Overtime, Leave and Holidays (Section 15)

Hours of work (Section 15 (1)): Section 15(1) of the Act deals with the number of working hours of an apprentice. According to this section, the weekly and daily hours of work of an apprentice while undergoing practical training in a workshop have to be such as may be prescribed.

1. The total number of hours per week must be 42 to 48 hours (including the time spent on related instructions).
2. Trade apprentices undergoing basic training ordinarily work for 42 hours per week including the time spent on related instructions.
3. Trade apprentices during the second year of apprenticeship must work for 42 to 45 hours per week including the time spent on related instructions.
4. Trade apprentice during the third and subsequent years of apprenticeship must work for the same number of hours per week as the workers in the trade in the establishment in which the trade apprentice is undergoing apprenticeship training.

It is to be noted here that no trade apprentice can be engaged on such training between the hours of 10 PM and 6 AM except with the prior approval of the apprenticeship adviser. The apprenticeship adviser must give his approval only if he is satisfied that it is in the interest of the training of the trade apprentice or in public interest.

Overtime (Section 15(2)): No apprentice can be required or allowed to work overtime except with the approval of the apprenticeship adviser. The apprenticeship Adviser grants such approval only when he is satisfied that such overtime is in the interest of the training of the apprentice or in the public interest.

Leave and holidays (Section 15(3)): An apprentice is entitled to as many leaves and holidays as prescribed and as are observed in the establishment in which he is undergoing training.

1. **Establishment not having proper leave rules:** The apprentice is entitled to follow the types of leaves if in the establishments in which he is undergoing training, proper leave rules do not exist or the total leave of different types admissible to their workers is less than 37 days in a year.
   a. **Casual leave:** Following are the rules to be observed in case of casual leaves:
      i. Casual leaves are admissible maximum period of 12 days in a year.
      ii. Any holiday intervening during the period of casual leave is not to be counted for the purpose of the limit of 12 days.

iii. Casual leave that is not utilized during any year stands lapsed at the end of the year.
iv. Casual leaves are not combined with medical leave. If casual leave is preceded or followed by medical leave, the entire leave taken is to be treated either as medical or casual leave. But it shall not be allowed to exceed the maximum period prescribed in respect of medical or casual leave, as the case may be.
v. Except in case of extreme urgency, applications for such leave are required to be made to the appropriate authority and sanction obtained prior to availing of leave.

b. **Medical leave:** Following are the rules to be observed in case of medical leaves:
   i. Medical leave up to 15 days is admissible for each year and the unused medical leaves are allowed to accumulate up to a maximum of 40 days.
   ii. Any holiday intervening during the period of medical leave is to be treated as medical leave and accounted for in the limits prescribed under clause (i) above.
   iii. The employer may require the apprentice to produce a medical certificate from a registered medical practitioner in support of his medical leave. A medical certificate is, however, necessary to be produced if the leave exceeds 6 days.
   iv. The employer is free to arrange a special medical examination of an apprentice if he has reason to believe that the apprentice is not really ill or the illness is not of such a nature as to prevent attendance.
   v. A female apprentice with one surviving child is entitled to be granted maternity leave for a period of 90 days from the date of its commencement without payment of stipend and the apprenticeship training period is extended accordingly. The monthly stipend is to be paid to the apprentice during such extended period.

c. **Extraordinary leave:** The extraordinary leaves are admissible up to a maximum of 10 days after he has exhausted the entire casual and medical leave, if the employer is satisfied with the genuineness of the grounds on which the leave is applied for.

2. **Establishment having proper leave rules:** In establishments where proper leave rules exist for workers, the leave to apprentices is granted by the employers in accordance with those rules. However, the grant of such leave is subject to the following conditions:
   a. Every apprentice engaged in an establishment which works for 5 days in a week (with a total of 45 hours per week) has put in a minimum attendance of 200 days in a year out of which one-sixth, namely, 33 days, are devoted to related instructions and 167 days to practical training;
   b. Every apprentice engaged in an establishment which works for 5.5 days or 6 days in a week has put in a minimum attendance of 240 days in a year, out of which one-sixth, namely 40 days, are devoted to related instruments and 200 days to practical training;
   c. An apprentice who for any reason is not able to undergo training for the period specified in clause (a) or clause (b) must be given an opportunity to make up for the shortfall in the following year. Such an apprentice will be eligible to take the test conducted by the National Council, if:
      i. He is engaged in an establishment referred to in clause (a) only if he has completed the period of training and has put in a minimum attendance of 600 days or 800 days accordingly as the period of training is 3 years or 4 years;
      ii. He is engaged in an establishment referred to in clause (b) only if he has completed the period of training and has put in a minimum attendance of 720 days or 900 days accordingly as the period of training is 3 years or 4 years.

Workers: Here, as defined under Section 2((r), 'worker' is a person who is employed for wages in any kind of work and who gets his wages directly from the employer but shall not include an apprentice referred to in clause (aa).

a. Is not less than 14 years of age, and
b. Satisfies such standards of education and physical fitness as may be prescribed.

Different standards may be prescribed in relation to apprenticeship training in different designated trades and for different categories of apprentices.

Test and Grant of Certificate (Section 21)

Every trade apprentice who has completed the period of training has to appear for a test to be conducted by the National Council to determine his proficiency in the designated trade in which he has undergone his apprenticeship training. The trade apprentice who passes the test referred to above is granted a certificate of proficiency in the trade by the National Council (Section 21(2)). The Section further provides that the progress in apprenticeship training of every graduate or technician apprentice technician (vocational) apprentice is to be assessed by the employer from time to time (Section 21(3)) and every such graduate or technician apprentice or technician (vocational) apprentice, who completes his apprenticeship training to the satisfaction of the concerned Regional Board, is granted a certificate of proficiency by that Board (Section 21(4)).

Offer and Acceptance of Employment (Section 22)

Section 22(1) mentions that it is not obligatory on the part of the employer to offer any employment to any apprentice who has completed the period of his apprenticeship training in his establishment. In a similar manner, it is not obligatory on the part of the apprentice to accept an employment under the employer.

However, if there was a condition in a contract of apprenticeship that, after the successful completion of the apprenticeship training the apprentice has to serve the employer, the employer is, on such completion, bound to offer suitable employment to the apprentice, and the apprentice will be bound to serve the employer in that capacity for such period and on such remuneration as may be specified in the contract. If in the opinion of the apprenticeship adviser, the period or remuneration specified in the contract of apprenticeship is not reasonable, he may revise such period or remuneration so as to make it reasonable, and the period or remuneration so revised is deemed to be the period or remuneration agreed to between the apprentice and the employee.

Records and Returns (Section 19)

Section 19 of the Act directs every employer to maintain records of the progress of training of each apprentice undergoing apprenticeship training in his establishment in such form as may be prescribed. Every such employer needs also to furnish such information and returns in such form to such authorities and at such intervals as may be prescribed.

LO4: Obligations of Employer and Apprentices

The obligations for the employer decided by the Act can be studied under the provisions of Sections 11, 13, 16 and 19. These provisions are discussed below:

1. **Obligations of employer (Sections 11)**: Section 11 states that following are the obligations for the employer:
   a. The employer has to provide training to apprentice in accordance with the provisions of the Act and the rules made thereunder;
   b. He has to ensure that a person possessing prescribed qualification is made in-charge of the training of the apprentice;
   c. The employer is required to provide adequate and qualified instructional staff for imparting practical and theoretical training and facilities for trade test of apprentices;
   d. The employer needs to fulfil obligations as agreed under the contract of apprenticeship.
2. **Obligation of payment (Section 13):** The employer is required to pay to every apprentice during the period of apprenticeship training such stipend at a rate not less than the prescribed minimum rate, or the rate which was being paid by the employer on 1 January, 1970 to the category of apprentices under which such apprentice falls, whichever is higher, as may be specified in the contract of apprenticeship. The stipend so specified is paid at specified intervals and subject to specified conditions. An apprentice is not required to be paid by his employer on the basis of piece work nor is he required to take part in any output bonus or other incentive scheme.
3. **Liability of employer to pay compensation for injury (Section 16):** In case of personal injury to an apprentice by accident arising out of and in the course of his training as an apprentice, his employer is liable to pay compensation. The compensation is decided in accordance with the provisions of the Workman's Compensation Act, 1923, subject to the modification specified in the Schedule (Apprenticeship Training Manual).

   It is to be noted that the ESI Act, 1948, does not apply to the apprentice under the Apprentices Act, 1961. However, there is no objection to an employer entering into a contract with an insurance in respect of his liability to pay compensation under Section 16 of Apprentices Act, 1961.
4. **Responsibility to maintain records and furnish information (Section 19):** Every employer is directed to maintain records of the progress of training of each apprentice undergoing apprenticeship training in his establishment in such form as may be prescribed. Every such employer is also bound to furnish such information and returns in a prescribed form, to prescribed authorities at specific intervals.

Obligations of Apprentices (Sections 12 and 17)

The obligations for the employer decided by the Act can be studied under the provisions of Sections 12 and 17. These provisions are discussed below:

1. **Obligations of trade apprentices (Section 12 (1)):** Every trade apprentice undergoing apprenticeship training is obligations to:
   a. Learn his trade conscientiously and diligently.
   b. Attend the practical and related instruction classes regularly.

c. Carry out his obligations under the contract of apprenticeship, to be executed by him at the time of admission.
d. Follow the rules and regulations of the establishments.

2. **Obligations of graduate or technician apprentices (Section 12(2)):** According to Section 12(2), every graduate or technician apprentice or technician (vocational) apprentice undergoing apprenticeship training is obliged:
   a. To learn his subject field in engineering or technology conscientiously and diligently at his place of training;
   b. To attend the practical and instructional classes regularly;
   c. To carry out all lawful orders of his employer and superiors in the establishment;
   d. To carry out his obligations under the contract of apprenticeship which shall include the maintenance of such records of his work as may be prescribed.
3. **Conduct and discipline (Section 17):** In all matters of conduct and discipline, the apprentice is governed by the rules and regulations applicable to employees of the corresponding category in the establishment in which the apprentice is undergoing training.

LO5: Administration and Authority

Authorities under the Act

In addition to the government, there are following authorities identified by the Act, namely:

1. The National Council.
2. The CAC.
3. The State Council.
4. The State Apprenticeship Council.
5. The All India Council.
6. The Regional Boards.
7. The Boards or State Councils of Technical Education.
8. The central apprenticeship adviser.
9. The state apprenticeship adviser.

Affiliation: Every State Council is affiliated to the National Council and every State Apprenticeship Council is affiliated to the CAC (Section 23(2)). On the other hand, every Board or State Council of Technical Education and every Regional Board will be affiliated to the CAC (Section 23(2A)). Each of the authorities specified above performs the functions as are assigned to it by or under this Act or by the government. It is further provided that a State Council also performs such functions as are assigned to it by the National Council and the State Apprenticeship Council, while the Board or State Council of Technical Education also performs such functions as are assigned to it by the CAC.

Central Apprenticeship Council (Section 24)

The central government, by notification in the Official Gazette, establishes the CAC (Section 24(1)). The CAC consists of a chairman and a vice chairman and such number of other members as the central government may think expedient, to be appointed by that government by notification in the Official Gazette from among the following categories of persons, namely (Section 24(2)):

1. Representatives of employers in establishments in the public and private sectors.
2. Representatives of the central government and of the state governments.
3. Persons having special knowledge and experience on matters relating to industry, labour and technical education.
4. Representatives of the All India Council and of the Regional Boards.

The number of persons to be appointed as members of the CAC from each of the categories specified above, the term of office of, the procedure to be followed in the discharge of their functions by, and the manner of filling vacancies among, the members of the Council are prescribed by the central government (Section 24(3)).

State Apprentices Council (Section 24)

The state government, by notification in the Official Gazette, establishes the State Apprenticeship Council (Section 24(1)).The State Apprenticeship Council consists of a chairman and a vice chairman and such number of other members as the state government may think expedient, to be appointed by that government by notification in the Official Gazette from among the following categories of persons, namely (Section 24(4)):

1. Representatives of employers in establishments in the public and private sectors.
2. Representatives of the central government and of the state government.
3. Persons having special knowledge and experience of matters relating to industry, labour and technical education.
4. Representatives of the Board or of the State Council of Technical Education.

The number of persons to be appointed as members of the State Apprenticeship Council from each of the categories specified above, the term of office of, the procedure to be followed in the discharge of their functions by, and the manner of filling vacancies among, the members of the Council are prescribed by state government (Section 24(5)).

The act further provides that the fees and allowances, if any, to be paid to the chairman and the vice chairman and the other members of the CAC are determined by the central government. In a similar manner, the fees and allowances, if any, to be paid to the chairman and the vice chairman and the other members of the State Apprenticeship Council are determined by the state government (Section 24(6)).

Central Apprenticeship Adviser and His Powers (Section 26 and 29)

Central apprenticeship adviser (Section 26): The central government, by notification in the Official Gazette, appoints a suitable person as the central apprenticeship adviser. The central apprenticeship adviser is the Secretary to the CAC.

Powers of central apprenticeship adviser (Section 29): Section 29 of the Act states that the central apprenticeship adviser or such other person, not below the rank of an assistant apprenticeship adviser, as may be authorized by the central apprenticeship adviser in writing in this behalf is authorized:

1. With such assistants, if any, as he thinks fit, to enter, inspect and examine any establishment or part thereof at any reasonable time.
2. To examine any apprentice employed therein or require the production of any register, record or other documents maintained in pursuance of this Act and take on the spot or otherwise statement of any person which he may consider necessary for carrying out the purposes of this Act.
3. To make such examination and inquiry as he thinks fit in order to ascertain whether the provisions of this Act and the rules made thereunder are being observed in the establishment.
4. To exercise such other powers as may be prescribed.

It is further provided in relation to establishments for which the appropriate government is the state government that a state apprenticeship adviser or such other person, not below the rank of an assistant apprenticeship adviser, as may be authorized by the state apprenticeship adviser in writing in this behalf is also authorized to exercise any of the powers specified in clauses (a), (b), (c) or (d) as mentioned above.

Despite having all the powers mentioned above, no person can be compelled by apprenticeship adviser the under this section to answer any question or make any statement which may tend directly or indirectly to incriminate him.

Apprenticeship Advisers to be Public Servants (Section 28)

Every apprenticeship adviser and every Additional, Joint, Regional, Deputy or Assistant Apprenticeship Adviser appointed under this Act is deemed to be a public servant within the meaning of Section 21 of the IPC (45 of 1860).

LO6: Penalties, Offences and Miscellaneous Provisions

Penalties (Section 30)

There are penal provisions under Section 30 of the act for the employer who contravenes the provision of the Act while engaging the apprentices is subject to a fine or imprisonment up to 6 months or both. Following are the acts of the employer attracting punishment under the Section.

If any employer:

1. Engages as an apprentice a person who is not qualified for being so engaged or
2. Fails to carry out the terms and conditions of a contract of apprenticeship or
3. Contravenes the provisions of this Act relating to the number of apprentices which he/she is
4. Required to engage under those provisions or
5. Refuses or neglects to furnish any information or return or false information or
6. Refuses or wilfully neglects the central/the state/assistant apprenticeship adviser.

Penalty where no specific remedy is provided (Section 31): If any employer or any other person contravenes any provision of this Act for which no punishment is provided in Section 30, he is punishable with fine which shall not be less than ₹1,000 but may extend to ₹3,000 (substituted by Act 4 of 1997, Section 7).

Offences by Companies (Section 32)

If the person committing an offence under this Act is a company, every person who, at the time the offence was committed, was in charge of, and was responsible to, the company for the conduct of business of the company, as well as the company, is deemed to be guilty of the offence and is liable to be proceeded against and punished accordingly.

It is further provided that nothing contained in this subsection renders any such person liable to such punishment provided in this Act if he proves that the offence was committed without his knowledge or that he exercised all due diligence to prevent the commission of such offence (Section 32(1)).

If an offence under this Act has been committed by a company and it is proved that the offence has been committed with the consent or connivance of, or is attributable to any negligence on the part of, any director, manager, secretary or other officer of the company, such director, manager, secretary or other officer is also deemed to be guilty of that offence, In this case, he is liable to be proceeded against and punished accordingly (Section 32(2)).

Cognizance of Offences (Section 33)

As provided under Section 33 of the Act, no court takes cognizance of any offence under this Act or the rules made thereunder except on a complaint thereof in writing made by the apprenticeship adviser or the officer of the rank of deputy apprenticeship adviser and above within 6 months from the date on which the offence is alleged to have been committed.

Protection of action taken in good faith (Section 36): Section 36 of the Act provides protection to any person for anything which is in good faith done or intended to be done under this Act, by disallowing any suit, prosecution or other legal proceedings against any such person.

Miscellaneous Provisions

Power to make rules (Section 37): The central government is authorized to, after consulting the CAC, by notification in the Official Gazette, make rules for carrying out the purposes of this Act. Rules made under this Act may provide that a contravention of any such rule will be punishable with fine which may extend to ₹50.

Rules to be laid before parliament: Every rule made under this section is to be laid before each House of Parliament for its approval and if both Houses agree in making any modification in the rule or both Houses agree that the rule should not be made, the rule must thereafter have effect only in such modified form or be of no effect, as the case may be. However, any such modification or annulment has to be without prejudice to the validity of anything previously done under that rule.

Delegation of Powers (Section 34): The appropriate government is authorized to notify in the Official Gazette, directing that any power exercisable by it under this Act or the rules made thereunder are exercisable also:

1. Where the appropriate government is the central government, by such officer or authority subordinate to the central government or by the state government or by such officer or authority subordinate to the state government, as may be specified in the notification; and
2. Where the appropriate government is the state government, by such officer or authority subordinate to the state government as may be specified in the notification.

Summary

1. To facilitate training and enhancing the employability of job seekers in private/corporate sectors, the Apprentices Act, 1961, was enacted.
2. The National Apprenticeship Scheme was launched in 1959, initially on a voluntary basis. However, the Act is applicable to the whole of India and the Act was subsequently amended in 1973 and 1986.
3. The employer of any establishment where trade, occupation or subject field in engineering or technology is carried out in terms of the Apprentices Act, 1961, as amended from time to time, is covered under the Act.
4. Anyone who is above 14 years of age and fulfils the requirements of the Apprentices Act, 1961, is an eligible apprentice under the Act.
5. An apprentice is a person who is learning a trade from a skilled employer, having agreed to work for a fixed period at low wages. The apprentice provides help to a skilled worker in order to learn the trade himself.
6. The employer and apprentice share a relationship of a master and servant.
7. Apprenticeship training course in each designated trade consists of three types: basic training, shop floor training or practical training and related instructions.
8. A person is eligible for being engaged as a trade apprentice if he satisfies the minimum educational qualifications as specified in Schedule I.
9. The number of training places to be reserved for the Scheduled Castes and the Scheduled Tribes has to be such as may be prescribed, having regard to the population of the Scheduled Castes and the Scheduled Tribes in the state concerned.
10. It is obligatory for the employer and the apprentice to enter into the contract of apprenticeship and no person can be engaged as an apprentice to undergo apprenticeship training in a designated trade without entering into a contract of apprenticeship with the employer.
11. Novation of contract of apprenticeship stands for the termination of contract of apprenticeship with one employer and continuation of apprenticeship training for the remaining period with another employer.
12. On the basis of the allotted trades, the period of apprenticeship training in the case of trade apprentices varies from 6 months to 4 years.
13. The Act empowers the central government to determine for each designated trade the ratio of trade apprentices to workers other than unskilled workers in that trade, after consulting the CAC, by order notified in the Official Gazette.
14. The contract of the apprenticeship gets terminated under three circumstances: on the expiry of the contract of apprentices, by the order of the apprenticeship adviser and on the novation of the contract of apprentices.

15. Every employer must make suitable arrangements in his workshop for imparting a course of practical training to every apprentice engaged by him in accordance with the programme approved by the apprenticeship adviser.
16. The weekly and daily hours of work of an apprentice while undergoing practical training in a workshop have to be such as may be prescribed.
17. No apprentice can be required or allowed to work overtime except with the approval of the apprenticeship adviser.
18. An apprentice is entitled to as many leave and holidays as prescribed and as are observed in the establishment in which he is undergoing training.
19. In establishments where proper leave rules exist for workers, the leave to apprentices is granted by the employers in accordance with those rules.
20. Every trade apprentice who has completed the period of training has to appear for a test to be conducted by the National Council to determine his proficiency in the designated trade in which he has undergone his apprenticeship training.
21. It is not obligatory on the part of the employer to offer any employment to any apprentice who has completed the period of his apprenticeship training in his establishment.
22. Every employer to maintain records of the progress of training of each apprentice undergoing apprenticeship training in his establishment in such form as may be prescribed.
23. The obligations for the employer decided by the Act can be studied under the provisions of Sections 11, 13, 16 and 19.
24. In case of personal injury to an apprentice by accident arising out of and in the course of his training as an apprentice, his employer is liable to pay compensation.
25. The obligations for the employer decided by the Act can be studied under the provisions of Sections 12 and 17.
26. In all matters of conduct and discipline, the apprentice is governed by the rules and regulations applicable to employees of the corresponding category in the establishment in which the apprentice is undergoing training.
27. Every State Council is affiliated to the National Council and every State Apprenticeship Council is affiliated to the CAC.
28. Every Board or State Council of Technical Education and every Regional Board will be affiliated to the CAC.
29. The central government, by notification in the Official Gazette, appoints a suitable person as the central apprenticeship adviser.
30. Despite having all the powers, no person can be compelled by apprenticeship adviser to answer any question or make any statement which may tend directly or indirectly to incriminate him.
31. There are penal provisions under Section 30 of the act for the employer who contravenes the provision of the Act, while engaging the apprentices is subject to a fine or imprisonment up to 6 months or both.
32. If the person committing an offence under this Act is a company, every person who, at the time the offence, was committed was in charge of, and was responsible to, the company for the conduct of business of the company, as well as the company, is deemed to be guilty of the offence and is liable to be proceeded against and punished accordingly.
33. The central government is authorized to, after consulting the CAC, by notification in the Official Gazette, make rules for carrying out the purposes of this Act.

Multiple Choice Questions

1. A person who agrees to work for a specified time in order to learn a trade, craft or profession in which the employer, traditionally called the master, assents to instruct him or her, is known as __________.
   a. Trainee
   b. Apprentice
   c. Employee
   d. None of the above

2. __________ is imparted to a learner for acquiring a reasonable ability to handle instruments/ machineries/equipment independently before he is moved to shop floor/work area for furthering trade skills.
   a. Basic training
   b. In-plant training
   c. Related instructions
   d. None of the above

3. __________ is imparted to an apprentice by the employer in the workshop for further enhancing his trade skills.
   a. Basic training
   b. In-plant training
   c. Related instructions
   d. None of the above

4. The trade apprentice who is undergoing apprenticeship training, in an establishment, during the period of training, is given a course __________ appropriate to the trade.
   a. Basic training
   b. In-plant training
   c. Related instructions
   d. None of the above

5. In the establishments employing less than __________, the employer must impart the basic training to the trade apprentices in training institutes set up by the government.
   a. 500 workers
   b. 200 workers
   c. 100 workers
   d. 50 workers

6. The total number of hours per week must be __________, including the time spent on related instructions.
   a. 12 to 18 hours
   b. 12 to 24 hours
   c. 42 to 52 hours
   d. 42 to 48 hours

7. Casual leaves are admissible up to a maximum period of __________ in a year.
   a. 10 days
   b. 12 days
   c. 15 days
   d. 20 days

8. Medical leaves up to 15 days are admissible for each year and the unused medical leaves are allowed to accumulate up to a maximum of __________.
   a. 20 days
   b. 30 days
   c. 40 days
   d. 45 days

9. The extraordinary leaves are admissible up to a maximum of __________ after he has exhausted the entire casual and medical leave.
   a. 10 days
   b. 15 days
   c. 20 days
   d. 1 month

10. There are penal provisions under Section 30 of the act for the employer who contravenes the provision of the Act while engaging the apprentices is subject to a ____________.
    a. Fine
    b. Imprisonment
    c. Both (a) and (b)
    d. Neither (a) nor (b)

True/False Questions

1. Anyone who is above 14 years of age and fulfils the requirements of the Apprentices Act, 1961, is an eligible apprentice under the Act.
2. The employer (master) is bound to instruct the apprentice by teaching him, bona fide, the knowledge of the art of which he has undertaken to teach him the elements.
3. The apprentice is entitled to payment for extraordinary services, when promised by the master and even when no express promise has been made, under peculiar circumstances.
4. Every apprentice undergoing apprenticeship training in a designated trade in an establishment is considered as an employee.
5. No apprentice can be required or allowed to work overtime except with the approval of the apprenticeship adviser.

Descriptive Questions

1. Write short notes on the following:
    a. Eligible employer under the Apprentices Act, 1961
    b. The Apprentices (Amendment) Bill, 2014
2. What do you understand by the term 'apprentice'? Discuss in detail the nature of the contract of apprenticeship.
3. Throw light on the provisions for the training of apprentices under the Apprentices Act, 1961.
4. Under what circumstances the contract of apprenticeship gets terminated? Discuss the related provisions of the Apprentices Act, 1961, in detail.
5. What type of leaves the apprentices are entitled to? Also discuss, how are the number of different types of leaves calculated as provided under the Apprentice Act, 1962?
6. What are the obligations decided by the Apprentices Act, 1961, for the employees and apprentices?
7. Write short notes on the following:
    a. Composition and authority of CAC
    b. Composition and authority of State Apprenticeship Council
8. What are different provisions dealing with the offences and penalties under the Apprentices Act, 1961?

18

CHAPTER

The Employment Exchanges (Compulsory Notification of Vacancies) Act, 1959

LEARNING OBJECTIVES

Upon completing this chapter, the reader would be able to:

LO1. Understand the objectives, scope and important definitions of the Act.
LO2. Gain insights into provisions dealing with the notification of vacancies.
LO3. Get the details of rules dealing with penalties for offences recognized the Act.
LO4. Understand some important miscellaneous provisions of the Act.
LO5. Know the highlights of the Employment Exchanges (Compulsory Notification of Vacancies) (EE) Amendment Bill, 2013.

Introduction

After the passage of few initial years of Independence, there emerged a requirement to have a system to gather important and reliable information about the employment trends in the country to enable the government to formulate its policy of training in technical education and to help the unemployed people of the country, both skilled and unskilled, to seek an appropriate employment. To meet that emerging requirement and enabling the government to access the employment potential in various categories of establishments, the Employment Exchanges (Compulsory notification of Vacancies) (EE) Act, 1959, was enacted.

LO1: Objectives, Scope and Important Definitions

Objectives

The EE (Compulsory notification of Vacancies) Act, 1959 (the Act), was enacted to provide for notification of vacancies to EE to be compulsory. It was enacted by the Parliament of the Union of India in the 20th year of the Republic of India. The main objective of this Act is to collect data on emerging employment trends and opportunities in different sectors of the economy to help the government to adopt suitable policies, and to provide guidance and information to unemployed youth.

After the enforcement of the Act, it is compulsory for all establishments, industries, trades in the public sector and offices in the private sector (except agriculture) which normally employ 25 or more employees to inform the government (the local EE) regarding the vacancies occurring in their establishment from time to time. The notification of vacancies in the manner prescribed by the Act provides important data and useful information to the government for formulation of employment policies. All concerned establishments, businesses, companies, production units and organizations employing 25 or more persons are required to register themselves with their local EE for this purpose.

Scope and Applicability of the Act

The EE (Compulsory Notification of Vacancies) Act, 1959, came into effect on 1 May 1960 and extended to whole of India as per Subsection (2) of Section 1 of the Act. However, it became effective on different dates in different states as central government decided by publishing under notification in the Official Gazette. For example, the Act was extended to and came into force in the Union Territories of Andaman and Nicobar Islands and Lakshadweep on 1 July 1978 vide particular notification in the Official Gazette of India.

The Act is applicable on all establishments in the public sector, and such establishments in the private sector excluding agriculture, where ordinarily 25 or more persons are employed. It is compulsory for these establishments to notify all vacancies (other than those exempted) to the appropriate EE as notified in the Official Gazette by the state government in the prescribed format. The establishments covered under the Act are also required to render quarterly employment return in Form ER-I for every quarter ending 31 March, 30 June, 30 September and 31 December and biennial occupational return in Form ER-II once in 2 years, namely, by private sector in odd years and by public sector in even years. The Act empowers the persons authorized by the government to have access to any relevant records of the employer. Such authorized persons can also inspect or take copies of relevant records or documents. Penal provisions of imposition of fine for any offence have been made for violation for various provisions of this act.

When the Act is not applicable (Section 3): Section 3 of the Act states that this Act will not apply to vacancies in any employment in:

1. Agriculture, horticulture and so on.
2. Domestic service.
3. Of which total duration is less than 3 months.

4. Unskilled office work.
5. Connection with the staff of Parliament.

Under Subsection 3(2), it is further provided that unless the central government otherwise directs by notification in the Official Gazette in this behalf, this Act will not also apply in relation to:

1. Vacancies which are proposed to be filled through promotion or by absorption of surplus staff of any branch or department of the same establishment or on the result of any examination conducted or interview held by, or on the recommendation of, any independent agency, such as the Union or a State Public Service Commission and the like;
2. Vacancies in an employment which carries a remuneration of less than ₹60 in a month.

Important Definitions

1. **Appropriate government (Section 2(a)):** 'Appropriate government' under the Act means:
   a. In relation to:
      i. Any establishment of any railway, major port, mine or oilfield, or
      ii. Any establishment owned, controlled or managed by:
         - The central government or a department of the central government,
         - A company in which not less than 51 per cent of the share capital is held by the central government or partly by the central government and partly by one or more state governments,
         - A corporation (including a co-operative society) established by or under a Central Act owned, controlled or managed by the central government;
   b. In relation to any other establishment, the government of the state in which that other establishment is situated.
2. **Employee (Section 2(b)):** Any person who is employed in an establishment to do any work for remuneration is an 'employee' under the Act.
3. **Employer (Section 2(c)):** An 'employer' is any person who employs one or more other persons to do any work in an establishment for remuneration and includes any person entrusted with the supervision and control of employees in such establishment.
4. **EE (Section 2(d)):** As per the Act, EE is any office or place established and maintained by the government for the collection and furnishing of information, either by the keeping of registers or otherwise, respecting:
   a. Persons who seek to engage employees,
   b. Persons who seek employment and
   c. Vacancies to which persons seeking employment may be appointed.
5. **Establishment (Section 2(e)):** 'Establishment' under the Act means:
   a. Any office, or
   b. Any place where any industry, trade, business or occupation is carried on.
6. **Establishment in public sector (Section 2(f)):** An establishment in the public sector is one which is owned, controlled or managed by:
   a. The government or a department of the government;

b. A government company as defined in Section 617 of the Companies Act, 1956 (1 of 1956);
c. A corporation (including a cooperative society) established by or under a central, provincial or state Act, which is owned, controlled or managed by the government; and
d. A local authority.

7. **Establishment in private sector (Section 2(g)):** An establishment in the private sector is one which is not an establishment in the public sector and where ordinarily 25 or more persons are employed to work for remuneration.
8. **Unskilled office work (Section 2(h)):** Unskilled office work is a work done in an establishment by any of the following categories of employees, namely:
   a. *Daftri.*
   b. *Jemadar*, orderly and peon.
   c. Dusting man or *farash.*
   d. *Bundel* or record lifter.
   e. Process server.
   f. Watchman.
   g. Sweeper.
   h. Any other employees doing any routine or unskilled work which the central government may, by notification in the Official Gazette, declare to be unskilled office work.

LO2: Notification of Vacancies

Notification of Vacancies to Employment Exchange (Section 4)

Section 4 of the Act makes it compulsory for every establishment in the public sector and private sector and every establishment pertaining to any specified class or category of establishment in the private sector to notify the vacancies to be filled in by that establishment to the prescribed EE. But there is no obligation to recruit any person through the EE only.

1. **In public sector (Section 4(1)):** After the enforcement of this Act in any State or area thereof, the employer in every establishment in the public sector in that State or area is required to, before filling up any vacancy in any employment in that establishment, notify that vacancy to such EE as may be prescribed.
2. **In private sector (Section 4(2)):** The appropriate government may direct by issuing a notification in the Official Gazette that from such date as may be specified in the notification, the employer in every establishment in private sector or every establishment pertaining to any class or category of establishments in private sector is required to, before filling up any vacancy in any employment in that establishment, notify that vacancy to such EE as may be prescribed, and the employer shall thereupon comply with such requisition.

The manner in which the vacancies referred to in Subsection (1) or Subsection (2) are notified to the EE and the particulars of employments in which such vacancies have occurred or are about to occur have to be such as may be prescribed. It is further provided that Subsections (1) and (2) do not impose any obligation upon any employer to recruit any person through the EE to fill any vacancy merely because that vacancy has been notified under any of those subsections.

Information and Returns by the Employer (Section 5)

According to Section 5 of this Act, in any state or area thereof, the employer in every establishment in the public sector in that state or area is required to furnish such information or return as prescribed in relation to vacancies. The appropriate government may direct by issuing a notification in the Official Gazette, that from such date as may be specified in the notification, the employer in every establishment in the private sector or every establishment pertaining to any class or category of establishments in the private sector needs to furnish such information or return as may be prescribed in relation to vacancies that have occurred or are about to occur in that establishment to such EE as may be prescribed, and the employer has to thereupon comply with such requisition (Section 5(2)). The required information is to be furnished in a prescribed form having prescribed particulars at the intervals of time as may be prescribed.

Right of Access to Records and Documents (Section 6)

The Act empowers an officer of government as may be prescribed in this behalf, or any person authorized by him in writing, to have access to any relevant record or document in the possession of any employer required to furnish any information or returns under Section 5. Such officers are also authorized to enter at any reasonable time any premises where he believes such record or document to be and inspect or take copies of relevant records or documents or ask any question necessary for obtaining any information required under that section.

LO3: Penalties

Section 7(1) of the Act states, if any employer fails to notify to the EE any vacancy as directed by Sections 4(1) and 4(2), he is punishable for the first offence with fine up to ₹500, and for every subsequent offence with fine up to ₹1,000.

If any person:

1. Required to furnish any information or return;
    a. Refuses or neglects to do so, or
    b. Knowingly furnishes or causes to be furnished any false information or return, or
    c. Refuses to answer, or gives any false answer; or
2. Impedes the right of access to relevant records or documents.

He shall be punishable for the first offence with fine up to ₹250, and for every subsequent offence with fine up to ₹500 (Section 7(2)).

LO4: Miscellaneous Provisions

Cognizance of Offences (Section 8)

The Act does not permit any prosecution for an offence under this Act to be instituted except by, or with the sanction of, such officer of government as may be prescribed in this behalf or any person authorized by that officer in writing.

Protection of Action Taken in Good Faith (Section 9)

Section 9 of the Act restricts any suit, prosecution or other legal proceedings to be lied against any person for anything which is in good faith done or intended to be done under this Act.

Power to Make Rules (Section 10)

The central government is empowered to, by notification in the Official Gazette and subject to the condition of previous publication, make rules for carrying out the purposes of this Act. In particular, and without prejudice to the generality of the foregoing power, such rules may be related to all or any of the following matters, namely (Section 10(2)):

1. The EE or EEs to which, the form and manner in which, and the time within which, vacancies are to be notified, and the particulars of employments in which such vacancies have occurred or are about to occur.
2. The form and manner in which, and the intervals at which, information and returns required under Section 5 are required to be furnished and the particulars which they must contain.
3. The officers by whom and the manner in which the right of access to documents and the right of entry conferred by Section 6 may be exercised.
4. Any other matter which is to be, or may be, prescribed under this Act.

Rules to be laid before Parliament (Section 10(3)): Every rule made under this Act has to be laid, as soon as may be after it is made, before each House of Parliament, while it is in session, for a total period of 30 days for their approval. If both the Houses agree in making any modification in the rule or both Houses agree that the rule should not be made, the rule shall thereafter have effect only in such modified form or be of no effect, as the case may be. However, any modification or annulment agreed by the Houses of Parliament has to be without prejudice to the validity of anything previously done under that rule.

LO5: The Employment Exchanges (Compulsory Notification of Vacancies) Amendment Bill, 2013

The EE (Compulsory Notification of Vacancies) Amendment Bill, 2013, was introduced by Minister of Labour and Employment on 22 April 2013 and is pending for the approval of Parliament. This bill seeks to amend the original Act and even seeks to change the short title of the Act, that is, from 'The EE

(Compulsory Notification of Vacancies) Act, 1959' to 'The Employment Guidance and Promotion Centres (EGPCs) (Compulsory Notification of Vacancies) Act, 1959'. The Bill proposes some changes in definition clause that includes the changes in the definition of terms 'Employee' and 'Employer'. Further, the Bill proposes to add the individuals seeking vocational careers and self-employment within the ambit of the Act. On the other hand, the Bill seeks exclusion of the employment in Parliament from the scope of this Act. Moreover, the amending bill advocates the enlarging of penalty, that is, maximum up to ₹10,000 for continuous commission of offences under the Act.

Following are the highlights of the Amendment Bill, 2013:

1. The Bill amends the EE (Compulsory Notifications of Vacancies) Act, 1959 (EE Act). The EE Act provides for the compulsory notification of vacancies to EE.
2. **Nomenclature:** The Bill amends the title of the Act to EGPC (Compulsory Notifications of Vacancies) Act, 1959. It changes the nomenclature of EE to EGPCs.
3. **Definitions:** The Bill proposes changes in the definition of an employee to include any person who is employed for a period 240 days or more in an establishment. It also changes the definition of an employer to include any person who employs one or more other persons to do any work for 240 days or more in an establishment.
4. **Inclusion to the Coverage of the Act:** The Bill advocates including individuals seeking vocational careers and self-employment within the ambit of the Act and adds plantations to the list of establishments that are covered under it. The Bill includes employment in unskilled office work within its ambit.
5. **Exclusions form the coverage of the Act:** The EE Act excluded employment in the Parliament from its ambit. The current bill also seeks to exclude state legislatures. Additionally, the Bill seeks to exclude vacancies carrying a remuneration of less than ₹60 per month.
6. **Notification of vacancies:** The Bill proposes that all employers in the public sector and those in the private sector employing 25 or more persons must notify any vacancies to the prescribed EGPCs.
7. **Furnishing information:** Employers are required to inform the EGPC within 30 days of filling up notified vacancies. The amendment requires employers in the private sector employing less than 25 people to furnish information required by the EGPCs for the collection of employment data. This information will be accessible to any authorized government official or a person authorized by him (or her) in writing.
8. **Penalties:** The amendment bill increases the penalty for non-notification of vacancies, or failure to furnish information from ₹500 up to ₹5,000 for the first offence. The fine for every second offence may extend to ₹10,000. Every subsequent offence may have a fine of ₹10,000 or lead to imprisonment which may extend to 1 month or both. Employers in the private sector employing less than 25 people are liable to pay up to ₹5,000 after two defaults, if they fail to furnish information to the EGPC. The Bill declares the person in charge of the conduct of business of the concerned company liable to be punished in case of an offence. Any other officer who is found responsible for the offence is also liable to be punished.

Summary

1. The EE (Compulsory notification of Vacancies) Act, 1959 (the Act), was enacted to provide for notification of vacancies to EE to be compulsory.

2. The Act is applicable on all establishments in the public sector and such establishments in the private sector excluding agriculture, where ordinarily 25 or more persons are employed.
3. It is compulsory for every establishment in the public sector and private sector and every establishment pertaining to any specified class or category of establishment in the private sector to notify the vacancies to be filled in by that establishment to the prescribed EE.
4. No employer is obliged to recruit any person through the EE to fill any vacancy merely because that vacancy has been notified under any of those subsections.
5. The Act empowers an officer of government as may be prescribed in this behalf, or any person authorized by him in writing, to have access to any relevant record or document in the possession of any employer required to furnish any information or returns under Section 5.
6. If any employer fails to notify to the EE any vacancy as directed by Sections 4(1) and 4(2), he is punishable for the first offence with fine up to ₹500, and for every subsequent offence with fine up to ₹1,000.
7. The Act does not permit any prosecution for an offence under this Act to be instituted except by, or with the sanction of, such officer of government as may be prescribed in this behalf or any person authorized by that officer in writing.
8. The central government is empowered to, by notification in the Official Gazette and subject to the condition of previous publication, make rules for carrying out the purposes of this Act.
9. The EE (Compulsory Notification of Vacancies) Amendment Bill, 2013, was introduced by Minister of Labour and Employment on 22 April 2013.
10. The Bill proposes some changes in definition clause that includes the changes in the definition of terms 'Employee' and 'Employer'. Further, the Bill proposes to add the individuals seeking vocational careers and self-employment within the ambit of the Act.

Multiple Choice Questions

1. All concerned establishments, businesses, companies, production units and organizations employing ____________ are required to register themselves with their local EE for the purpose of the Act.
   a. 15 or more persons
   b. 25 or more persons
   c. 50 or more persons
   d. 100 or more persons
2. The EE (Compulsory Notification of Vacancies) Act, 1959, was enacted by Parliament of Union of India in the ____________ of the Republic of India.
   a. 20th year
   b. 15th year
   c. 10th year
   d. 5th year
3. The EE (Compulsory Notification of Vacancies) Act, 1959, will not also apply in relation to
   a. Vacancies in an employment which carries a remuneration of less than ₹60 in a month.
   b. Agriculture, horticulture and so on
   c. Domestic service
   d. All of the above

4. Establishment in the private sector is an establishment which is not an establishment in the public sector and where ordinarily ________ are employed to work for remuneration.
   a. 100 or more persons
   b. 50 or more persons
   c. 25 or more persons
   d. 10 or more persons
5. Section 7(1) of the Act states, if any employer fails to notify to the EE any vacancy as directed by Sections 4(1) and 4(2), he is punishable for the first offence with fine up to ________.
   a. ₹100
   b. ₹500
   c. ₹2,500
   d. ₹5,000

True/False Questions

1. It is compulsory for all establishments, industries, trades in the public sector and offices in the private sector including agriculture which normally employ 25 or more employees to inform the government (the local EE) regarding the vacancies occurring in their establishment from time to time.
2. Section 3 of the Act states that this Act will not apply to vacancies in any employment in which total duration is less than 3 months.
3. Any person who is employed in an establishment to do any work for remuneration is an 'employee' under the Act.
4. Every employer of the establishment is obliged to recruit any person through the EE to fill any vacancy who are directed under Sections 4(1) and 4(2) to notify the vacancies.
5. An 'employer' is any person who employs one or more other persons to do any work in an establishment for remuneration, but it does not include any person entrusted with the supervision and control of employees in such establishment.

Descriptive Questions

1. Define the scope and objectives of the Employment Exchanges (Compulsory Notification of Vacancies) Act, 1959.
2. Write short notes on the following as defined under the EE (Compulsory Notification of Vacancies) Act, 1959:
   a. Employer
   b. Employee
   c. Establishments
   d. Provisions for penalty
   e. Power of appropriate government to frame rules
3. Throw light on major amendments proposed by the Employment Exchanges (Compulsory Notification of Vacancies) Amendment Bill, 2013.

Answer Key for Multiple Choice and True/False Questions

Chapter 2

MCQs
1. b; 2. a; 3. c; 4. d; 6. d; 7. c; 8. c; 9. a; 10. b

Chapter 3

MCQs
1. c; 2. d; 3. a; 4. b; 5. c; 6. a; 7. b; 8. c; 9. a; 10. a; 11. b; 12. d; 13. a; 14. c

True/False
1. True; 2. False; 3. False; 4. True

Chapter 4

MCQs
1. c; 2. b; 3. a; 4. b; 5. a

True/False
1. False; 2. True; 3. False; 4. True; 5. False

Chapter 5

MCQs
1. c; 2. a; 3. b; 4. c; 5. d

True/False
1. False; 2. True; 3. False; 4. True; 5. True

Chapter 6

MCQs
1. b; 2. a; 3. c; 4. d; 5. a; 6. c; 7. a; 8. b; 9. a; 10. a

True/False
1. True; 2. False; 3. True; 4. False; 5. False; 6. True; 7. True; 8. False; 9. True; 10. False

Chapter 7

MCQs
1. a; 2. b; 3. d; 4. a; 5. c; 6. c; 7. b; 8. a; 9. a; 10. b; 11. c; 12. b

True/False
1. False; 2. True; 3. True; 4. False

Chapter 8

MCQs
1. c; 2. d; 3. c; 4. c; 5. a; 6. b; 7. a; 8. a; 9. c; 10. b

True/False
1. False; 2. False; 3. True; 4. True; 5. False

Chapter 9

MCQs
1. d; 2. b; 3. d; 4. c; 5. b; 6. a; 7. a; 8. c; 9. a; 10; c

Chapter 10

MCQs

1. c; 2. a; 3. b; 4. d; 5. d; 6. b; 7. c; 8. b; 9. c;

True/False

1. True; 2. False; 3. True; 4. True; 5. False; 6. False

Chapter 11

MCQs

1. c; 2. a; 3. b; 4. d; 5. a; 6. c; 7. b; 8. c; 9. d; 10. a

True/False

1. True; 2. False; 3. True; 4. False; 5. True

Chapter 12

MCQs

1. c; 2. b; 3. a; 4. b; 5. a; 6. a; 7. d; 8. d; 9. d

True/False

1. True; 2. False; 3. True; 4. False; 5. True; 6. True

Chapter 13

MCQs

1. b; 2. c; 3. a; 4. b; 5. c; 6. d; 7. a; 8. d; 9. b; 10. c

True/False

1. False; 2. False; 3. True; 4. True; 5. False;
6. True; 7. True; 8. False; 9. True; 10. False

Chapter 14

MCQs

1. d; 2. b; 3. a; 4. b; 5. c; 6. d; 7. d; 8. c; 9. a; 10. c

True/False

1. True; 2. True; 3. False; 4. False; 5. False

Chapter 15

MCQs

1. d; 2. d; 3. a; 4. c; 5. b; 6. a; 7. c; 8. c; 9. a; 10. c

True/False

1. False; 2. True; 3. True; 4. False; 5. True

Chapter 16

MCQs

1. b; 2. a; 3. d; 4. c; 5. a; 6. a; 7. b; 8. b; 9. a; 10. c

True/False

1. False; 2. True; 3. False; 4. True; 5. True.

Chapter 17

MCQs

1. b; 2. a; 3. b; 4. c; 5. a; 6. d; 7. b; 8. c; 9. a; 10. c

True/False

1. False; 2. True; 3. True; 4. False; 5. True

Chapter 18

MCQs

1. b; 2. a; 3. d; 4. c; 5. b

True/False

1. False; 2. True; 3. True; 4. False; 5. False

Index